Francis Asbury

A COMPENDIOUS HISTORY OF AMERICAN METHODISM.

ABRIDGED FROM THE AUTHOR'S "HISTORY OF THE METHODIST EPISCOPAL CHURCH."

By ABEL STEVENS, LL.D.

NEW YORK:
PUBLISHED BY CARLTON & PORTER,
200 MULBERRY-STREET.
1867.

PUBLISHERS' NOTICE.

THE Book Concern has for some years been spending liberally to provide the Church with a *Standard History* of Methodism. It issued first a History of General Methodism in three volumes, giving an account of the denomination in all parts of the world, centralizing in the Wesleyan, or parent body, a work which has been reproduced by four or five competing publishers in England; second, a particular History of the Methodist Episcopal Church in four volumes—the fourth volume just out. These works have received the strongest indorsements not only by Methodists, but other authorities on both sides of the Atlantic. They meet a great want of the Church, and a demand of the general religious public. The author employed by the Concern to prepare them—Dr. Abel Stevens—has devoted his utmost power to them, and has, by thorough research, added more than one third to the data of our history, as given by preceding writers. These works are now a staple part of the property of the Church's own Publishing House: they have cost it much, and will yield much to its interest if properly patronized.

There are many of our people, however, who cannot spare the means for works as large as these. It has been our design from the beginning, therefore, to present them in cheaper form, that the whole Church may be supplied with them. When propositions were made by other parties to our author (with the most liberal offers of compensation) to prepare a smaller work for more popular circulation, he promptly declined them on the ground that it would be an indirect interference with the Book Concern's right of property in the work, and contrary to the understood rules of the trade in such cases, especially as the Concern designed in due time to issue an abridgment. That abridgment is presented in the present volume, by the author, with additions, bringing the narrative down to the Centenary of the Church, with full accounts of the results of the hundred years of its history, and life-like sketches of its representative men.

We feel that we can confidently call upon the Church to protect and promote the interests of its Book Concern by sustaining us in this undertaking. The larger work, in four volumes, should be obtained by all who can afford its price; but to the many who cannot, this re-edited form of it should be everywhere presented. The *History of the Church* ought to be known by all its people; there could be no better exposition or defense of Methodism. This volume is a connected *History* of the Church. Though much incident and many characters of the larger work are necessarily omitted, yet the narrative is unbroken, and its style and most interesting data are retained. The volumes of which it is a compend have received extraordinary commendations from the press generally. We append a few of these testimonials.

CARLTON & PORTER.
POE & HITCHCOCK.

October, 1868.

OPINIONS OF THE PRESS.

METHODIST.

We venture nothing in expressing our judgment that for profound interest, thrilling portraiture, charming style, beautiful diction, and soul-stirring narrative, it is incomparable. We are not alone in this opinion: in the judgment of the best minds who have read it, it is all we have stated it to be.—*(New York) Christian Advocate.*

After a careful reading, we pronounce the work a complete success. There is the same happy facility for grouping events and characters, the same beauty of description, the same masterly power in the delineation of character, which are found in his former work.—*(Boston) Zion's Herald.*

They have all the charm of romance. We say to all, Read these intensely interesting volumes.—*(Cincinnati) Christian Advocate.*

Dr. Stevens is the ecclesiastical Macaulay, and his works are as equally interesting and ever enchanting.—*(Chicago) Christian Advocate*

The senior bishop of the Methodist Episcopal Church (Morris) writes of the earlier portion of the work in the *(New York) Christian Advocate:* "It feeds the Christian's mind and warms his heart. I sincerely desire and pray that the author may live to complete the work, and bring it down to at least the first Centenary of American Methodism. Its value would be inestimable, not only to this generation, but also to those coming after us."

What Macaulay has done for England, Stevens has done for Methodism.—*William M'Arthur, Esq., of London.*

Entertaining and even fascinating by a style of thought and a variety of incident that never cease to please. The author has woven a narrative so thrilling and substantial that it deserves a place in every American family.—*(Pittsburgh) Christian Advocate.*

If there is another ecclesiastical historian who has given to the Church and the world so piquant, so readable, so eloquent a book as this, we have not read it.—*(New York) Methodist.*

Dr. Stevens has acquired just fame on this side the Atlantic, as well as in his own country, by his General History of Methodism. In addition to the copies of that work imported from America, four or five editions have been issued in England, and are on sale among us in various sizes. The volumes before us will not detract from the author's well-earned reputation. They contain the fruit of great research, presented in a very lively style, and are characterized by a truly Christian spirit.—*(London) Watchman.*

PROTESTANT EPISCOPAL.

We take up these new volumes wishing for the leeway of a Quarterly in which to find room for the reflections that naturally arise at their very sight. Their perusal would flood certain minds with light, and remove many a root of bitterness.—Dr. TYNG, in *(New York) Christian Times.*

Stevens is an excellent writer; he thinks clearly and writes strongly; he makes all of Methodism that can be made of it, and the field is fruitful. His delineations are admirable.—*Am. Quart. Church Review.*

CONGREGATIONAL AND LUTHERAN.

The *Congregational Quarterly* (Boston) speaks of "Stevens's fascinating History of Methodism."

"The researches of Dr. Stevens are exceedingly valuable, not only to the members of his own denomination, but to all who are interested in ecclesiastical history; and the author deserves the thanks of all the Churches in furnishing the public with so interesting and important a contribution.—*(Gettysburgh) Evangelical Quarterly Review.*

PRESBYTERIAN.

The author has bestowed years of patient thought and reading in the preparation of this work, and it is worthy of his previous reputation, which will hereafter be identified with these volumes. He has a mind that inclines him to look into the philosophy of things, and the growth of Methodism in the United States is a theme for a philosopher to study. No greater moral wonder has marked the present century. It is developed in these volumes. They are to be read by the many, to be studied by the few. The work will be studied by ministers and others who are not of his denomination.—*New York Observer.*

We take leave of the book, congratulating our Methodist friends that their history has been so carefully and attractively written. It has more than denominational interest.—*New York Evangelist.*

The *American Presbyterian and Theological Review* speaks of it as "a well-compacted and digested history. American Methodism is honored in and by its historian."

The *Princeton Review* says: "The author's elaborate History of Methodism has established his reputation as a faithful and able historian. His writings have taken the place of authorities, and have abiding importance for Christians of all denominations."

SECULAR AND LITERARY.

The *North American Quarterly* gives some nine or ten pages to the work, and speaks of it as "deserving high praise an important contribution to the ecclesiastical history of the United States."

The *Atlantic* gives it some four closely-printed columns, and says: "Dr. Stevens has displayed in the present volumes the same marked abilities which made his previous work so popular. The skill displayed in their arrangement and treatment, so as to make the narrative an absorbingly attractive one, is eminently praiseworthy. As a history, the work is not only creditable in a denominational and ecclesiastical point of view, but it is a valuable contribution to our national literature. Any ordinary ability would have made a readable story out of such materials; but to make a history worthy of the name required the hand of a master."

The New York Evening Post says: "The history of a great religious movement like this *must* be one of vast interest to all thinkers and statesmen. On the other hand, its romantic elements are such as to furnish material for popular interest to as great a degree as any legendary histories. We do not hesitate to say that this grand subject has found its fitting master in Dr. Stevens. No public man can afford to be ignorant of it; and it is also a book which unlettered readers will find more attractive than an ordinary novel. Dr. Stevens is carefully accurate in his researches. His book is, in fact, a gallery of pictures, in the same sense, at least, in which we may say the same thing of Milman or Macaulay. But it is not merely a series of illustrations, as, to a large extent, the histories of Milman and Macaulay are. The due proportions of men and facts are never lost sight of in Dr. Stevens's book; the whole field is in his eye as he describes any particular portion of it. He does not simply describe the facts as they are, but shows us why they are. His narrative of the origin of the Methodistic movement in the last century is indeed a picture of the age; yet he not only paints it, but also detects its spirit and traces it to its springs."

It is well done. It will be appreciated both in and out of his Church.—*(New York) Journal of Commerce.*

The narrative is marked by clearness and vivacity of statement, abounding in graphic biographical sketches, many of which exhibit not a little skill in that branch of composition.—*New York Tribune.*

It is not too much to say, that in comprehensiveness of detail, in distinctive portraiture of character, in broad, ingenuous philosophy of facts, in brilliance, purity, and vigor of style, it is worthy to be compared with the productions of the best English or American historians. "Truth, stranger than fiction," invests the work with romantic attraction.—*(Boston) Evening Transcript.*

This work will have readers among all denominations.—*(New York) National Review.*

CONTENTS.

CHAPTER I.

METHODISM—ITS SPECIAL ADAPTATION TO THE NEW WORLD.

CHAPTER II.

FOUNDERS OF THE METHODIST EPISCOPAL CHURCH.

CHAPTER III.

RISE OF METHODISM IN MARYLAND.

CHAPTER IV.

EARLY LAY EVANGELISTS.

CHAPTER V.

WESLEY'S FIRST MISSIONARIES TO AMERICA.

CHAPTER VI.

WESLEY'S MISSIONARIES: CONTINUED.

CHAPTER VII.

THE FIRST CONFERENCE—RETURN OF ENGLISH PREACHERS.

CHAPTER VIII.

NATIVE EVANGELISTS.

CHAPTER IX.

PRINCIPAL EVANGELISTS: 1773–1784.

CHAPTER X.

TRIALS AND PROGRESS DURING THE REVOLUTIONARY WAR: 1775–1784.

CHAPTER XI.

LABORS AND TRIALS DURING THE REVOLUTIONARY WAR.

CHAPTER XII.

CONFERENCES AND PROGRESS, FROM THE BEGINNING OF THE REVOLUTIONARY WAR, TO THE ORGANIZATION OF THE METHODIST EPISCOPAL CHURCH.

CHAPTER XIII.

ORGANIZATION OF THE METHODIST EPISCOPAL CHURCH.

CHAPTER XIV.

PROGRESS FROM THE ORGANIZATION OF THE CHURCH TO THE FIRST REGULAR GENERAL CONFERENCE: 1785–1792.

CHAPTER XV.

INTRODUCTION OF METHODISM INTO THE WEST.

CHAPTER XVI.

INTRODUCTION INTO THE NORTH AMERICAN BRITISH PROVINCES.

CHAPTER XVII.

INTRODUCTION OF METHODISM INTO NEW ENGLAND.

CHAPTER XVIII.

SUMMARY REVIEW: 1785–1792.

CHAPTER XIX.

FIRST REGULAR, OR SECOND GENERAL CONFERENCE—METHODISM IN THE SOUTH: 1792–1796.

CHAPTER XX.

METHODISM IN THE MIDDLE AND NORTHERN STATES: 1792–1796.

CHAPTER XXI.

METHODISM IN THE EASTERN STATES: 1792–1796.

CHAPTER XXII.

METHODISM IN THE WEST: 1792–1796.

CHAPTER XXIII.

GENERAL CONFERENCE OF 1796—METHODISM IN THE SOUTH: 1796-1804.

CHAPTER XXIV.

MIDDLE AND NORTHERN METHODISM: 1796-1804.

CHAPTER XXV.

METHODISM IN THE EASTERN STATES: 1796-1804.

CHAPTER XXVI.

METHODISM IN THE WEST: 1796-1804.

CHAPTER XXVII.

GENERAL CONFERENCES OF 1800 AND 1804: REVIEW.

CHAPTER XXVIII.

METHODISM IN THE SOUTH: 1804–1820.

CHAPTER XXIX.

METHODISM IN THE MIDDLE AND NORTHERN STATES: 1804–1820.

CHAPTER XXX.

METHODISM IN THE EASTERN STATES: 1804–1820.

CHAPTER XXXI.

METHODISM IN THE WEST: 1804–1820.

CHAPTER XXXII.

GENERAL CONFERENCES OF 1808, 1812, AND 1816—SUMMARY REVIEW—DEATHS OF WHATCOAT, COKE, LEE, AND ASBURY.

CHAPTER XXXIII.

PROGRESS AND TRIALS FROM THE GENERAL CONFERENCE OF 1820 TO THE CENTENARY JUBILEE 1866.

CHAPTER XXXIV.

AUXILIARY PLANS AND INSTITUTIONS—LITERARY, EDUCATIONAL, MISSIONARY, ETC.

CHAPTER XXXV.

REPRESENTATIVE MINISTERIAL CHARACTERS — SUMMERFIELD — MAFFITT — COOKMAN — OLIN.

CHAPTER XXXVI.

CENTENARY JUBILEE—RESULTS—THEIR CAUSES.

APPENDIX.

HISTORY

OF THE

METHODIST EPISCOPAL CHURCH.

CHAPTER I.

METHODISM — ITS SPECIAL ADAPTATIONS TO THE NEW WORLD.

IN the year 1757 John Wesley, traveling and preaching, night and day, throughout the United Kingdom, arrived in Glasgow. He "walked to its College, saw the new library, with the collection of pictures," and admired examples of the art of Raphael, Vandyke, and Rubens. Had he possessed the foresight of the Hebrew seers, he would have paused, as he crossed the University quadrangle, to admire a coming and nobler proof of genius; for it was in this same year that a young man, destined to become recognized as a chief benefactor of the human race, came to Glasgow to seek employment as an artisan, where, failing to find it among the citizens, he found sympathy in the learned Faculty of the University, and was allowed a humble chamber within its walls. The room is reached from the quadrangle by a spiral stairway, and is still preserved in its original rudeness, as too sacred to be altered. In the court below he put out a sign as "Mathematical Instrument Maker to the University." He lived on poor fare, and eked out his subsistence by combining, with his work for the Faculty, the manufacture of musical instruments; he made organs, and repaired flutes, guitars, and violins; but meanwhile studied assiduously the laws of physics, that he might apply them in an invention which was to produce the "greatest commercial and social revolution in the entire history of the world;" a revolution with which Methodism was to have important relations.

James Watt, the artisan of Glasgow University, gave to the world the Steam-Engine, and to-day the aggregate steam-power of Great Britain alone equals the manual capability for labor of more than four hundred millions of men; more than twice the number of males capable of labor on our planet. Its aggregate power throughout the earth is equal to the male capacity, for manual work, of five or six worlds like ours. The commerce, the navigation, the maritime warfare, the agriculture, the mechanic arts of his race have been revolutionized by the genius of this young man.

The invention of the steam-engine was more important to the new than to the old world. Is was vastly important to the latter through the former, for it was the potent instrument for the opening of the boundless interior of the North American continent to the emigration of the European populations, and the development of that immense commerce which has bound together and enriched both worlds. The great rivers of the new world, flowing with swift current, could convey their barges toward the sea, but admitted of no return. The invention of Watt, applied by the genius of Fulton, has conquered their resistance, and opened the grand domain of the Mississippi valley for the formation of mighty states in a single generation, and marshaled the peoples of Europe to march into the wilderness in annual hosts of hundreds of thousands.

Wesley, who might have saluted, in the quadrangle of Glasgow University, the struggling and dependent man whose destiny it was to achieve these stupendous changes, was himself actually preparing the only means that could supply the sudden and incalculable moral wants which they were to create. Methodism, with its "lay ministry," and "itinerancy," could alone afford the ministrations of religion to the overflowing population; it was to lay the moral foundations of many of the great states of the West. The older Churches of the colonies could never have supplied them with "regular" or educated pastors in any proportion to their rapid settlement. And in the sudden growth of manufacturing cities in both England and America, occasioned by Watt's invention, Methodism was to find some of the most urgent necessities for its peculiar provisions.

Watt and Wesley might well then have struck hands and bid each other godspeed at Glasgow in 1757: they were co-workers for the destinies of the new world.

The rapid settlement of the continent, especially after the Revolution, presented indeed a startling problem to the religious world. Philosophers, considering only its colonial growth, anticipated for it a new era in civilization. Hume perceived there "the seeds of many a noble state—an asylum for liberty and science." Montesquieu predicted for it freedom, prosperity, and a great people; Turgot, that "Europe herself should find there the perfection of her political societies and the firmest support of her well-being." Berkeley pointed to it as the seat of future empire. Locke and Shaftesbury studied out a constitutional polity for a part at least of its empire. The fervid spirit of Edwards, seeing, with Bossuet, in all history only the "History of Redemption," dreamed, in his New England retirement, of a millennium which was to dawn in the western hemisphere, and thence burst upon the nations and irradiate the globe.

The Revolution strengthened these anticipations, and in its train came events quite anomalous in the religious history of nations. No Protestant prelate had hitherto lived upon the continent; it now presented not merely a Church without a bishop, and a state without a king, but a state territorially larger than any other in the civilized world without an ecclesiastical Establishment. The State separated from the Church, enfranchising it by divorcing it. Religion was to expect no more legal support, except temporarily, in a few localities where the old system might linger in expiring. The novel example was contrary to the traditional training of all Christian nations, and might well excite the anxiety of Christian thinkers for the moral fate of the new world. How were

Christian education, Churches, and pastors to be provided for this boundless territory and its multiplying millions of souls? If the "voluntary principle" were as legitimate as its advocates believed, yet could it possibly be adequate to the moral wants of the ever-coming armies of population which, under the attractions of the new country, were about to pour in upon and overspread its immense regions; armies far surpassing the northern hordes whose surging migrations swept away the Roman empire, and with which was to be transferred to the new world much of the worst barbarism of the old?

The early training of the country had been, providentially, to a great extent religious, as if preparatory for its future history. Most of the colonies were founded in religious motives, their infancy moulded by religion, their adolescence invigorated and hardened by war—the preparation for their independence and liberty, and for a new civilization which should be based on the sovereignty of the people, and should emancipate the new world from the ecclesiastical and political traditions of the old.

But now came a solemn crisis in the history of these providentially trained populations, scattered almost from the frozen zone to the tropics, treading a virgin soil of exhaustless resources, and flushed with the consciousness of a new development of humanity. Their territory was to enlarge more than two thirds; their population beyond any recorded example. Though, in their colonial growth, Edwards, inspired by the "Great Awakening," saw the vision of the millennium flashing upon their mountains and valleys, yet the Revolution and national consolidation, endowing them with new and unexampled powers, oppressed them with new problems. A state may exist without a king, a Church without a bishop, a nation without an ecclesiastical establishment; but a people cannot be without religion, without God; they had better cease to be. And where now, with a political system which recognized no one religion by tolerating all, which made no provision for the spiritual wants of the people, should men, who believed religion to be the fundamental condition of civil righteousness and liberty, look for the safety of the marvelous destiny that had opened upon the new world?

The Revolution ended with the treaty of peace in 1783, and then commenced a national progress never anticipated in the most sanguine dreams of statesmen.' The inventive genius of Watt and Fulton was to wave a wand of miraculous power over the land; and not only the Valley of the Mississippi, stretching over twenty degrees of latitude and thirty of longitude, with millions of souls in our day, was to open, like a new world, to navigation and settlement; but the thirty-five thousand miles of principal rivers—above a third more than the circumference of the globe—besides the minor streams, making, with the former, more than forty thousand miles of navigable waters, were to be thrown open as the highways of population and commerce. The masses of Europe, in millions, were to enter these highways. The one million and a quarter (including blacks) of 1750, the less than three millions of 1780, were to be nearly four millions in 1790; nearly five and a third millions in 1800; more than nine and a half millions in 1820; nearly thirteen millions in 1830. Thus far they were to increase nearly thirty-three and a half per cent. in each decade. Pensioners of the war of the Revolution were to live to see the "Far West" transferred from the valleys of Virginia, the eastern base of the Pennsylvania Alleghanies, and the center of New York, to the great deserts beyond the Mississippi; to see mighty states, enriching the world, flourish on the Pacific coast, and to read, in New York, news sent the same day from San Francisco. Men, a few at least, who lived when the population of the country was less than three millions, were to live when it should be thirty millions. If the ratio of increase should continue, this population must amount, at the close of our century, but thirty-three years hence, to one hundred millions; exceeding the present population of England, France, Switzerland, Spain, Portugal, Sweden, and Denmark. A step further in the calculation presents a prospect still more surprising: by the year 1930, which not a few, living in our day, shall see, this mighty mass of commingled races will have swollen to the aggregate of two hundred and forty-six millions, nearly equaling the present population of all Europe.

This growth of population, could it take place in an old country, supplied for ages with religious and educational foundations, would suggest anxious moral questions to the reflections of the philosopher and Christian; but here it was to occur in the wilderness of savage life. "Westward the star of empire takes its way," sang Berkeley, as he contemplated the grand prospect; to the West this overwhelming flood was to sweep, and thither was to move with it the power of the nation, the political forces which were to take their moral character from these multitudes and impart it to the nation, if not to much of the rest of the world. Obviously then the ordinary means of religious instruction—a "settled" pastorate, a "regular" clergy, trained through years of preliminary education—could not possibly meet the moral exigencies of such an unparalleled condition. Any unfavorable contingencies, hanging over the federal organization or unity of the nation, could hardly affect these exigencies, except to exasperate them. A religious system, energetic, migratory, "itinerant," extempore, like the population itself, must arise; or demoralization, if not barbarism, must overflow the continent.

Methodism entered the great arena at the emergent moment. It was preparing to do so while Wesley stood in the quadrangle at Glasgow beneath the window within which Watt was preparing the key to unlock the gates of the Great West. In the very next year Wesley was to find the humble man who was to be its founder in the United States. About the same time a youth in Staffordshire was preparing, through many moral struggles, to become its chief leader and the chief character in the ecclesiastical history of the new world, the first resident bishop of Protestantism in the western hemisphere. Methodism was not to supersede here other forms of faith, but to become their pioneer in the opening wilderness, and to prompt their energies for its pressing necessities. It was to be literally the founder of the Church in several of the most important new states, individually as large as some leading kingdoms of the old world. It was to become at last the dominant popular faith of the country, with its standard planted in every city, town, and almost every village of the land. Moving in the van of emigration, it was to supply, with the ministrations of religion, the frontiers from the Canadas to the Gulf of Mexico, from Puget's Sound to the Gulf of California. It was to do this indispensable work by means peculiar to itself; by districting the land into Circuits which, from one hundred to five hundred miles in extent, could each be statedly supplied with religious instruction by but one or two traveling evangelists, who, preaching daily, could thus have charge of parishes comprising hundreds of miles and tens of thousands of souls. It was to raise up, without delay for preparatory training, and thrust out upon these Circuits thousands of such itinerants, tens of thousands of Local or Lay Preachers and Exhorters, as auxiliary and unpaid laborers, with many thousands of Class-leaders who could maintain pastoral supervision over the infant societies in the absence of the itinerant preachers, the latter not having time to delay in any locality for much else than the public services of the pulpit. Over all these circuits it was to maintain the watchful jurisdiction of traveling Presiding Elders, and over the whole system the superintendence of traveling Bishops, to whom the entire nation was to be a common diocese. It was to govern the whole field by Quarterly Conferences for each circuit, Annual Conferences for groups of circuits, quadrennial Conferences for all the Annual Conferences. It was to preach night and day, in churches where it could command them, in private houses, school-houses, court-houses, barns, in the fields, on the highways. It was to dot the continent with chapels, building them, in our times at least, at the rate of one a day. It was to provide academies and colleges exceeding in number, if not in efficiency, those of any other religious body of the country, however older or richer. It was to scatter over the land cheap publications, all its itinerants being authorized agents for their sale, until its "Book Concern" should become the largest religious publishing house in the world. The best authority for the moral statistics of the country, himself of another denomination, Dr. Baird, was at last to "recognize in the Methodist economy, as well as in the zeal, the devoted piety, and the efficiency of its ministry, one of the most powerful elements in the religious prosperity of the United States, as well as one of the firmest pillars of their civil and political institutions."

It has been said that Methodism thus seems to have been providentially designed more for the new world than for the old. The coincidence of its history with that of the United States does indeed seem providential; and, if such an assumption might have appeared presumptuous in its beginning, its historical results, as impressed on all the civil geography of the country and attested by the national statistics, now amply justify the opinion. Here, if anywhere, its results appear to confirm the somewhat bold assertion of a philosophic thinker (Isaac Taylor) not within its pale, who affirms "that, in fact, that great religious movement has, immediately or remotely, so given an impulse to Christian feeling and profession, on all sides, that it has come to present itself as the starting-point of our modern religious history; that the field-preaching of Wesley and Whitefield, in 1739, was the event whence the religious epoch, now current, must date its commencement; that back to the events of that time must we look, necessarily, as often as we seek to trace to its source what is most characteristic of the present time; and that yet this is not all, for the Methodism of the past age points forward to the next-coming development of the powers of the Gospel."

But what was this phenomenon of modern religious history, this "religious movement of the eighteenth century, called Methodism?"

It was not a new dogmatic phase of Protestantism. They err who interpret its singular history chiefly by its theology. Its prominent doctrine of justification by faith was the prominent doctrine of the Reformation. Its doctrines of the "witness of the Spirit" and of "sanctification" had been received, substantially, if not with the verbalism of Methodism, by all the leading Churches of Christendom. Wesley, Fletcher, and Sellon appealed to the standards of the Anglican Church in support of their teachings in these respects. Wesley taught no important doctrine which is not authorized by that Church, unless it be what is called his Arminianism. But even this was dominant in the Anglican Church in certain periods of its history. In fine, none of the important doctrines taught by Wesley and his followers were peculiar to them. That their theology was necessary to their system, of course, cannot be denied; but it had existed, every one of its essential dogmas, in the general Church, without the remarkable efficacy of Methodism. Calvinistic Methodism was powerful, alike with Arminian Methodism, in the outset, and failed at last only by the failure of its ecclesiastical methods. Methodism differed from other religious bodies, in respect to theology, chiefly by giving greater prominence, more persistent inculcation, to truths which they held in common, particularly to the doctrines of Justification by Faith, Assurance, and Sanctification. These were the current ideas of its Theology, but they were rendered incandescent by its spirit, and effective by its methods.

In these two facts—the spirit, and the practical system of Methodism—inheres the secret, if secret it may be called, of its peculiar power.

The "Holy Club" was formed at Oxford in 1729, for the sanctification of its members. The Wesleys there sought personal purification by prayer, watchings, fastings, alms, and Christian labors among the poor. George Whitefield joined them for the same purpose; he was the first to become "renewed in the spirit of his mind;" but not till he had passed through a fiery ordeal, till he had spent "whole days and weeks prostrate on the ground in prayer;" and he was saved at last "by laying hold on the cross by a living faith;" receiving "an abiding sense of the pardoning love of God, and a full assurance of faith." He was hooted and pelted with missiles in the streets by his fellow-students, but was preparing meanwhile to go forth a sublime herald of the new "movement;" a preacher of Methodism in both hemispheres; the greatest preacher, it is probable, in popular eloquence, of all the Christian ages.

John and Charles Wesley continue the ineffectual ascetic struggle, poring over the pages of the "Imitatione," and the "Holy Living and Dying;" in all things "living by rule;" fasting excessively; and visiting the poor and the prisoner.

They find no rest to their souls, untroubled, as yet, by any dogmatic question, but seeking only spiritual life. "Holiness, without which no man shall see the Lord," is the cry of Wesley's spirit, but he still finds it not. "I am persuaded," he writes, "that we may know if we are *now* in a state of salvation, since that is expressly promised in the Holy Scriptures to our sincere endeavors, and we are surely able to judge of our own sincerity." Taylor's Holy Living and Dying teaches him utter purity of motive; "instantly he resolves to dedicate *all* his life to God; all his thoughts and words and actions; being thoroughly convinced there is no medium." The dedication is made, but the light does not come. The two brothers determine to seek it in the wilderness of the new world—to "forsake all," become missionaries to the colonists and savages, and perish, if need be, for their souls. They accompany Oglethorpe to Georgia, and on the voyage they witness the joyous faith of Moravian peasants and artisans in the perils of storms; they are convinced that they themselves have no such faith. They question the Moravians, and get improved views of the spiritual life, but still grope in the dark. They learn more from the Moravian missionaries in the colonies, but sink into deeper anxiety. They preach and read the Liturgy every day to the colonists, and teach their children in schools. They fast much, sleep on the ground, refuse all food but bread and water. John goes barefooted, to encourage the poor children who had no shoes. The colonists recoil from their severities, and they return to England defeated.

In sight of Land's End John writes in his Journal: "I went to America to convert Indians, but O, who shall convert me? who is he that will deliver me from this evil heart of unbelief?" "The faith I want is a sure trust and confidence in God, that through the merits of Christ my sins are forgiven, and I reconciled to the favor of God." The Moravians meet him again in London, where they maintain several religious meetings in private houses. Both the Wesleys, turning away from St. Paul's, Westminster Abbey, the dead Churches, seek light from heaven in these humble assemblies. They become the associates of Peter Böhler, a

Moravian preacher, and later a Moravian bishop, a man of learning from the University of Jena, who, in good Latin, converses with them on divine subjects. John Wesley cleaves to him. The Moravian expounds to him faith, justification by faith, sanctification by faith; he begins to "see the promise, but it is afar off." Böhler says, "He wept bitterly while I was talking upon this subject, and afterward asked me to pray with him. I can freely affirm that he is a poor broken-hearted sinner, hungering after a better righteousness than that which he has hitherto had, even the righteousness of Christ." "I entreated him to believe in the Lord Jesus Christ, for that then *not only he but many others with him would be saved*"—a prophetical intimation of the future career of Wesley, says a Moravian authority. Thus prepared, Wesley attends a Moravian meeting and hears Luther's Preface to the Epistle to the Romans read; the truth breaks upon his mind. "I felt," he writes, "my heart strangely warmed; I felt I did trust in Christ alone for salvation, and an assurance was given me that he had taken away my sins, even mine, and saved me from the law of sin and death." Charles Wesley had three days before experienced the same change; "I now," he writes, "found myself at peace with God. I went to bed still sensible of my own weakness; I humbly hope to feel more and more so; yet confident of Christ's protection." Such is "regeneration," according to Methodism; such the first great truth of its proclamation to the world.

The next month John Wesley preaches "Salvation by faith" before the University of Oxford. He has begun his career. The Churches of London are startled by his sermons; by no new truth, but the emphasis and power with which he declares old and admitted truths of the Anglican theological standards, the "new birth," the "witness of the Spirit," and, subsequently, the doctrine of "sanctification," a doctrine which, as taught by Wesley, is in accordance with the highest teachings of the Anglican Church, "is," says a strict Churchman, "essentially right and important; combining, in substance, all the sublime morality of the Greek fathers, the spiritual piety of the Mystics, and the divine philosophy of our favorite Platonists. Macarius, Fénélon, Lucas, and all their respective classes, have been consulted and digested by him, and his ideas are essentially theirs." * His doctrine of faith seemed like a new truth to the apathetic formalism of the Church, but it was the doctrine of its Homilies and of its best theologians.

The genius of Methodism was, then, evangelical life; and, in theology, its chief concern was with those doctrines which are essential to personal religion. "What was the rise of Methodism?" asked Wesley in his conference of 1765. He answered, "In 1729 my brother and I read the Bible; saw inward and outward *holiness* therein; followed after it, and incited others so to do. In 1737 we saw this holiness comes by *faith*. In 1738 we saw we must be *justified* before we are sanctified. But still *holiness* was our point; inward and outward holiness. God then thrust us out to raise a *holy* people."

Whitefield had startled the metropolitan Churches before Wesley's arrival, and, flaming with apostolic zeal, had left for Georgia, the vessel which bore him passing in the channel that which brought Wesley; but he soon returned, and now the Methodistic movement began in good earnest. Its apostles were excluded from the pulpits of London and Bristol; they took the open field, and thousands of colliers and peasants stood weeping around them. They invaded the fairs and merrymakings of Moorfields and Kennington Common; ten, twenty, sometimes fifty, and even sixty thousand people, made their audiences. Their singing could be heard two miles off, and Whitefield's voice a mile. The lowest dregs of the population were dragged out of the moral mire and purified. The whole country was soon astir with excitement; the peasantry of Yorkshire, the colliers of Kingswood and Newcastle, the miners of Cornwall, gathered in hosts around the evangelists, for they saw that here were at last men, gowned and ordained, who cared for their neglected souls. Societies were organized for their religious training. Terms of membership in these societies were necessary, and thus originated the

* Knox: "Bishop Jebb's Thirty Years' Correspondence," Letter xix.

"General Rules," a purely catholic document, with not one dogmatic proposition: the terms of Methodist communion throughout the world. Places for their assemblies must be provided, and on the 12th of May, 1739, the foundations of a building were laid in Bristol: the first chapel founded by Methodism in the world. On the 14th of November the "Old Foundry," in London, was opened for worship by Wesley. Methodism thus early began its edifices, its material fortifications. In this year also its first hymn book, its virtual Liturgy, was published. It is the recognized epoch of the denomination.

The societies need instructors in the absence of Wesley, who now begins to "itinerate" through the kingdom, for the clergy will not take charge of them, and exclude them from the communion table. Wesley appoints intelligent laymen to read to them the Holy Scriptures. One of these, Thomas Maxfield, sometimes explains his readings; he is a man of superior talents; the Countess of Huntingdon (now an influential Methodist) hearing him often, encourages him to preach; and thus begins the lay ministry of Methodism, whose ten thousand voices were soon to be heard in most of the ends of the earth. The societies multiply faster than the lay preachers; these must, therefore, travel from one assembly to another, and thus begins the "itinerancy." The travels of the itinerants must be assigned definitive boundaries, and thus arises the "circuit system." The societies must provide for their chapel debts and other expenses; the members of that of Bristol are distributed into companies of twelve, which meet weekly to pay their "pennies" to a select member, appointed over each, and thus originates the financial economy of Methodism. They find time, when together, for religious conversation and exhortation, and thus begins the "class-meeting," with its "leader," the nucleus of almost every subsequent Methodist society in the world, and a necessary pastoral counterpart to the itinerancy. Many men of natural gifts of speech, who are not able to travel as Preachers, appear in the societies; they are licensed to instruct the people in their respective localities, and thus arise the offices of "Local Preachers" and "Exhorters," laborers who have done incalculable service, and have founded the denomination in the United States, the West Indies, Africa, and Australia. Wesley finds it necessary to convene his itinerants annually for consultation and the arrangement of their plans of labor, and thus is founded (June 25, 1744) the Annual Conference. Several of these bodies have to be formed in the extended field of the Church in the United States, and, for their joint action on important measures, it becomes necessary to assemble them together once in four years, and thus arises the American General Conference.

The Methodists, Wesley insisted, were raised up to spread "scriptural holiness over these lands." Their mission being purely spiritual, their practical or disciplinary system was founded purely in their spiritual designs. An Arminian himself, Wesley admitted Calvinists to membership in his societies. "One condition, and only one," he said, "is required—a real desire to save their souls." "I desire," he writes to the Methodistic Churchman, Venn, "to have a league, offensive and defensive, with every soldier of Christ." "We do not impose," he declared, "in order to admission, any opinions whatever;" "this one circumstance is quite peculiar to Methodism." "We ask only, 'Is thy heart as my heart? If it be, give me thy hand.'" "Is there any other society in Great Britain or Ireland so remote from bigotry?—so truly of a catholic spirit? Where is there such another society in Europe or in the habitable world?" In organizing the Methodist Episcopal Church, he gave it Articles of Religion abridged from the English Articles; but he did not insert or require them in the General Rules, or terms of membership.

Such, then, was Methodism—such its spirit and its methods. It was a revival Church in its spirit, a missionary Church in its organization.

It spread rapidly over Great Britain, into Scotland, into Ireland, to Nova Scotia, the United States, the West Indies, France, Africa, India, and was to achieve its most remarkable triumphs among the Cannibal Islands of the Southern Ocean. Wesley became almost ubiquitous in the United Kingdom, preaching daily. His lay preachers soon filled the land with the sound of the Gospel. Chapels rose rapidly in most of the country. Howell Harris, amid storms of persecution, planted Methodism in Wales, where it has elevated the popular religious condition, once exceedingly low, above that of Scotland, and has in our day more than twelve hundred churches, Arminian and Calvinistic. Wesley traversed Ireland as well as Great Britain. He crossed the channel forty-two times, making twenty-one visits; and Methodism has yielded there some of its best fruits. Whitefield, known as a Calvinist, and forming no societies, was received in Scotland. His congregations were immense, filling valleys or covering hills, and his influence quickened into life its Churches. He aided Harris in founding Calvinistic Methodism in Wales. The whole evangelical dissent of England still feels his power. With the Countess of Huntingdon, he founded the Calvinistic Methodism of Great Britain; but such was the moral unity of both parties, the Arminian and the Calvinistic, that the essential unity of the general Methodistic movement was maintained, awakening to a great extent the spiritual life of both the national Church and of the Nonconformists, and producing most of those "Christian enterprises" by which British Christianity has since been spreading its influence around the globe. The British Bible Society, most of the British Missionary Societies, Tract Societies, the Sunday-school, religious periodicals, cheap popular literature, negro emancipation, Exeter Hall with its public benefits and follies, all arose directly or indirectly from the impulse of Methodism.

Whitefield crossed the Atlantic thirteen times, and journeyed incessantly through the colonies, passing and repassing from Georgia to Maine like a "flame of fire." The Congregational Churches of New England, the Presbyterians and the Baptists of the Middle States, and the mixed colonies of the South, owe their later religious life and energy mostly to the impulse given by his powerful ministrations. The "great awakening" under Edwards had not only subsided before Whitefield's arrival, but had reacted. Whitefield restored it, and the New England Churches received under his labors an inspiration of zeal and energy which has never died out. He extended the revival from the Congregational Churches of the Eastern to the Presbyterian Churches of the Middle States, and throughout the Southern colonies. "The stock from which the Baptists of Virginia and those in all the South and Southwest have sprung was also Whitefieldian." The founder of the Freewill Baptists of the United States was converted under the last preaching of Whitefield.

Though Whitefield did not organize the results of his labors, he prepared the way for Wesley's itinerants in the new world. When he descended into his American grave they were already on his tracks. They came not only to labor, but to organize their labors; to reproduce amid the peculiar moral necessities of the new world both the spirit and the methods of the great movement as it had at last been organized by Wesley in the old, and to render it before many years superior in the former, in both numerical and moral force, to the Methodism of the latter.

Such is a rapid review of the early development both of the United States and of Methodism preparatory for those extraordinary advancements which both have made. The next year, as has been remarked, after Wesley stood in the quadrangle of Glasgow University, where Watt about the same time hung out his sign, the Methodist apostle stood preaching in the open air in an obscure village of Ireland to the people who were destined to form the first Methodist Church in the United States. In two years more they arrived at New York, in six years more they were organized as a society, and thenceforward, coincidently with the opening of the continent by the genius of Watt and Fulton, Methodism has maintained Christianity abreast of the progress of immigration and settlement throughout the states and territories of the Union.

We are now prepared to trace the humble beginnings and extraordinary progress of its mission.

CHAPTER II.

FOUNDERS OF THE METHODIST EPISCOPAL CHURCH.

IN the year 1758 Wesley visited the county of Limerick, Ireland. His Journal reports there a singular community, settled in Court Mattress, and in Killiheen, Balligarrane, and Pallas, villages within four miles of Court Mattress. They were not native Celts, but a Teutonic population. Having been nearly half a century without pastors who could speak their language, they had become thoroughly demoralized; noted for drunkenness, profanity, and "utter neglect of religion." But the Methodist itinerants had penetrated to their hamlets, and they were now a reformed, a devout people. They had erected a large chapel in the center of Court Mattress. "So did God at last provide," writes Wesley, "for these poor strangers, who, for fifty years, had none who cared for their souls." At later visits he declares that three such towns as Court Mattress, Killiheen, and Balligarrane were hardly to be found anywhere else in Ireland or England. There was "no cursing or swearing, no Sabbath breaking, no drunkenness, no ale-house in any of them." "They had become a serious, thinking people, and their diligence had turned all their land into a garden. How will these poor foreigners rise up in the day of judgment against those that are round about them!"

But the most interesting fact respecting this obscure colony was not yet apprehended by Wesley, or he would have wondered still more at their providential history. The Methodism of the New World was already germinating among them; in about two years the prolific seed was to be transplanted to the distant continent, and at the time of Wesley's death (about thirty years later) its vigorous boughs were to extend over the land from Canada to Georgia, from the Atlantic to the Mississippi. In about thirty years after Wesley's death (1820),

American Methodism was to advance to the front of the great "movement," with a majority of more than seventeen thousand over the parent Church, including all its foreign dependencies, and thenceforward the chief numerical triumphs of the denomination were to be in the western hemisphere.

But how came this singular people, speaking a foreign tongue, into the west of Ireland?

The troops of Louis XIV. devastated, in the latter part of the seventeenth century, the Palatinate, on the Rhine. Its population was almost entirely Protestant, the strongest reason for the relentless violence of the bigoted monarch and his army. The whole country was laid waste; the Elector Palatine could see from the towers of Manheim, his capital, no less than two cities and twenty-five villages on fire at once. The peaceable peasants fled before the invaders. Queen Anne sent ships to convey them from Rotterdam to England. More than six thousand arrived in London, reduced to dependent poverty. About fifty families emigrated to Ireland, where they settled, near Rathkeale, in the county of Limerick. A list of those who "settled contiguous to each other on Lord Southwell's estates" has been published; on it are the names of Embury, Heck, Ruckle, Switzer, Gier, and others associated with the original Methodists of New York.

Such was the origin of the "Irish Palatines," and thus did the short-sighted policy of Louis XIV. scatter these sterling Protestants of the Rhine to bless other lands, as his bigoted folly, in the revocation of the Edict of Nantes, had sent half a million of his own best subjects to enrich, by their skill and virtues, Switzerland, Germany, England, and the North American colonies. His attempt to suppress Protestantism in the Palatinate led, through the emigration of these Irish settlers, to one of the most energetic developments of Protestantism recorded in the modern history of religion.

Philip Embury was born in 1728 or in 1730. His family seem not to have been among the original German settlers in Ireland, but to have arrived there some years later. He bore among his neighbors the character of an industrious, sober, honest, and obliging young man. Gier, an aged Palatine, was schoolmaster to the little community of Balligarrane, and taught Embury the elements of knowledge in German. He afterward studied in an English school of the neighborhood. He was apprenticed to a carpenter, and became skillful in his craft. Without remarkable talents, he was esteemed not only an upright, but an intelligent youth. There remain fragmentary manuscripts from his pen which show that he was an elegant writer. His orthography is faultless; the punctuation, and certain abbreviations customary at that day, are given with perfect accuracy. One of these records, in a bold if not beautiful chirography, is of vital significance in his history. It reads thus: "On Christmas day, being Monday, the 25th of December, in the year 1752, the Lord shone into my soul by a glimpse of his redeeming love, being an earnest of my redemption in Christ Jesus, to whom be glory for ever and ever. Amen."

It was in this year, of his conversion, that he first saw Wesley, who was then traveling in the west of Ireland. With Gier he ministered faithfully to his neighbors, as a local preacher, in the intervals of the visits of the itinerant preachers on their circuit. There was apparently a tone of deep pathos in his quiet and somewhat melancholy nature. He was diffident; he shrank from responsibilities, and wept much while preaching. With a party of his brethren he emigrated to the New World. The company included his wife, Mary Switzer; two of his brothers and their families; Peter Switzer, probably a brother of his wife; Paul Heck and Barbara his wife; Valer Tettler; Philip Morgan and a family of the Dulmages. The vessel arrived safely in New York on the 10th of August, 1760.

It can hardly be doubted that, on arriving in New York, Embury, a Class-leader and also a licensed Local Preacher in Ireland, attempted some religious care of the few Methodists who had accompanied him; but they fell away from their steadfastness in the temptations of their new condition, and he, yielding to discouragement, appears not to have used his office as a Preacher till the autumn of 1766. One of our best authorities in Methodistic antiquarian researches says: "The families who accompanied him were not all Wesleyans—only few of them; the remainder were members of the Protestant

Church in Ireland, but made no profession of an experimental knowledge of God, in the pardon of sin and adoption. After their arrival in New York, with the exception of Embury and three or four others, they all finally lost their sense of the fear of God, and became open worldlings. Some subsequently fell into greater depths of sin than others. Late in the year 1765 another vessel arrived in New York, bringing over Paul Ruckle, Luke Rose, Jacob Heck, Peter Barkman, and Henry Williams, with their families. These were Palatines, some of them relatives of Embury, and others his former friends and neighbors. A few of them only were Wesleyans. Mrs. Barbara Heck, who had been residing in New York since 1760, visited them frequently. One of the company, Paul Ruckle, was her eldest brother. It was when visiting them on one of these occasions that she found some of the party engaged in a game of cards; there is no proof, either direct or indirect, that any of them were Wesleyans, and connected with Embury. Her spirit was roused, and, doubtless emboldened by her long and intimate acquaintance with them in Ireland, she seized the cards, threw them into the fire, and then most solemnly warned them of their danger and duty. Leaving them, she went immediately to the dwelling of Embury, who was her cousin. It was located upon Barrack-street, now Park Place. After narrating what she had seen and done, under the influence of the Divine Spirit and with power she appealed to him to be no longer silent, but to preach the word forthwith. She parried his excuses, and urged him to commence at once in his own house, and to his own people. He consented, and she went out and collected four persons, who, with herself, constituted his audience. After singing and prayer he preached to them, and enrolled them in a class. He continued thereafter to meet them weekly. Embury was not among the card-players, nor in the same house with them."

The little company soon grew too large for Embury's house; they hired a more commodious room in the neighborhood, where he continued to conduct their worship, its expenses being met by voluntary contributions. In a few months there were two "classes," one of men, the other of women, including six

From an Original print in possession of G.P. Disosway Esq.

or seven members each. No little excitement began soon to prevail in the city on account of these meetings, and they were thronged with spectators.

About February, 1767, the little assembly at Embury's house were surprised, if not alarmed, by the appearance among them of a stranger in military costume, girt with his sword. He was an officer of the royal army. "All eyes were upon him; had he come to persecute them, to interrupt their religious services, or prohibit them from worshiping?" He soon relieved their apprehensions by his devout participation in their devotions. When they sung he rose with them, when they prayed he knelt. At the conclusion of the service he introduced himself to the preacher and his leading brethren as Captain Thomas Webb, of the king's service, but also "a soldier of the cross, and a spiritual son of John Wesley. They were overjoyed, and hailed him as a 'brother beloved.'" He had been authorized by Wesley to preach; they offered him their humble desk, and thenceforward Captain Thomas Webb was to be one of the chief founders of American Methodism.

A very interesting character is this "good soldier of the Lord Jesus." "The brave are generous," says the old maxim. Thomas Webb's benignant face showed that he had both qualities. It presented the lineaments of a singularly tender, a fatherly heart, and there was no little "fire" and pathos in his elocution. He wore a shade over one of his eyes, a badge of his courage; for he had been at the siege of Louisburg, and had scaled with Wolfe the Heights of Abraham, and fought in the battle of Quebec. He had lost his right eye at Louisburg, and was wounded in his right arm at Quebec. About eight years after the battle of the Plains of Abraham he heard John Wesley preach in Bristol; he now became a decidedly religious man, and, in 1765, joined a Methodist society. Entering a Methodist congregation at Bath, which was disappointed by its circuit preacher, he advanced to the altar, in his regimentals, and addressed them with great effect, chiefly narrating his own Christian experience. Wesley, ever vigilant for "helpers," licensed him to preach, and through the remainder of his life he was indefatigable in Christian labors both in the New World and in the Old; preaching, giving his money, founding societies, and attending Conferences. There must have been an eminent power of natural eloquence in the preaching of this zealous man. John Adams, the statesman of the American Revolution and President of the Republic, heard him with admiration, and describes him as "the old soldier—one of the most eloquent men I ever heard; he reaches the imagination and touches the passions very well, and expresses himself with great propriety." By another hearer he is spoken of as "a perfect Whitefield in declamation." A high Methodist authority, who knew the captain well, says, "They saw the warrior in his face, and heard the missionary in his voice. Under his holy eloquence they trembled, they wept, and fell down under his mighty word."

Such was the stranger in uniform, whose sudden appearance startled the little assembly of Embury's hearers. He had heard of them at Albany, where he had lived a short time before as Barrack-master, and where he had opened his house for religious services, conducted by himself. He had hastened to New York to encourage the struggling society. Following the custom of the times, he always wore his military dress in public. He preached in it, with his sword lying on the table or desk before him. The populace were attracted by the spectacle, and soon crowded the preaching room beyond its capacity. A rigging loft, sixty feet by eighteen, on William-street, was rented in 1767. Here Webb and Embury preached thrice a week to crowded assemblies. "It could not contain half the people who desired to hear the word of the Lord."

Webb saw the necessity of a chapel; but he was anticipated in the design by Barbara Heck, who was really the foundress of American Methodism. This "elect lady" had watched devoutly the whole progress of the infant society thus far. She was a woman of deep piety. From the time that, "falling prostrate" before Embury, and "entreating him with tears to preach to them," she had recalled him to his duty by the solemn admonition, "God will require our blood at your hand," she seems to have anticipated, with the spirit of a prophetess, the great possible results of Methodism in the New World. Seeing the growth of the cause and the importance of a permanent temple, "she had made," she said, "the enterprise a matter of prayer; and, looking to the Lord for direction, had received with inexpressible sweetness and power the answer, 'I the Lord will do it.'" In the fervor of her wishes and prayers, an economical plan for the edifice was devised in her mind. She considered it a suggestion from God. It was approved by the society, and the first structure of the denomination in the western hemisphere was a monumental image of the humble thought of this devoted woman. Webb entered heartily into the undertaking. It would probably not have been attempted without his aid. He subscribed thirty pounds toward it, the largest sum by one third given by any one person. He was one of its original trustees, Embury being first on the list—first trustee, first treasurer, first Class-leader, and first Preacher. They leased the site on John-street in 1768, and purchased it in 1770.

The chapel was built of stone, faced with blue plaster. It was sixty feet in length, forty-two in breadth. Dissenters were not yet allowed to erect "regular churches" in the city; the new building was therefore provided with "a fireplace and chimney" to avoid "the difficulty of the law." Though long unfinished in its interior, it was "very neat and clean, and the floor was sprinkled over with sand as white as snow." Embury, being a skillful carpenter, "wrought" diligently upon the structure. He constructed with his own hands its pulpit; and on the memorable 30th of October, 1768, mounted the desk he had made, and dedicated the humble temple by a sermon on Hosea x, 12: "Sow to yourselves in righteousness, reap in mercy; break up your fallow ground, for it is time to seek the Lord, till he come and reign righteousness upon you." The house was soon thronged. Within two years from its consecration we have reports of at least a thousand hearers crowding it and the area in its front. It was named Wesley Chapel, and was the first in the world that bore that title. Seven months after its dedication a letter to Wesley, concerning Embury and Webb, said, "The Lord carries on a very great work by these two men." The city at this time contained about twenty thousand inhabitants, the colonies but about three millions. Methodism was thenceforward to grow alike with the growth of the city and of the continent.

Webb was practically an itinerant preacher. Being at last on the retired list, with the title and pay of a captain for his honorable services, he had leisure for travel. The kindred of his wife lived at Jamaica, L. I. He went thither, hired a house, and preached in it, and "twenty-four persons received justifying grace." He passed repeatedly through New Jersey, forming societies at Pemberton, Trenton, Burlington, and other places. He was the founder of Methodism in Philadelphia, where he first preached in a sail-loft, and formed a class of seven members in 1767 or 1768. He continued to preach in that city more or less till Wesley's itinerants arrived, and was there to welcome them in person in 1769. He aided in the purchase of the first Methodist church of Philadelphia, St. George's, in 1770, contributing liberally for it. He introduced Methodism into Delaware in 1769, preaching in Newcastle, Wilmington, and in the woods on the shores of the Brandywine. Still later he labored in Baltimore.

Having thus founded the new cause on Long Island, in New Jersey, Pennsylvania, and Delaware, and prominently helped to found it in New York, he appealed to British Methodism for aid, urging Wesley to send out preachers. In 1772 he returned to England, apparently to promote the interest of the Wesleyans for the colonies. He made a spirited appeal for missionaries at the Conference in Leeds, and led back with him, to America, Shadford and Rankin; Pilmoor and Boardman having been previously sent in response to his urgent letters. Re-embarking with his two missionaries in 1773, he continued his travels and labors with unabated zeal till the breaking out of the Revolution, when he returned finally to Europe.

Embury continued to minister faithfully in his chapel twice or thrice a week. "There were at first no stairs or breastwork to the galleries;" they were ascended by a rude ladder. "Even the seats on the lower floor had no backs." The "singing was congregational; some one set the tune, the rest joined in, and they made melody to the Lord." There was no vestry nor class-room; "the classes met in private houses." A parsonage, adjacent to the chapel, was erected in 1770—a small house, furnished chiefly with articles given or lent by the people. Wesley's first missionaries, Pilmoor and Boardman, arrived in the colonies in the autumn of 1769, and not long after the faithful carpenter retired from the city to Camden, a settlement in the town of Salem, Washington county, New York. Thither he was accompanied by Peter Switzer, Abraham Bininger, a Moravian, who had crossed the Atlantic to Georgia with Wesley in 1735, and others of his companions. He there continued to labor as a local preacher, and formed a society, chiefly of his own countrymen, at Ashgrove—the first Methodist class within the bounds of the Troy Conference, which in our day reports more than 25,000 communicants, and more than 200 traveling preachers. He was held in high estimation by his neighbors, and officiated among them not only as a preacher, but as a magistrate. While mowing in his field in 1775, he injured himself so severely as to die suddenly, aged but forty-five years, "greatly beloved and much lamented," says Asbury. Some of his family emigrated to Upper Canada, and, with the family of Barbara Heck, were among the founders of Methodism in that province. Thus we end reluctantly the meager narrative of what knowledge remains respecting this humble but honored man, whose name will probably never be forgotten on earth "till the heavens be no more." Barbara Heck lived and died a model of womanly piety—"a Christian of the highest order; she lived much in prayer, and had strong faith; and therefore God used her for great good." Some of her descendants have been conspicuous in the progress of Methodism.

CHAPTER III.

RISE OF METHODISM IN MARYLAND.

ROBERT STRAWBRIDGE was born at Drumsnagh, near the river Shannon, in the county of Leitrim, Ireland. Being an Irishman by nativity and education, if not by blood, he had the characteristic traits of his countrymen: he was generous, energetic, fiery, versatile, somewhat intractable to authority, and probably improvident. He came to America to secure a more competent livelihood—"which object, however, he never accomplished"—and plunged at once, with his young wife, into the "backwoods;" for Frederick county, where he settled on "Sam's Creek," had but recently been reclaimed from the perils of savage invasion. He opened his house for preaching; formed in it a Methodist Society; and, not long after, built the "Log Meeting-house" on Sam's Creek, about a mile from his home. He buried beneath its pulpit two of his children. It was a rude structure, twenty-two feet square, and, though long occupied, was never finished, but remained without windows, door, or floor. "The logs were sawed on one side for a doorway, and holes were made on the other three sides for windows."

He became virtually an itinerant, journeying to and fro in not only his own large county, (then comprehending three later counties,) but in Eastern Maryland, Delaware, Pennsylvania, and Virginia; preaching with an ardor and a fluency which surprised his hearers, and drew them in multitudes to his rustic assemblies. He seemed disposed literally to let the morrow, if not, indeed, the day, take care of itself. "During his life he was poor, and the family were often straitened for food; but he was a man of strong faith, and would say to them on leaving, 'Meat will be sent here to-day.'" His frequent calls to preach in distant parts of the country required so much of his time that his family were likely to suffer in his absence, so that it became a question with him "who will keep the wolf from my own door while I am abroad seeking after the lost sheep?" His neighbors, appreciating his generous zeal and self-sacrifice, agreed to take care of his little farm, gratuitously, in his absence.

The Sam's Creek Society, consisting at first of but twelve or fifteen persons, was a fountain of good influence to the county and the state. It early gave four or five Preachers to the itinerancy. Strawbridge founded Methodism in Baltimore and Harford counties. The first society in the former was formed by him at the house of Daniel Evans, near the city, and the first chapel of the county was erected by it. The first native Methodist Preacher of the continent, Richard Owen, was one of his converts in this county; a man who labored faithfully and successfully as a Local Preacher for some years, and who entered the itinerancy at last, and died in it. He was long the most effective co-laborer of Strawbridge, traveling the country in all directions, founding Societies and opening the way for the coming itinerants.

Owen's temperament was congenial with that of Strawbridge. He clung to the hearty Irishman with tenacious affection, emulated his missionary activity, and at last followed him to the grave, preaching his funeral sermon to a "vast concourse," under a large walnut-tree. "Richard Owen, the first Methodist Preacher raised up in America," says Lednum, our best chronicler of these dim, early times, "was a Local Preacher in Baltimore Circuit. At the time of his death he had been preaching fifteen or sixteen years. Though he had charge of a large family, he traveled and preached much as a Local Preacher, in what was then the back settlements, when Methodism was in its infancy. He was a man of sound heart, plain address, good utterance, and solid judgment; and for the last two years of his life he gave himself up wholly to the work of saving souls."

Several Preachers were rapidly raised up by Strawbridge in his travels in Baltimore and Harford counties: Sater Stephenson, Nathan Perigau, Richard Webster, and others; and many laymen, whose families have been identified with the whole subsequent progress of Methodism in their respective localities, if not in the nation generally. We have frequent intimations of Strawbridge's labors and success in the early biographies of Methodism, but they are too vague to admit of any consecutive narration of his useful career. We discover him now penetrating into Pennsylvania, and then arousing the population of the Eastern shore of Maryland; now bearing the standard into Baltimore, and then, with Owen, planting it successfully in Georgetown, on the Potomac, and in other places in Fairfax county, Virginia; and by the time that the regular itinerancy comes effectively into operation in Maryland, a band of Preachers, headed by such men as Watters, Gatch, Bonham, Haggerty, Durbin, Garrettson, seem to have been prepared, directly or indirectly through his instrumentality, for the more methodical prosecution of the great cause. At last we find his own name in the Minutes (in 1773 and 1775) as an itinerant. He seems to have become settled finally as Preacher to the Sam's Creek and Brush Forest Societies; the latter being in Harford county, and its chapel the second built in Maryland. We trace him to the upper part of Long Green, Baltimore county, where an opulent and generous public citizen, Captain Charles Ridgely, who admired his character and sympathized with his poverty, gave him a farm, free of rent, for life. It was while residing here, "under the shadow of Hampton," his benefactor's mansion, that, in "one of his visiting rounds to his spiritual children, he was taken sick at the house of Joseph Wheeler, and died in great peace;" probably in the summer of 1781. Owen, as has been remarked, preached his funeral sermon in the open air, to a great throng, "under a tree at the north-west corner of the house." Among the concourse were a number of his old Christian neighbors, worshipers in the "Log Chapel," to whom he had been a Pastor in the wilderness; they bore him to the tomb, singing as they marched one of those rapturous lyrics with which Charles Wesley taught the primitive Methodists to triumph over the grave. He was of "medium size, of dark complexion, black hair, had a sweet voice, and was an excellent singer." He will be for ever memorable as the contemporary of Embury and Webb, in founding the denomination.

Thus did Methodism begin simultaneously, or nearly so, in the north and in the middle of the opening continent. Its first two chapels were befittingly humble; their very humbleness being not only an adaptation to its peculiar mission among the poor, but giving, by contrast with the grandeur of its still advancing results, a peculiar moral sublimity, a divine attestation, to the great cause of which they were the first monuments. Each was in its lowly sphere an evangelical Pharos, shedding out a pure though modest light, the rays of which extended, blended, and brightened, till they streamed, a divine illumination, over the whole heavens of the nation, and fell in scattered radiance, like the light of the morning, on many of the ends of the earth.

CHAPTER IV.

EARLY LAY EVANGELISTS.

THE introduction of Methodism into America, demanded by the great movement of transatlantic immigration, was an incident of that movement. The new and urgent necessity thus evolved a moral provision for itself. Embury and the Palatines, Strawbridge, and scores, probably hundreds, of other Methodists, individually scattered through the colonies, had been floated, as it were, by the insetting current to the shores of the New World, and soon became the centers of religious societies among its Atlantic communities. Borne along by the irresistible stream, apparently submerged at times in its tumultuous course, many of them reappeared in the remote interior settlements and became the germs of early Methodist Churches in the desert. The Emburys, the Hecks, and some of their associates, bore Methodism not only to Northern New York, but at last to Upper Canada, years before any regular itinerants penetrated that province. The Preachers and laymen of Maryland bore it to the South and across the Alleghanies, and scattered the precious seed over the valleys of the Ohio and the Mississippi.

The little society in New York, worshiping in their unfinished temple, without a choir, without backs to their seats, and climbing a rude ladder to their galleries, seemed instinctively conscious of their great coming history. Letters were sent by them to England calling for missionary pastors. Thomas Taylor, one of their original Church officers, wrote to Wesley in their name as early as 1768; "We want," he said, "an able and experienced Preacher, one who has both gifts and graces necessary for the work. With respect to money for the payment of the Preachers' passage over, if they cannot procure it we will sell our coats and shirts to procure it for them. Great numbers of serious persons come to hear God's word as for their lives; and their numbers have so increased that our house," still the Rigging-loft, "for these six weeks past could not contain half the people." They were now planning for the erection of Wesley Chapel, and spent "two several days of fasting and prayer for the direction of God, and his blessing on their proceedings." Send us a Preacher, they cry to Wesley, "for the good of thousands send one at once," "one whose heart and soul are in the work;" and they predict "that such a flame should be soon kindled as would never stop until it reached the great South Sea." Even Wesley's faith might have been startled at the geographical reach of the sanguine prophecy; but it has long since been fulfilled. American Methodism has planted its standard in the Sandwich Islands, and if it has not borne it thence to Polynesia it is because British Methodism had taken possession of the "great South Sea," and raised among its cannibal populations the purest Churches now to be found on the earth, with native chieftains and kings in their ministry.

These and other appeals could not fail of effect in England. The rapid progress of Methodism there had impressed most minds, in its own communion, with a vague but glowing anticipation of general if not universal triumphs. The news of the dawn of their cause in the New World spread among the people before the Annual Conference was called upon to recognize and provide for it; and before the itinerant missionaries could be dispatched across the Atlantic, humbler men, imbued with the enthusiasm of the new movement, were ready to throw themselves upon the hazards of the distant field, that they might share in its first combats. One of these, Robert Williams, applied to Wesley for authority to preach there; permission was given him on condition that he should labor in subordination to the missionaries who were about to be sent out. Williams's impatient zeal could not wait for the missionaries; he appealed to his friend Ashton, who afterward became an important member of Embury's society. Ashton was induced to emigrate by the promise of Williams to accompany him. Williams was poor, but, hearing that his friend was ready to embark, he hastened to the port, sold his horse to pay his debts, and, carrying his saddle-bags on his arm, set off for the ship with a loaf of bread, a bottle of milk, but no money for his passage. Ashton "paid the expense of his voyage, and they landed in New York (1769) before the missionaries arrived." Ashton took an active interest in the welfare of Embury's little charge, and removed with him at last to Ashgrove, (named after himself,) in Camden, N. Y., where he was the first member and chief pillar of the "Ashgrove Methodist Society," his house being later the home of the itinerants. He left a legacy of three acres of land for a parsonage, and an annuity to the end of time for the oldest unmarried member of the New York Conference, the payment of which still reminds the preachers annually of his eccentric Irish liberality.

Williams immediately began his mission in Embury's Chapel, and thenceforward, for about six years, was one of the most effective pioneers of American Methodism, "the first Methodist minister in America that published a book, the first that married, the first that located, and the first that died." We have but little knowledge of his career, but sufficient to show that he had the fire and heroism of the original itinerancy. He was stationed at John-street Church some time in 1771. He labored successfully with Strawbridge in founding the new cause in Baltimore county. In the first published Conference Minutes he is appointed to Petersburg, Va. "He was the apostle of Methodism in Virginia." He followed Strawbridge in founding it in 1772 on the Eastern shore of Maryland. In the same year he appeared in Norfolk, Va. Taking his stand on the steps of the Court-house, he collected a congregation by singing a hymn, and then preached with a plainness and energy so novel among them that they supposed he was insane. No one invited him home, in a community noted for hospitality; they were afraid of his supposed lunacy: but on hearing him a second time their opinion was changed. He was received to their houses, and soon after a Society was formed in the city, the germ of the denomination in the state. In 1773 he traveled in various parts of Virginia. Jarrett, an apostolic Churchman, and afterward a notable friend of the

Methodists, encouraged his labors, and entertained him a week at his parsonage. Williams formed the first circuit of Virginia. A signal example of his usefulness (incalculable in its results) was the conversion of Jesse Lee. He was "the spiritual father" of this heroic itinerant, the founder of Methodism in New England. "Mr. Lee's parents opened their doors for him to preach. They were converted. Two of their sons became Methodist ministers, and their other children shared largely in the blessings of the Gospel, which he proclaimed with such flaming zeal, holy ardor, and great success." The religious interest excited by Williams's labors soon extended into North Carolina, and opened the way for the southward advancement of Methodism. He bore back to Philadelphia, says Asbury, a "flaming account of the work in Virginia—many of the people were ripe for the Gospel and ready to receive us." He returned, taking with him a young man named William Watters, who was thus ushered into the ministry, and has ever since been honored as the first native American itinerant. Leaving him in the field already opened, Williams went himself south-westward, "as Providence opened the way." Subsequently he bore the cross into North Carolina. He formed a six weeks' circuit from Petersburg southward over the Roanoke River some distance into that state, and thus became the "apostle of Methodism" in North Carolina, as well as Virginia. Like most of the itinerants of that day, he located after his marriage, and settled between Norfolk and Suffolk, where, and in all the surrounding regions, he continued to preach till his death, which occurred on the 26th of September, 1775. Asbury was now in the country, and at hand to bury the zealous pioneer. He preached his funeral sermon, and records in his Journal the highest possible eulogy on him. "He has been a very useful, laborious man. The Lord gave many seals to his ministry. Perhaps no one in America has been an instrument of awakening so many souls as God has awakened by him." He did for Methodism in Virginia and North Carolina what Embury did for it in New York, Webb in New Jersey, Pennsylvania, and Delaware, and Strawbridge in Maryland.

Another humble English Methodist appeared on the scene a few months after Williams's arrival. John King's name will never die in the records of the Church in the Middle States. He came from London to America in the latter part of 1769. He first appears in Philadelphia, where he proclaimed humbly but courageously his first message in the humblest of sanctuaries, over the graves of the poor, in the Potter's Field, and thus began a career of eminent usefulness. Thence we trace him into Maryland, where Strawbridge greets him with hearty welcome, and they work zealously together in Baltimore county, Robert Williams sharing their toils and sufferings. King was a man of invincible zeal. "It was the indomitable King who first threw the banners of Methodism to the people of Baltimore." His first pulpit there was a blacksmith's block at the intersection of Front and French streets. His next sermon was from a table at the junction of Baltimore and Calvert streets. His courage was tested on this occasion, for it was the militia training-day, and the drunken crowd charged upon him so effectually as to upset the table and lay him prostrate on the earth. He knew, however, that the noblest preachers of Methodism had suffered like trials in England, and he maintained his ground courageously. The commander of the troops, an Englishman, recognized him as a fellow-countryman, and defending him, restored order, and allowed him to proceed. Victorious over the mob, he made so favorable an impression as to be invited to preach in the English Church of St. Paul's, but improved that opportunity with such fervor as to receive no repetition of the courtesy. Methodism had now, however, entered Baltimore—down to our day its chief citadel in the New World. In five years after King stood there on the blacksmith's block, it was strong enough to entertain the Annual Conference of the denomination.

King was afterward received into the regular itinerancy. He was a member of the first Conference of 1773, and was appointed to New Jersey. He soon after entered Virginia, and with two other preachers traveled Robert Williams's new six weeks' circuit, extending from Petersburg into North Carolina.

"They were blessed among the people, and a most remarkable revival of religion prevailed in most of the circuit," says Lee, the contemporary historian of the Church. Still later we trace him again to New Jersey; he located during the Revolution, but in 1801 reappeared in the itinerant ranks in Virginia. He located finally in 1803.

John King did valiant service in our early struggles. He seems, however, to have been often led away by his excessive ardor; he used his stentorian voice to its utmost capacity, and it is said that when he preached in St. Paul's, Baltimore, he "made the dust fly from the old velvet cushion."

Such were the first lay evangelists, the founders of Methodism in America, Embury, Webb, Strawbridge, Owen, Williams, and King. In the year in which the last two arrived, Wesley responded to the appeal of the New York society, and his first two regular itinerants appeared in the New World. Let us now turn to them.

CHAPTER V.

WESLEY'S FIRST MISSIONARIES TO AMERICA.

SEND us "an able and experienced Preacher," wrote the New York Society to Wesley; "we importune your assistance;" "send us a man of wisdom, of sound faith, a good disciplinarian, whose soul and heart are in the work;" and, as we have seen, they call unto him with the glowing vision of "a flame kindled, which shall never stop until it reaches the great South Sea." Webb wrote; Embury, it is said, wrote; Thomas Bell, a humble mechanic, who had "wrought six days" upon their new Chapel, wrote. Dr. Wrangle, a good Swedish missionary, afterward chaplain to his king, sent out by his government to minister to its emigrants in Philadelphia, appealed to Wesley in person at a dinner-table, on his way home through England. The zealous and catholic doctor had been preparing the way for Methodism in Philadelphia. John Hood had been converted under his ministry there; and the missionary had recommended him to the friendship of Lambert Wilmer, who was then a devoted young man of St. Paul's Church. The two youths became like David and Jonathan, and after years of Christian co-operation they mutually requested that they might rest in the same grave. Their Swedish friend, obtaining from Wesley the promise of a preacher, wrote back to them the good news, and advised them to become Methodists. They accordingly became founders of the new Church in Philadelphia, where their names are still venerated, and where they now sleep in one tomb under the Union Methodist Church.

In Wesley's "Minutes of Conference" for 1769 are nine brief lines pregnant with volumes of history. On the 3d of August, in the Conference at Leeds, he said from the chair, "We have a pressing call from our brethren of New York (who have built a preaching house) to come over and help them. Who is willing to go? Richard Boardman and Joseph Pilmoor. What can we do further in token of our brotherly love? Let us now take a collection among ourselves. This was immediately done, and out of it £50 were allotted toward the payment of their debt, and about £20 given to our brethren for their passage."

Richard Boardman was now about thirty-one years of age, vigorous and zealous. He had preached in the itinerancy about six years. Wesley pronounced him "a pious, good-natured, sensible man, greatly beloved of all that knew him." His Irish brethren, when, thirteen years later, they laid him in his grave, said that "with eloquence divine he preached the word," and "devils trembled when for Christ he fought."

He set out for America mourning the recent loss of his wife, but courageous for his new career. He preached as he journeyed toward Bristol to embark. In the Peak of Derbyshire he stopped for the night, and preached on Jabez, (1 Chron. iv, 9, 10.) A young lady converted under this discourse became, after some years, the mother of one of the most distinguished leaders of Wesleyan Methodism, and gave him a name from the memorable text, Jabez Bunting.

Boardman, continuing to preach on his route, at last joined Pilmoor at Bristol, to embark in the latter part of August.

Pilmoor had been converted in his sixteenth year through the preaching of Wesley, had been educated at Wesley's Kingswood School, and had now itinerated about four years, being admitted to the Conference in 1765. He was a man of good courage, commanding presence, much executive skill, and ready discourse. The two evangelists arrived at Gloucester Point, six miles south of Philadelphia, on the 24th of October, 1769, after a boisterous passage of nine weeks.

The Methodists of the city were expecting them, Dr. Wrangle, the Swedish missionary, having written to Hood and Wilmer of their appointment. Captain Webb was there to receive them. They immediately began their mission, Pilmoor opening it from the steps of the old State-house on Chestnut-street. Soon afterward he was preaching from the platform of the judges of the race-course on the Common, now Franklin Square, Race-street. In seven days after reaching the city he wrote to Wesley that he "was not a little surprised to find Captain Webb in town, and a society of about one hundred members. This is the Lord's doing, and it is marvelous in our eyes. I have preached several times, and the people flock to hear in multitudes. Sunday night I went out upon the Common. I had the stage, appointed for the horse-race, for my pulpit, and I think between four and five thousand hearers, who heard with attention still as night. Blessed be God for field-preaching! There seems to be a great and effectual door opening in this country, and I hope many souls will be gathered in." Boardman, who acted as Wesley's "assistant," or "superintendent," in America, preached in the city "to a great number of people," and quickly departed for New York, where he met a hearty reception and began his mission in John-street Church.

It is an interesting coincidence that while Boardman and Pilmoor were tossed on their tempestuous voyage, Whitefield was borne through the same storms on his final visit to America, his thirteenth passage over the Atlantic. Arriving at his Orphan house in Georgia, his seraphic soul seemed to receive a presentiment of his approaching end, and to anticipate the joys of heaven. "I am happier," he wrote, "than words can express—my happiness is inconceivable." He started to preach northward, and on the evening of his departure recorded the prophetic words, "This will prove a sacred year for me at the day of judgment. Halleluiah! Come, Lord, come!" "Halleluiah! halleluiah!" he wrote to England; "let chapel, tabernacle, heaven, and earth resound with halleluiah! I can no more; my heart is too big to speak or add more!"

Arriving in Philadelphia, he hailed Wesley's itinerants and "gave them his blessing: it has never failed them." His soul had always, since his conversion, glowed with a divine fire, but it now seemed to kindle into flame. No edifices could contain his congregations; he preached every day. He made a tour of five hundred miles up the Hudson, proclaiming his message at Albany, Schenectady, Great Barrington. "O what new scenes of usefulness are opening in various parts of this world!" he wrote as he returned. "I heard afterward that the word ran and was glorified. Grace! grace!" He had penetrated nearly to the north-western frontiers. He saw the gates of the North-west opening, those great gates through which the nations have since been passing, as in grand procession, but he was not to enter there; the everlasting gates were opening for him, and he was hastening toward them. He passed to Boston, to Newburyport, to Portsmouth, still preaching daily. Seized with illness, he turned back; at Exeter he mounted a hogshead and preached his final sermon to an immense assembly. His emotions carried him away, and he prolonged his discourse through two hours. It was an effort of stupendous eloquence—his last field triumph—the last of that series of mighty sermons which had been resounding like trumpet blasts for thirty years over England and America. He hastened, exhausted, to Newburyport; the people gathered about his lodging in throngs to see and hear him once more; they pressed into the entry of the house. Taking a candle, he attempted to ascend to his chamber, but pausing on the stairs, he addressed them. He had preached his last sermon; this was to be his last exhortation. It would seem that some pensive misgiving, some vague presentiment, touched his soul with the apprehension that the moments were too precious to be lost in rest. He lingered on the stairway, while the crowd gazed up at him with tearful eyes, as Elisha at the ascending prophet. His voice, never perhaps surpassed in its music and pathos, flowed on until the candle, which he held in his hand, burned away and went out in its socket. The next morning he was not, for God had taken him.

He died of asthma on the 30th of September, 1770, and sleeps beneath the pulpit of the Federal-street Church, Newburyport. He had introduced the general Methodistic movement into America, and had finished his providential work. The great cause was now to assume an organic form.

On the 4th of November, 1769, Boardman wrote to Wesley: "Our house contains about seventeen hundred people. About a third part of those who attend get in, the rest are glad to hear without. There appears such a willingness in the Americans to hear the word as I never saw before. They have no preaching in some parts of the back settlements. I doubt not but an effectual door will be opened among them. O! may the Most High now give his Son the heathen for his inheritance. The number of blacks that attend the preaching affects me much."

Williams, who had been supplying Wesley Chapel, gave up the charge to Boardman and went southward, joining Strawbridge and King, and extending his labors into Virginia, as we have seen. Embury, relieved of further responsibility for the Society, formed with Ashton, Bininger, Switzer, the Hecks, and others, his little colony for Camden—the founders of the Ashgrove Church. Boardman's labors were immediately effective. He preached, at least, four sermons weekly, and "met the Society on Wednesday night." He had but two leisure evenings a week. The Church, still poor, provided him with board and about fifteen dollars a quarter for clothing. Among the first-fruits of his labors was the conversion of John Mann, who became a useful preacher and supplied the pulpit at John-street during the Revolutionary War, when the English preachers had either returned home, or gone into retirement. He also became one of the founders of Methodism in Nova Scotia, and died there, in the peace of the Gospel, after nearly half a century of faithful service.

After spending about five months in New York, Boardman exchanged with Pilmoor. They seem to have alternated between the two cities three times a year, in the spring, summer, and autumn; the winter term being five months. We can dimly trace Boardman's labors in New York, through considerable intervals, for four years: from 1769 to 1773; during which "his ministry was blessed to hundreds." In April, 1771, he wrote to Wesley from that city: "It pleases God to carry on his work among us. Within this month we have had a great awakening here. Many begin to believe the report; and to some the arm of the Lord is revealed." He was equally successful in Philadelphia. He made missionary excursions into Maryland, and preached in Baltimore. We have intimations that in the spring of 1772 he journeyed to the north-east, through Providence, as far as Boston, preaching wherever he found opportunity, and forming a small Society in the latter city. He therefore preceded Lee in New England by seventeen years. Pilmoor, meanwhile, was abundant in labors in Philadelphia and New York. He wrote to Wesley from the former city that "there seems to be a great and effectual door opening in the country. Many have believed the report, and unto some the arm of the Lord has been revealed. There begins to be a shaking among the dry bones, and they come together that God may breathe upon them. The Society here consists of about a hundred members, besides probationers; and I trust it will soon increase much more abundantly." In the summer of 1770 he went to Baltimore and other parts of Maryland, to aid Strawbridge, Owen, King, and Williams. He preached in that city, standing on the sidewalk; and, being a man of commanding appearance, and withal an able and convincing Preacher, he was heard with much interest. The next year we trace him again to New York, where Williams labored with him. They made an excursion to New Rochelle, where they found a little company gathered for worship, at the house of Frederick Deveau. A clergyman present refused Pilmoor the privilege of addressing the meeting; but the wife of Deveau, lying sick in an adjacent room, saw him through the opened door, and gave him a mysterious recognition. During her illness she had had much trouble of mind; she had dreamed that she was wandering in a dismal swamp, without path, or light, or guide; when, exhausted with fatigue and about to sink down hopeless, a stranger appeared with a light and led her out of the miry labyrinth. At the first glance she now identified Pilmoor with the apparition of her dream, and appealed to him, from her sick bed, to preach to her and the waiting company. He did so; and while "he was offering to all a present, free, full salvation," the invalid was converted, and in a few days died "triumphant in the Lord!" These singular events awakened general attention; Pilmoor preached again to the whole neighborhood, and Methodism was effectively introduced into New Rochelle, where, not long after,

Asbury was to form the third Methodist Society of the state, after those of John-street and Ashgrove. The beautiful town became the favorite resort of Asbury and his compeers for occasional repose from their travels, though not from their labors; the fountain whence Methodism spread through all Westchester county; its easternmost outpost, whence it, at last, invaded New England. There are allusions in our early records to several expeditions of Pilmoor to the South. He preached in Norfolk, traveled through the southern parts of Virginia and through North Carolina, to Charleston in South Carolina. He reached, at last, Savannah, Georgia, and made a pilgrimage to Whitefield's Orphan house, scattering the good seed over all his route. He spent nearly a year in this excursion, but left no record of its events. It is said, however, that he had many hair-breadth escapes of life and limb. He encountered the violence of the elements and of persecutors. At Charleston he could obtain no place for preaching but the Theater, where, while fervently delivering a sermon, "suddenly the table used by him for a pulpit, with the chair he occupied, disappeared," descending through a trap-door into the cellar. Some wags of the "baser sort" had contrived the trick as a practical joke. Nothing discouraged, however, the preacher, springing upon the stage with the table in his hands, invited the audience to the adjoining yard, adding pleasantly, "Come on, my friends, we will, by the grace of God, defeat the devil this time, and not be driven by him from our work," and then quietly finished his discourse. The fruits of his Christian labors appeared in the conversion of many souls. Wherever he went large crowds attended his ministry, and listened to his message.

Other messengers, from Wesley, were on the sea, hastening to the help of these laborers. One of them was destined to become the most notable character in the ecclesiastical history of North America, and was soon to eclipse all his predecessors in that great scheme of itinerancy which was to extend its network of evangelization over the continent.

CHAPTER VI.

WESLEY'S MISSIONARIES, CONTINUED.

THE name of "America" appears, in 1770, for the first time in Wesley's list of appointments. Four preachers are recorded as composing the little corps of its Methodist evangelists, Joseph Pilmoor, Richard Boardman, Robert Williams, and John King. In the minutes of the next year America appears for the first time in the list of returns of members of Society. It reports three hundred and sixteen. Captain Webb was still abroad laboring in the middle colonies, and was appealing to Wesley for more preachers. Pilmoor and Boardman also wrote to him, calling for recruits. Their reports of success, with the returns of more than three hundred members in their infant Churches, could not be resisted by Wesley. "Our brethren in America call aloud for help," he said to the Conference of 1771; "who are willing to go over and help them?" Five responded, and two were appointed. They were all that could be spared from the urgent work at home, supplied as yet by but about a hundred and twenty effective itinerants.

One of them was a young man who was the only son of an intelligent peasant of the Parish of Handsworth, Staffordshire, and of a pious mother who trained him with religious care. He never "dared an oath or hazarded a lie." His youthful associates were addicted to the usual vices of their age, but he "often retired from their society uneasy and melancholy." He could read the Bible when but seven years of age, and "greatly delighted in its historical parts." "God," he says, "sent a pious man, not a Methodist, into our neighborhood, and my mother invited him to our house. By his conversation and prayers I was awakened before I was fourteen years of age. I began to pray morning and evening, being drawn by the cords of love as with the bands of a man." "I then held meetings frequently at my father's house, exhorting the people there, as also at Sutton Coldfield, and several souls professed to find peace through my labors. I met in Class a while at Bromwich-Heath, and met in Band at Wednesbury. I had preached some months before I publicly appeared in the Methodist meeting-houses, when my labors became more public and extensive; some were amazed, not knowing how I had exercised elsewhere. Behold me now a Local Preacher, the humble and willing servant of any and of every preacher that called on me by night or by day; being ready, with hasty steps, to go far and wide to do good, visiting Derbyshire, Staffordshire, Warwickshire, Worcestershire, and indeed almost every place within my reach, for the sake of precious souls; preaching, generally, three, four, and five times a week, and at the same time pursuing my calling. I think, when I was between twenty-one and twenty-two years of age I gave myself up to God and his work after acting as a Local Preacher nearly five years."

He was only about seventeen years old when he began to hold public meetings, not eighteen when he began to preach, and about twenty-one when he started out as an itinerant, supplying the place of an absent traveling preacher, though not yet received by the Annual Conference. When appointed by Wesley to America he was about twenty-six years of age. He had been in the traveling ministry only about five years, and but four years on the catalogue of regular appointments, but had seen hard service on Bedfordshire, Colchester, and Wiltshire circuits. He was studious, somewhat introspective, with a thoughtfulness which was tinged at times with melancholy. His was one of those minds which can find rest only in labor; designed for great work, and therefore endowed with a restless instinct for it. He was an incessant preacher, of singular practical directness; was ever in motion, on foot or on horseback, over his long circuits; a rigorous disciplinarian, disposed to do everything by method; a man of few words, and those always to the point; of quick and marvelous insight into character; of a sobriety, not to say severity, of temperament, which might have been repulsive had it not been softened by a profound religious humility; for his soul, ever aspiring to the highest virtue, was ever complaining within itself over its shortcomings. His mind had eminently a military cast. He never lost his self-possession, and could therefore seldom be surprised. He seemed not to know fear, and never yielded to discouragement in a course sanctioned by his faith or conscience. He could plan sagaciously, seldom pausing to consider theories of wisdom or policy, but as seldom failing in practical prudence. The rigor which his disciplinary predilections imposed upon others was so exemplified by himself, that his associates or subordinates, instead of revolting from it, accepted it as a challenge of heroic emulation. Discerning men could not come into his presence without perceiving that his soul was essentially heroic, and that nothing committed to his agency could fail, if it depended upon conscientiousness, prudence, courage, labor, and persistence. "Who," says one who knew him intimately, "who of us could be in his company without feeling impressed with a reverential awe and profound respect? It was almost impossible to approach him without feeling the strong influence of his spirit and presence. There was something in this remarkable fact almost inexplicable and indescribable. It appeared as though the very atmosphere in which he moved gave unusual sensations of diffidence and humble restraint to the boldest confidence of man." Withal his appearance was in his favor. In his most familiar portrait he has the war-worn aspect of a military veteran, but in earlier life his frame was robust, his countenance full, fresh, and expressive of generous if not refined feelings. He was somewhat attentive to his apparel, and always maintained an easy dignity of manners, which commanded the respect if not the affection of his associates. The appeals from the American Methodists had reached him in his rural circuits, for he had never left his ministerial work to attend the Annual Conference. Two months before the session of 1771 his mind had been impressed with the thought that America was his destined field of labor. He saw in the New World a befitting sphere for his apostolic aspirations.

Such was Francis Asbury. These great qualities, made

manifest in his subsequent career, were inherent in the man, and Wesley could not fail to perceive them. He not only accepted him for America, but, notwithstanding his youth, appointed him, at the ensuing conference, at the head of the American ministerial itinerancy.

Receiving his appointment, he returned from the conference at Bristol to take leave of his friends. He arrived at last at Bristol to embark, but without a penny for his expenses. "Yet," he writes, "the Lord soon opened the hearts of friends, who supplied me with clothes and ten pounds: thus I found, by experience, that he will provide for those who trust in him." The ship sailed on the 4th of September. He had but two blankets for his bed, and slept with them on the hard boards during the voyage. "I want," he writes, "faith, courage, patience, meekness, love. I feel my spirit bound to the New World, and my heart united to the people, though unknown, and have great cause to believe that I am not running before I am sent."

His companion, Richard Wright, had traveled but one year in England when he set out on his voyage to America. We know but little of his history; scarcely more, indeed, than that he accompanied Asbury; that he spent most of his time, while here, in Maryland and Virginia, and a part of it, in the spring of 1772, in New York city; that in the early part of 1773 he was again in Virginia, laboring in Norfolk; and that in 1774 he returned to England, where, after three years spent in the itinerancy, he ceased to travel, and totally disappeared from the published records of the denomination.

After a voyage of more than fifty days they reached Philadelphia, "and," says Asbury, "were brought in the evening to a large church, where we met with a considerable congregation. Mr. Pilmoor preached. The people looked on us with pleasure, hardly knowing how to show their love sufficiently, bidding us welcome with fervent affection, and receiving us as angels of God." There were now probably about six hundred Methodists in the colonies, and at least ten preachers, (including Embury, Webb, Williams, King, and Owen,) besides Wesley's missionaries. The "large church" in which Asbury heard Pilmoor preach on the evening of his arrival was St. George's, still standing, and revered as the "Old Cathedral" of Methodism in Philadelphia. It had been built by a German Reformed Society, but its projectors failed, and sold it in 1770 to Miles Pennington, one of the first members of the first class, of seven persons, formed in the city by Captain Webb in 1768. It was probably at the instance of Webb that Pennington obtained it, for the veteran soldier knew the value of fortified fields. He gave liberally from his own funds toward it. The same year it was conveyed to the captain and others as trustees of the Methodist Society. For a long time it was unfinished and unfurnished, only half floored with rough boards, its pulpit a rude square box on the north side. The house was not plastered till Dr. Coke came to America, and the Methodists were organized into a Church. There was no church in the connection that Asbury labored as much for as St. George's. It was for nearly fifty years the largest place of worship that the Methodists had in America. It was their cathedral. Such was the first of that series of Methodist chapels in Philadelphia, which has ever since grown more rapidly than the chapel provisions of any other denomination in the city, orthodox or heterodox, and amounts in our day to seventy-two places of worship, more than one sixth of all the city churches.

Having refreshed themselves among these fervent brethren, the missionaries took their departure for new fields; Asbury to the North, Wright to the South.

Asbury arrived in New York on the 12th of November. "Now," he wrote as he entered it, "Now I must apply myself to my old work—to watch, and fight, and pray. Lord, help." Boardman, "a worthy, loving man," welcomed him. He opened his commission the next day with a characteristic sermon on the text, "I am determined to know nothing among you save Jesus Christ and him crucified." He could not be content, however, with stationary labors. He had always, since the commencement of his ministry, been an itinerant, and he must always continue such. Boardman and Pilmoor confined themselves mostly to the cities of Philadelphia and

New York. In about a week after reaching New York Asbury writes: "I have not yet the thing which I seek—a circulation of preachers. I am fixed to the Methodist plan; I am willing to suffer, yea, to die, sooner than betray so good a cause by any means." Supremely important was this disposition. Wesley had rightly estimated his man when he commissioned Asbury for the Western world. For however expedient modifications of the itinerancy might become in the maturity of the denomination, it was now the great necessity of the country and the special work of Methodism in it. But there was already spreading among the young Societies a disposition to localize their few pastors. Many of the oldest itinerants, during the remainder of the century, favored this tendency, and ceased to travel. The Church and the nation owe the maintenance of the itinerancy, with its incalculable blessings, chiefly to the invincible energy of Francis Asbury. "At present," he writes, "I am dissatisfied. I judge we are to be shut up in the cities this winter. My brethren seem unwilling to leave the cities, but I think I shall show them the way. I am in trouble, and more trouble is at hand, for I am determined to make a stand against all partiality." It was soon seen that he was not to be shaken in his purpose. There must be a winter campaign, and henceforth, while he lived, no cantonments, no winter-quarters. In a short time he had formed an extemporary circuit in the country around the city, including Westchester County and Staten Island. He continued thus to travel till the latter part of March, 1772, when he again passed over the scenes of Webb's labors in New Jersey, preaching almost daily till he arrived in Philadelphia, where he was refreshed by meeting Webb and Boardman. The latter, as Superintendent, sketched a plan of labor for some ensuing months. Boardman, himself, was to go eastward on his visit to Boston, Pilmoor to Virginia, Wright to New York, and Asbury was to stay three months in and about Philadelphia. They pursued this course energetically. In July, 1772, Boardman renewed his Plan of Appointments, taking charge himself of Philadelphia, with excursions to Delaware and Maryland; sending Asbury again to New York;

Wright to Maryland, to assist Strawbridge, King, and Williams; and Pilmoor to Virginia. Such are the sparse details we can glean of the early itinerancy; limited almost to meager names and dates, and yet signifying much. Asbury was evidently giving propulsion to the work. In his unintermitted excursions he was waking up preachers, societies, and the population generally. He preached mostly in private houses, sometimes in court-houses, less frequently in churches, sometimes in the woods, at others in prisons, especially where there were culprits condemned to death; and that was a day of much hanging. Sometimes he mounted a wagon at the gallows, impressing with awe the hardened multitude. Thus was he "instant in season and out of season." His sermons were now, frequently, two or three a day; yet he exclaims, "How is my soul troubled that I am not more devoted! O my God, my soul groans and longs for this!" "My way is to go straight forward!" "Hitherto the Lord hath helped me!" "I want to breathe after the Lord in every breath." Such are the ejaculations that almost continually break from his ardent soul in these unceasing labors. His remarkable subsequent career, the "giants of those days" who rose up in all parts of the itinerant field, and the great outspread of Methodism over the continent, have much of their explanation in these early indications of the great man who had thus suddenly appeared in the arena.

It was under the impulse of Asbury's example that Robert Williams now went to Virginia and preached on the steps of the Norfolk Court-House, and that Pilmoor went preaching southward as far as Savannah.

In the autumn of 1772 Asbury was again laboring in and all around New York. He there received a letter from Wesley appointing him "Assistant" or Superintendent of the American Societies, though he was yet but about twenty-seven years of age. He thus took charge of all the Churches and the appointments of the Preachers, subject to the authority of Wesley. He now turned southward, scattering the good seed as he went, and inspiriting the Societies and Preachers. He preached sometimes as early as five o'clock in the morning. He passes on rapidly through Philadelphia and Delaware, and in Maryland finds the cause spreading in all directions. He reaches the house of Henry Watters, "whose brother is an exhorter, and now gone with Mr. Williams to Virginia." Young Watters we shall soon meet, and find him sustaining worthily his distinction as the first native Methodist Itinerant of America. Asbury preached at the house of "friend Gatch," another name which was to become conspicuous in the early history of the Church. We trace him further to the home of Richard Owen, the first native Local Preacher, "where the Lord enabled" him "to preach with much feeling to a great number of people;" and to the Sam's Creek "Log Meeting-house" of Strawbridge. He entered Baltimore and preached there, but was soon away again, hastening from town to town. At last he "came to his Quarterly Conference at J. Presbury's, in Christmas week, 1772." There had been no Annual Conference yet in America, and this was the first Quarterly Conference of which we have any account. Asbury says, "Many people attended, and several friends came miles." By this time ten or twelve native Local Preachers and Exhorters had been licensed in Maryland, such as Richard Owen, William Watters, Richard Webster, Nathan Perigau, Isaac Rollins, Hezekiah Bonham, Nicholas Watters, Sater Stephenson, J. Presbury, Philip Gatch, and, probably, Aquila Standford and Abraham Rollins.

Asbury began the new year, 1773, at Baltimore, as his head-quarters. A local authority says: "The happiest event which could have occurred to Methodism in Baltimore, as well as to the cause of religion generally, was the arrival of Asbury in the fall of 1772, when he preached for the first time, in the morning at the Point, and in town at three o'clock in the afternoon and at six o'clock in the evening. Down to this period there had been no disposition shown, on the part of the people, to open their houses for Methodist preaching, or to extend to the Preachers those hospitalities which are now so characteristic of the city. But it was far otherwise in 1772: the good seed which had been sown by Strawbridge, Williams, and others, in the surrounding country, had been productive; while that scattered by King, Pilmoor, and Boardman was beginning to spring up in Baltimore, so that Asbury found a people prepared to his hands. A sail-loft, at the corner of Mills and Block streets, was provided free of charge, and was soon filled to overflowing, many coming from the country a distance of six miles before some of the people of the town had risen from their beds. Something like a permanent arrangement being made for perpetuating Methodism in Baltimore, Asbury set about in good earnest to regulate the Societies by *settling*, as he says, the classes, and thereby giving to Methodism that form and consistency which it had in England; and no man knew better how to do this than he did. On the 3d of January, 1773, he says, after meeting the Society, 'I settled a class of men,' and on the following evening, after preaching with comfort, 'I formed a class of women.' The formation of these two classes, and the addition of others soon after, together with the difficulty of finding room for those who were willing to hear the word of God preached, made it necessary to provide other than mere private accommodation; and, accordingly, in November following, Asbury, assisted by Jesse Hollingsworth, George Wells, Richard Moale, George Robinson, and John Woodward, purchased the lot, sixty feet on Strawberry Alley and seventy-five feet on Fleet-street, for a house of worship, where the church now stands—the only *original edifice* of the kind, of our religious denomination, in Baltimore. The following year William Moore and Philip Rogers took up two lots, and erected a church in Lovely Lane; Moore collecting £100 to assist in paying for it. Which of these two churches was first finished is not quite certain; tradition says the latter. The one in Strawberry Alley was commenced in November, 1773; that in Lovely Lane the 18th of April, 1774. Captain Webb, in writing to Asbury, then in New York, said that the church in Lovely Lane was so far finished by the middle of October that he preached in it."

The first Methodist chapel in Baltimore, that of Strawberry Alley, was on Fell's Point, where an hospitable Irishman, Captain Patten, had been the first citizen to open his house for the preaching of Asbury; thereby adding another instance to the extraordinary services of his countrymen in the early history of the denomination. It was built of brick, forty-one feet and six inches in length and thirty feet in width. The pulpit was in the old style, tub fashion, and very high; while over the Preacher's head hung, suspended by a cord, the inevitable sounding-board. Back of the pulpit there was a semicircle of blue ground, on which was emblazoned in large gilt letters the motto, "Thou, God, seest me." In 1801, when the Milk-street Church was built, the Strawberry Alley Church was given to the colored people for their exclusive use and benefit.

Such was the beginning of that series of Methodist chapels in Baltimore which has since increased so rapidly, that, in our day, they are more than double the number of those of any other communion, Protestant or Papal, in the city, and nearly a third of all its churches, though it has a larger supply of such edifices, in proportion to its population, than any other city on the continent.

Asbury's circuit, projecting from Baltimore, extended about two hundred miles; he traveled over it every three weeks. It comprised about twenty-four appointments; he moved among them continually, assisted by King, Strawbridge, Owen, and other preachers and exhorters.

Meanwhile Captain Webb had gone to England to appeal again to Wesley for help, and was now returning on the ocean with his recruits. Wesley wrote, in 1772, to a friend in Ireland, "Captain Webb is now in Dublin: he is a man of fire, and the power of God constantly attends his word." He was the right man to appeal to British Methodism for America, for he could tell his own story about it, and his military ardor gave a singular inspiration to his words. He went to the Conference, which began on August 4, 1772, at Leeds, and he there addressed the preachers with an eloquence that kindled the assembly into enthusiasm. George Shadford heard him, and says, "When he warmly exhorted preachers to go to America I felt my spirit stirred within me to go; more especially when I understood that many hundreds of precious souls were perishing through lack of knowledge, scattered up and down in various parts of the country, and had none to warn them of their danger. Mr. Rankin and I offered ourselves to go the spring following."

Thomas Rankin was one of the commanding men of the Wesleyan ministry. Wesley appointed him at once General Assistant or Superintendent of the American Societies, for he was not only Asbury's senior in the itinerancy, but was an experienced disciplinarian. Asbury had probably asked to be relieved by such a successor, and welcomed him with sincere gratification. He was a clear-headed and honest-hearted Scotchman; trained in his infancy to strict religious habits. "I bless God," he says, "that I was mercifully preserved from open wickedness. I do not know that ever I swore an oath in my life." Whitefield, flying over the realm, came across his path at Edinburgh. "I heard him," writes Rankin, "with wonder and surprise, and had such a discovery of the plan of salvation as I had never known before. I remembered more of that sermon than of all the sermons I ever had heard. From this time I was truly convinced of the necessity of a change of heart. I began to wrestle with God in an agony of prayer. I called out, 'Lord, I have wrestled long, and have not yet prevailed: O let me now prevail!' The whole passage of Jacob's wrestling with the angel came into my mind; and I called out aloud, 'I will not let thee go unless thou bless me!' In a moment the cloud burst, and tears of love flowed from my eyes, when these words were applied to my soul many times over, 'And he blessed him there.' They came with the Holy Ghost, and with much assurance; and my whole soul was overwhelmed in the presence of God. I could declare that the Son of man still had power on earth to forgive sins, and that he had pardoned my sins, even mine.'" It was not long before he was laboring as a local preacher. Wesley called him into the itinerancy in 1761.

George Shadford, like Rankin, had a somewhat strict early religious training, but was ebullient with the spirits of healthful childhood, and having a conscience more tender but less strong than that of Rankin, he was continually indulging in pranks of childish mischief, and as continually repenting of them as guilty and perilous to his soul. "When I was very young," he says, "I was uncommonly afraid of death. As I grew up I was very prone to speak bad words, and often to perform wicked actions; to break the Sabbath, and, being fond of play, took every opportunity on Sunday to steal away from my father. At fourteen years of age my parents sent me to the bishop to be confirmed, and at sixteen they desired me to prepare to receive the blessed sacrament. For about a month before it I retired from all vain company, prayed, and read alone, while the Spirit of God sent home what I read to my heart. I wept much in secret, was ashamed of my past life, and thought I would never spend my time on Sundays as I had done. But I had not a single companion that feared God. Nay, I believe at that time the whole town was covered with darkness, and sat in the shadow of death. I gave way to Satan, and, by little and little, lost all my good desires and resolutions, and soon became weak as in times past. I was fond of wrestling, running, leaping, football, dancing, and such like sports; and I gloried in them because I could excel most in the town and parish. At the age of twenty I was so active that I seemed a compound of life and fire, and had such a flow of animal spirits that I was never in my element but when employed in such kind of sports." He turned soldier, and was tossed about the country in the army, tempted by the vices of his comrades, but escaping most of them, and repenting with tears when overcome. At Gainsborough he went with a sergeant to hear a Methodist preach in a hall. He was exceedingly entertained and surprised at the services, and deeply smitten in his conscience by the discourse. "In Kent," he says, "the Lord arrested me again with strong convictions, so that I was obliged to leave my comrades at noonday, and, running up into my chamber, I threw myself upon my knees and wept bitterly. I thought, 'sin, cursed sin, will be my ruin!' I was ready to tear the hair from my head, thinking I must perish at last, and that my sins would sink me lower than the grave." "Wherever I traveled I found the Methodists were spoken against by wicked and ungodly persons of every denomination; but the more I looked into the Bible the more I was convinced that they were the people of God."

On his release from the militia service he returned home, musing much about this "sect everywhere spoken against." A Methodist farmer moved into the neighborhood, and opened his house for preaching. Shadford could not stay away. "I was now determined," he says, "to seek God, and therefore I went constantly to church and sacrament, and to hear the Methodist preachers, to pray, and read the Scriptures. I thought, 'I will be good. I am determined to be good.'" At last, while hearing an Itinerant in the cottage, "I cried out," he says, "being pierced to the heart with the sword of the Spirit, 'God be merciful to me a sinner.' No sooner had I expressed these words, but by the eye of faith (not with my bodily eyes) I saw Christ my Advocate, at the right hand of God, making intercession for me. I believed he loved me, and gave himself for me. In an instant the Lord filled my soul with divine love, as quick as lightning. Immediately my eyes flowed with tears, and my heart with love. I sat down in a chair, for I could stand no longer, and these words ran through my mind twenty times over: 'Marvelous are thy works, and that my soul knoweth right well.' I lay down at night in peace with a thankful heart, because the Lord hath redeemed me, and given me peace with God and all mankind." Thus had George Shadford become a Methodist; four of his family were converted in less than a year, and the little Society of the town grew vigorous by his humble labors. He became a Local Preacher. Wesley met him, summoned him into the itinerant field, and sending him to America in 1772, wrote to him, "I let you loose, George, on the great continent. Publish your message in the open face of the sun, and do all the good you can. I am, dear George, yours affectionately." Captain Webb and his wife were on the deck, and had made all necessary provisions for the little band. On Good Friday, April 9, 1773, accompanied by Joseph Yearbry (another preacher) and other passengers, they set sail. On the 1st of June they came to anchor in the

Delaware, "opposite Chester, about sixteen miles south of Philadelphia," after a passage of seven and a half weeks. On the 3d they were cordially received by Asbury and the Methodists of the city; "and now," wrote Rankin, "as I am by the providence of God called to labor for a season on this continent, do thou, O Holy One of Israel, stand by thy weak and ignorant servant! Show thyself glorious in power and in divine majesty. Let thine arm be made bare, and stretched out to save, so that wonders and signs may be done in the name of thy holy child Jesus." Asbury had been anxiously expecting them; "they have arrived," he writes, "to my great comfort." Rankin preached that night on an appropriate text, "I have set before thee an open door, and no man can shut it." On Saturday, 12th, accompanied by Asbury, he reached New York city, and was met by many Methodists on the dock where they landed. Rankin had thus successfully begun his career in the new world. Captain Webb passed up the Hudson, and Asbury went forth over his old New York circuit exclaiming "Glory to God! he blesses me with the graces and comforts of his Spirit in my soul!" Shadford had hastened from Philadelphia to New Jersey. By the middle of July the scattered itinerants were gathering at Philadelphia; an important event was about to occur there—the first American Methodist Conference.

CHAPTER VII.

FIRST CONFERENCE — RETURN OF ENGLISH PREACHERS.

THE first American Methodist Conference began its session in Philadelphia on Wednesday, the 14th, and closed on Friday, the 16th of July, 1773. Rankin says, "There were present seven Preachers, besides Boardman and Pilmoor who were to return to England." Asbury, detained on his New York Circuit, did not appear till the second day of the session; he was the tenth member, making the number the same as at Wesley's first Conference in England, held twenty-nine years before. The members were all Europeans; they were Thomas Rankin, Richard Boardman, Joseph Pilmoor, Francis Asbury, Richard Wright, George Shadford, Thomas Webb, John King, Abraham Whitworth, and Joseph Yearbry.

The first reports of members in Society were made to this Conference: there were 180 in New York, 180 in Philadelphia, 200 in New Jersey, 500 in Maryland, 100 in Virginia; nearly half were therefore in Maryland, the most fruitful soil that the denomination has found in the country. The aggregate returns were 1,160. These, however, were only its members of classes; there were many more adherents who considered themselves members of its Societies. The preachers had formed Societies without classes; the exact discipline of English Methodism had not, in fact, been yet fully introduced into America. Asbury labored hard to conform the American Societies to Wesley's model, but had met with no little resistance from both the preachers and laymen; Rankin had been sent out for this purpose, and to these two thorough disciplinarians we owe the effective organization of the incipient Methodism of the New World.

The proceedings of the session had direct reference to the establishment of the genuine Wesleyan Discipline as the only guarantee of Methodism in the country. The published report of these proceedings forms but one page of those annual "Minutes," which have swollen, by our day, into a dozen stout octavo volumes. It consists of the following questions, answers, and appointments, besides the returns of members already cited.

"1. Ought not the authority of Mr. Wesley and that Conference to extend to the Preachers and people in America as well as in Great Britain and Ireland? Yes.

"2. Ought not the doctrine and Discipline of the Methodists, as contained in the Minutes, to be the sole rule of our conduct, who labor in the Connection with Mr. Wesley in America? Yes.

"3. If so, does it not follow that if any Preachers deviate from the Minutes we can have no fellowship with them till they change their conduct? Yes.

"The following rules were agreed to:

"1. Every Preacher who acts in connection with Mr. Wesley and the brethren who labor in America is strictly to avoid administering the ordinances of baptism and the Lord's supper.

"2. All the people among whom we labor to be earnestly exhorted to attend the Church, and to receive the ordinances there; but in a particular manner to press the people in Maryland and Virginia to the observance of this minute.

"3. No person or persons to be admitted into our love-feasts oftener than twice or thrice, unless they become members; and none to be admitted to the Society meetings more than thrice.

"4. None of the Preachers in America to reprint any of Mr. Wesley's books without his authority (when it can be gotten) and the consent of their brethren.

"5. Robert Williams to sell the books he has already printed, but to print no more unless under the above restrictions.

"6. Every Preacher who acts as an assistant, to send an account of the work once in six months to the general assistant."

Wesley, being thoroughly loyal to the Established Church of England, had trained his people to humble submission to its arrogant policy toward them; Rankin enforced a like submission in this country, as the English Church was still recognized here in some of the colonies, particularly in Maryland and Virginia, where it was established by law; hence the rules numbered first and second. But the Revolution was already looming over the country. The English clergy were deserting it; and many that remained were of very questionable moral character. A great proportion of the colonists had no traditional attachment to the Anglican Church; the submissive policy of Wesley in England was therefore irrelevant in America. He was too distant to perceive the fact, and his representatives were too Anglican to recognize it; but many of the American Methodists, and some of their Preachers, were wiser. They insisted upon their right to the sacraments from their own Pastors. Theoretically none of us, now, can dispute their claim; practically Wesley himself conceded it, after the additional and decisive argument of the Revolution, by constituting them an independent Church, with full powers to consecrate the sacraments. The men who then seemed radical, in this respect, were so simply because they had a superior foresight of the predestined importance and needs of American Methodism. Robert Strawbridge contended sturdily for the right of the people to the sacraments, and could not be deterred by Asbury or Rankin from administering them. He had founded the Church in the regions whence now nearly one half of its members were reported; he had administered to them the sacraments before any English itinerants appeared in the country; and being an Irishman, he shared not in the deferential sympathies of his English brethren for the Establishment: as for any other sentiments, the actual character of the representatives of the Establishment, clerical and lay, around him, could claim none from him but pity or contempt. Its clergy were known chiefly as the heartiest card-players, horse-racers, and drinkers of the middle colonies. Strawbridge was doubtless imprudent in the Irish resolution with which he resisted the policy of the English itinerants; for the intuitive foresight with which he anticipated the necessity of the independent administration of the sacraments, should have suggested to him the certainty of their concession in due time, and therefore the expediency of patient harmony in the infant Church till that time should come. Discord was extremely perilous at this early stage of the denomination. He was firm, however; and though the first "rule" adopted by this Conference seems absolute, yet we learn from Asbury that it was adopted with the understanding that "no preacher in our connection shall be permitted to administer the ordinances at this time except Mr. Strawbridge, and he under the particular direction of the assistant." A concession so singular shows the extraordinary consideration in which Strawbridge was held, the influence he had obtained over the Societies of Maryland and Virginia, perhaps also the conscious necessity of the independent administration of the sacraments in that chief field of the denomination. As we shall hereafter see, this just claim of American Methodism could not be effectually refused; it led to increasing contention, and at last, providentially, gave birth to the organization of the "Methodist Episcopal Church in the United States of America."

"We parted in love," writes Rankin. The first differences of opinion noticed by Asbury seem to have yielded to a unanimous sense of the importance of harmony.

The appointments for the ensuing ecclesiastical year were: New York, Thomas Rankin, and Philadelphia, George Shadford, to exchange in four months; New Jersey, John King, William Watters; Baltimore, Francis Asbury, Robert Strawbridge, Abraham Whitworth, Joseph Yearbry; Norfolk, Richard Wright; Petersburg, Robert Williams.

Boardman and Pilmoor do not appear in this list, though they continued in the country nearly six months. They had labored in it about four years. When they saw the terrible certainty of war they quietly retired, embarking together for England on Sunday, the 2d of January, 1774, "after commending the Americans to God." They left 2,073 members in the Societies, 10 regularly organized circuits, and 17 preachers. Though no minute accounts of the labors of these first Methodist itinerants, in America, remain, and we are left to the mere allusions of contemporary records for an estimate of their services, these scattered notices suffice to show that, in co-operation with their assistants, they laid substantially and broadly the foundations of the denomination, preaching from Boston to Savannah, and preparing, effectively, during more than four years, the work which their successors were to prosecute with a success which has had no parallel since the Apostolic Age.

Richard Wright also returned to Europe in the early part of 1774. Captain Webb lingered in the Colonies a year or more, after the departure of Boardman and Pilmoor, laboring with his might to extend and fortify the young Societies, notwithstanding the increasing tumults of politics and war. But the contemporary records give us, further, only allusions to this noble man and devoted evangelist. We may here, therefore, properly take our final leave of him. He devoted at least nine years to the promotion of American Methodism, the periods of his absence in Europe being spent there in its behalf. On his return to England he secured a home for his family in Portland, on the heights of Bristol, but still traveled, and preached extensively in chapels, in market-places, and in the open air, attended by immense congregations. An English preacher writes: "Wednesday, December 1st., 1796. Last night, about eleven o'clock, Captain Webb suddenly entered into the joy of his Lord. He partook of his supper, and retired to rest about ten o'clock in his usual health. In less than an hour his spirit left the tenement of clay to enter the realms of eternal bliss. He professed to have had some presentiment that he should change worlds during the present year, and that his departure would be sudden." The venerable soldier and evangelist was laid to rest in a vault under the altar of Portland Chapel, Bristol, by "a crowded, weeping audience." The "Society showed him great respect; the chapel was hung in mourning;" and the trustees erected a marble monument to his memory within its walls, pronouncing him "Brave, Active, Courageous,—Faithful, Zealous, Successful,—the principal instrument in erecting this chapel." His name will be forever illustrious in the ecclesiastical history of the New World.

CHAPTER VIII.

NATIVE EVANGELISTS.

WHILE some of the laborers were retiring from the field, others were entering it—more important, because native evangelists. William Watters's name appears in the list of appointments made at the first American conference, and to him is now universally conceded the peculiar distinction of being the first native American itinerant of Methodism; an honor never to be shared, never impaired. He was born in Baltimore county, Maryland, on the 16th of October, 1751. When sixteen or seventeen years of age he was considered by his associates "a very good Christian," but he thought of himself quite otherwise. Strawbridge, King, and Williams were abroad around him, preaching in private houses, and in 1770 he had frequent opportunities of hearing them. "I could not conceive," he writes, "what they meant by saying we must be born again; and, though I thought but little of all I heard for some time, yet I dared not despise and revile them, as many then did. It was daily my prayer that God would teach me the way of life and salvation, and not suffer me to be deceived. After being uncommonly uneasy for several days concerning the state of my soul, I went with my eldest brother and family to a Methodist prayer-meeting in his neighborhood on a Sabbath day; and while one was at prayer I saw a man near me, whom I knew to be a poor sinner, trembling, weeping, and praying, as though his all depended on the present moment; his soul and body were in an agony. I went home much distressed, and fully determined, by the grace of God, to seek the salvation of my soul with my whole heart. Yet I could not shed one tear, neither could I find words to express my wretchedness before my merciful High Priest; I could only bemoan my forlorn state, and I wandered about through the afternoon in solitary places, seeking rest but finding none." That night, however, in another prayer-meeting, both his heart and eyes melted. The next day he was unfit for any business: he spent it in retirement. "I refused to be comforted," he says, "but by the Friend of sinners." For three days and nights eating, drinking, and sleeping in a measure fled from me, while my flesh wasted away and my strength failed. Having returned in the afternoon from the woods to my chamber, my eldest brother, (at whose house I was,) knowing my distress, entered my room with all the sympathy of a brother and a Christian. To my great astonishment he informed me that God had that day blessed him with his pardoning love. After giving me all the advice in his power, he kneeled down with me, and with a low, soft voice (which was frequently interrupted by tears) he offered up a fervent prayer to God for my present salvation." Young Watters received "a gleam of hope," but was not content with it. The next day several "praying persons," who knew his distress, visited him. He requested them to pray with him, and the family was called in, though it was about the middle of the day. "While they all joined in singing, my face," he says, "was turned to the wall, with my eyes lifted upward in a flood of tears, and I felt a lively hope that the Lord, whom I sought, would suddenly come to his temple. My good friends sung with the spirit and in faith. The Lord heard and appeared spiritually in the midst of us. A divine light beamed through my inmost soul, and in a few minutes encircled me round, surpassing the brightness of the noonday sun. My burden was gone, my sorrow fled, all that was within me rejoiced in hope of the glory of God; while I beheld such fullness and willingness in the Lord Jesus to save lost sinners, and my soul so rested in him, that I could now, for the first time, call Jesus Christ 'Lord, by the Holy Ghost given unto me.' The hymn being concluded, we all fell upon our knees, but my prayers were all turned into praises."

Such was the spiritual birth of the first regular Methodist preacher of the New World. This "memorable change," he says, took place in May, 1771, in the twentieth year of his age.

He immediately joined a Methodist class. All Methodists were, in those days, laborers in the evangelical vineyard. On the Lord's day, he says, they commonly divided into little bands and went out into different neighborhoods, wherever there was a door open to receive them, two, three, or four in company, and would sing their hymns, pray, read, talk to the people, "and some soon began to add a word of exhortation." "We were weak, but we lived in a dark day, and the Lord greatly owned our labors. It was astonishing to see how rapidly the work extended all around us, bearing down opposition as chaff before the wind. Many will praise God forever for our prayer-meetings." Two of his brothers were converted through his instrumentality; one of them becoming a zealous Local Preacher, and later, a Traveling Preacher.

In 1772, when he was twenty-one years old, William Watters began to preach. Robert Williams perceived his capacity for usefulness, and took him, in the autumn, to Norfolk, Va. The scene of his departure for an itinerant life was deeply affecting. His mother, whom he loved tenderly, offered him all her possessions if he would abandon his purpose. Many of his friends "wept and hung around" him; "but," he adds, "I found such resignation and so clear a conviction that my way was of the Lord, that I was enabled to commit them and myself to the care of our heavenly Father, in humble confidence, that if we never met again in this vale of tears, we should soon meet where the wicked cease from troubling and the weary are at rest." And now he began in earnest his itinerant career. The two evangelists journeyed and preached, almost daily, through Baltimore, Georgetown, and other places, and arrived at last in Norfolk, where, under many discouragements, Watters soon formed a circuit, extending some distance among the neighboring towns. He was seized with the measles, but continued his labors. Pilmoor had been preaching in Norfolk; he was now released by Watters to pursue his southern tour to Charleston. Williams also left the young itinerant and hastened to Portsmouth and further; Jarratt and M'Roberts, "two English clergymen," received him with open arms, and welcomed him to their parishes. Jarratt became a staunch friend to the Methodist itinerants and the confidential friend of Asbury: his name often occurs in the early Methodist publications. His zealous labors produced a wide-spread sensation. "Revivals" prevailed around him for fifty or sixty miles during about twelve years. He held frequent meetings, and, like the Methodists, formed numerous societies. He gratefully acknowledges that in the counties of Sussex and Brunswick "the work, from the year 1773, was chiefly carried on by the labors of the people called Methodists." He that year received Williams to his house and his church. "Many," he says, "in these parts who had long neglected the means of grace now flocked to hear not only me and the traveling preachers, but also the exhorters and leaders. And at their meetings for prayer some have been in such distress that they have continued therein for five or six hours. It has been found that these prayer-meetings were singularly useful in promoting the work of God. The outpouring of the Spirit which began here soon extended itself, more or less, through most of the circuit, which is regularly attended by the traveling preachers, and which takes in a circumference of between four and five hundred miles. Many were savingly converted to God, and in a very short time not only in my parish, but through several parts of Brunswick, Sussex, Prince George, Lunenburg, Mecklenburg, and Amelia Counties." Williams formed, in 1774, the old Brunswick Circuit, extending from Petersburg into North Carolina, the first reported in Virginia. Jarratt requested that his parish might be included in this circuit, that "all who chose it might have the privilege of meeting in Class and of being members of the Society."

This good work, the result as much of the catholic coöperation of the rector as of the labors of the itinerants, continued down to 1775, when Shadford had charge of the circuit. He reported no less than "two thousand six hundred and sixty-four persons in the Societies, to whom eighteen hundred were added in one year. The revival spread through fourteen counties in Virginia, and through Bute and Halifax Counties in North Carolina."

In the absence of Williams, on his visit to Jarratt, Watters was prostrated with nervous fever, and for some time he seemed suspended between life and death. He returned to his home after an absence of eleven months, in which he had been thoroughly initiated into the hardships and triumphs of the itinerancy. He met Asbury for the first time, and journeyed on horseback with him some miles; Rankin also came across his path, and he saw in these apostolic men the highest models of ministerial character.

After the Conference of 1773, he went to Kent, on the Eastern Shore of Maryland. "In this circuit, which," he says, "was a two weeks' one, and the only one then between the two bays, I continued four or five months, with greater freedom and success in preaching than ever before."

The Eastern Shore was thenceforth to be a "fruitful garden of Methodism." At the next Conference "Kent" was reported in the Minutes as a circuit, the first formed on the Peninsula, and in the same year its first church, "Kent Meeting-house," was erected. The chapel rose amid hostility; the timbers prepared for it were carried away at night and burned; but the Society persisted, and at last entered, with prayer and praise, their humble temple. It has since been known as "Hinson's Chapel." On retiring from the Eastern Shore, Watters labored, till the next Conference, in Baltimore and its vicinity.

Another native preacher, destined to become noted in the Church, entered the itinerancy in 1773, though his name, Philip Gatch, does not appear in the Minutes till the next Conference. He was born near Georgetown, Md., in the same year as Watters, 1751; they began their public labors as Exhorters the same year, and they were the first two native Methodist preachers reported in the "Minutes." They were remarkably similar also in character, being early and deeply susceptible of religious impressions, a fact that, perhaps, more than any other, is the pledge of an upright life, of conscientious decision of character, and of distinguished usefulness. "Indeed," he writes, "from a child, the Spirit of grace strove with me; but great was the labor of mind that I felt, and I did not know the way to be saved from my guilt and wretchedness. It pleased God, however, to send the Gospel into our neighborhood, in January, 1772, through the instrumentality of the Methodists. Previous to this time Robert Strawbridge had settled between Baltimore and Fredericktown, and under his ministry three others were raised up, Richard Owen, Sater Stephenson, and Nathan Perigau. Nathan Perigau was the first to introduce Methodist preaching in the neighborhood where I lived. He possessed great zeal, and was strong in the faith of the Gospel. I was near him when he opened the exercises of the first meeting I attended. His prayer alarmed me much; I never had witnessed such energy nor heard such expressions in prayer before. I was afraid that God would send some judgment upon the congregation for my being at such a place. I attempted to make my escape. I was met by a person at the door who proposed to leave with me; but I knew he was wicked, and that it would not do to follow his counsel, so I returned. The sermon was accompanied to my understanding by the Holy Spirit. I was stripped of all my self-righteousness. Three weeks from this time I attended preaching again at the same place. My distress became very great; my relatives were all against me, and it was hard to endure my father's opposition."

The early Methodists were singularly exact in the matter of conversion, and the contemporary memoirs abound in grateful commemorations of dates in their spiritual history. Philip Gatch records that "on the 26th of April I attended a prayer-meeting. After remaining some time, I gave up all hopes, and left the house. I felt that I was too bad to remain where the people were worshiping God. At length a friend came out to me, and requested me to return to the meeting; believing him to be a good man I returned with him, and, under the deepest exercise of mind, bowed myself before the Lord, and said in my heart, If thou wilt give me power to call on thy name how thankful will I be! Immediately I felt the power of God to affect me, body and soul. I felt like crying aloud. God said, by his Spirit, to my soul, 'My power is present to heal thy soul, if thou wilt but believe.' I instantly submitted to the operation of the Spirit of God, and my poor soul was set at liberty. I felt as if I had got into a new world.

I was certainly brought from hell's dark door, and made nigh unto God by the blood of Jesus. I was the first person known to shout in that part of the country. A grateful sense of the mercy and goodness of God to my poor soul overwhelmed me."

His father had threatened to drive him from his home, and the young convert now expected a harsh reception. "There is your elder brother," the father had said to him in his deep contrition, "he has better learning than you: if there is anything good in it why does he not find it out?" But this elder brother was "powerfully converted" at the same meeting with young Gatch, and the father was now disarmed of his opposition. The brothers introduced family prayers immediately into the household, and Philip Gatch's first exhortation was at the altar of his home. "The Lord blessed me," he says, "with a spirit of prayer, and he made manifest his power among us. I rose from my knees and spoke to them some time, and it had a gracious effect upon the family. Thenceforward we attended to family prayer." They soon had Perigau preaching in the house. Classes were formed; Gatch's parents, most of their children, a brother-in-law and two sisters-in-law, were, in a few weeks, recorded among the class-members. "The work was great, for it was the work of God."

In the latter part of 1772 Philip Gatch was abroad, a zealous Exhorter; he had formed "a humble circuit" of three appointments beyond the Pennsylvania line. In the following year he preached his first sermon at "Evans's Meeting-house, the oldest Society of Baltimore county." At a Quarterly Meeting in that county Rankin met him, and, commissioning him as a traveling preacher, sent him off to "the Jerseys." The humble but successful John King, first Methodist preacher in Baltimore, had been designated to New Jersey. He now met Gatch to introduce him to his new field and his untried life. John King was prompt and energetic, pausing not for ceremonious attentions. "In company with Mr. King," says Gatch, "I crossed the Delaware. He preached and held a love-feast. On the following morning he pursued his journey, leaving me a stranger in a strange land." King was immediately away to distant regions, and Gatch was now alone in the whole state, as a ministerial representative of Methodism, a stripling of twenty-one years, of small stature and very youthful appearance, the first preacher sent as a regular itinerant to New Jersey. "The Lord was with me," he says, "and my labors on the circuit were crowned with some success. Fifty-two united with the Church, most of whom professed religion. Benjamin Abbott's wife and three of her children were among the number. David, one of the children, became a useful preacher." He continued in this extensive field till the Annual Conference of 1774.

About the year 1773 another notable evangelist appeared in New Jersey, who, though he was not yet recorded in the Minutes, equaled his itinerant brethren in labors if not in travels. The name of Benjamin Abbott is in our day inscribed on a monument under the shadow of a Methodist Church in Salem, N. J., one of the principal scenes of his usefulness; thousands of Methodists have visited it in devout pilgrimage, and thousands will as long as the denomination lasts, pondering the wonders of his strangely eventful life. He was thoroughly original, unique in mind and character: religious biography hardly records his fellow except in the story of the "evangelical tinker" and "glorious dreamer" of Bedford jail. Like Bunyan, he had a rude, robust, but holy soul, profound in the mysteries of spiritual life; a temperament deeply mystic, and subject to marvelous experiences which baffle all scientific explanation, unless we resort to the doubtful solutions of clairvoyance and somnambulism. He was a great dreamer, and his "visions of the night," recorded with unquestionable honesty, were often verified by the most astonishing coincidences. He was an evangelical Hercules, and wielded the word as a rude irresistible club rather than a sword. His whole soul seemed pervaded by a certain magnetic power that thrilled his discourses and radiated from his person, drawing, melting, and frequently prostrating the stoutest opposers in his congregation. It is probable that no Methodist laborer of his day reclaimed more men from abject vice. He seldom preached without visible results, and his prayers were overwhelming.

Like Bunyan, his early life had been riotously wicked. He first appears as an apprentice in Philadelphia, "where," he says, "I soon fell into bad company, and from that to card-playing, cock-fighting, and many other evil practices. My master and I parted before my time was out, and I went into Jersey, and hired with one of my brothers, where I wrought at plantation work. Some time after this I married. All this time I had no fear of God before my eyes, but lived in sin and open rebellion against him, in drinking, fighting, swearing, gambling, etc.; yet I worked hard and got a comfortable living for my family. Thus I continued in a scene of sin until the fortieth year of my age; yet many were the promises I made, during that period, to amend my life, but all to no purpose; they were as often broken as made. A Methodist preacher came to preach in our neighborhood, and I went to hear him. It being a new thing in the place many came together to hear him. The word reached my heart in such a manner that it shook every joint in my body; tears flowed in abundance, and I cried out for mercy, of which the people took notice, and many were melted into tears." And now, as with Bunyan, ensued a struggle with despair itself; "Satan suggested to me that my day of grace was over; therefore I might pray and cry, but he was sure of me at last." In passing through a lonely wood at night he was tempted to commit suicide; but, while looking for a suitable place for the deed, he was deterred by an inward voice, which said, "This torment is nothing compared to hell." This was logic too clear to be resisted; he forthwith mounted his wagon, and believing the tempter to be immediately behind him, drove home "under the greatest anxiety imaginable," with his hair "rising on his head." His mind had evidently become morbid under its moral sufferings. Hastening the next day to a Methodist meeting, "I went in," he writes, "sat down, and took my little son upon my knee; the preacher began soon after. His word was attended with such power that it ran through me from head to foot; I shook and trembled like Belshazzar, and felt that I should cry out if I did not leave the house, which I determined to do, that I might not expose myself among the people; but when I attempted to put my little son down and rise to go, I found that my strength had failed me; I was utterly unable to rise. Immediately I cried aloud, *Save, Lord, or I perish!* That evening I set up family prayer, it being the first time I ever had attempted to pray in my family."

Thus did this rough but earnest soul struggle as in "the hour and power of darkness." The next day, accompanied by his sympathetic wife, he went more than ten miles to a Methodist assembly. That night (the 11th of October, 1772, for he is minute in such memorable dates) he awoke from terrible dreams, and saw, as in a vision of faith, the Lord Jesus, with extended arms, saying, "I died for you." He wept and adored God with a joyful heart. "At that moment," he says, "the Scriptures were wonderfully opened to my understanding. My heart felt as light as a bird, being relieved of that load of guilt which before had bowed down my spirits, and my body felt as active as when I was eighteen, so that the outward and inward man were both animated." He rose, and calling up the family, expounded the Scriptures and prayed, and then set off to spend the day in telling his neighbors what God had done for him. Benjamin Abbott had thus placed his feet securely in "the path of life." He had reached it indeed through darkness and terrors, stumbled into it, it may be said, through errors, morbid agitations, if not temporary insanity; but had evidently attained, at last, the fundamental truth of the Reformation and of Christianity, justification by faith; and he now and henceforth, till his last hour, stood out in the light, with unshakable steadfastness, on this rock of divine truth, a saved, a consecrated, a triumphant man. He devoted himself to the study of the Bible, and to "exhort all that" he "had any intercourse with." From "exhorting" he at last began to preach; his first sermon was over the coffin of a neighbor. His word was now uniformly "with power;" the sturdiest sinners trembled, or escaped in alarm from his mongrel assemblies. He was a man of great natural courage, and though there was an unction of habitual tenderness and humility in his manners, often revealing itself in tears, yet woe to the man who dared in his presence to treat religion with ridicule or irreverence. His indignant exhortations overwhelmed and swept before him any such offender. He was an example of what the evangelical historians report of the apostolic ministry: "Now when they saw the boldness of Peter and John, and perceived that they were unlearned and ignorant men, they marveled; and they took knowledge of them, that they had been with Jesus."

A Society was now formed in his neighborhood, he becoming its Class Leader; it was soon included in the circuit, and Methodism was permanently established in that region. Abbott spread it out in all directions. He broke up the ground around him for fifteen miles. He worked for his livelihood on week-days, held prayer and class meetings at night, and preached on Sundays. No itinerant in New Jersey did more to found securely the denomination in the State. He was its first Methodist convert that preached the Gospel. Asbury said, "He is a man of uncommon zeal, and of good utterance; his words come with great power."

Still another native preacher began his labors in 1773, though his name was not recorded in the list of Conference appointments till the following year. Daniel Ruff was converted in Harford County, Maryland, in the great religious excitement which prevailed in that and in Baltimore counties during 1771. The next year his house, near Havre de Grace, became a "preaching-place" for the itinerants, and the year following Ruff himself became noted as an Exhorter and Local Preacher, warning his neighbors to "flee from the wrath to come, and bringing many of them to the Saviour." He was a man of sterling integrity, great simplicity, and remarkable usefulness. Asbury, visiting his neighborhood, March 4, 1774, rejoiced over his success, and preached on the appropriate text, "The Lord hath done great things for us, whereof we are glad." "Honest, simple Daniel Ruff," he wrote, "has been made a great blessing to these people. Such is the wisdom and power of God that he has wrought marvelously by this plain man that no flesh may glory in his presence." Joining the Conference in 1774, Ruff traveled Chester Circuit, which then comprised all the Methodist appointments in the State of Delaware and in Chester County, Pa. He labored also in New Jersey. Freeborn Garrettson, one of the most successful preachers of Methodism, was converted after hearing one of his sermons, and Ruff first called him into the itinerancy. Ruff was the first native preacher appointed to Wesley Chapel in New York.

Such were the principal native evangelists who began to appear in the field about the time of the first American Conference.

CHAPTER IX.

PRINCIPAL EVANGELISTS, 1773-1784.

Of the labors of the principal evangelists during the ecclesiastical year following the Conference of 1773 we have but scanty intimations; enough, however, to show that they resumed their work with a strong consciousness that it had now become an established fact in the religious history of the country; that, being organized and put under the rigorous military discipline of Wesley, it was destined to deepen and widen, and assume the same importance which Methodism had acquired in the parent land. They went forth therefore to their circuits with the increased zeal, not to say enthusiasm, which such confidence was suited to inspire; "with a full resolution," wrote Rankin, "to spread genuine Methodism in public and in private with all our might."

Rankin and Shadford were appointed, as we have seen, respectively to Philadelphia and New York, but were to exchange during the year. Rankin's spirit glowed with renewed ardor as he closed the Conference. "For some days past," he wrote, "I have felt the Redeemer's presence in a most sensible manner; I want more life, light, and love; I want to be entirely devoted to God, and to walk before him as Enoch and Abraham did. O how I long to see the work of God break out on the right hand and on the left!" Though superintendent of the whole American field, he gave faithful attention to the local and particular interests of the Societies, "visiting all the classes" while in New York in October. He returned to Philadelphia, and in the latter part of the month set out southward. At the beginning of November he was holding a quarterly meeting at the Watters' homestead. The regions round about poured out their people on the occasion. "Such a season," he says, "I have not seen since I came to America. The Lord made the place of his feet glorious."

"*Wednesday, November* 3. After breakfast we finished our temporal business, and spent some time with the local preachers and stewards. At ten o'clock our general love-feast began. It was now that the heavens were opened and the skies poured down divine righteousness. I had not seen such a season as this since I left my native land."

In March, 1774, we trace Rankin to New York, still exulting in the success of his work. On the 6th he writes: "The congregations were large, and the presence of the Holy One of Israel was in our midst. I observed that the labors of my fellow-laborer, Mr. Shadford, have not been in vain." On May 23d he was on his way to Philadelphia, "to meet the brethren in our second little Conference." His headquarters being alternately in Philadelphia and New York, did not limit him to those cities; he itinerated not only between them, exchanging every four months, but around them on extensive circuits. He adopted fully Asbury's views of the itinerancy, not only enforcing them in his administration as Wesley's "General Assistant," but exemplifying them in his own labors.

Meanwhile Shadford had begun his work for the ecclesiastical year in New York with an ardor equal, if not superior, to that of Rankin. He had a soul of flame, and was singularly effective in his preaching. "A volume might be written," says Wakeley, the chronicler of John-street Chapel, "concerning Mr. Shadford. He had a great harvest of souls in America." Exchanging with Rankin, he went to Philadelphia, where he says, "I had a very comfortable time for four or five months that I spent with a loving, teachable people. The blessing of the Lord was with us of a truth, and many were really converted to God. They had kept prayer-meetings in different parts of the city for some time before I went to it, which had been a great means of begetting life among the people of God as well as others." He preached in the streets and lanes of the city, and left it at the end of the year, with two hundred and twenty-four members in its Society. His first year's labor in America had added nearly two hundred to the Church, "while hundreds had been benefited in various ways under his labors."

With his usual promptness Asbury was in the saddle, on the last day of the Conference of 1773, leaving Philadelphia for his great Baltimore Circuit, and praying, "May the Lord make bare his holy arm, and revive his glorious work!" He continued his travels on this circuit during the ecclesiastical year with no little success, but with much physical disability, suffering most of the time from fever and ague, going to and fro among his twenty-four appointments, and preaching in the intermissions of his disease. His spirit was exalted meanwhile with religious fervor. "The spirit of holy peace reigns in my heart," he writes, "glory be to God!" "My soul longs for all the fullness of God. When shall it once be? When shall my soul be absorbed in purity and love?" "My soul longs and pants for God!" Such are the ever-recurring phrases of his Journals. Occasionally, however, he records deep dejection, the effect of his malady and of the peculiar embarrassments of the incipient condition of the Societies he was almost everywhere forming. Baltimore itself contained about this time five Churches, Roman Catholic, Episcopal or English, Lutheran, and Quaker. The Rev. Mr. Otterbein, of the Lutheran Church, whose name occurs frequently in the early history of Methodism, was settled over a new congregation, partly through the influence of Asbury, early in the following year. Rev. Mr. Swoop, whom Asbury describes as a "good man," was pastor of the Lutheran, and Rev. Mr. Chase of the Episcopal Churches. St. Paul's, in which the latter ministered, was built in 1744, and was the first church in the city. Such was the ecclesiastical *status* of the town of Baltimore at this period. The first Methodist chapel was not yet opened, but was begun. In the last week of November, 1773, Asbury writes: "I have been able to officiate at the town and Point every day, and the congregations rather increase. Lord, make me humble and more abundantly useful; and give me the hearts of the people that I may conduct them to thee! I feel great hopes that the God of mercy will interpose, and do these dear people good. This day we agreed with Mr. L. to undertake the brick-work of our new building at the Point. Many are under some awakenings here, and they are very kind and affectionate to me. My heart is with the Lord. He is my all in all." "The Lord giveth me great patience, and all things richly to enjoy, with many very kind friends, who pay great attention to me in my affliction. Among others, Mr. Swoop, a preacher in high Dutch, came to see me. He appeared to be a good man, and I opened to him the plan of Methodism."

Swoop and Otterbein now became his steadfast friends. In May, 1774, he records that he "had a friendly intercourse with Mr. Otterbein and Mr. Swoop, the German ministers, respecting the plan of Church discipline on which they intended to proceed. They agreed to imitate our method as nearly as possible." A significant allusion is this, foreshadowing a new and important development of Methodism which has continued, with advancing prosperity, to our day, achieving no little usefulness, especially among the German population of the Middle and Western States, and well deserving here an episodical notice at the risk of some delay in our narrative.

Otterbein, under the influence of Asbury, soon became the founder of "The United Brethren in Christ," sometimes called "The German Methodists." His zeal was ardent, and his preaching eloquent. He held special prayer-meetings, a custom unknown in his Church at that day. "God was pleased to call to his help Martin Boehm, George A. Gueting, Christopher Grost, Christian Newcomer, Andrew Zeller, George Pfeimer, John Neidig, Joseph Huffman, Jacob Bowlus, and other holy men. The purity and simplicity with which these reformers preached the Gospel induced many to hear the word, and numbers became the happy subjects of converting grace. Large meetings were appointed in Pennsylvania, Maryland, and Virginia. Their first Conference was held at Baltimore in the year 1789, the following preachers being present: William Otterbein, Martin Boehm, George A. Gueting, Christian Newcomer, Adam Lohman, John Ernst, Henry Weidner."

Asbury and his Methodist coadjutors co-operated harmoniously with these good men. Otterbein assisted Coke in the episcopal consecration of Asbury. The German brethren increased rapidly, numerous Societies were formed, and in 1800 an Annual Conference assembled in Maryland. Otterbein and Boehm were elected Superintendents, or Bishops, of the infant Church. "Otterbein was large, and very commanding in his personal appearance, with a prominent forehead, upon which the seal of the Lord seemed to be plainly impressed. He was a ripe scholar in Latin, Greek, Hebrew, philosophy, and divinity. Bishop Asbury thus spoke of him when preaching the funeral sermon of Martin Boehm: "Pre-eminent among these is William Otterbein. He is one of the best scholars and greatest divines in America, . . . and now his sun of life is setting in brightness. Behold the saint of God leaning upon his staff, waiting for the chariots of Israel.'"

On receiving word of his death Asbury exclaimed, "Great and good man of God! An honor to his Church and country; one of the greatest scholars and divines that ever came to America or was born in it."

Following from the beginning some of the special methods of Methodism, the "United Brethren" have at last grown into a considerable denomination, quite analogous to the Methodist Episcopal Church. "Their sixteenth Annual Conference was held at Mount Pleasant, Westmoreland county, Pa., on the 6th of June, 1815, when they adopted a Discipline which was mainly an abridgment of that of the Methodist Episcopal Church, as will appear from the facts, that they have Quarterly, Annual, and General Conferences, with Bishops, presiding elders, probation, and course of study, the following forming a part of the course: Wesley's Sermons, Watson's Institutes, Fletcher's Appeal and Checks, Powell on Apostolical Succession, Clarke's Theology, etc., etc. The duties of the preacher having charge of the circuit, the questions asked and the instructions given, are Methodistic. In our day the "United Brethren in Christ" report 30 Conferences, nearly 1,300 Preachers, more than 82,000 Communicants, nearly 900 chapels, 357 districts, 208 missions, about 1,300 Sunday-schools with 50,000 scholars, a university named after Otterbein, and a Book Concern, with three periodical publications. Asbury then was doing far-reaching good in Maryland in these early times. Assisted by several local preachers and exhorters, he kept his extensive circuit active with interest, and such was his success that by the end of the year the number of Methodists in his Societies was more than doubled, being 1,063, a gain of 563. At a Quarterly Meeting in February, 1774, the large field was divided into four Circuits, Baltimore, Baltimore Town, Frederick, and Kent; and eight laborers were designated to it. No less than five chapels were built about this time, two of them in Baltimore, one at the Point, and the others in the town proper. The first, on Strawberry Alley, has already been noticed; the second was on Lovely Lane, a small street which ran east and west between Calvert and South streets. The location was a good one at the time, about a square and a half from the present Light-street Church, which sprung from it. In March, 1775, Asbury had the satisfaction of seeing it completed, and on the 21st of May, 1776, the Conference met there, for the first time in Baltimore. Asbury left at least thirty Societies in Maryland. Preachers and Exhorters were rising up numerously among them. The denomination had struck its roots ineradicably into the soil of the state.

Wright had been successfully at work, meanwhile, in Virginia, and on the 9th of May, 1774, on his return, he cheered Asbury with good news. "He gave us a circumstantial account of the work of God in those parts. One house of worship is built, and another in contemplation; two or three more preachers are gone out upon the itinerant plan; and in some parts the congregations consist of two or three thousand people." The first church here mentioned became famous in after years as "Yeargon's Chapel," the first Methodist edifice in Virginia; it was located near the southern line of the State, and was the outpost of the denomination, at this time, for the farther South. The other structure was in Sussex County, the second in the state, well known as "Lane's Chapel."

Williams also traveled in Virginia during this "Conference year," having been appointed to Petersburg Circuit. It extended into North Carolina, and took the title of Brunswick Circuit at the next Conference, a name of renown in the early Methodist annals. He reported from it at the Conference 218 members.

It was about the present period that an important family, converted under Jarratt's ministry, joined the Methodists, on Williams's Circuit, and opened their house as one of his preaching stations. A youthful son of the household was preparing to become one of the chieftains of the new cause, its founder in the New England States, and its first historian. Jesse Lee was converted in 1773, and the next year his name was enrolled among the members of Williams's Societies.

About the same time another young man, in Maryland, was struggling with his awakened conscience, for God was summoning him to eminent services in the Methodistic movement. "The Spirit of the Lord," he says, "at times strove very powerfully with me, and I was frequently afraid that all was not well with me, especially when I was under Methodist preaching. To these people I was drawn." Freeborn Garrettson's mind was thus irresistibly directed to a life of religious self-sacrifice and labor, which have rendered his name forever memorable. In a short time we shall meet him again, as one of the most successful itinerant champions of the Methodistic movement. For more than half a century the record of his life is to be substantially a history of his denomination.

In the Spring of 1774 the dispersed itinerants wended their way again toward Philadelphia for their second Conference. It met on May 25, and continued till Friday, the 27th. The disciplinary views of Rankin, enforced during the preceding year upon the Preachers and Societies with a rigor which seemed to some of them hardly tolerable, had produced salutary effects generally, as evinced by the growing efficiency of the denomination, and an unexpected increase of its members. Rankin says of the session, "Everything considered, we had reason to bless God for what he had done in about ten months. Above a thousand members are added to the Societies, and most of these have found peace with God.

We now labor in the provinces of New York, the Jerseys, Pennsylvania, Maryland, and Virginia. A reinforcement of seven preachers was received on trial." Five candidates were admitted to membership. The statistical returns showed 10 circuits, 17 preachers, and 2,073 members. There had been an increase since the last Conference of 4 circuits, 7 preachers, and 913 members. The members reported at the previous session had been nearly doubled. New York reported 222; Philadelphia, 204; New Jersey, 257; Maryland, 1,063; Virginia, 291. Maryland had gained 563; she had more than doubled her number of the preceding year; Virginia had gained 191, and had nearly trebled her previous returns. Maryland now included more than half the members of the entire denomination; Maryland and Virginia together included more than two thirds of them. Methodism was centralizing about the center of the colonies. The itinerancy was under a stern regimen at that day. Hitherto, it transferred the preachers from New York to Philadelphia every four months; now it was more rigorous toward the laborers of the cities than before, for while the preachers on the country circuits exchanged semi-annually, those of Philadelphia and New York exchanged quarterly. The itinerancy was prized not only as affording variety of ministerial gifts to the Societies, but as a sort of military drill to the Preachers. It kept them energetic by keeping them in motion. No great captain has approved of long encampments. The early Methodist itinerants were an evangelical cavalry; they were always in the saddle; if not in line of battle, yet skirmishing and pioneering; a mode of life which conduced not a little to that chivalric spirit and heroic character which distinguished them as a class.

On Friday, the 27th of May, the little band dispersed again to their circuits.

Asbury hastened to New York. He was bowed with disease, and though fervent in spirit, the record of his labors for the year is but meager. It is, however, pervaded with devout aspirations, and with an energy impatient of rest. Additional missionaries arrived from England about the middle of November; they relieved him and he hastened southward. He spent three months in Philadelphia, but was disabled much of the time by sickness. "I had," he writes, "some conversation with Captain Webb, an Israelite indeed, and we both concluded that it was my duty to go to Baltimore. I feel willing to go, if it is even to die there."

In the latter part of February he was on his way to Baltimore, preaching as he went. And now, with gradually returning health, he becomes himself again; he preaches, almost daily, at the Point or in the town, and incessantly hastens to more or less distant parts of the circuit, proclaiming his message along his route, and again we read of "the divine energy going forth among the people;" of "much of the power of God" in the assemblies; of their bowing "under the weight of the word;" of "rich and poor" thronging them and "melting under the truth." Otterbein accompanies him, and they have "a blessed and refreshing season." Williams arrives from Virginia and cheers him with increasingly good news from that province, still, as in the previous year, the scene of the greatest religious interest in America. He reports "five or six hundred souls justified by faith, and five or six circuits formed; so that we have now fourteen circuits in America, and about twenty-two Preachers are required to supply them."

Asbury's usefulness in the Baltimore Circuit in 1775 had permanently important results. He gathered into the young Societies not a few of those influential families whose opulence and social position gave material strength to Methodism through much of its early history in that city, while their exemplary devotion helped to maintain its primitive purity and power. Henry Dorsey Gough and his family were distinguished examples. Gough possessed a fortune in lands and money amounting to more than three hundred thousand dollars. He had married a daughter of Governor Ridgeley. His country residence—Perry Hall, about twelve miles from the city—was "one of the most spacious and elegant in America at that time." But he was an unhappy man in the midst of his luxury. His wife had been deeply impressed by the Methodist preaching, but he forbade her to hear them again. While reveling with wine and gay companions, one evening, it was proposed that they should divert themselves by going together to a Methodist assembly. Asbury was the preacher, and no godless diversion could be found in his presence. "What nonsense," exclaimed one of the convivialists, as they returned, "what nonsense have we heard to-night!" "No;" replied Gough, startling them with sudden surprise, "No; what we have heard is the truth, the truth as it is in Jesus." "I will never hinder you again from hearing the Methodists," he said, as he entered his house and met his wife. The impression of the sermon was so profound that he could no longer enjoy his accustomed pleasures. He became deeply serious and, at last, melancholy, "and was near destroying himself" under the awakened sense of his misspent life; but God mercifully preserved him. Riding to one of his plantations, he heard the voice of prayer and praise in a cabin, and, listening, discovered that a negro from a neighboring estate was leading the devotions of his own slaves, and offering fervent thanksgivings for the blessings of their depressed lot. His heart was touched, and with emotion he exclaimed, "Alas, O Lord! I have my thousands and tens of thousands, and yet, ungrateful wretch that I am, I never thanked thee, as this poor slave does, who has scarcely clothes to put on or food to satisfy his hunger." The luxurious master was taught a lesson, on the nature of true contentment and happiness, which he could never forget. His work-worn servants in their lowly cabins knew a blessedness which he had never found in his sumptuous mansion. He returned home, pondering the mystery, with a distressed and contrite heart. He retired from his table, which was surrounded by a large company of his friends, and threw himself upon his knees in a chamber. While there he received conscious pardon and peace. In a transport of joy he went to his company, exclaiming, "I have found the Methodists' blessing, I have found the Methodists' God!" Both he and his wife now became members of the Methodist Society, and Perry Hall was henceforth the chief asylum of the itinerants in the Middle States and a "preaching place." The wealthy convert erected a chapel contiguous to his house; the first American Methodist church that had a bell, and it rang every morning and evening, summoning his numerous household and slaves to family worship. They made a congregation, for the establishment comprised a hundred persons. The Circuit Preacher supplied it twice a month, and Local Preachers every Sunday. He built another chapel for the Methodists in a poor neighborhood. His charities were large; and he was ever ready to minister, with both his means and his Christian sympathies, to the afflicted within or without the pale of his Church. He preached at times, and, during the agitations of the Revolution, was brought before the magistrates for his public labors. He died in 1808, while the General Conference of his Church was in session in Baltimore. Asbury, who had led him to the cross, was present to comfort him in his final trial, and says, "In his last hours, which were painfully afflictive, he was much given up to God. When the corpse was removed, to be taken into the country for interment, many of the members of the General Conference walked in procession after it to the end of the town." "Perry Hall," says a Methodist chronicler, "was the resort of much company, among whom the skeptic and the Romanist were sometimes found. Members of the Baltimore bar, the *élite* of Maryland, were there. But it mattered not who were there; when the bell rang for family devotion they were seen in the chapel, and if there was no male person present, who could lead the devotions, Mrs. Gough read a chapter in the Bible, gave out a hymn, which was often raised and sung by the colored servants, after which she would engage in prayer. Take her altogether, few such have been found on earth." Asbury called her a "true daughter" to himself; and Coke, "a precious woman, of fine sense." "Her only sister became a Methodist about the same time that she did. Most of her relations followed her example of piety. Many of them were Methodists cast in the old die." Her only daughter became, under her parental training, a devoted Methodist, and her marriage into the Carroll family, memorable in our revolutionary history, did not impair, but extended her religious influence. We shall have occasion often to return to Perry Hall, and shall at last meet there Asbury and Coke, Whatcoat and Vasey, from England, and Black from Nova Scotia, constructing under its hospitable roof the organization of the M. E. Church prior to the "Christmas Conference." Asbury continued his successful labors on the Baltimore Circuit till May, 1775, when he departed for the Conference at Philadelphia.

Rankin has left but brief notices of his labors during this ecclesiastical year. He remained apparently about six months in Philadelphia, making expeditions to New Jersey and other adjacent regions. In the autumn of 1774 he went into Maryland to hold a Quarterly Conference. Shadford, and several of his fellow-laborers in the state, were present, and Williams had come two hundred miles from Virginia to encourage them with the good news with which he had refreshed Asbury.

Shadford was appointed by the Conference of 1774 to Baltimore Circuit, with three other preachers, Robert Lindsey, Edward Dromgoole, and Richard Webster. Lindsey, an Irishman, was admitted on trial at the Conference of 1774. He continued to itinerate in this country about three years, after which he returned to Europe, and labored in the Wesleyan ministry till 1788. Dromgoole was also an Irishman. He had been a Papist, but was led, in 1770, by Methodist influence in his native country, to renounce Popery, by reading, publicly in a church, his recantation. In the same year he arrived in Baltimore with a letter of introduction to his countryman, Robert Strawbridge. He heard Strawbridge preach, and induced him to visit Fredericktown. Methodism was thus introduced into that community. Dromgoole still deemed himself an unregenerate man; but after a period of deep mental distress he received the peace of God while upon his knees on a Sunday evening. He began to preach in 1773. He labored in various places, but chiefly in Virginia and North Carolina, till 1786, when he located on the Brunswick Circuit, where he continued to be useful. Richard Webster, Shadford's other colleague, was one of the earliest Methodist converts of Harford County, Maryland, where he joined the Church under

Strawbridge in 1768; in 1770 his house was a "preaching place" of the denomination; about the same time he became a public laborer in the cause; in 1772 Asbury sent him out to travel with John King, on the Eastern Shore of the state. He seems to have been an unpretentious "Helper;" for though his name appears in the appointments for 1774 and 1775, he was never received on trial, but traveled under direction of the "preacher in charge."

Led on by the ardent Shadford, these new laborers (all of them for the first time on the list of appointments) were, with their coadjutors on the two other Maryland Circuits, greatly successful. The number of Methodists in the state was increased, by more than one third, before the ensuing session of the Conference.

Among their fellow-laborers in the state was Philip Gatch, who traveled the Frederick Circuit some months, and Kent Circuit most of the remainder of the year. Gatch writes: "These were trying times to Methodist preachers. Some endured as seeing Him who is invisible; others left the field in the day of conflict." He had several severe rencounters with persecutors on this circuit. At one of his appointments a man entered the door while he was preaching, whose menacing aspect excited his suspicion. He gradually approached the preacher, and at the last prayer seized the chair at which the latter was kneeling, evidently intending to use it as a weapon with which to attack him; but Gatch took hold of it and prevented the blow. The contest now became violent, and the assailant "roared like a lion," while the evangelist "was upon his knees reproving him in the language of St. Paul." But the ruffian was soon seized by persons in the congregation, and thrown with such energy out of the house that his coat was torn entirely down his back. While in the yard he "roared like a demon;" but Gatch escaped without injury. He rejoiced over one of his best trophies won in this contested place: Philip Cox, afterward a useful traveling preacher, was converted there.

In accordance with the rule of the Conference, Gatch was transferred, before the close of the year, back to Frederick, "where," he says, "we had to labor hard." He reports "persecutions" as "prevailing" on this circuit. Storms were gathering around the whole horizon of the country. Political agitation and war were about to relax all its moral ties, and the Methodist itinerants were to suffer severely in the general tumult; to be mobbed, tarred and feathered, imprisoned, driven into exile or concealment; but they were not men who could be defeated by such hostilities, and in their worst trials they showed their greatest strength and won their greatest triumphs. "We had," says Gatch on Frederick Circuit, "this consolation, that though in some places indifference and persecution prevailed, yet in others the cause was prosperous, and many joined the Church." The increase on this circuit, for the year, was over one hundred and sixty. Before the Conference he was transferred again, as far as New Jersey.

Meanwhile the rough energy but saintly devotion and apostolic zeal of Abbott were awaking large portions of the State of New Jersey. Though he was the Class Leader and practically the Pastor of the Society in his own neighborhood, he was preaching at large on Sundays and at nights. He went to Deerfield, where a mob assembled and threatened to tar and feather any itinerant who should appear there. He was met by a friend on the road and admonished to turn back. "At first," he says, "I thought I would return; consulting with flesh and blood, I concluded that it would be a disagreeable thing to have my clothes spoiled, and my hair all matted together with tar." But he recalled the sufferings of his Lord, and immediately "resolved to go and preach if he had to die for it." He found a large congregation filling the house and crowding the neighboring premises. "I went," he continues, "in among them, and gave out a hymn, but no one sung; I then sung four lines myself, while every joint in my body trembled. I said, 'Let us pray,' and before prayer was over the power of God fell on me in such a manner that it instantly removed from me the fear of man, and some cried out. I arose, took my text and preached with great liberty; before the meeting was over I saw many tears drop from their eyes, and the head of the mob said that 'he had never heard such preaching since Robert Williams went away;' so I came off clear. Glory be to God, who stood by me in this trying hour!" He soon found his way into Salem, where his bones now rest, and where he is still venerated as the tutelary saint of its Methodist community. "A large congregation," he writes, "assembled, to whom I preached, and God attended the word with power; some cried out, and many were in tears. After the sermon I made another appointment for that day two weeks. There being an elder of the Presbyterian Church present, he asked me if I would come and preach at his house; I told him that I would, on that day two weeks, at three o'clock. Another said it was the truth I had spoken, but in a very rough manner. At the time appointed I attended, and found many people at both places. At the first, I felt much freedom in speaking, and after sermon found that both the man and his wife were awakened. At the second, great power attended the word; several cried aloud, and one fell to the floor."

Abbott, after his own hard struggles with the "great adversary," felt a sort of bold defiance of him, and was prepared always to invade his strongest holds. He now made a Sabbath expedition to a place which, for its notorious depravity, was called "Hell Neck." "One sinner there," he writes, "said he had heard Abbott swear, and had seen him fight, and now would go and hear him preach. The word reached his heart, and he soon after became a convert to the Lord. After meeting he invited me home with him, and several others invited me to preach at their houses, so that I got preaching places all through the neighborhood, and a considerable revival of religion took place, although it had been so noted for wickedness. Among others, a young lad, about fifteen years old, was awakened, and in a few weeks found peace; his father, being a great enemy to religion, opposed him violently, and resolved to prevent his being a Methodist, and even whipped him for praying. This soon threw him into great distress, and on the very borders of despair. I heard of it and went to see him. He told me his temptations." Abbott perceived his morbid anxiety, and comforted him. "The son," he adds, "then cried out, 'The Lord is here! the Lord is here!' The father then wept. I went to prayer, and the family were all in tears; after this the son went on joyfully. After I left this house I went to another of the neighbors, and after some conversation with them I went to prayer; the man kneeled, but the woman continued knitting all the time of the prayer. When I arose I took her by the hand and said, 'Do you pray?' and looking steadfastly at her, added, 'God pity you.' This pierced her heart, so that she never rested until her soul was converted to the Lord. The whole neighborhood seemed alarmed."

Such quaintly told incidents abound throughout the narrative of this good man's life. He thus "went about doing good," and in his devout simplicity and earnestness rescued more souls than all the more formal pastors for miles around him. The simple but degenerate people understood his artless words. All denominations gathered in his congregations, and often an individual conversion became the germ of a flourishing society. "A Quaker," he says, "who one day came to hear me, asked me home with him; when I entered his house I said, 'God has brought salvation to this house.' At prayer, in the evening, his daughter was struck under conviction, and soon after the old man, his wife, three sons and two daughters, were all brought to experience religion, so that we formed a considerable Society."

He reached Woodstown, where he had a crowded house. He was mobbed there, and bayonets were presented at his breast; "the people fled," he says, "every way; a man presented his gun and bayonet as though he would run me through; it passed close by my ear twice. If ever I preached the terrors of the law, I did it while he was threatening me in this manner, for I felt no fear of death, and soon found he could not withstand the force of truth; he gave way and retreated to the door. They endeavored to send him back again, but in vain, for he refused to return."

He moved his family to a new home, near Salem; "here," he continues, "I had many doors opened for me to preach, and a powerful work of religion took place, attended with several remarkable conversions."

His fame was now general, and "the work," he says, "became general; we used to hold prayer-meetings two or three times a week, in the evening; sometimes we would begin preaching at eleven o'clock, and not part till night; many long summer days we thus spent. Sometimes we used to assemble in the woods and under the trees, there not being room in the house for the people that attended. Often, some of them would be struck to the ground in bitter lamentations. The Lord wrought great wonders among us."

Thus the labors of this energetic man went on from village to village, town to town, county to county, till the whole state felt, more or less, his influence, and acknowledged that he was a strange but indisputable power among the people, turning scores and hundreds "from darkness to light, and from the power of Satan unto God."

William Watters was also abroad, in New Jersey, during most of this ecclesiastical year. "The latter part of the winter," he says, "and through the spring, many in the upper end of the circuit were greatly wrought on, and our meetings were lively and powerful." John King traveled, this year, the Norfolk Circuit, Va., and nearly doubled its members. Robert Williams, and three other preachers, labored on the Brunswick Circuit, in the same colony. We have already had allusions to his success. "In the latter part of the year there was a remarkable revival of religion in most of the circuits. Christians were much united, and much devoted to God, and sinners were greatly alarmed." "Indeed, the Lord wrought wonders among us during that year," writes the early historian, Jesse Lee. He wrote from his own observation, for it was in this year that the house of his father, Nathaniel Lee, was opened as a "preaching place" for the itinerants. The father became a Class Leader, and two of his sons, John and Jesse, traveling Preachers, taking rank among the most effective itinerants of their day. Young Jesse Lee was now going "many miles on foot," by night and by day, to attend the meetings of the circuit. Jarratt, the evangelical Rector, was active in this revival; it was, in fact, but a continuance, with increased intensity, of that extraordinary religious excitement which has already been noticed as prevailing the preceding year throughout this part of the state. "In the spring of 1774, it was," says Jarratt, "more remarkable than ever. A goodly number were gathered in, this year, both in my parish and in many of the neighboring counties. I formed several societies of those which were convinced or converted." The power of this "Great Revival" was seen in the return of members from Virginia at the end of the ecclesiastical year. The two circuits of the province became three; its less than three hundred Methodists multiplied to nearly a thousand.

Though some of the English Preachers had returned to England, and war between that country and the Colonies was now imminent, Wesley sent out recruits to the small company of itinerants, for he believed that, whatever might be the issue of the political struggle, Methodism was now a permanent fact in the moral destiny of the New World, and should be thoroughly fortified for the future, the more so as the political troubles of the country would tend to retard its progress. Accordingly in 1774 James Dempster and Martin Rodda arrived, accompanied by William Glendenning, who appears to have come with them as a volunteer, like Yearbry, the companion of Rankin and Shadford. They appeared in the latter part of the year, in time to relieve Asbury, in New York, as we have seen, for his labors in Philadelphia and Baltimore.

It was now a time that tried men's souls. "The dreadful cloud," writes Watters, "that had been hanging over us continued to gather thicker and thicker, so that I was often bowed down before the God of the whole earth." In two or three years more all the English missionaries had fled from the country, or had left the denomination, except Asbury, whose loyalty to the Church was superior to his loyalty to the British throne. Providentially, however, a native ministry had not only been begun, in time for this exigency, but was about to be reinforced by some of the ablest men with which American Protestantism has been blessed. Not a few of them were already preparing, in comparative obscurity, for their great careers. They were to attain an impórtance in their own denomination, if not in the general Christianity of the land, hardly less imposing than that which at last distinguished their contemporaries, the rising statesmen, the great founders of the Republic; and Asbury himself was, by his steadfastness, his administrative ability and success, to become, in the regards of the former, what Washington became in the regards of the latter.

Darker days were at hand. The country was rife, not only with political clamors, but with the preparations of war. Methodism was to pass from its feeble infancy into vigorous adolescence, tested and strengthened by severest trials. The necessity of its mission in the New World was to be demonstrated, and its providential career fully opened by the most momentous revolution of modern states. We shall behold it hesitating not before the fiery ordeal which is to try it, but entering it courageously, and communing there with "a form like the Son of God," and coming forth at last renewed in all its energies, "rejoicing as a strong man to run a race."

CHAPTER X.

TRIALS AND PROGRESS DURING THE REVOLUTIONARY WAR: 1775–1784.

THE American Revolution was now impending and inevitable. It was to have a profound effect on Methodism, for American independence implied the independence of American Methodism. The latter virtually became independent at the breaking out of the war, and the constitution, which organized it into the "Methodist Episcopal Church," was to be adopted in about one year after the treaty of peace with Great Britain, and to precede the adoption of the Federal Constitution by about five years. The new Church was to be the first religious body of the country which should recognize, in its organic law, by a solemn declaration of its Articles of Religion, the new Republic; the first to pay homage, in the persons of its chief representatives, its first Bishops, to the supreme Magistracy.

The Revolution was the normal, the necessary, that is to say, the providential consequence of the geographical condition and colonial training of the American people. Most of them had come to the New World for relief from religious oppressions or disabilities—Puritans and Quakers from England, Scotch Presbyterians from the north of Ireland, Palatines from the Rhine, Huguenots from France, Waldenses from Piedmont, Methodists from Ireland. It was impossible that such a people, when grown to social maturity, their settlements expanded to such contiguity that they blended, their various tongues nearly lost in a common language, should not become conscious of a community of interests in religious toleration and liberty, and a common hostility to the foreign system which had oppressed them and banished them from the homes of their fathers. They needed but to hear the tocsin of revolt sounded through the land, to rise and rend the remaining shreds of traditional attachments which connected them with the foreign world.

Thus considered, the American Revolution bore a moral character to which the American Methodists could not be indifferent. Neither they nor their native teachers were opposed to it, though the presence and controlling authority of their English missionaries held them somewhat in check and provoked against them public suspicion. War is always a crime on one side or the other of the contestants, and a crime of such contagious enormity that it is always demoralizing, temporarily, at least, to the communities which suffer from it, as well as to those who inflict it. The contemporaneous influence of the Revolution on the religious condition of the colonies was generally bad. Political and military events absorbed the public attention. Infidelity, especially through the influence of Thomas Paine, a conspicuous leader of the revolt, spread rapidly. The colonial clergy of the English Church were mostly foreigners, and were loyal to the British Crown. They quite generally deserted the country. The Evangelical Virginian Rector, Jarratt, wrote to Wesley, as late as 1773, that the colony then had ninety-five parishes, all of which, except one, were supplied with clergymen. But he knew of but one, besides himself, who entertained evangelical sentiments, and the alarm of war was the signal for their general abandonment of their people. It was this prostration of the English Church in the colonies that rendered necessary—providential, it may be said, without uncharitableness—the organization of the Methodist Episcopal Church, as we shall hereafter see.

Meanwhile the latter was relieved, by the Revolution, of its foreign missionaries and of foreign control. It was launched upon the tide of events to be managed by native men, except one, Asbury, whose far-seeing wisdom and generous sympathy with the colonial cause, if they could not at first completely counteract his British loyalty, so far qualified it as to restrain him from any rash concession to it, and kept him in the country, till the providential course of events fully revealed to him his duty to remain with the infant Church, and at last to recognize heartily the liberation of the colonies as the beneficent will of God. The imitation of the example of the Anglo-American clergy by the Anglo-American Methodist preachers, brought severe trials upon the Methodist ministry generally. ' They had," says one of them, who witnessed their afflictions, "almost insupportable difficulties, violent oppositions, bitter persecutions, and grievous sufferings to endure. So many of the preachers being Englishmen, and Wesley, who was considered the founder and chief ruler of the Methodist Societies, being in England, and known to be loyal to his king, and of course unfriendly to the American measures, occasioned jealousies and suspicions that the Methodists were, politically, a dangerous people. The way of the preachers on every side was almost hedged up; and for a considerable time it was with the utmost difficulty, and at the greatest risk of personal safety, that they could travel and preach at all.

When the times were about the worst, Asbury and Shadford agreed to make it a matter of fasting and prayer for direction, in their straits and difficulties, what to do; whether to stay in the country, or return to England. Shadford concluded that he had an answer to leave the country and return to England; but Asbury, who received an answer to stay, replied, 'If you are called to go, I am called to stay; so here we must part.' Accordingly they parted, to meet no more on earth. From that moment he made America his country and his home."

This same authority draws a dark picture of the sufferings of the ministry during these trying times. "I shall," he says, "principally confine myself to Maryland, my native state, where I was best acquainted, and where probably their sufferings were as great, perhaps greater, than in any other state. Some of the preachers were mulcted or fined, and others were imprisoned, for no other offense than traveling and preaching the Gospel; and others were bound over in bonds, and heavy penalties, and sureties, not to preach in this or that county. Several were arrested and committed to the common county jail; others were personally insulted and badly abused; some were beaten with stripes and blows nigh unto death, and carried their scars down to the grave. Garrettson was, for preaching the Gospel, committed to prison in one county; and severely beaten and wounded, even to the shedding of blood, in another. In the city of Annapolis, the capital of the state, Jonathan Forrest and William Wren, and I believe two or three others, were committed to jail; three of the men who were principally concerned in taking up and committing Wren afterward became Methodists, among whom was one of the magistrates who signed the mittimus for his commitment. I knew them well, and shall never forget the serious and solemn time when Wren and myself, with the man who arrested him, dined at the magistrate's house after they joined the Methodists. In Prince George County a preacher was shamefully maltreated by a mob; 'honored,' according to the cant of the times, 'with tar and feathers.' In Queen Anne, Joseph Hartley was bound over in penal bonds of five hundred pounds not to preach in the county. In the same county Freeborn Garrettson was beaten with a stick by one of the county judges, and pursued on horseback till he fell from his horse and was nearly killed. In Talbot County, Joseph Hartley was whipped by a young lawyer, and was imprisoned a considerable time. He used to preach, during his confinement through the grates or window of the jail, to large concourses of people on Sabbath days. They frequently came from ten to fifteen miles to hear him, and even from other counties. His confinement produced a great excitement, and God overruled it for good to the souls of many. Christ was preached, and numbers embraced religion. Even his enemies at length were glad to have him discharged. In Dorchester, Caleb Pedicord was whipped and badly hurt on the public road; he carried his scars to the grave. We might, perhaps, with propriety notice some other cases in different counties and states, both North and South, of the sufferings both of preachers and members; but time would fail."

The Revolution prepared them, it has been said, for their organization as a distinct denomination, and opened before them that career of success which at last advanced them to the van of the Protestantism of the nation. It may indeed be affirmed that American Methodism was born, and passed its whole infancy, in the invigorating struggle of the Revolution. In the year (1760) in which Embury and his fellow Palatines arrived, the Lords of Trade advised the taxing of the colonies, and the agitations of the latter commenced. The next year James Otis, the "morning star" of the Revolution, began his appeals in Boston for the rights of the people. The following year the whole continent was shaken by the royal interference with the colonial judiciary, especially at New York; and Otis attacked, in the Massachusetts legislature, the English design of taxation as planned by Charles Townshend. Offense followed offense from the British ministry, and surge followed surge in the agitations of the colonies. The year preceding that in which the John-street Church was formed is memorable as the date of the Stamp Act; the Church was founded amid the storm of excitement which compelled the repeal of the act in 1766—the recognized epoch of American Methodism. The next year a new act of taxation was passed which stirred the colonies from Maine to Georgia, and "The Farmer's Letters," by John Dickinson of Pennsylvania, appeared—the foundation rock of American politics and American statesmanship. In two years more the Massachusetts legislature "planned resistance." Samuel Adams approved of making the "appeal to heaven"—of war—and British ships and troops were ordered to Boston. The first Annual Conference of American Methodism was held in the stormy year (1773) in which the British ministry procured the act respecting tea, which was followed by such resistance that the ships bringing that luxury were not allowed to land their cargoes in Philadelphia and New York; were only allowed to store them, not to sell them, in South Carolina, and were boarded in Boston harbor and the freight thrown into the sea. In the next year the Boston Port Bill inflamed all the colonies; "a General Congress" was held; Boston was blockaded; Massachusetts was in a "general rising;" then came the year of Lexington, and Concord, and Bunker Hill, introducing the "War of Revolution," with its years of conflict and suffering. Thus Methodism began its history in America in the storm of the Revolution; its English missionaries were arriving or departing amid the ever increasing political agitation; it was cradled in the hurricane, and hardened into vigorous youth, by the severities of the times, till it stood forth, the next year after the definitive treaty of peace, the organized "Methodist Episcopal Church in the United States of America." Its almost continual growth in such apparently adverse circumstances is one of the marvels of religious history. In 1776 it was equal, in both the number of its preachers and congregations, to the Lutherans, the German Reformed, the Reformed Dutch, the Associate Church, the Moravians, or the Roman Catholics. At the close of the war it ranked fourth or fifth among the dozen recognized Christian denominations of the country. During the war it more than quadrupled both its ministry and its members.

In less than a month after the conflicts of Lexington and Concord, while the whole country resounded with the din of military preparations, the little company of American itinerants wended doubtfully their way again to Philadelphia for their third annual Conference.

CHAPTER XI.

LABORS AND TRIALS DURING THE REVOLUTIONARY WAR.

ASBURY prudently determined not to compromise himself, with either the home or colonial government, in the contest now beginning. His work was one: "to promote the kingdom of heaven," the kingdom of peace, and he wished to pursue his single task with such circumspection that, whatever might be the issue of the struggle, he should remain unimpeachable, and his ability to continue his evangelical labors unimpaired.

From the Conference at Philadelphia in 1775 he went by sea to Norfolk, Virginia, his new appointment. "Here," he says, "I found about thirty persons in Society after their manner; but they had no regular class meetings." A subscription was started for a chapel. Discipline was enforced, though "some of the members seemed a little refractory in submitting" to it. "But," he characteristically remarks, "without discipline we should soon be a rope of sand; so that it must be enforced let who will be displeased." Following the example of Wesley, he preached frequently at five o'clock in the morning, though, he says, "I have constant inward fever and drag a cumbersome body with me." He was now in the scene of Robert Williams's labors, the founder of Methodism in Virginia. Williams had married in the preceding year, and settled on the road between Norfolk and Suffolk. He continued to preach far and near, and his house was a home and preaching place for Asbury. In the autumn of 1775 he died; Asbury laid him to rest, with a funeral sermon, and pronounced upon him, as we have seen, the emphatic eulogy "that probably no man in America had been equally successful in awakening souls." The loss of this useful man was a saddening addition to the calamities of the times in the little communion of the Virginia Methodists. During Asbury's stay in this region he systematized the circuit work, and established rigid disciplinary order among his Societies. But in the next winter Norfolk was burned down by the royalists, and Methodism was extinguished there till the beginning of the present century. In 1803 Asbury found in the city a new chapel, the best in the state; in Portsmouth no Methodist Church was erected till 1800. Methodism took deep root in Virginia, but the ravages of war retarded all its plans for permanent edifices. Its people were content to worship in barns and private houses till the hurricane had passed.

In November he left Norfolk for the Brunswick Circuit, still the scene of extraordinary religious activity.

At the Conference of 1775 Shadford and four other laborers had been appointed to this field, and were now sweeping, like flames of fire, over its extensive range. "We added," he says, "eighteen hundred members, and had good reason to believe that a thousand of them were converted to God."

Young Jesse Lee witnessed this "remarkable" interest, as his home was one of the preaching stations of the circuit. He writes that, "In the course of this year there was a gracious work in several places, but in none did it equal that on Brunswick Circuit, where George Shadford was traveling at that time. It was quite common for sinners to be seized with trembling and shaking, and to fall down as if they were dead. This work in a very short time spread through Dinwiddie, Amelia, Brunswick, Sussex, Prince George, Lunenberg, and Mecklenberg Counties. It thus increased on every side; more preachers were soon wanted; and the Lord raised up several young men, who were exceedingly useful as local preachers." Lee himself was one of the most conspicuous of these local evangelists. Such was the success with which the militant Preachers of Methodism pushed forward their conquests amid the tumults of the Revolutionary War. This "Great Revival" was as remarkable, in some respects more remarkable, than the "Great Awakening," under Edwards, in New England. It was more durable.

Early in January Asbury meets Jarratt, who reports still a

"great work" under Shadford's preaching. The good Rector unites with the Itinerant in holding a Watch Night, at which they "stand about two hours each," preaching to an eager throng, among whom, says Asbury, "there appeared a great degree of divine power." Jarratt is with him also at the Quarterly Conference of the Circuit, where the Rector preaches, and administers the Lord's Supper. Asbury, soon after, visits his parsonage and finds in him "an agreeable spirit." After spending about a month in itinerating with him, Asbury set out for the North, called thither by Rankin. On arriving in Baltimore the alarms of war met him again; he found the city in commotion, caused by a report that a ship-of-war was approaching. Many of the inhabitants were hurrying out of town. "The congregations," he wrote, "were but small, so great has the consternation been. But I know the Lord governeth the world; therefore these things shall not trouble me. I will endeavor to be ready for life or death." He was welcomed to the tranquil retreat of Perry Hall by his friend Gough, and preached there to a great congregation. On the 19th of March, 1776, he reached Philadelphia, having "rode about three thousand miles" since he left it, on the 22d of the preceding May.

After spending some months in Philadelphia, rallying the Society from the public distractions, and making excursions into New Jersey and other parts of the country, where he found the young Churches desolated by the agitations of the war, he passed southward again on the last day of May, 1776. He is welcomed in Baltimore, and finds temporary shelter at Perry Hall; is refreshed by good news "of the glorious spread of the work of God in Virginia and North Carolina, where the Lord is still fulfilling his promise, and pouring out his Spirit on the people." He preaches for Otterbein, and remarks that "there are very few with whom he can find so much unity and freedom in conversation as with him." In one of his excursions he is arrested, taken before a magistrate, and "fined five pounds for preaching the Gospel." His health again fails, through excessive travel and preaching. He goes to the Warm Sulphur Springs of Virginia, accompanied by Gough, of Perry

Hall; there he holds a meeting every night, and preaches often in the open air.

His plan of relaxation and recuperation here is singular enough. He reads about a hundred pages a day; usually prays in public five times a day; preaches in the open air every other day; and lectures in prayer-meeting every evening. "And," he adds, "if it were in my power I would do a thousand times as much for such a gracious and blessed Master. But, in the midst of all my little employments, I feel myself as nothing, and Christ to me is all in all."

Having spent six weeks at the Springs, he left them for his Baltimore Circuit, where he resumed his travels with unresting energy. His journals are characteristically laconic; they abound in abbreviations which obscure, at this late day, their allusions; we are perplexed in tracing his journeyings, as he hurries us along from place to place; but we are kept in excited interest and wonder, at his hardly intermitted movements, his continual preaching, in the morning at a chapel, in the afternoon at a barn or school-house ten or fifteen miles distant, in the evening at a private house twenty miles further. The next day he is early in the saddle and again away to other fields; and so, day after day, week after week, year after year, for nearly half a century; for with him ministerial zeal was not a paroxysm, but a divine fire which kept his whole life incandescent until he dropped at last in the pulpit, consumed by it, or rather borne by it away, as if ascending, like the Hebrew prophet, in a chariot of fire. Neither Wesley nor Whitefield labored as energetically as this obscure man. He exceeded them in the extent of his annual travels, the frequency of his sermons, and the hardships of his daily life. His temperament was less buoyant than theirs, he was often depressed by a constitutional sadness, if not melancholy; but he had an iron will, a profound conscience, an ineffable sense of the value of the human soul, and an invincible resolution to attain the maximum availability of his life for the eternal welfare of himself and his fellow-men. He studied hard on his long routes, and, by his unaided endeavors, became able to read the holy Scriptures in the original Hebrew and Greek, and was familiar with ecclesiastical and general history and scientific theology. He visited Annapolis often about this time, preaching in an old theater. The war spirit menaced him in this region, and his friends could not protect him. His chaise was shot through, but he escaped unharmed. It became necessary, however, for him to think of means of safety. A pause is reported in his career of two or more years, during which he is usually represented as sequestered from the storms of the Revolution; but though it seemed to him such, it was but a partial retirement, for he still had a whole state for his parish most of the time. While pursuing his zealous course on the Baltimore Circuit, he received word of the return of Rankin to England; Shadford, to whom he clung as David to Jonathan, was persuaded to tarry, but he also soon departed; at last all Wesley's English missionaries but himself had left the country or the denomination. He bowed his head in profound dejection, but his will could not be bowed. He still pursues his work, though daily expecting to be arrested, for he hears from various directions of the mobbing and imprisonment of his itinerant brethren, though none but native preachers now remain with him. As Methodists they are held responsible for Wesley's opposition to the Revolution; and the mob and petty magistrates, swayed by political excitement, and many of them by sectarian jealousy, listen to no remonstrances or entreaties. The test-oaths require a pledge to take up arms, if called upon to do so by the authorities. Asbury, though well affected toward the colonial cause, cannot consent to such a contingency. His conscience as a preacher of the Gospel forbids him. The peril at last comes nearer home to him. In March, 1778, he writes, in concealment, at the house of his friend, Judge White, of Kent County, Del., "I intend to abide here for a season till the storm is abated." On the 2d of April the light horse patrol came to the house, and seizing Judge White, bore him off, leaving his wife and children with Asbury in great alarm. They observed together the next day as an occasion of fasting and prayer. On Saturday, April 4, Asbury says: "This was a day of much divine power and love to my soul. I was left alone, and spent part of every hour in prayer; and Christ was near and very precious." He retreated into a neighboring swamp for some days, but returned to his hospitable shelter. "From this place of retreat," says Cooper, "he could correspond with his brethren who were scattered abroad. He could also occasionally travel about, visiting the Societies, and sometimes preach to the people. He was accessible to all the preachers and his friends who came to see him; so that by means of correspondence and visits they could communicate with one another for mutual counsel, comfort, and encouragement. In some of their movements they had to be very cautious; for they were watched as the partridge is watched by the hawk on the mountains. Among those whose particular confidence he secured we might mention, with Judge White, the pious Judge Barrett, both of whom opened their houses for the brethren as homes, and protected the preachers, and exerted their influence in support of religion. Each of them was instrumental in having a preaching house built in his respective neighborhood, which to this day are called White's Meeting-house and Barrett's Chapel. We may also mention the late Richard Bassett, Esq., well known as a distinguished character, not only in the state but in the United States. At different times he filled high and honorable stations. He was a lawyer of note, a legislator, judge, and a governor of Delaware. He was also a member of the convention which framed the Constitution of the United States, a senator in the first Congress, and a judge of the United States Court for the Circuit comprising the Districts of Pennsylvania, New Jersey, and Delaware. They found Asbury to be a safe and a good citizen, a circumspect Christian, and a faithful minister of the Gospel, worthy of confidence as a friend to the country of his choice, of which he had voluntarily become a citizen."

Asbury's retirement, so called, was a period of no little labor. He was closely confined only about five weeks, and there were but eleven in which he did not travel more or less. Through the first year he ventured not far from home; but, besides preaching occasionally, he frequently held meetings for prayer and exhortation among his friendly neighbors. The preachers often met him in the hospitable family of Judge

White, and he privately held with them there a Conference in 1779. He gradually ventured to preach more openly; and during the second year of what he considered his confinement, the whole state of Delaware was his Circuit; the Conference which had furtively met at Judge White's house having appointed him to it and designated the appointment in the Minutes. The mansion of his friend was his head-quarters; it was not expedient for him to be absent for a long time from it; it was usually his shelter by night, but his ministerial excursions were made almost daily. The family which thus gave refuge to him and to not a few of his brethren during this stormy period was notable in the early days of Methodism. Like that of Gough, at Perry Hall, of Bassett, at Bohemia Manor, and of Barrett, at "Barrett's Chapel," its name continually recurs in the Journals of Asbury, Coke, Garrettson, Abbott, and in other early Methodist publications.

Protected by his influential friends, Asbury was at last enabled to emerge out of his comparative obscurity in Delaware, after spending there two years and one month. He came forth to be the hero of American Methodist history through all the remainder of his life. He had been found faithful when all his British associates had retreated from the stormy arena. The native preachers now not only revered, but loved him. Some of them had penetrated to his retreat, as we have seen; they there declared him their "general assistant" or superintendent, as Rankin had abdicated that office by leaving the country. And now began those incredible tours over the continent, averaging two a year, for the remainder of his life, which, with his daily preaching in chapels, court-houses, barns, private houses, or the open air, present perhaps the most extraordinary example of ministerial labor in the history of the Church, ancient or modern. His meager Journals give us few details; the biographer or historian is at a loss to sketch his courses from the slight jottings of the record; the reader is bewildered with the rapidity of his movements; but through them all the tireless, the invincible, the gigantic apostle appears, planning grandly and as grandly executing his plans; raising up hosts of preachers; forming new Churches, new

Circuits, and new Conferences; extending his denomination north, south, east, west, till it becomes, before his death, coextensive with the nation, and foremost, in energy and success, of all American religious communions.

He hastens southward and averts a schism likely to have been occasioned by the clamorous demand of people and preachers for the sacraments. He journeys to and fro in Virginia and North Carolina. He finds it necessary to use two horses on this difficult route. He returns northward through Virginia, Maryland, Delaware, Pennsylvania, New Jersey, meeting his fellow-laborers in Quarterly and Annual Conferences, and inspiriting the Churches. He rejoices to greet Jarratt again, but still more to find, all along his route, zealous native preachers rising up to extend the Church. He sees Abbott for the first time, and says "his word comes with great power; the people fall to the ground under it, and sink into a passive state, helpless, motionless; he is a man of uncommon zeal, and (although his language has somewhat of incorrectness) of good utterance." He learns as he presses onward that "there is daily a great turning to God in new places, and that the work of sanctification goes on in our old Societies." In about ten months he travels about four thousand miles, over the worst roads, and preaches upon an average a sermon a day. In May, 1781, he hastens southward again, and is soon penetrating the wilderness. He continues during the ensuing three years to fly like the apocalyptic angel, "having the everlasting Gospel to preach" over all the central parts of the continent, from New York to North Carolina. "The Lord," he writes, "is my witness that if my whole body, yea, every hair of my head, could labor and suffer, they should be freely given up for God and souls."

In November, 1784, weary and worn by travel and preaching, he arrived, on Sunday, during public worship, at his friend Barrett's Chapel. A man of small stature, ruddy complexion, brilliant eyes, long hair, feminine but musical voice, and gowned as an English clergyman, was officiating. Asbury ascended the pulpit and embraced and kissed him before the whole assembly, for the itinerant recognized him as another

BARRATT'S CHAPEL, KENT COUNTY, DELAWARE.

messenger from Wesley, come to his relief after the desertion of all his English associates; a man who, though of dwarfish body, had an immeasurable soul, and had become a chieftain of Methodism in England, Ireland, and Wales, only second to Wesley himself. Asbury knew not yet the full import of his mission; but after his labors and sufferings, as Wesley's solitary representative in America, any such visitor was to him like an angel from heaven, and he knew the man too well to doubt that his presence in the New World would make an era in its struggling Methodism. This little man, of gigantic spirit, whom Asbury, mourning his death years afterward, was to characterize as "the greatest man of the last century in Christian labors," not excepting Whitefield or Wesley, represented, in the humble pulpit of Barrett's Chapel, the most momentous revolution in American Methodism. He was the "Rev. Thomas Coke, LL.D., late of Jesus College, Oxford," but now the first Protestant bishop of the western hemisphere. Great events were at hand; but before introducing the stranger more fully upon the scene, it is expedient that we cast our glance repeatedly back again over our present period, for other and extraordinary men were abroad, laying deeply and widely the foundations of the coming reconstruction; men, some of whose once humble names become more and more illustriously historical as the results of their self-sacrificing labors still develop in the progress of the denomination.

Young Watters was abundant in labors and patient in trials during this troubled period. He went from the Philadelphia Conference of 1775 to the Frederick Circuit, Md. It extended over a region which might still be called the frontier. The roads were difficult, the settlements very scattered, the habitations mostly log-cabins, without conveniences for the sojourner. Watters went to proclaim his message through this wilderness, desponding often on his route, but he was refreshed at last by unexpected success. About midsummer a spiritual awakening appeared in almost every appointment of his circuit.

The changes of preachers from circuit to circuit were still semi-annual. After six months of unremitted labors, during which scores of converts were gathered into the Church, Watters departed for Fairfax Circuit, Va., where, notwithstanding the prevalent political and military agitations, his powerful ministrations bore down all before him over at least two thirds of his circuit, a flame of "revival kindling and spreading from appointment to appointment." "In less than a quarter," he writes, "we had the greatest revival I had ever seen in any place. If ever I was enabled to labor for the salvation of souls, it was now." There were some "very astonishing instances of the mighty power of God in the conversion of respectable persons;" among whom he mentions, as one of his trophies, Nelson Reed, destined to be a standard-bearer in the itinerant ministry. Down to the end of 1783 he continued to travel in Maryland and Virginia with a zeal that knew no abatement, and a success hardly excelled by any evangelist of the denomination—often in new circuits in mountainous regions, his lodging in log-cabins, his chapels barns, his health broken so much that, three or four times, his brethren expected to bury him, a martyr to his work. He was one of the few itinerants who had families, and in 1783 he was compelled to locate, but he still labored indefatigably, one of his regular appointments being at least forty miles distant from his home, another thirty. Not only many, but most of the itinerants of those early times had, sooner or later, to locate on account of their worn-out health or domestic embarrassments; but they continued to perform more laborious service in the ministry than most of their itinerant successors, and the early outspread of Methodism through the land is scarcely less attributable to their zeal than to that of the "regular" Preachers. Hardly had Watters located when he was cheered by news of the arrival of Coke, with authority from Wesley to organize the Church. The first native itinerant, he had served faithfully through most of the forming period of the young denomination; he was now to see it take organic and permanent form.

It was in the present period that Freeborn Garrettson began that memorable ministerial career which was to extend over more than half a century, and to leave historical and ineffaceable traces on the Church from North Carolina to Nova Scotia. He was of an influential family of Maryland, a descendant of the first settlers of that province; the possessor of lands and slaves; a young man of firm but amiable character. Strawbridge, as we have seen, was abroad in Maryland, and Garrettson met him and other itinerants. Their message was, at first, a mystery to him; yet he believed "they preached the truth," and he "dared not to join with the multitude in persecuting them." Asbury passed through the neighborhood, and the awakened youth heard him with delight, following him from place to place, "fully persuaded that he was a servant of God," and surprised to hear him preach in a manner that seemed to imply a knowledge of the inmost troubles of his own soul. Watters, Webster, Rollins, and other evangelists crossed his path; "revivals" broke out and persecutions followed. Garrettson's father became alarmed for him, and the young man's "name was already cast out as evil though he had made no open avowal of Methodism." Under the preaching of Daniel Ruff, he was "so oppressed that he could scarcely support his burden;" and riding homeward through a lonely wood, agonized by the sense of his sinfulness, and of the necessity of regeneration, he dismounted and began to pray. But his prayer was for forbearance that he might yet delay till a more convenient season. Resuming his ride, he was again arrested with an overpowering consciousness that "now is the accepted time, now is the day of salvation." "I threw," he says, "the reins of my bridle on the horse's neck, and, putting my hands together, cried out, 'Lord, I submit!' I was less than nothing in my own sight, and was now, for the first time, reconciled to the justice of God. The enmity of my heart was slain, the plan of salvation was open to me. I saw a beauty in the perfections of the Deity, and felt that power of faith and love that I had been a stranger to. My soul was so exceeding happy that I seemed as if I wanted to take wing and fly away to heaven."

On reaching home he called his family together for prayer, and not many days after, while about to lead their devotions, he gave one of the best proofs of the genuineness of his new faith. He declared to all his slaves their freedom, convinced that "it is not right to keep our fellow-creatures in bondage."

"Till then," he adds, "I had never suspected that slavekeeping is wrong; I had never read a book on the subject, nor been told so by any one. It was God, not man, that taught me the impropriety of holding slaves, and I shall never be able to praise him enough for it. My very heart has bled since that time for slaveholders, especially those who make a profession of religion; for I believe it to be a crying sin." It was while standing in the midst of his family and slaves, with a hymn book in his hand, beginning their family worship, that he pronounced his servants free. They all knelt before their common God as his common children. The devout young man, following thus a conscientious intuition of his purified mind, experienced at once the inexpressible consolation of such well-doing; "a divine sweetness," he says, "ran through my whole frame." "Had I the tongue of an angel I could not describe what I felt."

And now, like most Methodists of that day, he "went about doing good," with no definite idea of preaching, but "bearing his testimony" for what God had done for him. He held meetings at his own house, at that of his brother, and at others; he thus became an Exhorter even before he had formally joined the Church. He formed classes. Rodda took him at last out upon his circuit, and he thus undesignedly became a Preacher. He was attacked by ruffians, smitten on the face, mobbed, and summoned to drill as a soldier. When carried before a military officer he told his "experience," and sat on his horse "exhorting with tears" a thousand people; the court martial dismissed him with a fine of twelve dollars and a half a year, but he was never called upon to pay it. He soon had appointments in every direction.

At the Conference of 1776 Garrettson was received on trial, and appointed to Frederick Circuit. Three different times he turned his horse toward his home, from his new field, desponding under his diffidence and the hardships of his work; but prayer in the solitary woods, extraordinary impressions of his discourses awakening his hearers, or providential impediments, deterred him, and at last confirmed him in his lifelong mission of labor and sacrifice. A score were sometimes converted and added to the feeble Societies of the circuit at a single meeting. In six months he went to Fairfax Circuit. He extended his travels far up the Potomac to what was called New Virginia, where his labors were greatly successful. He was sent, the next year, to the famous Brunswick Circuit, with Watters; there of course he had triumphant times, large congregations, overwhelming effects of the word, meetings held in barns, or under the trees, which reminded him of the Pentecostal assembly of the Apostles. He penetrated southward into North Carolina. He failed not to inculcate his opinions of slavery, and preached often to the slaves, weeping with them in their wrongs, rejoicing with them in their spiritual consolations. He was menaced by persecutors, interrupted sometimes in his sermons, threatened by armed men, and one of his friends was shot (but not mortally) for entertaining him; "but," he says, "the consolations afforded me were an ample compensation for all the difficulties I met with wandering up and down." His next circuit was Kent, Md., where he was exposed to those political and military hostilities which prevailed against the Methodists. One of his colleagues, Hartley, was imprisoned, the others were dispersed, and he was left alone to bear the brunt of the persecution.

"God enabled me to go forward," writes Garrettson, "through good and through evil report; he stood by me, and I went on without fear." His friends in Kent entreated him not to hazard his life by traveling at large; but he "traveled through the country preaching once, twice, thrice, and sometimes four sermons a day to listening multitudes bathed in tears."

At one time he was near receiving the honors of martyrdom. Being unmolested in the congregation he deemed himself safe, notwithstanding he had been threatened privately with imprisonment. But on riding away he was met by an opposer, formerly a judge of the county, who struck him on the head with a bludgeon. The itinerant attempted to escape, but was overtaken by the swifter horse of his assailant, and, struck again, fell senseless to the ground. He was carried to a neighboring house and bled by a person, who, passing by, providentially had a lancet. It was supposed he could live but a few minutes; "the heavens," he writes, "seemed in a very glorious manner opened, and by faith I saw my Redeemer standing on the right hand of the Father pleading my cause. I was so happy that I could scarcely contain myself." The ruffian who assailed him seemed to relent, and sat by his bedside listening to his exhortations, and offered to carry him in his own carriage wherever he wished to go. The itinerant was cited, however, before a magistrate, who boisterously charged him with violating the laws. "Be assured," replied Garrettson, "this matter will be brought to light in an awful eternity." The pen dropped from the magistrate's hand, and the preacher was allowed to retire. Taken into a carriage by the friendly passenger who had bled him, he was safely borne away, and that night was again preaching in a private house, though his bed was his pulpit. He suffered very little opposition in the county afterward. The next day he rode many miles and preached twice, his "face bruised, scarred, and bedewed with tears;" his hearers were deeply affected, and his own soul was triumphant with grateful joy that he could suffer for Christ. "It seemed," he writes, "as if I could have died for him." In a few days he returned courageously to the place of his sufferings, and preached to a numerous and deeply affected concourse of people. He had conquered the field.

He afterward traversed the State of Delaware, preaching with remarkable power. Again he returned to Maryland, "and the work of the Lord went on prosperously." He founded societies, introduced Methodism into many new fields, and such was the peculiar energy and pathos with which he preached, that his journal is almost a continuous record of "melted congregations," "powerful awakenings," (in which not a few hearers were smitten down to the ground,) conquered opposers, and prolonged meetings, from which the eager multitude could hardly be persuaded to retire.

He began his labors in Dover amid a storm of opposition in the latter part of 1778. He had been invited thither by a gentleman who had been profited by his ministry elsewhere.

Hardly had he dismounted from his horse when the mob gathered, crying out, "He is a Tory; hang him, hang him!" while others shouted in his defense. Hundreds of clamorous voices resounded around him. "I was in a fair way," he says, "to be torn in pieces." He was rescued, however, by some friendly gentlemen, one of whom, taking him by the hand and leading him to the steps of the academy, bade him preach, and declared he would stand by him. The evangelist cried aloud to the multitude. He was heard through most of the town. The crowd wept. One person sitting in a window, a quarter of a mile distant, was alarmed by the truth, and afterward converted. More than twenty of his hearers were awakened. The ringleader of the mob repented and betook himself to the reading of the Bible, and "never again persecuted the children of God." Garrettson preached repeatedly in the town, formed a Society, and "the Lord was with them, spreading his word and converting many souls."

He went into Sussex County, and at Broad Creek preached to hundreds in a wood. They were a notoriously vicious people: "swearers, fighters, drunkards, horseracers, gamblers, and dancers." They now wept around him, as he declared, "I saw the dead, both small and great, stand before God," etc. More than thirty "were powerfully awakened," all of whom were joined in a Society. One of his hearers afterward attempted to shoot him, coming into the audience with a pistol for the purpose, but was prevented. The whole neighborhood was reformed, and Methodism effectually planted there. A hearer from Salisbury was converted, and opened the way for his preaching in that town. Garrettson was threatened by leading townsmen with imprisonment. The sheriff came to seize him, but was confounded and left him. Methodism was thus founded in Salisbury.

After spending some fifteen months on the Peninsula, at the end of which nearly thirteen hundred members of Society were returned to the Conference from Delaware and Kent County, Garrettson passed northward. In 1780 he was appointed, with two colleagues, to New Jersey. He there preached from ten to twelve sermons a week. In the autumn we find him again on the Peninsula founding the denomination in Dorchester County. A young lady of the county, sister-in-law to Bassett, of Bohemia Manor, had been converted while visiting his family, and on her return had borne good and effectual testimony for her new faith among her kindred. Henry Airey, a gentleman of influence and a magistrate, was awakened by her conversation, and further led into a religious life by his friend Judge White. The way was thus opened for the establishment of Methodism in the county. Garrettson visited Airey's home and preached with great effect. The lady of the house and many of the black servants were converted. After spending several days with them he resumed his journey, accompanied by Airey, but was attacked on the highway by a mob, who beat his horse, and clamorously assailed him with blasphemies. After dark they bore him before a magistrate, who ordered him to prison. Airey and some of his friends started on before toward the jail. As his assailants were conducting Garrettson along the highway, a sudden flash of lightning dispersed them and he was left alone. "I was reminded," he says, "of that place of Scripture where our Lord's enemies fell to the ground, and then this portion of Scripture came to me, 'Stand still and see the salvation of God.' It was a very dark, cloudy night, and had rained a little. I sat on my horse alone, and though I called several times there was no answer. I went on, but had not got far before I met my friend Airey returning to look for me. He had accompanied me throughout the whole of this affair. We rode on, talking of the goodness of God, till we came to a little cottage by the roadside, where we found two of my guards almost frightened out of their wits. I told them if I was to go to jail that night we ought to be on our way, for it was getting late. 'O no!' said one of them, 'let us stay until the morning.' My friend and I rode on, and it was not long ere we had a beautiful clear night. We had not gone far before the company collected again, from whence I know not. However, they appeared to be amazingly intimidated, and the leader rode by the side of me, and said, 'Sir, do you think the affair happened on our account?' I told him that I would have him judge for himself; reminding him of the awfulness of the day of judgment, and the necessity there was of preparing to meet the Judge of the whole earth. One of the company swore an oath, and another immediately reproved him, saying, 'How can you swear at such a time as this?' At length the company stopped, and one said, 'We had better give him up for the present;' so they turned their horses and went back. My friend and I pursued our way. True it is, 'The wicked are like the troubled sea, whose waters cast up mire and dirt.' We had not gone far before they pursued us again, and said, 'We cannot give him up.' They accompanied us a few minutes, again left us, and we saw no more of them that night." The next day, Sunday, they reappeared, twenty in number, headed by an aged man "with locks as white as a sheet," and a pistol in his hand. They seized the evangelist while preaching. He was borne away to Cambridge jail, where, during a fortnight, "I had," he says, "a dirty floor for my bed, my saddle-bags for my pillow, and two large windows open, with a cold east wind blowing upon me; but I had great consolation in my Lord, and could say, 'Thy will be done.' Sweet moments I had with my dear friends, who came to the prison window. Many, both acquaintances and strangers, came to visit me from far and near, and I really believe I never was the means of doing more good for the time. The word of the Lord spread through all that country, and hundreds, both white and black, have experienced the love of Jesus. Since that time I have preached to more than three thousand people in one congregation, not far from the place where I was imprisoned, and many of my worst enemies have bowed to the scepter of our sovereign Lord." In fine, this county presented, at first, the most formidable resistance to Methodism of any in the state, but was the most completely conquered. After about two years' labors, it reported nearly eight hundred Methodists; "and," says a late authority, "Methodism has long been honored here; there are but few professors of religion that belong to any other than the Methodist Episcopal Church."

In 1780 Garrettson labored on Baltimore Circuit with his

usual success. In the same year he made an excursion to Little York in Pennsylvania, and there, amid a mixed population of German, and English, with a greater variety of religious sects than he had ever found elsewhere, and no small amount of disputation and hostility, he preached for two months, with extraordinary results, in more than twenty places, and more than three hundred people were awakened. The next year he was sent into Virginia, where Jarratt received him cordially. At Maybery's Chapel he addressed two thousand people, not forgetting to remonstrate with them about slavery; he formed new circuits, hastened about among the old circuits, and, wherever he went, spread a quickening sensation among the suffering Societies. In 1781 he traveled about five thousand miles, preached about five hundred sermons, visited most of the circuits in Virginia and North Carolina, and opened one new circuit, "in which the Lord began a blessed work, so that many, both rich and poor, joined the Society."

During the remainder of our present period he traveled and preached incessantly in Pennsylvania, Maryland, and Delaware, and found the Churches prospering in the hard-fought fields which he had won, through so many persecutions, within the preceding six or eight years. At Dover, the scene of one of his severest trials, he rejoiced, in 1783, over a successful Church, Bassett and his family being now among its chief supporters. In the autumn he was about to depart to the Carolinas, determined to push the triumphs of the Gospel to the furthest South; but he was suddenly arrested by the news of Coke's arrival, and the important events which were immediately to follow. Coke soon reached him, at the house of Bassett, in Dover, and says: "Here I met with an excellent young man, Freeborn Garrettson. He seems to be all meekness and love, and yet all activity. He makes me quite ashamed, for he invariably rises at four in the morning, and not only he, but several others of the preachers. Him we sent off, like an arrow, from north to south, directing him to send messengers to the right and left, and to gather all the preachers together at Baltimore on Christmas eve."

During most of the period now under review (1775–1784) Philip Gatch was "abundant in labors" and sufferings. Though he escaped imprisonment, "he was, perhaps, the subject of as much, or more, persecution for his Master's sake than any of his contemporaries." He was sent by the Conference of 1775 to Kent Circuit, in Maryland. His colleague was John Cooper, a young man whom he first met on Frederick Circuit, and had recommended to the Conference; a "man of a solemn, fixed countenance, who had suffered much persecution." Cooper's family had opposed him. His father, seeing him once on his knees in a chamber, threw a shovel of hot embers upon him, and afterward expelled him from his home. His trials only confirmed him in his faith; he joined the itinerant band of evangelists, and lived and died in their ranks. Gatch was soon sent to Frederick Circuit. Between Bladensburg and Baltimore two men seized the bridle of his horse and stopped him; others, till then in concealment, hailed the assailants, and the preacher was led up to the mob. They had made preparations for him, and proceeded to tar him, "beginning at his left cheek." "I felt," he says, "an uninterrupted peace. My soul was joyful in the God of my salvation. The man who officiated called out for more tar, adding that I was 'true blue.' He laid it on liberally. At length one of the company cried out in mercy, 'It is enough.' The last stroke, made with the paddle with which the tar was applied, was drawn across the naked eyeball, which caused severe pain, from which I have never entirely recovered. In taking cold it often becomes inflamed, and quite painful. I was not taken from my horse, which was a very spirited animal. Two men held him by the bridle, while the one, elevated to a suitable height, applied the tar. My horse became so frightened that when they let him go he dashed off with such violence that I could not rein him up for some time, and narrowly escaped having my brains dashed out against a tree. If I ever felt for the souls of men I did for theirs. When I got to my appointment, the Spirit of the Lord so overpowered me that I fell prostrate before him for my enemies." He again conquered, notwithstanding this outrageous treatment; for the leader of the mob, who had applied the tar, and several of his associates were afterward converted. But a conspiracy was formed by others to waylay, if not to murder the itinerant. A number of ruffians concealed themselves under a bridge with weapons to attack him when he should pass over it. The design was revealed to some of his friends, and one of them rode over the bridge, while he was sent around on another road. The conspirators rushed upon his friend, but were confounded when they discovered not the preacher, but one of their own neighbors. Gatch escaped, and went on his way rejoicing and preaching. No part of the country needed more such evangelical laborers as Gatch, for not a few of its population were in extreme demoralization. They had nearly destroyed the life of a young exhorter by waylaying and whipping him; the "shirt upon his back, though made of the most substantial material, being literally cut to pieces." Gatch and his fellow-itinerants were no cowards; they gathered courage from their trials; and though they followed the Scripture precept, when persecuted in one city to flee to another, yet it was their policy to return in due time to the scene of hostilities, and never finally succumb. In four weeks he rode again to the same appointment where he had been "tarred," and threatened at the bridge. His friends had formed a guard for him, but he had no need of their aid. "I never," he says, "missed an appointment from the persecutions through which I had to pass, or the dangers to which I was exposed. I sometimes felt great timidity, but in the hour of danger my fears always vanished." The persecutions on Frederick Circuit were thus ended.

Gatch's next appointment was on Hanover Circuit, Virginia. It extended along both sides of the James River through six counties. He had to preach mostly in the open air, for no house could contain his hearers. His health gave way. "It seemed at last," he says, "that my lungs were entirely gone. Frequently I would have to raise myself up in the bed to get my breath." Jarratt sheltered and consoled him. In 1777 he was sent to Sussex Circuit, Va., but his enfeebled health rendered him comparatively ineffective. Here also he had trials from persecutors. While riding to an appointment on a Sabbath morning he was seized by two strong men, who caught hold of his arms and turned them, in opposite directions, with such violence, that he thought his shoulders would be dislocated, causing a torture which he supposed must resemble that of the rack—the severest pain he had ever felt. His shoulders were so bruised that they turned black, and it was a considerable time before he recovered the use of them. His lungs were also worse than ever, and he was compelled to retreat; he was now a married man; and at the Conference of 1778 his name disappears from the list of appointments. He located his family on a humble farm in Powhatan County, Virginia, but continued to labor in the ministry as his health would allow. It was here that he liberated his slaves, nine in number, who had come into his possession by his marriage. He declared manfully in the deed of emancipation, "Know all men by these presents, that I, Philip Gatch, of Powhatan County, Va., do believe that all men are by nature equally free; and from a clear conviction of the injustice of depriving my fellow-creatures of their natural rights, do hereby emancipate and set free the following persons."

Asbury regretted the disappearance of Gatch's name from the Minutes, and frequently recommended its reinsertion. After his removal to the West, whither we shall hereafter follow him, it was restored to the record.

It is difficult to trace with exactness, through the present period, the labors of Benjamin Abbott, in many respects the most remarkable evangelist in the eventful field. This mighty but simple-minded apostle, intent only on the spiritual results of his humble mission, seldom pauses to note dates or localities. It is his "next appointment," and again, and still again, his "next appointment," with the marvelous effects of the truth, that he records; hurrying us forward with intense interest, with frequent and bewildering surprises at the mysterious power of the man, and at both the spiritual and physical phenomena which it produces. If we can pause at all over his exciting narrative, it is to wonder at the moral, the beneficent efficacy of his ministrations, the peculiar, the magnetic eloquence of his unpolished discourse, and the questionable if not inexplicable problems of its physical effects. Seldom does he preach without some of these "physical phenomena;" his hearers by tens and scores fall like dead men to the earth. If he is himself, at first, astonished at these wonders, his simple and honest mind has a very direct logic respecting them. They are "insanity," they are "demoniacal," cry out shrewd and self-possessed spectators. Wait, replies the evangelist, let us see how these slain come to life again. If they are insane they will show it; if these strange things are of the devil they will recover their self-possession, blaspheming and be worse than they were before. They "come to," not in general, but invariably, with words of praise upon their lips, with grateful tears, with resolutions and strength to live a new life. "Stand still," cried Abbott to gainsayers, "stand still and see the salvation of God." Intellectually he was incapable of other reasoning on the subject, and went forward preaching, swaying and prostrating his wondering congregations.

To the student of such marvels the autobiography of Abbott offers the most curious data; a magnetic power, if such it can be called, which, intensified by his piety, was as irresistible, to certain temperaments, as the electricity of lightning—a seemingly clairvoyant discernment, a somnambulic insight and foresight, in dreams; facts that would be incredible, were not his honesty absolutely unquestionable, and were they not so circumstantially given, and so well known in the community among whom his narrative was circulated, as to silence all denial.

He traveled and preached for years without one cent of compensation, except his hospitable entertainment among the people. Frugal and industrious, he sustained his family by tilling a small farm, hiring laborers that he might alternate his manual toils with itinerant excursions; and, when he preached within convenient proximity to his farm, he led his workmen to his meetings, paying them for their time at the rate that he payed for their labor. All his family were members of the Church, and shared his zeal; one of his sons went forth an itinerant; the remainder of the household made their home a sort of chapel. He had a church erected in his neighborhood, for which he begged money and timber from house to house. Though he was not yet fifty years old, his appearance was unusually paternal, if not patriarchal; his person was large, his countenance bland, his manners marked by religious tenderness. He dressed with Quaker-like simplicity, and his broad-brimmed hat and straight coat added not a little to the attraction of his devout temper among the numerous "Friends" of New Jersey. They frequented his appointments, entertained him at their homes, and urged him to preach in their Meeting-houses. "Thee appears so much like us we will welcome thee," said their own preachers to him. They liked him the more for his Quaker doctrine about war, then raging in the land. He was a sound patriot, but could not approve fighting, though in early life a formidable pugilist. "My call is to preach salvation to sinners," he said; "to wage war against the works of the devil." He was sometimes assailed by troops. Then more than ever he blew the "trumpet of the Gospel," and never failed of victory. A major angrily attacked him for not "preaching up war." "I related to him," he says, "my conviction and conversion, and he was calm and wished me well." While the State was distracted with the marching and countermarching of troops, he was allowed to go on, in his own evangelical warfare, through its length and breadth.

He went to Trenton, but found the Methodist Chapel used as a stable by the army, and preached in the Presbyterian Church. He went forward and "preached in the evening to a crowded congregation," he writes, "and God poured out his Spirit in such a manner that one fell to the floor. A captain and some soldiers came to take me up, but the Spirit of God took him up in such a manner that he returned home crying to God for mercy. I saw him some time after, happy in God. We spent a precious time together, and parted in love. This meeting was a time of God's power; many were awakened to a sense of their danger, and the people of God were happy, and, for my part, I was very happy." He continues: "I went to my next appointment, where they had threatened to tar and feather me. Some advised me to go some other way; but when I arrived at the place I found a large congregation assembled, to whom I preached, and God attended the Word with power—many shed tears in abundance." They were now unwilling to let him go away. "As I was about to depart two young men came to me; one took hold of my leg, and the other held my horse by the neck, and said, 'Will you go?' I sat on my horse for some time, exhorting them to persevere, and the Lord would bless them. Many more stood weeping; so we parted, and I went to the New Mills, (Pemberton,) where the people came out by hundreds, to whom I preached my farewell sermon. I returned home, and by Thursday night a letter was sent, informing me that sixteen were justified, and two sanctified. I received a letter from a Presbyterian in Deerfield, that his house and heart were open to receive me, adding, 'When you read these lines look upon it as a call from God.' I accordingly wrote to him to make an appointment for me on the Sunday following. I attended, and found a large congregation, to whom I preached, and some few wept. I attended again that day two weeks, and we had a melting time. I then made an appointment for the traveling preacher. This and several other places in the neighborhood were taken into the circuit. The Lord began to work in a powerful manner, and we soon had two classes; then the devil roared horribly; but God worked powerfully, and blessed the word, and sent it with power to many hearts; many fell under it like dead men, being alarmed of their danger. We appointed a watch-night. This brought so many to see what it meant that the house could not contain the people. One of our preachers preached, and then an exhortation was given; the Lord poured out his Spirit in such a manner that the slain lay all over the house; many others were prevented from falling by the crowd, which stood so close that they supported one another. We continued till about midnight; some stayed all night, and in the morning others came; several found peace, and many cried to God for mercy; it was a powerful time to many souls."

These extraordinary effects sometimes spread through nearly his whole congregation, few escaping, except such as rushed out of the doors, or leaped out of the windows. If a temporary tumult ensued it was soon allayed, while the moral impression seemed to be permanent and salutary; many of the most noted reprobates of the county being reformed and converted at once into good Christians and good citizens.

His labors in all the region about Salem, noted at that time for its demoralization, were surprisingly successful. Some able preachers were raised up by him. Often a single sentence in his conversation left an ineffaceable impression.

Such humble labors with such positive results (however fastidiously we may criticise their incidental irregularities) could not fail of a general impression. The Society in the neighborhood of his residence increased: hitherto he had preached to them under the trees of the forest; he now projected his chapel, and Methodism was thus securely founded in that vicinity, and spread out dominantly into many neighboring towns.

For some time Abbott had been intimate with James Sterling, Esq., of whom the historian of the denomination, in New Jersey, says that probably no layman in the state "ever did more to advance religion and Methodism." A merchant of rare ability and great wealth, an officer in the American Revolution, a citizen of universal esteem and influence, this zealous layman devoted himself to the new Church in the day of its deepest humility. He accompanied Abbott in many of his excursions, and often exhorted in his congregations. His house at Burlington was the home of not only Methodist itinerants, but of Christian ministers of all denominations.

In the latter part of 1780 Abbott writes: "I had been pressed in spirit for some time to visit Pennsylvania, and, in the love and fear of God, I set out with my life in my hand, it being a time when war was raging through the land." He crossed the Delaware at New Castle, and opened his mission in that town to "a pack of ruffians" who had met to mob him. One of them stood before him with a bottle of rum in his hand, threatening to throw it at his head. Abbott preached on, however, dealing out to them "the terrors of the law" in a manner he had seldom done before.

He soon penetrated to Soudersburg, a German settlement,

where "the Lord wrought wonders; divers fell to the floor, and several found peace. The people cried aloud, and continued all night in prayer." He was welcomed by Martin Boehm, in Lancaster County. Boehm, as we have seen, was one of the founders, and at last one of the bishops of the "German Methodists," or "United Brethren." Strawbridge had visited and labored with him;. Peter Albright, founder of the "Albright Methodists," was one of the good German's converts. Boehm had formed a sort of circuit, consisting of four appointments; one of these, near his residence, was made a regular preaching place for the Methodist itinerants, and his own house was their hospitable home. The region became a stronghold of Methodism. Asbury visited it often; Boehm was one of his most confidential friends and counselors, and his son, Henry Boehm, joined the Methodist itinerancy, and became the bishop's traveling companion.

Abbott was accompanied to Boehm's Village by quite a procession, twenty at least of the zealous Methodists of Soudersburg following him on the route. His introduction to this new scene was attended, in an extraordinary manner, by those "physical demonstrations" which had occurred under his preaching in New Jersey, and which were comparatively unknown among these quiet, rustic people. They began spontaneously as soon as he appeared among them. "When I came to my appointment," he says, "the power of the Lord came in such a manner that the people fell all about the house, and their cries might be heard afar off. This alarmed the wicked, who sprang for the doors." To tranquilize the excitement, he read a hymn and called upon a friend to raise the tune; but as soon as the latter attempted it he was struck down, and lay as a dead man. Another repeated the attempt, but fell in like manner. Abbott himself then began to sing, but, he says, "as soon as I began, the power of God came upon me in such a manner that I cried out, and was amazed. Prayer was all through the house, up stairs and down." The veteran Boehm looked on with wonder, and exclaimed that it was a return of the apostolic Pentecost. At sunrise the next morning some were still lingering in prayer. A sensation spread through all the regions round about, and scores of the people followed the wonderful itinerant to his next appointment. "God there laid to his helping hand. Many cried aloud for mercy; many wept around" him when he dismissed them: "some were truly awakened, and others deeply convicted." He had written to his friend James Sterling, giving an account of the wonders of his journey, and inviting him to hasten to his help. Sterling reached him at Upper Octararo, and, though a layman, worked energetically with him; and at times his own vigorous mind was so overpowered by the prevailing excitement that he too fell, as dead, among the many who were slain by the mighty word of the preacher.

Abbott and his companion, Sterling, continued their travels and labors without intermission, almost everywhere attended with such remarkable scenes. They passed over all the ground then cultivated by Methodism in Pennsylvania, except Philadelphia, Bethel, (Montgomery County,) and Germantown. In about thirty days he had preached twenty-nine sermons, and held nearly twenty other meetings. Scores, if not hundreds, of his hearers were awakened or converted. Large districts of Delaware and Pennsylvania were aroused with astonishment and religious interest. He returned by way of Wilmington and New Castle, so exhausted that when he reached his home his friends supposed he "could never preach again;" but it was not long before he was again crossing the Delaware, on his way to Kent Circuit, Maryland, now traveled by his son, David Abbott. There the same singular power attended his word, kindling extraordinary interest from town to town. Thus he continued, from place to place, with scarcely varying effect, till he arrived near Kent Meeting-house, (Hinson's Chapel,) where a still more remarkable scene occurred. Many hundreds were collected at a funeral service, which was conducted by a church clergyman, who, after the usual forms and a sermon, invited Abbott to address the assembly. A tempest had been rising, covering the heavens; "two clouds appeared to approach from different quarters and met over the house. The people crowded in, up stairs and down, to screen themselves from the storm. With some difficulty the evangelist made his way through the throng, and took his stand on one of the benches. Almost as soon as he began "the Lord out of heaven began also." The tremendous claps of thunder exceeded anything he had ever heard, and the streams of lightning flashed through the house in "a most awful manner. The very foundations shook, the windows jarred with the violence thereof." He lost no time, but "set before them the awful coming of Christ, in all his splendor, with all the armies of heaven, to judge the world, and to take vengeance on the ungodly." The people wept, cried aloud, and fell all through the house. One "old sinner" attempted to escape, but fell to the floor as dead. The lightning, thunder, and rain "continued for about one hour in the most awful manner ever known in that country," during which time he continued to "set before the people the coming of Christ to judge the world, warning and inviting them to flee to him." Many were "convinced and many converted" on that great day. Fourteen years later, while Abbott was passing through the same region, he met "twelve living witnesses," who informed him that they dated their salvation from it, and enumerated others who had died in the faith, and some who had moved out of the neighborhood, who began their Christian life at that memorable time. It was long an occasion of general interest in the neighborhood, and old Methodists of Kent County were accustomed to speak with wonder of what they called "Abbott's thunder-gust sermon." "Between the voice of the Lord from heaven and the voice of his servant in the house, the people had never known such a time." Sterling again joined him in this neighborhood, and they pursued together their travels and labors from town to town, among whites and blacks, attended constantly with these astonishing demonstrations.

In October, 1782, this tireless laborer was again in Delaware, relieving his son on Dover Circuit, and scenes, equally extraordinary with those already cited, were of almost daily occurrence, as he advanced from town to town; the same questionable physical effects, the same unquestionable moral results. He reached Judge White's house, where he met Asbury and a score of other preachers, on their way to a quarterly meeting at Barrett's Chapel. The itinerants were astonished at his simplicity and power. His sermon in the chapel was overwhelming; some of the hearers fell to the floor, and others fled out of the house; many sobbed and prayed aloud. His expedition ended here; it had been successful, and he returned home with a thankful heart. He was now known through much of the land as one of the most extraordinary preachers of Methodism—a Boanerges—before whom gainsayers, persecutors, mobs, either yielded or were prostrated. He was soon to leave house and lands, and, entering the "regular itinerancy," extend his labors and triumphs to other parts of the country, where we shall meet him again.

Meanwhile one of the most distinguished itinerants of the times had entered the field in the South. We have already seen the youthful Jesse Lee introduced into the Church, on Robert Williams's Circuit, in Virginia, a convert in the great revival which was so long maintained by Williams, Jarratt, and their fellow-laborers. Thus endued with power from on high, while yet in his eighteenth year, he was maturing for the great work before him. In 1779 he preached his first sermon in North Carolina. Endowed with quick sensibility and ready utterance, he immediately became a popular speaker. In 1780 his destined career, as a preacher of Methodism, seemed about to be defeated by an unexpected trial. He was drafted into the Revolutionary army, and was compelled to go into camp, but his conscience revolted from war. "I weighed the matter over and over again," he says, "but my mind was settled; as a Christian and as a preacher of the Gospel, I could not fight. However, I determined to go, and to trust in the Lord, and accordingly prepared for my journey." He was ordered on parade. The sergeant offered him a gun, but he would not take it; the lieutenant brought him another, but he refused it. The lieutenant reported the case to the colonel, and returned again with a gun and set it down against him; he still declined to take it; he was then delivered to the guard. The colonel came and remonstrated with him, but unable to answer his objections, left him again to the custody of the guard. He not only refused to violate his conscience by bearing arms, he remembered that he was panoplied for a higher warfare, and immediately set himself about it. A neighboring inn-keeper, while yet in bed, heard his early prayer, was affected to tears, and came entreating him to preach. In a short time the man of God was standing on a bench near the tent of his commanding officer, proclaiming as his text, "Except ye repent, ye shall all likewise perish." "I was enabled," he says, "to speak plainly and without fear. Many of the people, officers as well as men, were bathed in tears before I was done." When his colonel heard of his preaching, "it affected him very much," says Lee, "so he came and took me out to talk with me on the subject of bearing arms. He asked me if I would be willing to drive their baggage-wagon. I told him I would, though I had never driven a wagon before. He said their main cook was a Methodist, and could drive the wagon when we were on a march, and I might lodge and eat with him, to which I agreed. He then released me from guard."

For nearly four months was he detained in the army, suffering severe privations and trials, fatiguing marches, want of food, the clamorous profanity of the camp, and sickness that, in one instance, endangered his life. During these sufferings he continued to preach whenever circumstances admitted, and not without effect on his hardy hearers. Disease prevailed among the troops, and many died. He not only preached to them on Sundays, but practically became their chaplain, going among them where they lay ill in barns, talking to them about their souls, begging them to prepare to meet their God, attending the funerals of those who died, and praying at their graves.

For more than a year after his discharge from the army he was zealously occupied in preaching in his native neighborhood. Before the end of 1782 he was on his way, with a colleague, Edward Dromgoole, to North Carolina, to form a new and extensive circuit. The next year he was appointed to labor regularly in that state; and being now fully in the sphere of his duty, he was largely blessed with the comforts of the divine favor, and went through the extensive rounds of his circuit with continual success. His word was accompanied with the authority and power of the Holy Ghost. Stout-hearted men were smitten down under it, large congregations were often melted into tears by irrepressible emotions, and his eloquent voice was not unfrequently lost amid the sobs and ejaculations of his audience.

Such a spirit could not fail to captivate the multitude. It was characteristic of Lee through his long and successful career. Pathos was natural to him. Humor seems, in some temperaments, to be the natural counterpart, or, at least, re-action of pathos. Lee became noted for his wit; it served him with many a felicitous advantage in his rencounters with opponents, especially in the Northeastern States. It flowed in a genial and perennial stream from his large heart, and played most vividly in his severest itinerant hardships; but he was full of tender humanity and affectionate piety. His rich sensibilities, rather than any remarkable intellectual powers, made him one of the most eloquent and popular preachers of his day. One of his fellow-laborers, a man of excellent judgment, says that he possessed uncommon colloquial powers, and a fascinating address; that his readiness at repartee was scarcely equaled; that he was, moreover, a man of great moral courage.

During the year 1784 he labored on Salisbury Circuit, in the west of North Carolina, and here the same traits characterized, and the same results followed, his ardent ministry. His labors were indefatigable, his journeys incessant, his health at times prostrated, and his life endangered by exposure to the weather and the fording of rivers. Still we hear from him but one language, expressive of unabated fervor, triumphant faith, and yearning, weeping sympathy for souls. During these labors he was repeatedly transferred, for half a year or more, to other circuits. From Norfolk in Virginia to the southwest of North Carolina he hastened to and fro, sounding the alarm, reorganizing Societies which had been nearly destroyed by the disturbances of the war, pioneering Methodism into regions which it had not before penetrated, and raising up some energetic men for the itinerancy. By the latter part of 1784 he had become recognized as a representative man of his denomination.

We have followed, through the stormy period of the Revolution, the principal evangelists of Methodism by such imperfect traces as the scanty records of the times afford. Meanwhile scores of other laborers entered the field, many of them men of might, who have left historic impressions on the denomination and on the country; whose labors have been gigantic in results, but unrecorded in detail. The energy and progress of Methodism during these tumultuous times are surprising. Revivals prevailed in some places throughout the whole period of the Revolution, and the ministry was rapidly reinforced. But many of the Societies, says the contemporary historian, were dispersed or could not assemble, many of their male members were drafted, and when the militia were called out, had to go into the army to fight for their country. He assures us, however, that no sooner had the war ended than the evangelists saw the fruits of their former labors in most of the land, and that the sufferings and dispersion of so many of the Societies proved to be a signal advantage. Many Methodists had, through necessity, fear, or choice, moved into the back settlements, or new parts of the country, some even beyond the great mountain ranges. "As soon as peace was declared, and the way opened, they invited us to come among them; and by their earnest and frequent petitions, both oral and written, we went. They were ready to receive us with open hands and willing hearts, and to cry out, 'Blessed is he that cometh in the name of the Lord.'" In fine, the providential design and adaptation of Methodism, for the new nation, are revealed all through this period of its preparatory operations.

The erection of chapels was retarded, if not arrested, through most of these years. Asbury's project of a building in Norfolk was defeated, and the city laid in ashes; the other scattered chapels in Virginia were hardly more than wooden shells: the two in Baltimore had the rudest accommodations. Thé rural meeting-houses of Maryland could hardly shelter their congregations from the weather. St. George's, in Philadelphia, was used as a riding-school by the British cavalry; but the military authorities, probably through respect for Wesley and the English itinerants in America, gave the Society the use of the First Baptist Church, on Lagrange Place, Front-street. The chapel in Trenton, N. J., was occupied by troops. That of Salem was not projected till about the close of the war; it was the fourth in the state after Bethel, Pemberton, and Trenton, and was hardly better than a barn. It was often besieged by mobs, till at last the magistrates interfered and protected the feeble Society. A profane club of the town continued the persecution, in burlesque imitations of the Methodist worship, but was suddenly arrested by an appalling occurrence in one of their assemblies. While they were amusing themselves with jocular recitations of hymns and exhortations, a female guest rose on a bench to imitate a Methodist class. "Glory to God!" she exclaimed; "I have found peace, I am sanctified; I am now ready to die!" At the last word she fell to the floor a corpse. The club, struck with consternation, never assembled again, and Methodism became eminently influential in the town and all its vicinity. It has been erroneously supposed that John-street Chapel, in New York, was occupied by the British troops during a part of the Revolutionary War. Seven Annual Conferences were, indeed, held without an appointment to that city. The chapels of most denominations in the city were appropriated by the enemy; but John-street was spared, through deference to Wesley and his English representatives in the colonies. The Methodists were allowed to use it themselves on Sunday nights; the Hessian troops, with their chaplain, occupied it in religious services on Sunday mornings. The little flock, though much reduced by the dispersion of many of its members, met regularly, and was providentially provided with pastors. We have already seen that John Mann was converted and received into the Society under the ministry of Boardman. He had graduated, as Class Leader and Exhorter, to the rank of an effective Local Preacher, by the time that the Revolution rendered his services most indispensable to his suffering brethren. They now placed him in charge of their deserted pulpit; he preached in it all through the war, and during the same time acted as Class Leader, Trustee, and Treasurer. His services were of the highest importance in this critical period. They probably saved the Methodism of New York city from at least temporary extinction.

During the war, after the battle of Long Island, no other itinerant crossed the Hudson. The little church in New York was totally isolated from the rest of the Methodist communion. Before the war it reported more than two hundred members; at its close but sixty. Occasionally some of the more important men of the army, from mischief, perhaps, rather than malice, interrupted their humble worship. "Upon a Christmas eve, when the members had assembled to celebrate the advent of the world's Redeemer, a party of British officers, masked, marched into the chapel. One, very properly personifying their master, was dressed with cloven feet and a long forked tail. The devotions of course soon ceased, and the chief devil, proceeding up the aisle, entered the altar. As he was ascending the stairs of the pulpit, a gentleman present, with his cane, knocked off his Satanic majesty's mask, when, lo, there stood a well-known British colonel! He was immediately seized and detained, until the city guard was sent to take charge of the bold offender. The congregation retired, and the entrances of the church were locked upon the prisoner for additional security. His companions outside then commenced an attack upon the doors and windows, but the arrival of the guard put an end to these disgraceful proceedings, and the prisoner was delivered into their custody."

During most of the war Methodism had its chief successes in its southern fields. Abbott and his fellow-laborers kept it alive and moving in New Jersey, and at the peace that state reported more than one thousand members; but, out of the nearly fourteen thousand returned in 1783, more than twelve thousand were in Delaware, Maryland, Virginia, and North Carolina. There were more within the small limits of Delaware than in Pennsylvania, New Jersey, or New York. At the end of the war there was probably not a Methodist in the Eastern States; for the Society formed by Boardman, in Boston, had become extinct. It was to achieve its chief triumphs, for some time yet, southward and westward, and to encounter in those directions adventures and hardships for which the ardent and generous spirit of its présent people and ministry peculiarly fitted it. It went forward, not only preaching and praying, but also "shouting," infecting the adventurous and scattered populations of the wilderness and frontiers with its evangelic enthusiasm, and gathering them by thousands into its communion. It pressed northward, at first, with the same zealous ardor, but became there gradually attempered with a more deliberate, a more practical, yet a hardly less energetic spirit. The characteristics of both sections blended, securing to it at once unity, enthusiasm, and practical wisdom, especially in its great fields in the West, where, for the last half century, and probably for all future time, it was destined to have its most important sway.

CHAPTER XII.

CONFERENCES AND PROGRESS FROM THE BEGINNING OF THE REVOLUTIONARY WAR TO THE ORGANIZATION OF THE METHODIST EPISCOPAL CHURCH.

For some years the infant Churches of American Methodism were content with humble "Quarterly Conferences" as their only judicatories or synods. These were held mostly in obscure places, their sessions occupying but a day or two, their members consisting of a few Itinerants, Local Preachers, Exhorters, and subordinate officials, gathered from neighboring circuits, and their records so slight, or deemed so unimportant, that I am not aware that an official copy of any of them remains. Not till Rankin arrived, as "assistant" of Wesley, did they hold an Annual Conference. But two of these annual sessions were held prior to our present period, both in Philadelphia, the first in 1773, the second in 1774. The printed records of both scarcely cover a page and a half of the octavo Minutes. Both have already been noticed. In the ten years now under review one session at least was held annually; in five of these years (1779–1783) ten took place; in the last year of the period (1784) there were no less than three, the final one being the memorable epoch of the Episcopal organization of Methodism.

Seventeen sessions were held in these ten years, and yet their records do not exceed fifteen pages in the printed Minutes. The contrast of their original humility with the greatness of their historical results can hardly fail to strike us as sublime. In obscurity, if not ignominy, amid poverty, persecutions, and strifes of politics and arms that swept over them like tempests, they were laying, stone by stone, the foundations of an ecclesiastical edifice whose dome was to cover the continent from the Atlantic to the Pacific, from the frozen zone to the Gulf of Mexico. Some of their obscure laborers were to see this grand consummation. The humble coral builders work in the obscure depths of the seas, but lay the foundations of beautiful and extended lands, upon which nature may rear her magnificent growths, and man his communities; and science traces their work, in the foundations of the globe, so far back as the Silurian period, and, in heavenward monuments, thousands of feet above the level of the seas.

All these Annual Conferences, and all subsequent sessions down to the organization of the General or Quadrennial Conference, were considered adjourned meetings of the undivided ministry, held at different places, often widely apart, for the local convenience of the scattered itinerants. The enactments of no one session were binding, till they had been adopted at all the other sessions of the same ecclesiastical year, and had thus become the expression of a majority of the ministry.

The Conference of 1775 began in Philadelphia on the 17th of May, not quite one month after the outbreak of hostilities at Concord and Lexington, and but a few months after the session of the Colonial Congress in the same city. The country was surging with agitation and martial preparations. Three candidates were admitted on trial, six probationers were received into full membership, and nineteen preachers were enrolled on the list of appointments. The returns of members amounted to 3,148, the increase was therefore 1,075, more than a third of the whole number. The only proceedings of this Conference, aside from the reception and appointment of preachers, related to the exchange of circuits, in some instances to take place quarterly, in others semi-annually; to the expenses of preachers from the session to their circuits, which was to be paid out of the public collections; and to a general fast in behalf of the prosperity of the Church and the "peace of America." The latter was repeated in the three ensuing years.

The next session was begun in Baltimore on the 21st of May, 1776. Asbury was not present; he set out on horseback for the city, but in such exhausted health that he had to return. Rankin makes no reference to the session, except in a later allusion to its Love-feast. Watters was present, and says: "It was a good time, and I was much refreshed in meeting with my brethren and companions in tribulation, and in the kingdom of Jesus Christ. We were of one heart and mind, and took sweet counsel together. We had a powerful time in our Love-feast a little before we parted, while we sat at our divine Master's feet, and gladly heard each other tell what the Lord had done, for and by us, in the different places in which we had been laboring." This was the first Conference attended by young Freeborn Garrettson; he entered it with insupportable anxieties; he had been preaching irregularly; but the question of the consecration of his whole remaining life to the labors and trials of the itinerancy was now to be decided, and he recoiled at the prospect. "The exercise of my mind," he writes, "was too great for my emaciated frame. I betook myself to my bed and lay till twelve o'clock; then I rose up and set off. I got into Baltimore about sunset. The Conference was to begin the next day: I attended, passed through an examination, was admitted on trial, and my name was, for the first time, classed among the Methodists. I received of Mr. Rankin a written license. My mind continued so agitated, for I still felt an unwillingness to be a traveling preacher, that, after I went from the preaching house to dinner, I again fainted under my burden and sank to the floor. When I recovered I found myself in an upper chamber on the bed, surrounded by several preachers. I asked where I had been, as I seemed to be lost to all things below, appearing to have been in a place from whence I did not desire to return. The brethren joined in prayer, and my soul was so happy, while everything wore so pleasing an aspect that the preachers appeared to me more like angels than men. And I have praised the Lord ever since, that, though unworthy of a seat among them, I was ever united to this happy family."

The Conference began on Tuesday, and concluded on Friday. It was held in the second Methodist Chapel built in the city, on Lovely Lane. This edifice had been erected about two years, but was yet hardly furnished; the seats had no backs; it had no provision for warming, and no galleries. It was still "the day of small things," though of vast hopes, with American Methodism. Rankin presided as Wesley's "Assistant." The aggregate membership reported was 4,921; the increase for the year was 1,773, the largest gains yet recorded. Twenty-five itinerants were on the roll of the Conference, a gain of five. Four new circuits were recognized; all in Virginia, except one, which was in North Carolina, and is the first appearance of that state in the Minutes. Methodism had been energetically pushing its conquests into the state for about three years; Pilmoor, as we have seen, passed through it preaching in 1773; Robert Williams entered it the same year, and, in the next, formed Societies within its bounds. Nine candidates were received on trial, and five probationers were admitted to full membership. Among the former was Nicholas Watters, brother to the first native itinerant, William Watters; he died an itinerant in Charleston, S. C., in 1804. Also Francis Poythress, who became one of the itinerant heroes of these times; and though his last years were darkened by clouds, he is still recalled by aged Methodists with vivid interest. He was a Virginian of large estate, but of dissipated habits in his youth. The conversations and rebukes of a lady of high social position arrested him in his perilous course. He returned from her house confounded, penitent, and determined to reform his morals. Hearing of the devoted Jarratt, he hastened to his parish, and was entertained some time under his hospitable roof for instruction. There he found purification and peace about the year 1772. It was not long before he began to co-operate with Jarratt in his public labors amid the extraordinary scenes of religious interest which prevailed through all that region. Thus, before the arrival of the Methodist itinerants in Virginia, he had become an evangelist; when they appeared he learned with delight their doctrines and methods of labor, and joining them, became a giant in their ranks. In 1775 he began his travels, under the authority of a quarterly meeting of Brunswick Circuit, and, the present year, appears, for the first time, on the roll of the Conference. Henceforth, in North Carolina, Virginia, Maryland, and Kentucky, he was to be a representative man of the struggling cause. In 1783 he bore its standard across the Alleghanies to the waters of the Youghiogheny. His name stands in the Minutes of 1802 for the last time among the elders, but without an appointment, for he had become incurably insane, by excessive labors and anxieties for a Western Methodist Seminary.

The session of 1777 began on the 20th of May, at a "preaching house," say the Minutes, "near Deer Creek, in Harford County, Md." It was the "preaching house" of John Watters, at this time one of the chief rural centers of Methodism in the state. Though the storm of war was now howling through the land, "and there were," says the historian, "fears within and fightings without in all directions," the small ministerial band assembled, not only in peace, but with gratulations over the evangelical victories of the last year. The returns showed a gain in the ministry of fully one third, and in the membership of considerably more than one third. "It was submitted," says Watters, "to the consideration of this Conference whether in our present situation, of having but few ministers left in many of our parishes to administer the ordinances of baptism and the Lord's supper, we should not administer them ourselves, for as yet we had not the ordinances among us, but were dependent on other denominations for them. After much conversation on the subject, it was unanimously agreed to lay it over for the determination of the next Conference, to be held in Leesburgh the 19th of May. I never saw so affecting a scene as the parting of the preachers. Our hearts were knit together as the hearts of David and Jonathan, and we were obliged to use great violence to our feelings in tearing ourselves asunder."

The membership amounted to 6,968, its increase being 2,047, the largest yet reported. The ministerial roll recorded thirty-eight names; there were fourteen circuits supplied by thirty-six preachers. The ministry already felt strong in its native men; Watters, Poythress, Garrettson, Dromgoole,

Cooper, Gatch, Ruff, and others now joining their ranks, Pedicord, Tunnell, Gill, Dickins, besides not a few who, like Abbott, were strenuously active, though not yet in the Conference: these, headed by Asbury, formed a force which rendered the denomination independent of England. Some of them were men of essential greatness of intellect and character, swaying the popular mind, through much of the middle states, for years, and recognized, at the beginning of our century, throughout the whole range of Methodism as its leaders. The "question of the sacraments" was again discussed, as the citation from Watters intimates. It was asked, "What shall be done with respect to the ordinances?" "Let the preachers pursue the old plan as from the beginning," was the answer. It appears, however, that already the sacramental party were too strong to be thus peremptorily silenced; and, to appease them, the possibility of an accommodation was admitted, for it was further asked, "What alteration may we make in our original plan?" And the answer was, "Our next Conference will, if God permit, show us more clearly." The subject was not allowed to sleep, as we shall hereafter see.

Fourteen preachers were received on trial, and eight admitted to membership. Among the former was Caleb B. Pedicord, one of the saintliest men of his age. His personal appearance is remembered as peculiarly interesting; his aspect was beautiful in its combined expression of intelligence, and moral refinement. His voice, in both singing and preaching, had a dissolving power of tenderness. Marvels are told of the quiet, pathetic force of his sermons. He continued in the itinerancy till his death, traveling and preaching with great popularity in Maryland, Delaware, New Jersey, and Virginia. Soon after he had entered upon his circuit, in Dorchester County, Md., he was attacked, on the highway, till the blood dripped down his person. He took shelter in the house of a friend, and, while his stripes were being washed, a brother of his assailant entered, and ascertaining the cruel grievance, mounted his horse and hastily rode away, indignantly threatening to chastise the persecutor. The latter was soon overtaken, and so severely beaten that he promised never to trouble another itinerant. Pedicord could not approve such a vindication; but he might well rejoice afterward over one of those striking coincidences which so often attended the labors and sufferings of the early itinerants, for both these brothers were subsequently seen sitting, "in their right minds," in the communion of the persecuted Methodists. The itinerant bore the scars of his wounds to his grave.

A memorable instance of his usefulness occurred on this circuit. He was an excellent singer; while riding slowly on the highway to an appointment at Mount Holly he was singing,

"I cannot, I cannot forbear
These passionate longings for home;
O! when shall my spirit be there?
O! when will the messenger come?"

A young soldier of the Revolution, wandering in a neighboring forest, heard him, and "was deeply touched not only with the melody of his voice, which was among the best he ever heard, but with the words, especially the last couplet." "After he ceased," writes the listener, "I went out and followed him a great distance, hoping he would begin again. He, however, stopped at the house of a Methodist and dismounted. I then concluded he must be a Methodist Preacher, and would probably preach that evening." That evening the youthful soldier heard him, and Caleb B. Pedicord thus became "the spiritual father" of Thomas Ware, one of the most pure-minded and successful of early Methodist itinerants—for fifty years a founder of the denomination from New Jersey to Tennessee, from Massachusetts to the Carolinas, and, by his pen, one of the best contributors to its early history.

John Tunnell was received on probation at the Conference of this year; a name fragrant to the Methodists of that early day, though familiar to few of our times. "He was truly an apostolic man; his heavenly-mindedness seemed to shine on his face, and made him appear more like an inhabitant of heaven than of earth." After several years of indefatigable labors in the Middle States, he was sent, by the Conference in 1787, with four itinerants, among whom was young Thomas Ware, beyond the mountains, to the "Holston country, now called

East Tennessee." He thus scaled the Alleghanies, and, though comparatively forgotten by us, takes historical rank among the founders of Methodism in the great valley of the West, its most important arena. He died near "Sweet Springs," in July, 1790; his brethren bore his remains over the mountains, about five miles east of the Sweet Springs. Asbury preached his funeral sermon at Dew's Chapel, and interred him there, among the hills of Western Virginia, where he sleeps without a memorial.

William Gill was the bosom friend of John Tunnell, and one of the most eminent itinerants of his times; yet, like his heroic friend, is hardly known in our day. He was a native of Delaware, and the first Methodist traveling preacher raised up in that state; a man of superior intellect and acquisitions, which so impressed Dr. Rush, who attended him during a period of sickness in Philadelphia, as to dispose that great man ever afterward to defend the Methodist ministry against the prevalent imputations of ignorance and fanaticism. His last field was Kent Circuit, Md., in 1788, where he died declaring "all is well," and closed his eyes with his own hands as he expired. Of these men, once so deservedly eminent, but now so slightly known, one of their best contemporaries (Thomas Ware) says that next to Asbury, "in the estimation of many stood the placid Tunnell, the philosophic Gill, and the pathetic Pedicord."

These were not the only important men who appeared in the itinerancy at this period. Reuben Ellis was another; he was born in North Carolina, and was one of the earliest itinerants raised up in that state. During nearly twenty years he traversed the colonies from Pennsylvania to Georgia, "sounding the alarm" amid the din of the Revolutionary War. He fell at his post in Baltimore, in 1796, "leaving few behind him who were, in every respect, his equals." John Dickins was also a notable Evangelist of these times. He traveled extensively in Virginia and North Carolina from 1777 till 1782, when he located, but continued to labor diligently in the latter state. Asbury met him there in 1780, when Dickins framed a subscription paper for a seminary, on the plan of Wesley's

Kingswood School; the first project of a literary institution among American Methodists. It resulted in Cokesbury College. At the close of the war Asbury induced him to go to New York, where he took charge of John-street Church in 1783. In 1789 he was stationed in Philadelphia, and there began one of the greatest institutions of American Methodism, its "Book Concern;" there also he departed to heaven by a triumphant death, in the memorable outbreak of the yellow fever in 1798. He was one of the ablest preachers of the early Methodist ministry; a good scholar; singularly wise and influential in counsel, and mighty in the pulpit—"one of the greatest and best men of that age; as it was said of Whitefield, he preached like a lion."

In reviewing the recruits of the ministry for this year, a Methodist historian remarks that "never before had such a class of strong men, such talented and useful preachers, entered into the itinerancy, to labor in the American field of Methodism."

The sixth Annual Conference began at Leesburgh, Va., on the 19th of May, 1778. It was the first session held in that province, then the chief field of Methodism, comprising nearly two thirds of its members. But a graver reason led the Conference to this interior and comparatively remote locality. It was a desolate year to both the country and the Church. Philadelphia and New York were both in possession of the British; the waters of Maryland were occupied by the royal fleet, and general dismay prevailed. All the English itinerants, save Asbury, had fled, and he was in confinement at the house of Judge White. The statistics of the Conference show the effect of the public troubles. Its Minutes barely occupy a page in print; the returns of the individual circuits are not given; the aggregate membership is hastily inserted, and is but 6,095, showing a loss of 873. The ministry has diminished from 38 to 30; the list of circuits indicates important changes: New York, Philadelphia, Norfolk, and others are omitted, amounting to no less than five; but there is an addition of six, making fifteen, a gain of one.

As Rankin had retreated and Asbury was in seclusion, William Watters, the senior native itinerant, presided at this

Conference, though he was not yet twenty-seven years old. Watters says of the session that, "As the consideration of the administration of the ordinances was laid over, at the last Conference, till this, it of course came up and found many advocates. It was with considerable difficulty that a large majority was prevailed on to lay it over again till the next Conference, hoping that we should, by that time, be able to see our way more clear in so important a change." The controversy will soon culminate, amid general alarm and no little peril, but it will finally prove itself to have been one of the most providential events of the incipient history of the denomination, the provocation and reason of its effective and permanent organization. About half the probationers, received at this time, traveled but two or three years. Some of the others became more or less distinguished in the Church. One of them, James O'Kelly, will hereafter appear in an unfortunate contest with the denomination; in these early times, however, he was highly esteemed for his talents and his fervent devotion.

Henry Willis is another pre-eminent name. He was the first man that Asbury ordained deacon and elder after the Christmas Conference. After years of apostolic labors his lungs failed, but he had such an estimate of the ministerial vocation that he deemed it his duty never to abandon his post till death should cancel his commission. The Minutes speak of him as "a great man of God, who extended his labors from New York, in the North, to Charleston, in the South, and to the Western waters. In these stations the name of Willis will be held in venerable remembrance." He was the first Methodist preacher stationed in Charleston, and one of the first who pioneered Methodism across the Alleghanies.

Two Conferences were held in the year 1779. The first was at the house of Judge White, Kent County, Del., on the 28th of April, to accommodate Asbury (who was confined there) and the preachers east of the Potomac; the second at Fluvanna, Va., on the 18th of May. Though their records are distinct in the Minutes, they have been deemed one Conference. The sacramental controversy was still rife among the preachers in Virginia, and Asbury doubtless hoped, by the more northern, anticipatory session, to forestall its threatened issues. Sixteen preachers, probably the whole number present, including Asbury and Watters, pledged themselves "to take the station this Conference shall place them in, and continue till the next Conference;" implying, it would seem, an apprehension that the regular session at Fluvanna might dissent from the proceedings at Kent. Preachers were ordered to meet the classes, at all their appointments if possible, and to meet the children once a fortnight, and counsel parents "with regard to their conduct toward them." The term of ministerial probation was changed from one year to two. Anticipating, probably, the proceedings at Fluvanna, the question was asked, "Shall we guard against a separation from the Church direct or indirect?" and answered, "By all means." Asbury was recognized as "General Assistant in America."

The statistics of the year are given only in the Minutes of the Fluvanna session. Eleven preachers were reported on trial. The whole number of traveling preachers was forty-four,* a gain of fourteen. The circuits numbered twenty, a gain of five. The returns of members amounted to 8,577, the increase to 2,482. The success of the year had been unexpectedly great, considering the tumults of the period. Lee says that "in some places the work of the Lord spread rapidly, and bore down all before it. But in many places the Societies were thrown into great disorder and confusion, by reason of the war which continued to rage through the land." We have, from the manuscript Journal of Gatch, the leader of the Fluvanna session, a fuller view of the sacramental controversy; the great fact in its proceedings, though entirely omitted in its published Minutes. This momentous question had been broached in the first American Conference, 1773. At the session of 1777 it was not dismissed, but only postponed to the ensuing session; at the latter it was again postponed until the session of 1779. The Fluvanna Conference being the "regularly appointed" session of this year, had the question therefore legitimately before it—referred directly to it by the

* The Minutes say forty-nine; but repeat those on Baltimore and Frederick Circuits.

preceding session. As a further reason for determining the controversy, they said, "The Episcopal Establishment is now dissolved in this country; and, therefore, in almost all our circuits the members are without the ordinances." They appointed "a committee"—Gatch, Foster, Cole, and Ellis—and constituted it "a Presbytery:" "first, to administer the ordinances themselves; second, to authorize any other preacher or preachers, approved by them, by the form of laying on of hands." The committee, or presbytery, ordained one another, and afterward such of the preachers present "as were desirous of receiving ordination." Such were the proceedings of the Conference on this important question. They were not only legitimate but harmonious. The Fluvanna Conference not only included a majority of the preachers and circuits, but comprised, in the list of its appointments, a very preponderating majority of the membership of the Church. "Most of our preachers," says Lee, "in the South fell in with this new plan; and as the leaders of the party were very zealous, and the greater part of them very pious men, the private members were influenced by them and pretty generally fell in with their measures; however, some of the old Methodists would not commune with them, but steadily adhered to their old customs. There was great cause to fear a division, and both parties trembled for the ark of God, and shuddered at the thought of dividing the Church of Christ. But, after all, they consented, for the sake of peace and the union of the body of Methodists, to drop the ordinances, for a season, till Mr. Wesley could be consulted." Most of the preachers who entered the itinerancy at these two sessions retired after a few years. The Fluvanna session had adjourned to Manakintown, Powhatan County, Va., May 8th, 1780. But the Minutes give none of the proceedings of this Conference; it is unmentioned in all our contemporary official documents; the indirect indications of its session are so obscure that few Methodists are to-day aware that any such Conference was ever held. It did meet, however, and, notwithstanding the efforts made during the preceding year to counteract the measures of the Fluvanna session, the session at Manakintown represented fully one half the circuits and nearly one half the preachers and membership of the denomination. Asbury, designated by the informal session in Kent to the office of General Assistant, called a Conference of the more northern preachers at Baltimore, on the 24th of April, and thus anticipated the Manakintown session by two weeks. Garrettson justly says, "The next Conference was appointed to be held at Manakintown, Va., May, 1780. Prior to this Conference we northern preachers thought it expedient, for our own convenience, to hold one in Baltimore, at which Messrs. Asbury, Watters, and Garrettson were appointed, as delegates to the Virginia Conference, to bring them back if possible to our original usages. The proposition that we made to them was, that they should suspend the administration of the ordinances for one year; in the mean while we would consult Mr. Wesley; and in the following May we would have a union Conference in Baltimore, and abide by his judgment. To this proposal they unanimously agreed; and a letter, containing a circumstantial account of the case, drawn up by Mr. Dickins, was sent to Mr. Wesley. In May, 1781, we met and received Mr. Wesley's answer, which was, that we should continue on the old plan until further direction. We unanimously agreed to follow his counsel, and went on harmoniously." We have the proceedings only of the Baltimore session of 1780, except the list of appointments made at Manakintown, which, after the fortunate reconciliation of the parties, was inserted in the Minutes of the year, though apart from the list made at Baltimore.

The Baltimore session was held in the new church on Lovely Lane; Asbury, who now finally ventured out of his retirement, presided. The minutes show twenty circuits; some old ones disappear, merged in new ones, of which there are three. There are forty-three traveling preachers, including Asbury, a decrease of one. Five are recorded as received on trial, and five "into full connection." The members returned are 8,504; showing a loss of seventy-three. The Conference resolved to "disapprove the practice of distilling grain into liquor, and disown all who would not renounce it." Preachers holding slaves were required to "give promises to set them free." It was declared that "this Conference acknowledges that slavery is contrary to the laws of God, man, and nature, and hurtful to society; contrary to the dictates of conscience and pure religion, and doing that which we would not that others should do to us and ours;" and that "we do pass our disapprobation on all our friends who keep slaves, and advise their freedom." Methodism thus early recorded its protest against negro slavery, anticipating its abolition in Massachusetts by three years, in Rhode Island and Connecticut by four years; the thesis of Clarkson, before the University of Cambridge, by five years; and the ordinance of Congress against it, in the Northwestern Territory, by seven years. Respecting the proceedings at Fluvanna, it was declared that "this whole Conference disapproves the step taken by the brethren in Virginia;" that "we look upon them no longer as Methodists, in connection with Mr. Wesley and us, till they come back;" and Asbury, Watters, and Garrettson were appointed to "attend the Virginia Conference, to inform them of their proceedings, and receive their answer." The "conditions of union with the Virginia brethren" were, that the latter should "suspend all their administrations, and all meet together in Baltimore the next year." The three delegates visited the Fluvanna brethren. Watters says, "After waiting two days, and all hopes of an accommodation failing, we had fixed on starting back early in the morning; but late in the evening it was proposed by one of their own party in Conference (none of the others being present) that there should be a suspension of the ordinances for the present year, and that our circumstances should be laid before Mr. Wesley, and his advice solicited; also that Mr. Asbury should be requested to ride through the different circuits, and superintend the work at large. The proposal, in a few minutes, took with all but a few. In the morning, instead of coming off in despair, we were invited to take our seats again in the Conference, where, with great rejoicings and praises to God, we, on both sides, heartily agreed to the accommodation. I could not but say it is of the Lord's doing, and it is marvelous in our eyes."

Few of the preachers who began their ministerial travels

this year continued long in the itinerant service. Half of them at least retired, in from two to five years. Some, however, were eminent in their day either for talents or for services before or after their location.

In 1781 a preparatory Conference was held by Asbury and about twenty preachers at Judge White's, in Delaware, on the 16th of April; but the regular session began in Baltimore on the 24th. The restoration of harmony seemed now nearly complete. Asbury wrote at the Baltimore session: "All but one agreed to return to the old plan and give up the administration of the ordinances. Our troubles now seem over from that quarter, and there appears to be a considerable change in the preachers from North to South. All was conducted in peace and love." Their restored harmony was confirmed by the evident blessing of God upon the labors of the past year. No less than 10,539 members were reported, showing an increase of 2,035. Lee records that "the Lord had wonderfully favored the traveling preachers, so that we spread our borders, and our numbers increased abundantly." There were twenty-five circuits, a gain of five; and fifty-five preachers, including Asbury, a gain of twelve. Deducting the "locations," the ministerial additions were no less than seventeen. Thirty-nine preachers, probably all who were present save one, subscribed a declaration of their determination "to discountenance a separation among either preachers or people," and "to preach the old Methodist doctrine, and strictly enforce the Discipline, as contained in the Notes, Sermons, and Minutes published by Wesley." Of the more than 10,500 Methodists now reported in the country, there were but 873 north of the southern boundary of Pennsylvania; 9,666 were below it.

Philip Bruce, of North Carolina, was now received on probation. He was of Huguenotic descent, a soldier of the Revolution, and one of the most laborious founders of the Church in the South. For thirty-six years he bore faithfully the standard of the Gospel as an itinerant. He closed his useful life the oldest traveling preacher in the Methodist Episcopal Church in the United States, except Freeborn Garrettson. He was a man of high and firm character and intellect.

Joseph Everett, a native of Maryland, now also joined the itinerancy. He was long known in the Middle States as one of the veterans of Methodism; a man of unique character, of exhaustless energy, profound piety, and extraordinary success. He has been called "the roughest-spoken preacher that ever stood in the itinerant ranks." He describes himself as having been one of Bunyan's "biggest Jerusalem sinners." An historian of Methodism (Bangs) who knew him, and who pronounces him "a remarkable man," says, "he was indeed anointed of God to preach the Gospel. He was eminently distinguished for the boldness, the pointedness, and energy with which he rebuked sin and warned sinners of their danger. And these searching appeals to the consciences of his hearers made them tremble under the fearful apprehension of the wrath of God, and their high responsibility to him for their conduct. Great was the success which attended his faithful admonitions; for wherever he went he was like a flame of fire." For about thirty years it may be said that he thundered the truth through New Jersey, Pennsylvania, Delaware, Maryland, and Virginia. The Conference, in recording his death, said that wherever he traveled he "proclaimed the thunders of Sinai against the wicked, and the terrors of the Lord against the ungodly. Few men in the ministry were ever more zealous and laborious. He feared the face of no man. He spent his time, his talents, his all, in the service of the connection." The closing scene of his life is recorded as "very remarkable." He died in 1809, in his seventy-eighth year, under the roof of his friend Dr. White, where he had often found an asylum. About midnight he awoke from a tranquil slumber, and "immediately his devout and pious soul entered into an uncommon ecstasy of joy; with exclamations of adoration, in raptures, he shouted for twenty-five minutes, 'Glory! glory! glory!' and then ceased to shout and ceased to breathe at once."

The ministry, now more than half a hundred strong, was fast becoming a great power in the land. It already included men of gigantic moral and intellectual stature, and they kept most of the middle and southern colonies astir with their ceaseless proclamations of the truth amid the distractions of the war. No thoughtful observer could fail to perceive that the energies and materials of a mighty ecclesiastical structure, probably to be coextensive with the continent, were being gathered and consolidated, and must, if overtaken by no early disaster, assume before long firm foundations and impregnable strength. Happily the war was now ending; the British forces surrendered in the autumn at Yorktown, and with the return of peace the whole land was to open as the arena of the heroic evangelists.

The Conference of 1782 held two sessions; the first on the 17th of April, at Ellis's Chapel, Sussex County, Va., the second on the 21st of May, at Baltimore. They are recorded in the Minutes as one Conference. It was, in fine, now understood that two sessions should be held annually for the accommodation of the widely-dispersed preachers; but the legislative power of the body was limited to the oldest or more northern portion of the ministry.

Asbury says of the Virginia session that "as there had been much distress felt by those of Virginia, relative to the administration of the ordinances, I proposed, to such as were so disposed, to enter into a written agreement to cleave to the old plan in which we had been so greatly blessed, that we might have the greater confidence in each other, and know on whom to depend. This instrument was signed by the greater part of the preachers without hesitation. Next morning I preached on Phil. ii, 1–5. I had liberty, and it pleased God to set it home. One of the preachers, James Haw, who had his difficulties, was delivered from them all; and with the exception of one, all the signatures of the preachers present were obtained. We received seven into connection, and four remained on trial. At noon Mr. Jarratt spoke on the union of the attributes." His Journal affords us but few intimations of the Baltimore session. On Monday, the 20th of May, he says: "A few of us began Conference in Baltimore; next day we had a full meeting. The preachers all signed the agreement proposed at the Virginia Conference, and there was a unanimous resolve to adhere to the old Methodist plan. We spent most of the day in examining the preachers. We had regular daily preaching. Wednesday, 22, we had many things before us. Our printing plan was suspended for the present for want of funds. Friday, 24, was set apart for fasting and prayer. We had a love-feast; the Lord was present, and all was well. We have now fifty-nine traveling preachers, and eleven thousand seven hundred and eighty-five in Society. Our young men are serious, and their gifts are enlarged." The statistics of the year show continued prosperity. The membership, amounting to 11,785, showed an increase of 1,246. There were sixty preachers, including Asbury, a gain of five; thirteen candidates were received on trial, and twenty-six circuits were recorded on the roll of appointments.

The Conference unanimously recognized Asbury as General Assistant, "according to Mr. Wesley's original appointment" before the arrival of Rankin. It was ordained, for the first time, that a certificate of membership should be required of laymen removing from one Society to another. The times and places of the sessions of the ensuing year also occur, for the first time, in the Minutes.

In 1783 the Conference held its two sessions again at Ellis's Preaching-house, Sussex County, Va., and Baltimore, Md., the former on the 7th, the latter on the 27th, of May. Asbury says of the former, "Some young laborers were taken in to assist in spreading the Gospel, which greatly prospers in the North. We all agreed in the spirit of African liberty, and strong testimonies were borne in its favor in our love-feast; our affairs were conducted in love." Of the Baltimore session he merely remarks that on Tuesday "we began our Conference with what preachers were present. On Wednesday we had a full assembly, which lasted until Friday. We had a love-feast, and parted in peace." Garrettson says there "were about sixty preachers" at Baltimore," "all of whom appeared to be in the spirit of the Gospel." The year had been prosperous; 13,740 members were reported, showing an increase of 1,955. There were now but 1,623 Methodists north of Mason and Dixon's line, 12,117 south of it. There were thirty-nine circuits. The corps of itinerants had increased from sixty to eighty-two, including Asbury. The most important measures of this Conference were, like those of the preceding year, initiated at the Virginia session, though dependent for their validity on that of Maryland. It took high "temperance" ground. We have seen that in 1780 the distillation of ardent spirits was denounced, and all Methodists who would not "renounce the practice" were to be "disowned." This year the Conference declared the manufacture, or sale, or use of them "as drams," to be "wrong in its nature and consequences," and ordered its preachers "to teach the people to put away this evil." It took another bold position, strikingly significant for the time and the place. Asbury's allusion to the Virginia session shows that there was no little popular ardor for "African liberty," among both preachers and people, in that region. At the session of 1780 slavery was denounced, and "traveling preachers," owning slaves, were required to emancipate them. At Ellis's Preaching-house it was now required that "Local Preachers" should follow this example, wherever the civil laws would allow them. The Revolutionary struggle of the country had produced a general sentiment in favor of the liberty of all men. Methodism was now imbued with this sentiment, and gave at this time, and for some years, a more articulate expression of it than any other religious community of the land, not excepting the Society of Friends; but it at last fatally compromised its primitive convictions, and thereby entailed lamentable disasters upon itself, if not upon the whole nation. There were some married preachers in the itinerant ranks, and it became necessary to provide better support for their families. Eleven "preachers' wives" are named "to be provided for." They probably were most, if not all, who pertained to the ministry, a fact which indicates that about seventy-one, out of the eighty itinerants, were yet practically bound to celibacy, the necessity of their hard lot.

Twenty preachers are recorded, for the first time, in the appointments of this year. Most of them traveled but few years. Jesse Lee, the first historian of American Methodism, and its founder in New England, was received at this Conference. The itinerancy made one of its most important acquisitions, this year, in Thomas Ware, of New Jersey, a man of admirable character, and an able and faithful laborer, who lived far into our own century. At the breaking out of the Revolutionary War he responded to the call of his country, and entered the army. Though he had not yet made profession of a religious life, he began his new career with manly and even devout sentiments. He was resolutely temperate in the camp, pouring upon the ground the strong drink given with his rations. He continued in the service till dismissed, as an invalid, suffering from "camp fever," which "cost him several years of the prime of his life." One day he observed Pedicord riding into Mount Holly, singing a hymn, as we have noticed. He followed the itinerant a "great distance," fascinated by the pathos of his voice, and that night heard him preach. "When the meeting closed," he says, "I hastened to my lodgings, retired to my room, fell upon my knees before God, and spent much of the night in penitential tears. Pedicord returned to our village. I hastened to see him, and tell him all that was in my heart. He shed tears over me, and prayed. I was dissolved in tears. He prayed again. My soul was filled with unutterable delight. He now rejoiced over me as a son, 'an heir of God, and a joint heir with Christ.'" He joined the Methodists, was made a Class Leader, and, not long after, an Exhorter. He possessed lively faculties, readiness of speech, and a pathos which gave him "the eloquence of tears."

About three months after the Conference of this year, Asbury, rejoicing over the increasing prosperity of the denomination, wrote to his old fellow-laborer, George Shadford, then in England, a letter which affords us some historical intimations of the times. "Long has been thy absence," he says; "many, many have been the thoughts I have had about thee, and my trials and consolations in losing and gaining friends. We have about 14,000 members, between 70 and 80 traveling preachers, between 30 and 40 circuits. Four clergymen have behaved themselves friendly in attending Quarterly Meetings, and recommending us by word and letter. They are, Mr. Jarratt, in Virginia, as you know; Mr. Pettigrew, North Carolina; Dr. M'Gaw, Philadelphia; and Mogden, in East Jersey.

You have heard of the divisions about that improper question proposed at Deer Creek Conference: 'What shall be done about the ordinances?' You know we stood foot by foot to oppose it. God has brought good out of evil, and it has so cured them that I think there will never be anything formidable in that way again. I admire the simplicity of our preachers. I do not think there has appeared another such a company of young devoted men. The Gospel has taken a universal spread. I travel 4,000 miles in a year, all weathers, among rich and poor, Dutch and English. O my dear Shadford, it would take a month to write out and speak what I want you to know. The most momentous is my constant communion with God as *my* God; my glorious victory over the world and the devil. I am continually with God. I preach frequently, and with more enlargement of heart than ever. O America! America! it certainly will be the glory of the world for religion!"

The Conference held two sessions in the year 1784, the first at Ellis's Preaching-house, Virginia, on the 30th of April, the second in Baltimore on the 25th of May. An extraordinary session, forever memorable as the "Christmas Conference," was also held at the close of the year in Baltimore, but its momentous proceedings claim separate consideration. The two regular sessions are reported, as one Conference, in the official Minutes. Asbury alludes but briefly to the Virginia session. On the 29th of April he writes that he "rode to Ellis's Chapel, in Sussex County, where we held our Conference the two ensuing days. Brother O'Kelly gave us a good sermon: 'I keep under my body, and bring it into subjection,' etc. Mr. Jarratt gave us a good discourse on 1 Tim. 1, 4. Our business was conducted with uncommon love and unity. From this Conference I proceeded on and crossed James River, on my way to the North, and was led to cry to God to go with us and meet us there." He reached Baltimore on the 20th of May, after a ride of fifty miles, and on the 25th opened the second session. Young Thomas Ware was present. He says: "It was the first I attended. There was quite a number of preachers present. Although there were but few on whose heads time had begun to snow, yet several of them appeared to be way-worn and weather-beaten into premature old age. I doubt whether there ever has been a Conference among us in which an equal number could be found, in proportion to the whole, so dead to the world, and so gifted and enterprising as were present at that of 1784. They had much to suffer at that early period of our history, and especially during the Revolutionary struggle. Among these pioneers, Asbury, by common consent, stood first and chief. There was something in his person, his eye, his mien, and in the music of his voice, which interested all who saw and heard him. He possessed much natural wit, and was capable of the severest satire; but grace and good sense so far predominated that he never descended to anything beneath the dignity of a man and a Christian minister. In prayer he excelled." "He prayed," says Garrettson, "the best, and prayed the most, of any man I ever knew."

The returns of members amounted to 14,988, showing an increase of 1,248. There were but 1,607 Methodists north of Mason and Dixon's line, and 13,381 south of it. There were eighty-four itinerant preachers, a gain of but two, though at least fifteen new laborers were received. Thirteen, or nearly one sixth of the whole ministry of the preceding year, must, therefore, have retired from the ranks. Forty-six circuits were reported; their increase was seven. It was ordered at these sessions that subscriptions for the erection or relief of chapels should be made on all the circuits, the preachers to "insist that every member who is not supported by charity" should "give something;" that members who "buy and sell slaves," if "they buy with no other design than to hold them as slaves, and have been previously warned, shall be expelled, and be permitted to sell on no consideration;" and that "Local Preachers who will not emancipate their slaves in states where the laws admit," shall be called to account; those in Virginia "to be borne with another year," those in Maryland, Delaware, Pennsylvania, and New Jersey to be suspended; that "traveling preachers who now are or hereafter shall be possessed of slaves, and shall refuse to manumit them, where the laws permit," shall "be employed no more." Asbury's "allowance," as General Assistant or Superintendent, was fixed at twenty-four pounds ($60) per annum, "with his expenses for horses and traveling."

Lee states that there was "a gracious revival this year in many of the frontier circuits, and the way was opening fast for us to enlarge our borders, to spread the Gospel through various places where we had never been before. The call of the people was great for more laborers to be sent into the harvest." Some of the new circuits indicate this extension of Methodism on the frontiers. In the preceding year Jeremiah Lambert had charge of the Holston Circuit, with sixty members of Society, at the head waters of the Holston River; Henry Willis followed him there the present year. Redstone Circuit now appears, as the first organized form of the ministerial work of the denomination beyond the Pennsylvania Alleghanies. Braddock's Road over the mountains had opened that ultramontane region, and emigration naturally took this prepared route. About three years before this Conference Methodism had crossed these mountains; but John Cooper and Samuel Breeze were now appointed to the first circuit in Western Pennsylvania; and, before the year closed, Asbury scaled the Alleghanies for the first time, to counsel and encourage them. Poythress, Haw, Roberts, and others, who had been laboring for two or three years on the "Alleghany Circuit," had reached the Redstone region, and opened the new field for their itinerant successors. Many Methodists had emigrated, during the war, to the mountains of Pennsylvania, Maryland, and Virginia; and Local Preachers among them were the real founders of Methodism in these Alpine regions, as they were in so many other parts of the world.

As early as 1768, John Jones, of Maryland, built his cabin on Redstone Creek; Robert Wooster, a Local Preacher, was the first Methodist that he heard in those then remote regions. About 1781 Wooster seems to have been casually preaching there. Jones went ten miles to Beesontown or Uniontown, to hear him, was awakened under his first sermon, invited him to his own house, and was there converted while the humble lay evangelist was conducting family worship. Jones gave a son to the Western itinerancy in the early part of the century, and became a pillar in the Church at Uniontown, the first Methodist Society in Western Pennsylvania. We shall hereafter see that as early as 1788 the second Conference west of the Alleghanies, comprising seven members and five candidates, was held by Asbury in Uniontown.

Among the mountaineer Local Preachers, founders of the denomination in the wilderness, were William Shaw, Thomas Lakin, and John J. Jacob; they were all ordained by Asbury on the same day, and were familiarly known as "the three bishops," a title won by "their indefatigable labors." Lakin was a native of Maryland, and a Methodist from the year 1780. A few years before the present Conference he emigrated beyond the Tuscarora Mountains, to Bedford County, Pa., and there became one of the frontier founders of the Church. He had superior talents as a preacher, was diligent in visiting the sick and dying, and was a sort of chaplain of that distant region on funeral occasions and other public solemnities. He often mounted his horse and went preaching from appointment to appointment over a six weeks' circuit, and attended every Quarterly Meeting in his own and many on the neighboring circuits. In fine, this good man was a pioneer of religion on the frontier, doing more effective work than most regular preachers of later times. As population pressed westward he moved with it, and died at last, in Ohio, aged more than seventy years. He left a sanctified name in the Church.

John J. Jacob was also a native of Maryland, a brave and good man, at the age of twenty a lieutenant in the American army, and a hero in the battles of Brandywine, Germantown, Monmouth, and Camden. He became a Methodist at Old Town, Md., in 1783. He refers to his conversion as attended by remarkable circumstances and "an indescribable ecstasy." "My whole frame," he adds, "especially my heart, seemed penetrated and wrapped in a flame of fire and love; and I think I felt like Peter, James, and John on the mount." Of course his susceptible spirit rendered him one of the most zealous of the "three bishops" of the mountains. He lived and preached in the rugged regions of Hampshire County, Va. He was "abundant in labors." "In the latter part of his life he gave up the world, and yielded his soul entirely to the service of his Saviour. It may be said that his life was full of benevolence, and that he lived only to glorify God. When he was nearing the heavenly country he took tender leave of his wife and children, saying, 'I shall soon meet Bishops Asbury and George. Now, Lord, receive me to thyself. I have fought a good fight, I have finished my course!'" He expired exclaiming, "All is well—safe!" in 1839, a veteran of more than eighty-two years.

Simon Cochrane was also a frontier pioneer of the local ministry. He was born in Harness Fort, in 1755, was a soldier in Dunmore's War, and also through the Revolutionary struggle. After eight years of military service, he joined the Methodists and devoted the remainder of his long life to "fighting the good fight of faith," a mountaineer champion of his Church, though always in its "local ranks," He began to preach in 1781. Asbury ordained him, and in the latter part of the century he emigrated to the wilderness of Kentucky, and thence, some years later, to Ohio, where, after sixty-four years of diligent ministerial labors, accompanied with the privations and perils of the frontier, he died in the faith, nearly ninety years old.

The Juniata Circuit, Pennsylvania, appears for the first time, this year, in the list of the appointments. It lay among the Tuscarora Mountains. As early as 1775, only about nine years after the epoch of American Methodism, Michael Cryder, a Local Preacher, penetrated to near the present town of Huntington, on the Juniata River, built himself a mill, and labored diligently at his humble avocation, and as diligently to found Methodism among the scattered settlers of his wild and beautiful neighborhood. "From this Society Methodism was propagated through the valleys and hills of this part of Pennsylvania. Circuits and stations have been growing up from it for the last seventy-five or eighty years." To the north-east of this mission field of Cryder lies Penn's Valley, "one of the most famous in the state." Robert Pennington, one of the earliest Methodists of Delaware, emigrated to this romantic region and settled in Center County, where he founded Methodism. He is honored among its people as "the first Methodist of this valley." He built a log chapel among the mountains, which is still familiarly known as "Father Pennington's Church." From this obscure source refreshing streams have gone forth through the whole valley; all the Methodism of that region dates from the labors of Robert Pennington.

It may be affirmed that not only was Methodism founded in the New World by Local Preachers—by Embury in New York, Webb in New Jersey and Pennsylvania, Strawbridge in Maryland, Neal in Canada, Gilbert in the West Indies, and Black in Nova Scotia—but that nearly its whole frontier march, from the extreme north to the Gulf of Mexico, has been led on by these humble laborers; that in few things was the legislative wisdom of Wesley more signalized than in providing in his ecclesiastical system the offices of local preacher and class-leader, a species of lay pastorate which, alike in the dense communities of England and the dispersed populations of America, has performed services which can hardly be overrated. The history of the denomination affords a lesson in this respect that should never be forgotten by Methodists while Christendom has a frontier anywhere on our planet. They have been accustomed to consider their "itinerancy" the pre-eminent fact of their history; they have demanded that all things should bend in subordination to this, and they have never exaggerated its importance; but they have failed to appreciate both the historical and prospective value of these humbler functions of their system. Most, if not all the early itinerants did inestimable service for the denomination as local preachers before they entered the itinerancy; most of them again became local preachers and labored on faithfully for the common cause. Their intervals of "regular" service have secured them historical recognition; but hundreds of their "irregular" and hardly less useful colaborers have been forgotten.

Of the fifteen preachers received on trial at the Conference of 1784, a third retired from the itinerancy in less than three years; nearly another third in about five years; some of the remainder became men of renown by their faithful and successful services.

We have thus gleaned and adjusted, into what orderly arrangement has been possible, the scattered fragments of the history of these obscure times. Again we are brought to the epoch of Asbury's interview with Coke at Barrett's Chapel, the epoch of events which were to give a new and formal development to American Methodism. Hitherto its progress has been but preliminary; hereafter it takes a more historic shape. From gathering the broken materials of its annals, dispersed over an indefinite field, we come now to witness the spectacle of the laying of the broad and permanent foundations of its ecclesiastic and historic structure. We shall see its walls rise in massive strength, and, entering its gates, shall find ourselves walking symmetrical streets, not only in a suburb, but in a citadel of the "city of God." If not perfect, if here and there marred by marks of both internal and external combat, yet shall we find it not altogether unworthy of the vision of the *Civitas Dei* which illuminated the studious vigils of Augustine, and continues to illuminate the hopes of Christendom.

HOLY BIBLE

CHAPTER XIII.

ORGANIZATION OF THE METHODIST EPISCOPAL CHURCH.

In the year 1776, while pursuing his daily travels and ministrations in Somersetshire, England, John Wesley was saluted by a clergyman who had come twenty miles to meet him. "I had much conversation with him," says Wesley, "and a union was begun then which, I trust, shall never end." The stranger was Thomas Coke, LL.D., a man who was destined to become a chief character in the history of Methodism in both hemispheres.

The only child of a wealthy house, Coke began early his education for one of the learned professions. In his seventeenth year he entered Jesus College, Oxford, as a Gentleman Commoner. He there chose the Church as the future sphere of his life; but he did not escape the infection of the speculative infidelity then prevalent in the English universities. Sherlock and other writers rescued him from doubt, but failed to teach him genuine personal religion. He entered upon his office as incumbent of South Petherton Parish, Somersetshire, an unregenerate man, but a conscientious inquirer. An interview with Thomas Maxfield, Wesley's first lay itinerant, afforded him better views of evangelical Christianity. Visiting a family in Devonshire, he found among its laborers an untutored but intelligent Methodist, a Class Leader of the rustics of the neighborhood. He sought this good man's conversation, and was surprised at his knowledge of divine truth. The nature of faith, justification, regeneration, and the evidences which attend them—the "unsearchable riches of Christ"—were themes upon which the clergyman found he could be instructed by the unlettered peasant. They not only conversed but prayed together. The educated divine obtained from the lay Methodist his best knowledge on the profoundest subjects, and acknowledged that he owed to him greater obligations, "with respect to the means of finding peace with God and tranquillity of mind, than to any other person."

His increased earnestness now surprised his parishioners; his church was crowded; its vestry declined to erect in it a gallery for the accommodation of the throng, but he had it put up at his own expense; he preached no longer with notes; he held numerous evening meetings in distant parts of his parish, introduced the singing of hymns, and testified to his people his personal experience of "the forgiveness of sins," attained while preaching at one of his neighboring appointments, where his "heart," he says, "was filled with joy unspeakable and full of glory." A clamor was raised against him as "a Methodist," though he had yet no relations whatever with Wesley, or any of his Societies. His bishop admonished him; his rector dismissed him; mobs of his own parishioners menaced him; he was "chimed" out of his church; but on the two ensuing Sundays he took his stand in the street, near the church door, and preached with power. Stones had been collected in heaps for an assault upon him, but he was protected by some of his pious people. He was compelled to abandon his parish. On the day he departed the bells were merrily rung, and the mob was treated with hogsheads of cider. Petherton celebrated as a jubilee its deliverance from a Methodist curate; but it gave to the world a man who was to rank second only to Wesley in the history of Methodism, and to be the first Protestant bishop of the New World. In later years the Petherton bells were to ring again for him as he flew over the country, one of its greatest evangelists; ring for him a hearty welcome to his old pulpit.

It has been remarked that Coke's appearance in the Methodist movement, at this time, was one of those noteworthy providences which mark its early history. Wesley, advanced in years, had hoped that Fletcher might be his successor in his great work; but the saintly vicar of Madeley was fast declining in health, and was to precede him to the grave. Coke, thrust out of Petherton, found refuge in the Wesleyan Conference at the opportune moment. Wesley needed now a practical, an energetic, an administrative coadjutor. He had himself legislated and matured the disciplinary system of Methodism, Whitefield had stirred the conscience of England and America for it, Fletcher had settled its theology, Charles Wesley had provided for it a psalmody which was to become its virtual liturgy throughout the world. The field of Wesley's operations and responsibilities had enlarged beyond his expectations and his powers; Methodism had already extended to foreign lands, and the time had come for grand foreign plans; the American Revolution was preparing the way for an American organization of the denomination. Coke now appeared by the side of the great but aged founder as the providentially commissioned man for the times. In travel and preaching he became as indefatigable as Wesley or Whitefield. He was to traverse continually the United Kingdom, the United States, and the West Indies. He was to have virtual charge, for years, of the Irish Conference, presiding at its sessions oftener than Wesley himself. He was to win the title of the "Foreign Minister of Methodism." He was to cross the Atlantic eighteen times, defraying himself his expenses; to organize, under Wesley, the Methodist Episcopal Church, as its first bishop; to originate the constitutional organization of English Methodism by Wesley's Deed of Declaration; to found the Wesleyan Missions in the West Indies, in Africa, in Asia, in England, Wales, and Ireland; to represent, in his own person, down to his death, the whole missionary operations of Methodism, as their official and almost their sole director; lavishing upon them his affluent fortune, and giving more money to religion than any other Methodist, if not any other Protestant of his times. Dying at last, a veteran of nearly seventy years, a missionary himself, on his way to the East, he was to be buried beneath the waves of the Indian Ocean, "the greatest man of the last century," says Asbury, "in labors and services as a minister of Christ." Like most, if not all, great men, he had peculiar faults, as we shall have occasion to see; but they hardly mar the noble proportions of his character.

Such was the man that Wesley was now to send to America to introduce a new era in its struggling Methodism. He was to go as a "Superintendent" or Bishop, and to be accompanied by two Assistants, as Elders, that he might thus conform, in his ordinations, to the usage of the English Church, which required in that solemnity the co-operation of at least two presbyters with the bishop. These assistants were Thomas Vasey and Richard Whatcoat. The former had traveled about nine years when Wesley ordained him as one of Coke's presbyters. He labored in America about two years, when he returned to England.

Richard Whatcoat was one of the saintliest men in the primitive itinerancy of Methodism. Had he been a Papist, he might have been canonized. His biographer adds that it might be said of him, as of St. Basil, "that so much divine majesty and luster appeared in him it made the wicked tremble to behold him. In him were seen majesty and love. His whole deportment was beautiful, and adorned with personal graces."

During eight or nine years he labored humbly but effectively as a Band and Class Leader in Wednesbury, Staffordshire, where Methodism was "tried as by fire" in terrible persecutions. In 1767 he began to hold public meetings, as an Exhorter, in rural neighborhoods. In 1769 the devoted John Pawson, who knew how to estimate his character, proposed him as an itinerant at the memorable Leeds Conference which sent the first Methodist missionaries, Boardman and Pilmoor, to America. The Conference might well have received their obscure young probationer with peculiar interest, could they have anticipated that he was providentially destined to follow their missionaries, and become one of the early bishops of the wide-spread Church they had thus been humbly founding in the distant West. After traveling two years in England he was sent to Ireland. In 1773 he was sent to travel among the mountains of Wales, where he continued two years. The remainder of his services, down to the time of his departure to America, were on various circuits in England. Shadford, who well knew the wants of the American Church, urged him to go with Coke; he hesitated, and observed a day of fasting and prayer for divine guidance. At last "my mind," he says, "was drawn to meditate on the subject; the power of God came upon me, and my heart was remarkably melted with love to God and man." He offered himself to be sacrificed, if need be, for his distant brethren.

These were the men whom Wesley selected to share with him the grave responsibility he was now about to assume, of organizing the "Methodist Episcopal Church in the United States of America." We have seen the necessity of this momentous measure. Methodism had extended greatly in the New World. It was the only form of religion that had thrived there during the Revolution. It now comprised more than eighty traveling preachers, besides many local preachers, hundreds of class leaders and exhorters, thousands of members, and tens of thousands of regular hearers. It possessed chapels in most of the principal communities of the Middle States, and in many of the rural towns. It was rapidly extending its network of ministerial plans over the land. Its members could not be called "communicants," for they had not the sacraments. It received its converts into its Churches without baptism, in many places, and the children of its families were growing up without that holy rite, except where the brief measures of the Fluvanna Conference had provided it. It was a Church without a sacramental altar, though as pure and valid as any then on the American continent. Its early but precarious dependence upon the English clergy for the sacraments had almost entirely failed since the outbreak of the Revolution. The colonial English Church had been generally disabled, if not extinguished; its clergy fleeing the country, or entering political or military life. It was in these circumstances that a majority, as has been shown, of the American itinerants, representing a majority of their circuits and people, attempted to provide the sacraments by the measures of the Fluvanna Conference of 1779, after years of compromise and delay. The temporary rupture of that year was healed by a further compromise and delay in 1780, till the counsel of Wesley could be obtained. The letters which Wesley received convinced him that something must be done, however extraordinary, for the relief of the distant and suffering Societies. He endeavored, nevertheless, to avert the necessity of "irregular" measures. Four years before the ordination of Coke, Whatcoat, and Vasey, he addressed two letters to Lowth, Bishop of London, entreating the ordination of at least one Presbyter to administer the sacraments among the American Methodists. "I mourn," he wrote, "for poor America; for the sheep scattered up and down therein; a part of them have no shepherds at all, and the care of the rest is little better, for their shepherds pity them not." Lowth declined his request.

In the year 1784 the Leeds Conference was again to be rendered memorable by its interest for America. Fletcher was there, and with his counsels the American question was brought to an issue. Wesley had already discussed it with Coke, representing to him the actual circumstances of the transatlantic Societies, their new relation and that of their country to the British Church and State; and the providential necessity that seemed to devolve upon him, as leader of the Methodistic movement, to venture on the extraordinary measure of ordaining men to supply them with the sacraments. He cited the example of the ancient Alexandrian Church, which through two hundred years provided its bishops through ordination by its presbyters. Coke was already an ordained presbyter of the Church of England; Wesley now proposed to ordain him a bishop under the unpretentious, but synonymous title of "Superintendent," and to send him to the relief of the American Methodists. Coke required time to consider a proposal so momentous; after about two months he wrote to Wesley, acceding to it, though still suggesting delay, or, if possible, some modification of the plan. Wesley summoned him, with Rev. James Creighton, a presbyter of the Establishment, to meet him and Whatcoat and Vasey at Bristol, and there, on the first day of September, 1784, assisted (according to the custom of the English Church) by the two presbyters, Creighton and Coke, Wesley ordained Vasey and Whatcoat deacons, and on the next day ordained them elders or presbyters. On the latter day he also ordained Thomas Coke superintendent or bishop of the Methodist Societies in America. By this solemn measure American Methodism was to take precedence of the Colonial Episcopal Church in the dates of their reorganization after the Revolution. The Methodist bishops were the first Protestant bishops, and Methodism was the first Protestant Episcopal Church of the New World; and as Wesley had given it the Anglican Articles of Religion, (omitting the seventeenth, on predestination,) and the Liturgy, wisely abridged, it became, both by its precedent organization and its subsequent numerical importance, the real successor to the Anglican Church in America.

On the 3d of November they landed at New York, and were conducted to the house of Stephen Sands, an influential member and trustee of the John-street Church, who entertained them with liberal hospitality. John Dickins, the Methodist preacher of the city, was soon introduced to them, and welcomed them heartily. Coke stated to him the scheme which he brought from Wesley. Dickins, being one of the Fluvanna brethren, emphatically approved it, and requested that it might at once be announced to the public, assured that it would be received with joy. Coke deemed it expedient to disclose it no further till he could consult Asbury. By the latter part of the week they were traveling southward, and on Saturday were received by Bassett at Dover, where the latter was now erecting a Methodist chapel. Coke met Garrettson at Bassett's house and admired him as "an excellent young man, all meekness, love, and activity." On Sunday, 14th of November, he arrived with Whatcoat at Barrett's Chapel, "so called," he says, "from the name of our friend who built it, and who went to heaven a few days ago." "In this chapel," he adds, "in the midst of a forest, I had a noble congregation, to whom I endeavored to set forth the Redeemer as our wisdom, righteousness, sanctification, and redemption. After the sermon, a plain, robust man came up to me in the pulpit and kissed me. I thought it could be no other than Mr. Asbury, and I was not deceived. I administered the sacrament, after preaching, to five or six hundred communicants, and held a love-feast. It was the best season I ever knew, except one at Charlemont in Ireland. After dinner Mr. Asbury and I had a private conversation on the future management of our affairs in America. We sent off Freeborn Garrettson, like an arrow, from north to south, directing him to send messengers to the right and left, and to gather all the preachers together at Baltimore on Christmas eve.

Asbury knew not that Coke was present till he arrived at the chapel. The occasion was a regular Quarterly Meeting of the Circuit, and fifteen of the preachers and a host of the laity were there. A spectator of the scene (Ezekiel Cooper) says: "While Coke was preaching, Asbury came into the congregation. A solemn pause and deep silence took place at the close of the sermon, as an interval for introduction and salutation. Asbury and Coke, with hearts full of brotherly love, approached, embraced, and saluted each other. The other preachers, at the same time, were melted into sympathy and tears. The congregation also caught the glowing emotion, and the whole assembly, as if struck with a shock of heavenly electricity, burst into a flood of tears. Every heart appeared overflowing with love and fellowship, and an ecstasy of joy and gladness ensued. I can never forget the affecting scene."

Thus we reach again the memorable interview at Barrett's Chapel; and here, in the forest solitude, the momentous scheme of Coke's mission was fully disclosed, the first General Conference of American Methodism appointed, Garrettson "sent off like an arrow" to summon it together, and the project of Dickins, for a Methodist college, revived. It was with prayerful counsels, sacramental solemnities, liberal devisings, and with singing and shouting, that the young denomination prepared, in this woodland retreat, to enter upon its new and world-wide destinies.

At Abingdon, Md., they were joined by William Black, an English preacher, who had been founding Methodism in Nova Scotia, and had wended his way through Boston, New York, and Philadelphia, seeking ministerial reinforcements for that distant province. On the 17th of December all the travelers, except Whatcoat, arrived under the roof of Gough at Perry Hall, "the most elegant house," says Coke, "in this state." "Here," he adds, "I have a noble room to myself, where

Mr. Asbury and I may, in the course of a week, mature everything for the Conference." Black alludes to Perry Hall as "the most spacious and elegant building" he had seen in America. Whatcoat, who had delayed in order to preach on the route, arrived on the 19th. The next day they began the revision of "the Rules and Minutes," and made other provisions for the approaching session. Four days were spent in this task, relieved by frequent religious exercises in Gough's numerous family, and by the social hospitalities of the neighborhood.

On Friday, the 24th of December, 1784, the apostolic little company rode from Perry Hall to Baltimore, and at ten o'clock A. M. began the first "General Conference," in the Lovely Lane Chapel. The latter was still a rude structure, and Coke commended gratefully the kindness of the people in furnishing a large stove, and backs to some of the seats, for the comfort of the Conference. Garrettson had sped his way over twelve hundred miles in six weeks, calling to Baltimore the itinerants, and preaching as he went, and had returned to find sixty present. Coke, on taking the chair, presented a letter from Wesley, dated Bristol, September 10th, 1784, and addressed "To Dr. Coke, Mr. Asbury, and our Brethren in North America." It said that "by a very uncommon train of providences, many of the provinces of North America are totally disjoined from the British empire, and erected into independent states. The English government has no authority over them, either civil or ecclesiastical, any more than over the states of Holland. A civil authority is exercised over them, partly by the Congress, partly by the state Assemblies. But no one either exercises or claims any ecclesiastical authority at all. In this peculiar situation some thousands of the inhabitants of these states desire my advice, and in compliance with their desire I have drawn up a little sketch. Lord King's Account of the Primitive Church convinced me, many years ago, that bishops and presbyters are the same order, and consequently have the same right to ordain. For many years I have been importuned from time to time to exercise this right, by ordaining part of our traveling preachers. But I have still refused, not only for peace' sake, but because I was determined, as little as possible, to violate the established order of the national Church, to which I belonged. But the case is widely different between England and North America. Here there are bishops who have a legal jurisdiction. In America there are none, and but few parish ministers; so that for some hundred miles together there is none either to baptize or to administer the Lord's supper. Here, therefore, my scruples are at an end; and I conceive myself at full liberty, as I violate no order and invade no man's right, by appointing and sending laborers into the harvest. I have accordingly appointed Dr. Coke and Mr. Francis Asbury to be joint *superintendents* over our brethren in North America. As also Richard Whatcoat and Thomas Vasey to act as *elders* among them, by baptizing and ministering the Lord's supper. If any one will point out a more rational and Scriptural way of feeding and guiding those poor sheep in the wilderness I will gladly embrace it. At present I cannot see any better method than that I have taken. It has indeed been proposed to desire the English bishops to ordain part of our preachers for America. But to this I object, 1. I desired the Bishop of London to ordain one only, but could not prevail; 2. If they consented, we know the slowness of their proceedings; but the matter admits of no delay; 3. If they would ordain them now they would likewise expect to govern them. And how grievously would this entangle us! 4. As our American brethren are now totally disentangled, both from the state and from the English hierarchy, we dare not entangle them again, either with the one or the other. They are now at full liberty simply to follow the Scriptures and the primitive Church. And we judge it best that they should stand fast in that liberty wherewith God has so strangely made them free."

In accordance with this document "it was agreed," says Asbury, "to form ourselves into an Episcopal Church, and to have superintendents, elders, and deacons." Asbury declined ordination to the superintendency, unless, in addition to the appointment of Wesley, his brethren should formally elect him to that office. Coke and he were unanimously elected superintendents. Whatcoat's notes of the occasion, though brief, are more specific than any other contemporary document relating to it. He says: "On the 24th we rode to Baltimore; at ten o'clock we began our Conference, in which we agreed to form a Methodist Episcopal Church, *in which the Liturgy* (as presented by the Rev. John Wesley) *should be read*, and the sacraments be administered by a superintendent, elders, and deacons, who shall be ordained by a presbytery, using the Episcopal form, as prescribed in the Rev. Mr. Wesley's prayer book. Persons to be ordained are to be nominated by the superintendent, elected by the Conference, and ordained by imposition of the hands of the superintendent and elders; *the superintendent has a negative voice*." * He further states that on the second day of the session Asbury was ordained deacon by Coke, assisted by his presbyters, Vasey and Whatcoat; on Sunday, the third day, they ordained him elder; on Monday he was consecrated superintendent, his friend, Otterbein, of the German Church, assisting Coke and his elders in the rite. Tuesday, Wednesday, and Thursday were spent in enacting rules of Discipline, and the election of preachers to orders. On Friday several deacons were ordained; on Saturday, January 1st, 1785, the project of Abingdon College was considered; on Sunday, the 2d, twelve elders (previously ordained deacons) and one deacon were ordained; "and we ended," adds Whatcoat, "our Conference in great peace and unanimity."

The session was a jubilee to the Methodists of Baltimore and its vicinity. Coke preached every day at noon, two of his discourses being especially on the ministerial office, and afterward published; there was preaching, by other members of the body, every morning and evening; Otterbein's Church, and the Methodist chapels in the town and at the Point, were occupied by them. Coke says: "Our Conference continued ten days. I admire the American preachers. They are indeed a body of devoted, disinterested men, but most of them young."

Coke's sermon at the Episcopal consecration of Asbury produced a vivid impression, and presents some eloquent passages.

* Memoirs, p. 21. The italics are his own.

"Keep that which is committed to thy trust," he said to him; "be not ashamed of the testimony of our Lord, but a partaker of the afflictions of the Gospel according to the power of God: endure hardships as a good soldier of Jesus Christ: do the work of an evangelist, and make full proof of thy ministry, and thy God will open to thee a wide door, which all thy enemies shall not be able to shut. *He will carry his Gospel by thee from sea to sea, and from one end of the continent to another.*" Watters says that Wesley's plan was adopted "in a regular formal manner, with not one dissenting voice." Black, from Nova Scotia, gazed upon the scene with admiration. "Perhaps," he says, "such a number of holy, zealous, godly men never before met together in Maryland, perhaps not on the continent of America."

In compliance with the call from Nova Scotia, Garrettson and James O. Cromwell were ordained elders for that province. Jeremiah Lambert was ordained to the same office for Antigua, in the West Indies. For the United States the elders were John Tunnell, William Gill, Le Roy Cole, Nelson Reed, John Haggerty, Reuben Ellis, Richard Ivey, Henry Willis, James O'Kelly, and Beverly Allen. Tunnell, Willis, and Allen were not present, but received ordination after the session. John Dickins, Ignatius Pigman, and Caleb Boyer were chosen deacons. Boyer and Pigman were ordained in June following at the Conference in Baltimore.

Though no "Journal" of the doings, in the usual form, was published or preserved in manuscript, its enactments were embodied in a volume "composing a form of Discipline for the ministers, preachers, and other members of the Methodist Episcopal Church in America," published in Philadelphia in 1785, and bound up with the "Sunday Service," and "Collection of Psalms and Hymns," which Wesley had prepared for the American Societies, and had sent over in sheets. In 1786 a new edition of the whole, in one book, was printed in London, under Wesley's eye. Hitherto, what are called the "Large Minutes" of Wesley had been recognized as the authoritative Discipline of the American Societies, with the special enactments of the American Conferences superadded.

The Large Minutes were a compilation, made by Wesley from the Annual Minutes of the British Conference. In the preliminary deliberations at Perry Hall they were revised and adapted to the new form of the American Church, and being adopted by the Christmas Conference, were incorporated with the "Sunday Service" and Hymns, and published in 1785 as the Discipline of American Methodism.

The Articles of Religion prepared by Wesley, and adopted by this Conference, are an abridgment of the Thirty-nine Articles of the English Church. The institution of slavery was again considered, and stringent and comprehensive measures were adopted for its "extirpation." The Conference declared that "We view it as contrary to the golden law of God, on which hang all the law and the prophets, and the inalienable rights of mankind, as well as every principle of the Revolution, to hold in the deepest debasement, in a more abject slavery than is perhaps to be found in any part of the world except America, so many souls that are all capable of the image of God. We, therefore, think it our most bounden duty to take immediately some effectual method to extirpate this abomination from among us." They then require every Methodist to "execute and record within twelve months after notice from the assistant" a legal instrument emancipating all slaves, in his possession, at specified ages. Any person concerned who should not concur in this requirement had liberty to leave the Church within one year, otherwise the preacher was to exclude him. No person holding slaves could be admitted to membership, or the Lord's supper till he had complied with this law; but it was to be applied only where the laws of the state permitted. Methodists in Virginia were allowed two years "to consider the expedience of compliance or non-compliance." Buying, selling, or giving away slaves, unless to free them, was forbidden on penalty of expulsion from the Church. These rules produced much hostile excitement, and were suspended in less than six months. Not a few emancipations, however, occurred before their suspension.

The Conference defined the salary or allowance of preachers and their families. It amounted to sixty-four dollars to each, the same sum to each wife of a preacher, sixteen dollars to each child under the age of six years, and about twenty-two dollars to each over six and under eleven years. No provision was made for children above eleven years old. It also ordained that a "General Fund for carrying on the whole work of God" should be provided by "a yearly collection, and, if need be, by a quarterly one," in "every principal congregation." It was a contingent fund, chiefly for the expenses of preachers sent into new or distant fields of labor. It was further enacted that it should be recommended to communicants to receive the eucharist kneeling, but they were to be allowed to receive it standing or sitting. None but members of the Church, or such persons as received "tickets" from the preacher, were to be "admitted to the communion." Baptism was to be administered according to the choice of the candidate, or, if a child, of his parents, either by sprinkling or immersion. Rebaptism of such as had scruples respecting their baptism in infancy was to be allowed. Persons who continued to attend divine service, and to receive the Lord's supper in other Churches, were to "have full liberty as members" of Methodist Societies while they "comply with our rules." Members who should persistently neglect their class meetings were to be excluded from the Church, after suitable warning. Members marrying "unawakened persons" were also to be expelled—a rule which was modified in 1804 by changing the penalty to "putting back on trial for six months." Subsequently all penalty was abolished, and the Church pledged only to "discourage" such marriages.

Such are the most important additions to, or modifications of, the previous American Minutes and Wesley's "Large Minutes," made by the Christmas Conference.

Wesley's abridgment of the Thirty-nine Articles of the Church of England reduced them to twenty-four,* and reduced and amended several of the retained articles. The positive

* There are, however, twenty-five articles in the Methodist Discipline; one, "Of the Rulers of the United States of America," being added by the Christmas Conference.

features of this compendium show that the theology of American Methodism is essentially that of the Anglican Church in all things which, according to that Church and the general consent of Christendom, are necessary to theological "orthodoxy," or the "doctrines of grace," unless his entire omission of the historically equivocal seventeenth article, on "Predestination and Election," be considered an exception. The negative features of these articles are, however, very suggestive, and the careful study of the document, in this respect, is necessary to a just estimation of the progress of Wesley's theological opinions. He obliterates nearly every trace of those Roman Catholic traditional opinions which the framers of the Anglican articles retained. The eighth article, recognizing the Nicene, Athanasian, and Apostles' Creeds, is totally omitted; though Wesley, with Christendom generally, approved the last as a good expression of Christian doctrine, and retained it in the baptismal formula of the new Church. But what is most noteworthy in the negative character of the American articles is, the fact that the opinions which are deemed most distinctive of Wesleyan theology have therein no expression, if indeed any intimation. Wesley eliminates the supposed Anglican Calvinism, but he does not introduce his own Arminianism, unless the thirty-first Anglican article on the "Oblation of Christ" be admitted to be Arminian in spite of the seventeenth article on "Predestination." In like manner we have no statement of his doctrines of the "Witness of the Spirit" and "Christian Perfection." And yet no doctrines more thoroughly permeate the preaching, or more entirely characterize the moral life of Methodism than his opinions of the universal salvability of men, assurance, and sanctification. He evidently designed the articles to be the briefest and barest possible symbol of expedient doctrines; and not even a requisite condition of Church membership, though a requisite functional qualification for the ministry. He consigned his other tenets, however precious to him, to other means of conservation and diffusion, for it was not his opinion that the orthodoxy of a Church can best guarantee its spiritual life, but rather that its spiritual life can best guarantee its orthodoxy.

The Arminianism of Wesley has been rightly so-called. It is essentially true to the teaching of the great theologian of Holland, though not fully true to the elaborations of his system by Episcopius and Limborch, and much less to its perversions by its later eminent representatives. His Arminianism was far from being that mongrel system of semi-Pelagianism and semi-Socinianism which, for generations, was denounced by New England theologians as Arminianism, until the most erudite Calvinistic authority of the eastern states (Stuart, of Andover) rebuked the baseless charge and bade his brethren be no longer guilty of it.

Of Wesley's doctrine of Assurance, founded upon the text, "The Spirit itself beareth witness with our spirits that we are the children of God;" and upon analogous Scripture passages, I have already said that it was not a peculiar opinion of Methodism, but common, in its essential form, to the leading bodies of Christendom, Greek, Roman, and Protestant; that, as a high theological as well as philosophical authority of our times (Sir William Hamilton) has declared, "Assurance was long universally held in the Protestant communities to be the criterion and condition of a true or saving faith; that Luther declares, 'He who hath not assurance spews faith out;' and Melancthon, that 'assurance is the discriminating line of Christianity from heathenism;' that assurance is indeed the *punctum saliens* of Luther's system, and unacquaintance with this, his great central doctrine, is one prime cause of the chronic misrepresentation which runs through our recent histories of Luther and the Reformation; that assurance is no less strenuously maintained by Calvin, is held even by Arminius, and stands essentially part and parcel of all the confessions of all Churches of the Reformation down to the Westminister Assembly." Wesley defines the doctrine clearly. "By the testimony of the Spirit," he says, "I mean an inward impression on the soul, whereby the Spirit of God immediately and directly witnesses to my spirit that I am a child of God; that Jesus Christ hath loved me, and given himself for me; that all my sins are blotted out, and I, even I, am reconciled to God. Meantime let it be observed, I do not mean hereby that the Spirit of God testifies this by any outward voice; no, nor always by an inward voice, although he may do this sometimes. Neither do I suppose that he always applies to the heart (though he often may) one or more texts of Scripture; but he so works upon the soul by his immediate influence, and by a strong, though inexplicable operation, that the stormy wind and troubled waves subside, and there is a sweet calm, the heart resting in Jesus, and the sinner being clearly satisfied that all his iniquities are forgiven and his sins covered."

For his doctrine of Sanctification, Wesley adopted the title of "Perfection," because he found it so used in the Holy Scriptures. Paul and John he deemed sufficient authorities for the use of an epithet, which he knew, however, would be liable to the cavils of criticism. The Christian world had also largely recognized the term in the writings of Clemens Alexandrinus, Macarius, à Kempis, Fénélon, Lucas, and other writers, Papal and Protestant. Fletcher of Madeley, an example as well as an authority of the doctrine, published an essay on it, proving it to be Scriptural as well as sanctioned by the best theological writers. Wesley's theory of the doctrine is precise and intelligible, though often distorted into perplexing difficulties by both its advocates and opponents. He taught not absolute, nor angelic, nor Adamic, but "Christian perfection." Each sphere of being has its own normal limits; God alone has absolute perfection; the angels have a perfection of their own above that of humanity, at least of the humanity of our own sphere; unfallen man, represented by Adam, occupied a peculiar sphere in the divine economy, with its own relations to the divine government, its own "perfection," called by Wesley Adamic perfection; fallen, but regenerated man, has also his peculiar sphere, as a subject of the mediatorial economy, and the highest practicable virtue (whatever it may be) in that sphere is its "perfection," is Christian perfection.

Admitting such a theory of perfection, the most important question has respect to its practical limit. When can it be said of a Christian man that he is thus perfect? Wesley taught that perfect Christians "are not free from ignorance, no, nor from mistake. We are no more to expect any man to be infallible than to be omniscient. . . . From infirmities none are perfectly freed till their spirits return to God; neither can we expect, till then, to be wholly freed from temptation; for 'the servant is not above his Master.' But neither in this sense is there any absolute perfection on earth. There is no perfection of degrees, none which does not admit of a continual increase. . . . The proposition which I will hold is this: 'Any person may be cleansed from all sinful tempers, and yet need the atoning blood.' For what? For 'negligences and ignorances,' for both words and actions, (as well as omissions,) which are, in a sense, transgressions of the perfect law. And I believe no one is clear of these till he lays down this corruptible body." Perfection, as defined by Wesley, is not then perfection, according to the absolute moral law; it is perfection according to the special remedial economy introduced by the atonement, in which the heart, being sanctified, fulfills the law by love, (Rom. xii, 8, 10,) and its involuntary imperfections are provided for, by that economy, without the imputation of guilt, as in the case of infancy and all irresponsible persons. The only question, then, can be, Is it possible for good men so to love God that all their conduct, inward and outward, shall be swayed by love? that even their involuntary defects shall be swayed by it? Is there such a thing as the inspired writer calls the "perfect love" which "casteth out fear?" (1 John iv, 18.) Wesley believed that there is; that it is the privilege of all saints; and that it is to be attained by faith. "I want you to be *all love*," he wrote, "this is the perfection I believe and teach; and this perfection is consistent with a thousand nervous disorders, which that high-strained perfection is not. Indeed, my judgment is, that (in this case particularly) to overdo is to undo; and that to set perfection too high is the most effectual way of driving it out of the world." He taught that this sanctification is usually gradual, but may be instantaneous; as, like justification, it is to be received by faith.

Methodism has in its Anglican Articles a general, though a very brief, platform, consisting of the leading dogmas of the universal Church. Aside from this, it preaches, especially,

Universal Redemption, Assurance, and Perfection. The latter are special to it, not so much as opinions, (for they are still, more or less, common to the Christian world,) but by the special emphasis with which Methodism utters them. They are the staple ideas of its preaching, of its literature, of its colloquial inquiries in its class meetings, prayer-meetings, and in the Christian intercourse of its social life. Though, as has been stated, the success of the denomination cannot be explained apart from its disciplinary system and its spiritual energy, yet unquestionably its spiritual life and its practical system could not long subsist without its special theology.

The clerical or ministerial bodies of the denomination were now the General, the Annual, and the Quarterly Conferences, the last, however, including its Official Laymen.

The Christmas Conference was the first General Conference; that is to say, all the Annual Conferences were supposed to be there assembled. It was, therefore, the supreme judicatory of the Church. It was not yet a delegated body, but the whole ministry in session. It made no provision for any future session of the kind; but for some years legislative enactments were made, as heretofore: every new measure being submitted to each Annual Conference by the superintendents, and the majority of all being necessary to its validity. Another General Conference was held, however, in 1792, no official minutes of which are extant. The third session was held in 1796, a compendium of the minutes of which was published. Thereafter a session has been held regularly every four years, and the minutes of each preserved. In the session of 1808 a motion was adopted for the better organization of the Conference as a "delegated" body. In 1812 it met in New York City as a "Delegated General Conference," under constitutional restrictions, which gave it the character of a renewed organization.

Until the appointment of stated or regular General Conferences, the Annual Conferences continued to be considered local or sectional meetings of the one undivided ministry, held in different localities for the local convenience of its members, every general or legislative measure being submitted, as we have seen, to all the sessions before it could become law. Down to 1784 there had been but two regular sessions a year announced, though more were sometimes irregularly held. The enlargement of the denomination now required more annual sessions; three were appointed for 1785: one in Maryland, one in Virginia, and one in North Carolina. These sufficed till 1788, when six were held. The next year they increased to eleven, and in 1790 to fourteen, two being held beyond the Alleghanies.

The proceedings of the Annual Conference were conducted in the form of questions and answers, as follows: "What preachers are admitted? Who remain on trial? Who are admitted on trial? Who desist from traveling? Are there any objections to any of the preachers? who are named one by one. How are the preachers stationed this year? What numbers are in the Society? What was contributed for the contingent expenses? How was this expended? What is contributed toward the fund for the superannuated preachers, and the widows and orphans of the preachers? What demands are there upon it? How many preachers' wives are to be provided for? By what circuits, and in what proportion? Where and when may our next Conference begin? How can we provide for superannuated preachers, and the widows and orphans of preachers?" The presiding bishop made out the appointments to circuits, for the next ecclesiastical year, of all the preachers within the territory of the Conference. At the close of the Conference, after singing and prayer, he read usually to a crowded house, and amid breathless stillness and solemnity, the "list of appointments;" most if not all the appointed preachers having had no previous knowledge of the fate thus assigned them for the ensuing year. The reading of the list was like the announcement of an order of battle. It was heard by the militant itinerants with ejaculations of prayer, with sobs, and shouts. Few, if any, revolted, for the post of greatest difficulty was considered the post of greatest honor.

The Quarterly Conference was a more local body, held, in accordance with its title, on each circuit once in three months, and was composed of the preachers of the circuit, its local preachers, exhorters, leaders, stewards, and later, its trustees and Sunday-school superintendents. It had, subordinately to the Annual Conference, jurisdiction over all the interests of the circuit: its finances, the authorization of its local preachers and exhorters, and, later, a class of judicial appeals, and the recommendation of candidates for the Annual Conferences. Its exercises were largely, mostly indeed, spiritual. It continued in session about two days, during which there were almost incessant sessions, sermons, prayer-meetings, or love-feasts.

The ministry now consisted of bishops, (instead of the former "general assistant,") "assistants," and "helpers;" for though the new titles of elders and deacons appear in the Minutes of the next year, the ordained men amount to but twenty-four, out of a hundred and four. These were designed to supply the sacraments to the Societies, as far as practicable; subsequently the elders were placed in charge of districts comprehending several circuits, and thence arose the permanent office of presiding elder, not for the administration of the sacraments, but for many and important executive functions. In time, all preachers on their admission to the Conference as members were ordained deacons, and, in two years more, elders. The titles "assistants" and "helpers" were then dropped.

The functions of the bishop have been mostly defined. His powers were extraordinary, almost plenary; but he was subjected to an extraordinary amenability. Besides presiding in the Conferences, he made absolutely the appointments, or annual distribution of the preachers, having yet no "cabinet" of presiding elders, a species of council which usage has since established, though it has no recognition in the Discipline. In the intervals of the Conference he could receive, change, or suspend preachers. He decided finally appeals from both preachers and people. Ordinations depended upon the vote of a majority of the Conference; but the bishop had a veto power over any such vote. He could unite two or more Annual Conferences, and appointed the times and places of their sessions. But he could be deposed and expelled from the Church not only for crime, but for "improper conduct," a liability to which no other preacher, nor the lowliest private member, was exposed. He had no higher salary than his ministerial brethren; he was allowed no local diocese, but must travel through the denomination.

The "assistant" was really the "preacher in charge" of the circuit, as he was subsequently called. He was esteemed the assistant of the bishop, and had charge of the other preachers on the circuit as his "helpers." His duties were minutely enumerated in 1784. He was "to see that the other preachers in his circuit behave well and want nothing; to renew the tickets quarterly, and regulate the bands; to take in or put out of the Society or the bands; to appoint all the stewards and leaders, and change them when he sees it necessary; to keep watch-nights and love-feasts; to hold Quarterly Meetings, and therein diligently to inquire both into the temporal and spiritual state of each Society; to take care that every Society be duly supplied with books, which ought to be in every house; to take exact lists of his Societies, and bring them to the Conference; to send an account of his circuit every half year to one of the superintendents; to meet the married men and women, and the single men and women in the large Societies once a quarter; to overlook the accounts of all the stewards; to take a regular catalogue of his Societies as they live in house-rows; to leave his successor a particular account of the state of the circuit; vigorously, but calmly, to enforce the rules concerning needless ornaments, and drams; as soon as there are four men or women believers in any place, to put them into a band; to suffer no love-feast to last above an hour and a half; everywhere to recommend decency and cleanliness; to read the rules of the Society, with the aid of his helpers, once a year in every congregation, and once a quarter in every Society."

All preachers, except the bishops and assistants, were called "helpers," whether members or probationers of the Conference. The Christmas session defined the duties of a helper to be, "1. To preach. 2. To meet the Society and the bands weekly. 3. To visit the sick. 4. To meet the leaders weekly."

It was added, "Let every preacher be particularly exact in this, and in morning preaching. If he has twenty hearers, let him preach!" The helper was not allowed, "on any pretense," to administer the Lord's supper; nor to "read the morning and evening service" in the congregation, except when authorized by a written direction from a bishop.

Besides this system of ministerial assemblies, functions, and regimen, American Methodism consisted, first, of local or individual Societies, composed of members and probationers, divided into classes of twelve or more persons, and meeting weekly under the care of a class leader for religious counsel and the contribution of money for the support of the Church according to the General Rules. The leaders were met at first weekly, afterward monthly, by the preacher. Each Society had its trustees holding the chapel property; its stewards having charge of its other finances; and, in many cases, its licensed exhorters and local preachers, men who pursued secular avocations but labored as public teachers whenever they found opportunity. The exhorter usually graduated to the office of local preacher, and thence to the traveling ministry. This, in fine, was the recruiting process of the Annual Conference. Secondly, of circuits composing a group of many local Societies, extending in some cases five hundred miles, requiring from two to six or more weeks to travel around them, and supplied by an "assistant" and two or three "helpers," who were aided by the local preachers, the class leaders maintaining a minute pastoral oversight in the Societies during the absence of the itinerants. Thirdly, (though at a somewhat later date,) of districts comprising several circuits and superintended by a presiding elder.

Thus had the new Church assumed an organic form: its series of synodal bodies, extending from the fourth of a year to four years, from the local circuit to the whole nation; its series of pastoral functionaries, class leaders, exhorters, local preachers, circuit preachers, district preachers or presiding elders, and bishops whose common diocese was the entire country; its prayer-meetings, band-meetings, class meetings, love-feasts, and almost daily preaching; its liturgy, articles of religion, psalmody, and singularly minute moral discipline, as prescribed in its "general rules" and ministerial regimen. Its system was remarkably precise and consecutive, and, as seen in our day by its results, as remarkably effective. Down to the Christmas Conference it had been for nearly a score of years in its forming process.

American Methodism is now to enter a new historic career, a career of unparalleled success. From its very birth till near the present date it has been struggling, advancing, or retreating, amid the agitations and obstructions of the American Revolution. Its whole history, before the arrival of Coke, wears an aspect of vagueness, of uncertainty. Hereafter it is to proceed with a definitive and more historic scope. Asbury and other men, heretofore only occasional or irregular leaders, rise into the character of heroes on the scene; great measures, great triumphs, great men crowd it—a series of apostolic bishops, not a few extraordinary "pulpit orators," missionaries to the savages, the slaves, and to foreign nations, an unequaled publishing agency, provisions of education, with academies and colleges in most if not all the multiplying states of the Union; the advance of the denomination into New England, into Canada, over the Alleghanies, through the length and breadth of the Valley of the Mississippi, over the Rocky Mountains, to the shores of the Pacific; foreign evangelization, reaching to many of the ends of the earth, and unequaled numerical growth. We have passed through about eighteen years, and the statistics of the forming denomination show less than fifteen thousand members, and about eighty preachers; in the next score they are to advance to more than a hundred and thirteen thousand members, and four hundred preachers; and the one Conference, with its two annual sessions, is to multiply into many, extending from Maine to Georgia, from the Atlantic to the Mississippi. In some single years, within this period, the increase of members is to equal the whole numerical force reported at the close of these years of preliminary labor and suffering.

CHAPTER XIV.

PROGRESS FROM THE ORGANIZATION OF THE CHURCH TO THE FIRST REGULAR GENERAL CONFERENCE: 1785–1792.

THE little ecclesiastical bark, built amid such troubled auspices, was now fairly launched upon the subsiding tumults of the country. Methodism presented itself to the new nation, an Episcopal Church, with all the necessary functions and functionaries of such a body; the only one, of Protestant denomination, now in the nation, for the colonial fragments of the English Establishment had not yet been reorganized.

The new Church had now eighteen thousand members and one hundred and four itinerant preachers,* besides some hundreds of local preachers and exhorters, who were incessantly laboring in its service. The number of its habitual hearers or adherents, aside from its members, was greater, in proportion to its actual members, than at any subsequent period of its history, for many of the members of the English Church in Delaware, Maryland, and Virginia now had no other ministry than that of the Methodist itinerancy. Its congregations were the largest in the country. It would be safe to estimate the Methodist community at this time at about two hundred thousand, including all habitual attendants on its worship. It had more than sixty chapels, the names of which are recorded. It had organized Societies in the state of New York as far north as Ashgrove, and on Long Island and Staten Island. In every county of West Jersey it had them, and in several counties of East Jersey. In Pennsylvania it had them, not only in Philadelphia, but in Bucks, Montgomery, Chester, Lancaster, Berks, and York Counties, and in the southern tier of counties as far as Bedford; and it had borne its standard across the Alleghanies and planted it in the Redstone settlement. It was

* Estimated from the next Minutes.

also extending its march rapidly up the Juniata. It had established itself strongly in every county of Maryland and Delaware, and was already the dominant popular religious power in these states. In Virginia it had not only unfurled its banner, but planted it in impregnable positions in almost every county east of the Alleghanies, and was bearing it successfully to the heights of the western mountains. It had crossed them at one point at least, and its joyous melodies were sounding at the headwaters of the Holston, and evoking welcoming echoes from its emigrant people in the primeval forests of Tennessee and Kentucky. With the exception of some of the southwestern, and a few of the southeastern counties of North Carolina, it had extended over that state, and had won important fields in South Carolina and Georgia, whither preachers were dispatched the next year.

With liberty and peace in the land, and organized order in the Church, the itinerants dispersed from the Christmas Conference to resume their labors with a confidence and hopefulness such as they had never known before. Coke spent five months in the states after the session, laboring incessantly. He was not content with the organization of the Church, but, as we have seen, projected, with Asbury, its first educational institution, and, while the Christmas Conference was yet in session, made arrangements and begged funds for the mission of Garrettson to Nova Scotia. After one of his sermons, at the session, he took up a collection of about a hundred and fifty dollars for it. On the 3d of January he left the city and rested for the night at Perry Hall, but was away the next morning for the North. Returning he passed southward to Charleston, S. C., and westward till he saw the Blue Ridge, and returning, traveled with Asbury to Mount Vernon, where they dined, by appointment, with Washington. "He received us," says Coke, "very politely, and was very open to access. He is quite the plain country gentleman. After dinner we desired a private interview, and opened to him the grand business on which we came, presenting to him our petition for the emancipation of the negroes, and entreating his signature, if the eminence of his station did not render it inexpedient for him to sign any petition. He informed us that he was of our sentiments, and had signified his thoughts on the subject to most of the great men of the State; that he did not see it proper to sign the petition, but if the Assembly took it into consideration, would signify his sentiments to the Assembly by a letter. He asked us to spend the evening and lodge at his house, but our engagement at Annapolis the following day would not admit of it." Such was the interest of the young Church against slavery; it seemed, as by a divine inspiration, to be conscious, from the beginning, of the importance of this question to the religious and political well-being of the new nation. Ever since its Conference of 1780, it had uttered its voice against the evil. Down to our day it has not failed one hour to bear its recorded testimony in favor of the "extirpation" of the unchristian institution.

On June 1st, Coke and Asbury met the preachers in Conference at Baltimore. As the doctor was to leave for Europe the next day, they sat till midnight. He preached before them at noon, urging ministerial faithfulness; and also early the next morning, on "St. Paul's awful exhortation to the elders of the Church at Ephesus, Acts xx." In a few hours he was sailing out of the harbor.

Asbury preached his first sermon, after his ordination, in the evening of the day on which the Christmas Conference adjourned, Jan. 3, 1785, at Baltimore, on Eph. iii, 8, "Unto me, who am less than the least of all saints, is this grace given, that I should preach among the Gentiles the unsearchable riches of Christ." The next day he was in the saddle, riding forty miles through the snow to Fairfax, Va. He traveled an average of thirty miles a day on horseback, preaching, reading prayers, and baptizing almost daily, and occasionally ordaining an itinerant. The fatigues of the route broke down his horse, but he obtained another. Jesse Lee and Henry Willis joined him, and accompanied him as far as Charleston, S. C. He found the people generally gratified by the Episcopal organization of the Church, and its provision of the sacraments. They were hospitably entertained in Charleston about two weeks, and preached every day. Before they departed their host was converted. Willis was left to maintain the Methodist standard in the city.

Leaving Charleston, Asbury returned through North Carolina and Virginia, proclaiming his message along the whole route, and attending Conferences. On Sunday, 5th of June, 1785, two days after the adjournment of the Baltimore Conference, he laid, with solemn forms, the corner-stone of Cokesbury College, at Abingdon, Md. As early as 1780, John Dickins suggested to Asbury, as has already been recorded, the plan of a Methodist academic institution. At the first interview of Coke with Asbury, at Barrett's Chapel, Asbury submitted the proposition to the doctor who zealously approved it, and procured from the Christmas Conference a vote that it should be immediately attempted as a collegiate establishment. Nearly five thousand dollars were quickly raised for the purpose. Coke had now contracted for the building materials, but could not stay to witness the beginning of the work. The site, about twenty-five miles from Baltimore, is one of the most commanding in the state; beautiful views extend in some directions twenty, in others fifty miles. The picturesque landscapes of the Susquehanna valley lay on either side of the river, and the magnificent Chesapeake Bay stretches away in the distance till lost in the ocean.

Abingdon soon became a favorite resort for families desiring a healthful locality, and the advantages of a good school. It accommodated the Conference in 1786; it became customary, indeed, for the Baltimore Conference to begin its session in the city, and adjourn to Cokesbury College for the conclusion of its deliberations.

During its ten years' history, Cokesbury College acquired an extensive fame. It was a shelter to the children of the preachers, a favorite resort of the itinerants, and an honor to the Church. But Asbury suffered hardly less trouble, in supporting and managing it, than Wesley did in sustaining Kingswood Seminary. It was destroyed by fire, at midnight, December 7, 1795.

Returning from the ceremonies at Abingdon, Asbury reposed a short time at Perry Hall, and then resumed his Episcopal itinerancy with his usual energy, preaching from Baltimore to New York, from New York to Charleston, and passing and repassing over the same route till he again met Coke in Charleston, in March, 1787, and found there a spacious chapel prepared for them.

Asbury provided the doctor with a vigorous horse, and they both set out together to travel and preach through nearly the length of the continent. They passed over three hundred miles in one week, preaching every day. Asbury says they had to "swim upon their horses several times." The roads were generally bad, the forests dense, the swamps frequent and frightful. "The preachers," writes Coke, "ride here about a hundred miles a week; but the swamps and morasses they have to pass through it is tremendous to relate. Though it is now the month of April, I was above my knees in water on horseback in passing through a deep morass, and that when it was almost dark. . . . In traveling, our rides are so long that we are frequently on horseback till midnight."

Coke returned to Philadelphia, whence he embarked again for Europe on the 25th of June, 1787.

Asbury, again alone in his vast Episcopal labors, paused not for rest. He hastened over much of Long Island, thence up the Hudson, crossing the romantic mountains of West Point to Newburgh. In four weeks more he had gone over the middle states as far as Bath, Va. He sometimes addressed a thousand people in the woods. He was often sick, dragging his infirm body along by an energetic will. "Faint," he says, "yet pursuing." His soul glowed meanwhile with the spiritual exhilaration of his labors. "O what a weariness," he exclaims, "would life be with without God and love and labor?" He hastened to the farther South, and wrote, as he journeyed, "I seldom mount my horse for a ride of less distance than twenty miles on ordinary occasions, and frequently have forty or fifty, in moving from one circuit to the other. In traveling thus I suffer much from hunger and cold." From Georgia he directs his course to the northwestward through the wilderness and ascends the Alleghanies. On April 28, 1788, he says: "After getting our horses shod we made a move for

Holston, and entered upon the mountains; the first of which I called steel, the second stone, and the third iron mountains; they are rough, and difficult to climb. This has been an awful journey to me, and this a tiresome day; and now I have thirty-five miles more to General Russell's. I rest one day to revive man and beast." He had thus scaled the grand barrier of the West; and the great Mississippi Valley, destined to become the chief theater of his Church and of the nation, lay below him in boundless range and primeval wilderness. He meets and encourages Tunnell, and, hastening into Tennessee, holds its first Conference; the first in the Valley of the Mississippi, at Half-Acres and Keyswoods, in May. "We held," he says, "our Conference three days, and I preached each day. The weather was cold, the room without fire, and otherwise uncomfortable. We nevertheless made out to keep our seats until we had finished the essential parts of our business." This is all his record of the first ultramontane Conference. There were "brethren from Kentucky" present, for on his route he had met them and preached before them. He proclaimed the Gospel continually among the scattered settlements, and, returning into North Carolina, passed into Virginia, still among the mountains, and at last reached Uniontown, Pa., where, with Whatcoat and eleven other preachers, he held a Conference on the 22d of July, and consecrated what is supposed to have been the first Methodist ordination beyond the Alleghanies. A pioneer preacher, (James Quinn,) then a youth, witnessed the session, and thus alludes to it: "Mr. Asbury officiated, not in the costume of the lawn-robed prelate, but as the plain presbyter in gown and band, assisted by Richard Whatcoat, elder, in the same clerical habit. The person ordained was Michael Leard, of whom it was said that he could repeat nearly the whole of the New Testament from memory, and also large portions of the Old. The scenes of that day looked well in the eyes of the Church people, for not only did the preachers appear in sacerdotal robes, but the morning service was read as abridged by Mr. Wesley. The priestly robes and prayer book were, however, soon laid aside at the same time, for I have never seen the one nor heard the other since."

The bishop continued to traverse the states from New York to Georgia, from the Atlantic to the Alleghanies, having the whole Episcopal care of the Societies till March, 1789, when Coke rejoined him in South Carolina. He held important Conferences in these years, but gives us little or no information of historical interest about them. Coke flew rapidly, and in repeated visits, over the continent; but Asbury had to bear the burden and care of the Churches.

Whatcoat has left us but brief notes of his travels and labors in the present period. Immediately after the Christmas Conference he took the field in Maryland and Delaware for about half a year, preaching "almost daily, sometimes twice a day," and administering the sacraments almost as frequently. In Kent County he records more than seventy-five baptisms on a single day—such had been the long privation of this ordinance among Methodist families! In 1786 he spent seven or eight months in Philadelphia and its neighborhood, and the next year penetrated to the west of Pennsylvania—to Alleghany, Bath, and Berkeley Circuits, where he spent nearly fourteen months supplying the settlements with the sacraments, and proclaiming the word in barns and woods. Again he was sent, in 1788–89, to Maryland and Delaware, the head-quarters of his charge, which was a district with no less than sixteen large circuits, extending from Philadelphia to Pittsburgh and Redstone, from the Maryland peninsula to Ohio. His manners were devoutly grave, but relieved by affectionate cordiality, and he was both revered and loved by the people. His preaching was often attended with overwhelming unction, and in the administration of the sacraments he was peculiarly impressive, rendering those solemnities, frequently, occasions of great effect. In 1789 he traveled with Asbury to the north as far as New York, and westward across the Alleghanies to Fort Pitt, (Pittsburgh,) and thence to Uniontown, Pa., where he assisted the bishop at the first ordination beyond the mountains. Returning to Baltimore, they held on their route to Charleston, S. C., where they met the South Carolina Conference, and thence into Georgia, where also they held a session. They then hastened westward to the Alleghanies, and passed into Tennessee and Kentucky. He was present when Asbury laid John Tunnell to rest in the grave among the mountains, on their return. On again reaching Uniontown, Pa., he records that "in the last fifteen months we have traveled six thousand miles." In 1790 he was flying to and fro through the middle states, supplying the sacraments and preaching continually. In 1791 he was stationed in New York city, where he stayed some months, and was then transferred to Baltimore, where he welcomed the first regular General Conference in 1792.

Benjamin Abbott continued his irregular but effective labors in New Jersey down to the early part of the year 1789, when he joined the Conference and gave himself wholly to the work of the ministry. He was appointed to Duchess Circuit, New York. It was a new field, and he encountered not a few difficulties in it. He was sometimes mobbed, and was often assailed by sectarian zealots, clerical as well as lay, who insisted on the discussion of his theology, especially his Arminianism. His righteous soul was vexed and wearied by such rencounters. The political revolution of the country had left the popular mind in an extraordinary fermentation. The agitations of the war being over, the people sought new excitements and new topics of discussion; wherever Abbott went he found them ready for polemical contests; they thronged his assemblies, some weeping, some falling down as dead men under his word, but many prepared to combat him, not only at the door after his meetings, but while he was in the act of preaching. Scenes were of daily occurrence which our modern sense of the decorum of public worship render almost inconceivable. The good man was sorely perplexed; he was compelled to become a polemic, a character which illy befitted him; but he sturdily fought his way forward, and at the end of the year reported about one hundred new members in his Societies. He penetrated as far north as Albany; "the alarm," he says, "spread far and wide," and in some of his assemblies "a dozen fell to the floor, and there was weeping and praising of God all through the house;" some were justified, some sanctified, and others "seemed lost in the ocean of redeeming love." The next year also he spent in traveling up and down the Hudson, and received into his young Societies about a hundred converts. The ensuing year he was sent to Long Island; he traversed his extensive circuit with the zeal and power of an apostle, triumphing over mobs, preaching the word daily with demonstrations that often overwhelmed his assemblies, prostrating many of his hearers to the floor. He formed numerous Societies, and labored especially to lead their members into the "deep things of God," his favorite theme being entire sanctification. He received between eighty and ninety souls into the communion of the Church during this year.

At the next Conference he requested Asbury to appoint him to the scenes of his early labors in New Jersey, that he might see his "children in the Gospel" on the Salem Circuit. On his way he paused at Philadelphia, and in St. George's Church, where he was to preach, the impression of his introductory prayer was so extraordinary that no preaching was possible after it. "The power of the Lord," he writes, "descended on the people in such a manner that some fell to the floor under the operation thereof; the cry of mourners, and the joyful acclamations of Christians, were so great that I could not be heard. Many cried aloud, and among them was Brother Cann, one of our preachers, who was wonderfully overcome by the divine power. When he came to, he stepped into the desk and publicly acknowledged that he had ever been an enemy to people's crying aloud, but that he then could not help it himself; that he could no more refrain from it than he could from dying if God were to send the messenger of death to arrest his body. Our meeting continued until near eleven o'clock. No doubt that meeting is well remembered by many of our friends in Philadelphia. O may its good effects be seen in eternity! It was a gracious time to many souls; several professed justification, and some sanctification."

Again among his former neighbors, he went from place to place like "a flame of fire." "There," he says, "I met many of my dear old friends whom I had not seen for about nine years; many of them were as happy as they could live." All felt that his mode of preaching, his peculiar power, was anomalous, mysterious, but also that it was beneficent. If it observed not the dignities of public worship, still it accomplished the ends of the Gospel, it awakened the heedless, reformed the profligate, led believers into a sanctified life—it awoke the dead in trespasses and sins, and not only crowded the chapels, but mightily recruited the Societies. Almost everywhere multitudes still fell, as dead men, under his marvelous power. If sober observers were disposed to revolt at the scene, they were yet afterward constrained to acknowledge that the moral result of his preaching was good, and permanently good. Even some of the quiet Quakers declared that his spirit was right, and his peculiar power an unquestionable inspiration. He preached in their meeting-houses; they attended his congregations in barns and private houses, and sometimes rose, amid the clamors of mobs, and bore their "testimony" that the power of God was with him. The rabble often beset him, sometimes with concerted plans of hostility; but he never feared them, and they always came off defeated.

The extraordinary events of his ministry, while they interest us, inexpressibly, as illustrations of his singular power and of the simple and rude character of the times, perplex us also with many problems, of which it is perhaps vain to attempt any explanation. One thing at least is clear, there could be no moral stagnation in any place which he entered. The whole community for miles around was stirred to its obscurest depths. All talked about him; the friendly defended and prayed with tears for him, the hostile disputed about him, assailed him, were prostrated by him. Few, if any, however indifferent or reckless about matters of religion, could, if within ten miles of his routes, remain undisturbed. They were compelled to share the general sensation of favorable or hostile interest—compelled to think or talk on the questions with which his presence startled the whole population. This, at least, was a blessing. By it hundreds, if not thousands, otherwise inaccessible to the Gospel, were brought to reflect, to pray, and to amend their lives; and it was especially true that the grossest sinners, the ignorant and degraded, who could be aroused to religious inquiry by none of the customary means, were seized, as it were, by this man's strange power and dragged up into the light out of their darkest abysses, and compelled to think, and often to pray and cry out in an agony of earnestness, "What shall we do to be saved?" He crowded the Methodist classes of New Jersey with such souls, reclaimed, purified, and not a few of them, for years after his death, models of the purest Christian life. In the latter years of his career we are, more than ever, startled by the anomalous records of his journals. He had been so accustomed to see his hearers fall insensible under his preaching, that, in his honest simplicity, he now evidently considered such demonstrations the necessary proofs of the usefulness of his ministry; he everywhere expected them, and, in fact, almost everywhere had them. Sometimes they took a character of undeniable extravagance; his own simple but Christian good sense could hardly fail to perceive this fact; but to him it was only proof of the mixture of human infirmity with the work of the divine Spirit; and his generous soul had no difficulty in excusing human weakness when redeemed, as he believed in these cases, by divine power and overshadowed by divine glory. Garrettson and Asbury deemed it proper at times to control, if not restrain him; but they seem at last to have concluded that he had a peculiar work to do, as an altogether peculiar man, and gave him free course.

His next circuit was that of Trenton, still within his old range. He had no sooner entered upon its territory than the usual effects attended his word. "On my way," he writes, "I attended the Quarterly Meeting at Bethel, and exhorted them to look for sanctification, for now was the day of God's power; and the power of the Lord fell on them in such a manner that they fell to the floor, all through the house, up stairs and down, so that speaking experiences was now at an end." The "public preaching" had to be dispensed with that morning; the preachers were employed in counseling and praying with the awakened multitude; the "slain and wounded lay all through the house," and the meeting lasted from nine o'clock in the morning till near sunset.

Abbott continued to labor in New Jersey with undiminished success. He formed the first Methodist Society of New Brunswick, consisting of nine members. At Princeton, also, he says, "the Lord raised up a Society of nine persons before I left the circuit, glory to God!" He subsequently went to Maryland, whither we shall follow him in due time.

Freeborn Garrettson was ordained at the Conference of 1784, and appointed to Nova Scotia. His labors in that province were extraordinary in their extent and success, but they will come under our notice hereafter. In April, 1787, he returned to the United States, by way of Boston, where he preached in private houses, not being admitted to its pulpits. At Providence and Newport he addressed large assemblies. Arriving in New York he hastened to the Conference at Baltimore. Wesley had been so impressed, by his success in Nova Scotia, that he sent a request to the Conference for his ordination as superintendent, or bishop, for the British dominions in America—a vast diocese, comprising not only the northeastern provinces and the Canadas, but also the West India Islands. But the Conference refused to spare him for this service. He was thus detained in the States, and resumed his labors in his old field of the Maryland Peninsula, where he traveled about twelve months, visiting, as elder, every circuit and nearly every congregation. "Multitudes," says his biographer, "flocked to hear the word, some excited from curiosity to see the man of whom so much had been said in former days, some from a desire to 'learn the way of the Lord more perfectly,' and numbers more to hear again from the lips of this flaming messenger of Christ those precious truths which they had found to be 'the power of God to their salvation.' So great, indeed, was the attention given to the 'words of this life,' that Mr. Garrettson observes, 'that it seemed as if they would all become Methodists.'"

In May, 1788, he passed to New York, designing to pioneer Methodism into New England; and he might thus have anticipated the great work and honor of Jesse Lee, had he not found Hickson, the preacher, in New York, dying. He was detained to supply his place. In Nova Scotia and on the Maryland Peninsula he had acted as presiding elder, traveling at large, superintending the circuit preachers, and administering the sacraments. Such were the functions of the elders ordained at the Christmas Conference, though the office, or at least the designation of presiding elders, proper, was not inserted in the Minutes till years later. He was now charged with this authority, to extend the march of the Church up the Hudson. Many young itinerants, stalwart, and flaming with the zeal of the Gospel, had appeared in the field about New York. Asbury requested Garrettson to take charge of a band of them and lead them up the river. Methodism had not extended northward further than Westchester County, if we except the Ashgrove Society, which was still solitary in the wilderness of Washington County, for Abbott's labors in Duchess County were at a later date. Garrettson was uneasy about his new commission, being an utter stranger to the country, knowing not one of its inhabitants, and unaware probably of the obscure Ashgrove settlement. His anxiety led him to "much prayer" for divine direction, and affected his sleep. He had in his dreams a sublime vision. "It seemed," he says, "as if the whole country up the North River, as far as Lake Champlain, east and west, was open to my view. After the Conference adjourned, I requested the young men to meet me. Light seemed so reflected on my path that I gave them directions where to begin, and which way to form their circuits. I also appointed the time for each quarterly meeting, requested them to take up a collection in every place where they preached, and told them that I should go up the river to the extreme parts of the work, visiting the towns and cities on the way, and, on my return, visit them all, and hold their quarterly meetings. I had no doubt but that the Lord would do wonders, for the young men were pious, zealous, and laborious." These young men were Peter Moriarty, Albert Van Nostrand, Cornelius Cook, Andrew Harpending, Darius Dunham, Samuel J. Talbot, David Kendall, Lemuel Smith, and Samuel Wigton. Some of them became historic characters in the Church. They formed six circuits, from New Rochelle to Lake Champlain, and thus was the denomination founded all along the Hudson, dotting, in our day, its beautiful towns and villages, on both banks, with Methodist edifices—a chapel and a parsonage in almost every hamlet.

Garrettson, having sent his young men up the river, soon after set out himself. He ascended its east bank through New Rochelle, North Castle, Bedford, Peekskill, to Rhinebeck, preaching in all the towns on his route. At Rhinebeck, destined to be the retreat of his last years, he was entertained by Thomas Tillotson, Esq., and preached repeatedly in a barn to constantly increasing congregations. On his return he found that his itinerants were almost everywhere prevailing over opposition, and forming prosperous Societies. "Many houses," he writes, "and hands and hearts were opened, and before the commencement of the winter we had several large circuits formed, and the most of the preachers were comfortably situated; sinners in a variety of places began to inquire what they should do to be saved. Satan and his children were much alarmed, and began on every hand to threaten us. Some said, 'They are good men;' others said, 'Nay, they are deceivers of the people.' A stranger from Vermont, on his way down the country, informed the people that we were spread all over the country through which he came. This sudden spread of our preachers caused some person to say, 'I know not from whence they all come, unless from the clouds.' Others said, 'The king of England hath sent them to disaffect the people, and they did not doubt but they would bring on another war;' while others gave it as their opinion that we were the false prophets spoken of in Scripture, who should come in the last days, and deceive, if it were possible, the very elect. The power of the Lord attended the word, a great reformation was seen among the people, and many were enabled to speak freely and feelingly of what God had done for their souls. My custom was to go around the district every three months, and then return to New York, where I commonly stayed about two weeks. In going once around I usually traveled about a thousand miles, and preached upward of a hundred sermons.

In 1789 he enlarged much the district, extending it westward to Schenectady. He penetrated to the little Society which had so long been hidden in Ashgrove, and reanimated it by his powerful preaching. They had recently erected their small chapel. John Baker, an Irish emigrant, had arrived among them about two years before Garrettson's exploration of the upper Hudson, and had endeavored to procure them a preacher from the Conference, but none could be spared till Garrettson sent to them one of his own band, Lemuel Smith, who placed the Society under good regulation, and made it the head-quarters of extensive evangelical labors for the surrounding country. "This Society," writes Garrettson's biographer, "may be considered the center of Methodism in this northern part of the country." A preacher who early traveled the circuit writes "that the Ashgrove Society was the hive of Methodism, and its common center to all this part of the country for many years. Ashton was a great friend to the preachers. He had one room in his house fitted up with a bed, a table, and chairs, for the special accommodation of the preachers. This room was known far and near by the appellation of the 'Preachers' Room.' Here the preachers were at home as if the dwelling had been their own. In his last will he gave a building lot for a parsonage and a burying-ground. He also gave the furniture of the Preachers' Room, and a cow for the benefit of the preachers who should be stationed on the circuit." Garrettson found not a few of the houses of the rich open for his entertainment on his long route. Gov. Van Courtlandt, near Croton River, especially became his ardent friend, and was long the hospitable protector of Methodist preachers.

In these three years' labor on the Hudson he opened nearly all its course for Methodism. He gathered into its Societies more than two thousand five hundred members. In 1791 he reported from it to the Conference twelve circuits. His district comprised nearly all the territory now included in the New York and Troy Conferences. He and his fellow-laborers not only traveled and preached indefatigably, but suffered severe privations, and sometimes formidable opposition. In one instance, at least, his life was periled. "On looking back," he writes, "I see the hand of a good God in my preservation last Thursday. I came to Mr. —— weary. and thirsty. I asked for something to drink, and my kind friend's wife went to fetch it. After staying about fifteen minutes, she returned with some small beer. As she advanced toward me I was as sensibly impressed as if some one had told me, That woman is not too good to put poison in the drink. As I was putting it to my lips the same impression was so strong that immediately I refused, and put it down on the table untouched. Shortly after dinner was brought on the table, but I could eat very little. The next morning she poisoned her husband and two others with the meat which had been set before me. I was informed not long since that she had said she would put an end to the Methodists. A skillful physician was at hand, or in all probability they would have lost their lives. She was immediately sent to the jail in Albany."

Methodism not only reached westward as far as Utica, but south-westward into the Valley of Wyoming, which is recorded in the Minutes, as a circuit, as early as 1791. It entered that beautiful region, however, some three years before a preacher was sent thither. Its real founder there was Anning Owen, a blacksmith, a brave pioneer, who went to the valley, with a company of adventurers, soon after the Revolutionary War broke out. Owen was one of the few courageous men who were overthrown by the superior savage force of Col. John Butler, and barely escaped the bloody slaughter which followed. Returning to the East, his providential escape led him to devout reflection. His conscience was awakened, and he was not content till he found out the Methodists, under whose influence he became a renewed man. He went again to Wyoming, and began to converse with his neighbors on religion. Full of enthusiasm, and as tender-hearted as he was courageous, he hastened from house to house, exhorting with tears, reproving vice, and seeking out all whose consciences were restless in sin. The historian of Methodism in that region, (Dr. George Peck) familiar with its earliest events, says, "He appointed prayer-meetings in his own house. The people were melted down under his prayers, his exhortations, and singing. He was invited to appoint meetings at other places in the neighborhood, and he listened to the call. A revival of religion broke out at Ross Hill, about a mile from his residence, and just across the line which separates the townships of Kingston and Plymouth. Great power attended the simple, earnest efforts of the blacksmith, and souls were converted to God. He studied the openings of Providence, and tried in all things to follow the divine light. He was regarded by the young converts as their spiritual father, and to him they looked for advice and comfort." He became, practically, their pastor, and formed among them the first Methodist class of the valley in 1788. Benjamin Carpenter, Esq., was one of its members. With him Owen had frequent and anxious conversations on the necessity of providing preaching for the little flock. "They agreed," says our authority, "to settle the question by opening the Bible and following the lead of the first passage which presented itself. Squire Carpenter handed the Bible to Owen, and, upon opening it, the first sentence his eyes fell upon was, 'Woe is me if I preach not the Gospel.' Squire Carpenter said, 'I cannot.' Owen said, 'I will.' The thing with him was settled, and he then began to meditate upon the measures necessary to carry into effect his resolution. He visited some point at the East, where Methodism had a local habitation and a name; and on returning, at a meeting of his Society, he said, 'I have received a regular license to preach, and now have full power to proceed in the work.' Upon an examination of the old Minutes it will be seen that Wyoming was not recognized until three years after the organization of the first class. Upon being asked what they did for preaching all this time, one of the first members answered, 'Father Owen hammered away for us, and we did very well. We were all happy in God, and were not so very particular.'"

During these three years the young Society kept its altar-fire burning without the aid of any other pastoral ministrations than those of the faithful blacksmith, and an occasional visit of Garrettson's preachers. "They set up," says one of them, "prayer-meetings and class meetings, and the Lord poured out his Spirit upon us. Saints rejoiced and praised God, and sinners fell on the floor and cried for mercy, and few were able to keep their seats. These meetings were held on Sundays, Sunday evenings, and Thursday nights. This disturbed the enemy's camp and raised persecution against us, and our names were cast out as evil; but the more they persecuted us the more the Lord blessed us. The first minister that was sent among us was Mr. Mills." Nathaniel B. Mills traveled the Newburgh Circuit, on Garrettson's District, in 1789. In that year he reached the Wyoming Valley—the first Methodist itinerant who entered it. In 1791 it was reported as a circuit, with James Campbell for its preacher. In the same year the Northumberland Circuit is recorded, but Methodism did not reach the valleys below till two years after its entrance into Wyoming. Richard Barrett had previously explored the Northumberland country, and now traversed it with Lewis Browning, forming classes and establishing "preaching places" in most of its settlements. They extended their labors till the Methodism of Northumberland met and blended with that of Penn's Valley, where we have already witnessed the pioneer labors of Robert Pennington. Soon after the General Conference of 1792, William Colbert, then on the Northumberland Circuit, carried the Methodist standard into the Tioga country. Thus had the denomination commenced its march, from Garrettson's great battle-ground on the Hudson, toward what was then the northwestern frontier. Anning Owen was the "apostle of Methodism in Wyoming Valley," and of its movements thence to the regions beyond. He joined the itinerant ranks a few years later, and labored successfully from Albany to the Chesapeake, from the Hudson far into the interior settlements of New York and Pennsylvania. He retired at last a worn-out veteran. His motto was, "Work! work! work! this world is no place for rest." His face was wrinkled, his head bald, and what of his hair remained was as white as snow. He died a blessed death the sixty-third year of his age.

CHAPTER XV.

INTRODUCTION OF METHODISM INTO THE WEST.

WE have already had several anticipatory glimpses of the advance of Methodism over the great Apalachian range. As early as 1783, Jeremiah Lambert is recorded in the Minutes as appointed to the Holston country—the first Methodist preacher designated to the ultramontane part of the continent. But in the same year that Lambert is supposed to have penetrated the Holston region, Francis Poythress, then on the Alleghany Circuit, Pa., extended his travels across the Alleghanies to the waters of the little Youghiogheny. The honor, however, of leading the march of Methodism into the great valley of the Mississippi belongs to the local ministry. Robert Wooster, a local preacher, labored in the Redstone country about the year 1781.* A venerable Methodist itinerant, (Quinn,) resident in that section three years later, and who witnessed the first Conference held there, at Uniontown, has left us a brief notice of this pioneer. Speaking of John Cooper and Solomon Breeze, who are first recorded in the Minutes for Redstone, (in 1784,) he says: "They made their entrance at Uniontown, in the immediate neighborhood of which were many Church people, and a few Methodists. But they had been preceded by Robert Wooster, a local preacher of piety and considerable talent. He had preached in many places, both in Fayette and Washington Counties. Souls had been awakened and converted to God by his preaching; but I am not sure that he formed any Societies. He came to one of my appointments in 1799, and preached for me a pure and powerful Gospel sermon. At that time his hair was as white as wool. I felt it a privi-

* The country into which our missionaries entered, and which they occupied under the name of Redstone, was of considerable extent, embracing parts of the states of Pennsylvania and Virginia.—*Quinn's Life*, p. 31.

lege to hear the first Methodist preacher, perhaps, whose voice was ever heard this side of the Alleghany Mountains. No doubt he is safe at home in paradise. He was an Englishman, and came to America about the time that Mr. Asbury did. He left the Redstone country early in the present century, settled in Bracken County, Ky., and removed from thence to Indiana, on White River, near Connersville, and died shouting." It was under Wooster's preaching that John Jones, who went ten miles to hear him, became the first Methodist convert, of whom we have any record, beyond the mountains. Cooper and Breeze went to and fro in their new and extensive field, reaping the harvest of Wooster's labors. "The first Society," continues Quinn, "was raised near Uniontown. I next found their steps on the Youghiogheny, near the Broad Ford;" he followed them down that river and discovered abiding traces of their labors at its forks in Westmoreland County, and indeed throughout much of the country.

In 1785 Peter Moriarty, John Fidler, and Wilson Lee were appointed to Redstone. "Moriarty," says Quinn, "was the first man I ever heard preach; I was then a lad in my eleventh year. His text was Hebrews xii, 1. Under that sermon I concluded myself a sinner. These men were greatly beloved by the people, and very useful among them; and the first generation of Methodists in that region of country loved, and thought, and talked about their endeared Cooper, Breeze, Moriarty, Lee, etc., as long as they lived. Blessed preachers! blessed people! they are now in paradise, and will be forever each other's joy and crown. At the close of 1785 the number of members from this field was five hundred and twenty-three, so that it appears they labored not in vain in the Lord. The next year, William Phœbus, John Wilson, and E. Phelps being appointed to Redstone, enlarged the circuit, passing up the several branches of the Monongahela above Morgantown, Va., namely, West Fork, Buckhannon, Tygart's Valley, and Cheat River, as far as settlements had been made by the whites. Some fifteen or twenty miles further up, toward Clarksburgh, a door was opened, and a good Society formed, at the house of J. Shinn, father of Rev. Asa Shinn. This man was of Quaker origin, but he believed and was baptized, and his household. Forty years have passed away since I preached and met the class in this good man's house. At that time Asa was seeking salvation with a broken spirit—a broken and a contrite heart; we prayed together in the woods, and I have loved him ever since. This young man was admitted on trial in 1801, although he had never seen a meeting-house or a pulpit before he left his father's house to become a traveling preacher. He had only a plain English education, yet in 1809 we find him, by the appointment of the venerable Asbury, in the Monumental City, as colleague of another backwoods youth, R. R. Roberts, afterward Bishop Roberts. Many souls were born of God. The patriarch in the membership here was old Moses Ellsworth, of German descent. He was great-grandfather to our Ellsworth of the Ohio Conference. On this circuit lived and labored, and died in holy triumph, Joseph Chieuvrant, a Frenchman by birth. He was converted from Catholicism, and converted to God, about the commencement of the Revolution, and had permission to exhort. He was called out by draft as a militia-man in the army; he became acquainted with and was instrumental in the conversion of Lasley Matthews, an Irish Catholic. These men were mighty in the Scriptures; they preached and loved, and lived holy. Chieuvrant was one of the most extensively useful local preachers I ever knew." In 1787 the number in Society in Redstone was seven hundred and fifty-six. From Uniontown, which was then the center of Methodism in the head of the great valley, the preachers continued to enlarge the field of labor on every side, and to every place whence the Macedonian cry was heard. In 1788 the Redstone field seems to have been divided into four circuits: Clarksburg, Ohio, Pittsburg, and Redstone. Seven preachers were appointed to it. "I knew them all," says Quinn; "they were considered pious men, and useful in their day, and some of them of very acceptable preaching talents." Jacob Lurton and Lasley Matthews stand for Redstone proper, and it was for them to enlarge the field to the east, and carry the Gospel to the sparse settlements interspersed through the mountains. They pushed on over all the neighboring country. Crossing the Laurel Hill, they made their way into the head of Ligonier Valley. Near old Fort Ligonier was raised a large and flourishing Society. Here the father of the memorable Bishop Robert and his extensive family joined the ranks of Methodism. The itinerants rallied many local preachers to their work, but a few noted traveling preachers were also raised up, and before the century closed all the Redstone country was pervaded with Methodism. It was the frontier field from which the denomination took its march at last over all the great northwestern territory.

The Holston region was the field whence it marched into the middle-western and south-western states. The "Holston country" was about the head-waters of the south fork of the Holston River, which extended as far east as Wythe and the borders of Grayson counties, and as far west as the Three Islands. It was in these rugged but sublime heights that the itinerants began their movements westward into Tennessee. At the Conference which appointed Lambert sixty church-members were reported. By whom had they been gathered? and by whom were the returns made? I cannot answer these questions, but conjecture that as early as 1777, when King, Dickins, and Cole labored in North Carolina, if not indeed in the preceding year, when Poythress, Dromgoole, and Tatum preached there, their travels were extended into these mountains. Henry Willis, whom we have lately left in Charleston, S. C., traversed these mountains in 1784, a man of whom Thomas Ware says that "he stood pre-eminent. He was a manly genius, and very intelligent. He well understood theology, and was a most excellent minister. I followed him to the south as far as North Carolina, to the east as far as New York, and to the west as far as Holston, and found his name dear to many of the excellent of the earth." The contemporary records of Methodism incessantly mention this able and useful itinerant.

Richard Swift and Michael Gilbert, Mark Moore and Mark Whitaker, John Tunnell, Jeremiah Mastin, Nathaniel Moore, Edward Morris, Joseph Doddridge, Philip Bruce, Thomas Ware, John M'Gee, William Burke, and others, followed, pressing further westward, before the close of our present period. An evangelist of those times, who well knew the country and its adventurous preachers, informs us that they "were under the care of an elder whose district included Salisbury and Yadkin Circuits in North Carolina, and Holston in the west. In 1787 the Holston Circuit was divided into two circuits, Holston and Nolachucky, and Philip Bruce was appointed elder. Two new preachers, Jeremiah Mastin and Thomas Ware, were sent in 1788, when two new circuits were made out of the old ones: the Holston Circuit, embracing all the settlements on the East and North Forks of Holston, and all the settlements on the Clinch River, including the counties of Washington and Russell in Virginia, and Blount County in 'the Western territory;' and French Broad, including all the settlements west and south of the main Holston to the frontiers bordering on the Cherokee nation." The same authority, Burke, speaking of Swift and Gilbert, who traveled among these mountains in 1785, says that the country at this time was new and thinly settled; that they met with many privations and sufferings, and made but little progress; that the most of the region through which they traveled was very mountainous and rough, and the greater part a frontier exposed to Indian depredations. They were followed by Mark Whitaker and Mark Moore, "who were zealous, plain, old-fashioned Methodist preachers," and were instrumental in raising up many Societies. Mark Whitaker in particular was a strong man. He laid a good foundation for his successors, and was followed by Jeremiah Mastin, Thomas Ware, and others. These men planted the standard of the cross in the frontier settlements of the French Broad, and numerous Societies were raised up, so that in 1791 they numbered upward of one thousand members. About this time William Burke arrived in the Holston country; he says the pioneers of Methodism in that part of Western Virginia and the Western territory suffered many privations, and underwent much toil and labor, preaching in forts and cabins, sleeping on straw, bear and buffalo skins, living on bear meat, venison, and wild turkeys, traveling over mountains and through solitary valleys, and sometimes lying on the cold ground; receiving but a scanty support, "barely enough to keep soul and body together, with coarse home-made apparel;" but "the best of all was, their labors were owned and blessed of God, and they were like a band of brothers, having one purpose and end in view—the glory of God and the salvation of immortal souls. When the preachers met from their different and distant fields of labor they had a feast of love and friendship; and when they parted, they wept and embraced each other as brothers beloved. Such was the spirit of primitive Methodist preachers."

Ware's departure, in 1787, to this distant section, at the call of his friend Tunnell, has already been recorded. He found, he says, the population of his circuit spread over a region equal in extent to East Jersey, almost wholly destitute of the Gospel. "Many were refugees from justice. Some there were who had borrowed money, or were otherwise in debt, and had left their creditors and securities to do the best they could; some had been guilty of heinous or scandalous crimes, and had fled from justice; others had left their wives, and were living with other women. Among these there were a few who had made a profession of religion, and two in particular who had been ministers of the Gospel and who opposed the Methodists violently. But, notwithstanding the opposition we had to contend with from these and other causes, God prospered us in our work. Societies were formed, and a number of log-chapels erected, and on the circuit three hundred members were received this year." He was attacked by mobs, and barely escaped with his life. Sick and weary, pursuing his route by marks on the trees, he was lost in the forest, wandering bewildered most of the night. He sometimes slept on the ground under the trees. His trials were as severe as perhaps were ever endured by an American pioneer preacher.

The first Methodist Conference beyond the Alleghanies is usually supposed to have been held at Uniontown, Pa., on the 22d of July, 1788; but a session was held, as we have seen, at Half Acres, Tenn., as early as the second week of the previous May. We have followed Asbury in his adventurous journey thither. Ware gives some further information of the memorable occasion. "As the road by which Bishop Asbury was to come was," he says, "infested with hostile savages, so that it could not be traveled except by considerable companies, he was detained for a week after the time appointed to commence it. But we were not idle; and the Lord gave us many souls in the place where we were assembled, among whom were General Russell and lady, the latter a sister of the illustrious Patrick Henry. I mention these particularly, because they were the first-fruits of our labors at this Conference. On the Sabbath we had a crowded audience, and Tunnell preached an excellent sermon, which produced great effect. His discourse was followed by a number of powerful exhortations. When the meeting closed, Mrs. Russell came to me and said: 'I thought I was a Christian; but, sir, I am not a Christian—I am the veriest sinner upon earth. I want you and Mr. Mastin to come with Mr. Tunnell to our house and pray for us, and tell us what we must do to be saved.' So we went, and spent much of the afternoon in prayer, especially for Mrs. Russell. But she did not obtain comfort. Being much exhausted, the preachers retired to a pleasant grove, near at hand, to spend a short time. On returning to the house we found Mrs. Russell praising the Lord, and the general walking the floor and weeping bitterly. At length he sat down, quite exhausted. This scene was in a high degree interesting to us. To see the old soldier and statesman, the proud opposer of godliness, trembling, and earnestly inquiring what he must do to be saved, was an affecting sight. But the work ended not here. The conversion of Mrs. Russell, whose zeal, good sense, and amiableness of character were proverbial, together with the penitential grief so conspicuous in the general, made a deep impression on the minds of many, and numbers were brought in before the Conference closed. The general rested not until he knew his adoption; and he continued a faithful and an official member of the Church, constantly adorning the doctrine of God our Saviour unto the end of his life." No name is recorded, in the biographies of the pioneer itinerants among these mountains, with more grateful affection than that of General Russell. His house was long their asylum, and Asbury always entered it with delight.

The appointments of this Conference for the Holston country were Edward Morris, Elder; Holston, Jeremiah Mastin, Joseph Doddridge; French Broad, Daniel Asbury; East New River, Thomas Ware, Jesse Richardson. Ware says that he and his colleague were instructed "to enlarge our borders from a two to a four weeks' circuit. This we did with great ease. There was not within the bounds of our circuit a religious meeting except those held by us. The hearts and houses of the people were open to receive us, so that we hesitated not to call at any dwelling which might first come in our way when we wanted refreshment." A succession of energetic men were rapidly dispatched to this new field, and thence to the further West. William Burke, a Virginian, was one of the mightiest among them. "In 1789," he says, "John Tunnell was presiding elder, and Bottetourt Circuit added. In 1790 two districts were formed; one was composed of West New River, Russell, Holston, and Green Circuits—Charles Hardy, presiding elder. This year John M'Gee and John West were on Green Circuit. Bottetourt, Greenbrier, and Kanawha Circuits made the other district—Jeremiah Able, presiding elder. This year the Little Kanawha Circuit was formed, and Jacob Lurton was the preacher in charge. He was an original genius, and a useful preacher. In 1791 Mark Whitaker was presiding elder, and Charles Hardy and John West were on the West New River Circuit. Mr. Asbury, on his return from the Kentucky Conference, met the Conference at Huffaker's, Rich Valley of Holston, on the 15th of April, 1792. Hope Hull, who had accompanied him from Georgia, and Wilson Lee, who was now returning from Kentucky to the East, were with him. Both preached at this Conference with great success. General William Russell, who had married the widow of General Campbell, and sister of Patrick Henry, and had embraced religion, together with his amiable lady, and who lived at the salt-works, on the North Fork of Holston, attended this session, and accommodated a number of the preachers. We had a good time for those days."

Burke had the usual perils and hardships of his ministerial brethren in these mountains, but saw many of the worst opposers reformed, and Churches founded in many settlements. "On Nolachucky there was," he says, "a rich and thickly-settled community, which afterward bore the name of Ernest's Neighborhood. It had but one Methodist, the wife of Felix Ernest, who attended preaching when she could, being about five or six miles distant from the appointment. Ernest was a very wicked man, and a drunkard. Being one day at a distillery, the Spirit of God arrested him. He immediately went home, and inquired of his wife if she knew of any Methodist meeting anywhere on that day. It happened to be the day that Brooks preached in an adjoining neighborhood, and Ernest immediately put off for the meeting. He arrived there after it had begun, and stood in the door, with his shirt-collar open, his face red, and the tears streaming down his cheeks. He invited Brooks to preach in his neighborhood. He consented, and in two weeks Brooks came round and found a good congregation. 'The word of God,' he says, 'had free course, and was glorified.' The whole family of the Ernests was brought into the Church, with many others, and by the first of September we had a large Society formed. I left the circuit in September, but the work continued." In a short time they built "Ernest's Meeting-House," and Ernest became a local preacher.

Meanwhile the itinerant heralds had entered Kentucky. It was only about ten years before the organization of the Methodist Episcopal Church that Colonel Daniel Boone penetrated this wilderness, and that the first emigrant families settled there. The luxuriant country invited immigration, and adventurers poured into its beautiful valleys. As early as 1784 Methodist local preachers began to enter it, both as settlers and as pioneers of their faith. In this year one of them, by the name of Tucker, while descending the Ohio in a boat with a number of his kindred, men, women, and children, was fired upon by Indians; a battle ensued; the preacher was mortally wounded; but, falling upon his knees, prayed and fought till, by his self-possession and courage, the boat was rescued. He then immediately expired, "shouting the praise of the Lord." Not long after the Revolutionary War, Francis Clark, a local preacher from Virginia, settled in the neighborhood of Danville, Mercer County, and was among the first Methodists that emigrated to the country. He was a man of sound judgment, and well instructed in the doctrines of Methodism. As a preacher he was successful in forming Societies, and lived many years to rejoice in the cause that he had been the instrument, under God, of commencing in the wilderness. He died at his own domicile, in the fall of 1799, in great peace. In 1786 the itinerants reached Kentucky. James Haw and Benjamin Ogden were the first that appeared there. In the years 1787, 1788, and 1789, "the holy flame spread all over Kentucky and Cumberland. Haw, Poythress, Wilson Lee, and Williamson were the chief instruments in carrying on this great work." Haw was a man of ardent soul. A letter written by him to Asbury, in the beginning of the year 1789, says: "Good news from Zion; the work of God is going on rapidly in this new world; a glorious victory the Son of God has gained, and he is still going on conquering and to conquer. Heaven rejoices daily over sinners that repent. Indeed, the wilderness and solitary places are glad, and the desert rejoices and blossoms as the rose, and, I trust, will soon become beautiful as Tirza and comely as Jerusalem. What shall I more say? Time would fail to tell you all the Lord's doings among us. It is marvelous in our eyes."

In 1787 Wilson Lee and Thomas Williamson joined these standard bearers. In 1788 they had three circuits, Lexington, Danville, and Cumberland, and reported 539 members. In 1792 they had four circuits, their membership had risen to 2,235, and there were eleven itinerants. "The reader," says Burke, "may have some kind of an idea what kind of pecuniary support they had: traveling and preaching, night and day, in weariness and want; many days without the necessaries of life, and always without those comforts that are now enjoyed by traveling preachers; with worn and tattered garments, but happy, and united like a band of brothers. The Quarterly Meetings and Annual Conferences were high times.

When the pilgrims came they never met without embracing each other, and never parted without weeping. Those were days that tried men's souls."

The itinerants devoted themselves not only to labor but to death. At a Conference it appeared that Cumberland must be left without a preacher. Henry Burchet said, "Here am I, send me." His friends remonstrated against his going; the distance was great; there was considerable danger from Indians; the small-pox prevailed in the country, and he was sick; but after asking the consent of Bishop Asbury and the Conference, he said, "If I perish, who can doubt of my eternal rest?" He labored with great success in Cumberland, and though much afflicted, he held on his way till late in the fall, when he was obliged to stop traveling. He was a welcome guest at the house of a rich planter, two miles west of Nashville, by the name of James Hockett, where he remained, enjoying the hospitality of the family and the visits of his numerous friends, till the month of February, 1794, when he died in hope of eternal blessedness. He was buried on the farm; but it has passed to other owners, and his grave is obliterated.

Asbury visited these frontier evangelists almost yearly for the remainder of his life, often convoyed by armed men, and suffering terribly. He records that he was strangely outdone for want of sleep, having been greatly deprived of it through the wilderness; "which is like being at sea in some respects, and in others worse. Our way is over mountains, steep hills, deep rivers, and muddy creeks; a thick growth of reeds for miles together, and no inhabitants but wild beasts and savage men. Sometimes, before I am aware, my ideas would be leading me to be looking out ahead for a fence, and I would, without reflection, try to recollect the houses we should have lodged at in the wilderness. I saw the graves of the slain. These are some of the melancholy accidents to which the country is subject for the present. As to the land, it is the richest body of fertile soil I have ever beheld." The local traces of the great Methodist bishop in these Western wilds are still sacred places of pilgrimage to Methodists. "I confess," says a traveler, visiting one of them in the Holston Mountains, "to a peculiar train of emotions as I walked amid the scenes once familiar to the apostle of American Methodism. One place is a quiet East Tennessee valley, a few miles north of the Paint Rock, on the French Broad River. Along the tortuous course of this headlong mountain-born stream the itinerant bishop used to travel, as you will see by reference to his Journal. Before he would ascend this stream from the valley of East Tennessee to the Carolinas he would here pause, as if to summon his energies for the difficult task; and then again, on his return through these lofty mountains, the most elevated in the Union east of the Rocky Range, he would pause again at this wayside home as if to rest from the fatigue of the way. Here he tarried and preached and wrote and refreshed himself, and thanked God and took courage. The house is a nondescript in modern architecture, and is venerable for its age. It was built in troublous times with the Indians, and in what were then the extreme borders of civilization. The Cherokees, in some respects the greatest tribe of aborigines, had their seat of empire but a few leagues distant, and at that time claimed all the country along these valleys as theirs. Hence the building was wisely put up of massive logs from the great forest, well hewn and strongly fitted together; the chimneys large, and built of limestone rocks obtained near by. They are two in number, and are placed outside the ends of the house. An old-fashioned porch runs the whole length of the building. There appears to have been originally no windows in the lower story for Indian eyes or bullets. The upper story is attic, very low. There are two rooms above corresponding with the two below, and are furnished with small fireplaces, the flues communicating with the chimneys. Each of these upper rooms is well ceiled, the ceiling overhead being fitted to the rafters. They are furnished with eight, though small, windows in the gable, there being one on each side of the chimneys, composed of eight panes. The south room in the attic still goes by the name of 'The Bishop's Room.' Here were his candlestick and table and bed, etc. The bed occupied a corner, and when the wayfaring bishop rested his weary head upon his pillow it was in close proximity to the roof. Here, I doubt not, he slept soundly to the music of the falling rain. Here he slept and roamed in dreams over all his wide-extended work, perchance back to his European home and friends, and then waked to the stern realities of the Western wilderness. Hard by the door of the bishop's wayside home springs from the earth a mammoth fountain of the purest water, abundant enough to supply a great city. It is environed with huge primitive limestone rocks, in the crevices of which ancient elms rear aloft their great forms, and spread wide their giant arms that have battled with the storms of many centuries. On these rocks, beneath these great trees, once sat the man of God, thankful for this cooling fountain, as he rested from the toils of his continent-circuit. To him such a retreat must have been exceedingly grateful. The host and hostess of Asbury have long since followed him to the region of the dead. The old homestead descended to a son, who retains a lively memory of the good old bishop. But the wayside home of Asbury, like the tombs of the prophets and the sepulcher of the Saviour, has passed into the hands of unbelievers and enemies."

Thus had Methodism broken through the mountain barriers of the West. Soon it was extending energetically over the great Valley of the Mississippi. By the close of this period there were nearly five thousand seven hundred recognized Methodists, and thirty-five traveling preachers, beyond the Alleghanies. It will not be many years before we shall see organized the great "old Western Conference," reaching from the Lakes to Natchez, with its giant itinerants, M'Kendree, Roberts, Scott, Kobler, Lakin, Sale, Parker, Blackman, Beauchamp, Collins, Young, Strange, Raper, Cartwright, Winans, Finley, Elliott, and hosts of others—the men who chiefly laid the moral foundations of the mighty states of the Mississippi Valley.

CHAPTER XVI.

INTRODUCTION OF METHODISM INTO THE NORTH AMERICAN BRITISH PROVINCES.

THE presence of William Black at the Christmas Conference, with his appeal for preachers for Nova Scotia, inspired the enthusiastic soul of Coke. He not only set apart Garrettson and Cromwell for the distant field, and begged and gave funds for their support, but returned to England to procure additional men and money for it. The storms of the ocean drove him with his ministerial recruits from near the shores of Nova Scotia to the British Antilles, and thus not only providentially led to the founding of the missions of the latter, but did not defeat his plans for the former. Garrettson and Cromwell embarked for Halifax about the middle of February, 1785. They had a boisterous passage of nearly two weeks. "I never," wrote Garrettson, "saw so dismal a time before; but through the amazing goodness of God we were brought safely to Halifax, and were very kindly received by a Mr. Marchington, a true friend to the Gospel." Marchington hired a house for public worship, and Garrettson immediately began his labors. In a few days he formed the first Methodist Society of Halifax, comprising seven or eight members. Cromwell set out for Shelburn, and Garrettson projected "a tour through the country." Before departing he wrote to Coke, "I am fully persuaded that our voyage to this part of the world was of God; the very time when preachers of our order ought to have come."

Garrettson was the founder of Methodism in Halifax, but not in the eastern British provinces. It is a noteworthy fact that it dates there from the year 1765, one year earlier than its epoch in the United States.* In that year John Coughland, a

* The true epoch of Methodism in the western hemisphere is 1760, when Gilbert formed the first Society in Antigua.

Wesleyan preacher, was, at the instance of Wesley and the Countess of Huntingdon, sent to Newfoundland by the Society for the Propagation of Christian Knowledge. During seven years he pursued his solitary labors, suffering much of the time severe persecutions. His health at last failed, and he returned to England. John M'Geary was subsequently sent by Wesley to occupy the vacant post. He found that the good work begun by Coughland had dwindled after his departure, and was nearly extinct. He labored in Carbonear, but with such slight results that he was about to abandon the field in despair, when, in 1791, William Black arrived from Nova Scotia. As the chief, though not the original, founder of Methodism in the eastern British provinces, Black's memory will forever be precious to the Church in those borean regions. In 1780 he began to exhort in public at Fort Lawrence, and with such success that two hundred persons were gathered into classes, one hundred and thirty of whom professed to have "passed from death unto life." He had, in fine, become a preacher, and before long was "itinerating," proclaiming the faith at Amherst, Fort Lawrence, Cornwallis, Horton, Falmouth, Windsor, and Halifax. Methodism was thus permanently founded in Nova Scotia. In 1784 his Societies were too numerous for him to supply them alone. He went to the United States to consult Coke, as we have seen, and procured the appointment of Garrettson and Cromwell. In 1786 his name occurs for the first time in Wesley's Minutes, though he had devoted himself exclusively to ministerial labors for five years, and his circuit embraced the whole province, extended to Newfoundland, and at last took in New Brunswick. On the arrival of the missionaries from the United States he did not relax his labors, but extended them further and further, till he reached M'Geary, who was desponding at Carbonear, and about to leave the field. "I have been weeping before the Lord," exclaimed M'Geary to him, "over my lonely situation and the darkness of the people, and your coming is like life from the dead." Black immediately began to preach in the town; an extraordinary revival ensued, and the mission was retrieved. He organized Methodism in the province, secured its church property, encouraged and fortified its classes, and obtained new laborers from Wesley. The people of Newfoundland had received him as a messenger from God, and dismissed him, at his return to Nova Scotia, with benedictions and tears. This apostle of Methodism in the eastern British provinces lived to see it generally and firmly established in those regions. He died in 1834, at the advanced age of seventy-four years, exclaiming, "God bless you! all is well!" and leaving in Nova Scotia, New Brunswick, and Newfoundland three Methodist districts, forty-four circuits, about fifty itinerant and many local preachers, with more than six thousand members.

John Mann, one of the earliest converts of Boardman in New York, and for some time during the Revolutionary War the pastor of the John-street Church, had gone to Nova Scotia, and was now an energetic colaborer there with Black and Garrettson. In his semi-centennial sermon the latter says that he traversed the mountains and valleys, frequently on foot, with his knapsack on his back, guided by Indian paths in the wilderness, when it was not expedient to take a horse; that he had often to wade through morasses half leg deep in mud and water; frequently satisfying his hunger with a piece of bread and pork from his knapsack, quenching his thirst from a brook, and resting his weary limbs on the leaves of the trees. But "thanks be to God!" he exclaims, "he compensated me for all my toil, for many precious souls were awakened and converted." He continued in Nova Scotia till the spring of 1787, when he returned to the United States, leaving about seven hundred Methodists in the classes of that province and Newfoundland. The Methodism of "Eastern British America" has, by our day, grown to mature strength; it ranks, in the Wesleyan Minutes, as a Conference with eight districts, nearly one hundred circuits, more than a hundred and twenty preachers, numerous chapels, many of them costly edifices, academies, a Book Concern and periodical organ, missions, and thousands of communicants.

Before the present term of our narrative closes, Methodism had penetrated the British North American possessions at another point, in what was then the remote Western frontier. We have seen that in Garrettson's great pioneer scheme for the Upper Hudson he projected, as his northernmost outpost, in 1788, the Lake Champlain Circuit, with Samuel Wigton as its solitary itinerant. The next year, William Losee, with David Kendall as his colleague, traveled this frontier territory. Their journeys brought them within sight of Canada. The circuit seems not, however, to have been successful, for in 1790 it was abandoned. It is supposed that Losee received permission from Garrettson (in the winter of 1789–90) to range at large, seeking a more eligible field. He had kindred in Upper Canada, and went among them preaching the Gospel; he thus became, so far as the regular ministry is concerned, the apostle of Methodism in that province, and 1790 is usually recognized as its epoch. In January of this year Losee crossed the St. Lawrence.

We have often been reminded, in the course of this narrative, of the adaptation of Methodism, by some of its providential peculiarities, for its self-propagation. Its class and prayer-meetings trained most, if not all, its laity to practical missionary labor, and three or four of them, meeting in any distant part of the earth, by the emigrations of these times, were prepared immediately to become the nucleus of a Church. The lay or local ministry, borne on by the tide of population, were almost everywhere found, prior to the arrival of regular preachers, ready to sustain religious services—the pioneers of the Church in nearly every new field. The year 1790 was not the real epoch of Methodism in Canada. The sainted Barbara Heck, foundress of the Church in the United States, went with her children, it is probable, into the province as early as 1774. The wife and children of Embury also went thither, and the names of these memorable families recur often in the primitive annals of the denomination, from Augusta to Quebec. Mrs. Heck and her three sons were members of a class at Augusta, under the leadership of Samuel, son of Philip Embury. In 1780 a local preacher, by the name of Tuppey, was a commissary of a British regiment at Quebec. He labored about three years, and some of his hearers and converts were left scattered through the settlements of the province. "We may regard this British soldier," says the Canadian historian, "as the first Methodist preacher in Canada." The second was George Neal, an Irish local preacher, and major of a cavalry regiment of the British army. Bangs, who early traveled the circuits of that region, says, "He was a holy man of God, and an able minister of the New Testament. His word was blessed to the awakening and conversion of many souls, and he was always spoken of by the people with great affection and veneration as the pioneer of Methodism in that country. Among those who first joined the Society may be mentioned Christian Warner, who lived near what is now called St. Davids, and became a class leader; his house was a home for the preachers and for preaching for many years. He was considered a father in Israel by all who knew him. The first Methodist meeting-house erected in that part of the country was in his neighborhood. Neal lived to see large and flourishing Societies established through all that country, and at length was gathered to his fathers in a good old age." For some time this military evangelist held up the Methodistic banner, alone, in all the province, but in 1788 two other pioneers entered the field. An exhorter by the name of Lyons came from the United States and opened a school at Adolphustown, in the Bay of Quinte country. He collected the people together on Sabbath days, in different neighborhoods, "and sung and prayed, and exhorted the people to flee from the wrath to come."

In the same year James M'Carty, an Irishman, from the United States, and a convert of Whitefield's ministry, reached Kingston, and passed on to Ernestown, where he found out Robert Perry and other lay Methodists, and began immediately to hold religious meetings in their log-cabins. Many were brought to a knowledge of the truth and the enjoyment of religion. His success provoked the hostility of leading Churchmen. A sheriff, a captain of militia, and an engineer combined to rid the country of his zealous labors, and M'Carty was destined to be honored as the protomartyr of Methodism in Canada. He was suddenly seized, thrust into a boat, and conveyed by four Frenchmen, hired for the purpose, down the St. Lawrence, to the rapids near Cornwall. He was landed on one of the numerous solitary islands of that part of the stream, and may have perished by starvation, or have been drowned in attempting to reach the main shore; but his fate has never been disclosed. The sad mystery has consecrated his name in the history of the Canadian Church. "Undoubtedly," says Playter, its historian, "M'Carty was a martyr for the Gospel, and so he was regarded by the early inhabitants."

In entering Canada (in 1790) Losee probably crossed the St. Lawrence at St. Regis, for it seems that he preached in Matilda, Augusta, and Elizabethtown, and then passed up to Kingston, and thence to Adolphustown, where his kindred resided. "He had but one arm; and yet with one hand to use, he could readily mount and dismount his horse, and guide him over the roughest roads and most dangerous crossways. He was a bold horseman, and usually rode his journeys on the gallop. Yet he was a man of very solemn aspect, with straight hair, a long countenance, and grave voice. His talents were not so much for sermonizing as for exhortation. He, and the preachers generally of that day, were of the revival class; laboring, looking, praying for immediate results. The man, his manner, and his style of preaching, caught the attention of the settlers, and young and old filled the houses where he preached."

In 1791 Losee formed a circuit. He was yet young, being but about twenty-seven years of age. He flamed with zeal for his new and great work, and had no cares but those of his office, being unmarried. The Methodist itinerancy was thus initiated in Canada. Its first Methodist chapel was erected at Adolphustown, in 1792. In the same month the second chapel was begun in Ernestown, for the accommodation of the eastern part of the circuit, the first being at its western end. Both structures were of the same size, thirty-six feet by thirty, two stories high, with galleries. Losee returned to the Conference of 1792 bearing cheering reports of his great field. The Minutes record a hundred and sixty-five members in his Societies; his circuit was divided into two, and he hastened back with Darius Dunham as his colleague. Vast results were to follow; gigantic laborers to appear in the opening wilderness; circuits and Societies to keep pace with the advancing frontier, and to reach eastward to Quebec; Indian missions to arise; Methodist chapels, many of them elegant edifices, to dot the country; a book concern, periodical organs, a university, and academies to be provided, and the denomination to become numerically the predominant faith of the people. Methodism in the British Provinces, especially in Canada, remained for many years under the jurisdiction of the Methodist Episcopal Church. It is, therefore, relevantly included in our early history, and, as we shall hereafter see, is one of its most important results.

CHAPTER XVII.

INTRODUCTION OF METHODISM INTO NEW ENGLAND.

NEAR the center of the Boston Park, or Common, stands a venerable elm, the crowning ornament of its scenery. Its decayed limbs are held together by clamps and rivets of iron, and a railing defends it from rude hands, for it is sacred in the traditions of New England. It is especially sacred to the Methodists of the eastern metropolis. On a serene afternoon of July, 1790, a man of middle age, of a benign but shrewd countenance, and dressed in a style of simplicity which might have been supposed the guise of a Quaker, took his stand upon a table to preach beneath its branches. Four persons approached, and gazed upon him with surprise while he sang a hymn. It was sung by his solitary voice; at its conclusion he knelt down upon the table, and, stretching forth his hands, prayed with a fervor so unwonted in the cool and minute petitions of the Puritan pulpits, that it attracted the groups of promenaders, who had come to spend an evening hour in the shady walks, and by the time he rose from his knees they were streaming in processions from the different points of the Common, toward him. While he opened his small Bible and preached to them without "notes," but with "the demonstration of the Spirit and of power," the multitude grew into a dense mass, three thousand strong, eagerly catching every utterance of the singular stranger, and some of them receiving his message into "honest and good hearts." A spectator who heard him at or about this time says: "When he stood up in the open air and began to sing, I knew not what it meant. I drew near, however, to listen, and thought the prayer was the best I had ever heard. When he entered upon the subject-matter of his text, it was in such a tone of voice that I could not refrain from weeping; and many others were affected in the same way. When he was done, and we had an opportunity of expressing our views to each other, it was agreed that such a man had not visited New England since the days of Whitefield. I heard him again, and thought I could follow him to the ends of the earth." This evangelist was Jesse Lee, the founder of Methodism in the Eastern states; and although the preceding year must be admitted as its true epoch, yet the year of his appearance in Boston, 1790, may be considered the period in which it assumed a definite and secure position. He had arrived in Connecticut in June, 1789, and preached at Norwalk, New Haven, and many other places, and toward the end of the year formed a class in Stratfield, a parish of Stratford, and another at Reading, but these were only preliminary movements. He was alone, surveying the ground. The classes in Stratford and Reading consisted, the first of but three, and the last of but two, members; the former was organized but about three months, and the latter only about three days, prior to 1790. It was in the latter year that a detachment of preachers, Jacob Brush, George Roberts, and Daniel Smith, arrived to prosecute the plans of Lee, and the labors of Methodism in New England were fairly begun. It was also in this year that the Annual Minutes report, for the first time, returns of members from New England towns.

After five years of delay, occasioned chiefly by the hesitancy of his brethren, Lee had at last accomplished his ardent wish of planting the Methodistic standard in the Eastern States. The denomination had spread into all the Atlantic States out of New England; it had penetrated into the primeval wildernesses of the West, and its itinerant heralds were marching in the van of that vast emigration which has since covered the immense regions of the Ohio and Mississippi with magnificent states. It had even entered Canada, and, passing along the waters of New England, had established itself in Nova Scotia. It now resolutely broke into this hard but fruitful field. Lee had been commissioned by the New York Conference of 1789 to bear thither its standard. During the first year he was alone in the new field, and when others came to his help he left them to occupy the posts he had already established, while he himself went to and fro in all directions, penetrating to the remotest northeastern frontier, preaching in private houses, in barns, on the highways, forming new circuits, and identifying himself with every advancement of the Church. On the 17th of June, 1789, he preached his first sermon in New England at Norwalk, Conn. Having spent about three months in Connecticut, and surveyed the ground for an extensive circuit, to be occupied by assistants whom he hoped would come from the South to his aid, he departed on another exploring tour through Rhode Island. He thus records his feelings on concluding this excursion: "I have found great assistance from the Lord of late. To-day I have preached four times, and felt better at the conclusion of my labor than I did when I first arose in the morning. I have found a great many Baptists in this part of the country who are lively in religion. They are mostly different from those I have formerly been acquainted with; for these will let men of all persuasions commune with them if they believe they are in favor with the Lord. I think the way is now open for our preachers to visit this part of the land. It is the wish of many that I should stay, and they beg that I would return again as soon as possible, although they never saw a Methodist before. I am the first preacher of our way that has ever visited this part of the country."

Returning to Connecticut, he preached, on Friday, the 25th, at Stratfield. It was a memorable day. After the sermon he conducted "a kind of class meeting," composed of about twenty persons. It was the first class meeting held on the circuit, and led to the formation, the next day, of the first class, composed of three women, who, he says, "appeared willing to bear the cross, and have their names cast out as evil, for the Lord's sake." Since his arrival in New England, three months of incessant labors and vexatious rebuffs had passed, and but three women were organized into the new Church, which was "to spread scriptural holiness over the land." But Lee had the faith which is the evidence of things not seen, and before its hopeful vision all the eastern hills and valleys stood forth white unto the harvest. He gave thanks, mounted his horse, the only companion of his laborious travels, and went forth to new trials and greater achievements. Monday, the 28th of December, though in these prosperous times it may appear a "day of small things," was another signal period in the history of his mission—the date of the second Society formed by him in the State. "I preached," he writes, "in Reading, and found great assistance from the Lord in speaking. I felt that God was among the people. One or two kneeled down with me when we prayed. The lion begins to roar very loud in this place, a sure sign that he is about to lose some of his subjects. I joined two in Society for a beginning. A man who has lately received the witness of his being in favor with the Lord led the way, and a woman, who, I hope, was lately converted, followed." The former was Aaron Sandford, who afterward became a local preacher, and lived to see his children and many of his grandchildren members of the Church, with a large and influential Society gathered around him. His name has been represented by a son and a grandson in the Methodist ministry.

About seven months of indefatigable toil had now passed, and but two classes, with an aggregate of five members, were formed. Reasoning from sight, and not by faith, the persistent preacher might well have despaired; but, "Glory be to God!" he writes, on forming this class of two members, "Glory be to God, that I now begin to see some fruit of my labor in this barren part of the world." And he departed on his way to other toils, exclaiming again, "Glory be to God that he ever called me to work in his vineyard, and sent me to seek and to feed the sheep of his fold in New England. The Lord only knows the difficulties I have had to wade through, yet his grace is sufficient for me. When I pass through the fire and water, he is with me; and rough ways are smooth when Jesus bears me in his arms." He was supported by the consciousness that Methodism was needed in New England, and would, therefore, sooner or later, be divinely prospered; and by remarkable communications of grace and consolation from on high, such as he records, amid the inclemencies of a bleak, wintry day, about this time, "I set out," he writes, "and my soul was transported with joy; the snow falling, the wind blowing, prayer ascending, faith increasing, grace descending, heaven smiling, and love abounding." On the 28th of January, 1790, he formed the third class of his circuit. "I preached," he says, "at Jacob Wheeler's, in Limestone, and after meeting formed a class, two men and two women. Perhaps these may be like the leaven hid in three measures of meal, that may leaven the whole neighborhood, and many may be brought to say, I will go with this people, because we have heard that God is with them."

By this time the whole state was rife with rumors of him as a strange man who had come from the South, and was traveling through its villages on horseback, and in a costume of Quaker-like simplicity; a very "remarkable man," who preached every day and several times a day, and went everywhere, without knowing any person; exceedingly good-humored, witty even; of a most musical voice, making his hearers smile or weep as he pleased, but mostly weep; "holding forth" in the court-houses, the school-houses, sometimes in the more liberal village churches, but oftener under the trees of the highway; that he frequently lighted the court-house himself, and then rung the bell to call out the people; that the pastors and deacons valiantly resisted him as a heretic, for he was an Arminian; that they turned his discourses into interlocutions by their questions and disputations, but that he confounded them by his tact, if not by his logic; that he scattered the village wits or wags by his irresistible repartees; and that many drunkards and other reprobates were reformed, and many a good man, despondent under the old theology, was comforted by his refreshing doctrines. Many who liked his theology could not approve his preaching, because he acknowledged that he was not an "educated minister." The pastor, and sometimes the village lawyer or doctor, tested him with Latin and Greek phrases; he responded in Dutch, a knowledge of which he had picked up in his childhood; they supposed this to be Hebrew, and retreated, or took sides with him as competent to preach. But above all, they saw that he was evidently an earnest and devout man. He prayed mightily, and preached overwhelmingly.

In one of the villages of Connecticut lived at this time an honest and intelligent blacksmith, who, when Lee appeared there, kept his family closely at home, lest they should become infected with the itinerant's supposed heterodoxy. One of his sons, about twelve years old, heard of the arrival of the stranger. He was not allowed to hear him preach, but never forgot him nor the marvelous rumors of his ministry. He was destined to become Lee's greatest successor in this very field, and to do more important services for American Methodism than any other man recorded in its history, save Asbury. Such was Dr. Nathan Bangs's first knowledge of Methodism.

Lee continued his untiring labors, journeying and preaching, without the aid or sympathy of a single colleague, until the 27th of February, 1790, when he received, at Dantown, the unexpected and joyful intelligence that three preachers were on their way to join him. After the preceding notices of his solitary labors and struggles, we can appreciate the simple but touching description of their arrival, which he recorded at the time: "Just before the time of meeting a friend informed me that there were three preachers coming from a distance to labor with me in New England. I was greatly pleased at the report, and my heart seemed to reply, 'Blessed is he that cometh in the name of the Lord.' When I saw them riding up I stood and looked at them, and could say from my heart, 'Thou hast well done that thou art come.' Jacob Brush, an elder, and George Roberts and Daniel Smith, two young preachers, came from Maryland, to assist me in this part of the world. No one knows, but God and myself, what comfort and joy I felt at their arrival. Surely the Lord has had respect unto my prayers, and granted my request."

He was holding a Quarterly Meeting, in a partly finished church, the second Methodist one begun in New England, at the time of the arrival of these brethren at Dantown. Mutually comforted and enlivened by the interview, they entered with renewed zeal upon their labors, and during the services the next day (Sabbath) "the power of the Lord," says a historian of Methodism, "was so manifested that many cried aloud for mercy; a thing so unusual in that part of the country that some were very much alarmed, and fled from the house in consternation; and others, who were in the gallery, jumped out on the ground. In the midst, however, of the confusion occasioned by these movements, those who had an experience of divine things rejoiced with exceeding great joy."

There were, then, in the spring of 1790, in the Methodist ministry of the Eastern States, four men. There were more preachers than classes, and scarcely more than two members to each preacher; but they looked and labored for the future, and tens of thousands of New England Methodists now testify to the wisdom of their hopes.

A part of Connecticut, and all the eastern and northern sections of New England, were yet unentered by the Methodist ministry. Cheered by the arrival of fellow-laborers, and accompanied by one of them, Lee started for these remoter regions. On Wednesday, March 3d, he says that Smith and himself set out to the eastward, leaving Brush to supply his two-weeks' circuit.

On Saturday, April 17, Lee penetrated into Windham County, Vermont, where he stayed two days, and passing through a portion of New Hampshire, entered Massachusetts. He records "many discouragements," and "not so much satisfaction in Massachusetts as in Connecticut." On the 10th of May he was again in the latter State, preaching, and consoling himself with his colaborer, George Roberts, at Middletown. He traveled to and fro, proclaiming daily the word of life, until the latter part of June, when he again set his face toward the east. On his route from Providence to Boston his attention was suddenly arrested by a sight as astonishing to him, in his peculiar circumstances, as a supernatural apparition could well have been. He saw at a distance on the road two men on horseback habited with the simplicity of Methodist preachers, and accompanied by that invariable symbol of the early itinerancy, the now obsolete saddle-bags. One of these horsemen was an intelligent but humble-looking colored man, who seemed to enjoy his position more than if he were attending a hero in a triumph; the other was a man of small but robust stature, neatly clad, of benignant aspect, and presenting to Lee's eye a startling resemblance to one of his old companions in the itinerant labors of the South. They appeared dusty and weary, as if they had journeyed far during the day. Lee quickened his pace, halted before them, and was soon clasping with delight the hand of his former friend and fellow-laborer, Freeborn Garrettson. His colored companion was the noted "Black Harry," who not only ministered to the temporal convenience of his master, but aided in his spiritual labors by frequently exhorting and preaching after him. The meeting of the two evangelists on the highway was too remarkable not to attract attention; a spectator approached them, and perceiving their character, and affected by their spirit, invited them to partake of his hospitality and preach at his house in the evening. Such interviews were too rare and too refreshing in that day not to be relished by the weary itinerants. They accepted the invitation, preached that night and the next morning in the house of their host, and tarried till after dinner in comforting conversations and devotions. On his return from Nova Scotia, in 1787, Garrettson passed through Boston, where he found three persons who had been members of the Society which was formed there by Boardman. The Society had expired for lack of pastoral care. Garrettson preached several sermons in private houses, and departed to the South, not, however, without the purpose of future efforts for the city. After laboring some time in Maryland, he started on his way to New England, in May, 1788; but on arriving at New York he was induced by Asbury to lead the pioneer expedition up the Hudson. He was thus prevented from anticipating Lee in the labor and honor of founding Methodism in New England. He kept a steady eye upon it, however, especially upon Boston, and in 1790, while yet superintending the northern district, he started on his present excursion to the eastern metropolis.

He entered the northwestern angle of Connecticut at Sharon, on the 20th of June, accompanied by "Harry," and preached under the trees to about one thousand people. Continuing his route, he and Harry preached almost daily till they arrived in Boston. Here they also labored hard, but with little success, and departing, met Lee, bound for the same difficult post. On parting from Garrettson, Lee pressed forward to Boston, where he arrived on the 9th of July. The impression produced by the brief visit of the former had already evanesced. The day was spent in useless attempts to procure a place, public or private, for preaching; "every expedient failed." But not discouraged, he took his stand, as we have seen, on the Common the next day and delivered his message to three thousand people. As the way seemed not yet open for him, he left the city the following day, to survey yet more extensively his eastern field. He made his way as far as Portsmouth, N. H., preaching continually, and returned to Boston, where he not only preached on the Common, but also in a private house; and, on one occasion, in a meeting-house belonging to the Baptists, which had been vacant. On the ensuing Sabbath he was again upon the Common, addressing a much greater multitude than on the two former occasions. Although there had been a considerable fall of rain that day, and the earth was quite wet, he calculated that there were not less than five thousand present. Having surveyed his new sphere of labor in the East, he departed on his way to the next Conference, in New York city. More than sixteen months had elapsed since his appointment to New England, about nine of them without the support of a single colleague. After traveling through portions of Connecticut, Rhode Island, Massachusetts, New Hampshire, and Vermont, proclaiming the word of life in fields, court-houses, private houses, and churches, by day and by night, and surmounting obstacles from which most men would have recoiled in disgust or despair, he entered the Conference in New York city, October 4, 1790, to solicit additional laborers for the east. What could he report of his services, since he left the same body, in June of the preceding year? A tale of as hard fare and as hard labors, doubtless, as any one there could relate, except possibly the venerable man who sat in the chair—the unequaled Asbury. But not of toils and trials alone could he speak; much had been achieved. Connecticut, Rhode Island, and Eastern Massachusetts had been thoroughly surveyed, for more definite plans of labor. He himself had proclaimed the principles of Methodism in all the five New England States. He had removed much prejudice, and put the whole country more or less in expectation of further efforts. Prior to his departure from Connecticut to Boston he had formed definitively two circuits, Stamford, or Reading, as it was afterward called, and New Haven, and subsequently the general outlines of another, in Eastern Massachusetts. His fellow-laborers had also extended their travels in many directions, so that five circuits were recorded on the Minutes at the Conference of 1790. Nearly two hundred souls had been united in classes; a remarkably large number, if we consider the formidable obstacles which obstructed every movement of the few laborers in the field. Two chapels, at least, had been erected; one in the parish of Stratfield, town of Stratford, by the society of Weston, (now Easton,) called *Lee's Chapel:* the first Methodist one built in New England; the second, in Dantown, partially built, when Lee welcomed into it his newly arrived assistants on the 27th February.

Such were the results, thus far; and with these for his arguments, he could not fail to intercede successfully for his new field. He spent three hours in a private interview with Asbury, discussing its claims. That good and far-seeing man not only complied with his wishes, so far as to dispatch with him additional laborers, but resolved to visit the Eastern States himself in the course of the ensuing year.

In the following schedule of the appointments made at this Conference for New England we have an outline of the field of Methodism within its limits: Jesse Lee, Elder; Fairfield, John Bloodgood; New Haven, John Lee; Hartford, Nathaniel B. Mills; Boston, Jesse Lee, Daniel Smith. Besides these circuits, under the nominal supervision of Lee, there was the Litchfield Circuit, Conn., traveled by Samuel Wigton and Henry Christie, and included in a district which lay mostly within the State of New York, under the presiding eldership of Garrettson. One district and part of a second, five circuits, and seven preachers, constituted, then, the ministerial arrangements of Methodism for New England during the ecclesiastical year 1790–91. Lee was preparing, at the Conference, to return to his eastern labors and struggles; but before he left melancholy news arrived, informing him of the death of his mother, whom he had not seen for two years and a half. He wept, was "confused in mind, scarcely knowing whether to return to New England or go home;" but his missionary zeal prevailed; he sent his brother to the afflicted family, "went with him to the ferry, stood and looked after him for a while, returned with a sorrowful heart," and, in less than a week, was sounding his evangelical trumpet again in the unfinished chapel, and receiving consolation in his sorrow from the little band of disciples, at Dantown, Conn. He also visited Stamford, Middlesex, Wilton, Reading, Newtown, Stratford, Putney, Milford, Wallingford, Middlefield, Middletown, South Farms, Wethersfield, and Hartford, at the last of which places he formed a Society. From Hartford he set out for Boston, and arrived there on the 13th of November. The next day was Sunday, but there was no place in which he could preach. At night he addressed a small company in a private house. His reception in the Puritan city at this time was, if possible, even more discouraging than at his previous visit. The description of it is chilling. "The following part of the week," he says, "I met with great and heavy trials. I took much pains in trying to get a house to preach in, but all in vain. A few of the friendly people made a little move also, but did not succeed. One of the greatest friends I had in the town, when I was here before, did not come to see me now; and when I went to see him would scarcely take any notice of me. I met with difficulties and troubles daily, yet I put my trust in God, and in general was confirmed in the opinion that God would bless my coming to Boston. The greater part of the week was wet, so that I could go out but little. My cry was, 'Lord, help me!'"

More than a wook had thus passed without affording a suitable house for preaching; and the Common, his resort at his former visit, was too exposed to the inclemency of the season to admit of an assembly under its trees. On Monday, the 22d, he "tried every prudent means" to obtain a house, but in vain. A second week passed without success, but a gleam of hope came from another quarter. "We had a letter," he says, "from a gentleman in Lynn, who desired me to come and see him, and gave me some encouragement, for he said he had a desire to hear some of the Methodists preach. I then began to think that the Lord was about opening a way for me there. I made some inquiry about a place in Boston, and told some of my best friends that if they could not get one I would go myself, and try and do the best I could. I began to think the Lord would grant me my request, and provide me a place to preach in." He could not leave Boston without further efforts. "A man went with me to the high sheriff, and we asked for liberty to preach in the court-house. He said he could not give leave himself, but that the clerk of the court had the disposing of the house, and we must apply to him. So we went to the clerk, but he very abruptly refused. After hearing him talk for a while we left him, and I felt more discouraged than ever; yet, if I am right, the Lord will provide for me. Thursday, 2d of December, at night, one of my friends came home with me, and told me he had used every means he could to get a particular school-house for me, but had at last received a plain denial, and it was given up. This, with all the other denials, bore pretty heavy upon my mind, and I began to doubt again whether I ought to be here or not."

More than four weeks had passed in these useless endeavors to obtain a place for preaching; it was time to look elsewhere.* "On Monday," he writes, "I left Boston, and went to Ben-

* Nothing, however, could chill his humor. It was on his way from Boston to Lynn that he had the famous trial of wit with two lawyers. While riding along he perceived them hastening after him on horseback, with evident expectations of amusement. They entered into conversation with him on extemporaneous speaking, one on each side of him. "Don't you often make mistakes?" "Yes." "Well, what do you do with them? Let them go?" "Sometimes I do," replied the preacher, dryly; "if they are very important, I correct them; if not, or if they express the truth, though differently from what I designed, I often let them go. For instance, if, in preaching, I should wish to quote the text which says, 'the devil is a liar and the father of it,' and should happen to misquote it, and say, he was a '*lawyer*,' etc., why, it is so near the truth I should probably let it pass." "Humph!" exclaimed the lawyer, "I don't know whether you are more a knave or a fool." "Neither," replied Lee, looking from one to the other, "I believe I am just between the two." The gentlemen of the bar looked at each other, and were soon in advance, hastening on their way.

jamin Johnson's, in Lynn, about twelve miles. I was very gladly received by him and his family. I felt as though I was at home as soon as I arrived. I had not been there long before he expressed a desire of having a Methodist Society set up in the town, though he had not heard a Methodist preach for nearly twenty years. In this place I found several persons that had heard some of our preachers in the South. Some of the people consider it as a very favorable providence that I have come to Lynn at this time, and they bid me welcome with a cheerful heart." The next day the news of his arrival was spread through the village, and in the evening he preached at Johnson's house, the first sermon delivered by a Methodist preacher in Lynn. "I had," he says, "a good many hearers, and great freedom in preaching. I maintained that Christ died for all men, without respect to persons. I felt much of the power and love of God, and earnestly begged the people to turn from their sins and come to Christ. The hearers were very attentive, and a few of them seemed to be somewhat affected." "Bless the Lord, O my soul," he adds, "for bringing me among this people." His friends at Lynn wished to form a Methodist Society immediately, but leaving with them copies of the General Rules, and directing them to reflect longer on their proposition, he returned again to Boston, determined not to abandon it without a further struggle. Pecuniary embarrassments were added to his other vexations, but he was not to be discouraged. "When I arrived in Boston," he remarks, "everything appeared as dark as when I left it, respecting my preaching. I had to get a new boarding-place. When I settled my past boarding I had two shillings and a penny left, which was all that I possessed. Some days before I felt concerned about my purse, not knowing that there was enough in it to discharge the debt due for my board. I was unwilling to let the people know that my money was just gone, for fear they should think it was money only that I was after. But I soon felt confidence in God that he would provide for me, though I knew not how. However, a man in Lynn offered to buy a magazine that I had for my own use. I very willingly parted with it, and by that means was enabled to discharge the debt. And if I can always have two shillings by me, besides paying all I owe, I think I shall be satisfied." Such discouragements would have been insupportable to any ordinary man; but, though among strangers, repulsed on every hand, reduced to but two shillings, he could not be driven from the city. "He lingered," says his biographer, "until he bore his testimony for Jesus. His preaching was not in vain in the Lord. Some were touched under the word, and brought to feel the force of divine truth. And let the Methodists of Boston, who now enjoy such distinguished privileges, recollect that they are indebted, under the blessing of God, to the indefatigable perseverance of Jesse Lee, amid neglect and insults, for their first establishment."

The remainder of this year, and the year following, until the latter part of the month of May, his labors were principally in Boston, Lynn, Marblehead, Danvers, Manchester, Beverly, Cape Ann Harbor, Ipswich, and Salem. On the 20th February, 1791, he formed the first Methodist Society of Massachusetts in Lynn. It consisted of eight members. On the 27th of the same month it amounted to twenty-nine members, and in the ensuing month of May more than seventy persons took certificates of their attendance on his ministry, a measure rendered necessary by the laws of that day, in order to secure them from taxation for the support of the clergy of the "standing order." On the 14th of June they began the erection of the first Methodist church in Massachusetts. It was raised on the 21st of the same month, and dedicated on the 26th. They entered it for public worship in less than two weeks from the day on which its foundation was laid. It may well be supposed that it was not finished with much fastidiousness. It was, in fact, but the shell of a frame building.

Lynn now became his head-quarters, until his departure to the next Conference at New York. His excursions from it were, however, incessant, and in all directions. He kept a steady eye on Boston, returning to it at frequent intervals.

On Monday, the 9th of May, he took his leave of Lynn for the New York Conference. "I met," he says, "the men's class in the morning, and they seemed lively and very humble. We had a sorrowful parting. It is not quite five months since I first preached in this place, and there are now in Society fifty-eight members. About ten o'clock, the men who generally attend on my preaching came to me and obtained certificates to show that they attended public worship with the Methodists, and contributed to the support of their ministry. After dinner I prayed with those that were present, and then bade them all farewell and set out for Conference at New York." About seven months had passed since the preceding Conference. Lee had made a strong impression in the region of Boston, Lynn, Salem, Ipswich, Newburyport, and other towns. Only a single Society, however, had been organized. An extensive circuit had, nevertheless, been formed, with posts of regular labor, and Boston itself, though no Society was formed there till the next year, had given an humble place to the indomitable evangelist; one which, however dubious its prospects might have appeared, could never again be wrested from a man of his vigor. He went to the Conference, then, reporting one circuit, one Society, and fifty-eight members. His colleagues, in the west of New England, had been cheered by visible success. Six circuits were reported bearing New England names. The returns of members in Society on these circuits exhibited an aggregate of four hundred and eighty-one, a gain of three hundred on the returns made eight months before. The good seed, so widely sown and laboriously nurtured, had taken root and was already bearing fruit. The experiment of Methodism in New England was determined. Thenceforth was the new denomination to take rank among the Christian bodies of the Puritan states, spreading the principles of a milder theology and a livelier piety through their length and breadth.

We have followed Lee and his fellow-laborers down to the end of the ecclesiastical year 1790–91. On the 26th of May, 1791, the Conference assembled in New York city. The Minutes report the plan of appointments in New England for the year: Jesse Lee, elder; Litchfield, Matthias Swaim, James Covel; Fairfield, Nathaniel B. Mills, Aaron Hunt; Middlefield, John Allen, George Roberts; Hartford, Lemuel Smith,

Menzies Rainor; Stockbridge, Robert Green; Lynn, John Bloodgood, Daniel Smith. One district and six circuits, four in Connecticut and two in Massachusetts, with eleven circuit preachers and one presiding elder, now constituted the ministerial corps and field of Methodism in the Eastern States.

Lee was appointed, as we have seen, presiding elder, with a district which comprehended the whole Methodist interest in New England, and the recently formed circuit of Kingston, in Upper Canada. He devoted his attention, however, chiefly to the region of the Atlantic coast, visiting but once the Societies in Connecticut. By the latter part of July he was again at Lynn, and labored for a month among the neighboring towns. He then departed for New Hampshire, but has left no important record of his journey. "I think," he wrote on his way back, "the time is near when the work of the Lord will begin to revive in this part of the world, and if the Lord work by us, our good mistaken brethren will be brought to say, 'Send, Lord, by whom thou wilt send.'" The next month he went to Rhode Island, where he projected a circuit in that State, which was recognized by the next Conference, and included most of those beautiful villages, on the shores of Providence River and Narraganset Bay, that now sustain vigorous Methodist Churches. Again he returned to Lynn, but on his arrival found Robert Bonsal, "just come from New York to preach the Gospel in these parts." Lee could now be spared from the circuit; leaving it, therefore, in the care of Smith and Bonsal, he immediately departed, proclaiming the word through the interior of Massachusetts and Connecticut. He found a prosperous Society formed at Enfield, and a visible improvement in the various appointments which he had established while laboring in Connecticut. "I see," he says, "that the Lord has prospered his work among the Methodists since I visited this part of the vineyard." In this excursion for a little more than one month (thirty-three days) he traveled five hundred and seventeen miles, and preached forty sermons. "I have reason," he says, on his return to Lynn, "to hope that the Lord has given me fresh strength and courage to go forward in his ways." During the last fourteen months he had preached three hundred and twenty-one sermons, besides delivering twenty-four public exhortations, and making almost continual journeys into New Hampshire, Massachusetts, Rhode Island, and Connecticut, and still he exclaims, "Forward! with fresh strength and courage."

A great man, both in word and deed, was this apostle of Methodism in the East; but a greater than he passed through these same regions in the period under review. Asbury entered Connecticut on the 4th of June, 1791. Though most repulsive vexations attended his visit, his notices of the country are expressive of that hopefulness which usually characterizes great minds—minds conscious of the energy that secures great results. On arriving at Reading, where Lee had formed his second class in Connecticut, he exclaims: "I feel faith to believe that this visit to New England will be blessed to my own soul, and the souls of others. We are now in Connecticut, and never out of sight of a house, and sometimes we have a view of many churches and steeples, built very neatly of wood." He moved on without cessation, preaching, as was his wont, wherever an opportunity offered—in churches, when allowed; where these were denied, in town-houses; and where these were closed, in private houses. On the 7th he arrived at Stratford, the town near which Lee formed his first New England Society. The time of trials had not yet passed. "Good news!" he exclaims, in a manner characteristic of himself; "they have voted that the town-house shall be shut. Well, where shall we preach? Some of the selectmen, one at least, granted access. Some smiled, some laughed, some swore, some talked, some prayed, some wept. Had it been a house of our own, I should not have been surprised had the windows been broken. We met the class, and found some gracious souls. The Methodists have a Society, consisting of about twenty members, some of them converted; but they have no house of worship." On the 23d he reached Boston. The prospects of Methodism had scarcely improved there. He records with emphasis his inhospitable reception: "I felt much pressed in spirit, as if the door was not open. As it was court time, we were put to some difficulty in getting entertainment. It was appointed for me to preach at Murray's Church—not at all pleasing to me, and that which made it worse for me was, that I had only about twenty or thirty people to preach to in a large house. It appeared to me that those who professed friendship for us were ashamed to publish us. On Friday evening I preached again; my congregation was somewhat larger. Owing, perhaps, to the loudness of my voice, the sinners were noisy in the streets. My subject was Rev. iii, 17, 18. I was disturbed, and not at liberty, although I sought it. I have done with Boston until we can obtain a lodging, a house to preach in, and some to join us." He had faith in the future, however, and the future has justified it. "The Methodists," he says, "have no house, but their time may come." In our day some ten churches, some of them among the best ornaments of the city, are occupied by his sons in the ministry, and are more numerous than its Puritan churches at that time. He tarried in Boston two days, and left it on the third for Lynn, where he was "agreeably surprised" to find "a Methodist chapel raised." After his discouraging reception in the metropolis he speaks with enthusiasm of Lynn, calling it the "perfection of beauty." He says, "It is seated on a plain, under a range of craggy hills, and open to the sea; there is a promising Society, an exceedingly well-behaved congregation; these things, doubtless, made all pleasing to me." He adds, with prophetic foresight, "Here we shall make a firm stand; and from this central point, from Lynn, shall the light of Methodism and truth radiate through the State." "I feel as if God would work in these States, and give us a great harvest." And again he predicts "that a glorious work of God will be wrought here." On the 13th of July he set his face toward the west, and again we trace him through a rapid passage, from Lynn to Springfield, where, on the 15th, he lifted up his voice, declaring, "It is time to seek the Lord, till he come and rain righteousness upon you;" the people were "moved," and one individual was "under deep conviction." He entered Connecticut, and, after preaching on the way, arrived at Hartford on the 19th, where he addressed an assembly from "Blessed is he, whosoever shall not be offended in me." He continued his route through Cornwall, New Britain, to Albany, preaching by night and by day. Such was the rapid tour through New England of this great apostle of American Methodism. It occupied less than eight weeks, but he had proclaimed his message in Connecticut, Rhode Island, and Massachusetts; had counseled with and directed the few laborers in the field, and had surveyed it sufficiently to guide him in his subsequent plans respecting it. He left New England with this reflection: "I am led to think the eastern Church will find this saying hold true in the Methodists, namely, 'I will provoke you to jealousy by them that are no people, and by a foolish nation I will anger you.'"

Thus much have we been able to ascertain respecting the laborers and labors of the ecclesiastical year, from May, 1791, to August, 1792. What were the results? We have but obscure intimations in the slight records of the times, but enough to show that it was the most prosperous of the three years which had passed since the introduction of Methodism into New England. Extensive revivals had occurred in several sections of the country. Lee informs us "that there was a considerable awakening among the people in different places, not far from Lynn;" that a door was opened for the outspread of Methodism through the Eastern States; that invitations for preachers multiplied in various directions; and, notwithstanding the general prejudice against the new Church, its members increased both in numbers and respectability. The circuits in Connecticut had been blessed with much prosperity. Of Reading, Asbury remarks: "God has wrought wonders in this town; the spirit of prayer is among the people, and several souls have been brought to God." On the Hartford Circuit an extensive reformation had prevailed. Demonstrations of the divine Spirit, like those witnessed in the days of Edwards and Whitefield, were again common among the towns on the banks of the Connecticut. At Tolland and the neighboring villages the interest was especially profound. Asbury estimates that one hundred and fifty souls were converted there, and that twice the number were under awakenings in the Societies around. "I felt," he says, "very solemn among them. Brothers Smith and Rainor have been owned of the Lord in these parts." He also speaks of a "melting among the people," at Pittsfield, where the "Lord was at work." About two hundred had been converted since the last Conference on the Albany district, which extended over this part of Massachusetts.

Three additional circuits, wholly or partly in New England, were reported this year, and the number of members returned from circuits bearing New England names was one thousand three hundred and fifty-eight, showing a gain of nearly nine hundred for the year. The few and scattered itinerants had made full proof of their ministry. Though still subjected to severe privations and annoying vexations, a goodly multitude of renewed souls now greeted and befriended them in their travels, and welcomed them, after the fatigues of the day, to humble but comfortable and consecrated homes. A Methodist people had been raised up; few, indeed, and feeble, but never to cease, we may trust, till the heavens and the earth are no more.

Lee arrived in Lynn, from his excursion to Connecticut, in the early part of May, 1792. He continued his labors in that town and its vicinity till the first week in August—a period memorable in the history of the denomination as the date of the first Conference held in the State of Massachusetts, and the first in New England. The preceding ecclesiastical year had included more than fourteen months. After so long a separation, and untold privations, labors, and sufferings, it was, indeed, a "holy convocation," a high festival, for the little company of itinerants, to meet in their first Conference. They assembled, as was befitting, in the first, and still unfinished, Methodist Chapel of Massachusetts. Asbury, who had now returned, speaks of it as a matter of congratulation, that "in Lynn we had the outside of a house completed." Had we the necessary data, it would be a grateful task to paint the picture of that first and memorable convention of New England Methodist preachers. We are able, however, to catch but a glimpse of it. We know the number, but hardly the names, of those who were present. "Our Conference," says Asbury, "met, consisting of eight persons, much united, besides myself." Asbury is himself the most imposing figure in the group. He was yet short of fifty years of age, and in the maturity of his physical and intellectual strength; his person was slight, but vigorous and erect; his eye stern, but bright; his brow began to show those wrinkles, the effects of extraordinary cares and fatigues, which afterward formed so marked a feature of his strongly characteristic face; his countenance was expressive of decision, sagacity, benignity, and was shaded, at times, by an aspect of deep anxiety, if not dejection; his attitude was dignified, if not graceful; his voice sonorous and commanding. By his side sat Lee, second only in the ranks of the ministry, for labors and travels, to its great leader. He was about the period of middle age, stout, athletic, full of vigor of muscle and feeling. His face was strongly marked by shrewdness, tenderness, and cheerfulness, if not humor; his manners, by unpretending dignity, remarkable temperance in debate, and fervid piety, mixed frequently, however, with vivid sallies of wit, and startling repartees. This trait of *bonhomie* was not without its advantages; it gave him access to the popular mind, and relieved the peculiar trials of his ministry. No man of less cheerful temperament could have brooked the chilling treatment he encountered while traveling the New England States without a colleague and without sympathy. This solitariness in a strange land, often without the stimulus of even persecution, but rendered doubly chilling by universal indifference or frigid politeness, was one of the strongest tests of his character. Those only can appreciate it who have endured it. He sat in the little band of his fellow-laborers with a cheerful aspect, for though he had gone forth weeping, bearing precious seed, it was now springing up, and whitening for the harvest, over the land. If it had been but as "a handful of corn in the earth, upon the top of the mountains," it now promised that "the fruit thereof would yet shake like Lebanon." In the group sat also the young and eloquent Hope Hull, the Summerfield of the time, attractive with the beauty of talent and of holiness; "that extraordinary young man," as

Thomas Ware called him, "under whose discourses the people were as clay in the hands of the potter." Asbury brought him, on his tour to this Conference, from the South, where he had been persecuted out of Savannah. There were, also, the youthful and talented Rainor, fresh from the revivals on Hartford Circuit, and undiverted yet from the labors of the itinerancy by the love of ease or domestic comfort, which was afterward too strong for him, and Allen, the "Boanerges," as his brethren called him. Besides these, it is probable that Lemuel Smith and Jeremiah Cosden were present.

Asbury introduced the occasion by a discourse on 1 John iv, 1–6. On Saturday he preached an ordination sermon to a "very solemn congregation." There was preaching every night during the session. The Sabbath "was the last day, that great day of the feast." A love-feast was held in the morning, after which Asbury preached on 1 Corinthians vi, 19, 20. In the afternoon John Allen preached, and the bishop gave a "farewell exhortation" to the people, who were deeply affected at his parting counsels. The next day he was away again, "making a hasty flight," as usual, and in four days he had passed over one hundred and seventy miles, on his way to other Conferences.

Lee was appointed this year presiding elder over a district that included eastern Massachusetts and Rhode Island, and the principal points of which were Lynn, Boston, Needham, and Providence. The General Conference was to convene on the first of the ensuing November, in Baltimore. But a brief interval of time remained, therefore, before it would be necessary for him to depart on his journey thither. He projected, however, a tour to Rhode Island, to attend to the further organization of the new Providence Circuit, which he had surveyed in his previous visit, and to which a preacher was assigned at the Conference of this year. In a few days after the adjournment of that body he was on his way thither. He visited Providence, Pawtuxet, Warren, and Bristol, preaching continually, putting in train the labors of the circuit for the newly arrived laborer, and re-entering Massachusetts after about one week's absence. On the 20th he was in Boston, and, at night, met the little class "which," he writes, "has been lately formed." In his history he records with exactness the date of its organization. "We had preached," he says, "a long time in Boston before we formed a Society, but on the 13th day of July, 1792, we joined a few in Society, and after a short time they began to increase in numbers. We met with uncommon difficulties here from the beginning, for the want of a convenient house to preach in. We began in private houses, and could seldom keep possession of them long. At last we obtained liberty to hold meetings in a school-house, but that too was soon denied us. We then rented a chamber in the north end of the town, where we continued to meet a considerable time regularly. The Society then undertook to get them a meeting-house, but being poor, and but few in number, they could do but little." Three years were yet to pass before the corner-stone of their first chapel could be laid. The next month he spent mostly in Lynn. He says: "Monday, 1st of October, I visited several friends in Lynn, and at night I preached my farewell sermon, on Phil. i, 27: 'Only let your conversation be as becometh the Gospel of Christ: that whether I come to see you, or else be absent, I may hear of your affairs, and that ye stand fast in one spirit, with one mind.' The Lord was with us of a truth; there was great weeping among the people, both men and women." With the leave-taking of Lee we must also take leave, for the present, of New England; but in thus reaching the limit of our present period, we perceive that his mission has been decisively successful. The tenacity of his purpose, the persistence of his zeal, have at last triumphed. Methodism has effectively taken its place in the ecclesiastical history of the Puritan States, and the name of its resolute pioneer must forever live in the records which commemorate those of the Mathers, Williams, Edwards, Channing, Ballou. The returns in the Minutes at the end of the conference year exhibit an advance in the membership of more than one fourth on the number of the preceding report. Four years had not yet elapsed since the formation of the first Society at Stratfield; the numerical gain of the infant Church thus far had been at the average rate of at least 435 per year, no small growth under the inauspicious circumstances of the times. A consciousness of the security and prospective success of their cause had spread through all their ranks, and while the violent and prejudiced began to deem it time for hostilities, the disinterested and devout began to open their hearts and their houses to welcome the itinerant evangelists as the "blessed" who "came in the name of the Lord," the men who "showed the way of salvation." Not only had their numbers augmented, but the field of travel and labor had extended in every direction. The number of circuits and stations had increased from nine to fourteen, and Lee began to cast his eye abroad for a new and more distant arena. He went to the Conference, determined to offer himself as a missionary to the "province of Maine," then a remote wilderness. Thither we shall hereafter follow him, to witness continued exhibitions of the moral heroism of his character while braving the inclemencies and perils of a new country, and achieving the sublime task of founding a religious organization which was to scatter, in our day, more than four hundred traveling and local preachers among its villages and cities, and enroll in them nearly twenty-five thousand members.

CHAPTER XVIII.

SUMMARY REVIEW: 1785-1792.

AFTER the General Conference of 1784 the Annual Conferences lose much of their historical importance. The organic measures of that session rendered much additional legislation unnecessary for a number of years. Down to that momentous assembly the two or more annual sessions were understood to be but one Conference, holding adjourned meetings. The Church, invigorated by its more thorough organization, now rapidly enlarged, and its Conferences multiplied. They were no longer considered to be adjourned sessions of the same body. But few grave matters of legislation were brought under their attention. It is probable, however, that any such matters were, as heretofore, submitted to the vote of each Conference before they were inserted in the laws of the denomination. A vague expectation of another General Conference seems to have been entertained, and important measures, which at any time appeared desirable, were mostly held in reserve for such a session. In the course of a few years, a general Council, the semblance of a General Conference, was attempted, and its failure providentially led to a regular Quadrennial Conference, which has ever since been the supreme body of the Church. The Minutes of these eight years afford but few items of historical interest. The only one recorded in 1785 is the suspension of the rules on slavery, accompanied, however, with the bold declaration that "we do hold in the deepest abhorrence the practice of slavery, and shall not cease to seek its destruction by all wise and prudent means." In 1786 the Minutes record nothing besides the usual routine questions and answers, and a few financial notices. In the ensuing year it is ordered that the children of the congregations shall be formed into classes; that register books shall be provided by the Societies for the record of baptisms and marriages, and an emphatic injunction on the preachers to leave nothing undone for the spiritual benefit and salvation "of the colored people" is inserted. We find in the Minutes of 1788 official provision made for the publication of books for the Church. John Dickins is appointed to Philadelphia, and designated as the "Book Steward;" and Philip Cox is left without a circuit, as "Book Steward" at large. The diffusion of religious literature had evidently become an important consideration with the Conference. The necessity of a General Conference was now univerally felt, but it seemed impossible to assemble the preachers, so widely dispersed over the country. The bishops therefore proposed, in the sessions of this year, the plan of a "Council," to be composed of "chosen men, out of the several districts, as representatives of the whole connection." The bishops were to have authority to convene the Council at their discretion, and its first meeting was appointed for the first day of December, at Cokesbury College. It held two sessions, in 1789 and 1790; and appointed a third for 1792, but the general opposition to it compelled the bishops to consent to substitute in its place a General Conference in the latter year. From the Christmas Conference to the sessions of 1790—somewhat more than five years—the statistical progress of the Church was remarkable. The returns of the year, which was closed by the Christmas Conference, showed about fifteen thousand members, (14,988,) and eighty-three preachers; the returns of the year 1790 amounted to more than fifty-seven thousand six hundred (57,631) members, and two hundred and twenty-seven preachers. The gains for these few years were, therefore, more than forty-two thousand six hundred (42,643) members, and one hundred and forty-four preachers. Estimating this period at six years, it yields an average annual growth of more than seven thousand one hundred members, and of twenty-four preachers. The latter item needs, however, very considerable qualification, for only the preachers actually on the list of appointments are reported; there is yet no supernumerary or superannuated list; and many every year retired from the itinerancy. Nearly all these entered the ranks of the local ministry, and continued to be habitual preachers. At least twenty-eight thus disappeared from the Minutes in the interval between the Christmas Conference and the year 1790; and besides these, not a few who were received on trial were not admitted into membership with the conferences, but were remanded to the local ranks, where they nevertheless did good service. We may safely estimate the increase of the ministry, in this brief interval, at one hundred and seventy-five, giving an annual average gain of nearly thirty. If we pass on, two years further, to the end of our present period, we meet an equally gratifying result. The aggregate returns for 1792 (all made before the session of the General Conference) swell to nearly sixty-six thousand (65,980) members, and two hundred and sixty-six preachers. The gains, then, since the returns last preceding the Christmas Conference, were nearly fifty-one thousand (50,992) members, and one hundred and eighty-three preachers. Estimating the interval at eight years, it exhibits an average annual gain of more than six thousand three hundred members, (6,374,) and of about twenty-three preachers. Qualifying the latter item, as above, the average ministerial gain must have been somewhat more than thirty.

Such was the statistical strength of American Methodism when its second General Conference assembled in Baltimore, in about eight years after its organization in that city, as "The Methodist Episcopal Church in the United States." Most of its founders were still living: Barbara Heck, Captain Webb, King, Watters, Gatch, Pilmoor, and Shadford.

About nineteen years had passed since its first Annual Conference was held in Philadelphia, when its first general statistical returns were made. It then reported eleven hundred and sixty members, and ten preachers; it had gained in the nineteen years nearly sixty-five thousand (64,680) members, and two hundred and fifty-six preachers. Its average annual gains had been more than thirty-four hundred (3,411) members, and more than thirteen preachers. There had been but two years in which the Minutes record a decrease of members: the first was 1778, when the Revolutionary War raged without, and the sacramental controversy within the Church—the loss amounted to eight hundred and seventy-three members, and five preachers; the second was 1780, the culmination of the sacramental contest, when a loss of seventy-three members was reported. It sterritorial extension had not only kept pace with the settlement of the country, but had transcended it; for Methodism was now established permanently in Nova Scotia and Upper Canada. At its first Conference of 1773 it reported but six circuits, reaching along a narrow line from New York city to Petersburg, Va. It now reported a hundred and thirty-six, extending from beyond the St. Lawrence, to Savannah, Ga.; from Lynn, Mass., to the most western settlements of Kentucky and Tennessee. The whole settled country was threaded with them. Seventeen Conferences were held in 1792, and twenty appointed for the next year, five at least of the latter beyond the Alleghanies.

In the Conference of 1773 all the preachers save one, William Watters, were foreigners; but since the Christmas Conference Wesley had dispatched no "missionaries" to America. All his former missionaries, except Asbury and Whatcoat, had returned to Europe; but American Methodism had now its native ministry, numerous and vigorous. Besides Asbury, Coke, and Whatcoat, it still retained many of the great evangelists it had thus far raised up: Garrettson, Lee, Abbott, O'Kelly, Crawford, Burke, Poythress, Bruce, Breeze, Reed, Cooper, Everett, Willis, Wilson Lee, Dickins, Ware, Brush, Moriarty, Roberts, Hull, Losee, and others. A host of mighty men, who will hereafter claim our attention, had recently joined these standard-bearers: M'Kendree, George, (both afterward bishops,) Roszel, Nolley, M'Gee, Smith, Gibson, M'Henry, Kobler, Fleming, Cook, Scott, Wells, Pickering, Sharp, Bostwick, M'Claskey, M'Combs, Bartine, Morrell, Taylor, Hunt, and scores more. These were to be soon followed, or rather joined, by another host of as strong, if not stronger representative men: Roberts, Hedding, Soule, Bangs, Merwin, Capers, Pierce, Winans, Kennon, Kenneday, Douglass, Redman, Thornton, Finley, Cartwright, Elliott, and many others equal to them; and amid an army of such were to arise in due time, to give a new intellectual development to the ministry, such characters as Emory, Fisk, Ruter, Summerfield, Bascom, Olin, and many others, some surviving into our day, men of not only denominational but of national recognition. Extraordinary indeed, a study full of inexpressible interest and profound lessons, is the history of that singular ministerial system of Methodism which we call the itinerancy. The development of character, of energy and success which it has revealed thus far in our narrative cannot fail to astonish us. Down to the final period of this record we shall find it as potent as ever. Its roll is glorious with heroes and martyrs. What clerical men since the apostolic age ever traveled and labored like these? What public men ever sacrificed equally with them the ordinary comforts of life? Their salaries or "allowance" (for they disclaimed the word salary) scarcely provided them with clothes. Asbury's allowance was sixty-four dollars a year. His horses and carriages were given by his friends, all donations of money from whom he assigned to his fellow-sufferers, his fellow-laborers. At one of the early Western Conferences, where the assembled itinerants presented painful evidences of want, he parted with his watch, his coat, and his shirts for them. He was asked by a friend to lend him fifty pounds. "He might as well have asked me for Peru," wrote the bishop; "I showed him all the money I had in the world, about twelve dollars, and gave him five." Most of the early itinerants had to locate, at last, on account of their broken health, or the sufferings of their families. Of six hundred and fifty whose names appear in the Minutes, by the close of the century, about five hundred died located, and many of the remainder were, for a longer or shorter interval, in the local ranks, but were able again to enter the itinerancy. Nearly half of those whose deaths are recorded died before they were thirty years old; about two thirds died before they had spent twelve years in the laborious service. They fell martyrs to their work.

If ever men presented the genuine credentials of Christian apostleship these men did. They were enthusiastic, sublimely so, but they were not fanatical. A remarkable seemliness and official decorousness characterized them as a body; an ecclesiastical dignity, which was the more commanding for being simple, unpretentious, laborious, and self-sacrificing. It was impossible that some eccentric, perhaps insane, minds, should not be drawn into the ever-widening circle of their enthusiastic movement; but the rigorous discipline and exhaustive labors of the denomination controlled or expended their morbid energy; or, if these failed, the rapid but steady motion of its ecclesiastical system threw them off, and so far off that they ceased to be dangerous. Into whatever position they found themselves thrown—from the itinerancy to the local ministry, from the conference to the class meeting—they found themselves bound by the tenacious "rules" of the Discipline. Hence, though untutored men, without a single collegiate graduate, besides Coke, in all their ranks thus far, no important doctrinal heresy had yet disturbed them. The theological symbol of general Christendom, the Apostles' Creed, and the Anglican Articles as abridged by Wesley, had never before had a purer or more effective promulgation among the masses of the people.

CHAPTER XIX.

SECOND GENERAL CONFERENCE—METHODISM IN THE SOUTH: 1792–1796.

ANOTHER important event in the history of American Methodism was at hand, the second General Conference. The first, called the Christmas Conference, (in 1784,) had been an extraordinary convention of the ministry, held, at the instance of Wesley, for the episcopal organization of the Church. No provision was made for any subsequent similar assembly. The rapid multiplication of sectional or "annual conferences" facilitated the local business of the denomination, but rendered legislation on its general interests difficult, if not impossible. Some other mode of general legislation was therefore necessary. The memorable assembly of 1784 presented the expedient example, and accordingly a General Conference was called for 1792.

Bishop Coke had left America, in May, 1791, on receiving the news of Wesley's death, and was absent about a year and a half. By the 31st October, 1792, he was again in Baltimore, where the General Conference began on the 1st of November. We have no "official" record of its proceedings; but Jesse Lee, who was present, has preserved an outline of its most important doings. He represents the gathering of preachers as numerous; "from all parts of the United States where we had any circuits formed." The first day was spent in considering the rules of the house. On the second, O'Kelly introduced a motion affecting radically the power of the episcopate, and indirectly reflecting on the administration of Asbury; it absorbed all attention for nearly a week, so that the revision of the Discipline, and the most needed legislation of the session, did not begin till Tuesday, the 6th.

On that day, of the second week, began the revision of the

Discipline. Regular General Conferences were ordained, and the Annual Conferences were distinguished, from these quadrennial assemblies, by the title of "District Conferences," as it was determined to hold one of them for each presiding elder's district. The office of presiding elder took, for the first time, a definitive form, and the title appears for the first time in the Discipline. Several minute regulations were adopted. In their preface to the next edition the bishops say: "We have made some little alterations in the present edition, yet such as affect not in any degree the essentials of our doctrines and discipline. We think ourselves obliged frequently to view and review the whole order of our Church, always aiming at perfection, standing on the shoulders of those who have lived before us, and taking advantage of our former selves."

But the chief subject of its deliberations was the proposition of O'Kelly to so abridge the episcopal prerogative that, "after the bishop appoints the preachers, at conference, to their several circuits, if any one thinks himself injured by the appointment he shall have liberty to appeal to the Conference and state his objections; and if the Conference approve his objections, the bishop shall appoint him to another circuit." The motion was obviously a reflection on his administration, but he bore it with admirable magnanimity. Having secured the organization of the body, with Coke for moderator, he retired anxious and sick, but his "soul breathing unto God, and exceedingly happy in his love." The discussion, as we have seen, occupied nearly a week; it was the first of those great parliamentary debates which have given pre-eminence to the deliberative talent of the body. It was led chiefly by O'Kelly, Ivey, Hull, Garrettson, and Swift for the affirmative, and by Willis, Lee, Morrell, Everett, and Reed for the negative, all chieftains of the itinerancy and eloquent preachers. Coke, however anxious for the issue of the controversy, sat in the chair rapt in admiration of the talent it elicited. "On Monday," says Lee, "we began the debate afresh, and continued it through the day; and at night we went to Otterbein's church, and again continued it till near bedtime, when the vote was taken, and the motion was lost by a large majority."

The next morning, after the decision of the question, the Conference was startled by a letter from O'Kelly and "a few other preachers," declaring that they could no longer retain their seats in the body, "because the appeal was not allowed." A committee of preachers was immediately appointed to wait upon them and persuade them to resume their seats. Garrettson, who had taken sides with them in the controversy, was on this committee. "Many tears," he says, "were shed, but we were not able to reconcile him to the decision of the Conference. His wound was deep, and apparently incurable."

After the withdrawal of O'Kelly peace and the old brotherly spirit again pervaded the Conference. On Thursday, the fifteenth and last day, the business being ended, Coke preached before the Conference. He left the city with a higher estimate of the American itinerants than he had ever formed before. "I had always entertained very high ideas of the piety and zeal of the American preachers, and of the considerable abilities of many; but I had no expectation, I confess, that the debates would be carried on in so very masterly a manner; so that on every question of importance the subject seemed to be considered in every possible light." O'Kelly returned to Virginia prepared to upturn the foundations he had helped to lay. Asbury hastened thither also, and held a conference in Manchester. Already O'Kelly had begun his pernicious work; some of the most devoted people and preachers had been disaffected; and, in this day, we are startled to read that William M'Kendree, afterward one of the saintliest bishops of the Church, and Rice Haggard, sent to Asbury "their resignations in writing." It was a period of general excitement in Virginia by the political contests of the Republicans and Federalists, the former being the dominant party. O'Kelly adroitly availed himself of these party agitations, and formed his associates into a Church with the title of "Republican Methodists." Their organization gave them a temporary power, and disastrous results followed. They held "conference after conference," devising a system of Church government; but insubordination reigned among them. In 1793 they had a number of Societies. "The divisive spirit," says Lee, "prevailed more in the south parts of Virginia than in any other place. There were some of our Societies in the northeast part of North Carolina who felt the painful effects of the division, and were considerably scattered and greatly injured. Several of our local preachers and many of our private members were drawn off from us, and turned against us. The Societies were brought into such troubles and difficulties that they knew not what to do. It was enough to make the saints of God weep between the porch and the altar, and that both day and night, to see how 'the Lord's flock was carried away captive' by that division."

In 1793 they held a conference in Mannakin Town, Va., the scene of a former dissentient Methodist assembly in the famous "sacramental controversy." They there framed a constitution, and O'Kelly, as their leader, ordained their preachers. In 1801 they discarded their laws and title, and assumed the name of "The Christian Church," renouncing all rules of Church government but the New Testament, as interpreted by every man for himself. It was impossible, however, that a schism so badly managed could long succeed. It broke into parties; several of its preachers fell away from it, and formed a new "plan of their own in Charlotte County, Va.;" many individual members and preachers, tired of the conflict, sought peace again in the parent Church; and Lee, writing in 1809, says: "They have been divided and subdivided, till at present it is hard to find two of them that are of one opinion. There are now but few of them in that part of Virginia where they were formerly the most numerous; and in most places they are declining." Ten years after O'Kelly's revolt Asbury met him again in Winchester, Va. "We met in peace," says the bishop, "asked of each other's welfare, talked of persons and things indifferently, prayed and parted in peace. Not a word was said of the troubles of the former times. Perhaps this is the last interview we shall have upon earth." Bangs supposes this interview was "near the close of O'Kelly's life," and expresses the hope that he died reconciled and "forgiven."

Asbury's Journals, however, show that for many years later the energetic seceder still fought his hopeless battle. He survived till the 16th of October, 1826, when he died in his ninety-second year, retaining "to the latest period of his life unabated confidence in the purity and power of his system."

Coke and Asbury parted after the General Conference of 1792, the former to the north, and thence to Europe; the latter to the south, to anticipate any schismatic measures of O'Kelly and his associates. He held conferences, love-feasts, class and band meetings, preaching once or twice and riding forty or fifty miles almost daily. He flew to all disturbed parts of the field in Virginia, and was successful in many, though in some he found incorrigible seceders. Not a few Societies were rent in pieces, and the enemies of religion and hostile sectarists exulted in the hope of the immediate and final downfall of the denomination throughout the State. He labored chiefly to promote among the distracted Societies a deeper religious feeling, spiritual unity, as the best means of ecclesiastical harmony. He not only traveled and preached, but wrote many letters. His usual correspondence averaged about a thousand a year, and was a heavy burden added to his many other cares.

He hastened through North and entered South Carolina, riding thirty, forty, fifty miles a day, "hungry," and "cold," for it was now December, but preaching at the close of nearly every day's journey in barns, private houses, and, occasionally, new chapels of "logs or poles," with "light and ventilation plenty." He was often drenched by storms; "the unfinished state of the houses, lying on the floor, thin clothing, and inclement weather, keep me," he writes, "in a state of indisposition." In Sumter District, S. C., he found, by Christmas day, shelter in one of those wealthy and hospitable houses which, like Perry Hall, were always open to welcome him as a prophet of God, at distant intervals of his great field. "Although the weather," he writes, "was cold and damp and unhealthy, with signs of snow, we rode forty-five miles to dear Brother Rembert's—kind and good, rich and liberal, who has done more for the poor Methodists than any man in South

Carolina. The Lord grant that he, with his whole household, may find mercy in that day!" A bishop of Southern Methodism, speaking of "Rembert Hall," so often and so gratefully mentioned in Asbury's Journals, says: "The proprietor of this estate, James Rembert, Esq., was a Methodist gentleman of large property, who was strongly attached to Asbury. There was a room in his mansion that was appropriated to the bishop's use. Here he commonly spent a week during his annual visitation to South Carolina. It was a sweet haven, where the weather-beaten sailor found quiet waters, and bright skies, and a season of repose. Here he brought up his journal, wrote his letters, and lectured of an evening to the family and visitors and crowds of servants. Mrs. Rembert was a lady of the kindest heart; she not only had the bishop's apartments always ready and commodiously furnished, but every year her seamstress made up for him a full supply of linen, which, neatly ironed, awaited the arrival of the bishop. Rembert Hall, in my time on the Sumter Circuit, was occupied by Caleb Rembert, Esq., his honored father and mother having long before gone to heaven."

Reaching Charleston, he found "the little flock in peace and a small revival among them," though here also the Church had been scathed by division. William Hammett, one of Coke's missionaries to the West Indies, had come to the United States, and had taken charge of the society in Charleston, where his remarkable natural powers of eloquence soon rendered him generally popular. He headed a secession from the young Church of the city in 1791, briefly anticipating and severely exasperating the revolt of O'Kelly and his followers in Virginia and North Carolina. Thus agitation prevailed through much of nearly one half of the territory of the Church, for the schismatic spirit spread infectiously, pamphlets were published, letters written, personal visitations made by disaffected preachers; even the new and feeble Churches beyond the Alleghanies felt the evil. Most of Hammett's Societies finally returned to the parent Church. He died in 1803, about eleven years after his secession, and the schism became extinct.

In this southern tour Asbury summed up the Minutes for the ecclesiastical year. "We have," he writes, "two hundred and seventeen traveling preachers, and about fifty thousand members in the United States. Glory to God in the highest!" We trace him among the western mountains of North Carolina, "wrestling with floods," his food "Indian bread and fried bacon," and his "bed set upon forks, and clapboards laid across, in an earthen floor cabin." He crossed the Alleghanies through perilous difficulties, and was again in the Great West, where he spent about six weeks among the emigrant settlements of Tennessee and Kentucky, convoyed sometimes by armed guards, and enduring the severest privations and fatigues. By the middle of May he was again among the heights of the Virginia mountains, sheltered in the comfortable home of the widow of General Russell, the sister of Patrick Henry, and one of the "elect ladies" of Methodism. The most romantic passages of his journals are his brief records of his adventures among the Alleghanies, and often at the close of weary days does he write, in log-cabins, that so many miles yet remain before he can reach "General Russell's," his longed-for resting-place. He now writes: "I am very solemn. I feel the want of the dear man who, I trust, is now in Abraham's bosom, and hope ere long to see him there. He was a general officer in the continental army, where he underwent great fatigue; he was powerfully brought to God, and for a few years past was a living flame, and a blessing to his neighborhood. He went in the dead of winter on a visit to his friends, was seized with an influenza, and ended his life from home. O that the Gospel may continue in this house! I preached on Heb. xii, 1–4, and there followed several exhortations. We then administered the sacrament, and there was weeping and shouting among the people; our exercises lasted about five hours." Such scenes often occurred there, for Mrs. Russell kept her mansion always open, not only for the shelter of the wayworn itinerants, but as a sanctuary for the mountaineer settlers, who flocked thither from miles around to hear the Gospel. "She was," says an itinerant who enjoyed her hospitalities, "eloquent like her brother, a woman of exemplary piety." Like most of the Methodist women of her day, she exhorted and prayed in public. Her home was a light-house shining afar among the Alleghanies.

By the middle of June Asbury was again holding a conference at Old Town, Md., but by the middle of September, 1793, he re-entered the southern field. Through all sorts of hardships he again penetrated South Carolina, to face the trials of Charleston, where he arrived on the 20th of January, 1794, and spent nearly a month preaching, visiting from house to house, and confirming the Church. On the 18th of June he once more found genial shelter in Baltimore, then the head-quarters of all his episcopal campaigns. He paused, however, but four or five days, and hastened on to the north and the east as far as Boston and Lynn. By the middle of October he was back again; a day of hospitable shelter at Perry Hall, a week of labor in Baltimore, at the conference, and the southern campaign is reopened. It was followed by another passage over the Alleghanies into Tennessee. On the 21st of May he was again in Baltimore, but saddened by the news of the death of one of his "best friends in America," Judge White, of Kent County, Md., whose important services to early Methodism have already been noticed. "This news," writes the bishop, "was attended with an awful shock to me. I have met with nothing like it in the death of any friend on the continent. Lord help us all to live out our short day to thy glory! I have lived days, weeks, and months in his house. O that his removal may be sanctified to my good and the good of the family! He was about sixty-five years of age. He was a friend to the poor and oppressed; he had been a professed Churchman, and was united to the Methodist connection about seventeen or eighteen years. His house and heart were always open; and he was a faithful friend to liberty, in spirit and practice; he was a most indulgent husband, a tender father, and a most affectionate friend. He professed perfect love and great peace, living and dying. I preached twice in town, and was delivered from my gloomy state of mind. I spent part of the week visiting from house to house. I feel happy in speaking to all I find, whether parents, children, or servants; I see no other way; the common means will not do; Baxter, Wesley, and our Form of Discipline, say, 'Go into every house:' I would go further, and say, Go into every kitchen and shop; address all, aged and young, on the salvation of their souls."

Again to the north and east, to Boston, Mass., and round about to Bennington, Vt., and back to Baltimore by the middle of October, for another southern campaign—journeying, preaching, holding conferences, meeting classes, and still visiting from house to house in the places where he had occasion to delay a few days—such are the events which crowd his journals, that extraordinary record which hastens us along with eager interest, while almost vexing us with the slightness, the brevity of its notes—so meager in details, yet so burdened with romantic significance. In his next southern tour he found that "the connection had regained its proper tone in Virginia, after having been kept out of tune for five years by the unhappy division." And at Charleston, S. C., also, he was cheered with improved prospects. "My soul," he says, "felt joyful and solemn at the thoughts of a revival of religion in Charleston." He continued there till the beginning of March, 1796. On the 3d of March he departed for Georgia, and after itinerating there over more than two hundred miles, set his face toward the northwest again, passed into the Alleghany mountains, and ranged about among them, sometimes in Tennessee, sometimes in North Carolina and Virginia, till he emerged on their west in Pennsylvania about the end of May. The difficulties of his way were incredible. Having no mercy on himself, he yet scrupled to impose such hardships on any one else. "I doubt," he says, as he escaped from them, "whether I shall ever request any person to come and meet me again at the levels of Green Briar, or to accompany me across these mountains again, as Daniel Hitt has now done. O how checkered is life! How thankful ought I to be that I am here safe, with life and limbs, in peace and plenty."

Many mighty men were Asbury's colaborers in the Southern States in the quadrennial period from 1792 to 1796; and many, destined to be pre-eminent at a later day, were rising up in the yet feeble and obscure conferences of that part of the continent.

Benjamin Abbott's appointments for the brief remainder of his life were in Maryland. His journals become more scanty than in the years through which we have already followed him, but they record the same extraordinary effects of his preaching, hearers falling under the word "like men slain in battle," the "opening of the windows of heaven, and the skies pouring down righteousness, so that the people fell before the Lord." We have referred to the astonishing physical and psychological phenomena which attended his ministrations, and stated the cautious interpretation of such anomalies given by the best Methodist authorities. Though not peculiar to his preaching, they were peculiarly powerful with him. They were indeed habitual, almost invariable, effects of his singular eloquence, for he was eloquent in the best sense of the word. Uneducated, rough, rude even, in speech and manner, his fervid piety and his genial human sympathy made his weather-worn features glow as with a divine light, and intoned his voice with a strange, a magnetic, an irresistible pathos and power. There may have been a psychological, perhaps a physiological, as well as a moral element in this marvelous power, a mystery which future science may render more intelligible; be this as it may, Benjamin Abbott led a divine life on earth, walking with God, like Enoch, from day to day, and the hardiest, the most ruffian men who came within his presence—the clamorous rabble that frequently thronged his congregations—fell back, or sank prostrate before him, seeing "his face as it had been the face of an angel;" and if they attempted, as they often did, to escape by the doors or the windows, his voice would sometimes smite them down like lightning. His casual conversation, always religious, his social or domestic prayers, had the same effect. We continually read not merely of "God attending the word, with the energy of the Holy Ghost, in such manner that numbers fell to the floor," that "the wicked flew to the doors," that "there was a shaking among the dry bones," but that at his temporary lodging-places, "in family prayer, the Lord was with him of a truth," and similar wonders attended him. If he went into a house to baptize a child, we hear of like effects—the "mother trembling in every joint, four persons falling to the floor, one professing that God has sanctified her soul." In some cases, as we have seen, most, or even all his congregation, save himself, were thus prostrated. And, however morally dangerous such scenes might seem to be, (physically they never were injurious,) they appear to have been uniformly followed with salutary results. Few preachers, perhaps no other one of his day, reclaimed more men from gross vice. His mission seemed especially to such.

He now kept the whole Eastern Shore of Maryland astir with religious interest. Even those whose religious education had taught them to associate quietude with piety were infected with the excitement. "In the morning," he writes, "we had a melting time; many wept. In the afternoon the Lord poured out his Spirit, and the slain fell before him like dead men; others lay as in the agonies of death, entreating God to have mercy on their souls; some found peace. 'Glory to God, many in this town seemed alarmed of their danger; may the Lord increase their number. A girl who lived with a Quaker was cut to the heart in such a manner that they did not know how to get her home; I went to see her, and found many round her, both white and black. She lay as one near her last gasp; I kneeled down and besought God for her deliverance, and in a few minutes she broke out in raptures of joy, crying out, 'Let me go to Jesus!' repeating it several times; then she arose and went home. Glory to God! for what my eyes saw, my ears heard, and soul felt that day of the blessed Spirit. The meeting continued from three o'clock until evening."

Family groups, bearing him in their carriages to their homes, from his meetings, were "awakened," "converted," "sanctified," "shouted the praises of God," "lost their strength," or consciousness, as he conversed with them on the route. In love-feasts, sometimes, not one could give the usual narration of Christian experience, but, under the introductory devotions, "the Lord so laid his hand upon them that sinners trembled and fell to the floor," and the customary exercises had to give way to prayer and praise. As the people returned to their homes they were heard praising God along the highways. And such scenes were not occasional or exceptional; nearly every day's record reports them, for there was hardly a day in which he did not hold a meeting, and hardly a meeting without immediate results. As facts of the times, not uncommon in any part of the Church, they are essential to a faithful record of its history, however our modern criticism, or more decorous ideas of religious life, may judge them.

On the more important or festival occasions of the Church, especially at the great quarterly meetings of the time, this spiritual enthusiasm kindled still higher, and spread out like a flame over whole circuits. They were jubilees to Abbott. On one of them he says: "Our meeting began at six o'clock in the morning, and when we had sung and prayed, the power of God came down in such a manner that the slain lay all through the house. We had to carry them out of the house, in order to make room that the people might come in for the public preaching; and when we had sung and prayed the presence of the Lord came down as in the days of old, and the house was filled with his glory; the people fell before him like men slain in battle." If he deviated for such special occasions to other circuits, the same extraordinary scenes attended him. "I went," he writes, "to quarterly meeting on Dover circuit; we had a happy day. The people fell and acknowledged the power of God; and the slain lay all about the house; some were carried out as dead men and women. The house was filled with the glory of Israel's God, who spoke peace to mourners, while sinners were cut to the heart. It was thought there were about fifteen hundred looking on with wonder and amazement at the mighty power of God, which caused the powers of hell to shake and give way."

Of course there could be no stagnation in the region through which such a man traveled sounding his trumpet daily; we read that "the flame spread around the circuit, and many were brought to the knowledge of God." He continued these labors till May, 1795, when failing in health, he returned to his home in New Jersey, and never was able to resume his travels on a circuit. He had been suffering, in Maryland, for three months from fever and ague. After re-entering New Jersey he frequently exerted his little remaining strength in religious meetings, until June, 1796, when he rapidly failed; but his soul remained unclouded to the last. He testified that "perfect love casteth out fear, and he that feareth is not made perfect in love. And for my part," he added, "I can call God to witness that death is no terror to me! I am ready to meet my God if it were now!"

On the 13th of August he was in "excrutiating pain," "which he bore with Christian patience and resignation. He appeared to possess his rational faculties to his last moments; and for some time previous was delivered from pain, to the joy of his friends; his countenance continued joyful, heavenly, and serene. 'Glory to God!' he exclaimed, 'I see heaven sweetly opened before me!'" The next day he was no more. He died as he had lived, "shouting!" "Glory! glory! glory!" are his last utterances recorded by his biographer, who attended him in death. He uttered them "clapping his hands, in the greatest ecstacies of joy imaginable." The ruling passion was strong in death.

Thus passes from the scene of our story one of its most remarkable characters. He had led hosts of souls from the lowest abysses of vice into a good life and into the Church, from the Hudson to the Chesapeake. He has been a problem to students of our history. I have already endeavored to give the solution of that problem; but his singular yet most effective life will ever remain a marvel, if not a mystery. An extraordinary individuality of character, sanctified by extraordinary endowments of divine grace, must be its chief explanation. They fitted him for a peculiar work, and he did it thoroughly, with all his might and to the end.

He died aged about sixty-four years, had been a Methodist nearly twenty-four years, a local preacher more than sixteen, a traveling preacher more than seven. His ministerial brethren characterized him in their Conference Minutes "as one of the wonders of America, no man's copy; an uncommon zealot for the blessed work of sanctification, he preaching it on all occasions and in all congregations, and what was best of all, living it. He was an innocent, holy man; he was seldom heard to speak anything but about God and religion; his whole soul was often overwhelmed with the power of God. He was known to hundreds as a truly primitive Methodist preacher, and a man full of faith and the Holy Ghost."

Whatcoat has left us but a page or two respecting his labors in this period. He was Abbott's presiding elder, most of the time, on the Maryland peninsula. Grave, but fervidly pious, he wondered while he rejoiced at the results of Abbott's preaching. An extraordinary revival spread over his extended district. "We had large congregations, and many blessed revivals in different parts of the district," he says: "Our quarterly meetings were generally comfortable, lively, and profitable. Some appeared extraordinary; souls were suddenly struck with convictions, and fell to the ground, roaring out for the disquietness of their souls, as though almost dead, and after a while starting up and praising God, as though heaven were come into their souls; others were as much concerned for a cleaner heart, and as fully delivered. I had to attend forty-eight quarterly meetings in the space of twelve months while on this district."

Henry Smith entered the field of the itinerancy in the present period—a man venerated throughout the Church; in our own day, familiar to most of its people by his long and widely-extended services, and his frequent published letters, dated from "Pilgrim's Rest," Baltimore county, on the early events of our history. When ninety-four years old he could say, "I am now, I believe, the only link in the old Baltimore Conference connecting our early preachers with the present race. Under a sermon, preached by Thomas Scott, (afterward Judge Scott, of Ohio,) I made up my mind to be a Christian in earnest, and joined the Methodists. In 1793 I was licensed to preach at a quarterly meeting. The late Joshua Wells signed my license. In the latter part of the summer I entered the itinerant work on Berkeley Circuit. On the 1st of June, 1794, I attended the first Conference at Harrisonburgh, Rockingham County. I was appointed to Clarksburgh Circuit, west of the Alleghany Mountains; in the following spring to the Redstone Circuit. In October, 1793, I attended my first Conference in Baltimore. From there I was sent to Kentucky; then to the far West. There was but one Conference then west of the

Alleghany Mountains, called the Western Conference, and that was small, though spread over a vast territory, namely, Western Virginia, New River and Holston, and East Tennessee, Cumberland and Kentucky. In October, 1799, I crossed the Ohio into the Northwestern Territory, and organized the Scioto Circuit. In the spring of 1800 I came to the General Conference in Baltimore, and by my own request was returned to Scioto, my newly-formed circuit. Thence I was returned to Kentucky, and ended my western labors on Nolachucky Circuit, Tennessee, March, 1803, having suffered much from bilious fever, ague and fever, dyspepsia, and rheumatism, being then quite a cripple. But being requested by the bishop I set out on horseback, and rode about four or five hundred miles in much pain, and came again to my mother Conference. I traveled seven years under the rule that allowed a preacher sixty-four dollars a year, including all marriage fees and presents, from a cravat down to a pair of stockings. I think our bishops were under the same rule. The last time I saw this rule imposed was at the Baltimore Conference, held at the Stone Chapel in May, 1800. In my mind I yet see the sainted Wilson Lee hand over his fees and presents. True, our traveling expenses were allowed if we could get them. The world never saw a more disinterested, cross-bearing, and self-sacrificing set of ministers than the early Methodist preachers."

He joined the Methodists about his twentieth year. He met soon after Francis M'Cormick, another memorable name, as we shall hereafter see. "I did not hesitate," says Smith, "to tell him seriously my whole and sole object in joining the Church, as he called it. He took me by the hand, and said, 'Farewell, I expect I shall join too after a while,' and went back into the house. He went to the meeting, was powerfully awakened, joined the Society, and that night began to pray in his family. He became a leader of a class, an exhorter, and finally a local preacher, and was a pioneer in the West. In the fall of 1779 I found him on the banks of the Little Miami, opening the way for the traveling preachers. He was my constant companion and true yoke-fellow while I remained at home."

Smith's friend, M'Cormick, became an ardent Methodist, and went forth with him to hold their first public meeting. It was at "Davenport's Meeting-House," in the wilderness of Western Maryland, and was a characteristic scene. "We found," writes Smith, "the lower part of the house full of people, and some in the gallery. There was no light but on the pulpit, and that was high; so we had to ascend the pulpit to see how to read a hymn. It was a trembling time with me, and no better with my companion. I opened the meeting. One poor sinner cried out for mercy under the prayer. I tried to exhort, but was, as I thought, amazingly embarrassed, and sat down in great confusion and distress of mind; for I felt as if I had done more harm than I should ever do good, and prayed to the Lord to forgive my presumption, and I never would do the like again. The poor woman was still crying for mercy. Brother M'Cormick gave a lively exhortation, and seemed to have great liberty, and concluded with singing and prayer. I was still so mortified that I wished to get out of the meeting-house and hide myself. But the people all seemed to be serious, and sat down, and some looked at the woman in distress. Presently Brother M'Cormick began to sing, 'Come on, my partners in distress,' in great spirit, for he was a fine singer, and the soul-melting power of the Lord came down upon us, and it was felt through all the house. My mind was relieved in a moment, and I soon found myself on a bench exhorting the people, and we had a most glorious time. This was a log meeting-house, and I had hauled the first log to it; and this was the first pulpit I ever opened my mouth in."

In 1793 Smith was licensed to preach, and began his itinerant career on Berkeley Circuit, Virginia. In the next year he was received on trial in the Conference, and sent beyond the Alleghanies; he thus took his place among the founders of Methodism in the valley of the Mississippi, where we shall hereafter meet him with his friend M'Cormick, both doing heroic service.

The name of M'Kendree has already appeared in our narrative—compromised with that of O'Kelly, but speedily redeemed. William M'Kendree was destined to be the fourth

REV. WILLIAM McKENDREE.

Bishop of the Methodist Episcopal Church.

bishop of the Methodist Episcopal Church, a chief founder of the denomination in the West, a preacher of transcendent power, an ecclesiastical administrator of scarcely rivaled ability, and a man of the saintliest character. Under the ministry of John Easter, famous for his eloquence and usefulness, his conscience was effectually awakened. "After a sore and sorrowful travail of three days," he says, "which were employed in hearing Mr. Easter, and in fasting and prayer, while the man of God was showing a large congregation the way of salvation by faith, with a clearness which at once astonished and encouraged me, I ventured my all upon Christ. In a moment my soul was relieved of a burden too heavy to be borne, and joy instantly succeeded sorrow." Easter induced him to accompany him on his circuit; but, after some attempts to preach, he returned home, fearful that he had run before he was called. Philip Cox was appointed to the Mecklenburg Circuit by the next Conference, and at the same session Easter, who knew M'Kendree's capacities better than his modesty allowed him to estimate them himself, had him received on probation and placed under the care of Cox, though he had not yet been licensed as a local preacher. Cox was a man of flaming zeal and indomitable energy, and bore along his diffident colleague. He made full proof of his ministry, and was successively appointed to Cumberland, Portsmouth, Amelia, and Greensville Circuits; to the latter as preacher in charge.

He was long under the powerful influence of O'Kelly, who was his presiding elder. M'Kendree did not know Asbury intimately enough to qualify, in his own mind, the charges made against him by O'Kelly; he yielded to the influence of his popular and ardent presiding elder, and, with Rice Haggard, sent in his resignation to Asbury. Regretting his sudden error, he resolved to ascertain, from personal acquaintance, the real character of Asbury, and for this purpose accompanied the bishop in his travels. He became satisfied that O'Kelly had misrepresented him, and resumed his work with a devotion which never again wavered. In 1795 his appointment was on Botetourt Circuit, still on the frontier, west of the Blue Ridge, for Asbury had discovered in him the qualifications of a pioneer and founder. He had four circuits under his care, traveling on each of them a quarter of a year. During the remainder of the century he traveled large districts as presiding elder, one of them extending along the Potomac, in Maryland and Virginia, and reaching from the Chesapeake to the Alleghanies. He had now become one of the leading men of the Church. He was nearly six feet high, with a robust frame, weighing about one hundred and sixty pounds, of extraordinary strength and activity, fair complexion, black hair and blue eyes. "His intellect, as a whole, was bright, and his thoughts diamond-pointed. He never said foolish things—never weak, never even common things. There was thought in all his words, and wisdom in all his thoughts. He was the man for the times and the age in which he lived, leading in triumph the Church in the wilderness."

Asbury judged him fit to be the leader of the western itinerancy. He passed into the valley of the Mississippi, where a grand career awaited him. He here had charge of the Western Conference, comprehending Ohio, Kentucky, Tennessee, Virginia, (west of New River,) and a circuit in Illinois. We shall find him at last worthily at the head of the American Methodist hosts.

Enoch George had also now become an effective evangelist. He came under the ministry of Jarratt, and was awakened, and afterward brought into the Church by Easter. His brethren encouraged him, and warned him that it was his duty to "exhort" the people. Philip Cox called him out upon a circuit, and Asbury sent him with a letter to a preacher who was breaking up the fallow ground and forming a circuit, at the head waters of the Catawba and Broad Rivers, in North Carolina, three hundred miles distant. The bishop knew that if anything could be made of the "beardless boy," presented to him by Cox, the heroic work of the frontier would make him. He was thus made an evangelic giant, and a worthy successor of Asbury.

It was in 1789 that Cox called him out; in 1790 he was admitted to the Conference on trial and sent to Pamlico Circuit, North Carolina; in 1791 to Caswell, where he had great success; but, in accordance with the "itinerancy" of the times, he was soon dispatched again to Pamlico Circuit, "embracing as sickly a region as any in North Carolina." "This sudden transition," he says, "from the foot of the Black Mountain to the margin of the sea, tried my faith. Thus I was made partaker in the afflictions of my brethren."

In 1792 he traveled Gifford County, North Carolina, where "it pleased the great Head of the Church to revive his work gloriously." He attended the General Conference of 1792, and witnessed afterward the schism of O'Kelly, as it desolated the neighborhood of his "relatives in Virginia, many of whom joined him." "I had sorrow upon sorrow," he writes. The secession spread into his North Carolina field, and required his utmost wisdom. In 1793 Asbury called, in a North Carolina Conference, for preachers for the further south, but they hesitated. "Here am I," said George; "send me. We set off, and when the expenses were paid nothing was left." He was rapidly tossed about the vast field, broke down in health, and had to locate, but resumed his itinerant labors in 1799 with restored vigor and increased zeal; and thenceforward, with a single intermission, passed through the denomination like "a flame of fire" for nearly thirty years, when he fell triumphantly in death in the highest office of the ministry. Like M'Kendree, he was large in stature, nearly six feet high, stout, with a tendency to corpulence, and full of energy; with a military erectness while standing, inclining forward when moving, with his hands usually thrown behind him, and habitually quick in his motions. His form was imposing by its expression of strength, his face broad, forehead prominent and expanded, nose large, eyes blue and deeply set, eyebrows dark and projecting, hair black, tinged with gray, and carelessly but gracefully hanging about his neck; his complexion sallow, the effect of his sufferings from the miasma of the South. His whole person, in fine, was stamped with character. His intellect was clear and sure, if not brilliant; calm, though always energetic; quiet energy pervaded all his acts and words. An extraordinary pathos melted his audiences and himself, and he often had to pause in his sermons and ask his hearers to join him in utterances of thanksgiving, while, with tears streaming down his weather-worn face, he would raise his spectacles, and, with uplifted eyes and hands, offer praise to God, bearing aloft his thronged congregations, thrilled, weeping, and adoring. The elder Methodists throughout the country still recall him with veneration as the "weeping prophet" of their episcopacy.

The two brothers, Coleman and Simon Carlisle, were successful evangelists of the South. The former joined the itinerancy in 1792. In the latter part of 1823 he "finally located, not from choice, but from absolute necessity." "He was," says one of his ministerial contemporaries, "a poor man, with a sickly, though truly good and excellent wife, and quite a number of little boys and girls. I have known him, after returning home from preaching several miles distant, after supper, take the same horse (having but one) and plow with him by moonlight until nearly midnight, and then go off next morning to his appointments. He neither owned nor hired servants." He was a very popular preacher, and, when local, was sent for far and near to preach funeral sermons. His brother, Simon Carlisle, preceded him in the ministry by two years, endured also the severest hardships of the itinerancy, and an additional and extraordinary trial from which, however, he had at last one of those providential vindications which so often occur in the annals of English and American Methodism, and which may well inspire with hope all innocent sufferers. After having labored with humble but intrepid devotion on some of the hardest fields of the South, he was arrested before the Church and expelled in 1794, and his name appears in the Minutes of that year branded with reproach as a fallen and outcast man. No affliction, no martyrdom could have been more appalling to a faithful Methodist preacher of those days of ministerial chivalry. The charge alleged against him was such as, if possible, to enhance the bitterness of his grief, by combining meanness with guilt, for it was theft! For two years the guiltless man bore, with bowed head, this great and, to him, mysterious sorrow; but his faith failed not. He had given offense by reproving a disturbance in one of his rude frontier congregations; under the provocation a young man went to his stopping place, placed a pistol in his saddle-bags, and the next day got out a search-warrant for him, making oath that he believed Carlisle had stolen his weapon. An officer hastened after him on his circuit, overtook him, and charged him with the crime. The astonished preacher, conscious of innocence, readily consented to have his saddle-bags searched. The pistol was found in them; he was thunderstruck; he knew not what to do, but calmly gave himself up to the law. He was found guilty, and had no way to clear himself: even the Church threw him off. But the criminal young man was cast on his death-bed: about an hour before he expired he frantically cried out, "I cannot die, I cannot die, until I reveal one thing: Mr. Carlisle never stole that pistol; I myself put it in his saddle-bags!" He then became calm, and so passed into eternity. Carlisle was restored to the ministry, and died in it with peace in 1838.

Stephen G. Roszel was now a young itinerant in Virginia, but rising continually in public influence by his flaming zeal and strong talents. For more than fifty years he was to be a chieftain of the Church in Virginia and Maryland, conspicuous as a presiding elder, an able debater in the General Conference, a leader in annual conferences, a revivalist in the pulpit, preaching often with great power through an hour and a half or two hours; "a man of mark, exerting a wide and powerful influence in his denomination." Joshua Wells was also abroad in the southern field at this period, in the full vigor of his young manhood. An able and successful laborer, and regarded by the Church with peculiar reverence through a singularly long life, he was nevertheless so modest, if not morbidly self-diffident, as scarcely ever to have spoken or written anything respecting himself. He was born in Baltimore County in 1764, joined the itinerancy when twenty-five years of age, and died more than ninety-seven years old. He had traveled and preached in Virginia, Maryland, Delaware, New York, Pennsylvania, Massachusetts as far as Boston, and became at last the oldest living preacher whose name was on the roll of the itinerancy. He was dignified and robust in person, his features strongly marked, and yet benignant. His sermons were noted for their perspicuity and brevity, their masculine sense, clear and vigorous argumentation, and effect. He was distinguished as a disciplinarian. Philip Bruce was energetically spreading out the denomination during these years on vast districts, as presiding elder, from Northern Virginia to Charlestown, N. C., and to Western Georgia; Nelson Reed was traversing large districts in Maryland and Virginia; Tobias Gibson in the Carolinas, and Valentine Cook and John Cole in the wilds of Virginia, were preparing, by the discipline of severest labor and hardship, for their great achievements in the new regions beyond the mountains, whither John Kobler, Barnabas M'Henry, Daniel Hitt, and other mighty men, had lately advanced from the same southern preparatory field. Thomas Scott, a memorable name in the West, was also there preparing for the same pioneer service, meanwhile leading into the Church, in Virginia, Edward Tiffin, afterward first governor of Ohio, a zealous preacher, and a founder, with Scott, of Methodism in the Northwestern Territory. Pickering, Bostwick, and other worthies were preparing for similar expeditions to New England, the latter also destined to bear part in the trans-Alleghany triumphs of the Church. In short, southern Methodism, at this early period, presented a surprising array of strong men; men who have impressed their names on the history of both the South and West, and who deserve to live forever in the grateful memory of the American people as the standard-bearers of Christian civilization along most of the southern and western frontier.

The Church had greatly extended in the South since the General Conference; no less than fourteen new circuits had been formed, reaching to the heart of Georgia, and into the Western mountains, across which preachers were penetrating into Kentucky and Tennessee. There were now in Maryland 12,416 Methodists; in Virginia, 13,779; in North Carolina, 8,713; South Carolina, 3,659; Georgia, 1,174; aggregately nearly 40,000 south of Delaware, exclusive of Kentucky and Tennessee. They amounted to considerably more than twice as many as in all the rest of the denomination.

CHAPTER XX.

METHODISM IN THE MIDDLE AND NORTHERN STATES: 1792–1796.

On his return from the South and West in 1793 Asbury entered New Jersey early in July, pressed forward in haste, and was holding a Conference at Albany in the third week of the month. "We had," he writes, "a melting season among the preachers. Great changes will be made among them from this Conference: some will be sent to New Jersey, others to Rhode Island and Massachusetts. We hope two hundred souls have been awakened, and as many converted, in Albany District the past year."

We get but mere glimpses of his episcopal pastorate from his meager journals; their records would seem a waste of paper were it not that they reveal so much, though so indirectly, the tireless man and the apostolic bishop. Ever regardful of the interests of the Church where they were most critical, he penetrated to the furthest tracks of his pioneer itinerants; hence his incessant return to the extreme South, to the ultra-Alleghany frontiers, to New England, and, before long, to the wilds of Upper Canada. In these journeys he must necessarily cross and recross the more settled central fields of the Church, and these he inspects with the minutest care, laboring as hard among them as their local pastors; but his records lose here much of their interest; they present little more than the briefest allusions—mere memoranda. He longed for the woods, the mountains, the excitements and hardships of the frontier. It is the fate of energetic men to be restless, to be unhappy without movement and achievement: the cause perhaps, and, in part, the effect of their activity. Asbury was constitutionally melancholy; unconscious, he often writes, "of any sin even in thought," yet in grievous dejection. No medical scholar can fail to observe in his journals, from beginning to end, and especially about this time, a profoundly morbid temperament. There is now scarcely a page in which we do not witness the heroic struggle of his invincible will with this formidable physical drawback. And the evil grows as he advances in life. He mentions, oftener than ever, his inward conflicts, alternations of joy and sadness, of mental freedom and oppression in the pulpit. He at last perceives the fact that his melancholy is "constitutional," and will end only with his life. This brave struggle with an unconquerable physical evil enhances inexpressibly the greatness of his character and of his unparalleled life. He had not, however, the sagacity or scientific knowledge to perceive that his excessive occupation caused much of his sufferings. It may be soberly affirmed that through all his ministerial career he was doing the work of ten if not twenty ordinary men. No human strength is adequate to such labors as his—journeys on horseback over the worst roads, thirty, forty, fifty miles a day, with almost daily preaching, class leading, visits from house to house, frequent and laborious sessions of conferences, a correspondence of a thousand letters yearly; for most of the year the poorest fare of log-cabins, with no other luxury than tea, which he always carried with him and often prepared himself beneath a tree; and almost continual sickness, chills, fevers, and rheumatism. Aristotle taught that the vices are the excesses of the virtues. Asbury erred in this respect. His life, effective as it was, might have been more effective if more healthful, physically and mentally. Johnson remarked to Boswell, that to interpret the Scripture command, "be instant in prayer," literally, were to abuse it; that no one could thus obey it without becoming a maniac. Asbury, besides his other extreme habits, was almost a literalist in this respect. He usually prayed with families at the close of each meal, at taverns, or wherever else he stopped. He prayed in all his pastoral visits. For years he prayed for each of his preachers by name daily; at every conference he prayed privately over each name on the list of appointments; on his rides he prayed ten minutes each hour, and he records that there were few minutes in the day in which his thoughts were not absorbed in prayer. He fasted every Friday, besides going without food from early morning till late evening several days in almost every week. We cannot wonder then that his life became abnormal, and we cannot but wonder that it was so mighty in spite of that fact. Nor can we be surprised that a tinge of severity, if not moroseness, overspread at times his really generous nature, and somewhat repelled his more diffident associates.

He ranged over the northern regions of New York with much of the zest of his western frontier adventures, preaching in log-cabins to multitudes gathered from great distances. "I find," he writes, "some similarity between the northern and western frontiers." He penetrated to Ashgrove, the seat of Embury's society, and refreshed the little band in a "solemn meeting." We trace him southward rapidly to "Coeyman's Patent," "weary, sick, and faint, after riding thirty-six miles. Dr. Roberts, however, was with him from New England, and kept up the incessant labors of the day. They reached the neighborhood of Rhinebeck, and were comforted with the society of Garrettson. "God," he says, "once put into Brother Garrettson's hands great riches of a spiritual nature, and he labored much; if he now does good according to his temporal ability he will be blessed by the Lord and men."

Garrettson, faithful in his prosperity, was "blessed by the Lord and men." His beautiful home at Rhinebeck often sheltered, in later years, Asbury and his fellow-laborers. The bishop delighted to call it "Travelers' Rest," and could write, "I do believe God dwells in this house." Through Garrettson he became intimate with, and exerted a salutary influence over, many distinguished families of the region—the Livingstons, Montgomerys, Sands, Rutsens, Van Courtlandts, and others, among whom were raised up memorable examples of the elder Methodism. Catharine Garrettson, a daughter of the Livingston family, was one of those elect "women of Methodism" who ministered to the bishop, like Mary and Martha to his divine Master, from Rhinebeck's "Travelers' Rest" to Perry Hall in Maryland, Rembert Hall in South

Carolina, and Russell's mansion among the Holston heights. He preached at Rhinebeck, but hastened on with Roberts. "We stopped," he says, "at Governor Van Courtlandt's, who reminds me of General Russell. We had all we needed, and abundantly more than we desired. Rest, rest, how sweet! yet how often in labor I rest, and in rest labor! Sunday, 20, I had a comfortable time at Croton Chapel, on Rom. i, 16. I returned to General Van Courtlandt's, and dined with my dear aged friends. Shall we ever meet again?"

The name of the good governor occurs often in the bishop's journals. He was a hearty Methodist, very rich, inheriting much of the old Courtlandt manor, and lived in a spacious mansion near the mouth of the Croton river. It was the home of many of the primitive itinerants, and had entertained Washington, La Fayette, Franklin, and Whitefield; the latter had preached from its portico to vast throngs. The governor's influence was an important aid to Methodism. He was the first lieutenant-governor of the State, was eighteen times elected to the office, and was president of the convention which formed the state constitution. He gave land for a Methodist church and cemetery, and died, as his epitaph says, "a bright witness of that perfect love which casteth out the fear of death."

After another tour over the South and West Asbury entered Pennsylvania, west of the mountains, in the first week in June, 1796, and held a Conference at Uniontown, where the pioneer evangelists of the Monongahela, the Alleghany, and Yohogany greeted him, and by the last week in July we find him again preaching and "meeting classes in the city" of Philadelphia. He prepared a subscription paper for the relief of suffering preachers and their families, and then "hasted with it from house to house." On the 15th of August he rode into New York to repeat the thorough work he usually performed there—in "meeting classes, and visiting from house to house a good deal of the time in the day, and frequently preaching at night." He spent more than two weeks there at this hottest part of the year, "generally walking three or four miles a day, praying ten or twelve times in the congregation, families, and classes," and closing the day with a sermon or a social religious meeting. On one Sunday we find him preaching three times and leading six classes. He ended the visit with a meeting of all the city class leaders "in close conference," another meeting of the trustees on the same day, and then, "after going hither and thither," preached in the evening. We cannot be surprised that, with such a leader, the ministry and people of early Methodism were kept continually astir. Asbury's own character and example, maintained with unwavering fidelity from the beginning to the end of his episcopal career, afford an obvious solution to the problem of the energy and success of the denomination. He passed again into New England, returned to Baltimore, holding Conferences at New York and Philadelphia, and prepared, at Perry Hall, for the next General Conference.

Methodism, in its denser communities of the Middle and Northern States, though prosperous during this period, presents few of those salient events which mark its history in its remoter fields. It was here established, and comparatively tranquil. At the beginning of the period George Pickering appears on the Dover Circuit, Delaware; and though he had, as already intimated, a brief previous training in the itinerancy of the South, yet he legitimately belongs at this time to the Church of the Middle States, being not only a laborer in its fields, but having entered it and begun to preach in Philadelphia. He was born in Talbot County, Maryland, in 1769, converted in St. George's Church, Philadelphia, when eighteen years old, and almost immediately began his public labors. In 1790 he was received on probation by the Conference. He lived to be the oldest active preacher in the itinerancy, and in his semi-centenary sermon remarked: "When I joined there were but about five conferences, two hundred and twenty-seven traveling preachers, forty-six thousand white, and eleven or twelve thousand colored members. Five or six only of those ministers are now living, and I only continue in the itinerancy. I am now an old man, and shall not labor much longer with you; but go on, my brethren; preach Jesus, preach with the Holy Ghost.

Preach to the people the blessed doctrine of holiness, it is the only thing that will bind the Methodist Church together. Pray for me, my brethren, and the blessing of an old man be upon you." He said this in 1840, in the far East, where he then stood a pillar of New England Methodism, and a patriarch of the denomination, venerated through all its borders.

In person he was tall, slight, and perfectly erect. His countenance was expressive of energy, shrewdness, self-command, and benignity; and in advanced life his silvered locks, combed precisely behind his ears, gave him a strikingly venerable appearance. The exactitude of his mind extended to all his physical habits. In pastoral labors, exercise, diet, sleep, and dress, he followed a fixed course, which scarcely admitted of deviation. In the last respect he was peculiarly neat, holding, with an old divine, that "cleanliness comes next to holiness." He continued to the last to wear the plain Quaker-like dress of the first Methodist ministry, and none could be more congruous with the bearing of his person and his venerable aspect. His voice was clear and powerful, and his step firm to the end. His personal habits had the mechanical regularity of clockwork. During his itinerant life he devoted to his family, residing permanently at one place, a definite portion of his time; but even these domestic visits were subjected to the most stringent regularity. In half a century of married life he spent, upon an average, but about one fifth of his time at home, an aggregate of ten years out of fifty. This rigor may indeed have been too severe. It reminds us of the noble but defective virtue of the old Roman character. If business called him to the town of his family residence at other times than those appropriated to his domestic visits, he returned to his post of labor without crossing the threshold of his home. In that terrible calamity which spread gloom over the land—the burning of the steamer Lexington by night on Long Island Sound—he lost a beloved daughter. The intensity of the affliction was not capable of enhancement, yet he stood firmly on his minis-ministerial watchtower, though with a bleeding heart, while his family, but a few miles distant, were frantic with anguish. Not till the due time did he return to them. When it arrived he entered the house with a sorrow-smitten spirit, pressed in silence the hand of his wife, and, without uttering a word, retired to an adjacent room, where he spent some hours in solitude and unutterable grief. Such a man reminds us of Brutus, and, in the heroic times, would have been commemorated as superhuman. He was seldom, if ever, known to occupy three minutes at a time in the discussions (usually so diffuse) of the Annual Conferences, and the directness of his sentences and the pertinence of his counsels always indicated the practical sage.

Ezekiel Cooper was, down to our own day, one of the representative men of Methodism, and was particularly prominent during most of the present period by his superior abilities in the pulpits of New York and Philadelphia. Like Wells and Pickering, he became one of the founders of the Church in New England, lived long enough to attain the distinction of being the oldest member of any Methodist conference in the western hemisphere, and only one survived in the old world who had preceded him. His personal appearance embodied the finest ideal of age, intelligence, and tranquil piety. His frame was tall and slight, his locks white with years, his forehead high and prominent, and his features expressive of reflection and serenity. A wen had been enlarging on his neck from his childhood, but without detracting from the peculiarly elevated and characteristic expression of his face. He was considered by his ministerial associates "a living encyclopædia" in respect not only to theology, but most other departments of knowledge, and his large and accurate information was only surpassed by the range and soundness of his judgment. He sustained a pre-eminent position in the Church during most of its history.

John M'Claskey during these times was leader, as presiding elder, of a host of powerful men on the Philadelphia and New Jersey Districts, the latter including all the state and a part of that of New York. He also occupied the stations of Baltimore and Philadelphia at intervals of this period. He was one of the Methodistic apostles of the Middle States till 1814, when his health failed, and he fell, with a triumphant death, at the head of the Chesapeake District. He held a high rank among the many gifted preachers which Ireland has given to American Methodism, and was a natural orator, with a fervid imagination, a warm heart, and a singular readiness of speech. His enthusiasm in the pulpit frequently rose into sublime and irresistible power. His voice had uncommon sweetness, and he could command it as a flute or a trumpet.

Lawrence M'Combs began his travels at the beginning of this period, a youth of twenty-three years, full of strength and ardor. His labors, for more than forty years, were in New England (for five years) and the Middle States as far as Baltimore. He became one of "the giants of those days." "No hostility could intimidate him in the course of duty, nor could any provocation betray him into petulance or resentment. In stature he was full six feet in height, with a finely developed form, though not corpulent; the breadth of his chest indicated the prodigious strength which enabled him to perform his almost gigantic labors. The general expression of his countenance betokened intelligence, gentleness, and energy; while his full, frank face was illumined by his ever-kindling eye. His voice was full, clear, and of great flexibility, sweeping from the lowest to the highest tone, and modulated in the most delicate manner, in beautiful harmony with his subject. In preaching in the field, which was his favorite arena, he was quite an approach to Whitefield."

Thomas Morrell is one of the most familiar names in our early records, as an able preacher, an itinerant of long and very general service, and a traveling companion of Asbury. At the very outbreak of the Revolution young Morrell harangued his fellow-youth of the town on the news from Lexington and Concord, formed a company of volunteers, and led them to the army. He was honored by Congress with commissions as captain and major. He was severely wounded in the battle of Long Island, and shared in other hard service of the war. He always retained the friendship of Washington, and personally conducted the official interview of the Methodist bishops with the great first president in 1789, in which the denomination was the first of American Churches to recognize publicly the new government. He was received by the Conference in 1787, and appointed to Staten Island Circuit, which included his native town. He subsequently labored in the cities of New York, Philadelphia, Baltimore, and Charleston. It was near the end of 1791 that he left his station at New York to accompany Asbury to the South. His experience as a soldier gave zest to the adventures which he had to share with the bishop on this tour. Coke, Asbury, and Wesley became his correspondents, and he stood forth now among the foremost men of American Methodism, occupying the most important stations of the Church till 1804, when, his health again failing, he was compelled to retire to Elizabethtown, where, however, he continued to labor as a supernumerary, "preaching as often as when he traveled," for sixteen years, and building up the denomination in all that region.

Thomas Ware was active in the itinerancy during our present period. After spending a part of 1792 on Staten Island Circuit, then reaching far into New Jersey, he was appointed presiding elder on the Susquehanna District, a vast and rugged field, comprising six large circuits. In 1793 he took charge of Garrettson's great field, or, at least, the northern part of it, then called the Albany District. It was, he writes, immensely large, and the country principally new. Accommodations for the preachers were, for the most part, poor, and the means of their support extremely limited. While passing through one of the circuits, soon after he came on the district, he called at the preacher's house, who happened at that time to be at home. It was near noon, and he, of course, must dine there. The poor itinerant had a wife and seven children; and their bill of fare was one blackberry pie, with rye crust, without either butter or lard to shorten it. After they had dined, and Ware was about to depart, he put a few dollars into the hands of his suffering brother, who, on receiving them, sat down and wept so heartily that Ware could not avoid weeping with him. "The Lord was with us," he adds, "in a very glorious manner, at some of our quarterly meetings, during the first quarter; and there appeared to be a general expectation that he would do still greater things for us throughout the vast field we had to cultivate. Here, as in Tennessee, there were multitudes of people wholly destitute of the Gospel, until it was brought to them by the Methodists." There were many small settlements without any religious provisions whatever till the itinerants reached them. They flew from one to another, preaching continually, and in our day we see the results of their labors and sufferings in prosperous Churches, studding all the "parts of four states" which, says Ware, were "embraced in my district." He had a corps of indomitable men under his command, such as Hezekiah C. Wooster, Elijah Woolsey, Aaron Hunt, James Coleman, Shadrach Bostwick, John Finnegan, and many others—men who could not fail to awaken a sensation of public interest, favorable or hostile, wherever they appeared. Through incredible labors and sufferings they were now laying the broad foundations of the Church along most of the extent of the Hudson.

We have already noticed the extraordinary rise of Methodism in the Wyoming, Cumberland, and Tioga regions, and the outspread of the Hudson River District, by Garrettson's and Ware's itinerants, to those then remote fields—the labors of Anning Owen, Nathaniel B. Mills, and William Colbert. Ware's trials among the Tioga wilds were fully shared by his associates. Colbert set out from the General Conference of 1792 for this wilderness, confronting wintry hardships most of the way, and arriving at Nanticoke, in Wyoming Valley, early in December. His story of privation and suffering seems almost incredible. We read of his breakfasting on a frozen turnip; sleeping at night in a wretched cabin, with his head "in the chimney-corner;" fording streams; living on the poorest fare; preaching in cabins, sometimes with "part of the congregation drunk," at others "with children about him bawling louder than he could speak;" and receiving, for the four months of his toil, "three dollars and fourteen cents." Ware reaches him ready to share his trials. "At one place," writes Colbert, "we could get no straw to sleep on; however, Brother Ware fixed himself on a chest, with a bunch of tow for his pillow, and I suppose thought himself well off. For my part, I had to get hay out of a boat for my bed, part of which a passenger begged." "Though the life of a Methodist preacher is very laborious and fatiguing," he adds, "it is what I glory in!" Such are mere examples of the primitive itinerancy of Methodism in the wilderness; but through such struggles has come the prosperity of later years. The Church is now ineradicably planted throughout most of these valleys. Chapels, schools, comfortable houses, all the blessings of advanced Christian civilization, enrich their romantic scenery; and from them have gone forth some of the ablest preachers of the denomination. Its most celebrated native pulpit orator, long a laborer in its institutions of learning, and a bishop in its Southern section, (Bishop Bascom,) received his first effective religious impressions at one of the humblest appointments of Colbert's Tioga Circuit.

Colbert passed to the Wyoming Circuit, and had similar, if not as severe, trials there. From Wyoming he went to Northumberland Circuit. Asbury appreciated such men. From not only a sympathy with their sufferings, but a real relish for their heroic kind of life, he seemed ever anxious to get among them, and in 1793 he plunged into these Pennsylvania valleys on his northward tour, accompanied by some of the nearest preachers on his route. Colbert exulted in the visit, "very much rejoiced to see four preachers in this part of the world." Only about five years had passed since Anning Owen, "the blacksmith" and itinerant preacher, had formed the first Methodist Society of that region at Ross Hill, Wyoming. Methodism had fought its way steadily from valley to valley. One hundred and seventy-seven members had been reported, and two circuits organized and supplied with itinerants, who kept the trumpet of the Gospel sounding through all the mountains, though, as Asbury wrote to Morrell from Wyoming, at this visit, "our poor preachers keep Lent a great part of the year here." They saved much of the rude population of that early day, and prepared the way for the reception of new settlers, some of whom came from the older fields of Methodism, and were fitted to fortify the incipient Church. Colbert was "a born pioneer;" he could not long remain in any one place. Thornton Fleming, a similar evangelist, came along through these yet obscure wildernesses as "elder," and bound on an evangelical exploration of the interior and western parts of New York, "the lake country." Colbert hailed him with gladness, and they went onward rejoicing and preaching together. He thus becomes transferred temporarily to a new scene, and we can trace him for some time founding Societies in that beautiful and flourishing region, now the garden of both the State and the Church, but then dotted with a few settlements "scattered through the wilderness, the hardy settlers sharing the country with the aboriginal inhabitants." Colbert returned; but in the year 1794 we find Fleming commanding a district with two long circuits, called Seneca and Tioga.

Another notable itinerant appears in this field in 1794 and 1795, Valentine Cook, whom we shall soon hail again in the far West. While Asbury was passing through these valleys he wrote to Morrell that he "had found a vast body of Dutch there," and wished him to dispatch Cook to them, because he could preach in their language. Cook appeared upon the scene, in Wyoming, in the stormy month of December, 1793, while Colbert retreated to his former field on the Western Shore of Maryland, but to return again in due time. Cook now went over the country rousing all its settlements. He was one of the wonders of the primitive Methodist ministry. He was born among the western mountains of Virginia, in the "Greenbrier country," now Monroe County, about 1765; became a famous hunter, but, having a mind of unusual vigor, devoted himself to study, as far as his limited means would admit, spent some time at Cokesbury College, and acquired the Greek and Latin languages, and such a knowledge of the German as to speak and preach in it with great fluency. The historian of Methodism in these wildernesses of Pennsylvania and New York says: "He had the reputation of a man of learning, and no one doubted that he was a man of decided talents. His sermons took the citadel of the heart by storm. The people in multitudes flocked to hear him, and the power of God attended his preaching in a wonderful manner." Methodism extended rapidly, under the labors of such men, among the new settlements east of the Cayuga, and between the Cayuga and Seneca Lakes. A circuit was this year formed, called after the latter. In the present day, with the hardly surpassed improvements and intercommunications of this part of New York, we can scarcely credit the Methodistic traditions of those early times: the poor fare of the preachers, the hard struggles of the infant societies, the long journeys through forests and over streams and mountains (sometimes on foot for twenty-five or thirty miles) to hear Colbert, Cook, Fleming, Brodhead, Turck, Smith, and other itinerants at quarterly meetings, and the vast sensation which spread out from these occasions over the new country, stirring up the scattered population to favor or hostility. A letter from Cook to James Smith, one of his preachers, remains, in which he says: "I have now walked near sixty or seventy miles, and am within ten miles of the head of the lakes, at Mr. Weiburn's, who I somewhat expect will lend me a beast, as I am obliged to leave my horse with but small hopes of his recovery. Yesterday I walked upward of thirty miles in mud and water, being wet all day without; yet heaven was within. Glory to God! I had three tempters to encounter, the devil, the mosquitoes, and my horse; and the rain and my wet clothes were my element, and God my comforter, and victory my white horse. Hitherto, O Lord, hast thou been my helper, and I trust thou wilt save to the end. Brother Fleming is to take my appointments through Tioga. I mean to overtake him if possible, and get him to attend the quarterly meetings downward in my stead, and so return to the Lakes Circuit in a few weeks, all which I shall have to do afoot if I can't get a horse. My trials are furious, but I am not discouraged."

The Minutes of 1796 reported three circuits in this westernmost region of the Northern Methodist field: Wyoming with two hundred and twenty-one members, Tioga with one hundred and thirty-eight, Seneca with two hundred and fifteen. It was yet "the day of small things;" the Church was feeble, but the country was new. Methodism was securing and breaking up the fallow ground, and to-day we witness the growth of both the Church and the country, "shaking like Lebanon."

The denomination extended into many new parts of these Middle States during the present period. The migration of Methodist families, especially of local preachers, founded it in many communities which it had not before reached. The itinerants were incessantly ramifying their circuits to new appointments. In the principal cities it was full of vigor. Philadelphia had reported, in 1792, but three hundred and twenty-eight members; in 1796 it reported five hundred and forty-four. New York had advanced from six hundred and forty-one to seven hundred and eighty-six. Its second or Forsyth-street Church was thronged, and it was already projecting a third, on Duane-street, which was begun in 1797. Little impression had been made on Albany, but it was surrounded by Methodist labors, and was the head of a circuit which reported three hundred and thirty-seven members. Garrettson had dedicated, in 1791, a small church, about thirty-two by forty-four feet, in the city, on the corner of Orange and Pearl streets, but it did not become a station till 1798. Meanwhile ministerial explorations were going on in all the more northern regions. One of the explorers, Richard Jacobs, sacrificed his life in his mission, in 1796. He belonged to a wealthy Congregational family, of Berkshire County, Massachusetts, which had cast him out and disinherited him at his conversion to Methodism. "With his young wife he was thrown penniless upon the world." He joined Garrettson's famous young band of northern pioneers, and, in 1796, left his family at Clifton Park, to make an expedition as far as Essex and Clinton Counties, proclaiming the Gospel among the scattered settlers of that remote region. Many were awakened and converted at Elizabethtown, and, promising them a pastor, he pushed along the western shore of Lake Champlain, preaching as he went, till, joined by a lay companion, he proposed to make his way back to his family, through the Schroon woods to the head of Lake George. For about seven days the two travelers were engulfed in the forests, suffering fearful privations, and struggling against almost insurmountable obstructions. "Their provisions failed; they were exhausted with fatigue and hunger; and, at last, in trying to ford the Schroon River, Jacobs sunk beneath the water and was drowned. All his family," adds the narrator of the sad event, "were converted, three of his sons became ministers, and two of his daughters married Methodist preachers."

There were about forty Methodists in the village of Brooklyn, the germ of a rich harvest; and there were now about 350 on Long Island. Methodism was extending from town to town on this beautiful island. From the labors of good Captain Webb to the present time it has found a fertile soil there, yielding in our day a harvest of 15,000 members, with 60 pastors.

At the close of the present period there were in the Middle States more than 11,600 Methodists. Delaware reported 2,228; Pennsylvania, 3,011; New Jersey, 2,351; New York, 4,044.

Meanwhile the struggling cause was advancing in still more northern fields. We have seen its providential introduction into Canada. John Lawrence, a devoted Methodist, who accompanied Embury from Ireland, and was one of the five persons in his first congregation in New York, married his widow, and with the Hecks, and others of the society at Ashgrove, left the United States, at the breaking out of the Revolutionary war, for Lower Canada, where they remained (mostly in Montreal) about eleven years. In 1785 they again journeyed into the wilderness, and settled on "Lot number four, third Concession," of what is now the town of Augusta, in Upper Canada. Here their peculiar work, their providential mission, as I have ventured to call it, was resumed. They were still pioneers and founders of Methodism; and in the house of John and Catharine Lawrence (the widow of Embury) was organized the first "class" of Augusta, and Samuel Embury, the son of Philip, was its first leader. Paul and Barbara Heck were among its first members, and their three sons were also recorded on its roll. They were thus to anticipate and, in part, prepare the way for the Methodist itinerancy in Canada, as they had at New York city and in Northern New York; for

William Losee, the first regular Methodist preacher in the province, did not enter it, as has been shown, till 1790. The germ of Canadian Methodism was planted by these memorable families five or six years before Losee's arrival.

We have traced the subsequent progress of the denomination, in Canada, through the labors of Tuppey, Neal, M'Carty, Lyons, and Losee, down to 1792. Losee, not being an elder, was accompanied to the province in the latter year by Darius Dunham, who was competent to administer the sacraments. Dunham worked mightily in this hard field, the difficulties of which he continued to brave, most of the time as presiding elder, down to 1800, when he located, through domestic necessities, and settled on the Bay of Quinte as a physician, but continued to preach till the end of his life. He "was a character: a man of small stature, but full of vigor, compact, formidable, with coarse, bushy eyebrows," and a tremendous voice, which often sent trembling through his rude congregations.

Methodism was now completely organized in the province, with three circuits, classes, societies, the sacraments, and all other essential provisions of a Church. It was under the jurisdiction of the General Conference, and the episcopal administration of Asbury. The denomination thus took actual precedence of the English Church there, as it had of the organization of the Protestant Episcopal Church in the United States. It was not till 1793 that the British government, reserving one seventh of the lands of Canada for an ecclesiastical endowment, sent out Dr. Mountain as bishop of Quebec, with spiritual jurisdiction over the province, and he found but three or four clergymen of his Church dispersed through the immense territory. No appointments appear in the Minutes for 1793; doubtless a clerical omission, as the returns of members (349) are given. In 1794 Dunham was appointed the first presiding elder of Canada, and two young itinerant recruits, James Coleman* and Elijah Woolsey, hastened to his solitary standard. At the close of the year the evangelists reported four hundred and eighty-three members, omitting those of Woolsey's circuit, which are not recorded. The little corps of itinerants had raised up a single recruit, Sylvanus Keeler, who appears with them in the Minutes this year (1795) as the colleague of Woolsey, on the Bay of Quinte Circuit. "He proved," says the Canadian chronicler of the Church, "a good and faithful minister of Christ." We trace him through about twelve years of hard labor on various circuits in the province, at the close of which he retires into the "local ranks," the fate of most of his ministerial brethren in those days of the poverty of the Church, when the necessities of their growing families compelled them to resort to other means of support, but seldom or never to abandon their Sabbath labors. Sylvanus Keeler retreated to a farm in Elizabethtown, near Brockville, where, and in the surrounding country, he continued to preach "all his days." He became a patriarch among the Societies, his hair "wool-white, long, flowing down upon his shoulders;" his "voice deep, yet soft as the roll of thunder in the distance." To him belongs, so far as I can ascertain, the enviable distinction of having been the first native Methodist itinerant of Canada, and he gave his whole ministerial life to its people.

In 1796 Dunham and Coleman returned to the province, accompanied by two new laborers, men of note, Samuel Coate and Hezekiah C. Wooster. Wooster was a man of extraordinary power. The rigors of the climate, and the excess of his labors, injured his health, and in 1798 he was seized with pulmonary consumption. Yet he did not immediately give up his ministrations, and his marvelous power over his hearers continued even when he could no longer speak loud enough to be heard except by those who stood immediately around him. It is authentically recorded, that when so far reduced as to be unable to speak above a whisper, his broken utterance, conveyed by another to the assembly, would thrill them like a trumpet, and fall with such power on the attention of the hearers that stout-hearted men were smitten down to the floor; and his very aspect is said to have so shone with "the divine glory that it struck conviction into the hearts of many who beheld it." With such men, of course, the whole region of their travels was soon in agitation. Bangs says that a great revival ensued which extended far into the States. The Societies were now rapidly multiplied, the circuits extended in every direction, and at the next Conference nearly eight hundred (795) members were reported—a gain of 321 for the year, averaging more than eighty for the labors of each preacher.

Methodism was thus spreading effectively through all these middle and northern sections of its vast field. It already arrayed within them an army of more than a hundred and twenty-four thousand (124,029) members. Its ministry had become a mighty force, in numbers and character. Humble edifices were rising rapidly, temporary sanctuaries, destined to give way in our day to commodious and beautiful temples. Its people were generally poor and illiterate, but there were not a few families of wealth and high social position interspersed among them. That its foundations, now laid, were substantial and broad, its subsequent history has attested.

CHAPTER XXI.

METHODISM IN THE EASTERN STATES: 1792-1796.

I HAVE recorded the progress of Methodism in the Eastern States from its origin in 1789 down to the first New England Conference in 1792. Lee went from this session to the General Conference at Baltimore, and afterward to his paternal home in Virginia, where he spent about five months preaching continually, and making excursions, to counteract the schism of O'Kelly. On the 20th of February, 1793, he re-entered Boston with horse and saddle-bags, in the fashion of the primitive Methodist itinerancy. He arrived after dark, much fatigued, "and with wet feet," from the wintry slush of the roads. His recollections of Boston could not be the most cheering, but he now found there a warm welcome, and "was comforted," he says, "with the Boston class, which met soon after I got at Mr. Burrill's." The next day he hastened with a glad heart to his "old friends" at Lynn, feeling "thankful to God for bringing him back again," and still more thankful to find "that religion had revived among the people" in his absence. He continued about three weeks in Lynn and its vicinity, but as it was supplied by the services of Rainor he departed on the 18th of March on another excursion to Rhode Island and to Connecticut. During this tour he visited Easton, Pawtuxet, Warwick, Greenwich, Weckford, Charlestown, New London; thence he journeyed to General Lippett's, in Cranston; to Providence, Needham, and on to Boston; after which he returned to Lynn. He continued to travel and preach almost daily until the Conference of the first of August ensuing, confining himself, however, (if indeed it can be called confinement,) mostly to Boston, Lynn, Marblehead, and Salem. Lynn was his favorite resort, "he being," says his biographer, "more attached to it than to any other place within the bounds of his district."

On the 21st of July Asbury again entered New England on his way to the second Lynn Conference. He was weary, and had been sick nearly four months, but pressed onward, attending to his responsible business, and traveling during these months of illness about three thousand miles. On the first day of August, 1793, the Conference convened. The preachers of the circuits in Western New England were not present, as a separate session had been appointed for their convenience at Tolland, Conn., to be held in about a week after the one at Lynn. Eight preachers were in attendance. Asbury remarks, "We have only about three hundred members in the district; yet we have a call for seven or eight preachers; although our members are few, our hearers are many." The business of the session closed on Saturday. The preachers addressed themselves forthwith with renewed zeal to their toils and sufferings, and none more so than Asbury, who now mounted his horse, and set his face toward the west. He passed a short time at Waltham, in the homestead of Benjamin Bemis, who was one of the first Methodists in that town, and whose mansion, sequestered among hills, and surrounded with fragrant orchards, became not only a sanctuary for the worship of his rustic neighbors, but the favorite home of the itinerants of Methodism. He was a man of wealth, and his hospitalities seemed only to enhance his prosperity. Nearly all the great men of the early Church were entertained beneath his roof, and proclaimed the "glorious Gospel" in the shade of his trees to the assembled yeomanry of the town. The conversion of many souls has consecrated the spot, and its old historical reminiscences still endear it to the Methodists of the Eastern States. It became the family residence of Pickering, who married the daughter of Bemis, and passed to heaven amid its venerable associations.

On Monday, August 11, the Conference met in Tolland, Conn. This town was about the center of the region included in what was then the Tolland Circuit. It was previously connected with the Hartford Circuit, and the great reformation, which had extended like fire in stubble through the latter, under the labors of Hope Hull, George Roberts, Lemuel Smith, and their colleagues, the preceding two years, had left distinct traces in Tolland. A small Society had been formed, and a chapel erected on the estate of an excellent townsman, Mr. Howard, who befriended the infant Church, and most of whose family were made partakers of the grace of life through its instrumentality. It was in this chapel, then but partially finished, that the Conference assembled. Most of the preachers, ten or twelve in number, were entertained at Howard's hospitable house, where, as with Bemis, Lippett, White, Barratt, Bassett, Gough, Rembert, and Russell, the itinerants of these times found sumptuous fare among the few "noble" who believed. The Lynn and Tolland Conferences formed an extensive scheme of labors; the itinerant field in New England comprehended two districts, and part of a third, fourteen circuits and stations, and twenty-five laborers. Enoch Mudge was received into the ministry at Lynn, and bore the distinguished honor of being the first native Methodist preacher of New England. He was born in this town on the 21st of June, 1776. He was one of the chief and most admirable characters of New England Methodist history. In stature he was below the ordinary height, stoutly framed, with a full round face healthfully colored, and expressive of the perfect benignity and amiability of his spirit. In advanced life his undiminished but silvered hair crowned him with a highly venerable aspect. In manners he would have been a fitting companion for St. John. He was distinguished by excellent pulpit qualifications, fertility of thought, warmth of feeling without extravagance, peculiar richness of illustration, and a manner always self-possessed and marked by the constitutional amenity of his temper. None were ever wearied under his discourses. He published a volume of excellent sermons for mariners, and many poetical pieces of more than ordinary merit.

Another well-known name occurs in the list of eastern appointments this year, that of Daniel Ostrander. His prominence, for many years, in the New York Conference—where he continued until our day, a representative of the earlier times—has identified him in the public mind with that body, and but few of the present generation of eastern Methodists know anything of his intimate connection with their early history. Daniel Ostrander was, nevertheless, one of the founders of Methodism in New England. He commenced his ministry within its limits, and spent the first thirteen years of it (save one) in sharing the trials and struggles of Lee, Roberts, Pickering, Mudge, Taylor, and their associates; laboring mightily in western Massachusetts, Connecticut, Rhode Island, and as far east as Boston. "From the year 1793 to the year 1843," say his brethren of the New York Conference, "a full term of fifty years, so remarkably did the Lord preserve him, that only three Sabbaths in all that time was he disabled from pulpit service by sickness. For fourteen years he was on circuits, eight years in stations, (New York, Brooklyn, and Albany,) and twenty-eight years in the weighty and responsible office of presiding elder. His high standing in the esteem of his brethren in Conference appears from the fact, that since the establishment of the delegated General Conference in 1808, they always elected him a member of that highest judicatory in our Church, down to the year 1840, inclusive; and never has his seat in an Annual Conference been vacant, during the forty-eight years that the writer of this article has known him, till called to his reward. The same is thought to have been the case from the time of his admission as a member of this body."

Zadok Priest, another of these itinerants, was a youthful martyr to the extreme labors of these times of struggle and victory. In 1795 he labored on Warren Circuit, where he was attacked with hemorrhage of the lungs, which terminated in consumption. He retired from his work to die. He went to his home, but his father, who was opposed to the Methodists, turned him away from the house. There resided at that time, and for many subsequent years, at Norton, Mass., a venerable Methodist, known as "Father Newcomb," whose home was ever open as an asylum for the itinerants. Thither Priest went in his affliction—"to die with them," as he said when the door was opened to receive him. He was confined there three weeks, and then passed down into the valley and shadow of death, expressing "a strong confidence in the favor of God, and no doubt of his salvation." He died on the 22d of June, 1796, in the twenty-seventh year of his age, and was buried on the estate of Newcomb. He was generally beloved, and a Christian brother now rests by his side, who esteemed him so highly in life as to request that he might sleep with him in death. The event occasioned a great sensation among his fellow-laborers and the infant societies in New England. His obituary may be seen in the Minutes for 1796; and Lee, who was his presiding elder at this time, also handsomely notices him in his History of Methodism.

Many other noted evangelists appeared now for the first time in the ranks of the New England itinerancy, such as Joshua Taylor, Joshua Hall, Aaron Hunt, and Hope Hull. Methodism had not yet reached the province of Maine. It was assigned as an appointment to Lee himself in the year 1793. It then, and for more than a quarter of a century afterward, pertained to Massachusetts, and its settlements were sparse, and mostly on the seaboard or principal rivers. Most of the interior regions were but occasionally favored with the ordinances of religion. Lee longed to sound the trump of the Gospel through its primeval forests and along its great rivers; and though he knew no one there to welcome him on his arrival, nor any one elsewhere to give him "a particular account of the place and the people," yet, as "it was commonly understood that they were in want of preaching," he took his horse and saddle-bags and directed his course toward it, not knowing what should befall him. His biographer has preserved but brief notices of this first excursion thither; it was, however, but a visit of observation. "He continued," says his Memoir, "in these settlements, traveling to and fro and preaching, with good hopes that his labor would be blessed of the Lord, until the latter part of October, at which time he returned to Lynn. In January, 1794, he repeated his visit to the settlements on the Kennebec and Penobscot Rivers, and enlarged his borders by preaching in many new places. His difficulties were many, but God gave him strength to bear all with becoming patience and resolution. He succeeded in forming a circuit in the province, which, by the way, is all that can be said of it, for we are not assured that there was a single Society of Methodists within its whole bounds." There was, in fact, no Society formed within its limits, or within the entire province, until after the ensuing Conference. The first class in Maine was organized at Monmouth about the first of November, 1794. Lee has given us, in his History of the Methodists, a brief sketch of this second tour. "I traveled," he says, "through a greater part of that country from September to the end of the year. I went as far as Castine, at the mouth of the Penobscot River; up the river to the upper settlements, which were then just below the Indian settlement called Old Town; thence I returned by the way of the Twenty-five mile Pond to Kennebec River; thence up the Sandy River, and back to Hallowell, and thence through to Portland." By tracing his route on the map it will be perceived that he surveyed quite thoroughly most of what was then the occupied portion of the province, namely, the region of the coast from Portsmouth to Castine, and the interior, between the Kennebec and Penobscot, as far up, and even further, than what has since become the site of Bangor on the latter, and Waterville on the former. "Although," he continues, "I was a perfect stranger to the people, and had to make my own appointments, I preached almost every day, and to crowded assemblies. After viewing the country, I thought the most proper place to form a circuit was on the Kennebec River. It was accordingly formed, and called Readfield. This was the name of the first circuit formed by the Methodists in that part of the country. It was about two hundred miles from any other which we had in New England. It extended from Hallowell to Sandy River."

The ecclesiastical year closed in the latter part of July. It had been a time of adversity and declension to the general Church; severe trials had also afflicted the small itinerant band in New England. They were hedged in on every side by a decayed Church, whose chief remaining vigor consisted in its pertinacity for its antiquated polemics, and its intolerance toward dissenting sects. They had reached, too, a degree of advancement where, more than at any earlier period of their history, the sectarian jealousy of the established Churches became excited and alarmed; but they surmounted all impediments and made good progress. The circuits were extended on all sides; eighteen were reported at the next Conference, a gain of more than one fourth on the number of the preceding year. Lee having surveyed extensively the wilderness of Maine, was now on his way to the Conference to solicit a laborer for that vast field, carrying with him a schedule of appointments, which, after personal inspection, he had definitively arranged into a circuit that extended along the Kennebec, quite into the interior of the province. New Hampshire and Vermont were also "stretching out their hands," and the itinerant corps resolved to extend its lines into those remoter regions at the approaching Conference. Thus the three remaining sections of New England were about to be permanently occupied by them. While the aggregate membership of the Church had decreased during the year more than 2,000, chiefly by the O'Kelly schism, the local membership of New England had advanced from 1,739 to 2,039, a small addition when compared with the progress of later years, but large for those days of trial and struggle.

The Conference commenced in Lynn, July 25, 1794. Another session had been appointed for the accommodation of the preachers in the western portion of New England, who, therefore, were not present at the one in Lynn. We have scarcely any information respecting the latter. Asbury has recorded but about half a dozen lines concerning it, with no intimation whatever of its business, except that difficulties had arisen which grieved him deeply, and rendered its termination grateful to his wounded feelings. He preached before the Conference and the Society of Lynn twice on the Sabbath, and departed for the Wilbraham session the next morning, passing, with his usual rapidity, a distance of forty miles the same day.

On the first of August he left his comfortable retreat at General Lippett's, and, after traveling and preaching daily, reached Tolland, Conn., by the tenth. He was now in the region of the "Association," which had arrayed itself against Methodism, under the leadership of Williams and Huntington. "Ah!" he exclaims, "here are the iron walls of prejudice; but God can break them down. Out of fifteen United States, thirteen are free; but two are fettered with ecclesiastical chains, taxed to support ministers who are chosen by a small committee, and settled for life. My simple prophecy is, that this must come to an end with the present century." He was too sanguine; the ecclesiastical oppressions of Connecticut were not abolished till 1816, and his own sons in the ministry had no unimportant agency in their removal.

By Sunday, August 17th, he was in Wilbraham, Mass., where he found a Methodist chapel, "forty by thirty-four feet, neatly designed." He was sick and weary throughout this trip, but, being accompanied by Roberts, they were able jointly to hold meetings continually. They made preaching excursions during a fortnight, and on September 2d returned to Wilbraham, lodged with Abel Bliss, a name still familiar to Massachusetts Methodists, and on Thursday, the 4th, opened the "Wilbraham Conference." Great men were there: Asbury, wayworn, but "mighty through God;" Lee, eloquent, tireless, and ambitious, like Coke, for "the wings of an eagle, and the voice of a trumpet, that he might proclaim the Gospel through the East and the West, the North and the South;" Roberts, as robust and noble in spirit as in person; Wilson Lee, "a flame of fire;" Ostrander, firm and unwavering as a pillar of brass; Pickering, clear and pure as a beam of the morning; young Mudge, the beloved firstborn of the New England itinerancy; the two Joshuas of Maine, Taylor and Hall, who, like their ancient namesake, led the triumphs of Israel in the land of the East; and others whose record is on high. The proceedings were what might have been expected from such evangelists: dispatch of business, incessant public devotions, and daily preaching. Sunday was a high festival. The services commenced at eight o'clock A. M. The first hour was spent in prevailing prayer, and in singing the rapturous melodies of the poet of Methodism, the doggerels of later days having not yet come into vogue. Asbury then mounted the pulpit, and addressed the throng, appealing to the ministry like a veteran general to his hosts on the eve of battle, calling on them to "put on the whole armor of God," and "endure hardness as good soldiers of Jesus Christ." Conflicts were before them, but their weapons were "mighty through God," and their brethren were moving on to victory through the land. Many might fall, but it would be amid the slain of the Lord, and with the shout of triumph.

After the stirring discourse, he descended to the altar and consecrated four young men to the ministry of the itinerancy, three as elders, one as deacon. Preachers and people then crowded around the altar, and with solemnity and tears partook of the Lord's Supper. Lee's ardent spirit was moved within him, for to him it was a "solemn time," "quickening" and "refreshing." The assembly was dismissed, but the people withdrew only for a few minutes. They again thronged the house, and were addressed in a series of exhortations by Lee, Thompson, and Ketchum. The exhortation of Lee was long spoken of as an example of overwhelming eloquence. "The crowd," says one who heard it, "moved under it like the forest under a tempest." "It was a time of God's power," says Lee. Stout hearts broke under the word, the fountain of tears was opened, and there was weeping in all parts of the house; the emotion at last became insupportable, and the overwhelmed assembly gave vent to their uncontrollable feelings in loud exclamations. The services finally closed after continuing seven hours and a half. "It was," exclaims Lee, "a blessed day to my soul." Asbury hastened away to attend the New York Conference. At one place on his route calls came to him to send preachers into New Hampshire and Maine, and at another he met Dunham, from Canada, beseeching him to send additional laborers into that opening region. Thus the field was enlarging in all directions, and whitening unto the harvest.

The new ecclesiastical year began with two districts and part of a third, eighteen circuits and stations, and thirty preachers; four circuits and five preachers more than in the preceding year. The names of New Hampshire and Vermont appear, for the first time, in the Minutes.

Of the itinerants who now, for the first time, appear in New England, twelve in number, more than half were recruits from Maryland or Virginia. Among them were conspicuous men, like Christopher Spry, long known in the "Old Baltimore Conference;" George Cannon, who founded Methodism at Provincetown and Nantucket; John Chalmers, who originated the first Methodist chapel of Rhode Island, (on Warren Circuit,) and fell in his work, as late as 1833, in Maryland, "full of faith and the Holy Ghost," say his brethren; David Abbott, son of the New Jersey "Boanerges," and Wilson Lee. Jesse Lee's appointment for the ensuing year was to the office of presiding elder; his district comprehended, nominally, Massachusetts, New Hampshire, and Maine, but virtually, the whole Methodist interests in New England. A year of extraordinary travels and labors was before him; but, sustained by a zeal as steady as it was ardent, he went forth upon it like a giant to run a race. He passed in a rapid flight through Connecticut, Rhode Island, Eastern Massachusetts, and far into the interior of Maine, amid snow-drifts and wintry storms; back again through Massachusetts, Rhode Island, and the islands of Nantucket and Martha's Vineyard, and again through Massachusetts and Maine into the British provinces, and back yet again to the interior of Connecticut. Philip Wager had been sent this year to Maine—the first Methodist preacher stationed in that section of New England. The first Methodist Class formed in that province comprised fifteen members. It was organized "about the first of November, 1794." The first lay Methodist in Maine was Daniel Smith, afterward a local preacher. He died in peace, October 10, 1846. Lee left the new society, praying that it might be as the "little cloud, which at first was like a man's hand, but soon covered the heavens." His prayer has prevailed, and in our day his denomination has become the strongest, numerically, in the State.

On Saturday, 15th of November, he reached Readfield, whither he was attracted by the recollections of his former cordial reception. Good news awaited him in that remote region; he found there the second Methodist society of Maine, recently formed—a people hungering for the word of life, and hanging on his ministrations with sobs and ejaculations—and the shell of the first Methodist chapel of Maine already reared. The class consisted of seventeen members. "Surely," he exclaims, "the Lord is about to do great things for the people. Even so; amen, and amen." Early on Wednesday, 26th, he was again pressing forward, on his way to Sandy River, over a lonely road, and through intense cold. December, with its Borean storms, had come upon the evangelist in what was then the heart of the wilderness province, but he still went forward. On a part of the way there were no traces of a path; his guide had to follow the "chops" on the trees; the snow was nearly a foot deep, and the traveling most difficult. He spent about two months in Maine, during which, undaunted by the driving storms of the north, he had penetrated on horseback to the frontier settlements, preaching the word, and encouraging the incipient societies, which could yet claim but one sanctuary in the province, and that scarcely more substantial than a barn, but have since multiplied themselves throughout the State, and studded its surface with temples. After laboring two or three weeks in Lynn and its vicinity, he sallied forth again, though amid the blasts of midwinter, on an excursion to Rhode Island, and the southeastern parts of Massachusetts. He returned for temporary shelter to his head-quarters in Lynn; but though it was now the most inclement period of the year, and especially unfavorable for travel, he longed to plunge again into the wilderness of Maine, and to bear the cross onward far beyond his former tours. He was soon away, and penetrated through the province to the Bay of Fundy. By the 21st of June he was back at Readfield dedicating the first Methodist chapel of Maine. Such is but a glance at the labors of this wonderful man during the ten months which had elapsed since his departure from the Wilbraham Conference. Similar journeys and labors, performed with our present conveniences for travel, would be considered extraordinary; how much more so were they at that day! How soon would the earth be evangelized were the whole Christian ministry of like spirit!

While Lee was approaching the seat of the next Conference from the north, Asbury was wending his course toward it from the south, where, as we have seen, he had performed unparalleled journeys and labors. The year had been a calamitous one for the Church generally; the Minutes reported an aggregate decrease of six thousand three hundred and seventeen members. "Such a loss," says Lee, "we had never known since we were a people." But while the desolating measures of O'Kelly were blighting the former rich growth of the South, the New England field was extending on every hand, and yielding an abundant increase. Its returns of members amounted to two thousand five hundred and seventy-five, an advance on the preceding year of five hundred and thirty-six, or more than one fourth. There was apparently a gain of but one circuit, or station, eighteen being reported the preceding year, and nineteen the present. One, however, of the former (Vermont) was merely nominal; Joshua Hall, who was appointed to it, being detained in Massachusetts. The gain was at least five; actually larger than in any former year. The remodeling of several western circuits diminished their number, but their real extent and importance were proportionably augmented by the change. Pomfret, in Connecticut; Provincetown and Marblehead, in Massachusetts; Portland and Penobscot, in Maine, were the new names reported among the appointments for the ensuing year. The gains in the membership were chiefly in Maine. A solitary preacher had been appointed, as we have seen, to that vast field, without a Society. Hundreds were awakened and converted under Lee's faithful labors and those of his coadjutor. Several societies were organized; the first Methodist chapel erected; the first returns of members made. Readfield Circuit reported 232; Portland, 136; and Passamaquoddy, (on the eastern boundary,) 50; an aggregate of 318. Methodism had unfurled its banners in Maine, with the hope never to strike them till the heavens are no more.

The Conference commenced its session at New London, Conn., on Wednesday, the 15th of July, 1795. Nineteen preachers were present. A small number of Methodists had been formed into a Society in the city about two years, but they were yet without a chapel in which to accommodate the Conference. It met in the house of Daniel Burrows. Though assembled without ostentation, and without a temple, sublime visions of the future rose before the contemplation of the men who composed the unnoticed body. Asbury looked forth from the private room in which they met, with the hope that their deliberations would be "for the good of thousands." Some of them were yet to see their little company grow into a host nearly a thousand strong, leading an evangelical army of nearly a hundred thousand souls. Asbury, Lee, Roberts, Pickering, Mudge, Taylor, Snethen, Smith, Ostrander, and M'Combs were among the rare men who composed the unpretending synod. The session continued until Saturday. The itinerants reviewed the successes and trials of the past year, planned new and more extended projects of labor for the future, united in frequent prayer that the word might run and be glorified, and preached it daily to each other and the gathered multitude in the court-house. Evan Rogers, who had been educated a Quaker, and combined much of the gravity of his first with the warm energy of his new faith, addressed the preachers particularly, and, it is said, very pertinently, on defects in their pulpit delivery, which were not uncommon at that date. His text, at least, was significant. It was 1 Cor. xiv, 19. Chalmers brought them glad tidings from Rhode Island, and reported the erection of the first Methodist chapel of that State. Ostrander brought good news from the Connecticut River; the cause was advancing slowly, but surely, along its banks, prejudice was yielding, the hostility of the established Churches had been defeated in several instances, and though the cry was that they were "turning the world upside down," yet numerous places in all directions were uttering to them the "Macedonian cry" to come over and help them, and hundreds were waking from their spiritual slumbers to a devouter life. Hill was there from New Hampshire, to report that innumerable doors were opening in that sparsely settled state for the new evangelists; but the laborers were few, and none could yet be spared. Lee, wayworn with his great travels, cheered them with surprising news from Maine. Encouraged by their mutual communications they sung a hymn, and bowed together in a concluding prayer, at noon, on Saturday. They tarried, however, through the Sabbath, the great day of the feast. Early on Monday morning, before the community were fairly astir, Asbury was away on his horse, and by eight o'clock A. M. was sounding the alarm in Norwich, while the preachers were urging their steeds in all directions to the conflicts of another year.

The programme of labor for the year, from July, 1795, to September, 1796, included one district and part of a second, nineteen circuits, and thirty preachers. Add to these about two thousand six hundred members, with some half dozen chapels, and we have a general outline of Methodism in New England at this date. Nearly one third of the preachers on the list of appointments this year were new laborers in New England. They were nine; and, of all this number, two withdrew from the ministry, and the remainder sooner or later located without again resuming effective service, so far as I can ascertain. It was a sad necessity of the times which compelled so many, at the maturest period of their energies, to seek bread for their families in secular pursuits. Lee returned to Boston, that he might assist in the ceremonies with which the founding of the Methodist chapel on Hanover Avenue was solemnized. Five years had he been laying siege to the almost inaccessible community of the metropolis, returning to the attack, ever and anon, from his distant excursions. His perseverance had conquered at last, and he now erected a battery in its midst. On the 28th of August he consecrated the corner-stone of the new temple, amid the rejoicings and thanksgivings of the humble worshipers, who had struggled to the utmost for its erection. It was located on a narrow lane in the poorest suburb of the city, but was for years a moral pharos, throwing an evangelical radiance over the population around it. Many of the greatest men of the Methodist ministry proclaimed the truth from its rude pulpit, and its humble communion has been adorned by some of the best samples of Christian character which have distinguished the denomination. Lee was three weeks in the city; during this time he took his stand, three successive Sabbaths, on the Common, where thousands heard the word of life from his lips, who would have gone nowhere else to hear it.

Leaving the work in Boston in charge of another, he went forth again on his travels, passing with rapid transitions in every direction. The unfortunate loss of his manuscripts has deprived us of the details of these tours. We know, however, that he passed over the whole length of Cape Cod, made two tours in Maine, and seemed almost omnipresent in his older eastern fields. In September, 1796, Asbury again entered New England. On reaching Old Haddam he wrote, "My body is full of infirmities, and my soul of the love of God. I think that God is returning to this place, and that great days will yet come on in New England." He read aright the signs of the times. He passed on to Thompson, Conn., where the Conference assembled on the 19th. The aggregate of the returns of Church members was now 2,519, showing a decrease of 56. On the other hand there had been a gain of 105 in Maine and New Hampshire, and numerous conversions in Vermont, which were not reported. The real loss was, therefore, probably smaller than it appears to be in the census. But if there was a slight numerical declension, there was an actual growth of the cause in the invigoration of its organized plans, and the extension of its scope of operations. Its laborers had formed two new circuits in Maine. They had penetrated into New Hampshire and Vermont, and had projected a long circuit in each. Lee had formerly preached the doctrines of Methodism in all the New England States, but before the present year its standards had been planted permanently only in Connecticut, Rhode Island, Massachusetts, and Maine; now they were reared, to be furled no more, in all the Eastern States. A network of systematic labors extended into them all, from Norwalk in Connecticut to the Penobscot in Maine, and from Provincetown in Massachusetts to Montpelier in Vermont; and hereafter the progress of the new communion is to have accelerated rapidity, in every direction.

At the Thompson, as at the New London Conference the year before, the itinerants had not the convenience of a chapel for their deliberations, but were entertained with hearty hospitality by the young Church, and assembled in an unfinished chamber in the house of Captain Jonathan Nichols.

In this humble apartment did these men of great souls devise plans which comprehended all these Eastern States, contemplated all coming time. About thirty were present, "some of whom," remarks Asbury, "were from the province of Maine, three hundred miles distant, who gave us a pleasing relation of the work of God in those parts." He preached to them in the chamber, enjoining upon them their ministerial duties to the people, from Acts xxvi, 18, 19: "To open their eyes, and to turn them from the power of Satan unto God; that they may receive forgiveness of sins, and inheritance among them which are justified." The sermon was heard with deep emotion by a crowded assembly, among whom sat the parish pastor, rapt in the interest of the occasion. To a late day its effect was often mentioned among the reminiscences of the olden times in the conversations of veteran Methodists. "We talked together, and rejoiced in the Lord," says Asbury. Enoch Mudge and Joshua Hall brought them refreshing reports from Maine. The former had witnessed the rapid spread of the Gospel along the banks of the Kennebec, where an additional circuit had been formed; the latter had been proclaiming it on both sides of the Penobscot, and had seen "the arm of the Lord made bare." They could both tell of hard fare, terrible winters, long journeys amid driving storms, and comfortless lodgings in log-cabins, through which the snow beat upon their beds; but also of divine consolations which had sanctified every suffering, and victories of the truth multiplying through the land. Lemuel Smith relieved the reports of declension from Massachusetts and Connecticut by news of an extensive revival on Granville Circuit, where nearly one hundred souls had been gathered into the Church since their last session. Lawrence M'Coombs reported severe combats and serious losses on New London Circuit, but was undaunted in his characteristic courage and sanguine hopes. Cyrus Stebbins brought the mournful intelligence that one of their number had fallen in the field since they last met, the youthful and devoted Zadok Priest. Asbury ordained seven deacons and five elders. Three itinerants, compelled, probably, by sickness or want, took leave of their companions and retired to the local ranks; but others, mightier men—Timothy Merritt, John Broadhead, Elijah Woolsey, etc.—stepped into their places, and the New England Methodist ministry presented a more imposing aspect of strength than had yet distinguished it. A man subsequently noted throughout the nation, offered himself for admission among them, the eccentric Lorenzo Dow; but the discerning eye of Asbury perceived the peculiarity of his character, and his application was declined. He lingered about the place during the session, weeping sincere tears. "I took no food," he says, "for thirty-six hours afterward." On Wednesday the little band again dispersed. Twenty-one circuits, one district, and a large portion of a second, together with thirty-one itinerant laborers and 2,519 members, constituted the force of New England Methodism for the year 1796–7.

CHAPTER XXII.

METHODISM IN THE WEST—1792–1796.

I HAVE recorded with some detail the early trans-Alleghany movements of Methodism from the labors of the local preacher, Robert Wooster, in the Redstone country, in 1781, down to the General Conference of 1792. We have witnessed the outspread of the Church in the then frontier regions now comprised in the Erie, Pittsburgh, and Western Virginia Conferences; the designation of Lambert to the Holston country, in 1783; the crossing of the Alleghanies, the same year, by Poythress; the first Western Conference, held among the Holston mountains, in 1788; the arrival in Kentucky of its first itinerants, Haw and Ogden, in 1786; Asbury's adventurous expeditions over the mountains; the first Kentucky Conference in 1790; and the perils and labors of the early evangelists, Poythress, Cooper, Breese, Haw, Ogden, Moriarty, Wilson Lee, Fidler, Phoebus, Chieuvrant, Matthews, Lurton, Willis, Ware, Tunnell, Maston, Bruce, M'Gee, Burke, Whitaker, Moore, Williamson, M'Henry, Tucker, Birchett, Massie, Daniel Asbury, and others: names which should never be forgotten in the West; for these men laid the foundations not merely of a sect, but of a moral empire, in that most magnificent domain of the New World.

Asbury passed almost yearly into this great field during the present period, convoyed often by armed friends, and enduring frightful sufferings and perils. We have seen that John Cooper and Samuel Breese were the first regular preachers sent to the Redstone country, whither they went in 1784, following in the tracks of Robert Wooster. John Cooper was the humble but memorable evangelist whose sufferings we have noticed as early as 1775, when he was the colleague of Philip Gatch, on Kent Circuit, Maryland—a man "who," Gatch says, "had suffered much persecution," whose father, detecting him on his knees, at prayer, threw a shovel of hot coals upon him, and expelled him from his house. He took up his cross, joined the itinerant host, and here we find him, at last, the first appointed standard-bearer of the Church beyond the Pennsylvania Alleghanies, the first regularly appointed one in the valley of the Mississippi, if the doubtful designation of Lambert to the Holston country the preceding year did not take effect, as I deem very probable. He labored in Maryland, Pennsylvania, Philadelphia, New Jersey, Virginia, North Carolina, and Western Pennsylvania, and died in 1789. Henry Willis was the first preacher stationed in Charleston, South Carolina, and was probably the first who had an effective appointment in the Holston mountains. Sinking under pulmonary consumption, he nevertheless persisted in his travels through years of suffering, and was one of the most dominant spirits of the times, energizing by his irrepressible ardor the work of the Church throughout two thirds of its territory. He labored mightily for the West, as if conscious of its prospective importance in the State and the Church. Quinn, who knew him in the Redstone country, describes him as about "six feet in stature," "slender," a "good English scholar," "well read," "an eloquent man, mighty in the Scriptures, and a most profound and powerful reasoner." Peter Moriarty, a laborer in the Southern, Northern, and Eastern States, a man of great power, also shared in the pioneer evangelization of the West, entering the Redstone country as early as 1785, with John Fidler and Wilson Lee, the latter of whom has also appeared repeatedly before us in most of the field. They were then the only itinerants on that side of the Alleghanies, except Henry Willis and the two preachers on his solitary Holston Circuit. We have seen John Tunnell leading, for years, a pioneer band of preachers among the Holston mountains, and buried, at last, by Asbury, among the Alleghany heights, a martyr to his work. We have also traced Poythress to the great western arena, where he became one of its most conspicuous champions, and broke down, physically and mentally, under superabundant labors. The itinerants in the Redstone country stood upon the frontier confronting the immense wilderness known as the Northwestern Territory. The scattered settlers had been slowly creeping across the mountains on the Braddock Military Road. Fort Pitt (Fort du Quesne) stood not far off, a memorial of French military adventure. A few huts nestled under its shelter; but Pittsburgh was not to be incorporated as a borough till a quarter of a century after the arrival of Wooster. The itinerants formed a circuit called Ohio, but it extended along the eastern bank of the river. The great wilderness gave no certain signs yet of the magnificent States which were soon to rise on its surface: Ohio, Michigan, Indiana, Illinois, and others, stretching to the Mississippi, and overleaping it to the Rocky Mountains. The evangelists looked across the Ohio with vague though sublime anticipations of the moral empire they were about to found in the boundless wilds. The first permanent settlement in Ohio, Marietta, was not made till 1788, seven years after Wooster began to preach in the Redstone region, and four after Cooper and Breese began their regular labors on the hither side of the Ohio River. More than twenty years were yet to pass, after Wooster's arrival, before Ohio was to become a State, thirty-five years before Indiana, and thirty-seven before Illinois.

The itinerants in the more southern trans-Alleghany field, the "Holston Country," were in even a more desolate region. "Straggling settlements" had been slowly extending, from the locality of Pittsburgh, up the Monongahela and its branches to the Greenbrier and the Neuse Rivers, where we have seen Asbury in some of his most romantic adventures. Thence they had reached to the upper valley of the Holston, "where the military path of Virginia led to the country of the Cherokees." Only seventeen years before the Methodist preachers penetrated to this valley, James Smith, accompanied by three fellow-adventurers, passed through it into Kentucky, then without a single settlement. Pushing down the Cumberland he reached the Ohio and the mouth of the Tennessee, but left no trace of his passage except the name of one of his little band, Stone, which he gave to a stream above the site of Nashville. Only about ten years (1773) before the appearance of the itinerants on the Holston, and but eleven before Methodist local preachers penetrated Kentucky, Daniel Boone, the "illustrious pioneer," after previous surveys, commenced his settlement of the latter county with six families, and began a road from the settlements on the Holston to the Kentucky River, harassed by the savages, who killed four of his men, and wounded as many more.

By our present period the current of emigration had strongly set in toward these western paradises, as they were esteemed, and as, in all natural attractions, they were worthy to be esteemed. But the privations and other sufferings of the first settlers were as yet only aggravated by the new accessions of population. The savages were rendered the more alarmed and relentless by the increasing probability of the inundation of their domain by the white race, and ambuscades and massacres prevailed everywhere. Asbury, as we have seen, had to travel with armed convoys, and keep anxious watch by night, and his preachers pursued their mountainous routes in continual hazard of their lives. Their fare was the hardest; the habitations of the settlers were log-cabins, clinging to the shelter of "stations," or stockaded "block-houses." The preachers lived chiefly on Indian corn and game. They could get little or no money, except what their brethren (themselves poor) of the more eastern Conferences could send them by Asbury. They wore the coarsest clothing, often tattered or patched. Their congregations gathered at the stations with arms, with sentinels stationed around to announce the approach of savages, and were not unfrequently broken up, in the midst of their worship, by the alarm of the warwhoop and the sound of muskets. The population was generally, though not universally, of the rudest character; much of it likely to sink into barbarism had it not been for the Gospel so persistently borne along from settlement to settlement by these unpaid and self-sacrificing men. We have already shown, from a contemporary author, that bankrupts, refugees from justice, deserters of wives and children, and all sorts of reckless adventurers, hastened to these wildernesses. It was soon demonstratively evident that the "itinerancy" was a providential provision for the great moral exigencies of this new, this strange, this vast western world, almost barricaded by mountains from the Christian civilization of the Atlantic States, but not barricaded from the civilizing power of Christianity as embodied in the indomitable ministry of Methodism. These first evangelists were immediately followed by some of the strongest men of the itinerancy. Barnabas M'Henry, a chieftain among them, entered the great field as early as 1789, and lives yet in its traditions as one of its most notable ecclesiastical founders. He has the peculiar honor of being the first Methodist preacher raised up west of the mountains. He became a chieftain of Western Methodism, braving its severest trials, and leading, on immense districts, bands of its ministerial pioneers. His excessive labors broke him down in 1795, and he retired to a farm near Springfield, Washington County, Ky., whence, however, he continued his ministry, as he had strength, in all the surrounding country, and sometimes to remote distances. He also established a school, in which he successfully taught, for he appreciated the importance of education to the young Commonwealth rising around him. He resumed his itinerant labors in 1818, and continued them, in important western appointments, till 1824, when he was returned "superannuated," in which honored relation to the Conference he remained till his death, seven years later. His ministry extended through forty-six years, twenty-three of them in the itinerancy, and twenty-three in the local ranks.

In the year 1792 Western Methodism reported three Districts—two in Western Virginia, Kentucky, and Tennessee, under Poythress and M'Henry, with such men as Wm. Burke, Wilson Lee, Henry Birchett, John Kobler, John Lindsey, and Stith Mead on their circuits; and one in Western Pennsylvania, under Amos Thompson, with Thornton Fleming, Daniel Hitt, and Valentine Cook as preachers.

Few men saw harder service there than William Burke. In the very outset his circuit led him through the thickest perils of Indian warfare. He was a courageous man, and as such was chosen to command bands of preachers and laymen who used to advance to meet Asbury and conduct him westward; he led such a band, consisting of sixty persons, in 1794, through terrible difficulties and dangers among the Cumberland mountains, to meet the bishop on the Holston, when four of the corps, who had advanced one mile, were killed and scalped. In 1794 we find him on Salt River Circuit, famous for its hardships. It was nearly five hundred miles in extent, comprising five counties, to be traveled every four weeks, with continual preaching. The sorely tried itinerant writes: "I was reduced to the last pinch. My clothes were nearly all gone. I had patch upon patch, and patch by patch, and I received only money sufficient to buy a waistcoat, and not enough of that to pay for the making." By the spring of 1795 this brave man had traveled all the Circuits of Kentucky, save a small one called Limestone, which lay on the north side of Licking River. From the time that the first Methodist missionaries entered the new field up to this spring there had been one continued Indian war, while the whole frontier, east, west, north, and south, had been exposed to the inroads and depredations of the merciless savages. In this spring was the noted Nickajack expedition, which terminated the Cherokee carnage. Wayne's treaty at Greenville, Ohio, put an end to the Indian wars, and the whole Western country, for once, had peace. We read, in Burke's autobiography, continually of incredible travels, labors, and sufferings; of journeys of upward of a hundred miles without a single house on the way, and of night campings in the woods; but also of the triumphs of the Gospel against the threatening barbarism of the wilderness. At the end of our present period (1796) he recrossed the mountains, being appointed to Guilford Circuit, North Carolina. But the next year he was back again. His fate was now fixed for the West. By the end of the century he had command of most of its Methodist interests; and in the summer of 1800 he "rode down two good horses," had "worn out his clothes," was "ragged and tattered," and had "not a cent in his pocket." He labored twenty-six years in the hardest fields of Virginia, Kentucky, Tennessee, and Ohio. As late as 1811 he organized and took charge of the first Methodist station in Cincinnati, the first indeed in Ohio; there his health failed, and he had to retire from the effective work of the ministry.

John Kobler appeared in 1792 among the rugged mountains of the Greenbrier, under the presiding eldership of Poythress, whose District comprehended much of Western Virginia, and Kentucky as far as Lexington. In 1793 he became presiding elder of the entire denomination in the Holston mountains, with three Circuits and five preachers; and now, in an adequate field, he displayed his full powers as one of the giant men of the itinerancy, by vast travels, powerful preaching, and the endurance of the worst trials of the ministry. The next year he retained command of his mountain corps, enlarged to seven men, with five Circuits. We find him there still in 1795, with seven Circuits and eleven men, among whom were such befitting associates as Benjamin Lakin, Tobias Gibson, and William M'Kendree. His great District reached to this side the mountains. He retained the laborious office till 1797, when he passed further westward, and presided over the whole field in Kentucky and Tennessee. He continued to traverse these wilds till 1798, when we shall meet him again, in Ohio, the first Methodist itinerant who entered the great Northwestern Territory—"a man," say his brethren, in their Minutes, "of saint-like spirit, dignified and ministerial bearing, untiring labors in preaching, praying, and visiting the sick;" of "preaching abilities above mediocrity;" tall, slender, with an energy of soul which far surpassed that of his body.

Among the really great men that begin now to rise like a host in Western Methodism is Thomas Scott, known and venerated throughout the West as Judge Scott. In 1794, at the command of Asbury, he descended the Ohio River from Wheeling, on a flatboat, to join the band of Kentucky itinerants, and met them in Conference at the Bethel Academy, in Jessamine County. He afterward labored on Danville and Lexington Circuits. Marrying in 1796, it became necessary, as usual with his fellow-laborers, to locate. To locate, however, was then, as we have often remarked, not to cease to preach. Preaching on Sundays, he applied himself to business on week days to support his family. Meanwhile, he studied law as best he could with the few facilities for such studies in the West. In 1801 he went to Chilicothe, Ohio, where by providential circumstances he became fixed for the remainder of his long and useful life. Years earlier, while traveling Berkeley Circuit, Va., he was invited to visit Charlestown, about four miles out of his usual route, a place where a few Methodists had been for some time molested by mobs. There Dr. Edward Tiffin was received by him into the Church. Now, eleven years later, as he wandered to Chilicothe, he found that Tiffin had also wandered thither from Virginia, and was already a commanding citizen, preaching the Gospel in all the surrounding country, organizing Churches, turning his medical practice into a means of religious ministration to the sick and dying, gratuitously dealing out medicines, with his characteristic liberality, to the poor, who came to him from great distances. His excellent wife "was," says a veteran itinerant, "one of the most conscientious and heavenly-minded women I ever saw—a mother in our Israel, indeed." She was one of those select "women of Methodism" who ministered to Asbury, and who were honored with his affectionate friendship. Asbury, on visiting Chilicothe, in 1808, went to her tomb and made the following record: "Within sight of this beautiful mansion lies the precious dust of Mary Tiffin. It was as much as I could do to forbear weeping as I mused over her speaking grave. How mutely eloquent! Ah, the world knows little of my sorrows; little knows how dear to me are my many friends, and how deeply I feel their loss; but they all die in the Lord, and this shall comfort me. I delivered my soul here. May this dear family feel an answer to Mary Tiffin's prayers."

The doctor became the chief citizen of Ohio; which was still a territory; he was one of its legislators; was elected a member of the convention which formed its state constitution, and soon after had the signal honor to be elected its first state governor "without opposition." Scott was welcomed to Chilicothe by his old friend and convert. He sent for his family, and settled there. Tiffin gave him employment in a clerkship, and promoted his legal business and studies. He was elected secretary to the convention for the formation of the state constitution. The Legislature appointed him a judge of the Supreme Court, whose chief justice he became one year later. His official rank secured him public influence, and this he, like his friend Tiffin, consecrated to religion. They were two of the strongest pillars of Methodism in Ohio, and to their public character and labors it owes much of its rapid growth and predominant sway in that magnificent State.

In following Scott northward, in order to complete, at one view, the outline of his career, we have anticipated, somewhat, important events of our narrative, for we leave him and Tiffin representative Methodists in Ohio before we have witnessed its introduction into the great "Northwestern Territory." The anticipation, however, is but brief; we have already seen Kobler, its first regular itinerant, tending toward that region; and before the close of our present period, its recognized founder in Ohio, a local preacher, had reached it. In the account of Henry Smith, a convert of Judge Scott, in Virginia, and himself a western pioneer, we have met, in Western Virginia, an obscure but most interesting character by the name of Francis M'Cormick. M'Cormick, "a powerful man" with the fist and the ax, was a young fellow-convert, and a fellow-exhorter, with Smith. We have seen both essaying their first ability as "exhorters" in "Davenport's Meeting-House," at the "head of Bullskin," a place where Tiffin also had often preached. The name of Francis M'Cormick was destined to become dear in the hearts, and great in the history, of his people as the founder of Methodism in the most important section of the North American continent, the Northwestern Territory. Like the martyr Tucker, and other local preachers of that day, he emigrated, in 1795, to Kentucky, more to preach the Gospel than to get gain. He settled in Bourbon County, but was soon dissatisfied with his position. He crossed the Ohio, and built his log-cabin at Milford, in Clermont County. Seven years afterward he removed to what is now known as Salem, but for many years was called "M'Cormick's Settlement," about ten miles from the site of

Cincinnati. At Milford he found the settlers thoroughly demoralized, for lack of the means of religion, and forthwith began his good work, inviting them to assemble to hear the word, which he proclaimed to them "as the voice of one crying in the wilderness." He formed a class there, the first Methodist Society organized in the Northwestern Territory. He went out preaching among the settlements, and soon established two other classes, one near the present town of Lockland, the other near Columbia. He made urgent appeals to the Kentucky itinerants, informing them of the new and open door of the great Northwest, and calling for immediate help. John Kobler soon responded, and became the first regular Methodist preacher north and west of the Ohio River. We shall have occasion, before long, to follow him, and thenceforward will rise before us the gigantic Methodism of the great northern states of the Mississippi Valley.

Henry Smith, our own venerated contemporary of "Pilgrim's Rest," was now also itinerating in the West, having gone, as we have seen, to Clarksburgh Circuit, on the Monongahela, Va., in 1794. He shared there the trials and the triumphs common to his ultramontane fellow-laborers. At his first appointment, about fifteen miles beyond Clarksburgh, he found "a good Methodist Society," under the care of the devoted Joseph Chieuvrant, "a respectable local preacher." The congregation came from miles around. "They were," says he, "all backwoods people, and came to meeting in backwoods style, a considerable congregation. I looked round and saw one old man who had shoes on his feet. The preacher wore Indian moccasins; every man, woman, and child besides was barefooted." They were still exposed here to the Indians, and Chieuvrant not only preached in moccasins, but shouldered his gun and followed the trail in pursuit of the murderous savages. In some places Smith saw the men "coming to meeting with their rifles on their shoulders, guarding their families, then setting their guns in a corner of the house till after meeting, and returning in the same order." "O what a poor chance," he exclaims, "these people had to be religious! and yet I found some very pious souls among them."

In 1795 he was sent to the famous Redstone Circuit. At the Baltimore Conference of 1796, "Asbury," he says, "called for volunteers to go to Kentucky, and fixed his eye upon me as one. I said, 'Here am I, send me.' I was ordained in a private room, before Conference opened; and in a few hours after my ordination John Watson and myself were on horseback, on our way to Kentucky, almost before any one knew we were going." He hastened into the interior and found Poythress, who sent him to Salt River Circuit. For some years he was a successful pioneer of the Church, "traveling round every Circuit in Kentucky and visiting every Society," sharing fully the trials and triumphs of the mighty men who were then abroad there, Poythress, M'Henry, Burke, Kobler, and their compeers. "Methodism," he remarks, "had spread, when I went out, nearly over the State, though opposed everywhere, and by nearly every sort of people." He passed also into the Northwestern Territory, and became a co-laborer of Kobler and M'Cormick.

In the great trans-Alleghany field we meet again Valentine Cook, that "wonderful man" of whom marvelous traditions are rife in the Church, from the interior lakes of New York, through the Wyoming and Tioga mountains, and Redstone and Holston countries, down to the remotest regions of Kentucky and Tennessee. He was on the Pittsburgh and Clarksburgh Circuits, and the Pittsburgh District, during these years, and afterward pushed into Kentucky, where he spent the remainder of his life. He was considered the most learned man of the American itinerancy of his day. His early education, at Cokesbury, and his devotion to biblical studies and the classic languages, together with a peculiar, original capacity of mind, very much like genius, gave him an intellectual vigor which, combined with extraordinary moral force and unction, rendered him a sort of prodigy among his brethren.

Besides the itinerants heretofore mentioned, many yet young, but destined to become historical characters, had already entered, or were about to enter, the great West, such as Daniel Hitt, John Lindsey, Tobias Gibson, Benjamin Lakin, William Beauchamp. William M'Kendree had been tending thither for some years, traveling a Virginia District which stretched beyond the Blue Ridge into the Greenbrier country; he was soon to enter Kentucky as the chieftain of Western Methodism, and to inaugurate a new era in its history. Robert R. Roberts was preparing for his episcopal career, in the woods, on the banks of the Little Chenango. James Quinn (who first led Roberts into public labors) was about to start on his first Circuit. John Sale was being trained on the hardest Circuit of Virginia, and was soon to make his way over the mountains. Thornton Fleming, whom we have met in the far North, was rapidly rising to that commanding influence which he long wielded in the old Pittsburgh Conference. John Collins, still in New Jersey, was seeking to save his soul, and leading his brother-in-law, the memorable Larner Blackman, into a holy life, both to become founders of the Church in the Northwest. James B. Finley, yet a youth, but a "mighty hunter," was pondering, in the Western woods, reports of the marvels of Methodism. Peter Cartwright, "naturally a wild, wicked boy, delighting in horse-racing, card-playing, and dancing," was studying, in the Kentucky wilderness, under Beverly Allen, and wondering at the strange news that reached him occasionally from the Methodist "Ebenezer" Church, a few miles to the south. Philip Gatch, whom we have so often met as one of the first two American itinerants, was preparing to leave his retreat in Virginia and plunge into the wilds of Ohio, where he was to do good service for the Church. Methodism was, in short, putting on strength all through the settled regions of the West. It had now spread entirely over Kentucky and Tennessee; there was hardly a "block-house station" or "settlement" where the itinerants did not, at longer or shorter intervals, sound their trumpets, and it had commenced that march, that triumphant march, into the Northwestern Territory, in which it has continuously gone on from conquering to conquer. Log chapels were rising through the wilderness; there was probably not yet a single church of higher pretensions; cabins, barns, and the sheltering woods were the most common sanctuaries. By the end of this period, the autumn of 1796, there were west of the mountains four Districts, twenty-three Circuits, thirty-six traveling preachers, and 6,500 Church members. The few Methodists of Ohio were yet unreported. Tennessee had about 550, Kentucky about 1,750; the remainder were in Western Pennsylvania and Virginia. The West had already much more than double the number reported from New England.

CHAPTER XXIII.

GENERAL CONFERENCE OF 1796 — METHODISM IN THE SOUTH: 1796-1804.

THE third General Conference was appointed to meet in Baltimore on the 20th of October, 1796. No difficult business, however, was pending, and it need not long delay the chronological course of our narrative. Coke had been in the West Indies, England, Ireland, and Holland, promoting his missions, writing his commentary, and preaching continually. He arrived in the Chesapeake Bay on the 3d of October, but was detained there five days by unfavorable winds. On the 18th October he reached Baltimore, two days before the Conference opened. Asbury was enjoying the hospitality of Gough at Perry Hall, but joined his colleague in the city on the 19th, where, he says, about a hundred preachers were in attendance; according to Lee, twenty more arrived later. The most important business done at this session was the definite arrangement of the whole Church in six yearly Conferences, to be no longer called "District," but Annual Conferences, namely, the New England, Philadelphia, Baltimore, Virginia, South Carolina, and Western Conferences; the adoption of a form of deed for the security of Church real estate, vesting its ownership in the Societies, to be held for them by their trustees, but guaranteeing the use of the pulpits to the authorized ministry; the establishment of the "Chartered Fund" for the relief of "distressed traveling preachers, the families of traveling preachers, superannuated and worn-out preachers, and the widows and orphans of preachers," an institution which still exists; the enactment of the rule that "if any member of our Society retail or give spirituous liquors, and anything disorderly be transacted under his roof on this account, the preacher who has the oversight of the Circuit shall proceed against him, as in the case of other immoralities, and the person accused shall be cleared, censured, suspended, or excluded, according to his conduct, as on other charges of immorality." Though defeated in their original provisions against slavery, the zeal of the ministry, on that question, was still unabated, and the Conference asked the question, "What regulations shall be made for the extirpation of the crying evil of African slavery?" and answered by some stringent regulations on the subject. The largest space devoted to any one subject in the journal of this session is that given to education, prescribing minute, though they are entitled "General Rules for the Methodist Seminaries of Learning." The session continued two weeks. Its aggregate membership shows a loss, since 1792, of more than nine thousand; it had been losing for three years,* the effect of the O'Kelly schism; but substantially it had never been more vigorous or more progressive. Away from the local disturbance, it was not only fortifying all its positions, but gaining in numerical strength. In New England it more than doubled its Circuits, and nearly doubled its preachers and communicants. It had now intrenched itself in all the Eastern States. In Canada it had trebled its Circuits, quadrupled its ministry, and nearly trebled its membership. The chief force of the denomination was now in Virginia; she reported nearly 14,000 members; more than three times the number of the State of New York. Maryland ranked next, and had nearly 12,500; more than four times as many as Pennsylvania, and more than three times the number of New York. New Hampshire ranked lowest on the list of the States, her Methodistic roll having yet but sixty-eight names. The aggregate membership throughout the republic and Canada was 56,664, the aggregate ministry 293; showing a loss, for the four years, of 9,316 members, and a gain of 27 preachers. The decrease, occasioned chiefly by the Virginia controversy, excited alarm. A General Fast was proclaimed for the first Friday in March, 1796, "to be attended in all the societies and congregations with Sabbatic strictness," and among the sins enumerated, as demanding this penitence, was

* It reported a diminution of white members as early as 1793, but the loss was then more than repaired by the gain of black members.

that of slavery. The declension of numbers ceased from this year; slowly but surely the returns increased until they rolled up in those grand aggregates which have astonished not only the denomination itself, but the religious world.

Asbury and Coke left the Conference together for the South on the 4th of November, 1795. They were soon among the scenes of the O'Kelly schism in Virginia. "I feel happy," wrote Asbury, "among the few old disciples who are left. My mind of late hath been in great peace. The Lord can give us children, 'that we shall have after we have lost our former,' who shall say in our hearing, 'Give place, that there may be room for us to dwell.' My dear aged friends told me their troubles and sorrow, which the divisions in the Societies had caused." He adds, after seeing a spot memorable to us all, "I had solemn thoughts while I passed the house where Robert Williams lived and died, whose funeral rites I performed." Coke rejoiced, in the Virginia Conference at "Maybery's Chapel," not only for the prospect in that State, but in the whole country, for his vivid faith was prophetic of American Methodism. Asbury's allusions to his illness and dejection are increasingly frequent. He was suffering under a violent attack of intermittent fever, his old foe, which perhaps was unavoidable while he exposed himself to all climates and weather of the continent, exhausted most of the time by travel, and much of it by scarcity of food. "My depression of spirits," he says, "at times is awful, especially when afflicted; that which is deeply constitutional will never die but with my body. I am solemnly given up to God, and have been for many months willing to live or die in, for, and with Jesus." He was, in short, unconsciously guilty of overworking himself, and all who were immediately associated with him, and had been doing so for years. Even his horse had to share in his sufferings. "My horse," he writes, "trots stiff, and no wonder, as I have ridden him, upon an average, five thousand miles a year for the last five years successively." He was at length compelled to rest for weeks, sending Jesse Lee to do his southern work. Lee left him, in repose, in Virginia, and passed rapidly along, having about five hundred miles to travel and twenty-five appointments to meet in thirty days. He reached Charleston by the beginning of 1798. He had been in the city, with Asbury and Willis, about thirteen years before, and preached the first sermon on that occasion; he now met there an Annual Conference, beheld two chapels, with seventy-seven white and four hundred and twenty-one black Methodists, while in the State were four thousand six hundred members. He penetrated into Georgia, where he preached twenty-one sermons in twenty-seven days. Returning northward he hastened along, preaching continually with an ardor and eloquence that stirred the Churches. He met Asbury again at the Virginia Conference, in Salem, where he preached the opening sermon, and says, "We had a most powerful, weeping, shouting time; the house seemed to be filled with the presence of God. Bishop Asbury exhorted for some time, and the people were much melted under the word. Several new preachers engaged in the work, and we had a very good supply for all the Circuits." Lee again met Asbury at the Baltimore Conference, where he dedicated a new church, and then hastened to his hard but favorite field of the East. But before the close of the year he was again abroad in the South. After traveling over the vast See of Asbury, in 1799, he says: "Our borders were greatly enlarged this year, and the way was opening for us to spread further, and to send forth more laborers into the vineyard of the Lord." In 1800 Asbury accompanied him, but Lee did most of the preaching. From three to six thousand people heard them weekly. Lee endured their hard fare as sturdily as the bishop; they often "had kitchen, house, and chamber all in one, and no closet but the woods;" or "found shelter in a log-cabin without doors, and with thirty or forty hogs sleeping under it." Their chief affliction, however, was the demoralization of the rustic population. There were "people grown to men's estate, and some that had families, who never heard a sermon till last summer," when the Methodist itinerants had reached them.

Down to the General Conference of 1804 Lee confined his labors to Virginia, where he was universally popular for not only his rare eloquence, but his unsparing devotion to his work. Withal, his characteristic and irrepressible humor gave him a species of power not without value. It attracted a class of minds which might not otherwise have come within his reach. It also enabled him to give effective rebukes, which rendered him a terror to evil-doers. "On one occasion," says his biographer, "when he was engaged in the opening services of public worship, he perceived the gentlemen intermixed with the ladies, and occupying seats appropriated to the latter. Supposing them to be unaware of the violation of our order, he respectfully stated the rule upon the subject, and requested them to take their seats on their own side of the house. All but a few immediately complied with the request. It was again repeated, and all but one left. He stood his ground as if determined not to yield. Again the rule was repeated, and the request followed it. But no disposition to retire was indicated. Leaning down upon the desk, and fixing his penetrating eye upon the offender for a moment, and then raising himself erect, and looking with an arch smile over the congregation, he drawled out, 'Well, brethren, I asked the gentlemen to retire from those seats, and *they* did so. But it seems *that man* is determined not to move. We must, therefore, serve him as the little boys say when a marble slips from their fingers—let him 'go for slippance.'" To say he slipped out of the house is only to describe the fact in language borrowed from the figure by which the rebuke was conveyed. At another time, while engaged in preaching, he was not a little mortified to discover many of the congregation taking rest in sleep, and not a little annoyed by the loud talking of the people in the yard. Pausing long enough for the absence of the sound to startle the sleepers, he raised his voice, and cried out, "I'll thank the people in the yard not to talk so loud; they'll wake up the people in the house!" This was "killing two birds with one stone" in a most adroit and effectual manner. Anecdotes of the wit of Lee are still current all through the denomination. It was usually very genial, but could be sufficiently arrowy to make opponents and wags keep at a due distance or approach him with deference.

Peace was now generally restored in the southern section of the Church, and its Societies were rapidly growing. The

Hammett schism had dwindled nearly away, and some of its pulpits were already occupied by the itinerants. The O'Kelly secession still occasionally disturbed the Societies of Virginia, but the leaders of the denomination, after having sturdily defended it, now adopted the wise policy of letting the recusants alone. Though the schism lingered, it gradually died from this period, and extraordinary "revivals" followed, not only in Virginia, but throughout the South. This renewed interest pervaded the whole city of Baltimore during the General Conference there in 1800. The Conference sat in a private room, while the local preachers, the young traveling preachers, and others were almost continually engaged in carrying on the meetings in the Church, and in private houses. "At one time the meeting continued," says Lee, "without intermission for forty-five hours, which was almost two days and nights." The excitement spread through most of Maryland and Virginia, and continued throughout the year. In 1801 it extended "greatly in most parts of the Connection," but prevailed chiefly in Maryland and Delaware. It overleaped the Western mountains, and prevailed in Kentucky and Tennessee like fire on the prairies. In 1802 the interest extended. At Rockingham a meeting continued nine days; "business was wholly suspended, merchants and mechanics shut up their shops," and "little else was attended to but waiting upon the Lord." The people crowded in from all the surrounding country, and hundreds were converted. In North and South Carolina and Georgia similar scenes occurred, and lasted through most of our present period. Many individual Societies were reinforced by a hundred additions at a time. Quarterly meetings were frequently turned into protracted camp-meetings, and it seemed, to the sanguine evangelists, that the whole population was about to bow before the power of their word. In short, the subsequent predominance of Methodism in the South can be traced to the impulse that it now received.

Southern Methodism was powerfully manned during this period. M'Kendree, Whatcoat, George, Everett, Bruce, Blanton, Spry, Mead, Jenkins, Lee, (the latter part of the time,) Hitt, Wilson Lee, Dougharty, M'Caine, were among its presiding elders; while such men as Sale, Harper, Gibson, Smith, Hill, Reed, Bloodgood, Sargent, Fleming, Lyell, M'Coy, Myers, Gassaway, Walters, M'Combs, Daniel Asbury, Wells, Cowles, Jones, Frye, Roberts, were among the circuit itinerants. George Dougharty occupies a conspicuous place in the early annals of Southern Methodism. "By application and perseverance he took," says one of his fellow-laborers, "a stand in the front rank of the South Carolina band of pioneers, marshaling the armies of the sacramental host from the sea-shore to the Blue Ridge." He was ungainly in his person; tall, slight, with but one eye, and negligent of dress; but his intellect was of lofty tone, his logical powers remarkable, and his eloquence at times absolutely irresistible. In 1801 he was attacked by a mob in Charleston, S. C., provoked by the antislavery action of the General Conference. They dragged him from the church to a pump, where they pumped upon him till he was exhausted, and would probably have perished, had not a heroic Methodist woman interfered, stopping up the mouth of the pump with her shawl. She held the mob abashed by her remonstrances till a courageous citizen threw himself into their midst with a drawn sword, rescued their victim, and led him to a place of shelter. He never recovered from this inhuman treatment, but lingered with consumption till the South Carolina Conference of 1807, when his voice was last heard, in that body, proposing and advocating a resolution, that any preacher who should desert his appointment "through fear in times of sickness or danger" should never again be employed by the Conference, a requisition necessary in that region of epidemics. He "spoke," says the old Minutes, "to the case with amazing argument and energy, and carried his cause like a dying general in victory." He died this year at Wilmington, N. C., where he was appropriately "buried in the African Church."

William Watters, the first native American Methodist preacher, reappears in the appointments for the year 1801, after having been located about eighteen years. During his location he preached habitually, and often at distances of many miles from his home. He was now fifty years old, mature in health and character, of extreme amiability, good sense, self-possession, and soundness of judgment. During most of our present period he labored at Alexandria, Georgetown, and Washington. He located again in 1806, and we get but few later glimpses of him. Boehm, the traveling companion of Asbury, says that in February, 1811, while in Virginia, they "rode to William Watters's. He was now living in dignified retirement on his farm on the Virginia side of the Potomac, opposite Georgetown, and was a stout man, of medium height, of very venerable and solemn appearance. Bishop Asbury and he were lifetime friends. When these aged men met on this occasion they embraced and saluted each other with 'a holy kiss.' Few holier ministers has the Methodist Church ever had than William Watters. In 1833, at the age of eighty-two, he died in holy triumph."

Enoch George resumed his itinerant labors in 1799 on Rockingham Circuit, Virginia, where, he says, "the windows of heaven were again opened, and grace descended upon us." In 1800 he had charge of a District extending from the Alleghanies to the Chesapeake Bay, and requiring from one thousand to twelve hundred miles travel quarterly. His excessive labors brought back his old infirmities, for "in those days," he says, "the preachers 'ceased not to warn every one night and day with tears' in doing the work given them, and exerted themselves not only to increase the numbers, but the holiness of the people. It was our duty to attend diligently to the Africans, in forming and establishing Societies; but as their masters would not allow them to attend the meetings during the day, we were obliged to meet them at night. Oftentimes this kept us up and out till late, in this unhealthy climate, which had a destructive influence upon our health." He broke down, was again located, and taught school in Winchester, Va., for his support. He preached meanwhile on Sabbaths, and having recovered sufficient strength re-entered the itinerancy in 1803, and labored successively and mightily on Frederick Circuit, Baltimore District, Alexandria District, Georgetown, Frederick, Montgomery, and Baltimore Circuits, and Baltimore and Georgetown Districts, till his consecration to the episcopate. William M'Kendree traveled during the present period, down to the end of the century, on vast Districts in Virginia. His labors were almost superhuman, interfering, he says, with his studies, and impairing his nervous system; but he rejoiced in the rapid extension of the Church. In 1800 he was again on his Richmond District, but had passed round it only once when Asbury and Whatcoat met him, with orders to pack up forthwith, and throw himself into the great Western field as leader of its itinerant pioneers. "I was," he says, "without my money, books, or clothes. These were all at a distance, and I had no time to go after them; but I was not in debt, therefore unembarrassed. Of moneys due me I collected one hundred dollars, bought cloth for a coat, carried it to Holston, and left it with a tailor in the bounds of my new District. The bishops continued their course: my business was to take care of their horses, and wait on them, for they were both infirm old men." They were soon descending the western slope of the Alleghanies, whither we shall hereafter follow them.

Tobias Gibson, also, after seven years of hardest service in Georgia and South Carolina, penetrating, in 1795, to the Holston region, departed in 1799 for the further West, the first Methodist pioneer of the Southern Mississippi Valley; we shall soon have occasion to greet him there.

By the close of this period the Minutes had ceased to return Church members according to States, but reported them according to Conferences. There were now three of these bodies in the South: Baltimore Conference, with 23,646 members; Virginia, with 17,139; and South Carolina, with 14,510. The aggregate of Southern Methodists was 55,295, of whom more than 14,000 were Africans. The gain for the last eight years had been 15,554, an average of nearly two thousand a year. The South had now nearly one half of all the membership of the Church including that of Canada. More than a hundred and sixty itinerants were abroad in its Conferences.

CHAPTER XXIV.

MIDDLE AND NORTHERN METHODISM: 1796–1804.

THE Church in the Middle States shared largely in the religious interest which we have noticed as prevailing throughout the South in the present period. It was indeed universal, if not simultaneous, from Maine to Tennessee, from Georgia to Canada. Some of our early authorities attribute it to the impulse given by the labors of Wooster in the latter section of the denomination. It seems, however, to have been one of those mysterious "times of refreshing" which appear at intervals in Christian communities, pass through their salutary cycle, and subside, to reappear in due time. Some excesses were incidental, if not unavoidable to the excitement. Watters was perplexed by them. Enoch George hesitated before them, and used repressive measures at first; but these prudent men, and their brethren generally, seem to have arrived at the conclusion of Wesley and his colaborers in similar cases, that such proofs of human weakness, or even folly, were not disproofs of the genuineness of the revival; it being natural, if not inevitable, that human infirmity should mingle even with a divine work among fallen men. They saw that the results of the excitement were salutary, that its general character was good, its defects exceptional. In Baltimore it prevailed mightily. It extended all through Maryland and Delaware; the chapels and meetings at private houses were crowded in the evenings, and by day the harvest fields, workshops, the forests where the woodmen were cutting timber, and the homes of the people, were vocal with Methodist hymns. It seemed, remarks a witness of the scene, that all the population were turning unto the Lord. About the beginning of the century the yellow fever prevailed in the Atlantic cities, and added much to the religious seriousness of the times. The Methodist preachers were steadfast at their posts through the period of the pestilence in New York, Philadelphia, and Baltimore. Some perished by it, but their Churches prospered greatly.

Asbury made no less than twelve passages over the Middle States in these years, going to and returning from the East; but, as usual in this mature portion of the Church, his notes are too meager to afford any historical information or interest. Thomas Ware, whom we have met in so many widely-apart sections, was sent at the beginning of this period to the Philadelphia District, which extended from Wilmington, Del., to the Seneca Lake, N. Y. "A glorious religious excitement," he writes, "commenced on Strasburgh and Chester Circuits, which spread through the whole peninsula, exceeding anything I have ever witnessed. This revival embraced all classes, governor, judges, lawyers, and statesmen, old and young, rich and poor, including many of the African race, who adorned their profession by a well-ordered life, and some of them by a triumphant death."

Dr. Chandler, studying medicine under Rush, of Philadelphia, was recalled to the itinerancy by Ware, and became one of its most influential members. He was eminently useful and popular on districts and in Philadelphia down to 1813, when he located, irrecoverably broken down in health. In 1822 his name was replaced upon the Conference roll, that he might die a member of the body, though unable to perform active service. He had preached as he had strength till 1820, when he was struck with paralysis in the pulpit of Ebenezer Church, Philadelphia. He went to the West Indies for relief, but suffered there a second attack, and hastened home to die. On a Sunday morning he said to his class leader, "Go to the meeting and tell them I am dying, shouting the praises of God!" Soon after this he sunk into a stupor, in which he remained to the last. In stature he was of medium height, his countenance was "fine and expressive," his manners bland and polished, but without affectation; his intellect much above mediocrity, and his preaching often of an enrapturing eloquence.

Solomon Sharp, whose name is still familiar throughout the

Churches of the Middle States, was one of the conspicuous itinerants of these times, traveling important Circuits in Delaware, large Districts in New Jersey, and closing the period in Philadelphia. He was an original, an eccentric, but a mighty man. His sermons were powerful, and delivered with a singular tone of authority, as if he were conscious of his divine commission. His form was tall, remarkably robust, and in his latter years he was one of the most noticeable and patriarchal figures in the Conference, with long white locks flowing upon his shoulders, and a bearing of no little dignity. His voice was powerful, and he sometimes used it to its utmost capacity, especially at camp-meetings; "but," says one of his friends, "there was nothing in his manner that savored of extravagance. He was noted for his courage, and it is supposed that he was hardly capable of feeling fear. He had occasion sometimes, at camp-meetings and elsewhere, to show this quality. No opponent challenged it a second time. In his old age a company of reckless young men attempted to play a 'practical joke' upon him by sending for him to come to their workshop, under pretense that one of their number was in great distress of conscience, and was desirous that he should converse and pray with him. Prompt to obey every call of duty, and especially such a call as this, he hastened to the place, where he found a person apparently in such a state of mind as had been represented. He listened with close attention to the sad recital, and was about to proceed to give the appropriate instruction, when something in the appearance of one or more of the men who were standing around awakened his suspicion that all was not right; and presently the whole company, not excepting the poor creature who had consented to be the subject of the impious farce, were exhibiting a broad grin at their imagined triumph. But the old hero was not at all at a loss how to meet such an emergency. He instantly closed the door and stood with his back against it; and, as there was no other way by which they could make their escape, they were obliged to listen, while he placed their characters and conduct in a light that was entirely new to them. He dwelt upon their meanness as well as their wickedness. He called them heaven-daring, heaven-provoking, hell-deserving sinners. He wrought himself up into a perfect storm of indignation, while he denounced upon them the threatenings of God, and brought vividly before them the terrors of the judgment. The infidel sneer and laugh soon gave place to the deepest concern; and it was not long before they actually trembled, like Belshazzar, when he saw the handwriting on the wall. And now they began to cry for mercy. 'Down on your knees, down on your knees,' said the veteran; and they actually fell upon their knees, praying, and begging the good old man to pray for them. He did pray for them, and some of them dated the beginning of a religious life from that period."

Thomas Smith was an effective laborer in the revival scenes of this period in the Middle States. He was converted in early life, and almost in the act of committing suicide. "I had caught up the rope," he says, "and had taken hold of the ladder, and put my foot on a round of it, when the thought rushed into my mind, 'It is an awful thing to die; you had better pray first!'" He dropped the rope at the foot of the ladder, fell on his knees, and continued praying until his disturbed mind was restored, and his troubled conscience found peace with God. In his eighteenth year he began to preach. Throughout our present period he labored in Delaware and New Jersey with great power; the demonstrations which had attended Abbott were repeated at almost all his appointments, and hundreds of souls were gathered into the Societies. He and his colleague, Anning Owen, the itinerant hero of Wyoming, suffered no little maltreatment. Though preaching with the utmost energy, Smith was remarkable for the shortness of his sermons, seldom exceeding twenty minutes. In these primitive times, when the congregations gathered from great distances, they demanded longer entertainment; and, strange as it may seem in our day, would sometimes remonstrate against its brevity. He never, however, would consent to prolong a single sermon, but sometimes would dispatch one, and, announcing a second text, discuss another subject, and formally concluding it, add even a third text and discourse.

His courage was unshakable, and he needed it all in his many encounters with persecutors. On one of his Circuits, in 1801, Ware was with him, preaching with overwhelming effect, while a band of young men waited at the door with bludgeons to attack Smith. When the meeting closed he boldly advanced through them, brushing their clothes, and seeing their clubs, but every arm hung down helpless. The next day he was fearlessly preaching among them in the open air to three thousand African slaves. A few days afterward he was "waylaid by four of his opposers, who had bound themselves under an oath to spill his blood that day." He appealed to God, "I will put my trust in thee," and rode bravely past them, hearing them curse one another behind him, with mutual accusations of cowardice. Nothing could deter him. "The work of the Lord," he wrote, "has been going on day and night for six months past, and Christ's kingdom is coming. On this Circuit we have no rest week. A pity we should, while souls are perishing for lack of knowledge. Let us be up and at our posts. We generally preach twice a day, meet two classes, and get up a prayer-meeting somewhere in the afternoon if we can. Our work on this Circuit is never done; we rest, and at it again." Such was Thomas Smith throughout these and many subsequent years, a man who preached with the utmost brevity, but with the utmost power. He had great physical vigor, was stout to corpulence, below the ordinary height, erect and authoritative in mien, fastidiously neat in dress, exceedingly sociable among his intimate friends, and preached always with intense excitement, moving through his twenty-minute discourse like a war-steed in a charge.

Henry Boehm began his long itinerant career in our present period. We have repeatedly alluded to the old homestead of his venerable father, Martin Boehm, who, expelled from the "Mennonites" for his "too evangelical opinions," became a bishop among the "United Brethren," or "German Methodists," a people founded, as we have seen, by the labors of Asbury's friend Otterbein. He lived and died a patriarch of Methodism in Lancaster County, Pennsylvania. His home at Conestoga is consecrated in the early Methodist records as the frequent shelter of Asbury, Whatcoat, and most of the Methodist leaders. We have noticed the achievements of Abbott in "Boehm's Chapel," and all through its neighborhood. Henry Boehm was converted in 1793, through the instrumentality of Chandler, but concealed the fact for five years. "These," he writes, "were lost years; lost to myself, lost to the Church, and lost to the world. There is nothing in my early history I regret so much as the loss of these five years." He heard Strawbridge and Abbott, and most of the itinerant "sons of thunder," at Boehm's Chapel. This famous structure was planned by Whatcoat, and built, in 1791, of limestone, on a hill which commands a magnificent view of the surrounding country. "There were wonderful gatherings," he says, "at Boehm's Chapel. The bishops and the great men of Methodism found their way there, and preached the word." In 1800 Thomas Ware called him out to travel Dorchester Circuit, Md., famous as the region into which Catharine Ennalls had introduced Methodism, and where Garrettson suffered his most memorable persecutions and imprisonment. His next circuit was Annamessex, where he labored with William Colbert. It has a singular history. An itinerant on his way to Accomac, beyond the line, in Virginia, inquired for his route, and was cruelly directed in a course that led him into Cypress Swamp, which extended many miles; plunging into it, he discovered that he had been deceived; but after wandering about in the mud, bogs, and water, in danger of sinking and perishing, he came out near the house of Jephthah Bowen, on the east side of the Pocomoke River. Bowen gave him a hearty welcome. The preacher prayed with so much effect in the family that he was invited to preach at the house. He did so, and the people were so pleased with his sermon that Bowen's house became a regular preaching place. Thus Methodism was providentially introduced into that region of the country. Jephthah Bowen and many of his neighbors were converted, and a Society was early formed at his house. He lived long enough to see the frame of a new chapel erected, which bore his name. "This led to the formation of several Societies in that region, and to the conversion of multitudes. His children and children's children were blessed, being the descendants of those who entertained the Lord's prophets."

Boehm afterward labored in Pennsylvania, and introduced Methodism into Reading and Harrisburgh, through much opposition. At the former, he says, "there was a shop in the neighborhood of the school-house, where some men used to meet together. One of the company, a young man, undertook to mimic the Methodists. He went on to show how they acted in their meetings. He shouted, clapped his hands, and then he would show how they fell down. (The Methodists in that day would sometimes fall and lose their strength.) He then threw himself down on the floor, and lay there as if asleep. His companions enjoyed the sport; but after he had lain for some time they wondered why he did not get up. They shook him in order to awake him. When they saw he did not breathe they turned pale, and sent for a physician, who examined the man and pronounced him dead. This awful incident did two things for us: it stopped ridicule and persecution; it also gave us favor in the sight of the people. They believed that God was for us. Little do the present Methodists of Reading know of our early struggles and difficulties. Now they have two churches, Ebenezer and St. Paul's, and Reading is the head of a District, which is not larger than my Circuit in 1803. German was the pioneer language, and prepared the way for the English. I could have accomplished but little there if I had not been able to preach in German." Boehm and Jacob Gruber, his colleague, were thus successfully bearing the standard of Methodism into the German regions of Pennsylvania before the close of our present period. The former was to survive till our day, and his personal life has been woven into our whole subsequent Church history.

Jacob Gruber was one of the unique "characters" of these times. Many of us still recall him: his prim clerical costume; his white locks sleekly combed behind his ears; his German accent, his glowing, genial face, with its quizzical play of humor and sarcasm, that at once attracted and held on anxious guard the interlocutor; his unrivaled power of quaint and apposite illustration; his aptness and humor in telling a story; his tireless readiness for labor, and his staunch tenacity for everything Methodistic. His colleague, Boehm, says he was at this time a fine, intelligent-looking man, and his countenance often expressed a thing before his tongue uttered it. "He had a German face and a German tongue, and often looked quizzical. He wore a drab hat, and a suit of gray cut in Quaker style. With a rough exterior, but a kind heart, it was necessary to know him in order to appreciate him. A more honest man never lived; a bolder soldier of the cross never wielded 'the sword of the Spirit.' As a preacher he was original and eccentric. His powers of irony, sarcasm, and ridicule were tremendous, and woe to the poor fellow who got into his hands; he would wish himself somewhere else."

He had been driven by his father from his home on account of his new faith. He took his leave, with his clothes in a knapsack, and wended his way on foot toward Lancaster, not knowing what should befall him. But on the route a Methodist preacher on horseback accosted him; a few minutes conversation sufficed to make known his forlorn case to the itinerant, who exhorted him to go out forthwith and preach the Gospel, recommending him to a vacancy on a Circuit. No advice could better suit Gruber's feelings at the moment. He immediately spent all his little means in purchasing a horse, and mounting him was away for the Circuit. Thus commenced, in about his twenty-second year, his long and never-slackened itinerant career of more than half a century, during the whole of which, it has been affirmed as "a remarkable fact," that there was not a gap or intermission of four consecutive weeks for any cause whatever. His appointments extended from New Jersey, through Pennsylvania, to the Greenbrier mountains of Western Virginia, from the interior lake regions of New York to the shores of the Chesapeake. He was presiding elder eleven years, was on Circuits thirty-two, and during seven filled important stations in Philadelphia, Baltimore, and Washington. He died an honored veteran of more than seventy-two years, and in a manner befitting his career. On being informed that he could not live through another night, "Then," he replied, "to-morrow I shall spend my first Sabbath in heaven! Last

Sabbath in the Church on earth—next Sabbath in the Church above!"

Peter Vannest was a worthy coadjutor of these faithful men. He labored some years in the Eastern States, then in Canada during two years, and subsequently for seventeen years in the Middle States, from Western New York to Maryland. Taking a "superannuated relation" in 1821, he resided in Pemberton, N. J., till his death in 1850. His death was not only peaceful, it was triumphant. Thomas Burch joined the Philadelphia Conference in the last year of our present period. His labors extended from Montreal to Baltimore, in the most prominent appointments of the Church. One of his familiar ministerial associates says: "He was one of the most amiable and sweet-tempered men I ever knew. As a preacher he always held a very high rank. The most remarkable attribute of his preaching, and indeed of his character generally, was a charming simplicity."

It was in the present period that the "Evangelical Association," sometimes called "German Albright Methodists," had its origin in Pennsylvania. This sect must not be confounded with the "United Brethren," or "German Methodists," of whom some account has been given in our pages. Jacob Albright was converted under the ministry of the elder Boehm, and became a local preacher among the Methodists in the year 1790. In 1796 he began to itinerate as an evangelist among the Germans, being convinced that "his call was exclusively to them." Asbury "esteemed him as a brother beloved," and doubtless the prevalent influence and example of Methodism in Pennsylvania prompted his extraordinary labors, and its practical system became the model of the organization of his people. In 1807 Henry Boehm procured, at his own expense, the translation and publication in German of the Methodist Discipline. The translator was an accomplished scholar, Dr. Romer, of Middletown, Pa., a physician, who had been educated in Europe as a Roman priest, but whose vigorous intellect had broken away from Popery and had fallen into philosophic skepticism. The devoutly exemplary life of a remarkable Methodist woman restored his faith. He became a Methodist in 1800, and his house was for years a home and a "preaching place" of the early itinerants. He prefixed to his version of the Discipline an admirable account of Methodism. This book had great influence on the Germans of not only Pennsylvania, but of other parts of the country, for Boehm and Asbury circulated it generally. We owe to it doubtless the Methodistic type so strongly impressed upon both the Otterbein and Albright communions; the "United Brethren in Christ," and the "Evangelical Association." The former, as we have seen, have the Methodistic economy in detail; the latter has equally adopted it, both in its ecclesiastical system and its articles of religion. Albright organized his converts in 1800. In 1803 their increase demanded more thorough care, and he was appointed their presiding elder. They were regularly organized as a Conference in 1807, the year of Romer's translation of the Discipline. Albright died six months after the Conference. In 1809 his people took the name of "Albrights," and at the same time one of their preachers framed their Articles of Faith and Discipline. In our day they are an important part of the German Methodistic Christianity of the country, reporting eight Conferences, three bishops, four hundred and five traveling, and three hundred and twenty-three local preachers, with more than fifty thousand communicants, and several educational institutions. Thus, while the denomination was spreading out, wave after wave, among the general population of the country, it was continually revealing special power or adaptation for special classes. Its peculiar "economy" and its spiritual vitality explain, in part, at least, this ever-varying and ever-growing success. Its ministerial itinerancy brought it into the presence, face to face, of every class in almost every locality. Its spiritual vitality met a profoundly felt want of earnest minds, in whatever class; a want that was not usually met by contemporary communions.

The New York Conference was still an immense territory, comprising New England west of the Connecticut and the Green Mountains, all the Methodist field of Canada, and New York along the Hudson and westward till it reached the incipient Circuits where the itinerants from the Philadelphia

Conference and from west of the Pennsylvania mountains were planting Societies. At the beginning of this period there was nominally no New York Conference, its territory being included (by act of the General Conference of 1796) in the New England and Philadelphia Conferences; but by the General Conference of 1800 it was defined as including much of Connecticut, New Hampshire and Vermont, Canada, and all New York east of the Hudson. It comprised during these years a host of able itinerants, many of whom have already been noticed.

A memorable character entered its ministerial ranks in 1798, Billy Hibbard, still familiar to the Church by his extraordinary wit, his devoted life, and useful labors. When his name was called in the Conference as William Hibbard, he gave no response. The bishop asked him if this was not his name. "No, sir," he replied. "What is it, then?" inquired the bishop. "It is Billy Hibbard." "Why," said the bishop, with a smile, "that is a little boy's name." "I was a very little boy when my father gave it to me," replied Hibbard. "The Conference was convulsed with laughter," says Boehm, for many of them knew him. When his character was examined, as was customary, it was objected to him that he practiced medicine. "Are you a physician, Brother Hibbard?" inquired the bishop. "I am not," he replied; "I simply give advice in critical cases." "What do you mean by that?" asked the bishop. "In critical cases," said Hibbard, "I always advise them to send for a physician." His humor seemed not to interfere with, but to enhance his usefulness. It attracted hearers which perhaps nothing else could bring within his influence. His meetings were usually thronged. A tenacious Quaker hung about him, charmed with his conversation, but not venturing to attend his preaching, objecting that the custom of "Friends" required him to wear his hat in the congregation. Hibbard sent him a hearty invitation to come and wear his hat, or two of them if he wished, offering to lend him his own for the purpose if the good man would accept it. He could resist the charm no longer, went, and became a zealous Methodist, and a useful class leader.

Hibbard labored in the Church about fifty years, devotedly and successfully. He died in 1844, in great peace, and in the forty-sixth year of his itinerant ministry. He was a very genial man, humorous, amiable, without learning, yet abounding in intelligence, fond of anecdote, and exceedingly happy in telling one: surprisingly apt in laconic remarks, richly endowed with the spirit of piety, ever ready for religious conversation, a thorough lover of his country, and staunchly republican in his politics; a tireless laborer in the pulpit, and one of the most useful men in our early annals.

Samuel Merwin will not soon be forgotten among the Methodist Societies of the Atlantic States from Canada to Maryland. Dignified in person, powerful in eloquence, generous in spirit, and mighty in labors, he was one of the most popular preachers of his day. His ministry extended through about forty years, and have rendered his name familiar through the Northern and Middle Churches. His person was large and commanding, and his voice musical and strong, swaying the greatest assemblies. Exceedingly graceful in his movements and lively in his affections, he was a perfect Christian gentleman. He possessed superior powers of government, and discharged the functions of the presiding eldership with special ability. The invaluable talent of reconciling discordant brethren or Societies was his in a rare degree, and the kindly, sympathetic spirit which usually accompanies that talent characterized him everywhere, and imparted to his ministrations a richly consolatory character. His pulpit appeals were accompanied by a flowing and sweeping eloquence, sometimes rising to wonderful power and majesty, and the living evidences of his usefulness are yet found throughout the whole extent of his pastoral labors.

Few men were more prominent in the service of the Church during this period than Sylvester Hutchinson; but as he located the next year after its close, the Minutes give him no other record than his appointments. Yet he traveled seventeen years in New Jersey, Maryland, New York, New England. When he had charge of Pittsfield District, he was the presiding elder of the youthful Elijah Hedding, afterward bishop. Hedding always spoke of him in the highest terms. "The District," says Bishop Clark, in his Life of Hedding, "was of gigantic proportions, and the presiding eldership no sinecure in those early days. It embraced New York city, the whole of Long Island, and extended northward, embracing the whole territory, having the Connecticut River on the east and Hudson River and Lake Champlain on the west, and stretching far into Canada. It included nearly the whole territory now included within three annual conferences. Hutchinson was a man of burning zeal and indomitable energy. Mounted upon his favorite horse, he would ride through the entire extent of his District once in three months, visiting each Circuit, and invariably filling all his numerous appointments. His voice rung like a trumpet blast; and with words of fire, and in powerful demonstration of the Spirit, he preached Christ Jesus. He was a small man, but had a very strong voice, and seemed never to be wearied; he lived in the Spirit, and was constantly ready for every good word and work."

With such itinerants were associated in the northern field, in these years, many congenial men: Garrettson, Bostwick, Arnold, Jewel, Draper, Crowell, Sawyer, M'Claskey, Morrell, Ostrander, Michael Coate, Jayne, Moriarty, Ryan, and others. The revivals which have been noticed as prevailing in the south and middle parts of the country, extended up the Hudson, and spread westward to the New York Lakes, and eastward over New England, greatly recruiting the Societies and the ministry. Joseph Sawyer, whom we shall soon meet in Canada, preached, in 1798, a discourse of great effect in Petersburgh, N. Y., under which Ebenezer Washburn, a school teacher, was awakened. He hastened to the nearest Society, in Hoosack, and joined it. His wife and several of his neighbors were converted, and they formed the first class in Petersburgh. Washburn became one of the holiest and most useful of the early itinerants. He began his successful career by exhorting among his neighbors, and it was not long before he reported thirty converts on the Petersburgh mountains. This was the beginning of nearly half a century of ministerial labors, sufferings, and triumphs. Before the end of our period Methodism was successfully planted in Troy. A class was formed there as early as 1801, but it had nearly expired, when, in 1804, John Wright, a lay Methodist, moving to the city, inquired for his brethren, and found "a small company worshiping in a private house." In three or four years they were able to build a humble temple in State-street. It became the headquarters of a "charge," including Troy, Albia, West Troy, Lansingburgh, and Brunswick, but for twelve or fifteen years the whole membership hardly exceeded one hundred. Troy now gives name to a powerful Conference. In 1802 William Anson was sent to plant the Church on Grand Isle, in Lake Champlain. He extended his Circuit to other islands, and even into Canada, and at the close of the year reported more than a hundred Church members. Before the end of the century Methodism had got a permanent footing in Warren County, near the head of the Hudson, a locality then called "Thurman's Patent." Josiah Woodward and Samuel Crane, with their families, formed the nucleus of the Society which gave origin at last to the "old Thurman Circuit." The first information they ever received of Methodism was the news of the drowning of Richard Jacobs, who, as we have seen, perished in Schroon Lake, while traversing, as an evangelist, this distant wilderness. His death led to inquiries about the "new sect;" the settlers were excited with curiosity to see and hear an itinerant. Henry Ryan arrived there in 1798, and lodged with Crane. Woodward invited him to preach at his neighboring house. Ryan stayed long enough to form a class, comprising these two families, seven members in all. The little Society was attached to the nearest Circuit, and supplied with preaching once in four weeks. Another class was soon formed at Johnsburgh, "and thus Methodism was introduced into that town." Subsequently "Thurman's Patent" became "Thurman Circuit," extending through ten towns, and comprehending all the Methodism in that region; it has, still later, grown to half a dozen Circuits.

Meanwhile the denomination was extending its lines in the interior regions of the Pennsylvania mountain valleys and New York lakes. In the spring of 1797 Colbert returned to the Wyoming Valley, and went preaching from settlement to settlement, attended by the old hardships and demonstrations of his ministry. He goes to Canandaigua, Seneca Lake, etc., and encounters great difficulties. "A man," he says, "needs to have a good constitution and a large stock of patience to travel this Circuit. May the Lord bless me with the latter!" He is sick also with chills and fever, the effect of his exposures, but drives on in his work. Numerous Societies are organized, the beginning of the Methodism that now flourishes in all the region like its rich harvests. The Circuit extended from the Skaneateles to the Canandaigua Lakes. Colbert names but two small villages upon it, Geneva and Canandaigua, and in neither of these had he yet permanent "appointments."

In 1798 he was again on Wyoming and Northumberland Circuits. The Conference rightly judged that he was the man for the mountains. The next year this interior field was rearranged, the northern portion being connected with a District that comprehended Albany and the Mohawk region, under the presiding eldership of William M'Lenahan. There were three Circuits: Seneca, with Jonathan Bateman for preacher; Tioga, with John Leach and David Dunham; Wyoming and Northumberland, with James Moore, Benjamin Bidlack, and David Stevens. These evangelists did valiant service; Bidlack especially was a noted hero, and was here in his own field. He had been in the Revolutionary army, being at Boston when Washington took command, and at Yorktown when Cornwallis surrendered; had been noted "for fun and frolic," for his love of strong drink and "good fellowship," and yet had a singular reverence for religion. He would attend gravely the preaching of the early evangelists, however drunk he might be at the time. "He sometimes sung with great gusto, and even raised the tune, when he could hardly stand without holding on to something." He once appeared in the congregation with his usual gravity, but with a bottle of rum in his pocket, its long neck visible to all around. Anthony Turck, a Dutch itinerant, fiery with zeal, and "bold as a lion," saw him, and poured forth a terrible denunciation against drunkenness. The congregation were alarmed, for they knew Bidlack's courage; but he trembled under the word, and "instead of resenting the attack, went home stung with remorse." He publicly confessed his vices, repented, became a Methodist, and, before long, was traveling with the itinerants, one of their most flaming fellow-laborers. He was a superior singer, an important advantage in the early ministry, and a preacher of acknowledged talents. "Bidlack has become a Methodist preacher rang through the country, and stirred up a mighty commotion." He was a gigantic man, over six feet high, with broad shoulders and strong limbs. He became at last the venerated "Father Bidlack," with white flowing locks, a face full of generous character, and universally beloved of the people. He died, in the peace of the Gospel, in 1843, aged eighty-seven years.

In 1800 Wyoming and Northumberland were attached to the Philadelphia District, under the presiding eldership of the veteran Joseph Everett, already familiar to us; while Oneida and Cayuga, Seneca and Tioga, were connected with the Albany District. Asa Smith, Bidlack, and Gruber were among the evangelists. "The word of God mightily grew and prevailed this year" throughout these regions, and the first meeting-house in Wilkesbarre was erected. The next year Owen was back again in this his old territory, where he had labored for about ten years. The evangelical blacksmith was in full strength, and kept all around him in motion. In 1800 the great revivals, prevailing in most other portions of the Church, swept over all this section; the societies rapidly enlarged, and nearly sixteen hundred members were reported from westward of the Albany and Saratoga Circuits. Powerful itinerants were traversing the country under M'Lenahan—Turck, Bidlack, Morris, Willy, Newman, Vredenburgh, Gruber, and others; and this year the first Methodist chapel within the limits of the Genesee Conference was erected at Sauquoit.

In 1802 Colbert became presiding elder of the Albany District, which took in all this county. His stentorian trumpet resounded all over it. The famous and erratic Lorenzo Dow broke into the region and worked mightily with the circuit evangelists. "He is tall," writes Colbert, "of a very slender form; his countenance is serene, solemn, but not dejected, and his words, or rather God's words delivered by him, cut like a sword." Colbert continued, through most of these years, to labor indefatigably in founding the Church throughout the interior parts of the State; he returned, in 1804, to Maryland, and took charge of the Chesapeake District. In this year we find Methodism well organized through all this new country, though strangely enough divided in its ecclesiastical arrangement among the New York, Philadelphia, and Baltimore Conferences. There was a "Genesee District," and we see already the forthcoming of the renowned "old Genesee Conference," and the mighty Methodism of interior and western New York. It is even now preparing to move westward of the Genesee River, where David Hamlin, a lay Methodist settler, is (in 1804) reading Wesley's sermons on Sundays to his neighbors in his own cabin, and waiting and watching for the coming of the itinerants. Of several of the stalwart evangelists who founded Methodism in these wilds I have already given some notices—of Owen, Mills, Colbert, Cook, Ware, Gruber, and Bidlack; but of most of them we have no other information than the vague but grateful traditions of the people, and the allusions of our early records. Anthony Turck was a rough German, who labored mightily for ten years, and died in the itinerancy, "a holy man," say the old Minutes; "indefatigable and successful;" James Paynter, a good preacher, a man of few words, exceedingly grave, yet as amiable, a great laborer, from these valleys to the valleys of Western Virginia; after preaching forty-eight years he died in Maryland, exclaiming, "I am not afraid to die;" Alward White, thirty-nine years in the ministry, a modest, unassuming, but acceptable preacher; Cornelius Mars, called "thundering Mars," for his manner of preaching; John Brodhead, of note in New England, now a young man of extraordinary power in the pulpit; he "hurled thunderbolts," says one of our authorities; Roger Benton, a "short, thickset man, a most excellent preacher," singularly "modest and meek," with a stentorian voice; he early broke down under his labors and exposures, and died in peace; John Leach, "a pious, circumspect man," of short and afflicted ministry, who died in "great peace" in New Jersey in 1802; James Moore, an Irishman of very precise manners, of shrewdness, and good preaching talents; David Stevens, from Baltimore, who "labored incessantly for the salvation of souls for thirty years, and," say the Minutes, "died full of faith and the Holy Ghost" in Maryland, 1825; James Polhamus, who spent twenty-six years in the ministry, popular, useful, a "great exhorter," his "appeals overwhelming," and "revivals following him wherever he went;" James Smith, called "Irish Jemmy," a "good preacher, but a little queer;" Morris Howe, "a great exhorter," twenty-seven years in the itinerancy, and spoken of as a very pathetic preacher; Robert Burch, brother to Thomas Burch, and his equal in the pulpit, excessively social, and abounding in Irish wit and true piety; Jonathan Newman, a great laborer, somewhat eccentric and vacillating, but honest and zealous, with a heavy voice, "capable of an immense compass; when he was fairly under way he slightly drew one corner of his mouth in the direction of his ear, and rolled out peal after peal, like the roaring of distant thunder;" Timothy Dewy, one of the founders of Methodism in New England, as well as New York, eccentric, firm to obstinacy, a grappler of theological problems, a great reader, and, it is said, "a profound thinker," often a tremendous preacher, "ardently pious, a true-hearted Methodist." These are but a portion of the primitive corps; their names are still precious to the elder Methodists that linger in the scenes of their hard toils. They were soon to be followed by men more familiar to our memory—Draper, Lane, Jewell, Ensign, Vannest, Puffer, Paddock, Bigelow, Chamberlayne, Fillmore, Lanning, Seager, Grant, Harmon, Mattison, Luckey, Peck, and other founders of the vigorous Conferences that now embody so much of the Methodism of interior New York and Pennsylvania.

Canadian Methodism still appertained to the New York Conference. It was considered, in fact, but an extension of that great interior field which we have just been surveying. Preachers of the interior, Draper, Jewell, and others, were laborers beyond the line. William Case, one of the first two presiding elders of the Genesee Conference, became a representative man of the Provincial Church, and for some time the Upper Province was an important portion of the territory of that Conference. We have traced its progress down to the close of 1796, and witnessed the labors and sufferings of Losee, Dunham, Coleman, Woolsey, Keeler, and Coate. In 1797 the Minutes record no additional laborers, nor indeed anything respecting its appointments. The historians of the Church assure us that great revivals prevailed among the settlements, chiefly through the instrumentality of Wooster, whose mighty ministry seemed to inflame its whole people.

In 1798 the itinerant band consisted of Dunham, Coate, Coleman, and Michael Coate. In 1799 the Minutes still show three Circuits, but eight hundred and sixty-six members. Michael Coate returns to the States; but Joseph Jewell enters the province, and takes charge of it as presiding elder. He was a good man, says one of our Canadian authorities, cheerful, fond of singing, and had the finest voice, it was said, that had ever been heard in the province. He went to Canada from Maryland, and braved its wintry storms for four years. By the next Conference nearly a thousand members (936) are enrolled. Samuel Coate and Coleman retire from the field, the latter after six years' toil in it; but he goes to encounter similar labors in Vermont. Dunham also disappears from the appointments, but settles in the country to become a useful local preacher. Four new laborers appear now on the roll: Joseph Sawyer, William Anson, James Herron, and Daniel Pickett. Sawyer began to travel, in the New York Conference, in 1797; he afterward itinerated in Massachusetts and Vermont, and, for a number of most useful years, devoted himself to this frontier work. He had led Washburn and Laban Clark into the Church, and was to find in the wilderness of Upper Canada Nathan Bangs, and send him forth on his long and memorable career of hardly rivaled services to American Methodism. Thirteen years Sawyer was a member of the Conference, four of them as a circuit preacher, four as presiding elder in Canada, the other five in the United States. He was a holy man, full of energy, of a vigorous mind, and great success.

NATHAN HALE [illegible]

In the next year he procured the erection of the first Methodist church in the Niagara country, where the faithful layman, Christian Warner, had long represented Methodism and entertained its preachers. There were now (1801) 1,159 Methodists in the province, and five circuits, supplied by ten preachers. Samuel Draper had come from the interior of New York, a man of excessive humor, but "in many places quite successful." Seth Crowell had come from New England; he was but about twenty years old, but of heroic character. Bangs says: "He was a young preacher of great zeal, and of the most indefatigable industry." Great revivals now prevailed, and as a consequence the returns of 1802 show more than fifteen hundred members, a gain of nearly three hundred and fifty in one year.

The important name of Nathan Bangs is now recorded on the roll of Canadian appointments. He was not only a public but a representative man in the Methodist Episcopal Church for more than half a century; during nearly sixty years he appeared almost constantly in its pulpits; he was the founder of its periodical literature, and of its "Conference course" of ministerial study, and one of the founders of its present system of educational institutions; the first missionary secretary appointed by its General Conference, the first clerical editor of its General Conference newspaper press, the first editor of its Quarterly Review, and, for many years, the chief editor of its monthly Magazine and its book publications; he may be pronounced the principal founder of the American literature of Methodism, a literature now remarkable for its extent, and of no inconsiderable intrinsic value. Besides his innumerable miscellaneous writings for its periodicals, he wrote more volumes in defense or illustration of his denomination than any other man, and became its recognized historian; he was one of the founders of its Missionary Society, wrote the Constitution and first Circular Appeal of that great cause, and through sixteen years, prior to the organization of its secretaryship as a salaried function, he labored indefatigably and gratuitously for the society as its vice-president, secretary, or treasurer, and during more than twenty years wrote all its annual reports. After his appointment as its resident secretary he devoted to it his entire energies, conducting its correspondence, seeking missionaries for it, planning its mission fields, pleading for it in the Churches, and representing it in the Conferences; and he was, withal, a man of profound piety, of universal charity, and much and admirable individuality. Few men, if any, have longer or more successfully labored to promote those great interests of the denomination which have given it consolidation and permanence.

Born in Connecticut, he had emigrated in his thirteenth year, with his family, to Stamford, N. Y., and thence, in his twenty-first year, as a school teacher and surveyor, to the Niagara region of Upper Cannada. He found a friend in Christian Warner, near St. Davids, and was brought under Methodist influence. In the month of August, 1801, about one year after he had joined the Church, and three months after he had been licensed as an exhorter, he received license to preach, and immediately departed for a circuit under the control of Sawyer. He labored from Quebec to Detroit, and received a thorough preliminary training for his subsequent eminent career in the States.

At the close of the period there were one district, seven circuits, ten preachers, and nearly eighteen hundred (1,787) members in the provincial Church. It had secured a permanent lodgment in both Canadas, though it could yet claim but little more than a hundred communicants in the lower province. Since our last notice of it, (in 1796,) it had advanced from seven hundred and ninety-five to one thousand seven hundred and eighty-seven members, gaining nearly a thousand, while its ministry had more than doubled. The period closed with the death of Barbara Heck, whose humble name will become increasingly illustrious with the lapse of ages, as associated with the founding of American Methodism in both the United States and British North America. She died at the residence of her son, Samuel Heck, in "front of Augusta," U. C., in 1804, aged seventy years. Her death was befitting her life. Her old German Bible, the guide of her youth in Ireland, her resource during the falling away of her people in New York, her inseparable companion in all her wanderings in the wildernesses of Northern New York and Canada, was her oracle and comfort to the last. She was found sitting in her chair dead, with the well-used and endeared volume open on her lap. And thus passed away this devoted and unpretentious woman, who so faithfully, yet unconsciously, laid the foundations of one of the grandest ecclesiastical structures of modern ages, and whose memory will probably last as "long as the sun and moon endure." The few Methodists of Canada who in 1804 bore her to her grave in the old Blue Churchyard, Augusta, might well have exclaimed, "What hath God wrought!" The cause which she had been instrumental in founding had already spread out from New York city over the whole of the United States, and over much of both Canadas. It comprised seven Annual Conferences, four hundred traveling preachers, and more than one hundred and four thousand members. But if we estimate its results in our day, we shall see that it has pleased God to encircle the name of this lowly woman with a halo of surpassing honor, for American Methodism has far transcended all other divisions of the Methodistic movement, and may yet make her name an endeared household word throughout the world.

CHAPTER XXV.

METHODISM IN THE EASTERN STATES: 1796–1804.

WE have traced the progress of Methodism in the Eastern States down to the Thompson (Conn.) Conference, held in September, 1796. Important laborers were now added to the small band of itinerants. John Brodhead's name, which we have incidentally met already, is endeared to the New England Church. He spent forty-four years in the ministry, forty-two of them in the East, laboring more or less in all the New England States. He was repeatedly elected to the Senate of New Hampshire and to Congress, yet was always personally averse to taking office; and though he spoke but seldom on political subjects, the soundness of his judgment, and the known purity of his life, gave much weight to his opinions. In the early days of his ministry he endured almost incredible fatigue and hardship in carrying the glad tidings of the Gospel to remote settlements, often swimming rivers on horseback, and preaching in his clothes saturated with water, till he broke down a naturally robust constitution and laid the foundation of disease, which affected him more or less during his after life. As a preacher, he possessed more than ordinary talents; his clear understanding, combined with quick sensibilities and a vivid imagination, could not but render him eloquent on the themes of religion. He was partial to the benigner topics of the Gospel, and often would his congregations and himself melt into tears under the inspiration of his subjects. When he treated on the divine denunciations of sin, it was with a solemnity, and at times with an awful grandeur, that overwhelmed his hearers. He was six feet in stature, with an erect and firmly-built frame. Though slight in person when young, in his maturer years he became robustly stout, and toward the end of his life somewhat corpulent, but retained to the last the dignified uprightness of his mein. His complexion was light, his features well defined, his forehead high and expanded, his eye dark, large, and glowing with the spontaneous benevolence of his spirit. In fine, his *tout ensemble* rendered him one of the noblest men in person, as he unquestionably was in character.

Timothy Merritt was "a prince and a great man in Israel." His judgment was remarkably clear and discriminating, grasping the subjects of its investigation in all their compass, and penetrating to their depths. He lacked fancy and imagination, but was thereby, perhaps, the better fitted for his favorite courses of thought—the investigation and discussion of the great doctrinal truths of religion. His predilection for such subjects was not a curious propensity to speculation, but an interest to ascertain and demonstrate the relations of fundamental tenets to experimental and practical piety. This was the distinguishing characteristic of his preaching. Like St. Paul, he delighted to discuss the "mystery of godliness," and illustrate its "greatness." Dangerous error shrunk in his presence. The doctrine of Christian perfection was his favorite theme, and he was a living example of it. "Holiness to the Lord was his constant motto," says his friend, Enoch Mudge. "When his physical energy gave way, his active mind felt the shock and totterings of the earthly tabernacle. This was the time for the more beautiful development of Christian resignation and submission. A calm submission spread a sacred halo over the closing scenes of life. Even here we had a chastened and melancholy pleasure in noticing the superiority of the mental and spiritual energies, which occasionally gleamed out over his physical imbecility and prostration. We saw a noble temple in ruins, but the divine Shekinah had not forsaken it." He did extraordinary service for Methodism. His preaching and devout life promoted it; he was continually writing for it, and some of his publications ranked high in its early literature; he was a champion in its antislavery contests, and was active in its efforts for missions and education. No man of his day had more prominence in the Eastern Churches for either the excellence of his life or the importance of his services.

After his visit to Virginia, Lee resumed his labors in the East at the beginning of 1797. His District comprised the whole Methodist field in Maine, New Hampshire, Vermont, Rhode Island, and Massachusetts, except two western Circuits in the latter; Ostrander, Pickering, Brodhead, Mudge, Snethen, and other strong men were under his guidance. He traversed his immense district with his usual rapidity, proclaiming the word, encouraging the preachers in the privations and toils of the remoter circuits, comforting feeble Churches, and inspiriting them to struggle with persecutions and poverty, to erect chapels, and spread themselves out into adjacent neighborhoods.

About September, 1797, Asbury sick and worn out with labors, was pursuing his way toward the East, to attend the New England Conference, which was to sit at Wilbraham on the 19th of that month; but on arriving at New Rochelle, N. Y., he was unable to go farther. He was "swelling in the face, bowels, and feet," and only after two weeks could he place his foot on the ground. On September 12th, when he was able to walk but once or twice across the room, he wrote a letter to Lee, instructing him to preside at the Wilbraham Conference, believing it would be impossible for himself to reach it. Though depressed with disease and exhaustion, his heart glowed with the idea of the great cause for which he labored. "Methodism," he exclaims in his letter, "is union all over: union in exchange of preachers; union in exchange of sentiments; union in exchange of interest: we must draw resources from the center to the circumference." Notwithstanding the arrangement made with Lee, the tireless bishop was on his route for Wilbraham the day after the date of his letter, but was unable to proceed, and returned to his comfortable lodgings at New Rochelle, where he went to bed with a high fever. He was disabled for several weeks, and "distressed at the thought of a useless and idle life." "Lord help me," he exclaims, "for I am poor and needy; the hand of God hath touched me." Lee proceeded to take his place at the Conference.

The labors of the year had been successful; extensive revivals had occurred on several of the Circuits. There was a gain of three Circuits. The returns of members amounted to 3,000, lacking one, showing an increase of 480—about one fourth of the gains of the whole Church for this year. Both the aggregate and the increase were doubtless larger, for there are no returns from Vermont, though a long Circuit had been formed within that State, and one of the New York Circuits, also, reached into it and included several incipient Societies.

On the 19th of September, 1797, the New England Conference convened, a second time, in Wilbraham, Mass. Lee presided, and made the appointments for the ensuing year. Five of the preachers located this year, broken down in health, or tired of the severities of an itinerant life; but able men, Shadrach Bostwick, Michael Coate, Peter Jayne, William Thacher, and others, took their places. Immediately after the Wilbraham Conference, Lee, agreeably to the vote of that body and the request of Asbury, hastened to New Rochelle, N. Y., where the bishop was awaiting him. Thence they journeyed southward, as we have seen, through all the Atlantic States as far as Georgia. Lee returned to New York, laboring night and day on the way, and on the 9th of July, 1798, left that city again for New England. On his route, Asbury and Joshua Wells overtook him. They pressed forward, holding meetings almost daily, through Rhode Island and Massachusetts into the heart of Maine. At Readfield they proposed to hold the first Conference in the province. The ecclesiastical year 1797-8 had been the most prosperous one recorded thus far in the history of Eastern Methodism. Extensive revivals had prevailed, and the struggling cause had everywhere advanced, augmenting its membership by more than one third. Many new Societies had been organized in all the New England States, several chapels erected, and a large band of local preachers formed and brought into effective co-operation with the traveling ministry. The plans, which had hitherto been incipient, now began to develop their power and results. There was a growing consciousness of stability and vigor in the new communion, of no small importance to its efficiency; and the doctrines of Methodism—so liberal and yet so vital—began to be more generally approved, except by those who were officially interested in the maintenance of the theology which had hitherto prevailed. The returns of members amounted to 4,155, a gain of 1,216. Connecticut had 1,455; Rhode Island, 162; Massachusetts, 1,194; Maine, 936; New Hampshire, 122; Vermont, 286. Connecticut had gained 254; Rhode Island had lost 15; Massachusetts had gained 281; Maine, 320; New Hampshire, 30; Vermont, (which had made no previous returns,) 286. The aggregate increase in New England this year was more than three times as great as that of all the rest of the Church throughout the republic and Canada. The local preachers scattered among the Societies amounted about this time to twenty-five at least. With such results the laborious itinerants gathered, with grateful hearts and good courage, at their Conferences at Readfield and Granville, in order to plan the work of another year.

The former is memorable as the first Methodist Conference held in Maine. It began the 29th of August, and was an occasion of no ordinary interest. Methodism, though recent in the province, had taken profound hold on the sympathies of the settlers, and hundreds flocked to the small village of Readfield to witness the first assembly of its pioneers in their new and wilderness country. The place was thronged with the devout, who came to enjoy the spiritual advantages of the occasion, and the worldly, who were there to reap gain from it. "Several came," says Lee, "in their carts, with cakes, etc., to sell. No one interrupted us in the meeting-house, but many were walking to and fro, and paid no attention to the meetings." The session lasted two days, Wednesday and Thursday. Ten preachers were present: Timothy Merritt, John Brodhead, Robert Yalleley, Aaron Humphrey, Roger Searle, Joshua Taylor, Jesse Stoneman, Enoch Mudge, and John Finnegan; Asbury made the tenth. Wednesday was a "great day," says Asbury. The Conference began its usual business very early, and closed it by eight o'clock A. M., in order that the rest of the time might be devoted to public exercises. An immense throng had gathered in the village. At nine o'clock the doors of the new and yet unfinished chapel (the first erected in Maine) were thrown open for the "large number of

Methodists, and none else." Shut in from the throng, they held a love-feast together. Representatives of their common cause were there from all the surrounding regions, and from several distant places. "It was a good time," says Lee; "they spoke freely and feelingly" of their Christian experience, and renewed their vows with God and each other. The multitude without heard their fervent ejaculations and exhilarating melodies, and waited impatiently for the public services.

At eleven o'clock the doors were opened. From "one thousand to eighteen hundred souls," says Asbury, attempted to get into the building; it was a solid mass of human beings. The galleries, which were yet unfinished, cracked and broke under the pressure, producing much alarm, and slightly injuring a few; but the services proceeded. Asbury ascended the rude pulpit and addressed his itinerant brethren from 2 Cor. iv, 1, 2: "Therefore, seeing we have this ministry, as we have received mercy, we faint not," etc. Well could their great leader, bearing in his own person the marks of his excessive labors, exhort the pioneers of Methodism in Maine to "faint not" in their extraordinary privations and toils. They gathered strength from the veteran's words, and welcomed the daily journeys, the incessant preaching, the wintry storms, and the spiritual victories of another year. Lee tells us that the bishop waxed "strong and courageous." The ordination services followed, and were witnessed with great interest by the throng.

The ordination being over, Lee, whose heart was full, mounted the pulpit, and proclaimed to the multitude of Methodists present, "The God of peace shall bruise Satan under your feet shortly." Rom. xvi, 20. A divine influence fell upon the assembly; tears flowed in all parts of the house. He could not but feel profoundly under the associations of the scene; only five years before he wandered a solitary evangelist through the province, without a single Methodist to welcome him; now multitudes of them were rising up over its length and breadth, and spreading into bands, and these were but the beginnings of a great work, which he unwaveringly believed would go on prosperously through all time. There was still another exercise before they dispersed. They partook of the Lord's Supper together. It was, Lee tells us, "a most solemn time. I stood astonished," he exclaims, "at the sight! to see so many people at the Lord's table, when it is not quite five years since we came into this part of the world."

Thus closed the first Conference in Maine. The preachers immediately hastened to their appointments. Asbury was away the same day. Lee tarried to complete some unfinished business, "thankful to God for the privilege of being at the first Conference ever held in the province."

The Conference at Granville began on Wednesday, September 19, 1798, three weeks after the session at Readfield. It was the largest assemblage of Methodist preachers which had ever been convened in New England, about fifty being present, many of them from the neighboring Circuits of New York. Ten new preachers were received at this session. "Praise the Lord, O my soul!" exclaims Lee as he records the fact. Among these young men were Epaphras Kibby, Daniel Webb, Asa Heath, and also those two remarkable men, so generally known alike for their great labors and great eccentricities, Billy Hibbard and Lorenzo Dow, the latter after no little opposition, as we have seen. Twelve were ordained. The public services were impressive; Lee speaks of "a blessed time in preaching," when preachers and people were melted into tears. The Conference closed on Friday, 21; the next day Asbury and Lee "began their flight," as the latter calls it. They were accompanied by twelve of the preachers, who had been designated to the neighboring Circuits of New York. By Sunday afternoon they had crossed the boundary, and the bishop was preaching the same evening at Dover.

Daniel Webb became the oldest effective Methodist preacher in the world. He early heard Mudge, Pickering, Bostwick, and Merritt, and often had serious reflections. At length, he writes, "A young woman, a member of the Methodist Episcopal Church, came to my father's house to work as a tailoress. She was faithful to her Lord, and religion was the theme of her conversation. Having an opportunity one day, she said to me, 'My young friend, what do you think of religion?' I replied, 'I think it to be a good and a necessary thing for all persons before they die.' 'Then,' said she, 'what objection have you to seeking it now?' 'If I could have my young companions with me I should be willing to seek it now,' I replied. She then said, 'My dear friend, do not wait for your companions; you may perhaps be in your grave before they will turn to the Lord.' These words were as a nail in a sure place. They arrested my attention. I was led to cry the more for mercy; and in about four weeks from the time of her faithfulness to me, in a little prayer-meeting, the Lord spoke peace to my soul; and the next day, in a woods, he gave me a sealing evidence of my acceptance with him, and I went on my way rejoicing. This was in the year 1797, and in the month of August."

In less than a year he was "exhorting" on the Circuit. Bostwick called him out to Middletown Circuit, (Conn.,) and there he preached his first sermon. In 1798, received by the Conference, he was appointed to Granville Circuit, which was then two hundred miles in circumference. "We had," he writes, "to cross the Green Mountains twice in each round. I frequently had to dismount my horse, and break through the snowbanks to get him along. We preached almost every day, besides visiting, and attending prayer and class meetings, so that our labors were very considerable." His subsequent appointments were in various parts of Massachusetts, Maine, and Rhode Island, and he lived, beloved and venerated for his unblemished character and long services, down to 1867, when he died in the full assurance of hope. He was noted for the brevity, perspicuity, systematic arrangement, and evangelical richness of his discourses, his unpretending but cordial manners, and his steadfast interest for his Church.

Epaphras Kibby survived down to our day, one of the patriarchs of the New England itinerants. He was converted under the ministry of George Roberts. "One sermon," he writes, "from this powerful, eloquent man was all-sufficient, under the Divine Spirit, to rouse my guilty soul, and to extort the cry, 'What shall I do to be saved?'" This was in 1793;

and in the sixteenth year of his age. In 1798 he was pressed into the itinerant service at the Granville Conference, though he had never attempted to preach a sermon, but had only "exhorted." "Go, my son," said Asbury to him, "and God be with you. Do the best you can; an angel cannot do better." His first appointment was on Sandwich Circuit, Mass., and thus began one of the longest ministerial careers in our annals. He traveled in Massachusetts, Rhode Island, New Hampshire, and Maine. He formed the first Methodist society in New Bedford, Mass., and also in Hallowell, Me., and occupied, with distinction, the stations of Boston, Portland, and New Bedford. He suffered the early hardships of the Maine Circuits courageously, and helped effectually to lay the foundations of Methodism through much of that country at the beginning of the century. When appointed there in 1800, it seemed a distant and appalling field to him; but he was accompanied and cheered on his way by a convoy of brave-spirited itinerants, Merritt, Heath, Webb, and others, all bound to eastern circuits. When he arrived he found a vast sphere of labor before him on Readfield Circuit. He preached and traveled every day, except one Saturday in each month. Frequently he was obliged to cross frozen streams when the ice would not bear his horse; but while he himself walked upon it, the latter, led by his hand, had to break a way, cutting himself with ice, and coming forth exhausted and bloody from the struggle. In other seasons these streams had to be forded or swam, often at the risk of life. In those remote regions he usually slept in log-cabins, through the roofs of which the stars shone upon his slumbers and the snow fell upon his bed, forming a cover by morning several inches thick. Again his spirit sunk within him. Such exposures and labors seemed impracticable; he felt that he must retreat, but God interposed for him. When about to give up in despair, a marvelous revival broke out in the Circuit; he took fresh courage and went on his way rejoicing.

This event was of too remarkable a character to be omitted here. While doubting and praying, respecting his duty to remain any longer, a young gentleman of Monmouth, of high position in society, heard him accidentally at a neighboring village, and on returning home reported among his neighbors an exalted opinion of the young preacher's talents and character, and particularly urged his own wife to go and hear him when he should arrive in their town. He himself made no pretensions to piety; his lady had been deeply serious some time before, but had apparently lost her religious convictions. Kibby went to Monmouth to preach in the Congregational Church. As he sat in the desk waiting, a divine afflatus seemed to descend on him and the gathering people. He has been heard to say that he never before nor since witnessed a more direct and remarkable agency of the Spirit of God. A well-dressed lady arrived, and took a seat, tremblingly, near the door, but where the whole assembly saw her. Without an audible expression her countenance and demeanor exhibited unutterable feeling, and the whole audience soon seemed to share it. The preacher proceeded with his discourse with unusual interest and solemnity. As he advanced, exhibiting the mercy of God, the feeling of awe which had hitherto absorbed the assembly seemed to change, a glad and grateful emotion sped through the mass, a bright and glowing expression shone on their faces; and the lady, with streaming tears and overflowing heart, found peace with God, and seemed transfigured before them. When they rose to sing, she fell insensible under her intense feelings; her husband, near her, was smitten down, and dropped upon his seat; the presence of God seemed to overshadow the place, and the assembly was overwhelmed. The lady herself became a devoted member of the Church; her husband, General M'Clellan, was the man who invited Kibby. He subsequently was converted, and their family was long known on the Kennebec for its affluent and Christian hospitality, and its devotion to the interests of Methodism. It afterward became the germ of the Methodist Church in Bath. The influence of this remarkable meeting spread like a flame through the town and neighboring villages, and, indeed, more or less over the Circuit. The sinking heart of the preacher was fortified forever.

These scenes at Monmouth led to the introduction of Methodism into Hallowell. A young man at the former, but belonging to the latter, entreated Kibby to visit the town and preach to its inhabitants. He consented, passed into the village, procured a school-house, and had a large congregation; but at the end of the service his hearers all retired, leaving him alone without an invitation to any of their homes, or an intimation of their approval or disapproval of his doctrines. He felt disappointed, mortified, and mounting his horse rode four miles to Augusta for a supper, believing that he had erred in going to Hallowell. On arriving at Augusta, some gentlemen of high respectability, who admired his talents, appointed a meeting for him in a hall. When he entered it he found an apparently selected audience. After the sermon one of the hearers rose and said, "I approve these doctrines and esteem this man;" and throwing a dollar on the table he added, "you, gentleman, may do likewise." A shower of silver dollars came down upon the table; the preacher refused them, but he was urged and compelled to receive them. It was no superfluous bounty, but a most opportune providence, meeting necessities which could hardly have otherwise been sustained. But a more cheering incident followed. Before he left the hall he was compensated, somewhat, for his mortifying treatment at Hallowell. A man, trembling with emotion, took him by the hand and inquired, "When, sir, are you coming again to Hallowell?" "Never, sir," replied the preacher. "Do, do come once more," rejoined the stranger, with tears, "for your discourse there to-day has awakened my guilty soul." Unexpected results of one day!

Kibby saw the hand of God in these things. He sent back by the stranger an appointment at Hallowell for four weeks afterward, the time of his next return to that part of the Circuit. When he arrived he found that the awakened man had been converted. The house was crowded, and he was embarrassed with invitations to hospitable homes; he tarried the next day, and spent it in visiting from house to house, and nearly every family he called upon he found under the awakening influence of the Divine Spirit. A revival broke out which spread through the whole population, and the first

Methodist Society of Hallowell was formed. The two first persons, a man and his wife, converted in this extraordinary reformation, presented their two sons to him for baptism. They were twins, and scarcely distinguishable. He offered them specially to God in prayer by that holy rite. One of them now sleeps in his grave in Africa, the first foreign missionary of the Methodist Episcopal Church. The other became a preacher of Methodism in New England.

In 1841 he was reported among the "superannuated" in the New England Conference, and remained on that honored roll till his death in 1865, when he departed, exclaiming, "Glory to God! glory to God!" after a ministry of sixty-seven years. He was tall, erect, and slight in person, extremely neat in dress, and venerable in appearance. His talents were of a very superior order. His imagination furnished him with vivid illustrations, always abundant, chaste, and appropriate; his reasoning was strikingly perspicuous, direct, and conclusive; his language remarkable for both elegance and force.

Joshua Soule, though not named in the Minutes till the next year, began to travel about this time, under the presiding elder of Maine District. About 1795 his family removed to Avon, then a recent settlement on Sandy River; the Readfield Circuit extended to this remote frontier, and Enoch Mudge and other traveling evangelists occasionally penetrated to it, sounding the word of life among its sparse habitations. "The settlement," says Mudge, "was new, and his father's house unfinished. Joshua had a precocious mind, a strong memory, a manly and dignified turn, although his appearance was exceedingly rustic." Youthful and untutored as he was, the doctrines of the Gospel, as exhibited by the preachers of Methodism, arrested his attention, and commended themselves to his opening intellect. In June, 1797, after seeking reconciliation with God through Jesus Christ, with a broken and contrite heart, he found peace in believing. The Divine Spirit selected and anointed him for signal achievements in the Church. Joshua Taylor, who was presiding elder in Maine about this time, perceived beneath the rudeness and rusticity of his appearance those elements of promise which have since distinguished his career, and encouraged him immediately to enter upon his ministerial labors. He was then (1798) but about seventeen years of age. He accompanied Taylor around the district, exhorting after his sermons, exciting general interest by his youth and devotion, and not a little by the contrast which he presented of rustic awkwardness with extraordinary though unpolished talents. He labored hard and rose rapidly in the ministry. In 1804 he took charge of and traveled two years as presiding elder the District of Maine. This was the only District in the province at that period; he had, therefore, the oversight of the entire Methodist interest of that large section of New England. Thirteen Circuits were under his superintendence. His sermons at this time are reported to have been distinguished by that breadth of view and majesty of style which, in later years, notwithstanding some abatement through the variety of his responsibilities, continued to mark with greatness his pulpit efforts. His word was oftentimes in irresistible power, bearing down upon the large assemblies which collected to hear him like the storm on the bending forest. He shared fully, during his presiding eldership in Maine, the sufferings of the early itinerancy: long journeys on horseback, over new roads, through vast forests, in the storms of winter; fording dangerous streams, lodging in exposed log-cabins, preaching almost daily, and receiving a pecuniary compensation scarcely sufficient for traveling expenses and clothing. These were the tests, however, which made strong men of the Methodist preachers of that day. He continued to travel in Maine and Massachusetts till 1816, when he was appointed Book Agent at New York. He did good service for the Church in this capacity during four years, especially by the publication of the Methodist Magazine, the appearance of which, "even at this late period," says the historian of the Church, "was hailed by the friends of literature and religion as the harbinger of brighter days to our Zion." Bangs took Soule's place at the Book Rooms in 1820, and the latter was stationed in New York city, where he labored two years with Hunt, Hibbard, Spicer, and Summerfield. The following two years he spent in Baltimore, and in

J. Pine pinx

J.F.E. Prudhomme Sc.

1824 was elected to the episcopacy in the forty-third year of his age and the twenty-sixth of his ministry. For forty-three years he sustained the onerous responsibilities of that office, traversing the continent from the Penobscot in Maine to the Colorado in Texas, presiding in Conferences, visiting in long and perilous journeys the Indian Missions, and energetically laboring, by the many facilities of his position, for the promotion of the Church.

In the discussions of the General Conference of 1844, which resulted in the division of the Church, he attached himself to the party formed by the representatives of the South. He was erect, tall, and slight in person, and dignified in his bearing; his forehead high, but narrow, his voice strong and commanding. In the pulpit he was slow, and long in his sermons—usually occupying an hour and a half for each; elaborate, almost entirely destitute of imagination or figurative illustrations, but strongly fortified in the main positions of his subject, and vigorous in his style. His discourses showed more breadth than depth, but were often overwhelmingly impressive. The dignity of his bearing, frequently verging on majesty itself, gave to his sermons, at times, an imposing solemnity; but on occasions less congruous with it, had the disadvantage of appearing, to the fastidious at least, pompous and repulsive. He did great services and endured great privations for Methodism. Northern Methodists, however they may regret his later measures, will ever recall him with gratitude and respect as one of their veteran pioneers, and a noble son of their soil. He died, near Nashville, Tenn., March 6, 1867, in the full assurance of faith.

There was no Conference in New England in 1799; the New York Conference made the appointments for the Eastern States. Elijah Hedding, though his name does not appear in the Minutes till a later date, commenced traveling this year by the direction of the presiding elder. He was born in Duchess County, N. Y., June 7, 1780, but removed with his parents, at about his tenth year, to Starksborough, Vt. The Methodist itinerants had not yet penetrated thither; but an aged Methodist and his wife, a "mother in Israel," had removed to that town from Connecticut, and, though remote from any members of their chosen communion, and several miles from any church whatever, they let their light so shine that their neighbors saw their good works, and glorified their Father which is in heaven. The Church is indebted for the services of this distinguished man to the instrumentality of that elect lady. Meetings were opened in her humble dwelling two or three years before the arrival of the itinerants. There was no one in the neighborhood, at first, capable of praying in public, except herself and her husband, who was a devoted Christian of moderate abilities. They induced young Hedding, then about sixteen years old, to assist them in their Sabbath services. Though uninterested in religion, he consented to read a sermon every Sunday to the assembled neighbors, the good man of the house beginning and concluding the exercises with singing and prayer. His first permanent religious impressions were produced by the conversations of the Christian matron. Joseph Mitchell, a man mighty in word and in doctrine, opportunely visited the place. Hedding heard him preach, his convictions were deepened, and as he returned to his home he retired into a forest, and, kneeling down by a large tree, covenanted with God to live and die in his service, whatever might be the sacrifice involved in the resolution. Soon after he heard Mitchell again; the discourse was one of remarkable power; it disclosed to him, in a manner he had never yet perceived, the exceeding sinfulness of sin, and the peril of the unrenewed soul. He looked with longing solicitude for the next visit of the itinerant evangelist, who soon arrived and preached in the house where the youthful penitent had been accustomed to read the sermons of Wesley. After the discourse a class meeting was held, as usual, by the preacher. On ascertaining the deep convictions of young Hedding, he proposed that special prayer should be made in his behalf; the itinerant and the pious cottagers bowed around him, and continued in supplications till peace dawned on his troubled spirit. This was on the 27th of December, 1798.

It was not long before he was licensed to exhort, and in about a year he was sent by the presiding elder to Essex Circuit, Vt., to supply the place of the eccentric Lorenzo Dow, who, after traveling and laboring with incredible diligence, had departed under a supposed divine impression to preach in Ireland. Hedding continued three months on the Circuit, exhorting, without a text, at all the appointments, holding a public meeting and leading a class daily. His word was in demonstration of the Spirit and of power, and revivals broke out around the whole Circuit. He soon after received license as a local preacher, and at the Conference of 1801 was accepted on probation, and dispatched to Plattsburgh. In 1802 he was appointed to Fletcher Circuit, a large field of labor, extending from Onion River, Vt., on the south, fifteen or twenty miles beyond the Canada line, and including the settlements east of Lake Champlain and west of the Green Mountains. Here he had to travel three hundred miles a month, preach once, and often twice, daily, besides attending classes and prayer-meetings. His colleague was Henry Ryan, "a brave Irishman," he says, a man, who labored as if the judgment thunders were to follow each sermon. The route of the Circuit was in the form of the figure eight. The two preachers usually met at the point of intersection, when Ryan, hastily saluting his young fellow-laborer, would exclaim as he passed, "Drive on! drive on, brother! let us drive the devil out of the land!" a significant though rough expression of the tireless energy which characterized the itinerant ministry of that day. Here, likewise, were encountered all the privations and exposures of a recent country; bad roads, long drives in wintry storms, through forests bound in ice, and sleepless nights spent in cabins through which the winds whistled and the rain dropped. More serious trials attended them and their successors in this region. In some places Hedding was hooted and threatened in the streets; Dow was struck in the face; Abner Wood was horsewhipped; and Elijah Sabin severely wounded on the head by the butt-end of a whip. Still they prevailed; their persecutors were often marvelously awakened, and now peaceful and prosperous Churches are spread all over that region, the fruits of the toils and sufferings of Hedding and his co-laborers. He continued to travel on circuits and districts in almost all parts of the East down to 1824, when he was elevated to the episcopate. The whole nation became his field. He stood firmly at his post in days of strife and peril, and aided in conducting the Church through exigencies which made the stoutest hearts tremble. From the time he commenced proclaiming the truth in the wilds of New Hampshire and Canada, he never wavered in the hope that God designed Methodism for enduring and universal triumphs.

Bishop Hedding, as remembered by most of the Church, was tall, stout, and dignified in person; his locks white with age, his face remarkable for its benign and intelligent expression, and his *tout ensemble* most venerable and impressive. His manners were marked by perfect simplicity and ease. In the pulpit he was always perspicuous, lucid, and instructive. His discourses were precisely arranged, delivered moderately, in a style of extreme plainness, and frequently with passages of affecting pathos. He was distinguished for his accuracy in the doctrines and discipline of Methodism, the exact discrimination of his judgment, the extraordinary tenacity of his memory, the permanence of his friendships, and his invariable prudence. The ecclesiastical year 1799–1800 included thirteen months, and had been attended with gratifying prosperity. There were now in Connecticut 1,571 Methodists; in Rhode Island, 227; Massachusetts, 1,577; Maine, 1,197; New Hampshire, 171; Vermont, 1,096; total 5,839.

We have reached the date of a new century, of the organization of the New England Conference by its separation from that of New York, and of the retirement of Lee, the chief hero of this part of our narrative, from the eastern field. We have seen him, solitary and friendless, begin his mission in New England by proclaiming "Ye must be born again," on the highway of Norwalk, June 17, 1789; eleven years have passed, years of vast labors, sore trials, of poverty and perplexity, yet of triumph. A host of great evangelists have entered the field: Roberts, Smith, Bloodgood, Mills, Hunt, Taylor, Mudge, Pickering, Ostrander, Mitchell, M'Combs, Brodhead, Merritt, Sabin, Bostwick, Beauchamp, Coate, Soule, Hedding, Kibby, Webb, and many others who were "mighty through God." They have confounded opposition, have preached the word "in demonstration of the Spirit and of power," from Fairfield in Connecticut to the furthest eastern settlement of Maine, and from Provincetown in Massachusetts to St. Albans in Vermont. They have laid securely the foundations of Methodism in the New England States, and at the close of eleven years we behold it spread into bands, comprising nearly fifty preachers and more than five thousand eight hundred members, an average of about one hundred and twenty to each preacher, and these members and preachers distributed over four Districts and thirty-one Circuits.

In the remainder of the period Asbury, accompanied by Whatcoat, made repeated tours through the Eastern States, penetrating to the interior of Maine. Their visits were high festivals to the young Churches, and the Conference sessions, especially, were jubilees. Lee also, in the summer of 1800, re-entered the great field for the last time, except a hasty visit some eight years later. It was his general leave-taking. He passed through its whole extent into Canada, and back by the Hudson, preaching farewell sermons amid the benedictions and tears of the people. His fellow-laborers and fellow-sufferers in the itinerancy parted with him, from place to place, with the deepest feeling, as from a hero who had led them to victory, and had secured for them the hard-fought field. During this circuitous and rapid journey his preaching averaged more than one sermon a day; he was continually occupied also in social prayer and counsels with the Societies. He now leaves New England to pursue his evangelic course, with unabated heroism, in other sections. The foundations of Methodism had been laid by him in all the Eastern States; a large Conference had been organized; chapels had sprung up; a powerful ministry was moving to and fro, proclaiming the "great salvation" through extended but organized Circuits, and thousands of converts were recorded on the roll of the Church. A great work had been achieved, and a great man had left his stamp upon the ecclesiastical history of all New England. His name, until recently, had been but little noted beyond the pale of his own denomination; but his instrumentality is developing broader and broader results as time elapses, and the future ecclesiastical historian of these Eastern States will place him among the foremost men of their religious annals.

The remaining four years were abundant in itinerant reinforcements: Daniel Fidler, a laborer from Virginia and the Redstone country, to Nova Scotia, and at last a patriarch of the New Jersey Conference; Ebenezer F. Newhall, an apostle of those memorable times; Philip Munger and Asa Heath, veterans of Maine Conference; Asa Kent, a patriarch of Providence Conference, and indeed of all New England, still remembered by many for the sanctity of his life, his small stature, halting gait, wenned neck, and grave aspect; Samuel Hillman, long a hard worker in Maine; Oliver Beale, a saint in the calendar of the Church; and many others equally worthy.

Thomas Branch was now a faithful and eminent itinerant, whose health broke down at last under the severities of the climate. He proposed to go to the southwest, and labor, while his dwindling strength should last, in the Western Conference, the only Conference then beyond the Alleghanies. He took leave of his Eastern brethren in much debility, and departed on horseback, with the usual itinerant accompaniment, the saddle-bags for his few books and rations, to penetrate through the forests to Marietta, on the Ohio. He never arrived, however; on passing from the western wilds of New York, down toward Ohio, along the southern shore of Lake Erie, he disappeared. News came at last that he had died somewhere among the log-cabins in the then remote forest of the northwestern angle of Pennsylvania; but even this vague information reached not most of those to whom he was dear in New England till fifteen years later, when one of his old fellow-laborers at the East, who had, meanwhile, been elevated to the episcopate, was pursuing his official visitations at the West, and accidentally discovering the place of his decease, sent home for publication information of his fate. "He fell," wrote his friend, "in the wilderness, on his way to this country, in the month of June, 1812. His grave is in the woods, in the state of Pennsylvania, near the shore of Lake Erie, between the states of New York and Ohio. As I came through that part of the country I made inquiry respecting the sickness, death, and burial of our once beloved fellow-laborer in the cause of Christ. An intelligent friend, who said he had frequently visited and watched with him in his last sickness, and attended his funeral, gave me, in substance, the following circumstances. When he came into the neighborhood where he died it was a new settlement, where there was no Methodist Society, and but few professors of religion of any name. He preached on a Sabbath, and at the close of the service stated to the strangers that he was on a journey, that he was ill, and unable to proceed, and desired that some one would entertain him till he should recover his strength sufficiently to pursue his way. There was a long time of silence in the congregation. At last one man came forward and invited him home. At that house he lingered many weeks, and finally expired. The accommodations were poor for a sick man—a small log-house, containing a large family, consisting in part of small children; but doubtless it was the best the place could afford. In his sickness (which was pulmonary consumption) his sufferings were severe; but his patience and his religious consolations were great also. He frequently preached, prayed, and exhorted, sitting on his bed, when he was unable to go out or even to stand. And so he continued laboring for the salvation of men while his strength would permit, and rejoicing in the Lord to the hour of his death. The above-named eye and ear witness informed me that he frequently said to him, 'It is an inscrutable providence that brought me here to die in this wilderness.' 'But,' said the witness, 'that providence was explained after his death; for, through the instrumentality of his labors, his patience, fortitude, and religious joys in his sickness, a glorious revival of religion shortly after took place, a goodly number of souls were converted to God, other preachers were invited to the place, and a large Methodist Society was organized after his death.' That Society continues to prosper, and they have now a good house for worship. After the soul of our brother had gone to heaven, his body was conveyed to the grave on a sled drawn by oxen. The corpse was carried to a log building in the woods, called a meeting-house; but the proprietors denied admittance, and the funeral solemnities were performed without. As I came through the woodland in company with a preacher, having been informed where the place of his interment was, leaving our horse and carriage by the road, we walked some rods into the forest, and found the old log meeting-house, which had refused the stranger the rites of a funeral; but it was partly fallen, and forsaken. Then following a narrow path some distance further through the woods, we came to a small opening, which appeared to have been cleared of the wood for a habitation for the dead. After walking and looking some time, a decent stone, near one corner of the yard, under the shade of the thick-set, tall forest, informed us where the body of our dear departed friend had been laid. A large oak tree had fallen, and lay across two of the adjoining tenants of that lonely place. We kneeled, prayed, and left the quiet spot, in joyful hope of meeting our brother again at the resurrection of the just."

Martin Ruter, who was born in Sutton, Mass., in 1785, but sleeps in a missionary grave on the banks of the Brazos, in Texas, entered the eastern itinerant ranks in 1801, called into them by Brodhead. He was one of the noblest sons of New England, a good debater and writer, an able preacher, a leader of the educational interests of the denomination in the East and in the West, one of its best representative characters for many years, and at last a pioneer evangelist on its furthest frontier.

Laban Clark also appears on the Conference roll, for the first time, in 1801. Born in Haverhill, N. H., in 1778, and early removing to Vermont, he heard some of the first evangelists who penetrated the latter state, and became a Methodist in 1799. In 1800 he was preaching about his neighborhood with John Langdon, a local preacher, and one of the principal founders of the Church in Vermont. Brodhead, who, the same year, had pressed Ruter into the itinerant service, now summoned out Clark, and thus presented to the Church two of its most important public men. Clark still lives, after more than sixty years of invaluable services; his life, like that of Ruter, has been so extensively identified with the general history of the Church as not to admit of its individualization here. A man of vigorous physical health, of strong and genial mind, of great practical capacity, of never-wavering enthusiasm for his Church and all its important enterprises, a living history of it for more than threescore years, and an able preacher, notwithstanding a marked vocal defect, he has been prominent among its most exponent characters.

These remaining four years were eventful to the Church all over the Eastern States. They began with the first session of the New England Conference, as a distinct organized body, at Lynn, Mass., July 8, 1800. Revivals prevailed generally, greatly increasing the congregations and societies. The itinerancy was not only largely recruited, but in a few places tested by severe persecutions. Elijah R. Sabin was mobbed on Needham Circuit, where he preached in the open air. Some of his brethren, at the Conference, would moderate his zeal; but Asbury approved him, affirming that "this is the way Methodist preachers began, and we need warm hearts to carry the work forward." The Boston Methodists suffered much from the rabble, who besieged their humble temple, begun on Hanover Avenue (then known as Methodist Alley) in 1795, but not completed till 1800, after which time, say its old records, "the troubled and persecuted society found, in some degree, rest to their souls;" it was yet only, however, in "some degree." They had still many a sore conflict before cultivated Boston properly recognized them. Hibbard fought his way through intolerable trials on Granville Circuit. He speaks of twenty-six sermons a month as "moderate labor," and only complains when he had twelve appointments a week, and "no rest-week in which to go home and visit his family." "Some days," he says, "when riding to my appointments, I was almost all the way in tears, often inquiring of the Lord, in ejaculatory prayers, 'What can I do to save these souls from delusion?' Some threw stones at me, and some set their dogs on me as I rode along; but the Lord defended me. I never had a stone to hit me, nor a dog to bite me. Some threatened to whip me, but I escaped all. I heard of many threats, but none laid hands on me." In Lancaster, Vt., Langdon, Clark, and Crawford were assailed by the mob. The ruffians cowered before the courage of Langdon, who was a gigantic and brave man; but they carried off Crawford, and ducked him in the river, with huzzas. In this same State, now so tolerant and so Methodistic, Washburn had similar trials, though better escapes. "I have had," he says, "stones and snowballs cast at me in volleys. I have had great dogs sent after me, to frighten my horse, as I was peacefully passing through small villages; but I was never harmed by any of them. I have been saluted with the sound of 'glory, hosanna, amen, halleluiah!' mixed with oaths and profanity. If I turned my horse to ride toward them, they would show their want of confidence, both in their master and in themselves, by scattering and fleeing like base cowards." Even in Middletown, Conn., (now the seat of their university,) the Methodists suffered such persecutions. Stocking, of Glastenbury, long a venerated local preacher, writes: "I have been stoned, and my life put in jeopardy, by the lawless mob. Open persecution continued there until put down by the strong arm of the law. Thanks to God, Middletown is renovated!" Ostrander, reporting a great revival there in 1802, says: "The spirit of persecution is much awake. The houses where we assemble are frequently stoned, and the windows broken to pieces; but all this does not move the young converts, who are as bold as lions."

Kibby was threatened with violence in Marblehead, and advised to leave the town, but stood his ground successfully. The Methodists of those days were in many places persecuted even to fines, the seizure of their goods, and, sometimes, imprisonment, by the dominant Church. They were denounced from the pulpits, maltreated in the courts, interrupted in the course of their sermons with charges of heresy, and assailed in the streets by the rabble. Washburn, as we have seen, was hooted through the villages; Hedding cursed with outcries on the highway; Dow's nose was publicly wrung; Sabin was knocked down, and struck on the head, to the peril of his life, with the butt of a gun; Wood was horsewhipped; Christie, summoned out of bed to answer to a charge of violating the laws, by marrying a couple of his people; Willard, wounded in the eye by a blow, the effect of which was seen through his life; Mudge, denied the rights of a clergyman, and arraigned before the magistrate for assuming them; Kibby, stoned while preaching, and Taylor drummed out of town. It requires more determination to endure such grievances than to meet graver trials; but the early Methodist itinerants were proof against both.

With all its poverty and persecutions the Church prevailed surprisingly during this period. There were, at its close, more than ten thousand Methodists in New England. It had about fifty Circuits, and moret han eighty itinerants. It had gained since 1796 more than seven thousand five hundred members, twenty-nine Circuits, and fifty-seven preachers.

CHAPTER XXVI.

METHODISM IN THE WEST: 1796-1804.

WE have seen the progress of Methodism in the West down to 1796, in its first field, the ultra-Alleghany region of Pennsylvania, called the Redstone country. The present period opens there with five Circuits and nine preachers, comprehended in one District. Valentine Cook commands the little band as presiding elder. We find in it James Paynter, who had pioneered among the Tioga Mountains, and Nathaniel B. Mills, whom we have met in the Wyoming Valley, its first itinerant preacher, and also an associate of Lee in the earliest struggles of the Church in New England. Such was the itinerancy of these days. Cook was the champion of the field. He flew over his District like a herald—a king's messenger—proclaiming the Gospel, night and day, directing his preachers, and rousing the scattered settlements.

The next year Daniel Hitt had charge of the vast district; a Virginian, who began to travel in 1790, and became distinguished throughout the Connection as an effective laborer, the traveling companion of Asbury and M'Kendree, and for eight years the Book Agent of the Church in New York city; and who died, after a ministry of thirty-five years, in Washington County, Md., in 1825, in the hope of the Gospel. James Quinn, to whom we have been already indebted for many historical reminiscences of this region, appears for the first time on the list of its appointments in 1799, and lived to be its most venerable representative in his Church. His family early moved to Fayette County, where they heard the first Methodist itinerants who crossed the Alleghanies, and became their disciples. It was not till the eleventh year of his age that young Quinn heard a sermon; he had then the great privilege of hearing the saintly Peter Moriarty. In his thirteenth year he witnessed the second Conference beyond the Alleghanies, at Uniontown, Pa. He was converted and joined the Methodists in 1792, under the ministry of Daniel Fidler and James Coleman, whom we have already met in far-off fields of labor. He was immediately pressed into active service in the Church, and in 1799 was received on probation by the Baltimore Conference, and appointed to Greenfield Circuit, which extended into three counties. Before the year ended he was tossed about on at least three similar Circuits. Thus began his long and faithful career. More than half a century after he began his ministry he stood in a Conference in Ohio, and could say, "And now here I am, 'a reed shaken with the wind,' a feeble old man, trembling as I lean upon the top of my staff; but where am I? In the midst of a Conference of ministers near one hundred and fifty in number, most of whom have been twice born since the time of which I speak. Among them are the sons, the grandsons, and great-grandsons of those who kindly received me, and to whom I ministered in their humble dwellings. No doubt I have taken some of these ministers in my arms, and dedicated them to God in holy baptism; and on some of them I have laid my hand in consecrating them to the sacred office and work of the ministry. O! why should my heart yield to fear? The Lord of hosts is with us, the God of Jacob is yet our help." As a preacher he was very instructive, and not unfrequently exceedingly powerful. His manners showed a singular blending of dignity and amenity, the truest style of the real gentleman; solemnity and pathos characterized him in his religious exercises; his form was manly, nearly six feet in height, and well proportioned; his forehead prominent and broad; his eyes dark, deeply set, and shaded by heavy brows.

Lasley Matthews was also a pioneer itinerant of these times, an Irishman and a Papist, who had served in the Revolutionary war. While in camp he was associated with Chieuvrant, who himself had been a Papist, but who now read to his comrade a small Bible, which he carried in his pocket, and thus led him to a religious life. Both became zealous preachers and founders of the Church in the West. We have met Chieuvrant repeatedly, and seen him last preaching in moccasins, and pursuing with his rifle the murderous Indians on the Monongahela, a brave man as well as a devoted evangelist. Matthews began to travel in 1786, and preached during twenty-seven years, mostly in the hardest parts of the work. After doing chivalric service he was crowned with a fitting victory. He died in 1813, on his way to meet his brethren in Conference. "When," wrote one of his friends, "he could no longer articulate, by putting my ear to his lips I could hear him attempting to say 'Glory! Praise him! My Jesus, come!'" Thornton Fleming had charge of the district in 1801. Born in Virginia in 1764, he joined the Methodists in about his twentieth year, and the itinerancy in his twenty-fourth year, and continued to labor with his might through a ministry of more than fifty-seven years; part of the time in Virginia, on some of its most mountainous Circuits; part as presiding elder, among the Tioga and Wyoming mountains and New York interior lakes, where we have already met him, but most of the time in the ultra-Alleghany region of Pennsylvania, where he did much to found the Pittsburgh and Erie Conferences, and was one of the first members of the former. For fifteen years he filled the laborious office of presiding elder. He was to suffer much, and perish at last, by a cancer in his left eye, but to die in the assured hope of the Gospel, the oldest member of the Pittsburgh Conference, a man "of rare endowments" and distinguished usefulness. Asa Shinn now also appears in the Redstone Circuit, a man of more than ordinary historic importance in the Church. We have already seen him struggling, in the western woods, for intellectual and moral improvement, under the aid of Quinn, and beginning to preach "before he had ever seen a meeting-house or a pulpit." He began to itinerate in 1800, on Pittsburgh Circuit, though he was not received in the Conference till the next year. He was a pioneer of Methodism in many regions, in Pennsylvania, Ohio, Virginia, and Kentucky, suffering much from miasmatic fevers and mobs. In his later ministry he occupied prominent appointments in the Eastern States. He wielded a strong and sharp pen, and became a champion of the secession which led to the organization of the Methodist Protestant Church. Throughout the remainder of the present period he did brave service for the Church on Redstone, Chenango, Hockhocking, and Guyandotte Circuits.

With such men were associated, through more or less of this period, Robert Manly, Jesse Stoneman, James Hunter, Joseph Shane, Thomas Daughaday, Thomas Budd, Shadrach Bostwick, and others, some of whom did notable service, to be hereafter recorded. By 1804 they had extended the Redstone District (now called after the Monongahela) far and wide; it reached into the Erie country, the wilds of Ohio and Western Virginia, and embraced nine vast Circuits, over which fourteen itinerants were heralding the Gospel and organizing Churches.

In penetrating into the more northern region, now the vigorous Erie Conference, Methodism had its usual frontier struggles. In 1798 a family by the name of Roberts settled in Chenango; about the same time two Irish local preachers, Jacob Gurwell and Thomas M'Clelland, ("very respectable preachers,") began to labor among the settlers, proclaiming the word in their cabins and in the open air under trees. They formed a class this year, and appointed a youth, Robert R. Roberts, its leader; he thus became the first leader of the first class in the Erie Conference, and was destined to become one of the most effective evangelists and bishops of the Church which had found him in these remote woods. He was a stalwart youth, wearing, says his biographer, the common backwoods costume: the broad-rimmed, low-crowned, white-wool hat, the hunting shirt of tow linen, buckskin breeches, and moccasin shoes. About 1800 Fleming gave him license to exhort; but his almost morbid diffidence kept him from using it; the next year Quinn called upon him often "to speak to the people," which he did with trembling, but with success. When he first presented himself in the Baltimore Conference he had traveled thither, from the western wilds, with bread and provender in his saddle-bags and with one dollar in his pocket; but his superior character immediately impressed Asbury and the assembled preachers. He passed in sixteen years from the humble position of a young backwoods itinerant to the highest office of the ministry. His episcopal appointment was providential for the great field of Methodism was in the West and he was a child of the wilderness; he had been educated in its hardy habits; his rugged frame and characteristic qualities all designated him as a great evangelist for the great West. No sooner had he been elected a bishop than he fixed his episcopal residence in the old cabin at Chenango; and his next removal was to Indiana, then the far West, where his episcopal palace was a log-cabin built by his own hands, and his furniture rude fabrications from the forest wood, made with such tools as he had carried in his emigrant wagon. The first meal of the bishop and his family in his new abode was of roasted potatoes only, and it was begun and ended with hearty thanksgiving. Here he lived in the true simplicity of frontier life, toiling, at his occasional leisure, in the fields. The allowance for his family expenses, besides two hundred per anum for quarterage, was, during most of his episcopal career, from two hundred to two hundred and fifty dollars per anum; at least this was the case till 1836.

Naturally cheerful and amiable, his piety was never gloomy, though seldom ecstatic. He was one of the most agreeable of companions; he could calmly endure afflictions, and compassionately forgive offenses; he was fitted for domestic life and permanent friendships.

As a preacher he was always interesting, and frequently eloquent, though his passions never had undue play in the pulpit. A thoroughly systematic arrangement of his subject, readiness of thought, fluent and generally correct diction, and a facile yet dignified manner, were his characteristics in the desk. His large person—corpulent, and nearly six feet in height, his strongly-marked features, elevated forehead, and manners of extreme simplicity and cordiality, gave to his presence the air of a superior man—one to be remembered, revered, and loved.

Methodism, beginning within the Erie Conference by the formation of Roberts's little class in Chenango, soon spread out to other settlements. Emigration poured into the country, bringing many Methodist families from the East. Settlements sprung up rapidly on each side of the Pennsylvania and Ohio line. By 1801 the Pittsburgh District, as this whole region was now called, took in all the present Erie, Pittsburgh, and West Virginia Conference. It reported two northern Circuits within the present Erie Conference, the Erie and Chenango, traveled by Quinn and Shane. Quinn's whole field had not yet a single Society or class. He went forth to organize it. Asbury, in appointing him to it at the Conference, called him forward, and, pressing him to his bosom, gave him a Discipline, and said, "Go, my son, and make full proof of thy ministry." Some half dozen classes were formed on his Circuit before the ecclesiastic year closed, and some sixty-five members reported; while the Chenango Circuit returned about sixty members: a hundred and twenty-five Methodists in all, the nucleus of a Conference which now (1866) reports nearly thirty thousand, and has covered the country with religious provisions.

The next year Asa Shinn labored with success through these regions, and Henry Shewel, a local preacher from New Jersey, who had lived some time in Redstone, penetrated (the last forty miles through an unbroken wilderness, without a settler) to Deerfield, Portage County, Ohio, and extended the Church thither, so that in 1803 we find Deerfield reported as the title of a new Circuit. By 1804 there were three Circuits, with three preachers, besides Fleming, the presiding elder, in these northern regions, and the membership had increased to more than five hundred. The whole district reported nine Circuits, fourteen preachers, and more than three thousand three hundred (3,327) members.

Meanwhile, farther southward, within Virginia, the denomination was pressing forward energetically. Reese Wolf, a local preacher, and Beauchamp, who lately left New England, had arrived on the banks of the little Kanawha, and founded it there.

Pushing still farther westward and southward, we are again among the evangelists of the Holston Mountains. These heights are as watch-towers to them, and we find them, during these years, now descending to the westward, now to the eastward, "sounding the alarm" through all the wilderness, from the Blue Ridge to the farthest Kentucky and Tennessee frontier. Already the Gospel was proclaimed, by Methodist itinerants, through most of the hither mountain valleys, those grand and fertile domains which stretch away, between their rocky barriers, from the interior of Pennsylvania through Virginia into North Carolina. Our present period opens with M'Kendree on a District which extends through Bottetourt County over the ridges and valleys to the Greenbrier, a stream that flows into the great Kanawha, and thence into the Ohio; and another District, under Philip Bruce, sweeping, in like manner, far westward over the more northward counties.

The year 1796 is memorable as the epoch of the formal designation of the Western field by the General Conference, as "The Western Conference," taking in Kentucky and Tennessee, and for years the only one in the valley of the Mississippi. In the Holston region itself we find now, in the outset, four immense Circuits, under the presiding eldership of Jonathan Bird, and traveled by six itinerants, Burke being chief among them. Beyond them lies the vast opening westward field, all yet comprehended in one District, which is traveled by Kobler, who has six Circuits and ten preachers under his care.

Among his itinerants is Benjamin Lakin, for many years an endeared name in the West. He was a giant amid those great revivals which prevailed in the West about the beginning of this century. One of his contemporaries says, that "in the greatest excitement the clear and penetrating voice of Lakin might be heard amid the din and roar of the Lord's battle. Day and night he was upon the watch-tower, and in the class and praying circles his place was never empty, leading the blind by the right way, carrying the lambs in his bosom, urging on the laggard professor, and warning the sinner in tones of thunder to flee the wrath to come. He preached his last sermon in M'Kendree Chapel, Brown County, Ohio, on the 28th day of January, 1848. In about a week afterward, visiting a Christian family, he sank down to the floor and quietly expired, in the eighty-second year of his age and the fifty-fourth of his ministry. He was of ordinary height, but of "spare habit," excessively given to fasting or abstinence, of singularly tender conscience; but, "though sedate, there was a spice of quiet humor in his conversation." "His appearance, in advanced life, was that of a cheerful, placid old man, and such indeed he was."

In 1798 Bird and Poythress lead, as presiding elders, the Holston corps, though there was yet but one District; and we meet again the tireless Valentine Cook at the head of the solitary District which comprises the more western field, with its six long Circuits and seven itinerants. Before the close of the century Cook was broken down in health. He married and settled in Kentucky, where he took charge of the Bethel Seminary, in Jessamine County, the first Methodist school of the West. He subsequently conducted a similar institution at Harrodsburgh, and, finally, located in Logan County, where he lived on a small farm about three miles from Russellville. He devoted himself to education, and was esteemed one of the best instructors in the West. Meanwhile he preached powerfully, not merely in his own vicinity, but often in extensive excursions through the State, and at quarterly meetings and camp-meetings. He was venerated as a saint for his singular piety; and it is probable that no man of his day wielded, in the West, greater power in the pulpit. In 1819 he was impressed with the thought that his end was near. He wished once more to visit some of his old fields, and "return home and arrange his affairs for an early departure to his inheritance above." He went preaching through Kentucky, parts of Ohio, and his old battle grounds in Pennsylvania. Passing on to Pittsburgh, New York, Philadelphia, he reached Baltimore, where he spent some time preaching "to vast crowds," and "scores and hundreds were converted through his instrumentality." He returned through the Greenbrier country of the Alleghanies, visiting his early friends, kneeling at the graves of his parents, giving his final warnings to the people, and re-entered his home in Kentucky singing a triumphant hymn. He settled his temporal affairs, and in the ensuing year died, uttering, as his last words, "When I think of Jesus, and of living with him forever, I am so filled with the love of God, that I scarcely know whether I am in the body or out of the body."

Good Henry Smith, whom we have so often met, was still braving the frontier trials of Kentucky. In 1798 he was under Poythress and Bird on Green Circuit, within the Holston District, and the next year reached Ohio, where he meets again his old friend, M'Cormick, and whither we shall soon follow him.

In 1799 the whole field, Holston, Kentucky, and Tennessee, and a Circuit in Ohio, was one immense District under Poythress, with an apostolic band of twelve preachers, including such men as Burke, Kobler, Smith, and Sale. John Sale was one of the most heroic evangelists and founders of western Methodism, though only five lines are given to his memory in the official Minutes, and we know not the precise place of his birth. During four years he labored indefatigably in the Holston Mountains and among the Kentucky settlements. In 1803 he passed into the Northwestern Territory, and now, for nearly a quarter of a century more, he alternates between Ohio and Kentucky, a successful circuit preacher, a commanding presiding elder. Worn out by his ministerial labors, he fell at last in his work, in 1827, crowned with the veneration of the Church, and exclaiming, "My last battle is fought, and victory sure! halleluiah!" Judge M'Lean says, "I have sometimes heard him, when, rising with the dignity and in the fullness of his subject, he seemed to me one of the noblest personifications of the eloquence of the pulpit."

The year 1800 was signalized in western Methodist history by the appearance of William M'Kendree at the head of the pioneer itinerants. Poythress, hitherto its chief representative man, was beginning to totter in both mind and body, and it now needed an able commander. Few of the early itinerants did more to lay the foundations of the Church both east and west of the Mountains than Poythress. He was one of the most zealous laborers for its educational interests, and fell a martyr to his devotion to that cause. He was the chief founder of the first Methodistic seminary in the West—the Bethel Academy, in Jessamine County, Ky. Its edifice was a large brick structure of two stories, and it had incurred a considerable debt, which weighed down his noble mind till it sunk in ruins. All efforts of himself, Valentine Cook, and other colaborers, to retrieve the institution failed, and Poythress lingered a wreck, like his favorite project. We have seen M'Kendree tending westward for some years among the mountain appointments of Western Virginia, and witnessed his departure on his transmontane route with Asbury and Whatcoat, without his "money, books, or clothes." They passed over the mountains, down the Holston River, into Tennessee, into the valley of Church River, where, reaching a "station" on the outskirts of the settlements, they combined with other travelers to form a company, and, on the 27th of September, 1800, began their course direct to Kentucky. Wearied and sick, they reached Bethel Academy, Jessamine County, and there held the Western Conference in the first week of October, the first session of that body of which there remains any correct record. Ten traveling preachers were present, including Asbury and Whatcoat; the session lasted but two days; two candidates were admitted on probation, one member located, fourteen local and four traveling preachers were ordained.

After the session Asbury, Whatcoat, and M'Kendree traveled and preached together, from the center of Kentucky to Nashville, in Tennessee, and thence to Knoxville, where they parted, M'Kendree returning to his great District, which comprised thirteen Circuits, over which he went preaching night and day with an ardor befitting so grand a sphere, and such sublime results as he could justly anticipate for the rising commonwealths around him, whose moral foundations Methodism was now effectively laying. An extraordinary religious excitement spread over all the country. It was largely attributable to the introduction of camp-meetings at this time—a provision which, however questionable in dense communities, seemed providentially suited to these sparsely settled regions. In the latter part of 1799, John and William Magee, who were brothers, the first a Methodist local preacher, the second a Presbyterian minister, started from their settlement in Tennessee to make a preaching tour into Kentucky. Their first labors were with a Presbyterian Church on Red River, where remarkable effects attended their labors, and excited such general interest that, at their next meeting, on Muddy River, many distant families came with wagons and camped in the woods. This was, in fact, the beginning of religious "camp-meetings" in the United States. They soon became general through all the Western Territories, and, at last, throughout the nation and Upper Canada. Ten, twenty, or more thousands attended them, devoting usually a week exclusively to religious exercises, living in tents or booths, which were arranged in circles around a rude pulpit or platform, and were illuminated at night by torches or pine-knots, and governed by prescribed rules and a temporary police. They soon bore the name of "general camp-meetings" from their catholic character, as combining all sects. As they were Presbyterian as well as, or even more than, Methodist, in their origin, Presbyterian clergymen were generally active in them. A great one was held in Cambridge, seven miles from Paris, Ky., soon after their introduction, which produced a general sensation; thousands of persons were present from all parts of the state, and even from Ohio; it continued a week. Hundreds fell to the earth as dead men under the preaching. At another, held at Cobbin Creek, Ky., twenty thousand were present; thousands fell as slain in battle, and the religious interest of the whole State seemed to be quickened by its results. Astonishing effects attended another on Desher's Creek, near Cumberland River; "the people fell under the power of the word like corn before a storm of wind."

M'Kendree, as he passed over his vast District, promoted these meetings, and it was not long before the Methodist itinerants were thus making their word resound in all parts of the State. New Societies were abundantly organized, and the Church assumed unprecedented vigor. At the close of his second year on the Districts even new Circuits had been formed, and the one District was divided into three. The mere handful of members, scattered here and there in the settlements, now numbered at least eight thousand, having increased more than five thousand in the last two years. The little Conference of twelve members had more than doubled its numbers. Much of the impetus which had been given to the Western work was through the preaching and superior wisdom of M'Kendree as the presiding elder.

One of the most interesting characters in Methodist biography was recorded in the appointments of 1802, Jacob Young, a man of such evangelical simplicity and purity, such good sense in counsel, and perspicuity and pertinence in speech, so entertaining in conversation, and of such cordiality of manners, and saintliness of character, that the most obstinate opposers and most fastidious critics were won by him, notwithstanding the faithfulness of his admonitions, and some obvious defects made the more obnoxious to criticism by the peculiar recitative tone of his preaching. He survived far into our day, not only revered by, but endeared to, all who knew him, by the peculiar charm of his character, as well as by his long and faithful public services.

In 1802 a very striking appointment appears on the roll of the Western Conference, that of "Natchez," with the solitary name of Tobias Gibson attached as preacher. Natchez, however, was obscurely recorded, with Gibson's name, two years earlier, as on the Georgia District, which fact only made the record appear the more extraordinary, for the immense territories which are now the two large States of Alabama and Mississippi, lay between Georgia and this point on the Mississippi River. The remote appointment appeared as a new sign in the far-off southern heavens; to the pioneer preachers of Kentucky and Tennessee it was as the constellation of the cross to mariners in the Southern Seas. It opened a boundless prospect of progress; and the word Natchez sounded like a new order of march to the itinerants and their cause—that march which they have since made over Mississippi, Louisiana, Texas, even to the Pacific boundary of California. Tobias Gibson was worthy of the pioneer mission, and was soon worthily to fall a martyr to his heroism, but not without opening the way, never to be closed, for the southwestern triumphs of the Church. He was a saintly man, of vigorous intellect, "greatly given to reading, meditation, and prayer;" very "affectionate and agreeable" in his manners. In 1799, after eight years' travel on southeastern Circuits, he volunteered to go to the distant southern banks of the Mississippi, though he was already broken in health by excessive labors and privations. With the approval of Asbury he started alone, and made his way on horseback to the Cumberland River, in Kentucky, traveling hundreds of miles through the wilderness, mostly along Indian trails. At the Cumberland he sold his horse, bought a canoe, and, putting his saddle-bags and a few other effects upon it, paddled down the river into the Ohio, and thence, six or eight hundred miles, down the Mississippi to his destination, where he immediately began his labors, eighteen years before the Mississippi Territory became a State of the Union. Four times he went through the wilderness, six hundred miles, among "Indian nations and guides," to the Cumberland, for the purpose of obtaining additional laborers from the Western Conference. In 1803 he presented himself before that body a broken-down hero, and, though needing recruits themselves, they spared him Moses Floyd, for the solitary veteran had gathered more than fourscore (87) members at Natchez, and the whole country was ready for the Gospel. By the next Conference there were more than a hundred Methodists reported from it, and Hezekiah Harriman and Abraham Amos were sent to aid the two evangelists; but the apostle of the little band was about to fall at his post; he had overworked. Harriman made his way thither through "thirteen days and twelve nights' toil in the wilderness," and soon witnessed a "revival" and formed the Washington Circuit; but he wrote back that Gibson was sinking; "his legs were swelled up to his knees," he had "violent cough," and had not been able to preach for months. "Tell my dear brethren, the young preachers," adds Harriman, "not to be afraid of this place, for God is here, and souls have been converted this winter in public and private, and others are inquiring the way to heaven. Here are also a great many souls that must die like heathens, except they are visited by faithful ministers of the Gospel. My hope revives that God will pour his Spirit on us more abundantly, and that our brethren will come and help us." Twenty days later Harriman wrote, "Brother Gibson has gone to his long home." He preached his last sermon on New Year's Day, 1804, "and it was profitable to many souls." After having suffered for three years with consumption, he "was seized with fever and vomited blood." He died in Claiborne County, on the 5th of April, 1804. He had "continued to labor in the vineyard of the Lord as long as he was able to preach or pray," and declared to his fellow-laborer that "he was not afraid to meet death," and "wished for the hour." His brethren, in the old Minutes, 1805, commemorate him with admiration, and say, "When Elijah was taken away there was an Elisha: we have two valuable men that will supply his place; but still Gibson opened the way; like a Brainerd he labored and fainted not, nor dared to leave his station till death gave him an honorable discharge." In the autumn of the year of his death Larner Blackman, one of the noblest itinerants of the West, went to take his place, and a succession of evangelists followed till Methodism spread out over all the country.

Of Larner Blackman we have had a transient glimpse, in New Jersey, his native State, where John Collins, his brother-in-law, and afterward his colaborer in the West, was guiding him in his early religious life. He now, and for some years, becomes almost ubiquitous in Western Methodism, south of the Ohio. After itinerating, with much success, three years in Kentucky, he was sent in 1804 to take the place of Gibson. After a journey of ten or eleven days, and lying out as many nights, making his saddle-bags his pillow, his blanket and cloak his bed, the heavens his covering, the God of Israel his defense, he arrived safe in the territory. At the time of his arrival Methodism was in its infancy in that country. In 1806 he was appointed to preside in the Mississippi District: God honored his ministrations with success, sinners were converted, and chapels were built and dedicated. When he left the Southwest it had a large District, five Circuits, six preachers, and more than four hundred (415) members. Returning to Tennessee he labored faithfully on various Circuits and Districts till 1815, when, crossing the Ohio in a ferry-boat, his horse was frightened and threw him into the river, where he perished, "an event which caused the heart of the whole Church to throb with sadness." He ranks as one of the great men of early Methodism. "He had the appearance, both in and out of the pulpit," says a contemporary authority, "of being quite a cultivated man." In stature he was about the middle height, well-formed, with a full face, and an eye which shone with the light of genius. Every feature became strikingly expressive while he was preaching or conversing.

While the range of Western Methodism was thus extending southward, it was also advancing in the opposite direction into the great Northwestern Territory. We have traced its introduction and first movements there under the agency of M'Cormick. Repeatedly did this faithful local preacher go over to Kentucky to solicit itinerants from the Conference, but none could yet be spared from their urgent work. Meanwhile laymen like himself were planting the Church. He met in Kentucky Ezekiel Dimmitt, a young emigrant from Berkeley County, Va., where he had been received into the Church by Joshua Wells. M'Cormick urged him to move into the Northwestern Territory, and help to found Methodism and a new State there. Dimmitt, full of religious and patriotic ardor, went in 1797, and built his cabin on the east fork of the Little Miami, not far below the present town of Batavia. He became a powerful coadjutor with M'Cormick. At last M'Cormick's appeal to the Conference was answered by the mission of Kobler, who, on the 2d of August, 1798, "preached the first sermon delivered in the Territory by a regularly constituted Methodist missionary." We have from Kobler's own pen an allusion to his expedition. In passing through the country he found it in its almost native, uncultivated state. The inhabitants were settled in small neighborhoods, few and far between, with little or no improvement about them. No house of worship had been yet erected. The site on which Cincinnati now stands was a dense forest, no improvement was to be seen but Fort Washington, which was built on the brow of the hill, and extended down to the margin of the river; around it were cabins, in which resided the first settlers of the place. When he crossed the Ohio in 1798, "at a little village called Columbia," he fell upon his knees upon the shore, and prayed for the divine blessing upon his mission. "That evening," he writes, "I reached the house of Francis M'Cormick. He lived ten or fifteen miles from Columbia, on the bank of the Little Miami River. On Thursday, August 2, I preached at his house to a tolerable congregation on Acts xvi, 9: 'And a vision appeared to Paul in the night: there stood a man of Macedonia and prayed him, saying, Come over into Macedonia and help us.' It was a time of refreshing from the presence of the Lord, who gave testimony to the word of his grace. The little band was much rejoiced at my arrival among them, together with the prospect of having circuit preaching and all the privileges and ordinances of our Church." His first Circuit embraced about one half the territory now included in the Cincinnati Conference. After seeing Methodism well established on the north bank of the Little Miami, M'Cormick once more changed his location, and settled in Hamilton County, about ten miles east of Cincinnati. A class was soon formed, and the neighborhood supplied with regular circuit preaching, M'Cormick pushing out in all directions to open the way for the itinerants. This class was the beginning of what has been long and widely known as the 'Salem Society,' and in early times became identified with the old White Oak Circuit, from the bounds of which nearly fifty preachers have been raised up for the regular work of the Methodist ministry."

Kobler labored and traveled night and day in the Territory for about nine months. He continued in the itinerancy till 1819, when he located; but the Baltimore Conference, without his solicitation, put his name upon its honored roll of superannuated preachers in 1836. He died in Fredericksburgh, Va., in 1843, aged 74 years. His last words were, "Come, Lord Jesus! come, Lord Jesus, in power! come quickly!"

On Kobler's return to Kentucky Lewis Hunt was sent to the Territory, and in 1799 the Miami Circuit, the first Methodist appointment in Ohio, appears in the Minutes, with the name of Henry Smith as preacher. Dimmitt's house was on Hunt's Circuit, and was made a preaching place; it was a cabin about sixteen feet square. Smith went on laboring unceasingly over his long Circuit, preaching twenty sermons every three weeks, and organizing small Societies in almost every settlement, for he found emigrant Methodists nearly everywhere.

Meanwhile an important acquisition was made by the struggling Society in the arrival on the scene of one of our earliest and most interesting heroes. Philip Gatch emigrated, with his family, to the Miami region, and appeared there but a few months after the coming of Kobler. He was born, as we have noticed, in the same year, and began to preach as early, as William Watters, who worthily ranks as the first native Methodist preacher of the United States, having anticipated Gatch a short time on the records of the Conference. But Gatch was more conspicuous than Watters for his sufferings and activity in the early history of the denomination. We have seen him, after his marriage, locate, but continue his labors, in Virginia. In 1798 he started for the West. He was now a neighbor of and a coworker with M'Cormick, and his home became a "preaching place" and a shelter for the itinerants. Most of his children were here gathered into the Church. Kobler, who had known him in the East, was delighted to meet him. For the remainder of his life he was a representative man of his Church in Ohio, preaching often, and promoting zealously its rising interests. He was made a magistrate, was a delegate to the convention which formed the Constitution of the State, and was appointed by the Legislature an Associate Judge. He became a most influential citizen, a patriarch of the Commonwealth as well as of the Church. Asbury, Whatcoat, and M'Kendree were often his guests, and his old eastern fellow-laborers, Watters, Dromgoole, and others, cheered him with letters. After invaluable services to his Church and country, he preached his last sermon on the day in which he was eighty-four years old, and died the next year (1835) "in great peace and unshaken confidence in Christ." His old friend, Kobler, revisited the country six years after his death. "Taking my hand," writes a son of Gatch, "he held it for some time in silence, looking me in the face with a most impressive expression of countenance, which produced in me a sensation that I shall not attempt to describe. At length, in the most emphatic manner, he said, 'Your father was a great man in his day. He fought many hard battles for the Church. May you be a worthy son of so worthy a father!' He visited the graves of my parents, took off his hat, and stood some minutes as if absorbed in deep thought; fell upon his knees for some time, arose bathed in tears, and walked out of the grave yard in silence." He was burdened with great memories, for the two veterans had shared in events which history, ages to come, may commemorate.

M'Cormick, Gatch, Tiffin, Scott, laymen and local preachers, with not a few others of like spirit, gave a character and impulse to Methodism in Ohio, to which must be ascribed much of its subsequent power over all the old Northwestern Territory. M'Cormick lived and died in a manner worthy of his historical position. In the latter part of his life he was absolved from active service by maladies which were the effects of the exposures and fatigues of his early preaching, but "the evening of his days was cloudless." He died in 1836, and his last words were, "Glory, honor, immortality, and eternal life!"

John Sale, from whom we have recently parted, was sent to the Scioto Circuit in 1803. The next year he was appointed, says his biographer, to Miami Circuit. These two circuits then embraced all the south and west portions of the State of Ohio. It was while traveling these regions that he organized the first Society of Methodists in Cincinnati. Kobler had visited it in 1798; he describes it as "an old garrison, (Fort Washington,) a declining, time-stricken, God-forsaken place." He wished to preach, but "could find no opening or reception of any kind whatever." Lewis Hunt and Elisha Bowman occasionally ventured into the demoralized scene, and preached without result. In 1804 John Collins, who had come the year before to the Territory, but was not yet in the itinerancy, went to it to purchase provisions. He inquired of a storekeeper, "Is there any Methodists here?" "Yes, sir," was the reply; "I am a

Methodist." The local preacher was taken by surprise at the joyful intelligence, and, throwing his arms around the layman's neck, he wept. He eagerly inquired if there were any more Methodists in the place. The response was equally cheering, "O yes, brother, there are several." The heart of Collins leaped for joy. "O," said the zealous young preacher, "that I could have them all together!" "In this you shall be gratified, my brother," rejoined the layman; "I will open my house, and call together the people, if you will preach." The upper room of Carter's (the merchant's house) was fitted with temporary benches, while every effort possible was made to give the appointment an extensive circulation. Only twelve persons attended, but "it was a memorable time for Methodism in Cincinnati. It was the planting of a handful of corn on the tops of the mountains, the increasing and ever-multiplying products of which were to shake like Lebanon." The next sermon to this infant Church was by Sale, in a house in Main-street, between First and Second streets. The congregation was increased to thirty or forty persons. After preaching, a Society was organized, and arrangements were made to have services regularly every two weeks by the circuit evangelists. In 1805 the small Society began to build their first church, the "Old Stone Chapel." Such was the humble origin of Methodism in Cincinnati.

We have already had occasion to note that it was, during these times, invading Ohio from the East as well as from the South, by the labors of Robert Manly. Jesse Stoneman followed him, and so enlarged the field, that Quinn and Shinn kept pace with the settlements extending back and up to Lake Erie, giving rise to scores of Circuits. Meanwhile, from the home of Roberts, in the Chenango and Erie regions, the itinerants made their way across the line, and Deerfield, in Portage County, is reported in the Minutes of 1803, with Shadrach Bostwick as its "missionary." Henry Shewel, a local preacher from Virginia, had preceded him, as we have recorded, and as early as 1801 a small Society had spontaneously organized in Deerfield. Methodism was, then, fully on its march into the Northwestern Territory, at nearly every accessible point, by the close of our present period. It had not only invaded Ohio, but reached hopefully beyond it. As early as 1802 Methodist preachers ventured within the present limits of Indiana, which then had but a few scattered settlers. Its first Methodist was Nathan Robertson, who moved from Kentucky to Charleston in 1799; three years later a small class was organized at Gassaway, near Charleston, in Clark County. The first chapel of the denomination in the State still stands, about two miles from Charleston; it was made of hewed logs. By 1807 we shall find in the State one Circuit, with one preacher and sixty-seven members; and by 1810, three Circuits, four preachers, and seven hundred and sixty members, the beginning of that great host, which is now a hundred thousand strong, led by four hundred itinerants. Before the close of our period Benjamin Young, brother of Jacob Young, was dispatched (1804) as a missionary to Illinois, which had but about two hundred and fifteen inhabitants in 1800, and was not admitted as a State of the Union till fourteen years after Young's appointment. In the first year he returned sixty-seven Church members from its sparse population. Methodism had already attempted to erect its standard as far north as Michigan. In 1803 a local preacher by the name of Freeman found his way far into the country, and preached at Detroit, where he left at least one awakened soul who welcomed his successors. In 1804 Nathan Bangs passed over from Canada and sounded the alarm in Detroit, though without apparent success; the place, woefully depraved with a conglomerate population of Indians, French, and immigrants, was subsequently invaded again, from Canada, by William Case, and soon after an Irish local preacher, William Mitchell, organized the first Methodist Society in the city, the first in the State. Methodism was never again totally dislodged from Michigan, though its progress was slow, and no Protestant Church of any denomination was erected within its bounds till 1818.

Asbury made five expeditions to the West in these eight years, though his health was more enfeebled, during most of this period, than in any other portion of his public life. His hardships were incredible. On recrossing the mountains, toward the end of the period, he writes: "Once more I have escaped from filth, fleas, rattlesnakes, hills, mountains, rocks, and rivers: farewell, western world, for a while!" In his habits of dress, manners, and all things, he was neat almost to precision; no one could be more at home than he in the opulent circles of Perry and Rembert Halls, the mansions of Russell, Bassett, and Lippett; but his preachers were suffering bravely the hardships of the frontier, and, if his presence was not absolutely necessary for their ecclesiastical affairs, still he willingly shared their trials for the moral advantage of his example. Under its influences some of the noblest men of the ministry plunged into these wildernesses to build up their Christian civilization. His example was hardly less important than his administrative ability in these early days of his Church.

There were, in 1804, nearly eleven thousand nine hundred (11,877) Methodists, and nearly fifty (46) preachers, reported in the Western Conference. It comprised four Districts and twenty-five Circuits. These statistics do not include, however, all the growing Societies of Western Pennsylvania and Western Virginia, which have been comprised in this survey of Western Methodism, for, in defining the West, I have regarded neither Conference nor State lines, but the natural geographical boundaries of the country. The Monongahela and Greenbrier Districts, had now nearly three thousand five hundred (3,438) Methodists and twenty-six preachers on fourteen Circuits. These, added to the statistics of the Western Conference, would give the denomination, west of the mountains, six Districts, thirty-nine Circuits, seventy-two preachers, and more than fifteen thousand three hundred (15,315) members; an estimate which still leaves out many Methodists beyond the Blue Ridge. It shows, however, remarkable prosperity for a newly and sparsely settled country. The Church had now been planted in Ohio, Illinois, Kentucky, Tennessee, and Mississippi, and Methodist itinerants were preaching the Gospel from Pittsburgh to Natchez. Western Methodism had gained in these last eight years two Districts, sixteen Circuits, thirty-six preachers, and about eight thousand eight hundred members. It witnessed already the presage of its later unparalleled triumphs.

CHAPTER XXVII.

GENERAL CONFERENCES OF 1800 AND 1804—REVIEW.

Two more General Conferences pertain to our present period, the sessions of 1800 and 1804. The former began at Baltimore on Tuesday, May 6, 1800. Its published journals give no roll of its members, and the briefest possible outline of its proceedings; but, happily, a spectator of the occasion (Henry Boehm) has recorded some account of it. He says: "It was one of the most remarkable in the history of our Church. The revival at that time was the greatest that has ever occurred at the session of any General Conference. The greatest displays of divine power, and the most conversions, were in private houses, in prayer-meetings. And yet the preaching was highly honored of God, for the ministers were endued with power from on high. The strong men of Methodism were there, and such a noble class of men I had never beheld. There were Philip Bruce, Jesse Lee, George Roberts, John Bloodgood, William P. Chandler, John M'Claskey, Ezekiel Cooper, Nicholas Snethen, Thomas Morrell, Joseph Totten, Lawrence M'Combs, Thomas F. Sargent, William Burke, William M'Kendree, and others. They elected Richard Whatcoat bishop, he having a majority of four votes over Jesse Lee. Sunday, the 18th, was a great day. The ordination sermon was preached by Rev. Thomas Coke, LL.D., in Light-street Church. Crowds at an early hour thronged the temple. The doctor preached from Rev. ii, 8: 'And unto the angel of the church at Smyrna write; These things saith the First and the Last, which was dead and is alive,' etc. After the sermon, which was adapted to the occasion, Richard Whatcoat was ordained a bishop in the Church of God by the imposition of the hands of Dr. Coke and Bishop Asbury, assisted by several elders. Never were holy hands laid upon a holier head." Asbury records a single paragraph of but fifteen lines respecting the session. "Two days," he says, "were spent in considering about Dr. Coke's return to Europe, part of two days on Richard Whatcoat for a bishop, and one day in raising the salary of the itinerant preachers from sixty-four to eighty dollars per year. We had one hundred and sixteen members present. The unction that attended the word was great; more than one hundred souls, at different times and places, professed conversion during the Conference." Lee writes, that "such a time of refreshing from the presence of the Lord has not been felt in that town for some years." He seems to have suffered little from his defeat in the episcopal election, for he was meanwhile as active as ever in the stirring scenes around him, preaching with great power in the churches and the streets. In reviewing the occasion he says, "I believe we never had so good a General Conference before. We had the greatest speaking and the greatest union of affections that we ever had on a like occasion."

There are some significant indications in the proceedings of this session which have hitherto been unnoticed by the historians of the Church. On the second day a motion was introduced to authorize the Annual Conferences to elect their own presiding elders. It was defeated, but was the beginning of a controversy which prevailed for years in the Conference and throughout the denomination. It was attempted also to make local preachers eligible to ordination as elders. The motion was adopted, but reconsidered and "withdrawn." William Ormond, who appears to have been the noblest "radical" of the body, tried it again, but failed. A motion to reorganize the General Conference, as a delegated body, was defeated by "a great majority;" but was an anticipation of a coming change. Coke attempted, without success, to obtain a rule by which the new bishop, in the absence of Asbury, should be required to read his appointments of preachers in the Annual Conferences, "to hear what the Conference may have to say on each station," in accordance with the English example. Joshua Wells was defeated in a motion to provide a committee of three or four elders, to be chosen by each Annual Conference, to aid the new bishop in making the appointments, an anticipation of a later function of the presiding elders. The motion was twice repeated by other members, but was negatived. These good men were fearful of innovations which have since become indispensable and most salutary in the Methodist system. A rule was recorded allowing the bishops to ordain "local deacons of our African brethren in places where they have built a house for the worship of God." Nine years later, Lee says that this concession was but "little known," and had never been published, owing to Southern opposition. Richard Allen, of Philadelphia, (afterward Bishop Allen,) was thus ordained on the 11th of June, 1799, the first colored preacher ever ordained by the Methodist Episcopal Church. But the most striking feature of the journals of this session (unnoticed by the Church historians) is the persistent antislavery interest of many of the most eminent men in the Conference. We have seen that ever since the Annual Conference of 1780 the subject had been kept before the Church; that the first General Conference (1784) had courageously faced it, and that the session preceding the present one declared itself "more than ever convinced of the great evil" of slavery. The question was soon again rife. Good William Ormond (though a Southerner) introduced it by moving that "whereas the laws now in force in two or more of the United States pointedly prohibit the emancipation of slaves, and the third clause of the ninth section of the Discipline forbids the selling of slaves, it is evident that the members of the Methodist Societies who own slaves, and remove themselves and families to another State, or to distant parts of the same State, and leave a husband or a wife behind held in bondage by another person, part man and wife, which is a violation of the righteous laws of God, and contrary to the peace and happiness of families. And it is further observed, that the rule now existing among us prevents our members increasing the number of their slaves by purchase, and tolerates an increase of number by birth, which children are often given to the enemies of the Methodists. My mind being seriously impressed with these and several other considerations, I move that this General Conference take the momentous subject of slavery into consideration, and make such alterations in the old rule as may be thought proper." Stephen Timmons moved, that if any of our traveling preachers marry persons holding slaves, and thereby become slaveholders, they shall be excluded our Societies, unless they execute a legal emancipation of their slaves, agreeably to the laws of the State wherein they live. Nicholas Snethen moved, that this General Conference do resolve, that from this time forth no slaveholder shall be admitted into the Methodist Episcopal Church. John Bloodgood moved, that all negro children belonging to members of the Methodist Society, who shall be born in slavery after the fourth day of July, 1800, shall be emancipated: males at —— years, and females at —— years. James Lattomas moved, that every member of the Methodist Episcopal Church, holding slaves, shall, within the term of one year from the date hereof, give an instrument of emancipation for all his slaves; and the quarterly meeting conference shall determine the time the slave shall serve, if the laws of the State do not expressly prohibit their emancipation. Ezekiel Cooper moved, that a committee be appointed to prepare an affectionate address to the Methodist Societies in the United States, stating the evils of the spirit and practice of slavery, and the necessity of doing away the evil as far as the laws of the respective States will allow; and that the said address be laid before the Conference for their consideration; and, if agreed to, be signed by the bishops in behalf of the Conference. William M'Kendree moved, that this General Conference direct the yearly Conferences to appoint a committee to draw up proper addresses to the State legislatures, from year to year, for a gradual abolition of slavery. The motion of Timmons prevailed. The Address to the Methodist Societies, proposed by Cooper, was prepared by a committee and sent forth; it provoked the resentment of Charleston, S. C., and led to the sufferings of Dougharty. The obnoxious documents were delivered by his colleague, Harper, to the authorities, and burned in presence of the mayor. The result of these enactments was the following additions to the Discipline at the next session of the Conference, in 1804: "When any traveling preacher becomes an owner of a slave or slaves by any means, he shall forfeit his ministerial character in our Church unless he execute, if it be practicable, a legal emancipation of such slaves, conformably to the laws of the State in which he lives. The Annual Conferences are directed to draw up addresses for the gradual emancipation of the slaves to the legislatures of those States in which no general laws have been passed for that purpose. These addresses shall urge, in the most respectful but pointed manner, the necessity of a law for the gradual emancipation of the slaves; proper committees shall be appointed, by the Annual Conferences, out of the most respectable of our friends, for the conducting of the business; and the presiding elders, elders, deacons, and traveling preachers shall procure as many proper signatures as possible to the addresses, and give all the assistance in their power in every respect to aid the committees, and to further this blessed undertaking. Let this be continued from year to year till the desired end be accomplished." The Methodist Church had thus far been the most active antislavery Society in the nation, and in spite of some reverses was still to remain such, till the barbarous evil should be swept away forever.

While these deliberations were going on in the Conference, the whole city seemed swayed by religious excitement; the great revival of the times, which prevailed over most of the nation, seemed to centralize there. The churches could not contain the people, and many private houses had to be occupied for preaching. I have recorded the name of Catharine Ennalls, (sister to Bassett's wife,) who introduced Methodism into Dorchester, Md. She had married William Bruff, a Methodist merchant of Baltimore, and was now most active in the extraordinary scenes of this revival. Her house was continually open for preaching; Lee, Bruce, M'Combs, Smith, and others preached there with wonderful success. Boehm, who, not being a member of the Conference, had leisure to share in these spiritual labors, describes the results as surprising. "The Lord," he says, "is at work in all parts of the town." "Christ the Lord is come to reign." Preachers and laymen passed from Bruff's house to the churches, "singing the praises of God along the streets. This greatly surprised the people, and hundreds came running out of their houses and followed us till we reached the house of God. There were wonderful exhibitions of power as we went through the streets, and we entered the house singing and shouting the praises of God."

The next General Conference assembled in Light-street Church, Baltimore, May 7, 1804. Coke, "as senior bishop," presided. John Wilson was elected secretary. The records present, for the first time, a list of the members, who amounted to a hundred and twelve; five, however, were "excepted" as not entitled to vote, not having traveled four years. The Philadelphia Conference was represented by thirty-seven, Baltimore by thirty, New England by but four, and the great Western field by three. Philadelphia and Baltimore had sixty-seven of the members, nearly two thirds of the whole Conference. It was obvious that a reorganization of the body, on the principle of delegation, had become necessary, but it was deferred to the next session. The Discipline was elaborately revised, section by section, Coke reading item after item, and the Conference debating with no little interest. Some changes were made. The bishops were not allowed to appoint preachers for more than two successive years to the same appointment; hitherto there had been no restriction, and some had been three years in one appointment. Asbury rejoiced in the new rule as a great relief to the appointing power. The title of "Quarterly Meeting Conference" was given to the quarterly assembly of the official members of the Circuits. The "Book Concern" was ordered to be removed from Philadelphia to New York. At the organization of the Church, in 1784, it was the first religious body of the country to insert in its constitutional law (in its Articles of Religion) a recognition of the new government, enforcing patriotism on its communicants. A very noteworthy modification (peculiarly interesting in our day) was made in this article at the present session. In the original article it was affirmed that the "Congress," etc., "are the officers of the United States of America, according to the division of power made to them by the General Act of Confederation," etc., the national constitution having not yet been adopted; but the present Conference, by a motion of Ezekiel Cooper, (a man noted for his sagacity,) struck out all allusion to the "Act of Confederation," inserting in its stead "the Constitution of the United States," etc., and declared that "the said States are a *sovereign* and independent *nation*." Methodism thus deliberately, and in its constitutional law, recognized that the "Constitution" superseded the "Act of Confederation," and that the republic was no longer a confederacy but a *nation*, and, as such, supreme and sovereign over all its States. It was at a period of no little political agitation on the question of State Sovereignty that this change was made: the Kentucky "Resolutions of 1798," and those of Virginia, 1799, had become the basis of a State Rights party. A contemporary Methodist preacher (Henry Boehm, still living) records that just previous to this time "there was great political excitement. Federalism and Democracy ran high. Such was the excitement that it separated families, and friends, and members of the Church. I was urged, on every side, to identify myself with one political party or the other, or to express an opinion. I felt sad to see what influence this state of feeling was producing in the Church." It was in such circumstances that the Methodist Episcopal Church took its stand for the National Constitution. After the adoption of that Constitution, Methodism never doubted the *sovereign* nationality of the republic, and never had the unstatesmanlike folly to recognize any state right of secession, or any sovereignty which is not subordinate to the National Sovereignty. During the late civil war it appealed to its Article, as expressing the loyal duty of all its people, and they responded to the appeal with a patriotic devotion surpassed by no other religious communion of the country.

The subject of slavery was discussed as usual. M'Caine introduced it by demanding that it be made the order of the day for a given time. At the appointed time Bruce brought it up by a petition from the Virginia Conference, when M'Caine made the motion "that the Question (in the Discipline) concerning it should run thus: 'What shall be done for the extirpation of the evil of slavery?'" which was "carried." The Journal then records that "a variety of motions were proposed on the subject; and, after a long conversation, Freeborn Garrettson moved, that the subject of slavery be left to the three bishops, to form such a section to suit the Southern and Northern states, as they in their wisdom may think best, to be submitted to this Conference. Carried. Bishop Asbury having refused to act on the last vote, the question was left open. Ezekiel Cooper moved, that a committee be formed, one from each Conference, to take the different motions, and report concerning slavery. Carried. George Dougharty, Philip Bruce, William Burke, Henry Willis, Ezekiel Cooper, Freeborn Garrettson, and Thomas Lyell were appointed." This committee reported a long statute in answer to the new question, "What shall be done for the extirpation of the evil of slavery?" retaining most of the act of 1796, but with modifying phrases; the adjective "African" is dropped and the word "slavery" alone retained. The clause providing for the expulsion of a member who should be guilty of selling a slave was qualified by the proviso, "except at the request of the slave, in cases of mercy and humanity, agreeably to the judgment of a committee of the male members of the Society, appointed by the preacher who has the charge of the Circuit." It was also provided that "if a member of our Society shall buy a slave with a certificate of future emancipation, the terms of emancipation shall, notwithstanding, be subject to the decision of the quarterly-meeting conference." Methodists in the States of North and South Carolina, Georgia, and Tennessee were exempt from the rules ont he subject, on account of the stringent laws of those States. The directions, to the Annual Conferences, to prepare forms of petition to the state legislatures for emancipation were omitted, and it was ordered that "our preachers, from time to time, as occasion serves, admonish and exhort all slaves to render due respect and obedience to the commands and interests of their respective masters." The treatment of their petitions and addresses in the South, and Dougharty's sufferings at Charleston, had evidently somewhat discouraged the preachers; their tone is more subdued, though the law, in its new form, is still very thorough, imposing the penalty of expulsion from the Conference upon any preacher who should "become, by any means, an owner of slaves," unless he should "execute their legal emancipation, if practicable, according to the laws of the State where he lives;" expulsion from the Church, on any member who should sell a slave, and conditional emancipation on any who should purchase one, except at the request of the slave.

The Conference adjourned on the twenty-third of May, having sat seventeen days. It "closed," says Lee, "in peace, and the preachers parted in much love." Coke embarked for Europe, and was to see his American brethren no more; and Whatcoat, the junior bishop by election, but senior by age, was to meet with them no more in a General Conference.

These eight years were the most prosperous in the history of the Church thus far, surpassing in numerical gains any equal period. They end with more than a hundred and fifteen thousand (115,411) members, and four hundred preachers. The denomination had gained nearly fifty-nine thousand (58,747) communicants, and more than one hundred (107) preachers, more than doubling its membership, and increasing its preachers by more than one third, notwithstanding the great number of "locations," which, as has been repeatedly shown, were not real losses to the ministry, nor hardly to the itinerancy. It gained more members in these eight years than it had reported at the end of the first twenty-four of its history. The Philadelphia Conference took the lead, numerically. It returned more than twenty-eight thousand seven hundred (28,712;) Baltimore ranked next, and Virginia third. The gain of a hundred and seven preachers is no indication of the actual ministerial growth of the Church; a host of its most commanding men retired to the local ranks in these years, but still to labor indefatigably. There were no less than two hundred and seventy-eight candidates received into full membership by the Conferences; there were but twenty-four deaths, and six expulsions or withdrawals; but there were two hundred and four locations, besides many who were put back into the local ministry from a probationary relation to the Conferences. Able local preachers, many of them veterans from the itinerancy, were now scattered over the whole country, and were among the chief founders of the Church in new regions. They were much more numerous than the traveling ministry. No reports of them were yet made in the statistical returns; but Lee, who had traveled in all its bounds with Asbury, endeavored to ascertain their number in 1799. His estimate was doubtless much short of the truth, but it gives eight hundred and fifty. There were then but two hundred and sixty-nine traveling preachers. About sixty of these local evangelists were beyond the Alleghanies. New England had twenty-five, and about a quarter of these were in the remote province of Maine.

Methodism was now intrenched in every State of the Union, and was penetrating every one of its opened territories. The few itinerants who had followed Gibson to the Natchez country invaded West Florida and East Louisiana. The germs of Churches now obscurely planted in Ohio, Indiana, and Illinois, were never to die, but to yield, in our day, the mighty harvest of 116,000 members and 600 preachers in Ohio; 90,000 members and 450 preachers in Indiana; 90,000 members and 560 preachers in Illinois; and to spread out sheltering boughs over all the West to the northern lakes and the Pacific coast. We shall hereafter see the yet feeble forces of Western Methodism, hitherto so scattered that we have hardly been able to make anything like a coherent record of them, consolidated into thirty-five powerful Conferences, with three thousand itinerants, and half a million communicants, aside from the Methodist Episcopal Church, South, and all other branches of the denomination. Though it began in the West nearly a quarter of a century after its beginning in the East, and was yet in the former but a dispersed and struggling band, it was destined to embody, in its ultramontane Conferences, by our day, fully one half of its ministerial strength, and to move forward in the van of all the other Protestant Christianity of the Valley of the Mississippi.

But in all other sections of the republic, not excepting New England, the inherent vitality and progressive energy of the denomination had now become indisputable, and it was henceforward to advance with a celerity unknown to any other form of Christianity in the nation. In the last decade of the last century (1790–1800) the ratio of increase of the population of the United States was 35·02 per cent., that of Methodism, meanwhile, was but 12·60 per cent.; but this disproportion between the growth of the nation and the denomination was to cease for our age, if not forever, with the close of the eighteenth century. Excepting the periods of the secession of the Methodist Episcopal Church, South, and of the southern Rebellion, the ratio of the increase of the Church has far outsped that of the nation. Even dating from 1790, and making no allowance for these two formidable drawbacks, the average ratio of the increase of the Methodist Episcopal Church has been, down to our day, (1865,) 56·85 per cent. for each ten years, while that of the population of the republic has been 35·82 per cent. The Church has led the nation at the rate of twenty-three per cent. each decade. And yet this statement gives no adequate estimate of the vigor of Methodism, for about half its force in the United States is outside of the Methodist Episcopal Church. The astonishing gains of the latter have been made in spite of secessions, by which half the actual strength of American Methodism stands organized beyond its ecclesiastical lines, though identical with it in doctrine and internal discipline, and nearly so in ecclesiastical economy.

We stand, then, at present (1804) in a most interesting stage of its progress, about midway of the decade in which, after faltering long, in the ratio of its growth, behind that of the country, it was about to wheel from its position in the rear and advance with its triumphant banner to the front, not only of all other denominations, but of the nation itself in the ratio of its increase; and thenceforward, for good or ill, lead the Christianity of the North American continent, adding to its ranks annually masses of population which not only astonished its own humble laborers, but the Christian world, and sometimes, in a single year, exceeded the entire membership of denominations which had been in the field generations before it.

CHAPTER XXVIII.

METHODISM IN THE SOUTH: 1804–1820.

During all the years from 1804 to 1820 Methodism was rapidly matured and consolidated throughout the South, which had now become its chief field, possessing nearly half its numerical strength. It reported at their beginning 13 Districts, 87 Circuits, 164 itinerant preachers, with more than 55,000 members, including, however, the ultramontane portions of the Baltimore and Virginia Conferences, which I have thus far geographically assigned to the West. At the close of the period it reported 23 Districts, 102 Circuits, and 272 preachers, with more than 101,500 members. Methodism had taken ecclesiastical possession of the South. It was now not only founded, but fortified, in all the principal Southern cities. Meanwhile it spread prevailingly through the interior towns and settlements. It had long been tending toward the Southwest. Early in the period it penetrated into Alabama, where it was destined to become the predominant religious power. The noted Lorenzo Dow had wandered into this wilderness in 1803, and was there also in 1804. The historian of the State acknowledges that he preached the first Protestant sermon delivered on its soil. Louisiana, ceded to the United States under Jefferson's administration, reached as far eastward as the Perdido River. The Indian title to some of the eastern lands was extinguished, and we early hear of white settlements on Tensas, Tombigbee, Buckatawny, and Chickasaw. It was to these frontier and semi-barbarous pioneers that Dow heralded Methodism. In 1807 Asbury called, in the South Carolina Conference, at Charleston, for missionaries to this then far western field, and among the appointments to the Oconee District, traveled by Josiah Randle, is Tombigbee Circuit, with Matthew P. Sturdevant as preacher. Randle's District must have been immense and perilous, for between the Oconee, from which it took its name, and the Tombigbee Circuit, lay an Indian country of four hundred miles extent. The next year Tombigbee still appears in the Minutes, with Michael Burdge and Sturdevant as preachers, but the latter bears the title of "missionary," implying, probably, that he was to push to "regions beyond." At the end of this second year they report eighty-six Church members, the germ of all the subsequent growth of Alabama Methodism. In 1809 John W. Kennon and Burdge were the whole itinerant force of the field. Their labor was hard and their success slow; but they returned to the Conference in 1811, reporting one hundred and sixteen members.

Meanwhile itinerants from Tennessee were entering the northeastern portions of the country. About the year 1807 the Indian title to the region north of the Tennessee River bounded on the east by Flint River, on the west by Indian Creek, and reaching to the Tennessee boundary line, was extinguished, and in 1808 Madison County was organized. It was reached by the Elk (Tenn.) Circuit, and the next year we read the title of "Flint Circuit," with no less than one hundred and seventy Methodists, to whom the Conference, assembled in Cincinnati, sent Jedediah M'Minn as preacher. Thus the itinerants of the Southeast and the far West met on the new field of Alabama. In 1811 the Western preachers at the North, and those of South Carolina at the South, returned an aggregate of about four hundred communicants in the country. The labors and sufferings of the earliest evangelist were as severe as any endured in the history of the Church, but they are unrecorded, and known now only by fragmentary traditions. John S. Ford, who was sent with Kennon to Tombigbee Circuit in 1810, relates that from the time they set out from the settlements in Georgia till they reached Fort Claiborne, on the Alabama River, they had to sleep under the trees thirteen nights. They carried their own provisions, except what they could occasionally obtain from the Indians, till they arrived among the whites on Bassett's Creek, now in Clark County Here their Circuit began, and crossing the Tombigbee at old Fort St. Stephens, continued thence up the Buckatawny over to

Chickasawha, and back through the Tensas settlements to Bassett's Creek. In the South Carolina Conference of 1810 Asbury called for volunteers for regions far beyond what was then called "the wilderness." The latter, for that day, was the country from the Ocmulgee River to near the Alabama. Beyond this lay still another "wilderness" of the Chickasaw and Choctaw Indians, and still beyond the latter lay the field to which the itinerants now began to move.

In 1811 the Western Conference, at Cincinnati, sent Thomas Stilwell and David Goodner to Richland and Flint, and at the close of the ecclesiastical year three hundred and forty-eight members are reported from Flint Circuit. The South Carolina Conference of 1811 ceases to report Tombigbee Circuit; but it reappears, in the Mississippi District, with one hundred and forty members, under the jurisdiction of the Western Conference. Alabama thus passes definitively into the ecclesiastical geography of the West, but with it went a company of strong South Carolina preachers, at whose head, as presiding elder, was Dunwody. His Mississippi District was to become, in the Minutes of 1817, the Mississippi Conference. Gibson, as we have seen, had reached the still remoter Southwest by the Ohio and Mississippi Rivers, and in 1812 a band of four young evangelists departed from South Carolina, on horseback, for the distant fields of Mississippi and Louisiana. They were Richmond Nolley, Lewis Hobbs, Drury Powell, and Thomas Griffin. We shall have occasion to notice hereafter some of their adventures in the far Southwest.

Of the host of able men whom we have heretofore seen in the Southern itinerancy, most were yet abroad, and still in their prime vigor; others, who have not yet come under our notice, were now mighty in labors; and still others, of later historical prominence, were about to appear.

William M. Kennedy began his career at the beginning of this period. Joining the South Carolina Conference of 1805, he filled its most important appointments for more than thirty years, half of the time as presiding elder. In 1839 he was struck with apoplexy; and his Conference placed him on its superannuated list, but he continued to labor. "I wish," he exclaimed, "the messenger of death to find me at my Master's work." Traveling in the service of the Church, he was suddenly struck down by another attack of his malady at the foot of a large oak in Newburgh District, S. C., and died in 1840, lamented as one of the noblest men of Southern Methodism.

One of the most memorable evangelists of the Southern itinerancy, a man of real and rare genius, James Russell, appeared in the same year with Kennedy. He had been refused license to exhort because of his ignorance, but his surpassing natural powers at last bore him above all opposition. He carried his spelling book with him along his Circuit, seeking assistance in its lessons even from the children of the families where he lodged. If the state of society in the far South at this early time would allow such a fact to detract from the ministerial character of ordinary men, it could not with him, for his extraordinary power in the pulpit armed him with a supreme authority. He was capable of the highest natural oratory, striking with awe or melting with pathos his crowded auditories. His self-culture advanced rapidly. He became a good English scholar, and a man of refined taste, commanding the admiration of the most intelligent as well as the most illiterate among his hearers, and "standing," says a bishop of his Church, "prominent among such men as Hope Hull, George Dougharty, John Collinsworth, and Lewis Myers. He was one of the fathers of the Southern Methodist Church, and famous in three States as among the most eloquent and powerful preachers of his time."

Lovick Pierce and his brother, Reddick Pierce, entered the itinerancy in the same year with Russell and Kennedy. The former still lives a representative of Southern Methodism after more than sixty years of labors and sufferings for it; a man of the soundest faculties, of unflagging energy, powerful in the pulpit, and of hardly paralleled public services, which, however, have yet had no such record as would admit of their just historic appreciation. In 1799 Methodist preachers on the old Edisto Circuit extended their travels to the obscure locality (on Tinker's Creek) in South Carolina, where the two brothers were growing up with hardly any opportunities of religious improvement. Their father "despised the Methodists with bitterness," but the itinerants were welcomed by some of his neighbors. The two youths obtained his permission to attend one of their meetings, at which James Jenkins preached. "This," Lovick Pierce writes, "was the first time we ever heard the Gospel preached with the Holy Ghost sent down from heaven, and that day we both resolved to lead a new life; then and there we commenced our life of prayer." In 1801 they joined the Church, and within three weeks all the family who were old enough were enrolled in it. The next year a Methodist chapel was erected near their house; both brothers began to exhort, and in December of 1804 both were received into the Conference at Charleston. Reddick Pierce was one of the purest of men, and his word was in prevailing power. "I myself," says his brother, "saw on one occasion, under one of his exhortations, eleven sinners fall from their seat—from one seat—to the ground, crying for mercy." Lovick Pierce as pastor, presiding elder, a leader in his Annual Conference, a representative in the General Conference, has hardly been surpassed in the South. He has led many a young hero into the ministerial ranks, and his early labors were honored by the conversion of one of the noblest martyrs of the itinerancy. Richmond Nolley was, by birth, a Virginian, but his parents removed with him early to Georgia, where he was soon left a poor and orphan boy. Captain Lucas, a Methodist of Sparta, Ga., gave him a home and employment. A camp-meeting, still famous in Georgia Methodist traditions, was held, near Sparta, in 1806, and attended by an immense crowd. It was impossible for all the people to hear the preacher, and Lovick Pierce was deputed to hold a separate meeting on adjacent ground. He stood upon a table and proclaimed the word with such power that a hearer, the daughter of Captain Lucas, fell, smitten by it, in the outskirts of the throng. The whole multitude was soon in commotion. A simultaneous movement was made toward the preacher. "The people fell upon their knees. This interest continued during the remainder of the day and the night. Over one hundred souls professed conversion around that table." Nolley, and a fellow-clerk in the store of Lucas, were among these converts.

He continued under the parental care of his friend Lucas a year longer, preparing himself for the ministry by exhorting in the neighborhood, and in 1807 was received by the Conference, and sent to Edisto Circuit, where he did good service among the slaves. In 1809 he was appointed to Wilmington, N. C., where he rejoiced in a general revival. The next year he was in Charleston, S. C., where he labored sturdily against no little persecution. Fire-crackers were often thrown upon him in the pulpit, and while he was on his knees praying; but he would shut his eyes, that he might not be distracted by menaces, and preach and pray on with overwhelming power, a habit which, it is said, lasted through the remainder of his life. His voice was as a trumpet, and no man of the South proclaimed the Gospel with greater energy than he. It was already manifest that his character was, in the highest sense, heroic, and that the bravest work of the itinerancy befitted him. Accordingly in 1812 we find him wending his way, with three other preachers, toward the Mississippi. Remarkable scenes and a martyr's death awaited him there. But we must part with him at present, to meet him soon again in his new field.

Samuel Dunwody also began his itinerant life in South Carolina early in this period, (in 1806,) though he was a native of Pennsylvania, born in Chester County in 1780. For forty years he traveled and preached like an apostle through much of Georgia and the Carolinas, greatly extending and fortifying the denomination. In 1846 he was compelled to retire to the superannuated ranks; and "fell asleep," in a most tranquil death, in 1854, a veteran of nearly seventy-four years. He was of Irish blood and energy; rough in features, in voice, in manners; resolute to the uttermost, having a "determined spirit, which would only require the influence of circumstances to render its actings truly heroic." All about him, "dress, horse, saddle-bags," were marked by poverty, by disregard of fashion, or even comfort; he seemed totally absorbed in his spiritual life and work; and "his external life," it is said, "so manifestly drew its powers from the spirit within, that there was dignity, it would hardly be too much to say sublimity, in his roughness." He attained commanding influence in his Conference as one of its principal, though one of its least polished representatives, and was charged by Asbury, in 1811, as we have noticed, with the leadership of the whole Southwestern field of Methodism, as presiding elder of the Mississippi District.

Alfred Griffith was brought into the Church in 1801, in a revival which began on Montgomery Circuit, Md., under the exertions of Wilson Lee, who had recently returned, broken in health, from his great western labors, but was preaching with his usual zeal as a supernumerary of the Circuit. At one of Lee's appointments (in a private house) lived a remarkably devoted colored Methodist by the name of Charles. The preacher having determined to open the campaign at this place, covenanted with the faithful African that at the next meeting, while he should be preaching in the principal room, Charles should be on his knees, in a shed-room opening into that in which the service was proceeding, engaged in supplication for the success of the word. "When the time came, and the itinerant, of whom men stood in awe while they admired him, arose in the crowded parlor, Charles, true to his engagement, was on his knees in the shed-room. There was present on that day in that place a power more than human. The people fell on every side. They prayed, they wept sore. Into the midst of this scene now came the pious negro. He had heard the Lord's answer, and, not venturing to rise, he entered the room walking on his knees, while the tears streamed down his black face, now made, if not white, at least intensely bright by the grateful joy which overspread it. Many souls were converted at that single meeting, which was the more glorious because it was only one of a glorious series, only the beginning of a widely-extended, long-continued revival of religion, reaching to Baltimore city and County, to Frederick County, to the Eastern Shore of Maryland, to Pennsylvania, and to Virginia, and lasting till 1808. In 1806 young Griffith was received into the Baltimore Conference, and sent to the Wyoming country. In his numerous subsequent appointments he has been an able contributor to the outspread of the Church in Pennsylvania, Maryland, and Virginia, a leader in the Baltimore Conference, and a venerated counselor in the General Conference. He is small in stature; like Paul, of unpretentious personal presence; of simple manners; of few words, but strikingly pertinent in debate; profound and statesmanlike in counsel; and in familiar conversation remarkably entertaining, anecdotal, and humorous.

A young man by the name of John Early was admitted to the Virginia Conference in 1807. His family belonged to the most influential class of society in Bedford County, Va., where he was licensed to preach in his twenty-first year. He had begun his public labors among Mr. Jefferson's slaves at Poplar Forest, in Bedford County, and, notwithstanding his adherence to the policy of the Church, South, respecting the slavery controversy, he has been noted from the beginning for his interest in the religious welfare of the colored race. His strong characteristics quickly marked him as a superior man. Possessing an iron constitution, a practical but ardent mind, a notably resolute will, and habits rigorously systematic and laborious, he became a favorite coadjutor, a confidential counselor, of Asbury, M'Kendree, Bruce, Jesse Lee, and their associate leaders of the denomination. He was a renowned, if not indeed a dreaded, disciplinarian. His preaching was simple, direct, and powerful; and few, if any, of his early fellow-itinerants gathered more recruits into the Church in Virginia. Possessing surpassing capacity for business, he was often called upon for important services by both Church and State. He took an active part in the measures that resulted in the division of the Church in 1844, and the organization of the Methodist Episcopal Church, South; shared in its convention at Louisville, Ky., in 1845; was the president *pro tempore* of its first General Conference at Petersburg, Va.; and was there elected its first Book Agent. In 1854 he was made one of its bishops at Columbus, Georgia. He still lives, after one of the most laborious careers in the history of the American Methodist itinerancy. One who has well known him says that "he has probably received more persons into the Methodist Church than any man in it. As a presiding officer we seldom see his equal for precision, dispatch, and business. His preaching is always dignified, simple, and impressive, and often perfectly irresistible; thousands of souls, on earth and in heaven, are the seals of his ministry."

The next year after Early's admission to the itinerancy another young man who was to attain episcopal dignity and national reputation, William Capers, entered the ministry in the South Carolina Conference. His temperament was vivid, brilliant, and generous. He loved society, and was gayest of the gay; but his Methodistic domestic training had touched the deeper susceptibilities of his soul. It had preserved him from youthful vices, and, in 1806, at a camp-meeting on the estate of Rembert, of Rembert Hall, (so historical in early Methodism,) his conscience was thoroughly awakened. After a short period of healthful religious progress he became the victim of a morbid delusion, (sanctioned by the current Calvinistic theology, but denied by Methodism,) under which he suffered for about two years, and which deterred him from an open profession of his faith. Meanwhile his father had also been led astray by the schism of Hammett in Charleston, and had lost the life, if not the form, of his piety. In 1808 his sister was converted at a camp-meeting in the Rembert neighborhood, and returned home exemplifying the power and peace of the Gospel. An affecting scene soon followed, which he describes: "It grew night; supper was over; it was warm, and we were sitting in a piazza open to the southwest breeze which fans our summer evenings. My sister was singing with a soft, clear voice some of the songs of the camp-meeting, and as she paused, my father touched my shoulder with his hand, and slowly walked away. I followed him till he had reached the furthest end of the piazza on another side of the house, when, turning to me, he expressed himself in a few brief words, to the effect that he felt himself to have been for a long time in a backslidden state, and that he must forthwith acknowledge the grace of God in his children or perish. His words were few, but they were enough, and strong enough. I sank to my knees and burst into tears at the utterance of them, while for a moment he stood trembling by me, and then bade me get the books. The Bible was put on the table; the family came together. He read the hundred and third psalm, and then he kneeled down and prayed as if he felt indeed that life or death, heaven or hell, depended on the issue. That was the hour of grace and mercy—grace restored to my father as in times of my infancy, and mercy to me in breaking the snare of the fowler that my soul might escape." He had been studying for the Bar, but his law books were now laid aside for the Bible. William Gassaway summoned him out to accompany him around a circuit. He went to Camden to meet Gassaway for the purpose, and diffidently took refuge in an inn, at the door of which the venerable Rembert, who was passing, met him, and exhorted him to go with Gassaway. He found Kennedy with the latter, and accompanied them to the church. Kennedy preached, and afterward beckoned him to the pulpit, where Gassaway, who sat in the desk, cried out to him, "Exhort!" He did so, and thus began his distinguished ministerial career.

In the last month of 1808 young Capers was received by the Conference, and appointed to the Wateree Circuit, on which he had to fill twenty-four appointments every four weeks. He had formidable labors and trials, and was well initiated. In 1809 he traveled Pee Dee Circuit, where he was especially devoted to the religious welfare of the colored people. He found many of them eminently pious, and some as eminently useful. One of his churches, at Fayetteville, had been founded by a faithful negro, whose name has thereby become historic in the annals of the Conference. "The most remarkable man," he says, "in Fayetteville when I went there, and who died during my stay, was a negro by the name of Henry Evans, who was confessedly the father of the Methodist Church, white and black, in Fayetteville, and the best preacher of his time in that quarter, and who was so remarkable as to have become the greatest curiosity of the town, insomuch that distinguished visitors hardly felt that they might pass a Sunday in Fayetteville without hearing him preach. Evans was from Virginia; a shoemaker by trade, and, I think, was born free. He became a Christian and a Methodist quite young, and was licensed to preach in Virginia. While yet a young man he determined to remove to Charleston, S. C., thinking he might succeed best there at his trade. But having reached Fayetteville on his way to Charleston, his spirit was stirred at perceiving that the people of his race in that town where wholly given to profanity and lewdness, never hearing preaching of any denomination. This determined him to stop in Fayetteville, and he began to preach to the negroes with great effect. The town council interfered, and nothing in his power could prevail with them to permit him to preach. He then withdrew to the sand-hills, out of town, and held meetings in the woods, changing his appointments from place to place. No law was violated, while the council was effectually eluded, and so the opposition passed into the hands of the mob. These he worried out by changing his appointments, so that when they went to work their will upon him he was preaching somewhere else. Meanwhile, whatever the most honest purpose of a simple heart could do to reconcile his enemies was employed by him for that end. He eluded no one in private, but sought opportunities to explain himself; avowed the purity of his intentions, and even begged to be subjected to the scrutiny of any surveillance that might be thought proper to prove his inoffensiveness; anything, so that he might but be allowed to preach. Happily for him and the cause of religion, his honest countenance and earnest pleadings were soon powerfully seconded by the fruits of his labors. One after another began to suspect their servants of attending his preaching, not because they were made worse, but wonderfully better. The effect on the public morals of the negroes, too, began to be seen, particularly as regarded their habits on Sunday, and drunkenness; and it was not long before the mob was called off by a change in the current of opinion, and Evans was allowed to preach in town. At that time there was not a single church edifice in town, and but one congregation, (Presbyterian,) which worshiped in what was called the State-house, under which was the market, and it was plainly Evans or nobody to preach to the negroes. Now, too, of the mistresses there were not a few, and some masters, who were brought to think that the preaching which had proved so beneficial to their servants might be good for them also; and the famous negro preacher had some whites as well as blacks to hear him. From these the gracious influence spread to others, and a meeting-house was built. It was a frame of wood, weather-boarded only on the outside, without plastering, about fifty feet long by thirty wide. Seats, distinctly separated, were at first appropriated to the whites, near the pulpit. But Evans had already become famous, and these seats were insufficient. Indeed, the negroes seemed likely to lose their preacher, negro though he was; while the whites, crowded out of their seats, took possession of those in the rear. Meanwhile Evans had represented to the preacher of Bladen Circuit how things were going, and induced him to take his meeting-house into the Circuit, and constitute a Church there. And now there was no longer room for the negroes in the house when Evans preached; and, for the accommodation of both classes, the weather-boards were knocked off, and sheds were added to the house on either side; the whites occupying the whole of the original building, and the negroes these sheds as a part of the same house. Evans's dwelling was a shed at the pulpit end of the church. And that was the identical state of the case when I was pastor. Often was I in that shed, and much to my edification. I have not known many preachers who appeared more conversant with Scripture than Evans, or whose conversation was more instructive as to the things of God. He was a Boanerges, and in his duty feared not the face of man. He died during my stay in Fayetteville in 1810. The death of such a man could not but be triumphant, and his was distinguishingly so. I was with him just before he died. His last breath was drawn in the act of pronouncing, (1 Cor. xv, 57,) 'Thanks be to God, which giveth us the victory through our Lord Jesus Christ.' On the Sunday before his death the little door between his humble shed and the chancel where I stood was opened, and the dying man entered for a last farewell to his people. He was almost too feeble to stand at all, but, supporting himself by the railing of the chancel, he said, 'I have come to say my last word to you. It is this: None but Christ. Three times I have had my life in jeopardy for preaching the Gospel to you. Three times I have broken the ice on the edge of the water and swum across the Cape Fear to preach the Gospel to you, and now, if in my last hour I could trust to that, or to anything else but Christ crucified, for my salvation, all should be lost, and my soul perish forever.' A noble testimony! worthy, not of Evans only, but St. Paul. His funeral at the church was attended by a greater concourse of persons than had been seen on any funeral occasion before. The whole community appeared to mourn his death, and the universal feeling seemed to be that in honoring the memory of Henry Evans we were paying a tribute to virtue and religion. He was buried under the chancel of the church of which he had been in so remarkable a manner the founder."

Capers's influence throughout the South, and throughout the denomination, became commanding. He was sent to the General Conference, and to England as representative of the American Church, appointed collegiate professor, and president, editor, missionary secretary, and at last, after the division of the denomination, elected bishop of the Methodist Episcopal Church, South, which office he maintained with unremitted labor till his death in 1855. He was five feet nine inches in stature, with delicately molded features, expressive of uncommon refinement, intelligence, and benevolence. His eyes were black and lustrous, his voice musical; his manners marked by perfect amenity. In the pulpit he was usually mild, suasive, and instructive, occasionally exceedingly impressive and powerful. He was a restless worker, and spent "a handsome patrimony for the Church," was often in want, and died without other resources than his ministerial salary. He was perhaps the most important, if not the most responsible, man in the division of the denomination in 1844.

Still another youth, destined to the episcopal office, was given to the itinerancy by the South the next year after that in which Capers entered the ministry. Beverly Waugh was born in Fairfax County, Va., in 1789, became a Methodist under the ministry of Dr. Thomas F. Sargent, in Alexandria, Va., in his fifteenth year, and joined the Baltimore Conference in 1809, when hardly twenty years old. He was repeatedly appointed to Washington, Baltimore, Georgetown,

Frederick, etc., down to 1828, when the General Conference elected him Book Agent at New York, where he conducted, with ability and energy, the momentous publishing business of the Church for eight years. He had now become one of the prominent men of the denomination, not so much by brilliant or popular qualities, as by his well-balanced faculties, his consummate prudence, his exalted character, his devout temper, Christian courtesy, and effective preaching. The Cincinnati General Conference of 1836 elected him to the episcopate, and for twenty-two years he sustained that most onerous office with extraordinary diligence. Notwithstanding his precarious health, impaired by his labors in the Book Concern, he never failed, in a single instance, to attend his Conferences. These were years of stormy controversies in the Church, and he was worn and wan with care and fatigue. It has been estimated that the average number of ministerial appointments made by him per annum was five hundred and fifty. He suddenly died in his work, by disease of the heart, at Baltimore in 1858. He was dignified in person, with calm, benign, though careworn features, brilliant eyes, shaded by heavy eyebrows, a voice of sonorous distinctness, and manners grave, but endearingly cordial and affectionate. He retained to the last the original plain costume of the ministry. In the pulpit he was often exceedingly powerful; in the episcopal chair prompt, without hurry; cautious, though firm.

John Davis joined the Baltimore Conference the year following Waugh's admission, and became, as his brethren testify, "a prince in Israel." He attributed his conversion in his nineteenth year, to the ineffaceable impression of a lesson of the Holy Scriptures, heard while sitting upon his father's knee while yet a child. His earliest appointments were on rugged Circuits of the western mountains; but he soon became eminent among his brethren, and occupied the most conspicuous stations in Baltimore, Washington, and elsewhere. He was presiding elder during many years; a delegate to the General Conference at every session, save two, after 1816, till his death, and a chief counselor there, though never given to speech-making. He was a practical and effective preacher, and gathered into the Church hosts of members. He persisted steadily in his itinerant career till his infirmities compelled him to retreat to the honored ranks of his "superannuated" brethren in 1846, and died in 1853, in the sixty-sixth year of his age and the forty-fourth of his ministry, exclaiming, "Happy! happy! peaceful! Tell the Conference all is peace!" In stature he was tall, slight, but vigorous. He was energetic in his movements, always appearing to have something to do. In familiar life he was exceedingly agreeable, a good converser, and given to anecdote, especially respecting the adventurous life of the primitive itinerancy. So sound was his judgment, that his clearly expressed opinion was usually deemed decisive of questions in the Conference without further argument.

As the period draws to its close, names familiar and dear to us all nearly half a century later begin to multiply, such as Tucker, Beard, Hamilton, Tippett, and others; within our present chronological limits they were graduating toward the orders of elders—modest young evangelists, trying their strength on hard Circuits, but full of promise.

Such are a few, and but a few, of the preachers of the South in our present period—the second generation of Methodist itinerants—worthy recruits of the elder corps, which was still mighty in the field, led by Lee, Bruce, Roberts, Wells, Everett, Daniel Asbury, George, Reed, Snethen, Shinn, Henry Smith, Roszell, Christopher Sprye, Gassaway, Douglass, Mills, and similar men. Many others of equal note, but of scantier record, might be mentioned, some of whom will be noticed at more apposite points of our narrative.

These were years of rife religious excitement through most of the South. The camp-meeting of the West was generally introduced, and from Bassett's Woods, in Delaware, to Rembert's, in South Carolina, and far beyond, in Georgia, these great occasions were of almost continual occurrence, attended sometimes, says Asbury, by ten thousand people, and three hundred traveling and local preachers. A thousand conversions in a week are sometimes recorded of a single meeting. A pervasive influence went forth from them through the Circuits and Districts, and Methodism spread into almost every city, town, and settlement of the South. The annual Conferences were often held at or near the camps, and the arrival of Asbury, sometimes with M'Kendree or Whatcoat, always with an able "traveling companion," and usually with a retinue of other preachers gathered on his route, became a sort of spiritual ovation, a triumphal march of the great leader, which put in motion the Methodist hosts all along his progress. The great man had become now a wonder to the nation, a hoary captain, with such a prestige as no other clergyman of the western hemisphere could claim. He had led his people to victory in all the land. His whole American life had been heroic, and now, tottering with years, he was as invincible in the field as ever. There was no faltering in his course. His character and example were a marvelous power. The people felt that a cause thus providentially conducted could not fail, but would probably take the whole country. The itinerants especially could not but grow strong in the presence of such a man. His continual passages among them inspirited them to emulate his wondrous energy. They almost universally took a chivalric character, a military *esprit de corps*, which kept them compactly united, exultant in labor, and defiant of persecution and peril. It may be doubted whether the Christian world ever saw a more laborious, more powerful, more heroic, or more successful band of evangelists than the Methodist itinerants who were now traversing the South from Chesapeake Bay to the Mexican Gulf. We are not, therefore, surprised that their communicants numbered, at the close of these years, more than ninety thousand; that they had gained rapidly, not only through the rural districts, but in all the cities, nearly trebling their numbers in Baltimore, nearly doubling them in Washington, more than doubling them in Richmond and Charleston, and gathering all they yet had in Savannah. Baltimore Conference now enrolled 33,289, Virginia 23,756, South Carolina 32,969.

CHAPTER XXIX.

METHODISM IN THE MIDDLE AND NORTHERN STATES: 1804–1820.

THE maturer fields of the Church, in the Middle and Northern States, had almost continual prosperity during the present period. It was a time of church building, in which the primitive temporary structures began to give place to more commodious but hardly more pretentious edifices; of local growth, in membership and influence, and of rapid and important accessions to the ministry. But these sections had not much frontier work, except in Western New York and Canada, and, therefore, fewer of those salient events, which still marked the progress of the denomination in the South and West, and to some extent in the yet reluctant States of New England. Their published records continue to be singularly scanty in historical data. Beginning the period with forty thousand four hundred and fifteen members, the two Conferences of this region ended it with three Conferences and eighty-two thousand two hundred and fifty-four members. They had more than doubled their numerical strength. In 1810 they detached a large and thriving portion of their territory, and formed of it the Genesee Conference, under which has grown up the flourishing Methodism of interior and Western New York. Asbury, in the summer of 1807, wrote: "Our Pentecost for sanctification is fully come in some places. Ten camp-meetings north of New York in about two months, and more laid out. Now, I think, we congregate two millions in a year, and I hope for one hundred thousand souls converted, convicted, restored, or sanctified. The whole continent is awake. I am on a route of three thousand miles from and to Baltimore. Such a work of God, I believe, never was known for the number of people."

Among the eminent men who entered the ministry in this period none attained a more important historical position in the Middle States than John Emory. In his seventeenth year he joined the Church, a consecrated youth. He was classically educated, and early devoted himself to the profession of the law. At the time he abandoned his ambitious hopes of wealth and honor for the Methodist itinerancy hardly any young man in his native State had more flattering prospects. An inflexible will, the most assiduous habits of study and application, thorough manliness and uprightness, remarkable self-possession, clearness, and comprehensiveness of mind, readiness of speech, in a style of equal perspicuity and vigor, and an extraordinary logical faculty, marked him as a man to whom success was beyond any other hazard than that of life itself. He was not eligible to the bar, according to usage, till his majority, but was admitted two years earlier, and soon had, says one of his legal contemporaries, "every prospect of wealth and fame" by a successful practice. He abandoned the bar for the ministry. His father, though a pious man, persistently opposed his resolution, refused him a horse with which to begin his itinerant career, and refused for two years to hear him preach, or to receive letters from him. Borrowing a horse from a friend, he went forth, however, and traveled, "under the presiding elder," till the session of the Philadelphia Conference in 1810, when he was received into its membership. His father at last became reconciled to his course, encouraged his labors, and, when dying, sent for him to attend and console his last hours. From 1810 to 1813 young Emory rode Circuits, but never afterward. His subsequent appointments were important "stations." In 1820 he was sent as representative of his Church to the British Conference; in 1824 appointed Book Agent, with Nathan Bangs; and in 1832 elected bishop, positions which identify him with important questions and advancements of the Church. In them all he showed the qualities of an extraordinary man, down to his sudden death in 1835, when he was found, bleeding and insensible, on the highway, having been thrown out of his carriage on his route from his home to Baltimore. He died the same day without the restoration of his consciousness. In person he was below the ordinary size, slight, not weighing over one hundred and twenty-five pounds, but well proportioned, and erect. His features were expressive of tranquil thoughtfulness, firmness, and kindliness. He was long a sufferer from gastric ailments, but was a persevering worker, a thorough student, an early riser, and rigorously systematic. Down to his day the Church had not possessed a more scholarly, a better trained intellect. He was pre-eminent as a debater in Conferences, especially in the General Conference, and his legal skill solved for it some of its most difficult legislative problems. Withal he was remarkably versatile, and successful in all that he attempted. His writings in defense of his denomination, both its theology and polity, were always authoritative and conclusive. His piety was profound, steady, yet fervent. He saw in his own Church the mightiest system of agencies for the evangelization, not only of the New World, but of the whole world, that Christendom afforded, and he consecrated himself entirely to the development and application of its forces.

Jacob Gruber's labors in this period down to 1814 were beyond the western mountains, but after one year more, spent in Baltimore, he had charge of the Carlisle District, Penn., which reached into Maryland. In the latter State he held a camp-meeting in 1818, at which he preached before three thousand hearers against slavery, no very uncommon thing among the leaders of the early itinerancy; but a warrant was issued, and he was arrested at one of his quarterly meetings. The grand jury, at Hagerstown, Md., produced an indictment against him, and in 1819 he was solemnly tried for felony in the Frederick County Court. The case produced general excitement, especially among the Methodists, now eminently influential in the State. Many of his chief ministerial brethren, especially Roszell and Snethen, zealously sustained him. Ignatius Pigman, once an itinerant, now an eloquent lawyer, and local preacher, Roger B. Taney, afterward chief justice of the Supreme Court of the United States, and two other lawyers, were employed to defend him. Hon. J. Buchanan, chief judge, Hon. A. Shriver, and Hon. T. Buchanan,

Painted by J. Nims Engraved by E. Mackenzie.

REV. M. RICHARDSON.

of the New York Conference

associate judges, composed the court. The trial proceeded with intense public interest. The jury, after a few minutes' retirement, pronounced a verdict of "not guilty." He went forthwith to the session of his Conference at Alexandria, D. C., and was appointed for the ensuing year to Frederick Circuit, named after, and comprehending, the town in which he had been tried.

Marvin Richardson was awakened at the old Sands-street Church, Brooklyn, in 1805, and, in the next year, converted at a camp-meeting held at Tuckahoe, Westchester County. William Thatcher presided over this gathering, and Asbury and a host of preachers were present. It was an extraordinary occasion. Asbury said that it exceeded any camp-meeting he had ever attended. "From it," writes Richardson, "revivals spread east, west, north, and south; the Spirit of the Lord was poured out upon the city of New York in an unusual manner." In 1808 Ostrander announced him to preach in Brooklyn without his knowledge. With great diffidence and agitation he thus began, when but nineteen years old, his long and successful itinerant life. The same year he was called out by his presiding elder to the Croton Circuit. Thomas Thorp, later a useful preacher, was one of the fruits of his first sermon on this Circuit; yet such was the self-distrust of the young evangelist, that he determined to give up preaching and return home, when Woolsey met him, and by urgent and fatherly admonitions forced him back to the Circuit. A second time he attempted to retreat; but his colleague, Isaac Candee, met him on his homeward route, and again turned him back. He was received into the Conference in 1809, and sent three hundred miles to Charlotte Circuit in Vermont, along the shores of Lake Champlain. He went to it on horseback, carrying his clothing and books, all that he possessed, in his portmanteau. He had formidable labors on his Circuit, but was sustained by a "powerful revival in Middlebury, Vt.," which so strengthened the Church there as to enable it to become a "station." Two hundred souls were added to the membership of the Circuit. During the remainder of these years he occupied laborious appointments. On some of his circuits he suffered severely, receiving but little salary, sometimes hardly enough to buy clothing for the year, having poor fare, impaired health, and terrible exposures in winter, with "face, hands, and feet frozen;" but he was faithful to his charge, and, as his subsequent appointments show, became one of the representative men of the New York Conference. He was called the "finest looking" member of that body—in person well-proportioned and dignified, with an expressive face, simple but most courteous manners, of few words, extreme modesty, great prudence in counsel, and a tranquil uniformity of temper and life—the perfect Christian gentleman, and unblemished Christian minister. "The oldest member of the New York Conference," says one of his brethren, "he has attended fifty-eight of its annual sessions, having never failed of one of them, and being forty-two years 'effective.' He has held a place in the front rank of his Conference, and in the regards of the people. He has been fourteen years on Circuits, thirteen in city stations, fifteen presiding elder, and eight times a delegate to the General Conference."

In 1808 Nathan Bangs returned from Canada, and was appointed to Delaware Circuit, N. Y., where, among many other fruitful incidents of his ministry, was the reception into the Church of his brother, Heman Bangs, who joined the Conference in 1815, and became one of its strongest men. Tall, robust, of powerful voice, and more powerful brain, an incessant preacher, and able disciplinarian, assiduously devoted not only to the perfunctory labors of the ministry, but to all the philanthropic undertakings of the Church, a man of fervent zeal, of great practical sense, of good humor, and no little adroitness, Heman Bangs has been one of the most successful Methodist preachers of the last half century. Nathan Bangs occupied important posts during this period: Albany Circuit, New York city, and Rhinebeck and New York Districts. His pen was busy in publications in defense of Methodism, and, with Emory, he was now beginning the literature of American Methodism. He was greatly useful in New York city from 1810 to 1812. Methodism had one Circuit in the city, with but little more than two thousand members, when he began there. A profound religious interest prevailed during both years of his appointment. More than two hundred and fifty members were added to the Church by the close of the first, and nearly one hundred and fifty more by the close of the second. On the Rhinebeck District he had almost continual revivals. By the end of his four years on the District its nine appointments had increased to thirteen, its nineteen preachers to twenty-five, and it had gained nearly a thousand members. Besides this numerical success, nearly all its economical interests had improved; chapels and parsonages were springing up all over its territory. Methodism had, in fine, secured in this extensive region not only a lodgment, but a strength which no subsequent adversities have been able to shake. He led many a useful laborer into the ministry during his presiding eldership in these years, some of whom were to take historical rank in the Church. It was toward the close of this period that he called out Robert Seney, his life-long, and perhaps his dearest friend, one of the first three graduates of college in the ministry, a man who sacrificed the profession of the law and high social rank for the heroism of the itinerancy, which he maintained for more than thirty years; "an excellent general scholar," writes Bangs, "a well-read theologian," a successful preacher in the most important appointments of New York Conference, a staunch friend, a perfect Christian gentleman, of extraordinary memory, intuitive discernment of character, rare humor, and profound modesty. It may be doubted whether Bangs's usefulness during these times was, in any other respect, greater than in his success in recruiting the ministry with similar men.

While Dr. Emory was in charge of the Union Station, Philadelphia, in 1814, he had a reluctant agency in the events which gave rise to the African Methodist Episcopal Church. As early as 1787 some colored Methodists in Philadelphia, withdrawing from the Church, undertook to build a chapel for themselves, and Bishop White, of the Protestant Episcopal Church, ordained a colored preacher for them. Richard Allen, once a southern slave but self-redeemed, had become wealthy and influential among his people in Philadelphia, and, in 1793, erected for them a church on his own land, which was dedicated by Asbury, and named Bethel. Allen and his brethren had entered in 1796 into an engagement, by a "charter," to remain under the disciplinary regulations of the Church and the jurisdiction of a white elder, appointed in the Philadelphia Conference; but contentions soon arose respecting their relations to the Conference; an appeal was made to the law, and the Supreme Court of Pennsylvania responded in favor of the Bethel Society. They thus became independent. Emory in 1814 addressed to them a circular letter, announcing that the white preachers could no longer maintain pastoral responsibility for them. They called a general convention of colored Methodists in April, 1816, to organize a denomination; and "taking into consideration their grievances, and in order to secure their privileges and promote union among themselves, it was resolved that the people of Philadelphia, Baltimore, and all other places, who should unite with them, should become one body under the name and style of the 'African Methodist Episcopal Church.'" Thus arose the most important Protestant body of Africans in the United States, or indeed in the world. It adopted substantially the Discipline and Doctrines of the parent Church, modified by lay representation through the local preachers. Allen was elected bishop by its General Conference in 1816, and consecrated by five regularly ordained ministers, one of whom was a presbyter of the Protestant Episcopal Church. He died in 1831; but the denomination has had a succession of able superintendents, some of whom have been remarkable for administrative talent and pulpit eloquence. Of its eight bishops, three of whom have died, all were slaves except one. One of them, Willis Nazrey, has episcopal charge of the Colored British Methodist Episcopal Church in Canada, now an independent body. In the United States they have (in 1867) ten Conferences, 550 preachers, including five bishops, but exclusive of 1,500 local preachers, and about 200,000 members, seven eighths of whom live in the Southern States. They have Church property to the amount of four millions of dollars, a Book Concern in Philadelphia, a weekly newspaper, and a college in Ohio. A later organization of colored Methodists has also acquired importance, reporting more than 90,000 members, with about 400 traveling and many local preachers. It sprung from the Methodist Episcopal Church in New York city. There were about eight hundred and forty Africans in the city Methodist Churches in 1818, but in 1821 only sixty-one remained. A schism had been working during the interval, and resulted in the second African Methodist Episcopal Church, distinguished usually by the prefix "Zion," as the first usually is by that of "Bethel," taken from the titles of their original Churches in the respective cities. The two denominations are quite distinct, though maintaining cordial relations with each other.

Methodism continued to extend up the Hudson through all this period. Nearly the whole Ashgrove District was astir with revivals. Camp-meetings were now in more general vogue than ever, and rekindled, summer after summer, religious interest throughout the whole territory of the Middle and Northern Conferences. In each year of the period able young men, besides those already mentioned, and destined to become generally recognized as ministerial leaders, but of most of whom no adequate records remain, entered the itinerancy: in 1805 Charles Giles, George Lane; in 1807, Peter P. Sandford, Phineas Rice, Lewis Pease, George Harmon; in 1808, Friend Draper, Thomas Neal, William Jewett; in 1809, Stephen Martindale, Isaac Puffer, Loring Grant, Coles Carpenter, George Gary; in 1810, Arnold Scolefield, Benjamin G. Paddock, Seth Mattison; in 1811, Joseph Lybrand, Manning Force, John B. Matthias, Benjamin Griffen, Marmaduke Pearce; in 1812, David Dailey, George Banghart, Tobias Spicer, Elisha Williams, William Ross, Gad Smith, Gideon Lanning; in 1813, John Potts, Israel Chamberlayne; in 1814, Joseph Rusling, Buel Goodsell, Elias Bowen; in 1815, Richard W. Petherbridge, Josiah Bowen; and in the remaining five years, John Dempster, George Peck, Fitch Reed, John J. Matthias, Charles Pitman, Noah Levings, Seymour Landon, Zachariah Paddock, Glezen Fillmore; men of pre-eminence in the pastorate, or in educational institutions, editorial positions, the missionary secretaryship, the American Bible Society, but who were yet in their youthful preparatory training.

Meanwhile the frontier movement of Methodism in the Middle and Northern States, which we have heretofore traced, was energetically advancing. The Susquehanna District, pertaining to the Baltimore Conference, with Owen, Griffith, Paynter, Christopher Frye, Draper, and a succession of similar men, as preachers, prospered greatly. In 1807 Draper was sent to form the Canaan Circuit, of ancient renown, and the Church advanced rapidly among the Cumberland, Tioga, and Wyoming mountains and valleys. In the more northerly interior the denomination extended among the New York lakes, planting itself in most of the small settlements which have since risen into flourishing towns and cities. It passed over the Genesee River, as we have seen, in 1804, represented by a useful layman, David Hamlin, who for three years gathered the settlers in his own house for religious worship. Peter Vannest, who had been tending in this direction for years as an itinerant, forded the Genesee River in 1807, near the present city of Rochester, and delivered his first sermon in what is now Ogden Center. The first class was organized the same year in Newstead, at the house of Charles Knight. The next year a youth, George Lane, afterward well known throughout the Church as a faithful itinerant, as Book Agent at New York, and as a saintly man, crossed the Genesee, and held the first camp-meeting of that region. He traveled Vannest's new Circuit laboring unceasingly, and spread out the cause in all directions, preaching as far as Buffalo. He reached at last the northernmost tracks of the ultra-Alleghany itinerants of Pennsylvania, in the region since known as the Erie Conference. In 1809 Glezen Fillmore, a young "exhorter," visited Clarence. "He had joined the Church in Westmoreland. He went to a place now called Skinnersville, to see a family with whom he had been acquainted at the East, where he was invited to hold a meeting, and left an appointment for the next Sabbath. On Sunday morning he went, and, on his approach, he saw people wandering about carelessly; but upon arriving at the place of meeting he found no one there except the family. Wright, the man of the house, seemed distressed at the disappointment, and, rising under the influence of considerable excitement, said, 'I cannot stand it.' He went out, and returned with two persons, a man by the name of Maltby, and his wife. The family and these two constituted the congregation; but Fillmore, nothing daunted, proceeded with his meeting. Maltby and his wife seemed considerably impressed. At the close of the exercises Maltby said it had been 'a solemn meeting,' repeating the words several times. He invited Fillmore to hold another at his house the next Sabbath, to which he gave his cordial consent. When the time arrived the house was full, and a good religious feeling prevailed. A revival immediately commenced, and a Society was formed. Maltby and his wife were among the converts, and he became a local preacher. Four of his sons were afterward members of the Erie Conference: grand results often follow what appear to be small causes. Fillmore was licensed to preach, and continued his labors in a local capacity for the space of nine years, preaching in the newly opening settlements, and preparing the way for the traveling preachers. This period he considers as one of the most useful and successful portions of his life." He was to have a prominent place in the subsequent history of the Church.

In 1805 Thomas Smith, whose notable adventures in New Jersey and more southern regions have been mentioned, was sent, with Charles Giles, to the Seneca Circuit, which comprised all the country between the Cayuga and Seneca Lakes, south and west of the latter, and north to Lyons, with few settlers scattered over it, and they extremely poor. Smith had his usual trials and success in this new field. He found Indians still numerous on his Circuit, and preached where "the shining tomahawk and glittering scalping knife" were within sight. He suffered from the diseases of the country, and at one time "lay six days, on three old chairs," in a log-cabin, sick with fever. He was, however, a dauntless itinerant. Opposers could not stand before him. He assailed them sometimes in quite original modes of attack. At Lyons lived a highly respectable Methodist, Judge Dorsey, whose wife, Eleanor Dorsey, was one of those "women of Methodism" who ministered to Asbury, and the other earliest itinerants in Maryland.* The general spirit of emigration had led them to this new country, and their house was now the home of Methodist preachers. Smith went to Lyons, and says: "Here we had a respectable Society, and a small meeting-house. But the people of Lyons were generally wicked. They took pleasure in unrighteousness, in deriding the ways of God, and in persecuting the humble followers of Jesus Christ. They interrupted and insulted us in our religious worship, and on this evening they were worse than usual. I paused until I got their attention, and then remarked that I should not wonder if Lyons should be visited on the morrow in a way that it never had been before, and perhaps never would be again to the end of time. We then had quietness to the close of the meeting. When the congregation was dismissed, and I had come out of the house, the people gathered around me, and with one voice cried out, 'For God's sake, tell us what is to happen here to-morrow!' I replied, 'Let to-morrow speak for itself.' I went home with Judge Dorsey, a short distance from the town. After breakfast the next day I said to Mrs. Dorsey, 'I wish you to go with me into Lyons this morning, as there are some families to which I cannot get access without you.' She, being acquainted with the place, readily consented. At nine o'clock A. M. we entered the town. Scores from the country were already there, and the place was in commotion. We went to the house of Mr. ——, where we were politely received. I knew if we could storm that castle the day was ours. After conversing some time, I remarked that Mrs. Dorsey and myself were on a visit to Lyons, and, if it were agreeable, we would pray before we parted. 'By all means, Mr. Smith; by all means, sir.' Before prayer was over there were scores of people at the door, and by this time the order of the day began to be understood, and they that feared God were at their posts, coming up to the help of the Lord against the mighty. We then went, in large procession, from house to house, entering every door in order, and praying for the souls of the families. Our little band soon increased to some three or four hundred. When

* "Women of Methodism," p. 250. New York, 1866.

we came near the tavern, where we had been derided, it was inquired, 'Will they admit us?' But the doors and windows being open, we entered, and was there ever such a shout while storming Lucifer's castle! At four o'clock in the afternoon we called a halt to see what was done, and, forming a circle on the green, the new converts were invited within the circle, when thirty-two came in who that day had found the pearl of great price, Christ in them the hope of glory. These thirty-two, and eight more, were added to the Church of God on that afternoon. Thanks be to God, this was another good day's work in the Lord's vineyard. This meeting produced a pleasing change in Lyons, and Methodism gained a footing in that place it never had before. To God be the glory!"

So rapidly had it spread through these interior regions that in 1810 Asbury organized it in a new Conference. On the twentieth of July the preachers of the Susquehanna, Cayuga, and two Canada Districts were convened at the barn of Judge Dorsey, in Lyons, and there formed the new organization, comprising all their recent territory, except Lower Canada. Increased efficiency was thus immediately given to its work. Its three Districts, thirty Circuits, and ten thousand seven hundred members of 1810 increased, by the end of the present period, to eight Districts, seventy-four Circuits, and nearly twenty-four thousand members, more than doubling all its forces in a decade. It included Canada during the whole period.

In the latter country now appeared, (in 1805,) for the first time, two very important men, Henry Ryan and William Case. The former we have already met in Vermont, where he began his ministry in 1800, an energetic Irishman, and one of the sturdiest itinerants of his day. William Case will ever rank as one of the noblest acquisitions of the ministry. He was one of the original members of the Genesee Conference, and one of its first three presiding elders in 1810; Draper and Ryan being the two others. For eighteen years he had charge of Districts--the Cayuga, Oneida, Chenango, Lower Canada, Upper Canada, and Bay of Quinte. In 1828 he was appointed superintendent of Indian missions and schools in Canada, and in 1830 general superintendent of the Methodist Societies in the province. In 1852 he was allowed to travel and preach at large through the province till his death in 1855. He was esteemed for years as the patriarch and leader of Canadian Methodism, the chief of its great mission field, a truly apostolic man, fervid, genial, prudent, attractive and effective in the pulpit, and singularly successful and beloved among the Indians.

In 1806 Canada has two Districts, and twelve Circuits, including two pertaining to New York Conference. Samuel Coate is at Montreal, and Nathan Bangs at Quebec. A Lower Canada District appears in the Minutes, and a mission to its French population is added to the appointments. In 1808 the first report of members in Quebec appears—hardly more than a single "class"—thirteen in number. Methodism, however, was destined to find a stronghold in that city, though long harassed by public prejudice and the coming war. In 1809 Detroit, Mich., is reached by Case. At the organization of the Genesee Conference in 1810 the Upper Canada District was placed under its jurisdiction, while that of Lower Canada was retained by New York Conference; there were not yet, however, two hundred members in all the five appointments of the latter. The whole country now became alarmed by the omens of the approaching war, and, in the next year, none of the preachers went to the Conferences in the States. No returns of members reached the Genesee Conference from the upper province, but, in the lower, Montreal reported more than fifty, Quebec about half that number, Ottawa Circuit about a hundred, and that of the St. Francis River one hundred and twenty. Bangs was appointed to Montreal, but did not reach it on account of the military obstructions between the two countries. Thomas Burch was sent to Quebec, and made his way thither; Luckey, appointed to St. Francis, failed to get there. Robert Hibbard, a native of New York, who had joined its Conference in 1809, and for two years had labored faithfully in Canada, where he had formed the St. Francis Circuit, gathering upon it more than a hundred members, consented to return notwithstanding the troubled times. He reached the Ottawa Circuit, and kept to his work, though the provincial government had, by proclamation, ordered all citizens of the United States to leave the country. Learning that the preachers for the St. Francis Circuit, so dear to him as his own work, had not arrived, he resolved to go thither and encourage the Churches under their new trials. He reached Montreal, but in his further progress was drowned in the St. Lawrence; his horse escaped to the shore, but the evangelical hero was borne away, and was seen "going down with his hands lifted toward heaven." His body was never found. He was a sanctified man, "studious," and "indefatigable," and, say his brethren in their Minutes, "entered the watery grave to rise again to a glorious immortality at the last day." Asbury delivered a "funeral sermon" on the event before the next New York Conference.

In 1813 the war had cut off all communication between the Churches of the two countries. The preachers could not attend the Genesee Conference, but they met together and made their own appointments as best they could. At the close of the contest, in 1815, the Genesee Conference resumed its care of the country. Case was appointed presiding elder of Upper Canada District, Ryan of that of Lower Canada. There were now but nine Circuits and twelve preachers. Montreal and Quebec were unsupplied; but the British Conference sent over three missionaries for these stations, and thus was brought on the question of territorial jurisdiction, which subsequently led to no small amount of discussion and negotiation, but was at last amicably settled, with more intimate relations between the two bodies than ever had existed since the organization of the American Church. The war ended with a loss of nearly one half the membership in Canada, the returns of 1815 amounting to but one thousand seven hundred and sixty-five. But Methodism was too vital to suffer long from such a cause. The next year the Minutes show eleven Circuits, with sixteen preachers, and two thousand five hundred members. They had yet but eleven churches or "meeting-houses," all built of wood, except that of Montreal, which was of stone, but small.

Freer scope than ever was now given to the denomination in the Canadas. In 1817 the Genesee Conference, many of whose preachers were curious to see their foreign territory, held its session at Elizabethtown, beyond the boundary. About eighty of them assembled there, including twenty-two Canadian itinerants. Enoch George presided, and the occasion was a jubilee to the Church in the wilderness. It was estimated that one hundred souls were awakened at the session, and a flame of religious excitement spread out among the Circuits, so that an increase of one thousand four hundred members the ensuing year was attributed to this first Canadian Conference. The Gospel was now preached in every English settlement of Upper Canada, for Methodism, besides its itinerants, traveling immense Circuits, had a large corps of local preachers and exhorters, who were kept incessantly at work. Meanwhile the British Conference continued to send out Wesleyan missionaries. There were nine of them in the country in 1818, who extended their labors even to Toronto and the Bay of Quinte, and thus further complicated the question of ecclesiastical jurisdiction. Correspondence between the American bishops and the Wesleyan Missionary Committee, London, followed; the relations of the two Churches were cordial, but unsettled in respect to the province, and could not be adjusted till the next General Conference, when Emory was dispatched to England for the purpose.

In 1820 the Genesee Conference again met in Canada. There were now in Upper Canada sixteen clergymen of the Church of England, fifteen Presbyterian and Congregational, and eighteen Baptist preachers. The Methodist itinerants (including the Wesleyan missionaries) were thirty-three, besides forty-seven local preachers and sixty-five exhorters. The actual working ministry of Methodism must now have constituted more than one half of the pastoral supply of the province. The number of Methodists in the country (including the Wesleyan charges) amounted to six thousand three hundred. They had much more than trebled in these sixteen years, though they had thus far only been planting in the wilderness the germs of that harvest which was to yield, in our day, nearly one hundred thousand members in the various Methodist communions, and nearly a thousand traveling preachers, with Indian missions, publishing houses, periodicals, colleges, academies, and churches, many of them costly edifices, adorning the whole settled country. They were to keep pace with emigration, and reach westward to the Pacific coast, and eastward, till they should blend with the Methodism planted by Coughland, M'Greary, Black, and Garrettson on the Atlantic coast, and the denomination become the most effective religious force of British North America.

The period closes then with a remarkable exhibit of strength and prospect for the middle and northern fields of the denomination. Not merely their numerical growth from two to three Conferences, from 40,415 to 82,215 members, and from 135 to 297 preachers, more than doubling their force in these sixteen years, in spite of secessions in Philadelphia and New York; but the intellectual advancement of their ministry, the rapid erection of church edifices, the ever memorable organization of the general Missionary Society, the beginning of periodical publications, and the recommencement of academic institutions, (all three events in New York city,) render this one of the most imposing epochs of American Methodism.

CHAPTER XXX.

METHODISM IN THE EASTERN STATES: 1804–1820.

THE present period (1804–1820) opens with a host of able men in the eastern itinerancy, most of whose names are already familiar to us: Moriarty, Crowell, Crawford, Beale, Brodhead, Ruter, Hedding, Soule, Ostrander, Washburn, Pickering, Kibby, Jayne, Snelling, Webb, Joshua Taylor, Munger, Heath, Hilman, Merwin, Chichester, Sabin, Kent, and many others. Recruits, not a few of whom have survived till our day, were to be rapidly added to the ranks: in 1804 Lewis Bates; in 1806 Joel Steele, Caleb Fogg, Solomon Sias; 1807 Charles Virgin, Joseph A. Merrill; 1808 Isaac Bonney, William Swayze, David Kilbourn; 1809 John Lindsay, George Gary, Benjamin R. Hoyt, Coles Carpenter, Amasa Taylor, Ebenezer F. Newell, Edward Hyde; 1811 Thomas Norris, Daniel Fillmore; 1812 Jacob Sanborn, John Adams, Thomas Tucker, Joseph Ireson; 1813 Van Rensselaer Osborn; 1814 Thomas C. Pierce, Bartholomew Otheman; 1815 John Lord, Nathan Payne; 1816 Daniel Dorchester, Moses Fifield; and, toward the close of the period, increasing numbers of familiar names, Jennison, Wiley, Hascall, Fisk, Taylor, Stoddard, Horton, Crandall, Baker—a bald list of names, but if of little interest to the general reader, yet all of them mementoes of precious memories to New England Methodists. Many others of the same dates, and of hardly less importance, could be added; not a few of the humblest of them men of heroic character, whose travels and labors, in many instances, extended through half a century, and from Canada to Long Island Sound.

The appearance of Wilbur Fisk in the ministry in 1818 may be said to have dated a new epoch in New England Methodism. A man of intrinsic greatness; of the highest style of Christian character; of rare pulpit eloquence, full of grace,

Engraved by E. Mackenzie

W. Fisk

dignity, and power, he was also the first Methodist preacher of the Eastern States who had the advantages of a collegiate education; a fact of no little importance among the people of New England. No man did more to redeem his Church from the imputation of ignorance, not to say the contempt, with which it had been branded among the trained clergy of those States; for, notwithstanding the ministerial competence and greatness of such men as Merritt, Ruter, Soule, and Hedding, their commission had been generally discredited, beyond their own people, for lack of academic diplomas. Fisk led up the whole Methodism of the East in educational enterprise, ministerial culture, and public influence; while his saintly life presented a model of Christian character, which impressed his entire denomination, not only in New England, but throughout all the land, for his usefulness and reputation became national. In 1830 he was called to the presidency of the Wesleyan University, Middletown, Conn., of which he was one of the founders. In 1835 his enfeebled health compelled him to make a voyage to Europe, where he officially represented American Methodism in the Wesleyan Conference. He was elected bishop of his Church while absent, but declined the episcopal office in favor of his function as an educator. Returning, he continued his labors in the Wesleyan University with declining health, but unabated devotion, till his death.

Wilbur Fisk's person bespoke his character. It was of good size, and remarkable for its symmetry. His features were harmonious, the contour strongly resembling the better Roman outline. His eye was nicely defined, and, when excited, beamed with a peculiarly benign and conciliatory expression. His complexion was bilious, and added to the diseased indication of his somewhat attenuated features. His head was a model not of great, but of well-proportioned development. It had the height of the Roman brow, though not the breadth of the Greek. His voice was peculiarly flexible and sonorous. A catarrhal disease affected it; but just enough, during most of his life, to improve its tone to a soft orotund, without a trace of nasal defect. It rendered him a charming singer, and was an instrument of music to him in the pulpit. Without appearing to use it designedly for vocal effect, it was nevertheless an important means of impression to his sermons. Few men could indicate the moral emotions more effectually by mere tones. It was especially expressive in pathetic passages. If genius cannot be claimed for him, nor the very highest order of intellect, yet he approached both so nearly as to command the admiration of the best cultivated minds, and the almost idolatrous interest of the people. Good vigor in all his faculties, and good balance of them all, were his chief intellectual characteristics. His literary acquisitions were not great. The American collegiate course in his day was stinted. After his graduation he was too busy to study much, and he was not a great reader. His resources were chiefly in himself; in his good sense, his quick sagacity, his generous sensibilities, and his healthy and fertile imagination. He possessed the latter power richly, though it never ran riot in his discourses. It was an auxiliary to his logic, an exemplification of Dugald Stewart's remark on the intimate relation between the imagination and the reasoning faculty in a well-balanced mind. Its scintillations were the sparkles that flew about the anvil on which his logic plied its strokes. His style, not being formed from books, was the natural expression of his vigorous and exact intellect; it was therefore remarkable for its simplicity and terseness, its Saxon purity and energy. A meretricious sentence cannot be found in all his published writings. His polemical writings were not only in good temper, but models of luminous and forcible argumentation. His sermon on Calvinism may be referred to as an example. That discourse, with his sermon and lectures on Universalism, his essays on the New Haven Divinity, his sermon on the law and the Gospel, his tract in reply to Pierrepont on the Atonement, etc., would form a volume which the Church might preserve as no ignoble memorial of both his intellectual and moral character. His Travels in Europe, though containing some examples of elaborate reflection and picturesque description, was not a volume of superior claims; it had too much of the ordinary guide-book character. His moral character was as perfect as that of any man whom it has been the writer's happiness to know. His intimate friends will admit that there is hardly a possibility of speaking too favorably of him in this respect. It has often been remarked by those who had years of personal relations with him, that they were literally at a loss to mention one moral defect that marred the perfect beauty of his nature. This is saying very much; it is saying what cannot be said of one man perhaps in a million; but it can be deliberately said of this saintly man. It was his rare moral character, more even than his intellectual eminence, that gave him such magical influence, and rendered him so successful in the government of literary institutions. All about him felt self-respect in respecting him. To offend him was a self-infliction which even the audacity of reckless youth could not brook. In 1839, in the forty-eight year of his age, Wilbur Fisk died in great peace. His chamber had been for days sanctified, as it were, by the glory of the Divine Presence, and his broken utterances were full of consolation, and triumph over death. "Glorious hope!" was the last and whispered expression of his religious feelings.

Another name has been mentioned, among the additions to the New England ministry, in this period, which has become as familiar to Eastern Methodists as that of Fisk; the name of a man whose life, like that of not a few others in the Methodist itinerancy, forces upon the historian the suspicion, not to say the discredit, of writing "romance" rather than fact. During the last war between England and the United States lived, in an obscure suburb of the city of Boston, a poor but devoted English woman, who, having lost her husband soon after her emigration, depended for her subsistence on the earnings of her needle. She opened her small front room several times a week for a prayer-meeting, and procured the aid of her Methodist associates in conducting it. Much of the good seed thus scattered with a faith that hoped against hope, and in a soil that seemed utterly arid, produced good fruit. Among the attendants at the meeting was a young mariner, with an intellectual eye, a prepossessing countenance, and the generous susceptibilities of a sailor's heart. Amid the corruptions of his associates he had been noted for his temperance and excellent disposition. And yet this child of the sea had been a wanderer on its waves from his earliest years; a natural superiority of head and heart had raised him above the moral perils of his lot. His fine traits interested much the English Methodist and her religious friends, and they could not but hope that God would make some use of him among his comrades. He had received no education, but could read imperfectly. She trusted that Providence would in some way provide for his future instruction; but he was suddenly summoned away to sea. He had been out but a short time when the vessel was seized by a British ship, and carried into Halifax, where the crew suffered a long and wretched imprisonment. A year had passed away, during which the good woman had heard nothing of the young mariner. Her hopes of him were abandoned as extravagant, in view of his unsettled life, and its peculiar impediments to his improvement. Still she remembered and prayed for him with the solicitude of a mother. About this time she received a letter from her kindred, who had settled in Halifax, on business which required her to visit that town. While there her habitual disposition to be useful led her, with a few friends, to visit the prison with Tracts. In one apartment were the American prisoners; as she approached the grated door a voice shouted her name, calling her "mother," and a youth beckoned and leaped for joy at the grate. It was the lost sailor boy. They wept and conversed like mother and son, and when she left she gave him a Bible, his future guide and comfort. During her stay at Halifax she constantly visited the prison, supplying him with religious books and clothing, and endeavoring, by her conversation, to strengthen the religious impressions made on his mind in Boston. After some months she removed to a distant part of the province, and for years she heard nothing more of the youth. It was her happiness to reside again in Boston, in advanced life, and to find her "sailor boy" the chief attraction of its pulpit, in times when Channing, the elder Beecher, Wainwright, and other men of national reputation, were its ornaments. Such was the beginning of the long and eminent ministry of Edward T. Taylor, a man whose fame for genius and usefulness became general, whose extraordinary character has been sketched in our periodicals, and the books of transatlantic visitors,* as one of the so-called "lions" of the city, whom a distinguished critic has pronounced the greatest poet of the land, though unable to write a stanza; and a mayor of Boston has publicly declared to be a more effectual protector of the peace of the most degraded parts of the city than any hundred policemen.

In a spacious and substantial chapel, crowded about by the worst habitations of the city, he delivered every Sabbath, for years, discourses the most extraordinary, to assemblies also as extraordinary perhaps as could be found in the Christian world. In the center column of seats, guarded sacredly against all other intrusion, sat a dense mass of mariners—a strange medley of white, black, and olive—Protestant, Catholic, and sometimes pagan, representing many languages, unable, probably, to comprehend each other's vocal speech, but speaking there the same language of intense looks and flowing tears, for the preacher could address them by his own, and his gestures, if not by words. On the other seats, in the galleries, the aisles, the altar, and on the pulpit stairs, crowded, week after week, and year after year, (among the families of sailors, and the poor, who had no other temple,) the *élite* of the city, the learned professor, the student, the popular writer, the actor, groups of clergymen, and the votaries of fashion, listening, with throbbing hearts and wet eyes, to the man whose chief training had been in the forecastle, whose only endowments were those of grace and nature, but whose discourses presented the strangest, the most brilliant exhibition of sense, epigrammatic thought, pathos, and humor, expressed in a style of singular pertinency, spangled over by an exhaustless variety of the finest images, and pervaded by a spiritual earnestness that subdued all listeners; a man who could scarcely speak three sentences, in the pulpit or out of it, without presenting a striking poetical image, a phrase of rare beauty, or a sententious sarcasm, and the living examples of whose usefulness are scattered over the seas.

* See the American Travels of Miss Martineau, Buckingham, Miss Bremer, Mrs. Jamieson, and Dickens.

He was born in Richmond, Va., about 1793; entered the American naval service, as surgeon's boy, in his childhood; was some time in the Spanish navy in the Mexican waters; served again in the American navy at New Orleans; went to Boston, where he joined a privateer in the war of 1812, and was taken prisoner by a British frigate while pursuing a British brig. After an imprisonment of six months he returned to Boston, and, under the ministrations of Hedding and Sabin, began his Methodist career. By the aid of an eminent Methodist layman, Colonel Binney, he had three months' instruction at New Market (N. H.) Seminary, the only academic education of his life.

His name appears in the Minutes, for the first time, in 1819, when he was received into the New England Conference, and appointed to Scituate Circuit, among his own seafaring people, under the presiding eldership of Pickering; it embraced seven towns. In 1820 he was at Falmouth and Sandwich; in 1821 at Sandwich and Harwich; 1822, Harwich and Barnstable; 1823, Fairhaven and New Bedford; 1824, Martha's Vineyard; 1825, Milford; 1826, Bristol; 1827 and 1828, Fall River and Little Compton. In his rapidly changed appointments he had a good initiation to the labors and trials of the itinerancy. His extraordinary and somewhat eccentric genius had attracted great congregations; but he had been found chiefly useful among seamen; the Church, therefore, with its usual policy of placing the right man in the right place, commissioned him, in 1829, as chaplain to mariners in the metropolis of New England. His impression on the public mind of Boston was immediate and most vivid. The high culture of many of its citizens fitted them the better to appreciate the unquestionable genius and marvelous eloquence of the uncultivated preacher. He projected a Mariner's Church, and, after he had labored hard in other parts of the country to collect funds for its erection, the people of Boston, without regard to sectarian distinctions, took it in hand, completed it, effectively endowed it, and gave it, a "Mariner's Home," thus securing to the preacher a life-long sphere of remarkable power to which the Church has ever since annually appointed him.

During most of this period, down to 1816, when Joshua Soule was appointed to the Book Concern, New York, he was the chief itinerant in Maine, traveling, in the outset, its only District, which comprehended all its Methodist territory; with Joshua Taylor, Munger, Heath, Hillman, Baker, Kibby, Virgin, Ruter, Newell, and similar men under him. The whole state was now resounding with the sound of the Gospel by their ministrations. Hedding labored during these times in Vermont, New Hampshire, Connecticut, Massachusetts, and Maine, mostly on immense districts, which extended over several of the states. About midway of the period he thus reviews his work: "I have averaged over three thousand miles travel a year, and preached on an average a sermon a day since I commenced the itinerant life. I have never in this time owned a traveling vehicle, but have ridden on horseback, except occasionally in winter, when I have borrowed a sleigh, and also a few instances in which I have traveled by public conveyance or a borrowed carriage. I have both labored hard and fared hard. Until recently I have had no dwelling-place or home; but, as a wayfaring man, lodged from night to night where hospitality and friendship opened the way. I have traveled many a day in summer and winter without dinner, because I had not a quarter of a dollar that I could spare to buy it. Such are some of the difficulties the Methodist preachers have been compelled to encounter, especially in New England, during the past ten years. But notwithstanding all, God has been with us. Revivals have spread through all the country, and multitudes have been added to the little and despised flock." Pickering labored mostly about Boston, and on the Boston District as presiding elder, his field in the latter appointment extending from the end of Cape Cod to Providence, R. I., from Marblehead to the interior of New Hampshire; Kibby, Snelling, Webb, Munger, Merwin, Kent, Hyde, Merrill, Sabin, Brodhead, Lindsay, and many more such men, being under his command. Ruter, returning from his Canadian labors, traveled in New Hampshire, Massachusetts, and Maine, but mostly in New Hampshire, where he followed Hedding in 1809, on a District so large that it bore the name of the State. New Hampshire's single District, with its five Circuits, nine preachers, and one thousand members of 1804, was to double all its numerical force before the close of these years. The period began in Vermont with some five Circuits, seven preachers, and a few scattered members, under the presiding eldership of Joseph Crawford, whose District extended into Massachusetts, on the one hand, and Canada on the other. It closed there with fully doubled strength. The two Districts which comprehended the earlier occupied fields—Massachusetts, Rhode Island, and Connecticut—at its beginning, much more than doubled all their statistics by its close.

Lee once more passed over the scene. After an absence of eight years in the South, he was anxious to revisit his early eastern battle-fields, and see how the contest still went on. His passage was a humble but exultant religious ovation. In the latter part of June, 1808, he arrived at Norwalk, Conn., the village on whose highway he had preached his first sermon in New England. "He was much gratified," says his biographer, "in saluting, in the name of the Lord Jesus, some of his friends of former days. Almost twenty years had passed away since he first, as a stranger, entered this part of the world." With tears and benedictions and last farewells, all along his route, he reaches Boston on Thursday, the 21st, and finds the same evening a congregation ready to hear him in the old church, and another, the next night, in the new. By Saturday he is with his first Society, in Massachusetts, at Lynn. They call on him at the parsonage in the evening. The next day being the Sabbath he preaches to them in the morning, with much effect, from Isa. xxxiii, 13. "It was," he writes, "an affecting time. When I put the brethren in mind of my first coming among them, and the difficulties that I, as well as they, had to go through, they could not forbear weeping." By Friday, the 30th, he is in Maine, the field of his hardest conflicts. The people flock to hear him on all his route, and have often to leave their chapels and turn into the woods for room. At Monmouth, where the first Society was formed, they cannot get into the house; many, after the service, come to the altar to give him their hands in pledge of meeting him in heaven. "They wept," he says, "and I could not refrain from weeping." Soule and Fogg are with him there. The preachers generally gather about him as he passes along, saluting him as an old leader and conqueror, and joining in the jubilatic gatherings of the people. Passing through many towns, with similar greetings, he enters New Hampshire, having spent forty-three days and preached forty-seven times in Maine. He gives nearly a week and seven farewell sermons to the former. After spending six days and delivering seven sermons in Connecticut, he reaches Garrettson's "Traveler's Rest," at Rhinebeck, on the last day of September. Thus ended Lee's personal connection with Methodism in New England. His historical connection with it will probably last till the consummation of all things. He survived this visit about eight years, during which he continued to labor indefatigably in the Middle and Southern States.

Through the remainder of this period the history of the Church in the Eastern States was a continuous repetition of such events and scenes as have been narrated: the holding of obscure Annual Conferences, where, however, great things were devised; gradual additions of Circuits, and reinforcements of the ministry by such men as have already been named; the building of churches, and frequent "revivals," sometimes extending over much of the country, especially now that camp-meetings were introduced; excessive travels, privations, and labors by the itinerants; not unfrequent persecutions and mobs; but continual triumphs. The first decade of the century ended with Methodism established in all the New England States. It had one extensive Conference, and a large portion of a Second. The four Districts with which it began the century had increased to eight; its thirty-two Circuits to seventy-one; its fifty-eight preachers to one hundred and fourteen, and its five thousand eight hundred and thirty-nine members to seventeen thousand five hundred and ninety-two. In ten years its Districts had doubled, its Circuits considerably more than doubled, its ministry lacked but two of being doubled, and its membership had more than trebled. It had gained in these ten years eleven thousand seven hundred and fifty-three members, an average increase of more than one thousand one hundred and seventy-five each year, or nearly one hundred per month. At the close of the second decade its membership numbered nearly twenty-five thousand, its ministry one hundred and twenty-five traveling, and some hundreds of local preachers. Such were the beginnings and early growths of that great harvest which, by the centenary of American Methodism, (1866,) was to yield in New England one hundred and three thousand four hundred and seventy-two members, and about a thousand traveling preachers, with nearly nine hundred chapels, more than a hundred thousand Sunday-school students, and thirteen educational institutions, including a university, a theological school, and boarding academies. The vitality of Methodism would be tested in New England, if anywhere; the result has been most satisfactory. The increase of members, from the beginning of the century, has been eighteenfold. Through every decade save one (1840–1850) the denomination has gained upon the growth of the population, notwithstanding the rapid ingress of foreign Papists. It has become, in our day, in New England aggregately, the second denomination in numerical strength, and the first in progress. In the metropolis itself it makes more rapid progress than any other Protestant denomination, and its churches are among the best architectural monuments of the city.

CHAPTER XXXI.

METHODISM IN THE WEST: 1804–1820.

AGAIN we turn to the "great West," the scene, in our day, of the greatest triumphs of Methodism. In the outset (1804) it is still the one "Western Conference," with its four Districts. In 1806 the Mississippi District appears in the Minutes, under Larner Blackman. The successors of Tobias Gibson, seven adventurous itinerants, are invading the great Southwest. In 1813 the Northwestern Territory becomes an Annual Conference, by order of the General Conference of 1812, under the title of Ohio. It comprehends much of Kentucky, and has six Districts. The name of the old "Western Conference" disappears, and that of Tennessee is first recorded, with seven grand Districts. In 1817, by the legislation of the General Conference of 1816, the Western field has four Conferences: Ohio, with five Districts, under Finley, Jacob and David Young, Moses Crume, and Samuel Parker; Missouri, with two Districts, under Samuel H. Thompson and Jesse Walker; Tennessee, with six Districts, under Marcus Lindsey, Thomas L. Douglass, John M'Gee, James Axley, Jesse Cunningham, and John Henninger; and Mississippi, with two Districts, under Thomas Griffin and Ashley Hewitt. The ecclesiastical arrangements of the vast field remained thus, with some local variations and a rapid multiplication of Districts, Circuits, preachers, and members, down to the expiration of our present period, when the General Conference of 1820 created the Kentucky Conference, with five Districts. Such was the geography of Western Methodism in these years. We are now prepared to look over it more in detail, though it must be with but glances. Extraordinary triumphs of the Gospel, and men of gigantic proportions, intellectual and moral, multiply too fast in the grand arena for our space.

I have recorded the rapid outspread of Methodism in the ultra-Alleghany regions of Pennsylvania, the "Redstone country." It advanced victoriously there throughout the present period, blending on the North with the southwestern appointments of the Genesee Conference; on the West with the Circuits of the itinerants from Kentucky, who were now ranging through nearly all the sparse settlements of Ohio; on the South with the labors of the mountaineer itinerants of the Holston country. It was still a presiding elder's District till 1825, when the Pittsburgh Conference was organized, comprehending all the appointments in two large Districts, the Erie and the Ohio. A renowned ecclesiastical body was this "old Pittsburgh Conference" to become; thronged with notable men, constituting the chief northern stronghold of Methodism between the East and the West, and yielding at last the Erie Conference on its north, and the Western Virginia on its south.

Methodism had effectually, though slowly, broken into the Western Reserve by the labors of Shewel and Bostwick. The former a local preacher, whom we have seen working for the Church in Western Virginia, and penetrating to the Reserve at the beginning of the century, now rejoiced in the spiritual harvest around him, and, after toiling through the week with his hands, went about on Sunday, usually on foot, to distant settlements, holding meetings and organizing societies. Like M'Cormick, of Ohio, and other lay evangelists, he was practically an apostle in the wilderness. He even moved his residence to extend his religious labors. Passing from Deerfield he settled in Hartstown, Portage County, Ohio, in 1814, and began preaching in all the neighboring regions, besides turning his own cabin into a Sabbath "appointment." He formed many classes. "Thus," says the local historian, "did this faithful old pioneer find his way into the new settlements, breaking up new ground, and after raising up Societies, he would hand them over to the preachers on the Circuit, and then seek out new places of labor." Jacob Young, whom we have met in Kentucky and the Holston Mountains, traveled this District for three years like a herald, directing, and inspiriting with his own energy, a powerful corps of preachers, who made their way to the obscurest settlements. They reached at last (about 1812) the place where Thomas Branch had met his affecting death in the wilderness on his way from New England to the far West, as heretofore recorded. It was called North East, and is in Erie County, Pa. There was not a Methodist within twenty miles of the dying hero, but Young's pioneers soon formed a Society on the spot, some of its members probably being the fruits of Branch's last exhortations and prayers. A local preacher from Canada built his cabin there, and did good service for the young Society. A chapel was erected, "and," says the historian, "the Church has maintained a prosperous existence ever since, and many happy spirits have gone up from that town to join the triumphant host in heaven." An important western character appeared in this field in 1816. Young failed to reach the District after the General Conference of that year; James B. Finley came to supply his place, and continued to superintend it till 1819 with extraordinary zeal and success. Few men have attained more distinction as evangelical pioneers of the West; he was, in all respects, a genuine child of the wilderness, one of its best "typical" men; of stalwart frame, "features rather coarse," but large benevolent eyes, "sandy hair, standing erect," a good, expressive mouth, a "voice like thunder," and a courage that made riotous opposers (whom he often encountered) quail before him. He did not hesitate to seize disturbers of his meetings, shake them in his athletic grasp, and pitch them out of the windows or doors. Withal his heart was most genial, his discourses full of pathos, and his friendships the most tender and lasting. All over the Northwest he worked mightily, through a long life, to found and extend his Church, traveling Circuits and Districts, laboring as missionary to the Indians, and chaplain to prisoners, and in his old age making valuable historical contributions to its literature. William Swayze succeeded Finley on the District in 1819. "He was," says a western historian, "emphatically a 'son of thunder,' attracting great crowds of people to his ministry, and speaking with a power and pathos that few have ever equaled, moving and exciting many, some to tears, others to cry for mercy, while others would shout for joy."

His fellow-laborers pronounce him "a martyr to his work." "He was," says our western authority, who knew him well, "a very remarkable man, differing greatly from Finley, Young, and Gruber, but in moving, melting eloquence not inferior to either of them. Himself full of feeling and interest, and possessing a wonderful command of the feelings of others, he would at times sway the multitude of astonished listeners like trees by a hurricane, carrying his congregation up with him, until they would rise from their seats and rush toward the speaker, some weeping, some shouting, and others falling like dead men. We will venture the opinion that more souls, along the southern shore of Lake Erie, have gone up to shine like stars in the heavenly sky through the instrumentality of William Swayze than by that of any other man dead or living."

He had many able young preachers under his authority on this District; among them was Charles Elliott, a man of extraordinary learning, of tireless labor through a protracted life, and of most genial character. He came from Ireland to the United States a local preacher in 1814, and plunged immediately into the woods of Ohio. For years he was a principal founder of the Church as circuit preacher and presiding elder in these regions, and one year he spent as missionary among the Upper Sandusky Indians. But his superior education fitted him for more exigent services, as professor in colleges, editor, and author. Besides his fragmentary writings, (almost innumerable editorials, and other contributions to the periodical literature of the Church,) he has written "Delineations of Roman Catholicism," a standard work, republished in England; "Sinfulness of American Slavery," an exhaustive investigation of the subject; and the "History of the Great Secession" of the Methodist Episcopal Church, South, from the parent body in 1844, a large volume, in which the history of that momentous proceeding and of the antecedent ecclesiastical controversy on slavery is thoroughly given.

By 1820 Methodism was thoroughly established in all this country, with Districts and Circuits belonging, some to the Genesee, some to the Baltimore, others to the Virginia, and still others to the Ohio Conferences; more than half a hundred itinerants were sounding the Gospel among the mountains and valleys from Lake Erie to far into West Virginia, and thousands of zealous members were rallying into classes and incipient Churches. They were laying the foundations of the Erie, Pittsburgh, and West Virginia Conferences.

Passing further westward, into the "great Northwestern Territory," we again meet Quinn, whom we have so often followed over the ground just surveyed, but who had now been borne away by the surges of emigration. On the Sciota Circuit he had about thirty appointments, the nearest being fifty miles from his family. Emigrants from Kentucky were now pouring into this region, and among them were many zealous Methodists. At one of his meetings "a very dignified and elderly looking" woman, a stranger, remained to attend the class, in which she said, "with a full soul, and with eyes swimming in tears, 'I am, through the infinite mercy of God, a child of his, and, by blessed experience, know I enjoy the pardoning love of the Saviour. I am a widow, recently from Kentucky. I have a large family of children. I have traveled nine or ten miles to enjoy this means of grace, and to invite you to preach in my cabin for the benefit of my children and my unconverted neighbors.' Her words were with power, and it was manifest that the love of Christ constrained her, that she was filled with the Holy Ghost. While she spoke, the same flame was kindled in the hearts of others, and some shouted aloud for joy. After the class Quinn learned that the stranger was Jane Trimble, mother to Governor Trimble, and grandmother to Joseph M. Trimble. On his next round he preached at her double cabin, on Clear Creek, three miles north of Hillsboro. At this meeting, it is probable, no professor of religion was present except the pious widow and the preacher. After the sermon, as there was no class to meet, he stated that it was his last round on the Circuit, and, as he had soon to leave for Conference, he could not preach to them any more, but that his successors would. He then sung one of the songs of Zion. At that period his voice was most melodious and sweet. The tones of the music, accompanied with a holy unction, melted every heart. While singing, he passed through the room, and shook hands with every one present. All were more or less affected. Young Mrs. Trimble, first wife of Allen Trimble, and mother of Joseph M., though once a professor of religion, became conscious of her backsliding and lukewarmness, and the absolute necessity of the reclaiming grace of God. Her anguish of spirit was so great that she could conceal it no longer. She first went out of the room; but, finding there no means of relief to her distressed soul, she soon returned, and kneeled down at a seat. Many hearts perhaps sympathized with her, but there were but two to pray for her. They were, however, efficient suppliants, and, having power with God, they soon prevailed. In a short time the earnest seeker was powerfully reclaimed; and such was the clear testimony of the Spirit, assuring her that her soul was restored to the favor of God, that she praised the Lord with but little intermission till midnight. In a few years she passed away in holy triumph, and now awaits the arrival of her friends in heaven."

The venerable Jane Trimble became a "mother in Israel" to the Methodists of the Northwestern Territory. Her family, that of her son, Governor Trimble, and of her grandson, Joseph M. Trimble, (one of the missionary secretaries of the Church,) have been identified with nearly the entire history of the denomination in Ohio. She was an extraordinary woman. Born in Virginia in 1755, on the very borders of civilization, she was familiar, from childhood, with the warwhoop of the savage. Several of her family perished in the Revolutionary and Indian wars. In 1784 she emigrated to Kentucky, whither her husband had gone to lay out a farm and build a log-cabin. "She traveled," says her biographer, "on horseback, carrying her eldest child behind her, and her little boy, Allen, eleven months old, in her lap. On reaching Clinch River the stream was found swollen by recent rains, and the swift current dashed over huge rocks. She was leading the company of females, and, trusting in God and committing all her interests to him, she urged her steed into the rapid stream, and reached the opposite shore in safety, amid the prayers and shouts of those who watched her progress. The remainder of the company crossed by a ford further up the river." General Knox, who convoyed the train, and witnessed the feat, and her noble conduct throughout the journey, applauded her as equaling in courage and presence of mind "the women of Sparta."

For fifteen years she lived, surrounded by Indian perils, about ten miles from a "station," near the site of Lexington, educating her children and servants with the ability and dignity of a true Christian matron. She possessed a remarkably vigorous mind, was familiar, there in the backwoods, with the great English poets, and had the four Gospels entirely in her memory, acquired when she was but fifteen years old. Some of the writings of Fletcher fell into her hands, and she became a Methodist in 1790. Her husband determined to push on further with the movement of emigration, and purchased lands in Ohio, but died before the family started for their new home. The noble widow led her eight children thither, and there, in Highland County, welcomed Quinn, and formed one of the first Sunday-schools in the State. Every interest of the Church, especially its missions to the aborigines, had her hearty co-operation through the remainder of her long life. She saw all the Northwestern Territory overspread by her denomination, her great State organized, the infant son, whom she had carried on her steed to the West, its chief magistrate, and died under his roof in 1839, aged more than eighty-four years, having been a devoted Methodist nearly fifty years. She was not only one of the best, but one of the ablest women who have adorned her Church or country, a befitting associate of Mary Tiffin, Mrs. General Russell, and similar "elect ladies" of the Church in the wilderness.

Burke, Shinn, Oglesby, Sale, Lakin, Parker, William Young, Lotspeich, Lasley, Manley, Cummins, and many other energetic men were colaborers of Quinn in these regions throughout these years. From Ohio the systematic work of the Church extended westward over Indiana, Illinois, and Missouri. Indiana territory was constituted in 1800; in 1805 it was divided by the organization of Michigan territory, and in 1809 that of Illinois was detached from it. In 1802 the first Indiana Methodist Society was formed at Gassaway, in "Clark's Grant," Nathan Robertson being the first Methodist of the territory. Two years later there was an Illinois mission. Whitewater Circuit was formed in 1807, with Thomas Hellams for its preacher, and sixty-seven members; Silver Creek in 1808, and Vincennes in 1810. In 1815 there were, in the entire territory, Whitewater, Silver Creek, Illinois, Little Wabash, Vincennes, and Lawrenceburgh Circuits, having one thousand seven hundred members and seven preachers. The latter were John Strange, W. M. Hunt, Shadrach Ruark, John Scripps, John Shrader, James Noland, and W. C. Harbesson. By the end of our present period there were in the same territory twenty-six preachers and eight thousand members. By the end of the first quarter of the century they had so increased that there were in Michigan four, in Illinois eighteen, and in Indiana twenty-eight itinerants, making forty preachers and fourteen thousand members. Seven years later the increase was, in Michigan, eight preachers and one thousand six hundred members; in Illinois, forty-four preachers, ten thousand members; and in Indiana, sixty preachers and twenty thousand members. In 1832 was formed the Indiana Conference. For twelve years the entire State was in one Conference, which was first divided in 1844, when it reported sixty-six thousand members, two hundred traveling preachers, and four hundred and eighty-eight local preachers. In our day (1866) it has four Conferences, four hundred traveling preachers, seven hundred local preachers, and ninety thousand members. "This State, though it bears a name signifying 'domain of the Indian,' has for its more than one million three hundred and fifty thousand inhabitants, two thousand nine hundred and thirty-three places of worship, one thousand two hundred and fifty-six of which are furnished by the Methodists, with accommodations for more than one million, and valued at nearly four million five hundred thousand dollars. It has six thousand five hundred free schools, one thousand one hundred and twenty-three Sabbath-schools, more than one hundred higher schools or academies and colleges, of which the Methodists furnish one third."

The extension of Methodism northwestward, into the Michigan Territory, was slow. The fruits of the labors of Bangs, Case, and Mitchell lingered in Detroit till Joseph Hickox was appointed to the Circuit in 1815; the recent war had demoralized the whole country, and Hickox could discover only seven Methodists in Detroit. A Society, which had been organized at Monroe in 1811, he found entirely broken up, and he was the only Protestant preacher in the territory for at least one year. There was not yet a single Protestant chapel in it. But, after the war, emigration, and, with it, Methodism, began to pour into the country. "As the population extended, our ministers," says a local authority, "followed them, wading through the swamps and marshes, and striking the Indian trails, so that the people have never been left for any considerable time without the Gospel. The first preachers were sent from the New York Conference, the next from the Genesee, the third from the Ohio. In 1836 the Michigan Conference was created—it included a part of Ohio; but in 1840 the Ohio portion was separated, leaving Michigan alone. At this time there were only seventy-eight ministers and preachers, and eleven thousand five hundred and twenty-three members. Though this seems small, we must consider that the population was sparse. Now we have about three hundred ministers, and thirty-two thousand members. The first Protestant church erected in Michigan was built near Detroit in 1818. It was made of logs, and was considered a fine affair; but now we find substantial churches dotting all the country."

We have seen the extension of the itinerant ministry to the Illinois Territory, by Benjamin Young, in 1804. He had been preceded, however, by less known laborers. The "real pioneer of the Church," says our best living Illinois authority, "was Capt. Joseph Ogle, who went thither in 1785. The first Methodist preacher was Joseph Lillard, who, in 1793, formed a class in St. Clair County, and appointed Captain Ogle leader. The next Methodist preacher was John Clarke, who originally traveled in South Carolina from 1791 to 1796, when he withdrew on account of slavery. He was the first man that preached the Gospel west of the Mississippi, in 1798. Hosea Riggs was the first Methodist preacher that settled in Illinois, and he revived and reorganized the class at Captain Ogle's, formed by Lillard, which had dropped its regular meetings. From 1798 there seems to have been no regular preacher in Illinois till 1804; then Benjamin Young was sent as a missionary. In the fall of 1805 he returned sixty-seven members, and Joseph Oglesby was appointed to succeed him on the Illinois Circuit."

A notable character, Jesse Walker, appeared on the scene in 1806, a man whose name is identified for years with the westward progress of Methodism. One of his contemporaries says: "He was a character perfectly unique; he had no duplicate. He was to the Church what Daniel Boone was to the early settler, always first, always ahead of everybody else, preceding all others long enough to be the pilot of the new-comers. The Minutes, in his case, are no guide, from the fact that he was sent by the bishops and presiding elders in every direction where new work was to be cut out. His natural vigor was almost superhuman. He did not seem to require food and rest as other men; no day's journey was long enough to tire him; no fare too poor for him to live on; to him, in traveling, roads and paths were useless things—he 'blazed' out his own course; no way was too bad for him—if his horse could not carry him he led him, and when his horse could not follow, he would leave him, and take it on foot; and if night and a cabin did not come together, he would pass the night alone in the wilderness, which with him was no uncommon occurrence. Every time you could hear from him he was still further on." His appointment to Illinois in 1806 was a mission to the whole territory. The region between Kentucky and the interior of this new field was yet a wilderness, and difficult to travel. M'Kendree, the presiding elder, set out, therefore, with his pioneer itinerant, to assist him on the way. They journeyed on horseback, sleeping in the woods on their saddle blankets, and cooking their meals under trees. Walker, at last left alone in the territory, moved over it courageously, till the winter compelled him to suspend his circuit plan, and commence operating from house to house, or rather from cabin to cabin, "passing none without calling and delivering the Gospel message. He was guided by the indications of Providence, and took shelter for the night wherever he could obtain it, so as to resume his labor early the next day, and he continued this course of toil till about the close of the winter. The result was a general revival with the opening spring, when the people were able to reassemble, and he to resume his regular plan. As the result of his first year's experiment in Illinois, two hundred and eighteen Church members were reported in the printed Minutes.

His next field was Missouri, and he continued to travel thenceforward, alternately in each territory, down to 1812, when, as presiding elder, he took command of all the Methodist interests of both; both appertaining to the Tennessee Conference. He had charge of Districts in one or the other till 1819, when he was appointed Conference missionary, that he might range about "breaking up new ground," a work for which he was singularly fitted, and in which he persisted for years. Before Walker's arrival, however, Methodism had penetrated Missouri, by the occasional preaching of Joseph Oglesby. The first intimation that the Minutes give of an appointment to Missouri is in 1806, when Walker entered Illinois. John Travis, then a youth, recently admitted to the Western Conference, was dispatched immediately to the Missouri wilds, when the whole country had but about sixteen thousand inhabitants. The young pioneer returned a hundred white and six African members at the next Conference, at which two Missouri Circuits were recorded, "Maramack and Missouri," and Walker and Edmund Wilcox sent to them. Slow but steady progress was made till the field was mature enough to be constituted a Conference in 1816, without a boundary on the West, "but including the last Methodist cabin toward the setting sun," and taking in all Missouri and Illinois and the western part of Indiana. Walker was a great sufferer as well as a great laborer in these fields. "I think it was in the fall of 1819," says Peter Cartwright, "that our beloved old Brother Walker, who had traveled all his life, or nearly so, came over to our Tennessee Conference, which sat in Nashville, to see us; but O how weather-beaten and war-worn was he! almost, if not altogether, without decent apparel to appear among us. We soon made a collection, and had him a decent suit of clothes to put on; and never shall I forget the blushing modesty and thankfulness with which he accepted that suit, and never did I and others have a stronger verification of our Lord's words, 'That it is more blessed to give than to receive.'"

Though Jesse Walker was not the first Methodist itinerant in Missouri, he ranks as the principal founder of the denomination there. No obstruction could withstand his assaults. As pioneer, circuit preacher, presiding elder, he drove all opposition before him, and inspirited his colaborers with his own energy, so that Methodism effectively superseded the original Roman Catholic predominance in that country. Having effectually broken the way open for it in Missouri, during sixteen years, Walker, eager for pioneer adventures, went, in 1823, to the Indian tribes up the Mississippi, where he labored till 1830, when the hero of so many fields was esteemed the man for other new work, and was appointed to the extreme North, to Chicago Mission, "where he succeeded," says Peter Cartwright, "in planting Methodism in that then infant city. In 1831 he was sent to the Des Plaines Mission, and organized many small Societies in that young and rising country." In 1832 there was a Chicago District formed, mostly of missionary ground. Walker was superintendent of this District, and missionary to Chicago town, and in 1833 was continued in the City Missionary Station. This year closed his active itinerant life. "He had," says Cartwright, "done effective service as a traveling preacher for more than thirty years, and had lived poor, and suffered much; had won thousands of souls over to Christ, and firmly planted Methodism for thousands of miles on our frontier border. We have fought side by side for many years, we have suffered hunger and want together, we have often wept and prayed and preached together; I hope we shall sing and shout together in heaven." He died, "in confident hope of a blessed immortality," in

1835. He was five feet seven inches high, of slender but vigorous frame, sallow complexion, light hair, prominent cheeks, small blue eyes, a generous and cheerful expression, and dressed always in drab-colored clothes, of the plainest Quaker fashion, with a light-colored beaver hat, "nearly as large as a lady's parasol." He had extraordinary aptness to win the confidence and sympathy of "backwoodsmen;" his friendships were most hearty, his courage equal to any test, his piety thorough, his talents as a preacher moderate. His great talent was his great character.

Methodism became mighty in Missouri Conference, numbering nearly twenty-four thousand members before the southern secession of 1844; but that event rent the Church to pieces; the war of the rebellion still further devastated the great field. Peace has restored the denomination, and the Missouri Conference still exists, with reorganized plans of usefulness.

During these years men of genuine greatness of character and talents were continually rising up in the western itinerancy. Samuel Parker was called the Cicero of the western ministry. His natural eloquence was remarkable. The people thronged from great distances to hear him; his word was irresistible, and "wherever he went," says one of his contemporaries, "wondering and weeping audiences crowded about him." He possessed an exceedingly musical voice, a clear, keen mind, an imagination which, though never extravagant, afforded frequent and brilliant illustrations of his subject, while his ardent piety imparted wonderful tenderness and power to his appeals. Withal, his personal appearance was striking before he became attenuated with disease. He was nearly six feet high, had a remarkably intellectual countenance, with a full forehead, and a black, piercing eye. In 1809 he became presiding elder on a district which included Indiana, Illinois, and Missouri. He continued north and west of the Ohio with increasing influence and success till 1815, when he was made presiding elder in Kentucky, where his great eloquence commanded general interest. In 1819 he was appointed to lead the itinerants who were extending the Church in the far southwest, on the memorable Mississippi District. They needed such a man;

but his health was broken, and it seemed but an appointment to martyrdom. He was ready for it, nevertheless, and when it was announced, at the close of the Conference, in Cincinnati, "it seemed," says a spectator, "that a wave of sympathy rolled over the whole assembly." He sank down and died on the District in 1819. Winans, whom he had called out to preach, in Ohio, attended him in death, and followed him to his grave, in Washington, Miss. "He died," says Winans, "not only peacefully, but triumphantly."

James Axley has left traditions of his character and work in the Church from Indiana to Louisiana. A fellow-laborer (himself one of the most genuine products of nature and the West) has said that Axley "was the most perfect child of nature I ever knew." He was tossed about, with singular rapidity, in his appointments, from Tennessee to Ohio, from Ohio to the Holston Mountains, from Holston to Opelousas, in Louisiana, back again to Holston, then to the Wabash District, in Indiana, back again to the Holston District for four years, thence to Green River District in Kentucky, and finally to French Broad District, among the Alleghanies of North Carolina. In 1822 he located, near Madisonville, Tenn., where he died in 1838. Through this vast range of his ministerial travels he was one of the most energetic, most popular, and most useful preachers of the times. His pulpit talents were not above mediocrity, his manners utterly unpolished; but he combined with profound piety and much tender sensibility the shrewdest sense, an astonishing aptness of speech, and an exhaustless humor. The latter, however, was usually so well directed that it seemed wisdom itself, arrayed in smiles. Few, if any, of his contemporaries drew larger audiences, for Axley was irresistible to the western people. He joined the Conference at the same time with Parker and Cartwright. To the latter he was of course a congenial mind. "We were always," says Cartwright, "bosom friends till he closed his earthly pilgrimage." Cartwright records "an illustration of Axley's extraordinary faith," which is an equal illustration of the character of the times and the country. They were at a camp-meeting in Tennessee, Axley endeavoring to sustain order among a crew of 'rowdies' while Cartwright was preaching. "They actually threatened to lay the cowhide over him," says the latter. "He replied with great calmness and firmness that that was not the place for an encounter, and that, if they were really bent on fighting, they must retire outside the encampment. Immediately he found himself in the midst of a crowd there. Axley remarked that he could not possibly go into the fight until he had prayed, and instantly knelt down. He poured forth his heart in a strain of uncommon fervor; the base fellows themselves were actually disarmed, and such an impression of reverence and solemnity came over them that they at once abandoned their impious design, and behaved themselves with perfect decorum. On the Monday following he preached a sermon, under which several of them were melted into tears. When the awakened came forward for the prayers of the Church, there were found among them a number of these persons, and, before the meeting closed, some of them professed to have become new creatures in Christ Jesus."

Peter Cartwright grew up in Kentucky thoroughly seasoned with western hardihood, but saved from many of the vices prevalent around him. In his ninth year he heard the itinerant, Jacob Lurton, preach in his father's cabin, and describes him as "a real son of thunder." "My mother," he adds, "shouted aloud for joy." A small class was formed at about four miles distance, to which his good mother walked every week. At last they built a little church, and called it "Ebenezer." In his sixteenth year, after dancing at a wedding, he went home with an awakened conscience. Unable to sleep, he spent much of the night on his knees with his praying mother, and, sometime afterward, was converted at a camp-meeting. In his nineteenth year, urged by his mother, but opposed by his father, he went forth as a circuit preacher "under the presiding elder." At the Conference of 1804, held at Mount Gerizim, Ky., he was received on probation. Of all the itinerants of that session he is the only survivor. The bare enumeration of his subsequent "appointments" would cover pages. In Tennessee, Kentucky, in almost every portion of the Northwestern Territory, he fought courageously the battles of his Church; not always with the voice, but sometimes, like Finley and others, he had to use his stout fist against the onset of semi-barbarous mobs. A frontier man, he knew the perils and necessities of frontier life; and when his appeals to the conscience of his sometimes half savage hearers could not prevail, and especially when the decorum of public worship, or the safety of his congregations were periled, he could show himself physically formidable, and make the mob recoil. We need to read the record of such a life as his with somewhat of the moral license of the early frontier spirit. "My voice," he says, "at that day was strong and clear, and I could sing, exhort, pray, and preach almost all the time, day and night." Some of his meetings lasted all night. His circuits were like lines of battle, continually in excitement, if not commotion. Some of his quarterly meetings were not only scenes of spiritual conflict and victory, but of "hand-to-hand fights" with the rabble. One of them, on Scioto Circuit, in 1805, was held in the woods. The mob, led on by two champions, who bore "loaded whips," invaded it. Cartwright called from the stand upon two magistrates in the assembly to arrest the leaders, but they replied that it was impossible. He came forward himself, offering to do it for them, but the assailants struck at him. The greatest tumult ensued; the congregation was in confusion; the whole mob pressed upon him and his friends. He seized one after another of the principal rioters, and threw them to the earth, including a drunken magistrate who had taken sides with them. "Just at this moment," he writes, "the ringleader of the mob and I met. He made three passes at me, intending to knock me down. The last time he struck at me, by the force of his own effort he threw the side of his face toward me. It seemed at that moment I had not power to resist temptation, and I struck him a blow in the burr of his ear, which felled him to the earth. Our friends now rushed by hundreds on the mob, knocking them down in every direction. In a few minutes the place became too strait for them, and they wheeled and fled; but we secured about thirty prisoners, marched them off to a vacant tent, and put them under guard till

Monday morning, when they were tried, and every man was fined to the utmost limits of the law. They fined my old drunken magistrate twenty dollars, returned him to court, and he was cashiered of his office. On Sunday, when we had vanquished the mob, the whole encampment was filled with mourning; and, although there was no attempt to resume preaching till evening, yet, such was our confused state, there was not then a single preacher on the ground willing to preach, from the presiding elder, John Sale, down. Seeing we had fallen on evil times, my spirit was stirred within me. I said to the elder, 'I feel a clear conscience, for under the necessity of the circumstances we have done right, and now I ask you to let me preach.' 'Do,' said the elder, 'for there is no other man on the ground can do it.' The encampment was lighted up, the trumpet blown, I rose in the stand, and required every soul to leave the tents and come into the congregation. There was a general rush to the stand. I requested the brethren, if ever they prayed in all their lives, to pray now. My voice was strong and clear, and my preaching was more of an exhortation and encouragement than anything else. My text was, 'The gates of hell shall not prevail.' In about thirty minutes the power of God fell on the congregation in such a manner as is seldom seen. The people fell in every direction, right and left, front and rear. It was supposed that not less than three hundred fell like dead men in battle, and there was no need of calling mourners, for they were strewed all over the camp-ground. Our meeting lasted all night, and Monday and Monday night; and when we closed on Tuesday there were two hundred who had professed religion, and about that number joined the Church. Brother Axley and myself pulled together like true yoke-fellows. We were both raised in the backwoods, and well understood frontier life."

Similar scenes were hardly rare on the western frontier. Irreconcilable as they may be to our sense of religious decorum, they are essential illustrations of the times. History cannot evade them, even if we should not feel a lurking sympathy with the rude courage which they too often provoked beyond all self-control.

For nearly seventy years Peter Cartwright has been a Methodist, for nearly sixty-five an itinerant preacher, for about fifty a presiding elder; twelve times he has shared in the General Conferences of his Church. In his long ministerial life he has not lost six months from his regular work for any cause whatever. "For twenty years of my ministry," he writes, "I often preached twice a day, and sometimes three times. We seldom ever had in those days more than one rest-day in a week, so that I feel very safe in saying that I preached four hundred times a year. I was converted on a camp-ground, and for many years of my early ministry, after I was appointed presiding elder, lived in the tented grove from two to three months in the year. I have lived to see this vast western wilderness rise and improve, and become wealthy without a parallel in the history of the world; I have outlived every member of my father's family; I have outlived every member of the class I joined in 1800; I have outlived every member of the Western Conference in 1804; I have outlived nearly every member of the first General Conference that I was elected to, in Baltimore, in 1816; I have outlived all my early bishops; I have outlived every presiding elder that I ever had when on circuits; and I have outlived hundreds and thousands of my contemporary ministers and members, as well as juniors, and still linger on these mortal shores. Though all these have died they shall live again, and, by the grace of God, I shall live with them in heaven forever." He has received into the Church some twelve thousand members, and led into the itinerancy scores, if not hundreds, of preachers. Rough and hardy as the oak; overflowing with geniality and humor; a tireless worker and traveler; a sagacious counselor, giving often in the strangest disguises of wit and humor the shrewdest suggestions of wisdom; an unfailing friend, an incomparable companion, a faithful patriot, and an earnest Methodist, Peter Cartwright has been, for nearly three generations, one of the most noted, most interesting, most unique men of the West and of Methodism.

David Young's labors, especially in Ohio, were long and

successful. He was born in Bedford County, Va.; was well trained at home, where he had the then rare advantage of a good library, and by becoming a studious youth, prepared an intelligent and effective manhood. From his seventh year he was seldom without religious reflection. In 1803 he emigrated to Tennessee, where he taught a grammar school; and in the same year was converted, and became a Methodist. The next year he was "exhorting," and in 1805 joined the Conference. His appointments were for some time in Tennessee; but in 1811 he was sent to Ohio, where he labored, with commanding influence, down to 1849, when he was placed on the "superannuated list." He suffered from disease most of his life, the effect of his early itinerant exposures. His self-education, improving good natural powers, secured him "the first rank among his brother ministers." * He was always master of his subject. "His logical method, associated with fervency of spirit, enchained his auditory. Sometimes his pathos was overwhelming, for he was often a weeping prophet. Fond of reading, he had in store a large amount of general literature, which gave great interest to his preaching. His voice was pleasant, though sometimes shrill and penetrating; his gesticulation graceful, and his whole manner peculiarly solemn and impressive." He led into the communion and ministry of the Church its present senior bishop, who describes him as "tall and slender, but straight and symmetrical. His step was elastic. He wore the straight-breasted coat, and the broad-brimmed hat usual among early Methodist preachers. His yellow hair, all combed back, hung in great profusion about his neck and shoulders, giving him an imposing appearance. His blue eyes were prominent, and exceedingly penetrating. I heard a Virginia lawyer say that he could withstand the direct contact of any preacher's eye in the pulpit he ever saw, except David Young's; but his always made him quail. In manners he was a finished gentleman of the Virginia school. He abounded in incident, and had a rare talent at narration, both in and out of the pulpit. Yet, as a minister, he was grave and dignified. No man conducted a public

* Rev. Dr. Trimble, in Sprague, p. 431.

religious service more solemnly or impressively than he did, especially in reading the Holy Scriptures or in prayer. His deep religious emotion was always apparent in his prayers and his sermons. On special occasions, while applying the momentous truths of the Gospel, he stood on his knees in the pulpit, and, with many tears, entreated sinners, as in Christ's stead, to be reconciled to God. Among the most celebrated Methodist preachers of the great West fifty years ago were William Beauchamp, Samuel Parker, and David Young, each of whom excelled in his own way. Beauchamp was the most instructive, Parker the most practical and persuasive, and Young the most overpowering. Under the preaching of Beauchamp light seemed to break on the most bewildered understanding; under that of Parker, multitudes of people melted like snow before an April sun; while, under the ministry of Young, I knew whole assemblies electrified, as suddenly and as sensibly as if coming in contact with a galvanic battery. I have myself, under some of his powerful appeals, felt the cold tremors passing over me, and the hair on my head apparently standing on end. On camp-meeting occasions, where the surroundings were unusually exciting, it has sometimes happened that vast numbers of persons have simultaneously sprung from their seats and rushed up as near to the pulpit as they could, apparently unconscious of having changed positions." He died at Zanesville in 1858. His descent to the grave was like a serene going down of the sun. "I am calmly," he said, "though through great physical suffering, nearing my better home."

John Collins has already appeared in our pages as founding the Church in Cincinnati. He was born in New Jersey in 1769, and was of Quaker parentage. When very young his attention was drawn to religious subjects by hearing a hymn sung as he passed the house of a neighbor. For several years he struggled against his convictions, living a moral life, but attaining no rest for his soul. He went to Charleston, S. C., in order to escape his local associations, and, if possible, become a more decided Christian away from the observations of his acquaintances, but failed, and, returning home, was converted in 1794. He soon began to preach, but with much self-distrust, and doubt of his divine call to the ministry. Larner Blackman, his brother-in-law, was saved by his first sermon, in New Jersey, and Collins now hesitated no more, especially as he further ascertained that ten or twelve of his kindred were awakened by the same discourse. His word, even his casual allusions to religion, seemed to have remarkable effect. He had been appointed major of militia, but now resigned the office, and sold his uniform to his successor, saying to him, "My friend, when you put these on, think of the reason why I laid them off." The brief sentence was "a nail fastened in a sure place." It so impressed the young officer that he also resigned the post and became a Methodist. Blackman went to the West, where he became a champion of the itinerancy from Ohio to Louisiana. Collins followed him in 1803, and located his family in Clermont County, about twenty-five miles west of Cincinnati. He thus became a colaborer with M'Cormick, Gatch, Tiffin, and Scott in founding the denomination in the Northwestern Territory. His appointments, with two intervals of "location," were all in Ohio for thirty years. In 1837 his infirmities required him to retreat into a "superannuated relation." He lived yet about seven years a serene Christian life, venerated by the Church, beloved for his memorable services, his gentle manners, his catholicity, his pathetic eloquence, and his cheerful piety. He died a blessed death, in 1845. "Happy! happy! happy!" were his last words.

The fruits of his ministry abounded in all parts of Ohio, for his superior character and talents gave him extraordinary influence among all classes of the population. Among other eminent citizens, he led into the Church John M'Lean, afterward judge of the Supreme Court of the nation, and the biographer of the itinerant. Born in New Jersey in 1785, M'Lean emigrated successively to Western Virginia, Kentucky, and Ohio. When eighteen years old he began his legal education, in Cincinnati, under Arthur St. Clair. He gave himself meanwhile to general studies in almost every department of science and literature. He became skeptical in religion, but, after his admission to the bar, at Lebanon, Ohio, in 1807, he was rescued by Collins. One of the judge's biographers says: "Collins had an appointment to preach in a private house at Lebanon. The people crowded the rooms, and many had to stand about the doors. Among these was M'Lean, who stood where he could hear distinctly, though, as he thought, unobserved by the speaker. During the discourse, however, he fell under the notice of Collins's keen eye, and his prepossessing appearance attracted, at the first glance, the notice of the preacher. He paused a moment, and mentally offered up a short prayer for the conversion of the young man. Resuming his discourse, the first word he uttered was 'eternity.' That word was spoken with a voice so solemn and impressive that its full import was felt by M'Lean. All things besides appeared to be nothing in comparison to it." He soon sought an acquaintance with Collins, and became a regenerated man. The United States never had a more upright or more honorable citizen, nor American Methodism a more faithful member than Judge M'Lean. He was commanding in person, tall, and symmetrical in stature, with a Platonic brow, thoughtful, tranquil features, and the most modest but cordial manners. He was an able statesman, almost infallible in his cautious judgment, a thoroughly devoted Christian, persevering and punctual in the minutest duties of his Church, and catholic in his regard for good men of whatever sect. Lawyer, member of Congress, supreme judge of Ohio, member of the cabinets of Monroe and Adams, and supreme justice of the Republic, he passed through a long life unblemished, and, above all his titles, gloried in that of a Christian. M'Lean says of Collins that as both a local and an itinerant minister it is supposed that the Methodist Church in the West has not had a more successful preacher. He was a marked man in his person. He always wore the primitive Quaker dress. His forehead was high, his eyes small, but very expressive, and over all his features was spread an air of refinement, a sort of intellectual and benevolent glow, that immediately won the interest of the spectator. And his spirit and manners corresponded with these indications.

John Strange, a Virginian, was one of the most successful evangelists of Methodism in Ohio, whither he went in his twentieth year. He commenced preaching in 1811; in many parts of the Northwestern Territory he labored powerfully, though oppressed with chronic disease, down to 1832, when he "died in great peace," at Indianapolis, while at the head of the Indianapolis District. "He was," says a fellow-laborer, "one of the brightest lights of the American pulpit, in the Valley of the Mississippi, in the early part of the present century. He was formed by nature to be eloquent. He was tall and slender, and stood remarkably erect. His bearing was that of one born to command; and yet, combined with this, there was a gentleness and softness of manner that never failed to win the hearts of those with whom he came in contact. His hair was raven black, and his eyes blue, and generally mild; but, when he was animated, they became remarkably brilliant and penetrating. His voice was unsurpassed, as far as my knowledge extends, for its compass, and the sweetness, richness, and variety of its tones. There were times when his audience were held spell-bound by his eloquence, and sometimes they were even raised *en masse* from their seats." A bishop of the Church describes his appearance in the pulpit as "peculiar, almost angelic. I should pronounce him, unhesitatingly, a man of the highest style of genius." Traditions of his eloquence and usefulness are rife through all Ohio. He was an accomplished and heroic soldier of the cross, and won innumerable trophies. Just before he died, his last words to a friend were, "Serve God and fight the devil."

Superior even to Strange, as a preacher, was Russell Bigelow, a man of inferior presence, but of astonishing eloquence, of which the elder Methodists of Kentucky, Indiana, and Ohio never tire of speaking, though they can only describe it as "indescribable." President Thomson, (afterward bishop,) when a young student, was attracted by his fame to hear him at a camp-meeting, and says: "He was below the middle stature, and clad in coarse, ill-made garments. His uncombed hair hung loosely over his forehead, came down to his cheeks, and concealed a broad and prominent forehead; the keen eye that peered from beneath his heavy and overjutting eyebrows beamed with intelligence; the prominent cheek bones, projecting chin, and large nose, indicated anything but intellectual feebleness; while the wide mouth, depressed at its corners, the slightly expanded nostrils, and the *tout ensemble* of his expression, indicated both sorrow and love. His words were pure and well-chosen, his accent never misplaced, his sentences grammatical, artistically constructed, and well arranged, both for harmony and effect. Having stated and illustrated his position clearly, he laid broad the foundation of his argument, and piled stone upon stone, hewed and polished, until he stood upon a majestic pyramid, with heaven's own light around him, pointing the astonished multitude to a brighter home beyond the sun. As he closed his discourse, every energy of his mind and body seemed stretched to the utmost point of tension. The audience were well-nigh paralyzed beneath the avalanche of thought that descended upon them. I returned from the ground dissatisfied with myself, and saying within me, 'O that I were a Christian!' He preached to audiences as large, and with results as astonishing, as I have ever witnessed. He was a perfect gentleman. His mind seemed filled with beautiful analogies, by which he could rise from the material to the spiritual, and make an easy path to heaven from any point of earth."

Among these extraordinary men young Henry B. Bascom appeared in the Western itinerancy in 1813. Down to 1823 he filled laborious appointments in Ohio, Western Virginia, Tennessee, and Kentucky. In the last year he was elected chaplain to Congress, through the influence of Henry Clay. In 1827 he was elected president of Madison College, in Uniontown, Pa. In 1832 he was elected professor of Moral Science and Belles-lettres, in Augusta College, Kentucky. He was a delegate in the General Conference of 1844, when the Church was divided, was prominently active in that event, and shared in the Southern Methodist Convention, at Louisville, in 1845, and also in the Southern General Conference of 1846, by which he was appointed editor of the Southern Methodist Quarterly Review. The General Conference of 1849 elected him bishop.

On the last Sunday of July, 1850, he preached his last sermon in St. Louis; an effort of great eloquence, occupying two hours. In the ensuing September he died at Louisville, aged fifty-four years. In person he was a model of physical dignity and beauty; tall, well-proportioned, with perfectly symmetrical features, black and dazzling eyes, and a forehead expanded and lofty, "a very throne of intellect." He was fastidious in his apparel, reticent in his manners, and habitually seemed morbidly self-conscious. He published a volume of sermons; but they give no explanation of his peculiar eloquence, and will hardly bear critical examination. He was self-educated, and, though very thoroughly so, escaped not the usual defects of self-training. His style was elaborate, abounded in new-coined words, and was sometimes grandiloquent; his imagination was exuberant, too often excessive; his argumentation complicated, his thoughts abrupt and fragmentary. His sermons were brilliant mosaics, apparently composed of passages which had been laboriously prepared, at long intervals, and without much relation to the discourse as a whole. They lacked simplicity; were artificial, without the facility or ease which characterizes the mastery of art by disguising its labor. But, in spite of his defects, his power has seldom been rivaled in the American pulpit; he was a wonder of genius to the people, and drew them in multitudes which no temple could accommodate.

Thomas A. Morris, a man entirely contrasted with Bascom, and destined to much more extensive service in the Church, joined the itinerancy in 1816. He was born on the west side of the Kanawha River, Kanawha County, five miles above Charlestown, in Western Virginia, in 1794, joined the Church in 1813, and was licensed to preach the next year. His itinerant ministry in the West was extensive and successful down to 1834, when he was appointed the first editor of the Western Christian Advocate, at Cincinnati, and issued the first number of that influential paper on the 2d of May. In 1836 he was elected bishop, which office he has continued to sustain with pre-eminent wisdom down to our day, being for many years the senior of the episcopate. During the perilous crises of the denomination, in the antislavery controversy and the southern secession, he has guided the Church with unwavering prudence. He is short in stature, corpulent, with a ruddy complexion, and an intellectual brow; extremely cautious in speech, and reserved in manners; brief in his sermons, not usually exceeding thirty minutes, but exceedingly pertinent in thought, and terse and telling in style; among his familiar friends a most entertaining talker, given to reminiscences of early itinerant adventures and humorous anecdotes; a man of most wholesome mind, tranquil piety, and soundest judgment. He has contributed considerably to the literature of the Church in a volume of sermons, remarkable for their condensed sense, practical appropriateness, and pure and vigorous style; a volume of biographical and historical sketches of the western ministry, and numerous editorial and other fragmentary productions. He lingers in broken health, but in the unbroken affection and veneration of the Church.

Another pre-eminent preacher, John P. Durbin, entered the western itinerancy in 1818, though his name does not appear in the Minutes till 1820. His education up to his fourteenth year was of the commonest kind of the frontier. In the autumn of 1818 he was converted. He soon felt that it was his duty to preach the Gospel, and was appointed to the northwest corner of Ohio. Here he began his studies in the cabins, where there was but one room, which served for chapel, parlor, kitchen, dining-room, and chamber for the whole family. He studied in the winter by firelight, which was made by pine-knots and dry wood, prepared by the boys, who used to wonder at him as a living marvel. The next year he was sent into Indiana, and had for his colleague James Collord, later, for many years, the printer of the Methodist Book Concern, New York. At Collord's instance he began to study English Grammar, and from him he received much instruction. Toward the close of the year he attracted the notice of Dr. Martin Ruter, who advised him to study Latin and Greek, and gave him a grammar or two. He studied indefatigably, and, as he was stationed the third year in Hamilton, Ohio, about twelve miles from the Miami University, (at Oxford,) he used to go to the university on Monday, stay all the week, pursuing his studies, and return on Friday evening to prepare for the Sunday. The next year he was stationed in Cincinnati, and was admitted to the Cincinnati College, with the personal countenance of Dr. Ruter and the late President Harrison. Here he finished his collegiate course, and was admitted to the degree of A. M. without being required to take first the degree of A. B. He subsequently occupied important positions as pastor, presiding elder, professor and president of colleges, editor and author. In 1850 he was appointed unanimously, by the bishops, missionary secretary, in the place of Dr. Pitman, who had resigned on account of ill health. The General Conference of 1852 reappointed him to the same post, which he has ever since occupied with admirable ability.

Dr. Durbin is distinguished both as a preacher and an executive officer. It is difficult to describe his preaching. He begins with a tone, look, and style which would at once damp all favorable expectation were it not for his general fame. The statement of his subject, and the outline of his discourse, are not usually remarkable; but as he advances some unique thought, or some ordinary thought strikingly presented, startles the interest of the hearer, and his attention is riveted through the remainder of the sermon. The entire self-possession and agreeable facility with which the preacher proceeds in his discourse delights the listener by the relief which his manner thus affords to his feeble and peculiar voice. The frequent occurrence of striking passages, striking often by their beauty, but often also by the mere manner of their utterance, yet always endued with a strange, a mystic power over the soul of the hearer, calls forth spontaneous ejaculations or sudden tears. He has also a habit of introducing into almost every sermon some odd or equivocal speculative suggestion which never fails to provoke thought on the part of his audience. His sermons are usually long, but no one tires of them; no one hears the last sentence without regret. He excels in illustration, in picturesque description, and in pathos. He has been distinguished by ability in every sphere of his public life; in no one of them has he ever failed. A capacity for details, practical skill, promptness, energy that never tires, because it moves always calmly, though incessantly, the power to carry with him the interest of the people, these have been the elements of his strength, and have rendered him one of the most capable officers in the Church.

Thus did the West raise up, in these years, men who were not only adapted to its own peculiar frontier work, but some of whom, by their genius and self-culture, were fitted to take the highest positions in the denomination, and to become the chief attractions of its eastern pulpits. They were now extending Methodism, with a sort of triumphal march, all over the "Redstone country," the Northwestern Territory, the Holston Mountain Valleys, Kentucky, and Tennessee. It had already become the predominant form of religion in these vast regions, and was molding into Christian civilization their rapidly growing populations. Meanwhile its itinerants were extending their victories southward in the Valley of the Mississippi. We have followed Gibson in his romantic and heroic mission to Natchez as early as 1799, and seen the labors and sufferings of his first humble itinerant reinforcements, and the arrival of Larner Blackman in 1804, as also the westward advance of the South Carolina Conference itinerants, and the southward progress of those of Eastern Tennessee into Alabama, all pushing southwesterly toward the standard planted on the distant Mississippi by Gibson.

From the Western Conference of 1805 Asbury dispatched Elisha W. Bowman to survey the still further South, and introduce Methodism among the English settlements of Louisiana. He made his way to New Orleans and Opelousas, and the next year the name of the latter appears, for the first time, in the annual Minutes, with Bowman as its Circuit preacher. It is placed under the control of Blackman, who had hitherto been traveling the solitary Circuit of the South Mississippi, that of Natchez, but who now became presiding elder of the "Mississippi District," which was first reported in 1806.

In 1807 Jacob Young was sent thither. Five Circuits, with as many preachers, were assigned him. They journeyed on, forty or fifty miles a day, through Indian tribes—the Chickasaws and Choctaws—and all kinds of frontier hardships. Arriving at Fort Gibson, they pitched their tent "on the Common," and soon after met Blackman, Bowman, and Lasley, the only three preachers of the country. These were about to return; but with Young were Richard Browning, John Travis, Zedekiah M'Minn, James Axley, (a host in himself,) and Anthony Houston. In two days the new itinerants had dispersed to their hard work.

About two years Young continued to travel this great District, through scenes of wild life the most incredible, often swimming rivers, losing himself in woods and swamps, making his way by Indian trails, lodging in filthy cabins, and encountering at many of his appointments the most godless, reckless, hardy, and degraded population of the whole American frontier; many of them men of high crimes, who had escaped thither from the retributions of justice in older settlements. Axley's field was the Opelousas Circuit, where he labored mightily, and was in great favor with many of the rudest settlers, though fiercely persecuted by others. He was "out of money," says Young, "and his clothing very ragged; we made him up some money to buy him some clothes, and sent it to him, but he paid the money out for flooring-boards. He then went into the forest and cut down pine-trees, and hewed them with his own hands; next, borrowed a yoke of oxen, and hauled them together; finally, he called the neighbors to raise the house, which he covered with shingles, made with his own hands. He built his pulpit, cut out his doors and windows, bought him boards, and made seats. He then gave notice that the meeting-house was ready, and if the people would come together he would preach to them. They all flocked out to hear him. He preached several times, then read the General Rules, and told them if they would conform to those rules he would take them into the Methodist Church. The first day he opened the church door eighteen joined." Axley thus built with his own hands the first Methodist Church in Louisiana. After toiling there alone many months "our beloved Brother Axley returned," says Young, "from Louisiana to the Mississippi Territory. When he went to Louisiana he was a large, fine-looking man; but his flesh had since fallen off, and he looked quite diminutive. His clothes were worn out, and when he saw his brethren he could not talk for weeping. The people soon clothed him, his health became restored, his spirits revived, and he came to our camp-ground in pretty good order." His fellow-laborers also suffered much. Travis was prostrated with typhoid fever, and had to be left on the route homeward to the North.

John M'Clure succeeded Young, and had charge of the District two years, when (1810) Miles Harper took command of it for one year, with a reinforcement of preachers, enlarging the little corps to ten. It was now that its most eminent evangelist, and one of the most notable men of the American ministry, William Winans, appeared there. When about eighteen years old he received "thirteen and a half days'" instruction at school, the only academic education of his life. He had heard Valentine Cook, and other celebrated itinerants, who had preached in his mother's cabin, and through most of his early life was addicted to religious reflection. In 1808 he was licensed to preach, and sent to Limestone Circuit, Ky. The Conference held at Shelbyville, Ky., in 1810, dispatched him to the Southern Mississippi, where he traveled the Claiborne Circuit. He made his way thither through the Indian and other dangers of the wilderness route, like Gibson, Blackman, Young, and their associates, and at once proved himself the right man for the peculiar exigencies of the country. None of his predecessors had borne to it more gigantic energies of mind or body. "And what changes," writes one of his friends, "he witnessed! In 1810 the work of the Mississippi preachers extended over what is now the territory of Louisiana, Mississippi, and Alabama Conferences. There were but ten itinerants in this great field of labor, and the whole number of Church members five hundred and nine. Now, in these Conference bounds there are more than three hundred itinerants, and between eighty and ninety thousand Church members! The number of preachers has increased thirtyfold, the Church members upward of one hundred and sixtyfold! Nor is this all. The Mississippi Conference has contributed largely to the

Memphis, Arkansas, Florida, and the Texan Conferences, and somewhat to the California Conference. In this great work William Winans has been, under Providence, mainly instrumental."

William Winans became the most representative character of Southwestern Methodism. His last appearance in the North was at the memorable General Conference of 1844 in New York, where the secession of the Southern Church, on account of slavery, was initiated. He took a chief part in that controversy, for he had himself become a slaveholder, under the plea of domestic necessity. He was then, next to Peter Cartwright, the most unique man in the assembly; tall, thin, weather-worn, and looking the very image of a frontier settler who had worn himself lean by the labors of the field and the hunts of the woods. He wore no stock or neckerchief, his shirt collar lay slouchingly about his neck, and his whole attire had the appearance of habitual neglect. And yet this rough backwoodsman was a "doctor of divinity." In discourse he was most intensely earnest, the tight features of his face became flushed and writhed with his emotions, his eye gleamed, and his voice (strong but harsh) thrilled with a stentorian energy and overwhelming effect. In contrast with these traits (unrelieved as they were by a single exterior attraction) was a mind of astonishing power—comprehensive, all grasping, reaching down to the foundations and around the whole circuit of its positions; not touching subjects, but seizing them as with the claws of an eagle. His style was excellent, showing an acquaintance with the standard models, and his scientific allusions proved him well read if not studied in general knowledge. With the secession of the South and the consequent civil war, much of the great work he had done in Mississippi and Louisiana was undone; but after the restoration of peace its germs were still found vital in the soil, and promise again to cover those extended regions with evangelical harvests.

The extraordinary history of Richmond Nolley has heretofore been sketched down to his departure from South Carolina for the southwest, whither he was sent, with Lewis Hobbs, Drury Powell and Thomas Griffin, in 1812. They set out together on horseback, and journeyed through the forests and Indian tribes three hundred and fifty miles, "swimming deep creeks, and camping out eleven nights," till they arrived at Nolley's appointment, the Tombigbee Mission. For two years he ranged over a vast extent of country, preaching continually, stopping for no obstructions of flood or weather. When his horse could not go on he shouldered his saddle-bags and pressed forward on foot. When Indian hostilities prevailed, and the settlers crowded into isolated forts and stockades, Nolley sought no shelter, but hastened from post to post, instructing and comforting the alarmed refugees. He kept "the Gospel sounding abroad through all the country," says our authority. It was in this wild country that happened the fact, often cited as an illustration of the energy of the primitive Methodist ministry: In making the rounds of his field Nolley came to a fresh wagon-track. On the search for anything that had a soul, he followed it, and came upon the emigrant family just as it had pitched on the ground of its future home. The man was unlimbering his team, and the wife was busy around the fire. "What!" exclaimed the settler upon hearing the salutation of the visitor, and taking a glance at his unmistakable appearance, "have you found me already? Another Methodist preacher! I left Virginia to get out of reach of them, went to a new settlement in Georgia, and thought to have a long whet, but they got my wife and daughter into the Church; then, in this late purchase, [Choctaw Corner,] I found a piece of good land, and was sure I would have some peace of the preachers, and here is one before my wagon is unloaded." Nolley gave him small comfort: "My friend, if you go to heaven you'll find Methodist preachers there; and if to hell, I am afraid you will find some there; and you see," he said, "how it is in this world; so you had better make terms with us, and be at peace."

By 1814 he had made his way into Louisiana to the renowned Opelousas and Attakapas Circuit, which lay far in the interior of that State, half way of the distance from New Orleans to Texas, and extended from the Red River to the Gulf. Wonderful things are still told of his labors there. He appeared in the next Conference an attenuated, worn-out man, yet it was deemed necessary to send him back to the same rugged field. "He went," says his presiding elder, "without a murmur." He was accompanied on his return by Griffin, his presiding elder. They crossed the Mississippi and a vast swamp. "The difficulties we had to encounter," says Griffin, "were almost incredible." Coming to a place where they must separate, after embracing each other, with mutual benedictions they parted. It was in the latter part of November, and a dark, cold, rainy day. Across his path there lay a large swamp and deep creeks, and not a single white man was to be found between him and the place of his destination. Alone he traveled on till evening, when he found himself at an Indian village. "Having to cross a creek before night, and apprehending from the rains that it would be swollen, he employed an Indian to go with him. When he arrived on its banks he found it, as he anticipated, a full and angry flood, rushing tumultuously along. There was no alternative but to cross or remain with the savages, so he chose the former; and, leaving his valise, saddle-bags, and a parcel of books with the Indian, he urged his horse into the stream. No sooner did his charger strike the current than he was beaten down the flood. The animal battled courageously with the stream, but before the other shore was reached, horse and rider were far below the landing-place of the ford, and, the banks being high, it was impossible for the horse to gain a foothold, or make the ascent of the other shore. In the struggle to do so the rider was thrown, and, grasping the limb of a tree which extended over the stream, he reached the bank. The horse swam back to the side of the stream whence he had started. The missionary directed the Indian to keep his horse till morning, and he would walk to the nearest house, which was distant about two miles. He traveled through the woods about one mile, wet, cold, and weary. Unable to proceed any further, and conscious perhaps that his work was done, and that he had at last fulfilled the errand of his Master, he fell upon his knees, and commended his soul to God. There, in that wild wood of the far West, alone with his God and the ministering spirits that encamp around the saints, Richard Nolley, the young missionary, closed his eyes on earth to open them in heaven. When he was found he was lying extended upon the wet leaves, his left hand upon his breast, and the other lying by his side. The eyes were closed, and the gentle spirit left a smile upon his pallid cheek ere it passed away to that bright and beautiful world, where the wicked cease to trouble, and the weary are at rest." His knees were muddy, and there were prints of them in the ground, showing that he had been praying in this last scene of his mortal life. He had evidently resigned himself calmly to his fate, selecting a place to die on, beneath a clump of pines, composing his limbs and closing his eyes. A traveler found him the next day, bore him to the nearest house, and on Sunday he was buried "in Catahoula Parish, near the road leading from Alexandria to Harrisonburg, and about twenty miles from the latter place." He was but thirty years old, tall, slender, emaciated by labors and fastings; had dark, radiant eyes, and a countenance full of determination and saintliness; was never married; "was always busy, rising at four o'clock at all times and places;" was a man of no extraordinary intellectual powers, but of extraordinary courage, self-denial, and labor, and yet achieved more perhaps by his death than by his life, for his name is consecrated in the heart of the Church as that of a martyr.

In 1817 appears in the Minutes, for the first time, the title of the "Mississippi Conference," ordered by the General Conference of 1816. It was organized at the house of William Foster, at Pine Ridge, Adams County, about seven miles above Natchez, Bishop Roberts presiding. A southern authority, writing in 1858, says: "The little company of pioneers then assembled were a feeble band, nine in number, all told. They had to provide for the spiritual wants of the people, so far as Methodism was concerned, from the Chattahoochee to the Tennessee River, and from the Cherokee nation east to the Sabine River west. The little company all slept under the same roof, and ate at the same hospitable table. From this nucleus have sprung the Alabama, Louisiana, two Texas Conferences, and a part of the Memphis Conference. It had now two Districts, Mississippi and Louisiana, nine Circuits, twelve preachers, and one thousand nine hundred and forty-one members. By 1820 it reported three Districts, all with State titles —Mississippi, Louisiana, and Alabama—comprising the State of Louisiana south of the Arkansas, all the Mississippi Territory south of the Tennessee River, and stretching over the present States of Mississippi and Alabama. It had yet but eleven "appointments" and seventeen preachers, but most of its Circuits were four or five hundred miles around, and the itinerants preached daily. Many mighty men were subsequently in their ranks, and influential local or "located" preachers co-operated with them extensively. Methodism here, as elsewhere in the West, was rapidly appropriating the country.

These powerful men were under the episcopal guidance of Asbury and M'Kendree; leaders worthy to command such a host. Asbury made through all these years, down to within four or five months of his death, his annual visit to the West; but, as now in all other parts of the country, his records give us hardly any available facts.

Toward the end of this period western Methodism, essentially a system of missionary evangelization, became more distinctively missionary, by turning its attention to the aborigines, thereby prompting at last the organization of the Missionary Society of the Church. Remarkably providential events gave it this new direction. While Marcus Lindsey was preaching on a Sabbath, in 1815, in Marietta, Ohio, a negro addicted to drunkenness, and on his way to the river at the time to drown himself, heard the voice of the itinerant, went to the door of the Church, and, after listening to the sermon, returned home with an awakened conscience. On the next Sunday he joined the society, and his neighbors soon saw that he was indeed a regenerated man. He endeavored, in a humble way, to do good, and resolved at last to go among the Indian tribes a witness for the Gospel. He could read, and was a superior singer. With his Bible and hymn book he traveled to the Delawares, on the Muskingum, thence to a tribe near Pipetown, on the Sandusky, thence to another tribe on the Upper Sandusky. In some places he was well received, in others fiercely repelled, and in peril of martyrdom by the tomahawk; but he usually allayed the violence of the savages by his melodious hymns, or by falling on his knees in prayer, an attitude which the Indians revered with wondering awe. On the Upper Sandusky he found, among the wigwams of the Wyandottes, a captive negro, Jonathan Pointer, who had been taken by them in Virginia when a child, and who could act as his interpreter. His first congregation consisted only of an old Indian man, "Big Tree," and an aged Indian woman, named Mary. But he soon had the whole clan under his influence; and thus went forth, from the first settlement in the North-western Territory, the first American Methodist "missionary," John Stewart, and he an African, the founder of that series of aboriginal missions which has since been extended over most of the Indian countries, which has rescued, amid the general decline of the tribes, thousands of immortal souls, and which opened the whole "missionary" career of the denomination.

These extraordinary facts excited no little interest in the western Churches. Assistance was bountifully sent to Stewart and his converts; Jane Trimble especially gave them her sympathies and aid. In 1819 the Ohio Conference adopted the mission, and sent James Montgomery as Stewart's colleague, both being under the presiding eldership of Finley. A school was established by the aid of the national government. Finley, Elliott, Gilruth, Henkle, and many other preachers, labored among the scattered communities of the tribe. Stewart was made a local preacher, and died in the faith in 1823. Converted Wyandottes bore, in 1820, the news of their evangelization to a portion of their tribe, near Fort Malden, in Canada; two Indian preachers went thither, converts were multiplied, and, twelve years later, there were nine aboriginal missionary stations in Upper Canada, with two thousand adult Indians, and four hundred youths were receiving instruction in eleven schools, and the names of John Sunday, Peter Jones, and other native evangelists, became eminent in the Church and in Europe.

The labors of Stewart and his white colleagues continued to prosper greatly. A saintly woman, Harriet Stubbs, sister-in-law of Judge M'Lean, went to their aid as teacher of Indian girls. "She possessed," says Finley, "more courage and fortitude than any one of her age and sex that I have been acquainted with. In a short time the intrepid female missionary was the idol of the whole nation. They looked upon her as an angel-messenger sent from the spirit-land to teach them the way to heaven. They called her the 'pretty redbird,' and were only happy in the light of her smiles. This most amiable young lady took charge of the Indian girls, and began to teach them their letters, and infuse into them her own sweet and happy spirit." It was not long before five leading chiefs, Big Tree, Between-the-Logs, Mononcue, Hicks, and Peacock, joined the Church. Big Tree was the first convert of his tribe. Between-the-Logs became a powerful preacher; but Mononcue excelled him in the peculiar aboriginal eloquence, and "was," says Finley, "a son of thunder." All these, and hundreds more, after useful lives, died in the faith, but not till they saw Methodist missions established among their people from Canada to the Gulf of Mexico. In about three years after Stewart went, solitary and unsupported, on his mission, the "Missionary Society of the Methodist Episcopal Church" arose. Its necessity had become obvious. It threw its protecting arms around all the Indian missions, and has since reached them out, with the Gospel of peace, to nearly all the ends of the earth.

With such men, led by such commanders as Asbury and M'Kendree, we are not surprised that western Methodism triumphed all over the settled regions of the Mississippi Valley; that the one Western Conference with which we began this period had increased to five by its close, each of them bearing the names of now mighty States—Ohio, Kentucky, Missouri, Tennessee, and Mississippi—that its six presiding elders' Districts were now twenty-seven, many of them individually comprehending the territory of a modern Conference; that its thirty-nine Circuits were now two hundred, striking the waters of the great lakes on the north, and of the Gulf of Mexico on the south, winding among the Alleghany fastnesses on the East, and threading the Indian trails to the farthest log-cabins on the West; and that its seventy-two preachers had increased to three hundred and forty, and its communicants from fifteen thousand three hundred and fifteen to ninety-eight thousand six hundred and forty-two. The men who were chief actors in these strange scenes saw in them "signs and wonders," but hardly dared to estimate their full significance; we now see that they were constructing one of the mightiest religious empires of our planet. Half the Methodism, nearly half the entire Protestantism, of the New World, lie now beyond the Alleghanies. Strenuous with life and energies, boundless in resources, continually rearing churches, academies, colleges, publishing houses, and, above all, noble men and women, this "great West," for which Methodism showed such a wise prescience and heroic devotion, seems destined soon to be the fountain-head, the reservoir, not only of material, but of moral resources for the western hemisphere, if not, indeed, for the whole earth.

CHAPTER XXXII.

GENERAL CONFERENCES OF 1808, 1812, AND 1816—SUMMARY REVIEW—DEATHS OF WHATCOAT, COKE, LEE, AND ASBURY.

I HAVE traced the legislative development of the Church, by the General Conference, down to the end of the session of 1804. The next meeting of that body was in Baltimore, May 6, 1808. It had been anticipated with no little interest, as the change of its organization, to a delegated assembly, was generally expected. A committee of two members from each Annual Conference, making fourteen in all, was now appointed to report on the subject. On the twenty-fourth the report of the committee was substantially adopted, "almost unanimously." It provided that one representative for every five members of the Annual Conferences shall be sent to the General Conference; that the latter shall have "full powers" to make "rules and regulations" for the Church under certain "restrictions," to wit, that it shall not change the Articles of Religion; nor allow more than one delegate for every five, nor less than one for every seven members of an Annual Conference; nor do away episcopacy or the itinerancy of the episcopate; nor change the "General Rules;" nor abolish the right of trial and appeal of accused preachers and members; nor "appropriate the produce of the Book Concern or Chartered Fund," except for the benefit of ministers and their families. These restrictions could, however, be suspended by the joint recommendation of all the Annual Conferences, together with a majority of two thirds of the General Conference. Such are what are usually called the Restrictive Rules of the Methodist Episcopal Church. With the "Articles of Religion," and the "General Rules," they compose the organic or constitutional law of the denomination. They are attributed chiefly to Joshua Soule. In their form, at this time, they leave open to change the fundamental interests of the Church, even its theology and terms of membership, without representation of the laity; but, in 1832, the proviso giving this power was modified, making the Articles of Religion unalterable, and requiring a vote of three fourths of the members of the Annual, and two thirds of the General, Conferences to effect any of the other specified changes. The ratio of representation has been repeatedly altered.

The ecclesiastical system of the Church had been so thoroughly developed and established by this time that the further proceedings of the Conference present little more than the enactment of administrative details. On the 12th of May M'Kendree was elected to the office of bishop by ninety-five votes out of a hundred and twenty-eight, and consecrated in Light-street Church on the 17th. The question of slavery, which had never failed to come up in the sessions of the General Conference, was again brought up by Roszell. M'Claskey and Budd were defeated in a motion to strike out "the whole section in the Discipline on the subject." Roszell and Ware carried a resolution to "retain the first two paragraphs of the section," and to authorize the Annual Conferences to "form their own regulations relative to buying and selling slaves." The Conference adjourned on the 26th of May, having sat twenty days.

On May 1, 1812, the first delegated General Conference assembled in the "old John-street Church," New York. M'Kendree submitted a written address or message to the Conference, the first example of the kind. "Upon examination," he said, "you will find the work of the Lord is prospering in our hands. At present we have about one hundred and ninety thousand members, upward of two thousand local, and about seven hundred traveling, preachers in our Connection, and these widely scattered over seventeen States, besides the Canadas and several of the territorial settlements." After protracted debate the ordination of local preachers, as elders, was voted; but only for localities where the "official services" of local elders might be necessary, and "provided that no slaveholder shall be eligible to the office of local elder in any State or Territory where the civil laws will admit emancipation, and suffer the liberated slave to enjoy his freedom." It was ordered that the Magazine, which had been published in 1789 and 1790, should be revived, but it was not, till six years later. Two days were spent in a great debate on the question of the election of presiding elders by the Annual Conferences. Lee, Shinn, and Snethen were the leaders of the affirmative, and many of the ablest delegates shared their opinions; but they were defeated, the bishops being known as profoundly opposed to it. At every session of the General Conference since 1784, down to 1828, (with the possible exception of that of 1804,) this question obtruded itself, arraying the chief men of the ministry against each other in formidable parties. In the session of 1812 the majority against the change was but three; the delegates of Philadelphia, New York, and Genesee were pledged to it; the southern and western members were mostly opposed to it. Lee, Cooper, Garrettson, Ware, Phœbus, and Hunt were its most strenuous advocates.

In 1816 the Conference again assembled on the first of May in Baltimore. The war with Great Britain had just closed, and left, as has been noticed, some disturbance between the Wesleyan and American Methodist bodies by the encroachment of Wesleyan missionaries on the Canadian appointments. A letter from the English Missionary Board was read, full of congratulations and cordial sentiments, but soliciting the cession of the Montreal appointment, and Lower Canada generally, to their control. A committee reported that the great majority of the Methodists, of both Upper and Lower Canada, wished the continuance of the jurisdiction of the American Church, and that therefore "we cannot, consistently with our duty to the Societies, give up any part of them." On the fourteenth Enoch George and Robert R. Roberts were elected bishops. A course of study, to be prepared by the bishops, or a committee appointed by them, for ministerial candidates, who were to be examined at the Annual Conferences, was ordered; the first example of any such requisition in the Church, though habits of reading and study had always been enjoined. Measures were adopted providing for the better support of the ministry; for repressing heretical opinions; for abolishing pews (which were yet confined to New England Churches) and assessments, or taxes, in support of preaching; and for the licensing of exhorters. Joshua Soule and Thomas Mason were elected Book Agents, and the order for the publication of the "Methodist Magazine" was repeated by a motion of Bangs, and about two years later obeyed. The question of the election of presiding elders was again elaborately debated, but lost. Pickering moved that the "unfinished business of the last General Conference so far as it relates to slavery" be referred to a select committee. It was "*Resolved*, That no slaveholder shall be eligible to any official station in our Church hereafter where the laws of the State in which he lives will admit of emancipation, and permit the liberated slave to enjoy freedom." A Book Depository at Pittsburgh was authorized, and the Missouri and Mississippi Conferences established. The Conference adjourned on the twenty-fourth of May.

The Church now advanced with increasing prosperity. The statistical exhibit of Methodism in 1820 astonished not only the Church, but the country. It was evident that a great religious power had, after little more than half a century, been permanently established in the nation, not only with a practical system and auxiliary agencies of unparalleled efficiency, but sustained and propelled forward by hosts of the common people, the best bone and sinew of the republic—and that all other religious denominations, however antecedent, were thereafter to take secondary rank to it, numerically at least, a fact of which Methodists themselves could not fail to be vividly conscious, and which might have critical effect on that humble devotion to religious life and work which had made them thus far successful. Their leaders saw the peril, and incessantly admonished them to "rejoice with trembling." The aggregate returns show that there were now 273,858 members in the Church, with between nine and ten hundred itinerant preachers.* In the sixteen years of this period there was

* An error in the Minutes of 1820 (vol. i, p. 346) is corrected by the Minutes of 1821, (ibid., p. 366.) The Minutes cannot be followed for the aggregates of any given calendar year, for the reason that the returns of the Western Conferences, printed in any given year, were made up the preceding year. I correct this defect in the estimate in my text. Bangs followed the Minutes without this modifi-

a gain of no less than 158,447 members, and of more than 500 preachers. In the twenty years of the century the increase was 208,964 members, and 617 preachers; the former had much more than quadrupled, and the latter much more than trebled.

The first native American Methodist preacher was still alive, and was to see both this large membership and its ministry more than doubled.

The comparative statistics of Methodism (if they may be given without the appearance of invidiousness) showed its peculiar energy; its communicants already lacked but about 13,000 to be equal to those of its elder sister, the regular Baptist Church, which dates its American origin more than a century and a quarter before it, and, in one decade later, they were to be nearly a hundred thousand in advance of them. They were already much more than double the number of those of the Presbyterian Church, and more than eleven times those of the Protestant Episcopal Church. In a few years more Methodism was to advance to the front of the Protestantism of the New World, and thenceforward, for good or evil, lead its van with continually increasing ascendency. It had advanced, by this year, to the front of the Methodist world, with a majority of 1,700 over the parent British denomination.

It had by 1820 a well-defined ecclesiastical geography, covering all the settled parts of the republic and Canada, with its eleven immense Conferences, subdivided into sixty-four presiding elders' Districts, and more than five hundred Circuits, many of the latter full five hundred miles in range; and it now possessed, in more or less organized form, nearly a complete series of secondary or auxiliary agencies of usefulness, literary, educational, and missionary. It seemed thoroughly equipped, and had only to move forward.

cation; Goss's "Statistical History" has followed Bangs. The preachers for 1820 are given in the Minutes as 904, but this includes the preachers of the West only for 1819. The Minutes of 1821 give the ministry as 977; this includes the western preachers of 1820, but also those of the East down to the end of the spring (and one Conference beyond it) of 1821. The statement in the text is sufficiently precise.

In casting a glance back over these sixteen years, so replete with great characters and achievements, we are reminded of events which might strike us as catastrophes were it not that they were in the order of Divine Providence, and therefore in "due season," and illustrations of the Methodistic maxim that "God calls home his workmen, but carries on his work." Among a host of men, many of them prominent, who fell by death in the ministerial field, Whatcoat, Coke, Asbury, and Lee have all disappeared from the scene as we close the period.

Whatcoat sustained his episcopal functions with continual disability from chronic disease, but was ever in motion throughout the whole extent of the Church North, South, East, and West. His beautiful character preached more effectually than his sermons. Peculiarly simple, sober, but serene and cheerful, living as well as teaching his favorite doctrine of sanctification, extremely prudent in his administration, pathetically impressive in discourse, and "made perfect through sufferings," he is pre-eminently the saint in the primitive calendar of American Methodism. In November, 1806, Asbury wrote to Fleming: "Dear Father Whatcoat, after thirteen weeks' illness—gravel, stone, dysentery combined—died, a martyr to pain in all patience and resignation to the will of God. May we, like him, if we live long live well, and die like him."

He had "finished his sixth episcopal tour through the work after his consecration," says his biographer, "or near that, and, after great suffering, he got an honorable discharge from the Captain of his salvation, and by his permission came in from his post, which he had faithfully kept for fifty years." He took refuge at the home of Senator Bassett, Dover, Del., where he died, "in the full assurance of faith," say the Minutes, July 5, 1806. "He professed," adds his brethren, "the justifying and sanctifying grace of God, and all that knew him well might say, If a man on earth possessed these blessings, surely it was Richard Whatcoat."

Nearly a year later Asbury reached Dover, and over his tomb declared that he "knew Richard Whatcoat, from his own age of fourteen to sixty-two years, most intimately—his holy manner of life, in duty at all times, in all places, and before all

people, as a Christian and as a minister; his long suffering as a man of great affliction of body and mind, having been exercised with severe diseases and great labors; his charity, his love of God and man, in all its effects, tempers, words, and actions; bearing, with resignation and patience, great temptations, bodily labors, and inexpressible pain. In life and death he was placid and calm. As he lived, so he died."

He was thirty-seven years an itinerant preacher, twenty-two of them in America, six in the episcopate, and died aged seventy.

We have witnessed Coke's final departure from the United States in 1804. On his return to England he was made president (in 1805) of the Wesleyan Conference. After his last visit to this country he seemed, for nine years, almost ubiquitous in the United Kingdom, administering the affairs of the Wesleyan Church, founding and conducting its Irish, its Welsh, its "Domestic," and its Foreign Missions, virtually embodying in his own person the whole missionary enterprise of English Methodism. When an old man of nearly seventy years he conceived the project of introducing Methodism into Asia. He presented himself before the British Conference, and, against great opposition, entreated, with tears, to be sent as a missionary to India, offering to defray the expenses of himself and seven chosen colleagues. The Conference could not resist his appeal, and at length, on the 30th of December, 1813, he departed with his little band, consisting of nine persons besides himself, (two of them wives of missionaries,) in a fleet of six Indiamen. Terrible gales swept over them. In the Indian Ocean his health rapidly declined. On the morning of the third of May, 1814, his servant knocked at his cabin door to awake him at his usual time, but heard no response. Opening the door he beheld the lifeless body of the missionary extended on the floor. A "placid smile was on his countenance." He was cold and stiff, and must have died before midnight. It is supposed that he had risen to call for help, and fell by apoplexy. His cabin was separated by only a thin wainscot from others, in which no noise or struggle had been heard, and it is inferred that he expired without violent suffering. Consternation spread among the missionary band, but they lost not their resolution. They prepared to commit him to the deep, and to prosecute, as they might be able, his great design. A coffin was made, and at five o'clock in the afternoon the corpse was solemnly borne up to the leeward gangway, where it was covered with signal flags; the soldiers were drawn up in rank on the deck; the bell of the ship tolled, and the crew and passengers, deeply affected, crowded around the scene. One of the missionaries read the burial service, and the moment that the sun sank below the Indian Ocean the coffin was cast into its depths. He died in his sixty-seventh year. Though the great leader was no more, his spirit remained; and the East Indian Missions of Methodism, "presenting in our day a state of massive strength and inexpressible utility," sprang from this fatal voyage. The news of his death struck a sensation through all the Methodist world. He was commemorated in funeral sermons in the principal Methodist churches of America. Asbury preached them in all his routes, before the assembled preachers, in Conference, and pronounced him a man "of blessed mind and soul; a gentleman, a scholar, and a bishop; and as a minister of Christ, in zeal, in labors, and in services, the greatest man in the last century." He had a leading agency in the greatest facts of Methodism, and it was impossible that the series of momentous deeds which mark his career could have been the result of mere accident or fortune. They must have been legitimate to the man. Neither Whitefield nor Wesley exceeded him in ministerial travels. It is probable that no Methodist of his day, it is doubtful whether any Protestant of his day, contributed more from his own property for the spread of the Gospel. His biographer says that he expended the whole of his patrimonial estate, which was large, on his missions and their chapels. He was married twice; both his wives were like-minded with himself, and both had considerable fortunes, which were used like his own. In 1794 was published an account of his missionary receipts and disbursements for the preceding year, from which it appeared that there were due him nearly eleven thousand dollars; but he gave the whole sum to the cause. Flying, during nearly forty years, over England, Scotland, Wales, and Ireland; crossing the Atlantic eighteen times; traversing the United States and the West Indies; the first who suggested the organization of English Methodism by Wesley's Deed of Declaration; the organizer, under Wesley, of American Methodism; one of the first, if not the very first, of Protestant bishops in the Western hemisphere; the founder of the Methodist missions in the West Indies, in Africa, and in Asia, as well as in Ireland, Wales, and England; the official and almost sole director of the missionary operations of the denomination during his long public life, and the founder of its first Tract Society, he must be recognized as one of the chief representative men of modern religious history.

On the 31st of March, 1816, Francis Asbury fell in death at the head of the hosts of Methodists who had been marshaled and led on, chiefly by himself, over all the republic for nearly half a century. If a distinct portraiture of his character had not been attempted, in the outset of his American career, it would now be superfluous, for he has thus far been the most familiar actor in our story, the dominant hero of American Methodist history. Though not the first, he was the chief, founder of the denomination in the New World. The history of Christianity, since the apostolic age, affords not a more perfect example of ministerial and episcopal devotion than was presented in this great man's life. He preached almost daily for more than half a century. During forty-five years he traveled, with hardly an intermission, the North American continent from North to South, and East to West, directing the advancing Church with the skill and authority of a great captain. Beginning his itinerant ministry in England when but seventeen years of age, he came to America in his twenty-sixth year, was ordained bishop of the Church when thirty-nine years old, when it comprised less than fifteen thousand members, and but about eighty preachers, and fell in his seventy-first year, commanding an army of more than two hundred and eleven thousand Methodists, and more than seven hundred itinerant preachers. It has been estimated that in his American ministry he preached about sixteen thousand five hundred sermons, or at least one a day, and traveled about two hundred and seventy thousand miles, or six thousand a year; that he presided in no less than two hundred and twenty-four annual Conferences, and ordained more than four thousand preachers. He was, in fine, one of those men of extraordinary—of anomalous—greatness, in estimating whom the historian is compelled to use terms which would be irrelevant, as hyperbole, to most men with whom he has to deal. His discrimination of character was marvelous; his administrative talents would have placed him, in civil government or in war, by the side of Richelieu or Cesar, and his success placed him unquestionably at the head of the leading characters of American ecclesiastical history. No one man has done more for Christianity in the western hemisphere. His attitude in the pulpit was solemn and dignified, if not graceful; his voice was sonorous and commanding, and his discourses were often attended with bursts of eloquence "which spoke a soul full of God, and, like a mountain torrent, swept all before it." With Wesley, Whitefield, and Coke, he ranks as one of the four greatest representatives of the Methodistic movement. In American Methodism he ranks immeasurably above all his contemporaries and successors. Notwithstanding his advanced age and shattered health he continued his travels to the last, till he had to be aided up the pulpit steps, and to sit while preaching.

In taking his last leave of the West, some six months before he died, he wrote: "My eyes fail. I will resign the stations to Bishop M'Kendree. I will take away my feet." Thence he journeyed southward, suffering from influenza, which resulted in pulmonary ulceration and consumption. He endeavored to advance northward, to meet, once more, the General Conference at Baltimore, preaching continually on the way. While passing through Virginia he wrote: "I die daily—am made perfect by labor and suffering, and fill up still what is behind. There is no time, no opportunity to take medicine in the day; I must do it at night. I am wasting away with a constant dysentery and cough." In the last entry of his journal (save a single sentence) he says: "My consolations are great. I live in God from moment to moment—broken to pieces." He reached Richmond, Va., and at three o'clock Sunday afternoon, March 24, 1816, preached there, in the old Methodist church, his last sermon. He was carried to and from the pulpit, and sat while preaching. His faithful traveling companion, Bond, took him to Spottsylvania, where he failed rapidly, and on Sunday, 21st, expired, raising both his hands, when unable to speak, in affirmative reply to an inquiry respecting his trust and comfort in Christ. His remains were disinterred, and borne to Baltimore, at the ensuing General Conference, where, with public solemnities, a sermon from M'Kendree, and an immense procession, they were laid to rest beneath the altar of Eutaw-street Church.

In that procession, including all the General Conference, and hundreds of other clergymen from the city and neighboring churches, walked Jesse Lee. Thrift, his biographer, who was by his side, says, "The scene was solemn and impressive; Lee's countenance bespoke his emotions. A dignified sorrow, such as veterans feel while following to the grave an old companion in arms, was evinced by his words and countenance. They had suffered together, and had long fought in the same ranks. The one had gained his crown, the other was soon to receive his." In less than six months Lee also had fallen. About the middle of August he went to a camp-meeting, near Hillsborough, on the Eastern Shore of Maryland. After preaching he was seized with fever, and carried to Hillsborough. All remedies failed. He suffered at first from depression; but, "for several days preceding his death he was filled with holy joy. Frequently he cried out, 'Glory, glory, glory! halleluiah, halleluiah! Jesus reigns!' At another time he spoke with great distinctness and deliberation for nearly twenty minutes, giving directions about his affairs, and sending the assurance he was 'dying in the Lord' to comfort his distant family. Nor did he forget his fellow-laborers. 'Give my respects to Bishop M'Kendree,' he said, 'and tell him I die in love with all the preachers; that I do love him, and that he lives in my heart.' Having finished his work, he said but little more; but fell asleep on the evening of the 12th of September, 1816." He was fifty-eight years old. A man of vigorous, though unpolished mind, of rare popular eloquence and tireless energy, an itinerant evangelist from the British provinces to Florida for thirty-five years, a presiding elder for many years, a chief counselor of the Church in its Annual and General Conferences, chaplain to Congress, founder of Methodism in New England, and first historian of the Church, he lacked only the episcopal office to give him rank with Asbury and Coke. Asbury early chose him for that position. Some two or three times it seemed likely that he would be elected to it, but his manly independence and firmness of opinion, in times of party strife, were made the occasions of his defeat. His staunch advocacy of an elective presiding eldership, and his opposition to the ordination of local preachers as elders, (questions of prolonged and spirited controversy,) cost him the suffrages of men who should have been superior to such party considerations, at least in the presence of such a man. But his historic position needed no such addition. No official distinction could enhance its dignity. In public services he may fairly be ranked next to Asbury, and as founder and apostle of Eastern Methodism he is above any other official rank. In this respect his historic honor is quite unique; for though individual men have, in several other sections of the continent, initiated the denomination, no other founder has, so completely as he, introduced, conducted, and concluded his work, and from no other one man's similar work has proceeded equal advantages to American Methodism.

Thus fell, in arms, but victorious, toward the conclusion of this period, one after another of the most conspicuous heroes of this grand Methodistic battle-field of the New World; the last two (and, perhaps, the two most important in the American history of the denomination) in the very year that completed its first half century, and all of them giving, by both their great deeds and sublime deaths, a sort of epic grandeur and completeness to the history of the Church down to this epoch.

CHAPTER XXXIII.

PROGRESS AND TRIALS FROM THE GENERAL CONFERENCE OF 1820 TO THE CENTENARY JUBILEE, 1866.

IN the outset of our narrative we noticed particularly the successive Annual Conferences, for they were, for some years, the highest assembly of Methodism. From the first regular General Conference, in 1792, down to 1820, we have duly recorded the sessions of that body; for it had become the supreme one of the denomination. By 1820, however, American Methodism may be said to have been completed in its organic structure. The delegated form of the General Conference, adopted in 1808, and exemplified, for the first time, in 1812, determined permanently its constitutional law, except as the Restrictive Rules were qualified by the session of 1832, as already shown, and occasional amendments of the "General Rules" on slavery and "temperance." Nearly all the important additions to its practical system—its auxiliary institutions of education, missions, Sunday-schools, "Book Concern"—had also been initiated before the date (1820) which we have reached. Hereafter the proceedings of the General Conferences are to have chief reference to these great interests. As, however, it will be most convenient to present the substance of such proceedings in summary and classified accounts of these important institutions, we need not delay by a minute record of the remaining sessions. Their other salient facts, as affecting the Church generally, can also be best treated apart from their chronological succession.

In nothing, perhaps, have these sessions shown greater caution and wisdom than in the supply of the episcopate. That office sustains the highest responsibility, and wields the greatest power of the denomination. The most reliable men have, therefore, ever been sought for it, and the Church has been providentially successful in finding them. Coke, Asbury, Whatcoat, M'Kendree, George, and Roberts have thus far been its episcopal standard-bearers, and more apostolic bishops have not been known in the modern history of Christianity, as our narrative fully shows. The later incumbents of the office have been Joshua Soule and Elijah Hedding, consecrated in 1824; J. O. Andrews and John Emory, in 1832; Beverly Waugh and Thomas A. Morris, in 1836; L. L. Hamline and E. S. Janes, in 1844; Levi Scott, Matthew Simpson, O. C. Baker, and E. R. Ames, in 1852; D. W. Clark, E. Thomson, and C. Kingsley, in 1864. Time has greatly augmented their official functions, and they can no longer pass, like Asbury and his immediate successors, over their long routes, locally inspecting the individual Churches. They must hasten from Conference to Conference through much of the year, and make journeys to the Pacific Coast, to Germany, Scandinavia, Bulgaria, Africa, India, and China, preaching as they go, but burdened by innumerable other duties. Notwithstanding the almost singular purity and integrity of its bishops, the Church has been peculiarly hesitant to multiply them. It has, for many years, had a less number, in proportion to its territory and membership, than it had in the first year of its organization.

After the schism of O'Kelly, which effectively began in the General Conference of 1792, the denomination had a long period of comparative peace and of continuous prosperity. But in 1820 began a new and graver disturbance, which reached its crisis in the session of 1828, and which gave birth to the "Methodist Protestant Church." The controversy was ostensibly on the subject of Lay Representation—a question which has seldom ceased to agitate more or less American Methodism from the first decade of its organization to our day. The "Reformers" published, in 1820, a journal—the "Wesleyan Repository"—in Trenton, N. J. A "Union Society" was formed in Baltimore to promote their designs. In 1824 they began a periodical, "The Mutual Rights," in the latter city, and the war now raged with perilous severity. Nicholas Snethen, Alexander M'Cain, and Asa Shinn, men of distinction in the ministry, became champions of the movement. Henry B.

Bascom wrote in defense of it. Disorders ensued which led to ecclesiastical trials and expulsions. Dr. Thomas E. Bond appeared in "An Appeal to the Methodists" as the defender of the Church. Compromises were attempted, but personal passions had become so commingled with the questions in debate that pacificatory counsels could not be heeded. Emory answered M'Cain in a memorable pamphlet, "The Defense of our Fathers." A new society, "The Associated Methodist Reformers," was organized in Baltimore, and about six months before the session of the General Conference—November, 1827—a convention assembled which prepared a memorial to the Conference, which, together with similar petitions from various parts of the country, brought the whole controversy before that body. Emory presented from the Committee on Petitions an elaborate review of the subject—a report written by Dr. Bond—and the demands of the petitioners were declined. The "Protestant Methodist Church" soon after arose from this unfortunate dispute, and, through many struggles, has continued to our day. The insurmountable difficulty of the controversy was the acrimonious spirit with which it was conducted. Bangs hesitates not to blame both sides, though he does not admit the principal charge of the "Reformers." He says, "Whoever will consult the writings of those days will find complaints, on the part of the 'Reformers,' that an attempt was made by the advocates of the present order of things to suppress inquiry, to abridge the freedom of speech and of the press, and that trials were instituted, in part, at least; as a punishment for exercising this freedom on the subjects that were then litigated. This was a great mistake. It was for an *abuse* of this freedom, for indulging in criminations injurious to individual character, that the delinquents were tried and finally condemned. This will appear manifest to every person who will impartially inspect the charges, the specifications, and the testimony selected from 'The Mutual Rights' to support the accusations, and also from the Report of the General Conference on petitions and memorials. It was indeed expressly disavowed at the time by the prosecutors, and by all who had written on the subject, that they wished to suppress freedom of inquiry, either in writing or speaking, provided only that the debaters would confine their discussions to an investigation of facts and arguments, without impeaching the character and motives of those from whom they dissented." The "Itinerant" was established by the Church party, in Baltimore, as an organ of its defense. "At last," says Bangs, "the spirit of contention, which had long been impatient of control, became wearied, and the combatants gradually retired from the field of controversy, the 'Itinerant' was discontinued, and the 'Christian Advocate and Journal,' which had, indeed, said but little on the subject, proposed a truce, which seemed to be gladly accepted by the dissentient brethren, and they were left to try the strength of their newly-formed system without further molestation from their old brethren."

The new denomination reported at its outset 5,000 members and 83 preachers. It extended rapidly into most sections of the country, but has encountered severe trials. The anti-slavery controversy rent it in 1858, when nineteen of its Conferences disowned "such Conferences and Churches as practiced or tolerated slaveholding," their General Conference having declined to respond to their petitions against slave-trading. Since the rebellion, and its solution of the problem of slavery, many of the Southern Churches have been merged in the Methodist Episcopal Church, South. In the North there is a growing disposition to return to the parent body, especially since the General Conference of the latter has expressed a willingness to accord Lay Representation whenever a majority of the Church shall demand it. The Protestant Methodists, however, still report more than 800 traveling, nearly 800 local preachers, and above 100,000 Church members. They sustain four weekly papers, two Book Concerns, a Mission Board, and seven colleges.

At the General Conference of 1828 also culminated, but amicably, the question of the independence of Canadian Methodism. We have already seen that as early as the British and American War of 1812 a controversy arose between the Wesleyan and the Methodist Episcopal Churches respecting the alleged intrusion of the former on the provincial fields of the latter. Though the dispute was concluded with the never-failing mutual cordiality of these bodies, by correspondence and the official visit of Emory to England, by order of the General Conference of 1820, yet the war had left no little disaffection in Canada toward the American Church, and its jurisdiction over its provincial societies subjected them to serious disabilities. The preachers in Canada, therefore, proposed, at their Conference of 1824, a separate organization of the provincial Church, and memorialized the General Conference to thus organize them. The latter body saw the expediency of the change, but, acknowledging that it had no constitutional power to divide the denomination, it seemed inextricably embarrassed with the question, till Emory suggested that, as it had a right to withdraw from any field, (a foreign mission, for example,) and as all preachers to Canada had hitherto been sent thither with their own consent, and not imperatively appointed, as in the States, the Church could cease to make appointments beyond the boundary line, and thus leave the Canadian brethren to organize and provide for themselves. The Conference facilitated the rearrangement of the distant field as much as possible, making liberal provisions for it, and recommending the adoption of the "form of government of the Methodist Episcopal Church in the United States." Canadian Methodism has ever since been independent, but the most friendly relations have subsisted between the parent Church and its vigorous offspring. The latter has passed through varied fortunes, but has greatly prospered. A portion of its preachers and people insisted on retaining the Episcopal system of the original Church, which was not finally established by the separated body. Much controversy prevailed, attended with the usual intermixture of passion and doubtful motives. A subdivision followed, and we have now "The Canadian Wesleyan Church," and the "Methodist Episcopal Church in Canada," the former reporting more than 56,000 members, 500 itinerant preachers, and 750 Sunday-schools, with about 45,000 scholars; a university, a female college, and a Book Concern with its weekly paper.

The Episcopal section reports three Annual Conferences, two bishops, 216 traveling and 224 local preachers, and 20,000 members; a seminary, a female college, and a weekly newspaper. Both bodies are in amicable relations with the General Conference of the Church in the States. There is also a "Canadian Wesleyan Methodist New Connection Church," in affinity with the New Connection Methodists of England; it reports 90 traveling and 147 local preachers, about 9,000 members, a theological school, and a weekly paper. The Primitive Methodists, from England, sustain in the Province Circuits and a weekly press. Methodism has, in short, become numerically the strongest form of Protestantism in the British North American Provinces.

The question of slavery came up, as we have seen, in the very first General Conference, and was found to be irrepressible. The early "testimony" of Methodism on the subject was worthy of the denomination; but, yielding to the exigencies of later times, it compromised that testimony, and was compelled at last to suffer the severest retribution. It is not yet time for an impartial record of the personal and party responsibilities of the later controversy, nor is it perhaps desirable, as, providentially, the question has reached its final solution, and the Church may indulge the hope, however yet contingent, that by the lapse of time and the tranquilization of passion its old and glorious unity may be restored, and its combined and almost boundless energies put forth in its common and peaceful work. The effects of this controversy in memorable secessions must, however, be noticed. By 1834 the contest was begun in good earnest, by the "Appeal" of a number of the New England preachers and the "Counter Appeal" of others. The New Hampshire Conference soon after passed decidedly antislavery resolutions. The refusal of the bishop to put these resolutions to vote originated a new question on "Conference rights," and the Eastern Conferences were soon rife with both. Meanwhile "Zion's Herald," the earliest journal of the denomination, and the most vigorous in all progressive measures, became the effective organ of these contests. The General Conference had attempted repressive measures, which only provoked greater energy in the agitation. At the session of 1836 delegates were formally rebuked for participating in an anti-slavery meeting at Cincinnati, the place of the session. The Conference condemned by resolutions "abolitionism," and in its pastoral address "disowned any right to interfere in the political relation of master and slave." The controversy now swept over the northern Church, and, in 1843, a convention was held at Utica, N. Y., for the organization of the "Wesleyan Methodist Connection." Some of the leaders of the antislavery movement entered heartily into the new organization, but many resolutely remained in the elder Church as the best field for the prosecution of the contest. Good and heroic men were thus divided, and in some instances turned their weapons against each other. Churches were rent, and strifes spread over most of the Northern States. Questions of Church polity, especially that of lay representation, were mixed with the controversy, and exasperated it. The new denomination adopted lay representation, and assumed an apparently formidable organization. It had not a few able men, and, as it proposed freedom and Church "reform," it bore with it no small amount of popular sympathy. The advancement of the parent Church in both these respects has, however, reclaimed from it much of that sympathy, and relieved it of most of the original reasons of its organization. Not a few, therefore, of its earliest leaders and most zealous supporters have returned to the elder denomination; and, having accomplished its mission, the "Wesleyan Connection" appears destined, sooner or later, to be absorbed in other Methodist bodies. It still reports, however, 236 itinerant and 164 local preachers, and 25,000 members. It has quite generally disappeared in the New England States, where it had its earliest sway.

Meanwhile the great controversy went on in the Methodist Episcopal Church, till it eventuated in what has justly been called the "Great Secession" of 1844, by which nearly all the vast territory and numerical force of the Southern States were rent away. At the preceding session the old usage of the Church, denying ordination to slaveholding preachers, and especially keeping the episcopate clear of the charge of slaveholding, was abandoned by a resolution that "mere ownership in slave property" constitutes no legal barrier to "the various grades of the ministry." This, of course, threw open the episcopate itself to slaveholders. At the next session it was found that one of the bishops had become the owner of slaves by marriage. He was required to relieve himself of the "impediment," or to be suspended from his functions. The Southern delegates protested, and after prolonged and remarkably able debates on both sides, they formally announced to the Conference that its jurisdiction over their Annual Conferences "would be inconsistent with the success of the Methodist ministry" in their States. A schism seemed now inevitable, and the Conference, to relieve as much as possible its disastrous effects, enacted "a plan of separation," defining boundaries, a division of the Church property, etc., to take effect in case of a separate organization. A Southern Methodist Convention was held at Louisville in May, 1845, and "The Methodist Episcopal Church, South," was there begun. In the next year its first General Conference was held at Petersburgh, Va., and its organization completed.

Methodism had become the chief religious denomination of the Southern States; this stupendous rupture, it cannot be doubted, was the effective beginning of the great national rupture which soon after startled the world with the greatest civil war of modern history. The Methodist Episcopal Church, South, has published no statistics since the Rebellion broke out; it has doubtless suffered disastrously by the war, but it reported the last year before the Rebellion nearly 700,000 members, 2,600 itinerant and 5,000 local preachers. It had a Book Concern, 12 periodical publications, 12 colleges, and 77 academies, with 8,000 students. Its Missionary Society sustained, at home and abroad, about 360 missionaries, and 8 manual labor schools, with nearly 500 pupils.

These successive events precipitated the "abolition controversy" in the Northern Church. It soon became the most energetic antislavery body in the nation; it reattained its original antislavery platform, and, in 1864, its General Conference inserted in its fundamental law (its "General Rules,") an absolute interdiction of slaveholding. It contributed more than a hundred thousand of its members to the armies of the war for the Union, thinned its congregations, and disbanded many of its Sunday-school and Bible classes by these patriotic contributions. Its pulpits resounded with enthusiastic pleas for the Constitution. Its entire denominational press (the most extensive in the land) was, without one exception, fervently and continually devoted to the national cause. The national flag waved from its spires and draped its pulpits, and its characteristic enthusiasm was kindled to the highest fervor by the national struggle. Many of its preachers entered the army as chaplains, others as officers, and others as privates. Thousands of Methodist martyrs for the Union sleep under the sod of southern battle-fields. In fine, Methodism, as the chief religious embodiment of the common people, felt that its destiny is identical with that of the country, and threw its utmost energy into the great struggle for the national life. The government recognized its services, and, at its General Conference of 1864, President Lincoln addressed it an emphatic testimonial, saying: "Nobly sustained as the Government has been by all the Churches, I would utter nothing which might in the least appear invidious against any. Yet without this it may fairly be said that the Methodist Episcopal Church, not less devoted than the best, is, by its greater numbers, the most important of all. It is no fault in others that the Methodist Church sends more soldiers to the field, more nurses to the hospitals, and more prayers to heaven than any. God bless the Methodist Church! bless all the Churches! and blessed be God, who in this our great trial giveth us the Churches!"

During all these years of strife and war, within and without, the march of the Church was almost continuously forward. These tests were, indeed, among the most striking demonstrations of its energy. Estimated by decades from our last considered date, (1820,) its statistics show but two instances of declension: one by the secession of the Church, South, the other by the civil war, and from both it quickly arose with surprising buoyancy. By 1830 it had 476,153 members, an increase for the decade of 216,263; by 1840 it had 801,784, an increase of 325,631. By the close of the next decade it had lost the whole Methodist Episcopal Church, South, but rallied so rapidly as to be able to report 689,682 members, a decrease of but 112,102; at the end of the following decade (1860) it had much more than recovered all the numerical force which it had lost by the division, and reported 994,447, a gain for the decade of 304,765. In the ensuing half decade it was again to be ravaged by the war, especially by the loss of its "Border Societies," whole Conferences of which were broken to pieces; it reported, therefore, (in 1865,) 929,259, a decrease of 65,188; but in the ensuing year it more than regained all this loss, and reported more than a *million* (1,032,184) members, while the other Methodist bodies of the New World were a million more. Such vitality has no parallel in the history of Christendom. Meanwhile its ministry had proportionately advanced. Its traveling preachers, numbering 904 in 1820, amounted, in 1830, to 1,900; in 1840, to 3,697; in 1850, to 4,129; in 1860, to 6,987; and in 1866, to 7,576.

Such are some of the salient events in the proceedings of the quadrennial Conferences, and in the general history of the Church through these later years. But, as much if not most, of the proceedings of that body, and of the general activity of the denomination, related during these times to those "benevolent enterprises" which we have seen incorporated into its practical system, we turn now to the more summary consideration of these important interests.

CHAPTER XXXIV.

AUXILIARY PLANS AND INSTITUTIONS; LITERARY, EDUCATIONAL, MISSIONARY, ETC.

THE practical, or Disciplinary, as well as the Theological, system of Methodism has been defined in its appropriate place. But a Church must, in this age, have other, not to say extra-ecclesiastical, means of labor if it would meet the ever-varying wants of the world, and not stagnate and die. Methodism has habitually been adding such auxiliaries to its working system. They have been noted in their due time, as they have, one after another, sprung up; but their fuller consideration has been reserved till the present stage of our narrative, when their series—literary, educational, and missionary—had become substantially complete. They afford some of the most important and startling facts of the history of the Church.

American Methodism from its organization, and even before that date, appreciated the importance of the Press. The example and injunctions of Wesley kept the denomination, not only in England, but wherever it extended, zealous in the diffusion not only of religious literature, but of "useful knowledge" in general. He was the founder of the system of "cheap publication;" cheap prices sustained by large sales.* The literary labors of Wesley would seem, aside from all his other services, to be sufficient for the lives of half a score of men. A German historian of Methodism classifies, with German elaborateness, the great variety of his literary works, as Poetical, Philological, Philosophical, Historical, and Theological. Though he probably wrote before Wesley's death, he states that many of these

* Lackington, the famous London publisher, claimed this distinction; but Wesley preceded him, at least in religious literature, and Lackington, who was a Methodist, was set up in the business by the aid of Wesley's "Fund," established at City Road for the assistance of needy business men.

writings, after ten or twenty editions, could not be obtained without difficulty, and the whole could not be purchased for less than ten guineas, notwithstanding they were published at rates surprisingly cheap. A catalogue of his publications, printed about 1756, contains no less than one hundred and eighty-one articles, in prose and verse, English and Latin, on grammar, logic, medicine, music, poetry, theology, and philosophy. Two thirds of these publications were for sale at less than one shilling each, and more than one fourth at a penny. They were thus brought within reach of the poorest of his people. "Simplify religion and every part of learning," he wrote to Benson, who was the earliest of his lay preachers addicted to literary labors. To all his itinerants he said, "See that every society is supplied with books, some of which ought to be in every house." In addition to his collected "Works," (fourteen octavo volumes in the English edition, and seven in the American,) his biblical "Notes" and abridgments make a catalogue of one hundred and eighteen prose productions, (a single one of which, "The Christian Library," contains fifty volumes,) forty-nine poetical publications by himself and his brother, and five distinct works on music. Not content with books and tracts, Wesley projected, in August, 1777, the Arminian Magazine, and issued the first number at the beginning of 1778. It was one of the first four religious magazines which sprung from the resuscitated religion of the age, and which began this species of periodical publications in the Protestant world. It is now the oldest religious periodical. It may be questioned whether any English writer of the last or the present century has equaled Wesley in the number of his productions.

American Methodism has always been true to this example of English Methodism, and in fact has far transcended it. Its "Book Concern" is now the largest religious publishing house in the Protestant world.

We have seen the beginnings of this literary agency in the printing and circulation of Wesley's sermons by Robert Williams, one of the earliest lay evangelists, who, according to Lee's history of the Church, "spread them through the country, to the great advantage of religion, opening the way for the preachers where these had never been before." But as early as the first Conference (1773) this individual or independent publishing was prohibited, the "consent of the brethren" being required, because, as Lee writes, "it now became necessary for all the preachers to be united in the same course, so that the profits ensuing therefrom might be divided among them, or applied to some charitable purpose." "Be active," commanded the Church to its ministry at its organization of 1784, "be active in the diffusion of Mr. Wesley's books. Every 'assistant' may beg money of the rich to buy 'books for the poor;'" and it was ordained at the same time that "they should take care that every society be duly supplied with books." The Conferences of 1787 made further provisions for the purpose, and "from this time," says Lee, "we began to publish more of our own books than ever before, and the principal part of the business was carried on in New York." No publisher or "Book Agent" was yet named, however; but, two years later, we find Philip Cox and John Dickins designated to that office in the Minutes. The former acted as a sort of colporteur at large for three years, the first American example of that useful office, and died in it, "after circulating," says his obituary in the Minutes, "many hundred books of religious instruction." Dickins, the only Methodist preacher in Philadelphia in 1789, began there, at that time, the "Methodist Book Concern," in addition to his pastoral labors. The only capital of the Concern was about six hundred dollars, lent to it by Dickins himself. The first volume issued by him was the "Christian Pattern," Wesley's translation of Kempis's celebrated "Imitatione." The Methodist Discipline, the Hymn Book, Wesley's Primitive Physic, and reprints of the first volume of the Arminian Magazine, and Baxter's Saint's Rest, followed. In 1790 portions of Fletcher's "Checks" were reprinted. In 1797 a "Book Committee" was appointed, to whom all books were to be submitted before their publication. In 1804 the Concern was removed from Philadelphia to the city of New York. As early as 1796 the General Conference ordered the publication of a "Methodist Magazine," in imitation of Wesley's periodical; it was not successfully attempted till 1818. It still prosperously continues, under the title of the Methodist Quarterly Review. Western Methodism had, however, anticipated it by the publication of Beauchamp's "Christian Monitor," at Chilicothe, Ohio, in 1815. In 1824 the Concern secured premises of its own on Crosby-street, with presses, bindery, etc. In 1823 the "Youth's Instructor," a monthly work, was begun. The same spirit of enterprise led to the publication of the Christian Advocate and Journal, which appeared, for the first time, on the ninth of September, 1826. But New England preceded the rest of the Church in providing for this want; in 1815 a publication was commenced, entitled, "The New England Missionary Magazine." It was edited by Martin Ruter, and printed at Concord, N. H., by Isaac Hill; but it ceased after four quarterly numbers had been issued. In 1821 the New England Conference formed an association, styled the "Society for Giving and Receiving Religious Intelligence." This gave rise to Zion's Herald, printed by Moore and Prouse, under the direction of the committee of the society, of which Elijah Hedding was president. The first number was issued January 9, 1823, on a small royal sheet, the pages measuring only nine by sixteen inches. Such was the origin of the first weekly publication of Methodism in the world, a paper which has had an unsurpassed power on the great questions and crises of the Church.

The success of the Advocate was remarkable. "In a very short time," writes Bangs, one of its original publishers, "its number of subscribers far exceeded every other paper published in the United States, being about twenty-five thousand. It soon increased to thirty thousand, and was probably read by more than one hundred and twenty thousand persons, young and old." It should be noticed also that, at the earnest request of Methodists west of the mountains, the General Conference of 1820 authorized the establishment of a branch of the Book Concern in Cincinnati, under Martin Ruter, a precedent which led to secondary branches in various parts of the country. The rapid increase of the business soon made it necessary to enlarge its buildings in New York. Accordingly all the vacant ground about its site in Crosby-street was occupied. But even these additions were found insufficient to accommodate the several departments of labor, so as to furnish the supply of books, now in constantly increasing demand. Five lots were therefore purchased on Mulberry-street, between Broome and Spring streets, and one building erected in the rear for a printing office and bindery, and another of larger dimensions projected. In the month of September, 1833, the entire establishment was removed into the new buildings. In these commodious rooms, with efficient agents and editors at work, every thing seemed to be going on prosperously, when suddenly in 1836 the entire property was consumed by fire at night. The Church thus lost not less than two hundred and fifty thousand dollars. The buildings, all the printing and binding materials, a vast quantity of books, bound and in sheets, a valuable library which the editor had been collecting for years, were in a few hours destroyed. Fortunately the "Concern" was not in debt, and by hiring an office temporarily, and employing outside printers, the agents soon resumed their business. The smaller works were put to press, and "the Church's herald of the news, the Christian Advocate and Journal, soon took its flight again (though the first number after the fire had its wings much shortened) through the symbolical heavens, carrying the tidings of our loss, and of the liberal and steady efforts which were making to reinvigorate the paralyzed Concern."

At the General Conference of 1836 the plan of a new building was submitted and approved. It went up with all convenient dispatch, in a much better style, more durable, and safer against fire, than the former structure. The front edifice is one hundred and twenty-one feet in length, and thirty in breadth, four stories high above the basement, with offices for the agents, editors, clerks, a bookstore, printing office, committee rooms, etc. The building in the rear is sixty-five feet in length, thirty in breadth, and four stories high, with a wing connecting it with the front edifice, and is chiefly used as a depository, bindery, etc. Large additions have since been made.

In our day (1866) the Methodist Book Concern, aside from that of the Methodist Episcopal Church, South, which was founded by a division of its funds, comprises two branches, eastern and western, and seven depositories, with an aggregate capital of more than $950,000. Four "Book Agents," appointed by the General Conference, manage its business. It has twelve editors of its periodicals, nearly five hundred clerks and operatives, and between twenty and thirty cylinder and power presses constantly in operation. It publishes about five hundred "General Catalogue" bound books, besides many in the German and other languages, and about fifteen hundred Sunday-school volumes. A Tract Society is one of its adjuncts, and its tract publications number about nine hundred in various tongues. Its periodicals are a mighty agency, including one Quarterly Review, four monthlies, (one of commanding circulation, for females, "The Ladies' Repository") one semi-monthly, and nine weeklies, with an aggregate circulation of over one million of copies per month. Its Quarterly and some of its weeklies have a larger circulation than any other periodicals of the same class in the nation, probably in the world.

The influence of this great establishment, in the diffusion of popular literature and the creation of a taste for reading among the great masses of the denomination, has been incalculable. It has scattered periodicals and books all over the valley of the Mississippi. Its sales in that great domain, in the quadrennial period ending with January 31, 1864, amounted to about $1,200,000. If Methodism had made no other contribution to the progress of knowledge and civilization in the New World than that of this powerful institution, this alone would suffice to vindicate its claim to the respect of the enlightened world. Its ministry has often been falsely disparaged as unfavorable to knowledge; but it should be borne in mind that its ministry founded this stupendous means of popular intelligence, and has continued to work it with increasing success up to the present time. They have been its salesmen, and have scattered its publications over their Circuits. Wesley enjoined this service, as we have seen, upon them in their Discipline. "Carry books with you on every round," he said; "leave no stone unturned in this work;" and thus have they spread knowledge in their courses over the whole land,

and built up their unparalleled "Book Concern." There has never been an instance of defalcation on the part of its "agents;" it has never failed in any of the financial revulsions of the country; and it is now able, by its large capital, to meet any new literary necessity of the denomination. Among its agents and editors have been some of the ablest men of the Church. Ten of them have been called from its service to the episcopate in the northern Church alone.

The Sunday-school system of the Church has been closely allied to its Book Concern. Methodism shared in the origin of the institution in England, and first incorporated it in the Church. Francis Asbury established the first school of the kind in the New World in 1786, at the house of Thomas Crenshaw, in Hanover County, Va.; and this first attempt prefigured one of the greatest later advantages of the institution by giving a useful preacher to the denomination. In 1790 the first recognition of Sunday-schools by an American Church was made by the vote of the Methodist Conferences, ordering their formation throughout the Church, and also the compilation of a book for them. Methodism for many years made no provision for the general organization or affiliation of its Sunday-schools. Its Book Concern issued some volumes suitable for their libraries, chiefly by the labors of John P. Durbin, who prepared its first library volume, and its first Question Book; but no adequate, no systematic attention was given to this sort of literature. It was obvious, on a moment's reflection, that an almost illimitable field for the enlargement of the business of the Concern, and the diffusion of useful knowledge, was at its command in this direction. Accordingly the "Sunday-School Union" was organized on the second of April, 1827. Bangs says that "the measure was hailed with grateful delight by our friends and brethren throughout the country. It received the sanction of the several annual Conferences, which recommended the people of their charge to form auxiliaries in every circuit and station, and send to the general depository in New York for their books; and such were the zeal and unanimity with which they entered into this work, that at the first annual meeting of the society there were reported 251 auxiliaries, 1,025 schools, 2,048 superintendents, 10,290 teachers, and 63,240 scholars, besides above 2,000 managers and visitors. Never, therefore, did an institution go into operation under more favorable circumstances, or was hailed with a more universal joy, than the Sunday-School Union of the Methodist Episcopal Church." This great success, however, could not save it from the misfortunes of bad management. Under "an injudicious attempt," continues Bangs, many years later, "to amalgamate the Bible, Tract, and Sunday-School Societies together, by which the business of these several societies might be transacted by one board of management," and by other causes, it declined, if indeed it did not fail, until resuscitated by the zeal of some New York Methodists, and by an act of the General Conference of 1840. It passed through modifications till it assumed its present effective form of organization, and grew into colossal proportions under the labors of its indefatigable secretaries, Drs. Kidder and Wise. It now (1866) has (aside from its offspring in the Methodist Episcopal Church, South) 13,400 schools, more than 150,000 teachers and officers, and near 918,000 scholars, about 19,000 of whom are reported as converted during the last year. There are in the libraries of these schools more than 2,529,000 volumes. They are supported at an annual expense of more than $216,000, besides nearly $18,000 given to the Union for the assistance of poor schools. There are circulated among them, semi-monthly, nearly 260,000 "Sunday-School Advocates," the juvenile periodical of the Union. The numbers of conversions among pupils of the schools, as reported for the last eighteen years, amount to more than 285,000, showing that much of the extraordinary growth of the Church is attributable to this mighty agency. The Union has four periodicals for teachers and scholars, two in English and two in German, and their aggregate circulation is nearly 300,000 per number. Its catalogue of Sunday-school books comprises more than 2,300 different works, of which more than a million copies are issued annually. Including other issues, it has nearly 2,500 publications adapted to the use of its schools. In fine, few if any institutions of

American Methodism wield a mightier power than its Sunday-School Union. These figures, however, show but partially the Sunday-school enterprise of American Methodism, as they do not include those of its several branches, which broke from the parent Church. These will hereafter be given.

We have already had frequent intimations in these pages of the interest of Methodism for education. The founders of the denomination in England were classically educated men, and it had its birth in a university. Wesley, in the very year which is recognized as its epoch, (1739,) began its noted "Kingswood School," and at his first Conference (1744) proposed a theological school, a "seminary for laborers," or lay preachers, a project which was at last realized by the present two "Theological Institutions" of English Methodism. American Methodism early shared this interest of the parent body in education. Dickins had proposed, in 1780, an academic institution for the denomination. In the year of the organization of the Church (1784) Coke and Asbury projected the Cokesbury College, and laid its foundations the next year at Abingdon, Md. In 1787 Asbury consecrated and opened it with public ceremonies. In 1795 it was destroyed by fire; but a second edifice was soon after provided in Baltimore; this, however, shared the fate of its predecessor in precisely one year. It has been supposed that these disasters not only discouraged Asbury, but led him fallaciously to infer that Providence designed not the denomination to devote its energy to education. It was far otherwise, however, with that great man. He did not believe that collegiate or pretentious institutions of learning should be attempted by the Church while yet in its infancy, but he never abandoned the design of secondary or more practically-adapted schools. He formed, indeed, a grand scheme for the establishment of academies all over the territory of the denomination, one for each "District," a District then being a Conference.

As far south as Georgia contributions in land and tobacco were received for the founding of a college there in 1789; and in the yet frontier settlements of Redstone, Pa., and Kentucky, seminaries were attempted under Asbury's auspices.

In 1789 overtures for an academy in Kentucky were approved by him and the Conferences, and the next year the Western Conference began subscriptions for it. At Bethel, Ky., an edifice and organization were really established, but financially broke down at last, prostrating the health and intellect of Poythress by its fall. At Uniontown, Western Pennsylvania, an academy was started in 1794 or 1795 by Asbury's influence, and survived some few years, educating Thomas Bell, Samuel Parker, and other eminent men. Thus in its primitive struggles of the last century did the Church show its appreciation of education. In 1792 Asbury was ambitious to place "two thousand children under the best plan of education ever known in this country."

Before the close of the last century Hope Hull established an academy in Wilkes County, Ga., and George, M'Henry, and Valentine Cook personally devoted themselves at intervals to the work of education. In 1818 Dr. Samuel K. Jennings and other Methodists attempted a college in Baltimore, but this also failed. No failures, however, no discouragement, could obliterate from the mind of the denomination the conviction of its responsibility for the education of the increasing masses of its people. In 1820 the General Conference recommended that all the annual Conferences should establish seminaries within their boundaries, thus proposing to supply the whole republic with such schools, though with considerable territorial intervals. This demonstration of interest for education in the supreme body of the Church was prompted by the spontaneous enterprise of the ministry and the people, who, three years before, had, chiefly under the guidance of Martin Ruter, started an institution in New England, (at New Market, N. H.,) still distinguished, in its later location, at Wilbraham, Mass.; and in 1819 another, chiefly under the guidance of Nathan Bangs, in New York city, afterward transferred to White Plains, N. Y. The impulse thus given not only produced numerous academies, but led, in 1823, to the beginning of Augusta College, Ky., whose edifice was erected in 1825, and commenced the series of modern collegiate institutions under the patronage of the denomination, so that by the General Conference of 1832, says the biographer of Hedding, "the Wesleyan University had been established at Middletown, Conn., and Dr. Wilbur Fisk, of the New England Conference, was at its head, and John M. Smith, of the New York Conference, one of the professors. Madison College, now extinct, but whose place has since been supplied by Alleghany College, had gone into successful operation in Western Pennsylvania; J. H. Fielding had succeeded H. B. Bascom as president, and H. J. Clark was one of the professors; both were members of the Pittsburgh Conference. Augusta College had been established under the patronage of the Kentucky and Ohio Conferences; Martin Ruter was president, and H. B. Bascom, J. S. Tomlinson, J. P. Durbin, and Burr H. M'Cown, were professors; all of them members of the Kentucky Conference except J. P. Durbin, who belonged to the Ohio. In the Southwest, Lagrange College had been established; Robert Paine was president, and E. D. Simms one of the professors. In Virginia, Randolph Macon College had been established, and M. P. Parks, of the Virginia Conference, was one of its professors, and Stephen Olin was soon after placed at its head. Thus it will be seen that no less than five colleges had sprung into existence in an incredibly short time, and were already in successful operation under the supervision of the Church. Several Conference seminaries also had been established; such were the Cazenovia Seminary, the Maine Wesleyan Seminary, Wilbraham Academy, Genesee Wesleyan Seminary, Shelbyville Female Academy, and others, which were in successful operation in different parts of the Church."

The Church could not pause here. Wesley, as we have seen, had proposed ministerial education at his very first Conference, and the British Methodists had embodied the proposition in two imposing "theological institutions." The New England Methodists agitated the question in their Church periodical, and in 1839 a convention was called, in Boston, to provide such an institution. It was founded with the title of the Biblical Institute; it struggled through many adversities, was at first connected with the Wesleyan University, Middletown, Conn., then with the Methodist Seminary, at Newbury, Vt., but at last was located in Concord, N. H., where it exerted no inconsiderable influence upon the character of the New England Methodist ministry. It has been removed to the vicinity of Boston. In 1845 John Dempster, of New York city, became its professor of theology. He threw his remarkable energy into the cause of ministerial education throughout the denomination, and not only forced along the New England institution against formidable discouragements, but became a leading founder of the northwestern seminary at Evanston, Ill., where a Chicago Methodist lady, by the gift of property amounting to $300,000, gave endowment and her name to the Garrett Biblical Institute.

Thus boarding academies, colleges, and theological seminaries have rapidly grown up in the denomination, till the Methodist Episcopal Church alone now (1866) reports no less than 25 colleges, (including theological schools,) having 158 instructors, 5,345 students, about four millions of dollars in endowments and other property, and 105,531 volumes in their libraries. It reports also 77 academies, with 556 instructors and 17,761 students, 10,462 of whom are females, making an aggregate of 102 institutions, with 714 instructors and 23,106 students. The southern division of the denomination reported before the Rebellion 12 colleges and 77 academies, with 8,000 students, making an aggregate for the two bodies of 191 institutions and 31,106 students.

The moral and social influence of such a series of educational provisions, reaching from the year of the organization of the Church to our own day, must be incalculable; and, could it point the world to no other monuments of its usefulness, these would suffice to establish its claims as one of the effective means of the intellectual and moral progress of the country.

American Methodism could not long fail to imitate the example of British Methodism in the "Missionary cause," for the parent Church had early become pre-eminent before the Christian world in this sublime enterprise. The idea of religious missions is as old as Christianity, and has been exemplified by the Papal Church through much of its history, and in the ends of the earth. The Moravians early embodied it in their system. In the Protestantism of England it had but feeble sway till the epoch of Methodism. That grand form of it which now characterizes English Protestantism in both hemispheres, and which proposes the evangelization of the whole race, appeared in the latter part of the eighteenth century. Societies for the propagation of the Gospel had previously existed in Great Britain, but they were provided chiefly, if not exclusively, for the Christianization of countries which, by reason of their political dependence upon England, were deemed to have special claims on British Christianity—the inhabitants of India and the Indians of North America. An historian of missions, writing in 1844, says: "It was not until almost within the last fifty years that the efforts of the religious bodies by whom Christian missions are now most vigorously supported were commenced." Methodism was essentially a missionary movement, domestic and foreign. It initiated not only the spirit, but the practical plans of modern English missions. Bishop Coke so represented the enterprise in his own person for many years as to supersede the necessity of any more formal organization of it, but it was none the less real and energetic. The historian just cited says: "The Wesleyan Missionary Society was formed in 1817, but the first Wesleyan missionaries who went out, under the superintendence of Coke, entered the British colonies in 1786. The Baptist Missionary Society was established in 1792, the London Missionary Society in 1795, and the Edinburgh or Scottish and the Glasgow Missionary Societies in 1796. The subject also engaged the attention of many pious persons belonging to the Established Church, besides those connected with the London Missionary Society, and by members of that communion the Church Missionary Society was organized, in the first year of the present century." The London Missionary Society, embracing most Dissenting bodies of England, arose under the influence of Calvinistic Methodism, and the Church Missionary Society sprang from the evangelical Low Church party which Methodism, Calvinistic and Arminian, had resuscitated in the Establishment,

Venn, the son of the Methodist Churchman Venn, being its projector.

Though Coke represented the Arminian-Methodist Mission interest, as its founder, secretary, treasurer, and collector, it really took a distinct form some six years before the formation of the first of the above-named societies. Coke spent more than a year in bringing the negro missions before the English people, immediately after his second visit to the West Indies. In 1786 a formal address was issued to the public in behalf of a comprehensive scheme of Methodist missions. It was entitled "An Address to the Pious and Benevolent, proposing an Annual Subscription for the Support of Missionaries in the Highlands and adjacent Islands of Scotland, the Isles of Jersey, Guernsey, and Newfoundland, the West Indies, and the Provinces of Nova Scotia and Quebec. By Thomas Coke, LL.D. 1786." It speaks of "a mission intended to be established in the British dominions in Asia," but which was postponed till these more inviting fields should be occupied. This scheme was called in the address an "Institution;" it was really such; though not called a society, it was one in all essential respects; and if the fact that it was not an extra-ecclesiastical plan, but a part of the system of Methodism, should detract from its claim of precedence in respect to later institutions of the kind, that consideration would equally detract from the Moravian missions, which were conducted in a like manner. The address filled several pages, and was prefaced by a letter from Wesley indorsing the whole plan. The next year (1787) the Wesleyan Missions bore the distinctive title of "Missions established by the Methodist Society." At the last Conference attended by Wesley (1790) a committee of nine preachers, of which Coke was chairman, was appointed to take charge of this new interest. Coke continued to conduct its chief business; but the committee were his standing counsel, and formed, in fact, a Mission Board of Managers two years before the organization of the first of British Missionary Societies. Collections had been taken in many of the Circuits for the Institution, and in 1793 the Conference formally ordered a general collection for it."

In this manner did Methodism early prompt the British Churches, and call forth the energies of the British people, in plans of religious benevolence for the whole world. Its previous missions in Scotland, Wales, Ireland, and the Channel Islands did much for the reformation of the domestic population. Besides its efforts in 1786 in the West Indies, it began its evangelical labors in France as early as 1791, and its great schemes in Africa in 1811; in Asia in 1814; in Australasia in 1815; in Polynesia in 1822; until, from the first call of Wesley for American evangelists, in the Conference of 1769, down to our day, we see the grand enterprise reaching to the shores of Sweden, to Germany, France, and the Upper Alps; to Gibraltar and Malta; to the banks of the Gambia, to Sierra Leone, and to the Gold Coast; to the Cape of Good Hope; to Ceylon, to India, and to China; to the Colonists and aboriginal tribes of Australia; to New Zealand, and the Friendly and Fiji Islands; to the islands of the Western as well as of the Southern Hemisphere; and from the Gulf of St. Lawrence to Puget's Sound. From 1803 to the present time Wesleyan Methodism has contributed more than twenty millions of dollars for foreign evangelization. In England the "Church Missionary Society" alone exceeds its annual collections for the foreign field; but the Wesleyan Society enrolls more communicants in its Mission Churches than all other British missionary societies combined. The historian of religion during the last and present centuries would find it difficult to point to a more magnificent monument of Christianity.

Coke, the first bishop of American Methodism, was to the end of his life the representative character of Methodist Missions. In his old age he offered himself, as we have seen, to the British Conference as a missionary to the East Indies. His death on the Indian Ocean struck not only a knell through the Church, but a summons for it to rise universally and march around the world. He had long entertained the idea of universal evangelization as the exponent characteristic of the Methodist movement. The influence of the movement on English Protestantism had tended to such a result, for in both England and America nearly all denominations had felt the power of the great revival not only during the days of Whitefield and Wesley, but ever since. Anglo-Saxon Christianity, in both hemispheres, had been quickened into new life, and had experienced a change amounting to a moral revolution. The magnificent apostolic idea of evangelization in all the earth, and till all the earth should be Christianized, had not only been restored, as a practical conviction, but had become pervasive and dominant in the consciousness of the Churches, and was manifestly thenceforward to shape the religious history of the Protestant world. The great fermentation of the mind of the civilized nations—the resurrection, as it may be called, of popular thought and power—contemporaneous in the civil and religious worlds, in the former by the American and French Revolutions, in the latter by the Methodist movement—seemed to presage a new history of the human race. And history is compelled to record, with the frankest admission of the characteristic defects of Thomas Coke, that no man, not excepting Wesley or Whitefield, more completely represented the religious significance of those eventful times.

Though American Methodism was many years without a distinct missionary organization, it was owing to the fact that its whole Church organization was essentially a missionary scheme. It was, in fine, the great Home Mission enterprise of the North American continent, and its domestic work demanded all its resources of men and money. It early began, however, special labors among the aborigines and slaves. The history of some of these labors would be an exceedingly interesting and even romantic record, but our limits admit but this passing allusion to them, after the account lately given of their singular origin by Stewart, the African. The year 1819 is memorable as the epoch of the formal organization of the American Methodist missionary work. Nathan Bangs, long distinguished as its secretary and chief representative, was also its chief founder. He made it the theme of much preliminary conversation with his colleagues and the principal Methodist laymen of New York city. Laban Clark introduced it by a resolution to the attention of the metropolitan preachers at their weekly meeting, "consisting," says Bangs, "of Freeborn Garrettson, Samuel Merwin, Laban Clark, Samuel Howe, Seth Crowell, Thomas Thorp, Joshua Soule, Thomas Mason, and myself. After an interchange of thoughts the resolution was adopted, and Garrettson, Clark, and myself were appointed a committee to draft a constitution. When this committee met we agreed to write, each, a constitution, then come together, compare them, and adopt the one which should be considered the most suitable. The one prepared by myself was adopted, submitted to the Preachers' Meeting, and, after some slight verbal alterations, was finally approved. We then agreed to call a public meeting in the Forsyth-street Church on the evening of the fifth of April, 1819, which was accordingly done. I was called to the chair, and, after the reading of the constitution, Joshua Soule moved its adoption, and supported his motion by a powerful speech. He was seconded by Freeborn Garrettson, who also pleaded in favor of the scheme from his experience in the itinerant field from Virginia to Nova Scotia." The constitution was unanimously adopted, and the following officers were chosen: Bishop M'Kendree, President; Bishops George and Roberts, and Nathan Bangs, Vice-presidents; Thomas Mason, Corresponding Secretary; Joshua Soule, Treasurer; Francis Hall, Clerk; Daniel Ayres, Recording Secretary. The following managers were also chosen: Joseph Smith, Robert Mathison, Joseph Sandford, George Suckley, Samuel L. Waldo, Stephen Dando, Samuel B. Harper, Lancaster S. Burling, William Duval, Paul Hick, John Westfield, Thomas Roby, Benjamin Disbrow, James B. Gascoigne, William A. Mercein, Philip J. Arcularius, James B. Oakley, George Caines, Dr. Seaman, Dr. Gregory, John Boyd, M. H. Smith, Nathaniel Jarvis, Robert Snow, Andrew Mercein, Joseph Moses, John Paradise, William Myers, William B. Skidmore, Nicholas Schureman, James Wood, Abraham Paul. The historian of the society says: "It is obvious that almost its entire business was conducted by Dr. Bangs for many years. In addition to writing the constitution, the address and circular, he was the author of every Annual Report, with but one exception, from the organization of the society down to the year 1841, a period of twenty-two years. He filled the offices of corresponding secretary and treasurer for sixteen years, without a salary or compensation of any kind, until his appointment to the first named office by the General Conference of 1836." In this single instance of his manifold public life he was to be identified with a grand religious history. He was to see the annual receipts of the society enlarged from the $823 of its first year to $250,374, (including its offspring of the Methodist Episcopal Church, South, to half a million,) and its total receipts, down to the last year of his life, more than four and a half millions, not including the southern society. He was to witness the rise (chiefly under the auspices of the Society) of American-German Methodism, an epochal fact in the history of his denomination next in importance to the founding of the Church by Embury and Strawbridge. Without a recognized missionary for some time after its origin, the society was to present to his dying gaze a list of nearly four hundred, and more than thirty-three thousand mission communicants, representing the denomination in many parts of the United States, in Norway, Sweden, Germany, Switzerland, Bulgaria, Africa, India, China, and South America. Assisting in this great work, and rejoicing in its triumphs, he was to outlive nearly all its original officers and managers.

The next General Conference (in 1820) sanctioned the scheme. Emory submitted an elaborate report on the subject. After reasoning at length upon it, he asked, "Can we, then, be listless to the cause of missions? We cannot. Methodism itself is a missionary system. Yield the missionary spirit, and you yield the very life-blood of the cause. In missionary efforts our British brethren are before us. We congratulate them on their zeal and their success. But your committee beg leave to entreat this Conference to emulate their example." The Conference adopted, with some emendations, the constitution prepared for the society by Bangs. He thus saw his great favorite measure incorporated into the structure of the Church. He writes: "These doings of the Conference in relation to the Missionary Society exerted a most favorable influence upon the cause, and tended mightily to remove the unfounded objections which existed in some minds against this organization." By the session of the General Conference of 1832 the society's operations had extended through the states and territories of the nation, and had become a powerful auxiliary of the itinerant system of the Church. Hitherto it had been prosecuted as a domestic scheme, for the frontier circuits, the slaves, the free colored people, and the Indian tribes; it had achieved great success in this wide field, and was now strong enough to reach abroad to other lands. It proposed, with the sanction of this Conference, to plant its standard on the coast of Africa. and send agents to Mexico and South America to ascertain the feasibility of missions in those countries. Thus were begun those foreign operations of the society which have become its most interesting labors.

Its domestic Indian missions were now numerous, and some of them remarkably prosperous; "attended," Bangs says, "with unparalleled success." In Upper Canada they numbered, in 1831, no less than ten stations, and nearly two thousand Indians "under religious instruction, most of whom were members of the Church. Among the Cherokees, in Georgia, they had at the same date no less than seventeen missionary laborers, and nearly a thousand Church members. Among the Choctaws there were about four thousand communicants, embracing all the principal men of the nation, their chiefs and captains." And, more or less, along the whole frontier, Indian Missions were established. Meanwhile the destitute fields of the domestic work proper were dotted with humble but effective mission stations, from the St. Lawrence to the Gulf of Mexico, and these stations were rapidly passing from the missionary list to the Conference catalogue of appointments as self-supporting Churches.

Melville B. Cox, whose baptism, and the reception of his family into the Church by Kibby, in Maine, have been noticed, sailed for Africa, the first foreign missionary of American Methodism. He organized the Liberia Mission. He fell a martyr to the climate, but laid on that benighted continent the foundations of the denomination, never, it may be hoped, to be shaken. About the same time a delegation from the distant Flathead Indians of Oregon arrived in the States soliciting missionaries. Their appeal was zealously urged through the Christian Advocate, and received an enthusiastic response from the Church. Bangs, who had been a leading promoter of the African Mission, now, in co-operation with Fisk, advocated this new claim with his utmost ability. Jason and Daniel Lee, and Cyrus Shepard, were dispatched as missionaries. An extraordinary scheme of labors was adopted, involving great expense; "but," writes Bangs, "the projection of this important mission had a most happy effect upon the missionary cause generally. The entire funds of the society up to this time had not exceeded eighteen thousand dollars a year; their amount more than doubled in the year in which the Lees and Shepard departed to their field. The surges of emigration have overwhelmed nearly all that grand ultramontane region; the aborigines are sinking out of sight beneath them; but the Oregon Mission became the nucleus of the Christianity and civilization of the new and important State which has since arisen on the North Pacific coast.

Meanwhile Fountain C. Pitts was sent on a mission of inquiry to South America. He visited Rio Janeiro, Buenos Ayres, Monte Video, and other places, and the Methodist South American Mission was founded the next year by Justin Spaulding. Thus had the Church borne at last its victorious banner into the field of foreign missions. It was to be tried severely in these new contests, but to march on through triumphs and defeats till it should take foremost rank among denominations devoted to foreign evangelization. The operations of the Missionary Society had now assumed such importance as to justify, in the judgment of the General Conference, the appointment of a "Resident Corresponding Secretary," who could devote his whole attention to them. Of course the mind of the Conference, as indeed of the general Church, turned spontaneously to Bangs as the man for such an office, and he was elected by a large majority. He entered with energy upon his new functions. The first year of his secretaryship was signalized by the first recognition and announcement, by the Missionary Society, of one of the most remarkable events in the history of modern missions, the beginning of the German Methodist Missions. Professor Nast, a young German scholar of thorough but Rationalistic education, had been reclaimed by Methodism to the faith of the Reformation. He labored for some time among his countrymen in Cincinnati, and later on the Columbus District, comprising a Circuit of three hundred miles, and twenty-two appointments. Thus originated the most successful, if not the most important of Methodist missions; and in the next Annual Report of the society the "German Mission," and the name of "William Nast," its founder and missionary, were first declared to the general Church. German Methodism rapidly extended through the nation; to Boston in the northeast, to New Orleans in the southwest. German Methodist Churches, Circuits, Districts, were organized. "In the brief space of fourteen years," says the historian of Methodist Missions, "the German Missions have extended all over the country, yielding seven thousand Church members, thirty local preachers, eighty-three regular mission circuits and stations, and one hundred and eight missionaries. One hundred churches were built for German worship, and forty parsonages. Primitive Methodism appears to have revived in the zeal and simplicity and self-sacrificing devotion of the German Methodists. May they ever retain this spirit! No agency has ever been employed so specifically adapted to effect the conversion of Romanists as that which is immediately connected with the German Mission enterprise. The pastoral visitations of the preachers bringing them into immediate contact with German Catholics, their distribution of Bibles and tracts, their plain, pointed, and practical mode of preaching, all combine to bring the truth to bear upon that portion of the population; and the result is the conversion of hundreds from the errors of Romanism." The chief importance of the German Mission has, however, been subsequently developed. It has not only raised up a mighty evangelical provision for the host of German emigrants to the New World, but, under the labors of Jacoby, it has intrenched itself in the

German "fatherland," and is laying broad foundations for a European German Methodism. German Societies and Circuits, a German Conference, a "Book Concern," with its periodicals, a Ministerial School, and all the other customary appliances of evangelical Churches, have been established; and, in our day, this Teutonic Methodism comprises, on both sides of the Atlantic, nearly thirty thousand communicants, and nearly three hundred missionaries.

It is impossible here to trace in detail the further outspread of this great interest, especially under the successful administration of its ablest secretary, John P. Durbin, nor is it appropriate to the limits of the present work. Suffice it to say that the annual receipts of the society, which, the year before his administration began, amounted to about $104,000, have risen to more than $700,000; and that, besides its very extensive domestic work, the Methodist Episcopal Church has now missions in China, India, Africa, Bulgaria, Germany, Switzerland, Denmark, Norway, Sweden, and South America. Its missions, foreign and domestic, have 1,059 circuits and stations, 1,128 paid laborers, (preachers and assistants,) and 105,675 communicants. The funds contributed to its treasury from the beginning amount to about $8,000,000. About 350 of the missionaries preach in the German and Scandinavian languages, and more than 30,000 of the communicants are German and Scandinavian. The Methodist Episcopal Church, South, had, in addition to these, before the Rebellion, missions in China, among our foreign settlers, among the American Indians, and the southern slaves. About three hundred and sixty of its preachers were enrolled as missionaries.

American, like British, Methodism, has become thoroughly imbued with the apostolic idea of foreign and universal evangelization. With both bodies it is no longer an incidental or secondary attribute, but is inwrought into their organic ecclesiastical systems. It has deepened and widened till it has become the great characteristic of modern Methodism, raising it from a revival of vital Protestantism, chiefly among the Anglo-Saxon race, to a world-wide system of Christianization, which has reacted on all the great interests of its Anglo-Saxon field has energized and ennobled most of its other characteristics, and would seem to pledge to it a universal and perpetual sway in the earth. Taken in connection with the London and Church Missionary Societies, the British and Foreign Bible Society, the London Tract Society, to all of which Methodism gave the originating impulse, and the Sunday-school Institution, which it was the first to adopt as an agency of the Church, it is not too much to say that it has been transforming the character of English Protestantism and the moral prospects of the world. Its missionary development has preserved its primitive energy. According to the usual history of religious bodies, if not indeed by a law of the human mind, its early heroic character would have passed away by its domestic success, and the cessation of the novelty and trials of its early periods; but by throwing itself out upon all the world, and especially upon the strongest citadels of Paganism, it has perpetuated its original militant spirit, and opened for itself a heroic career, which need end only with the universal triumph of Christianity. English Methodism was considered, at the death of its founder, a marvelous fact in British history; but to-day the Wesleyan missions alone comprise more than twice the number of the regular preachers enrolled in the English Minutes in the year of Wesley's death, and nearly twice as many communicants as the Minutes then reported from all parts of the world which had been reached by Methodism. The latest reported number of missionary communicants in the Methodist Episcopal Church equals nearly one half the whole membership of the Church in the year (1819) in which the Missionary Society was founded, and is nearly double that with which the denomination closed the last century, after more than thirty years of labors and struggles.

Such, then, are some of the results of Methodism. Nor are these all, for all the existing Methodist bodies of the country have sprung from it, and their combined strength alone properly shows the aggregate result. Half the Methodism of the country stands to-day beyond the ecclesiastical limits of the Methodist Episcopal Church.

CHAPTER XXXV.

REPRESENTATIVE MINISTERIAL CHARACTERS: SUMMERFIELD—MAFFITT—COOKMAN—OLIN.

THE first and second generations of Methodist preachers have been somewhat amply described in the preceding periods of our narrative; they present a type of ministerial character which has continued to be more or less characteristic of the mass of the itinerancy through the subsequent history of the Church. Not a few of the men described still linger in its pulpits. The present period begins with 904 traveling preachers, and ends with 7,576. It is impossible, therefore, to treat of them with any such detail as has been deemed proper to the ministry of the earlier or forming periods of the denomination. I have already, however, alluded to a new type or phase of ministerial character which had begun to appear before the present date, and which remains to be represented by a few of its eminent examples—a class of men who were to retain the spiritual power and unction of the original itinerants, but to combine with them a higher intellectual culture or the commanding attractions of genius, and whose example and influence have tended to elevate, intellectually and almost universally, the character of the pastorate, and to prepare it for those necessities which the maturer condition of the Church must create, and thus secure its future as well as its past.

From the beginning not a few of the itinerants had, by their moral energy and natural talents, wielded more than a denominational sway over the popular mind; but the new class were to attain a sort of national rather than denominational recognition, and to give their Church the highest vindication before the American people. Some of this class have already necessarily been noticed, such as Capers, Emory, Bascom, Ruter,

Durbin, Elliott, Fisk, but many remain unrecorded. Some appeared, for the first time, and died, in our present period; not a few are now living; of the former alone can we venture here to speak.

The peculiar unity of the Church, resulting from its itinerant episcopate, and the interchange of its pastors, has been highly favorable to the reputation of such men. They have been recognized as the common representatives and common favorites of the denomination. They have moved extensively through its territory, not as foreign visitors, but as honored members of one great family, leaders in the common pastorate. In no other denomination of the land has this sentiment of fraternity been so prevalent and so characteristic. It has been of no little practical value; a great idea, a great deed, or a great man, has always had a wider sway among Methodists than among other Churches. While the reputation of eminent preachers, in more localized or more restricted communions, has been analogous to that of leaders in the State governments, the fame of our distinguished preachers, and its moral power, have been analogous to the fame and influence of our great National Statesmen. With the increase and consolidation of the Church this advantage is disappearing—perhaps inevitably. It gave to the class of men referred to a standing among us, similar to that which the great preachers of the age of Louis XIV. occupied among the clergy of France. Methodism may have hereafter as great men intrinsically, but they can hardly wield as extended a sway over the general mind of the Church.

John Summerfield, if not the first of this general or extra-denominational fame, was unquestionably one of the very best. He joined the Irish Conference in 1819, and came to America in 1821. His fame was immediate through all the Atlantic States; no temples could accommodate the throngs which crowded to hear him in the great cities; they blocked the streets around the churches; his words of charity and power dissolved all sectarian repugnances, and the whole Protestant community gathered about him and regarded him as an unequaled representative of their common faith—regarded him with wonder, benedictions, and tears. His ministry was short, and presents no salient historical facts except its extraordinary pulpit power, and of this it is hardly possible to give a just idea to readers who never heard him. A chaste style; fertility of good but not extraordinary thought, adorned frequently, however, by apposite figures; the facility of a remarkably colloquial manner, which made his hearers feel as if they had a sort of interlocutory participation in the discourse; and, above all, an indescribably sweet spirit of piety—the very personality of the speaker sanctified, and revealing itself in his tones, looks, and gestures—were the traits of this extraordinary man. This manifestation of his personal characteristics had nothing, however, of egotism about it. It was not preaching himself instead of Christ, but Christ in himself, as well as in his subject; so that Christ was presented at once both "objectively" and "subjectively," and thus became "all in all." The fame of few men has depended less upon original talent, and more on personal dispositions, than that of Summerfield. Though the most transcendent in his reputation, he was at the same time the most imitable of the eminent preachers of Methodism. Simplicity, placidity, meekness, and a colloquial manner, combined with good but not great ideas, certainly would seem to be of easy acquisition. Still the imitation of the excellences of a model, however desirable, is often found exceedingly difficult. To copy a model entire is impracticable, and always results in absurd defects, for the moral idiosyncrasies of men give an individuality to their character and manner which must remain inexorably distinct from all resemblances, as the differences of faces show themselves notwithstanding any similarity of features. Only such as are similar in these idiosyncrasies could possibly imitate each other's excellences. Henry B. Bascom would have become ridiculous with the pulpit manner of John Summerfield.

The best judges who were familiar with Summerfield's preaching find it impossible to tell, precisely, in what its interest consisted. We venture to repeat that the solution of the problem is to be found mostly, if not wholly, in the consecrated *personality* of the man—the beautiful compatibility between the preacher and his preaching—a harmony that revealed itself in his looks, his tones, his gestures, and all the subtler indications of verbal style, mental aptitudes, and moral dispositions. We have only to suppose him strongly characterized by other traits than those mentioned, to perceive at once that he must have been an entirely different preacher. Had he possessed the same intellectual capacities, but been *brusque*, or denunciatory, or satirical—had he been tinged strongly with moroseness, misanthropy, or self-conceit—his pulpit characteristics would have been different; he never could have won the peculiar fame which attaches to his memory; he would probably have gone down to the grave without public distinction. With a mind susceptible of all graceful impressions, a heart whose sensibility was feminine—yet with such feminineness as we ascribe to angels, and think of as consistent with mighty though serene strength—he united the very sanctity of religion, and a simplicity of purpose which saved him utterly from the affectations or artifices that might have marred his character, and must have quite changed the effect of his preaching.

Montgomery the poet expressed a just critical estimate of him when he said: "Summerfield had intense animal feeling, and much of morbid imagination; but of poetic feeling, and poetic imagination, very little—at least there is very little trace of either in anything that he has left, beyond a few vivid but momentary flashes in his sermons." This "animal feeling," however, must be understood to have been refined and intensified by divine grace into the holiest moral affections; so that the sympathetic instincts of the heart became in him pure religious passions, and seemed such as might befit the bosom of a seraph. His appearance in the pulpit was expressive of his character, and contributed much to the effect of his discourse. Though his face possessed nothing at first and near view remarkably striking or agreeable, yet, when irradiated with the fervor of his feelings, it was angelically beautiful. The portrait which accompanied Holland's memoir is considered a good one, but it fails to represent the glowing life that played over his features and radiated from his eyes. The languor of disease could not mar this moral beauty; it rather enhanced it, by adding a delicacy which could not fail to associate with the hearer's admiration a sentiment of tender and even loving sympathy. His voice was not strong, but exceedingly flexible and sweet, and harmonized always with the vibrations of his feelings. His gestures did not violate the rules of the art, but seemed not the result of it. They were unexceptionably natural, and yet naturally conformed to the art. He was, in fine, so exempt from artifice—he so entirely surrendered himself to the occasion and its concomitants, whatever they might be—that he spontaneously fell into unison with them, and seemed naturally and immediately to acquire that mastery over them which the highest art cannot always command. This is the truest genius. Genius is not independent of art, but it is its prerogative often to assume it intuitively, reaching its results without its labors. Labor is an important aid to genius unquestionably; the latter is seldom notably successful without the former; and yet the great characteristic of genius is the facility, the apparent ease, with which it accomplishes what art, without genius, reaches only through elaborate assiduity. Genius suffers more than it labors, but it suffers not so much in action as in reaction. Its sensibility is what mainly gives it success, but it often inflicts misery also.

Though in the delivery of his sermons there was this facility —felicity we might call it—in their preparation he was a laborious student. He was a hearty advocate of extempore preaching, and would have been deprived of most of his popular power in the pulpit by being confined to a manuscript; yet he knew the importance of study, and particularly of the habitual use of the pen in order to success in extemporaneous speaking. His own rule was to prepare a skeleton of his sermon, and after preaching it, write it out in fuller detail, filling up the original sketch with the principal thoughts which had occurred to him in the process of the discourse. The first outline, however, took in the perspective of the entire discourse—the leading ideas, from the exordium to the peroration. He followed this method even in his platform speeches. Montgomery notices the minuteness of his preparations in nearly two hundred manuscript sketches. Besides this large number of sermons and sketches, filling seven post-octavo volumes, he left two considerable volumes, one "a counting-house ledger," filled with exegetical notes on the Scriptures, in such minute penmanship, and with so many abbreviations, that it is said they can scarcely be "deciphered without a glass."

A volume of his sermons and sketches of sermons has been published. They afford no evidence of the transcendent power of the preacher. The "skeletons" contained in this volume illustrate, however, his pulpit style; to such as heard him often they must recall the image and indescribable manner of the preacher, his facility of thought, his colloquial and abrupt style, the fervent variability of his feelings. They may be taken also as specimens of his outline preparations. Not only are the leading thoughts noted, but abundance of illustrative details also. The pithy Scripture allusions with which they abound are characteristic of his discourses; his own diction was sententious and Saxon, but its terseness and simple beauty were continually enhanced by remarkably apt biblical phrases. His style was a mosaic of pertinent and beautiful texts. The quotation of a single word would sometimes terminate a climax with brilliant effect, or conclude an illustration with epigrammatic significance.

He was taken from the Church while yet in his youth. What would have been the effect of years on his eloquence is a question which occurs to us very naturally, and is a curious one at least. We so spontaneously associate his juvenile delicacy and beauty with the impression of his preaching, that we can hardly conceive of him as the same man in middle life or old age. He was but about twenty years old when he began to preach, but twenty-three when he arrived in America, and only twenty-seven when he died. His personal appearance first excited the anxiety of the hearer, next won his sympathy, until he discovered in it at last, by the contrast of his mature and resplendent ability, only an additional reason for wonder and admiration. The circumstances under which his second appearance in public, after his arrival in this country, took place, very happily concurred to enhance this advantage. It was on the anniversary platform of the American Bible Society. A masterly address had just been pronounced by an eminent clergyman; murmurs of applause were audible in the assembly. Dr. Bethune, who was present, says: "The chair announced the Rev. Mr. Summerfield, from England. 'What presumption!' said my clerical neighbor; 'a boy like that to be set up after a giant!' But the stripling came in the name of the God of Israel, armed with 'a few smooth stones from the brook' that flows 'hard by the oracles of God.' His motion was one of thanks to the officers of the society for their labors during the year; and of course he had to allude to the president, then reposing in another part of the house; and thus he did it: 'When I saw that venerable man, too aged to warrant the hope of being with you at another anniversary, he reminded me of Jacob leaning upon the top of his staff, blessing his children before he departed.' He then passed on to encourage the society by the example of the British institution. 'When we first launched our untried vessel upon the deep, the storms of opposition roared, and the waves dashed angrily around us, and we had hard work to keep her head to the wind. We were faint with rowing, and our strength would soon have been gone, but we cried, "Lord, save us, or we perish!" when a light shone upon the waters, and we saw a form walking upon the troubled sea, like unto that of the Son of God, and he drew near the ship, and we knew that it was Jesus; and he stepped upon the deck, and laid his hand on the helm, and he said unto the winds and waves, "Peace, be still," and there was a great calm. Let not the friends of the Bible fear; God is in the midst of us. God shall help us, and that right early.' In such a strain he went on to the close. 'Wonderful! wonderful!' said my neighbor the critic; 'he talks like an angel from heaven.'"

"He talked like an angel," not merely because his thoughts were excellent, but because the visible man, clothed with physical delicacy and youthfulness, and glowing with moral beauty, seemed an embodiment of our ideal of an angelic apparition. Riper years would doubtless have modified this peculiar charm of his youthfulness; but it may be doubted that they could have marred the effect of his eloquence, for the good reason that his oratory was perfectly natural. Being natural, it would have been permanent as his nature, taking new hues from the changes of life, but only such as, being congenial with those changes, would render it congruous with them—would sustain his beautiful naturalness. If his eloquence had lost some of its juvenile traits in maturer years, it would probably have gained in riper and richer qualities, as good wine gains in zest, though it loses in sweetness, by age. Emanating as it did from the very nature of the man, we can imagine it to have retained its essential charm uninjured, though varied, even in old age; and if John Summerfield had lived to hoary years, we can conceive of him only as the St. John of his day--the beloved disciple, who still saw the visions of God, and upon whose lips, as was said of Plato, bees from the flowers had shed their honey.

In private life Summerfield was, if possible, still more interesting than in the pulpit. He was fertile in conversation. He had a flowing but delicate humor, quite Addisonian in its character, always appropriate but never sarcastic. His extraordinary memory rendered him familiar with the names of all who were introduced to him, even children and servants—he seldom or never forgot them. Above all, he had the happy faculty of introducing into all circles appropriate subjects of religious conversation. There was no cant about him, no overweening endeavor to impress the eager groups around him with a sense of his clerical scrupulousness, but an unaffected respectfulness, a confiding courtesy, which conciliated the listener and compelled him to look upon any devout remark as happily congruous to the occasion, and even felicitously befitting to the man.

An incurable malady reminded him that he must work while the day lasted, for the night was at hand. He was incessant in his labors, preaching often from five to ten discourses a week. Besides frequent addresses, in which he was remarkably happy, he delivered about four hundred sermons in the first year and a half of his ministry. Throughout his brief but laborious career he bore about with him that "morbid feeling" of which Montgomery speaks, and which seems indeed a usual pathological accompaniment of genius. His conversion had been clear and decided, yet in his subsequent religious experience he was subject to severe inward conflicts, and Holland has justly remarked that "the light of spiritual illumination in him (whatever may have been the case in others) did not uninterruptedly shine 'brighter and brighter unto the perfect day;' but clouds and darkness frequently intercepted the rays of that Sun of righteousness which had so evidently arisen on his soul. Indeed, the Lord seems to have led his servant, not with the shadow by day and the glory by night of the pillar of cloud and fire, but alternately amid perpetual natural gloom, presenting to him the light of the flame that cheered the Israelites on the verge of the Red Sea, and the darkness behind that frowned upon the Egyptians their pursuers. But God, who is 'love,' was equally present to him in the splendor and terror—in the hidings as in the revealings of his face—and by that mysterious dispensation, we cannot doubt, led him, as the best mode of guidance, through the sea and the wilderness, over Jordan to the Canaan and Jerusalem, which is above."

This was his discipline; he needed it amid the dangerous flatteries of his success. It was probably one of the most effectual causes of that profound humility which was at once the protection and the charm of his saintly character. Could we read the inmost history of most of the mighty men of God in the earth, we should find that they have been summoned by him to confront, like Moses, the fiery terrors of Sinai, or like Daniel, to call upon him from the lions' den, or like Paul, to bear with them to the grave the thorn in the flesh. The youthful hero, wounded in the well-sustained conflict, retired at last to his tent to die, in 1825. "Well—yes—well—all is well." "I want a change—a change of form—a change of everything," he said feebly as the last struggle approached. "All—though—sin—has—entered;" but his utterance failed in the quotation. Night came on; with increased energy he exclaimed, "All's perfection!" "Good-night!" were his last words.

John N. Maffit, an Irishman, joined the itinorancy in 1822, and for some thirty years was one of the most extraordinary and anomalous pulpit orators of the nation. As an elocutionist he may be said to have been perfect—in voice and gesture unrivaled. To the last, his arrival in any city produced a general sensation; and no preacher, not even Summerfield or Bascom, attracted larger multitudes. His style was Ossianic; too extravagant to be read, but, sustained by his elocution, seemed natural, and was even fascinating, in the desk, and his discourses were always wonderfully effective. He was eccentric; simple and indiscreet as a child; "a parodox," says one of his brethren, "of goodness, greatness, and weakness." The Spartan-like severity of the elder ministry was perplexed with wonder and doubt before his singularities, but these good men could not question his usefulness; they reluctantly tolerated his Hibernian peculiarities, and received, through his labors, thousands of converts into their Societies. He broke away from the "regular itinerancy," and for years traveled over most of the nation, streaking its whole sky as a comet. He was elected chaplain to Congress, and produced a powerful impression at the national capital. He abounded in illustrations and anecdotes, and could play on the sympathies of his hearers like an accomplished musician on the strings of his instrument. They seemed to yield themselves entirely to his magical power, alternately smiling and weeping, often sobbing aloud and nearly drowning his voice. He drew them in penitent crowds to the altars for prayers and religious counsels, and was everywhere successful as a "revivalist." A cloud came over his eccentric career at last. Checked in the Northern Church, he found refuge in the Southern, and died in Mobile, mourned by many, impeached by not a few, but the wonder if not the admiration of all.

George G. Cookman disappeared from the Church by a terrible disaster in the prime of his manhood, and at a period in his ministerial career when the star of his fame seemed to culminate, and attract the gaze not only of the Church but of the nation. He was born in 1800, at Hull, England, and came of a good Wesleyan stock. His father, a man of wealth and of high respectability, was a Methodist local preacher, and his early domestic education tended to form the son for the work of his life. While yet very young he gave evidence of his peculiar capabilities for public speaking, on the platform of Sunday-school and juvenile missionary anniversaries. Some of these efforts of his childhood are said to have excited extraordinary interest. In his eighteenth year the death of a young friend left a profound impression upon his mind, which resulted in his conversion. When about twenty-one years old he visited this country on business for his father, and while at Schenectady, New York, received the impression that it was his duty to devote his life to the Christian ministry. He began there his labors as a local preacher. In 1821 he returned to Hull, and entered into business with his father, exercising his talents meanwhile zealously in the Wesleyan local ministry. He continued in his father's firm during four years, but with a restless spirit; for his ardent heart panted for entire devotion to Christian labors. So profound was his conviction of his duty in this respect that it visibly affected him; and his father, prizing him, with an Englishman's regard, as his eldest son, and the representative of his family, but perceiving that he "*must go*," gave him up, and bade him depart with God's blessing. Having witnessed the labors and triumphs of the Methodist preachers on this continent, he resolved to join them, and forthwith took passage for Philadelphia. After laboring a few months in that city as a local preacher, he was received into the Philadelphia Conference in 1826. He continued in the itinerant ranks, without intermission, the remainder of his life, laboring with indomitable energy, and constantly increasing ability and success, in various parts of Pennsylvania, New Jersey, Maryland, and the District of Columbia.

He was slight, but sinewy in person, and capable of great endurance. His arms were long, and gave a striking peculiarity to his gestures. His eye was keen and brilliant, his craniological development good, but not remarkable, and his lean features were galvanic with an energy which, Englishman though he was, never allowed any obese accumulations to form beneath them. Every nerve and muscle of his lithe frame seemed instinct with the excitement of his subject; even the foot often had its energetic gesture, and he took no little perambulatory range when the limits of the desk or platform allowed it. The latter was his favorite place; never did popular orator revel more in the licensed liberties of the platform. All his powers were brought out there, and lavished upon the occasion with absolute prodigality—strong argumentation, dazzling imagery, satire, pathos, wit—holding his hearers in a spell of close, clear thought, shaking them with resistless strokes of humor, melting them suddenly into tears, or, by some energetic or heroic thought, throwing the whole assembly into tumultuous agitation, and provoking from it irrepressible responses. If at such times his manner tended to boisterousness, it seemed compatible with the scene: the zephyr may refresh, but the mighty rushing wind shakes and bends the forest.

There was in his voice a strenuous, silvery distinctness, and even music, which enhanced much the effect of his more powerful passages. In a large house, or at a camp-meeting, where he was usually the hero of the field, he could send its pealing notes, with thrilling effect, to the remotest hearer. The Hall of Representatives, at Washington, never echoed more eloquent tones or more eloquent thoughts than when he occupied its rostrum during his chaplaincy to Congress. He was peculiarly successful in these congressional ministrations. Notwithstanding the great variety of character and prejudice concentrated at the national capital during the legislative sessions, he was a universal favorite. All men about him felt that whether in the humble Methodist pulpit, or amid the magnificence of the national capitol, he was himself; and men will generally, if not always, waive their personal prejudices in the presence of talent which stands forth before them in its simple genuineness and sincerity. Cookman's sermons before Congress were thoroughly prepared; they were often truly great, but directly to the purpose, and stamped throughout with the honest, earnest individuality of the man. There was much of special adaptation in them. He was always apt in seizing on casual events for the illustration or enforcement of his subjects; but his congressional discourses were peculiarly distinguished by the success with which he availed himself of the exciting incidents of the place and season. These sermons had also a deep moral effect as well as oratorical interest. Several of his distinguished hearers, both in Congress and in the executive department of the government, were awakened to a personal interest in religion by his powerful appeals.

He was characterized by a sort of chivalry, a martial predilection, which gave him real bravery, and combative promptness and energy. This was one of the strongest elements of his nature. The military events which stirred all Europe during his youth, doubtless had an influence on his forming character. Be this as it may, there was a military fire in him which nothing could extinguish, and which, sanctified by religion, gave an heroic and invincible power to his ministrations. It influenced his imagery and his very language. It revealed itself in his sermons, in his exhortations, his very prayers, and most especially in his platform addresses. The first of the latter that we open upon in his published "Speeches"* is an example. It marshals the different evangelical sects of the country into a general missionary conflict, and is full of chivalric spirit. His martial temper rendered his assaults on error formidably vigorous. He liked right well a manful encounter, and relished a pungent sarcasm, or a humorous thrust that scattered in dismay sophistry or skeptical conceit. He had good sense, and a good amount of it; but his imagination was his dominant faculty. It furnished him incessantly with brilliant illustrations. Besides the minute beauties with which it interspersed his ordinary discourses, it sometimes led him into allegories which might have entertained the dreams of the "tinker of Bedford." The martial Bible Society address at New Brunswick, in 1828; the mission ship, in his famous Baltimore Conference speech of 1829; the widow and her daughters, in his American Sunday-School Union speech of 1831; and the personification of "Liberalism," (the prodigal son of the "spy Bigotry,") in his New York Sunday-school address of 1832, are examples. It can hardly be doubted that had he devoted himself to the production of

* Speeches delivered on Various Occasions by Rev. George G. Cookman, of the Baltimore Annual Conference, and Chaplain of the Senate of the United States. New York: Carlton & Phillips, 200 Mulberry-street.

a work in this rare and difficult kind of literature, he might have become a worthy disciple of the "glorious dreamer" of Bedford jail. This allegorizing mood, however, befits the poet better than the orator.

In his private life he had many attractions. His piety was deep, and he was always ready for any good word or work; but his religion never interfered with his enjoyment of life. He relished good fellowship, enlivening conversation, and the entertainment of books. He adhered through life to the primitive Methodist costume. It was not the most graceful for his lank person; but under this Quaker-like external primness he carried a large and generous heart—a heart which seemed ever juvenile in the freshness of its sentiments and the ardor of its aspirations. On the 11th of March, 1841, he embarked for Europe in the ill-fated steamer President, and was never heard of more.

Stephen Olin stands forth with commanding prominence and an imperial mien among the princes of our Israel. He was a shining light, a full orb—if not the most notable, yet, perhaps, the most intrinsically great intellect that American Methodism has possessed. So manifest and commanding were his traits, that this pre-eminence can be awarded him without the slightest invidiousness. He was chiefly distinguished as a preacher; though he chiefly served the Church as an educator, from Georgia to Connecticut, and died President of the Wesleyan University in the latter State. A New Englander by birth, a Southerner by long residence, a professor or president of colleges in both sections, he became a national character in his sentiments and influence.

His character—moral, social and intellectual—was, throughout, of the noblest style. In the first respect he was pre-eminent for the two chief virtues of true religion—charity and humility. With thorough theological orthodoxy he combined a practical, an unusual liberality. There was not an atom of bigotry in all the vast soul of this rare man. Meanwhile, it could be said of him as was said of Chalmers, "The most astonishing thing about him was his humility." He was one of the best examples of that childlike simplicity which Christ taught as essential to those who would enter the kingdom of heaven, and which Bacon declared to be equally necessary to "those who would enter the kingdom of knowledge." Like Fisk, he was a personal example of St. Paul's doctrine of "Christian perfection" as expounded by Wesley. Respecting the Methodistic hypothesis of that doctrine he at first entertained doubts; but as he advanced in life, and especially under the chastening influence of affliction, it became developed in his own experience. "I sunk into it," he remarked. "My children, my wife, my health, my entire prospect on earth, all were gone—God only remained; I lost myself, as it were, in him, I was hid in him with Christ—and found, without any process of logic, but by an experimental demonstration, the 'perfect love that casteth out fear.'" He was never obtrusive in the avowal of this great truth, but ever ready to give, with all lowliness and meekness, a reason of the hope that was within him. The marvelous grace that imbued his very greatness with unsurpassed humility was owing, in a great measure, to his faith in this sublime idea of Christianity.

His social character was attractive; he was ever ready, for not merely the cheerful remark, but the exhilarating pleasantry. Nor were these buoyant intervals rare or brief. Frequently through a prolonged but always fitting conversation, would this play of sunshine illuminate his presence, and with it would intermix, congruously, often most felicitously, a radiant play of thought or a happy expression of Christian sensibility—never, however, the meaningless twaddle of weakness. A truer and more forbearing friend could not be found. His domestic affections were warm, and the circle of his family was a sanctuary full of hallowed sympathies and enjoyments.

His scholarship was more exact and thorough within his professional sphere, than varied or comprehensive beyond that limit. At his graduation he was considered the "ripest scholar" who had been examined in his college. He was conservative in his views of classical education, and very decidedly opposed to the "modernized" system of training attempted and abandoned by some American colleges. A high and finished classical discipline was his ideal for the college over which he presided; and that institution has sent out, under his superintendence, as thorough students as have honored the education of the land. While he was a genuine scholar within his appropriate sphere, he possessed also a large range of general intelligence, though without that devotion to any favorite department of extra-professional knowledge which often relieves and adorns the professional life of studious men by becoming a healthful and liberalizing counterpart to their stated routines of thought.

With the current history of the world in politics, science, and especially religion, he had more than the usual familiarity. A remarkable memory, tenacious of even statistics and names, doubtless gave him, in this respect, an advantage over most intellectual men. The *original* powers of his mind were, however, his great distinction. And these, like his person, were all colossal—grasp, strength, with the dignity which usually attends them, a comprehensive faculty of generalization, which presented in conclusive logic grand summaries of thought. This comprehensiveness, combined with energy, was his chief intellectual characteristic; under the inspiration of the pulpit it often and indeed usually became sublime. It may be doubted whether any man of our generation has had more power in the pulpit than Stephen Olin; and this power was in spite of very marked oratorical defects. His manner was ungainly; his gestures quite against the elocutionary rules; his voice badly managed, and sometimes painful in its heaving utterances; but the elocutionist is not always the orator. While the hearer saw that there was no trickery of art with the preacher, he felt that a mighty, an irresistible mind was struggling with his own. He was overwhelmed—his reason with argument, his heart with emotion.

When he began his discourse, attention was immediately arrested by the dignity and sterling sense of his thoughts. It was perceived at once that something well worth most careful attention was coming. Paragraph after paragraph of massive thought was thrown off, each showing a gradually increasing glow of the sensibility as well as the mental force of the speaker. By the time he had fairly entered into the argument of the sermon, his audience was led captive by his power; but it would be difficult to say which was most subduing—his mighty thoughts or his deep feeling. Seldom or never were tears seen in his own eyes, but they flowed freely down the cheeks of his hearers. Ever and anon passages of overwhelming force were uttered, before which the whole assembly seemed to bow, not so much in admiration of the man, as in homage to the truth. Such passages were usually not poetic, for he was remarkably chary of his imagery; but they were ponderous with meaning. At suitable periods of the sermon, which usually occupied from an hour and a half to two hours, he would pause briefly to relieve his voice and his feelings. The mental tension of his audience could be perceived, at such times, by the general relaxation of posture, and the simultaneous, heaving respiration; but as soon as, with a peculiar, measured dignity, he resumed the lofty theme, all eyes were again fixed, all minds again absorbed.

Effective as was his preaching usually, it was not always so. His ill-health sometimes spread a languor over his spirit which no resolution could throw off. He sometimes alluded in conversation to these failures with much good nature, and remarked that his history as a preacher had taught him to expect the blessing of God on even such efforts. He used to relate an instance which occurred during his ministry in South Carolina. Preaching at a camp-meeting he was heard by a Presbyterian clergyman, who was to address the next session of his synod in Charleston, and who repeated there not only the text, but, substantially, the sermon before his clerical brethren, giving, however, full credit to its Methodist author. So remarkable a fact could not fail to excite great interest among the people of Charleston to hear the latter, who, at this time, occupied the Methodist pulpit of that city. The next Sunday evening his church was crowded with the *élite* of the community, including several clergymen. He preached long, and, as he thought, loudly and confusedly; and felt, at the close of the discourse, confounded with mortification. He sank, after the benediction, into the pulpit, to conceal himself from view till the assembly should be all gone, but espied some eminent individuals apparently waiting in the aisle to salute him. His heart failed, and noticing a door adjacent to the pulpit, he determined to escape by it. He knew not whither it led, but supposed it communicated with the next house, which had once been a parsonage, as he recollected having heard. Hastening to the door, he got it open, and, stepping out, descended abruptly into a graveyard, which extended beyond and behind the former parsonage. The night was very dark, and he stumbled about among the tombs for some time, but reached at last the wall which closed the cemetery in from the street, and which he found insurmountable. Groping his way to the opposite side, he sought to reach a back street by penetrating through one of the gardens which belonged to a range of houses there. It was an awkward endeavor in the darkness, and among the graves; at last he found a wicket-gate, but had no sooner passed through it than he was assailed by a house-dog. Having prevailed in this encounter, he pushed on and reached the street, with some very reasonable apprehensions that the neighborhood would be alarmed by his adventures. He now threaded his way through an indirect route to his lodgings, passed unceremoniously to his chamber, and shut himself up for the night, but slept little, reflecting with deep chagrin on the strange conclusion of the day. On the morrow he hardly dared to venture out; but while yet in his study, one of the first citizens in Charleston, and a leading officer in a sister denomination, called at the house; he was admitted to the preacher's study with reluctance; but what was the astonishment of the latter to hear him say that the sermon of the preceding evening had enabled him to step into the kingdom of God, after many years of disconsolate endeavors, during which he had been a member of the Church. The same day a lady of influential family came to report the same good tidings. Other similar examples occurred that morning; and this failure was one of the most useful sermons of his ministry.

His style was somewhat diffuse, and always elaborate—too much so for elegance. Johnson used to insist that his own pompous Latinism was an effect of the magnitude of his thoughts; its fantastic collocation, even in the definitions of his dictionary, stand out, however, inexorably and grotesquely against the fond conceit; the critics pronounce his verbiage a result of his early study of Sir Thomas Browne; but false, in part, as was the great author's apology, it was also, in part, true. He had a magnitude and Roman-like sturdiness of thought which demanded capacious expression, though the demand was exaggerated, and thus became a characteristic fault, as well as a characteristic excellence. Olin's style was affected by a similar cause, but not to such a faulty extent. The defect was perceptible in his ordinary conversation, and quite so in his extemporaneous sermons. In some of his later writings, however, like Johnson in his Lives of the Poets, he seemed to escape the excesses while he retained the excellences of his diction.

He was gigantic in person. His frame would have befitted a Hercules; his head was one of those which suggest to us superhuman capacity, and by which the classic sculptors symbolized the majesty of their gods. His gigantic structure was, however, during most of his life, smitten through and through with disease and enervation. The colossal head seemed too heavy to be supported, and appeared to labor to poise itself. The eye, somewhat sunken in its large socket, presented a languid expression, though relieved by a sort of religious benignity which often beamed with feeling. This great man must be added to the long and melancholy catalogue of self-martyred students. His infirmities commenced in his college life; they were exasperated by his labors as an instructor in a southern climate; and they were the burden of his later years, almost to the exclusion of any continuous labors. During these years his usefulness was confined mostly to occasional discourses, some of which have been published; to the quiet but inestimable moral power which the mere official presence of such a man cannot fail to exert over any responsibility to which he is related; and last, but not least, to the ministration of example under circumstances of suffering and personal religious development.

He was frankly independent in his opinions, and not without

what would be called strong prejudices—no uncommon accompaniment of powerful minds. He was decidedly conservative on most subjects, though early disposed to political liberalism. He inclined to stringent institutions of government in both Church and State, but at the same time deemed the polity of his own Church susceptible of many liberal changes, in order to adapt it to what he considered the demands of the times. He was especially interested in the intellectual improvement of her ministry, and was one of the warmest friends of theological education. Before a theological school was begun in the Church he wrote home from London, where he witnessed the experiment among the Wesleyans, a public letter, urging the subject upon the attention of the denomination, and inclosing a considerable donation toward it. He believed this, indeed, to be the capital want of Methodism in our day, and never disguised the conviction amid any prejudice to the contrary. He entertained sublime views of its missionary resources, and longed and labored to see its energies amply brought out and applied to this great work, especially in the foreign field. The evangelization of the world he deemed an achievement quite practicable to Protestant Christendom. Some of his discourses on the subject were signal efforts of intellect and eloquence.

On the night of the 15th of August, 1851, a small and silent circle stood at the death-bed of this good and great man. The herculean frame lay helpless and heaving in the last struggle. "I hope in Christ," (pointing with his finger upward,) "most certainly, in Christ alone. I believe I shall be saved, though as by fire," were among the last utterances of the dying sufferer. Early the next morning he was no more among men. He had been twenty-seven years in the ministry.

Thus have some of the most notable characters of the denomination in this period passed in review before us. Others might be selected from the dead; and there are, among the living, those who will take rank with such as I have recorded. But we are necessarily restricted to examples. Olin was unquestionably the greatest, but Fisk the most perfect man in this class. The former had both the largest and strongest intellectual grasp, the latter more versatility and practical skill. Olin had the highest, the philosophic genius; and if his health had allowed him a productive life, he would have taken rank where, by the title of his genius, he really belonged—among the first men of his day: Fisk had talent and tact rather than genius; he was the practical though not the technical logician in both speculation and in life. Olin had very little of the detail of practical logic, but in him the higher logic, the faculty of generalization, was predominant; it gave grandeur to his habitual conceptions, though it could not take those minute cognizances of events or truths which afforded Fisk an habitual mastery over any position in which he found himself placed, and gave more perfect proportions to the development of his character. Cookman had neither the philosophic comprehensiveness of the one nor the practical skill of the other, but more mental alertness and energy than either. Olin could have best planned the policy of a state; Fisk could have planned best the movements of its army; Cookman could have best executed those movements. Cookman had much of Bascom's imagination. His nature was too hardy, too Saxon, to admit of any resemblance to Summerfield. His allegorical skill was all his own. Summerfield's position in the group hardly admits of comparison. He had none of Olin's intellectual breadth, little of Fisk's tactical skill, not much more of Cookman's energetic vivacity or of Bascom's imagination. His distinction was almost entirely one of temperament, a temperament to which was subordinated, in the happiest manner possible, all his powers of intellect and of expression. His soul was not in his head, but in his heart. Never was the power of a public speaker more pure, more anomalous. It was not the power of logic, proceeding from the intellect; it was not poetic power, proceeding from the imagination; nor did it flow from the passions: it was a moral magnetism, a gentle suasive effluence from the inmost life of the man. His biographer, though he claims for him justly a second-rate kind of "genius," declares the "predominating" qualities of his mind to have been "good sense and good taste." Undoubtedly this was the case; but these qualities do not solve the problem of his power. There are thousands of men who have "good sense and good taste," but who have no such power. It proceeded, as has been affirmed, from his peculiar and sanctified temperament; his "intense animal feeling," as Montgomery somewhat equivocally calls it; and his "good sense and good taste" were but its regulators.

Such are a few of the superior intellects which have arisen within the pale of Methodism, and thus has its ministerial system been found suited to the highest pulpit talent, and at the same time capable of rallying and directing the ruder energies of thousands of uncultivated laborers, making them, by its peculiar discipline, "workmen that need not to be ashamed," and covering the continent with the fruits and signs of their apostleship.

CHAPTER XXXVI.

CENTENARY JUBILEE: RESULTS, AND THEIR CAUSES.

A GREAT occasion drew near; the hundreth year of the cause which, beginning in such feebleness, had achieved such triumphs, and had now attained national ascendency in the popular religious faith of the country. Though the Republic was still surging with an unparalleled civil war, the Church, which had given to its battle-fields a hundred thousand of her children, staggered not with a momentary doubt of the issue of the struggle, or of the destiny of the country. Both had seen a great past, both expected a greater future. The General Conference of 1864 assembled in Philadelphia May 1st, amid the continued tumults of the war, but with hymns of triumph. It received the grateful acknowledgment of the patriotic services of the denomination, from the President of the Republic, and proceeded confidently to ordain beneficent celebrations of the triumphs of the Church, and to provide for still larger triumphs. It reinforced, by one third, its Episcopate, for it believed that it must soon resume its old undivided national diocese, from Canada to the Mexican Gulf. It established a "Church Extension Society," for it doubted not that the "waste places" of the war were soon to be resupplied with chapels, and that the frontier domains were about to open more largely than ever. It placed in its organic law an unconditional prohibition of slavery. It repeated substantially its former expression of a willingness to regard the wish of its people respecting Lay Representation, should it become manifest that a majority of them demanded such a change in its Constitution. It extended the term of ministerial appointments from two to three years. But not the least important of its measures had reference to the practical improvement of the approaching Centenary Jubilee. By discussions in committee and in the Conference a munificent scheme for its celebration, and a "Centenary" Committee of twelve preachers, an equal number of laymen, and all the bishops, to mature and prosecute the scheme, were provided. It adjourned, hoping that two millions of dollars might be thus obtained in commemoration of this first hundred years of success, and in preparation for the achievements of another century.

The Centenary Committee met at Cleveland, Ohio, February 22, 1865, and issued a plan of contributions, most of which were to be devoted to education, in the domestic field, in Germany, and in Ireland. The whole Church was placed by districts under Centenary sub-committees. The first Sunday in the jubilee year was given to discourses in promotion of its beneficent designs. The successive Annual Conferences had special Centenary sermons delivered to crowded audiences. Two "Centenary Books," and a series of "Centenary Tracts," were issued. Centenary meetings were held in the cities and large towns, with a continually rising interest and unexpectedly large subscriptions of funds, till the last Sunday of October, when the Church throughout its thousands of Societies finally celebrated the great occasion with love-feasts, discourses, and pecuniary contributions. Instead of two millions of dollars, which at the beginning was deemed an extreme amount, more than five millions were pledged.* At the Centenary of Wesleyan Methodism, in 1839, the American Church had given about half a million; the difference made by about a quarter of a century was proof of the growth of the denomination in resources as well as numbers.

But its general statistics, as exhibited in its Centenary celebration, afforded more imposing proofs. On this memorable occasion the Methodist Episcopal Church alone was to see a full million of communicants within its pale,† and in its congregations four millions of the population of the Republic. But it had become several bands; yet all were identical, save in some points of ecclesiastical polity. Its first assembly, in

* Five millions have been officially reported, but the Conference reports have not yet (October, 1867) been completed.

† They amounted to 1,032,184.

Embury's private house, had multiplied to thousands and tens of thousands of congregations; its first chapel, of 1768, to at least twenty thousand churches, studding the continent from the northernmost settlements of Canada to the Gulf of Mexico. from the Atlantic to the Pacific. Its first two classes of 1766, recording six or seven members each, were now represented by 2,000,000 communicants;* its first congregation of five persons by about 8,000,000 of people; its three local preachers, Embury, Strawbridge, and Webb, who founded the whole cause, by at least 15,000 successors in their own order of the ministry; its first two itinerants, Boardman and Pilmoor, who reached the New World in 1769, by about 14,000 traveling preachers; its first educational institution, opened in 1787, by nearly 200 colleges and academies, with an army of 32,000 students; its first Sunday-school, started by Asbury in 1786, by at least 20,000 schools, 200,000 teachers, and over 1,500,000 scholars; its first periodical organ, begun in 1818, after a previous failure, by thirty periodical publications, the best patronized and among the most effective in the nation; its first Book Concern, with its borrowed capital of $600, begun in 1789, by four or five similar institutions in the United States and Canada. The festivities of the centenary jubilee of the denomination were to be tempered, as well as enhanced, by the startling fact that it bore the chief responsibility of Protestantism in the New World, its aggregate membership being about half the Protestant communicants of the country, its congregations between one fifth and one fourth of the national population; and that, if the usual estimate, by geographers, of the Protestant population of the globe (80,000,000) is correct, American Methodism, with its eight millions of people, is responsible for one tenth (with general Methodism, for one seventh) the interest and fate of the Protestant world.

The influence of this vast ecclesiastical force on the general progress of the New World can neither be doubted nor measured. It is generally conceded that it has been the most energetic religious element in the social development of the con-

* I give the aggregates of the different Methodist bodies in America. The details can be found in the "Centenary Book," cited mostly from official sources.

tinent. With its devoted and enterprising people dispersed through the whole population; its thousands of laborious itinerant preachers, and still larger hosts of local preachers and exhorters; its unequaled publishing agencies and powerful periodicals, from the Quarterly Review to the child's paper; its hundreds of colleges and academies; its hundreds of thousands of Sunday-school instructors; its devotion to the lower and most needy classes, and its animated modes of worship and religious labor, there can hardly be a question that it has been a mighty, if not the mightiest, agent in the maintenance and spread of Protestant Christianity over these lands.

The problem (so called) of this unequaled success has been the subject of no little discussion; but we may well hesitate to admit that there is any such problem. I have failed to interpret aright the whole preceding record if it does not present, on almost every page, intelligible reasons of its extraordinary events. A principal error in most of the discussions of this alleged problem has been the attempt to find some one fact or reason as its explanation. The problem (if such it may be admitted to be) is complex, and no single fact can suffice for its solution. Doubtless the theology of Methodism has had a potent influence on its history—its Arminianism, its doctrines of Regeneration, the Witness of the Spirit, and Sanctification. But it should be borne in mind that Calvinistic Methodism was, during most of the last century, as energetic as Arminian Methodism. It is as much so to-day in Wales, where it presents the best example of Sabbath observance and Church attendance in the Christian world. Whitefield was an ardent Calvinist, but was he less a Methodist, less a flaming evangelist than Wesley? Moravianism shared the theology of Methodism, especially its most vital, most experimental doctrines; but not its prosperity. Indisputably one of the greatest responsibilities of the denomination, for the future, is the maintenance and diffusion of its theology; but this cannot be assigned as the single, or the special cause of its success.

The legislative genius of Wesley, the practical system of Methodism, has been pronounced the chief cause of its progress; it has been, doubtless, hardly less important than its theology;

we have seen its power throughout this whole narrative. But neither of them explains the problem, for neither of them, nor both together, could have succeeded without something else. The whole Methodistic system, introduced into some of our comparatively inert modern denominations, could only result in a prodigious failure. Could they tear up their ministerial families by the roots every two or three years, and scatter them hither and thither? Could they drive out their comfortably domiciled pastors to wander over the land without certain homes or abiding places, preaching night and day, year in and year out? Could they throw their masses of people into class meetings for weekly inspection respecting their religious progress or declension? The system, momentous as it has been, presupposes prior and infinitely more potential conditions.

If we must narrow the explanation to the fewest possible conditions, it may be said that there have been two chief causes of the success of Methodism, one primary, the other proximate. First, it was a necessity of the times, a providential provision for the times. The government of God over our world is a unit; the history of his Church is a unit; and however unable we may still be to correlate its divers parts, yet in ages to come, perhaps after hundreds of ages, the world will behold its perfect symmetry. History, if not as much under the sway of laws as physics, is nevertheless a providential process. The apostolic ministry founded the kingdom of Christ in the world, but the apostles themselves predicted the rise of Antichrist and the great "falling away." The medieval night, a thousand years long, followed; the Renaissance, with the Reformation, began the modern history of the world. The Reformation proclaimed the right and responsibility of the individual conscience in the interpretation of the word of God, and reproclaimed the apostolic doctrine of justification by faith. It went far, if not so far as it might have gone; but in the eighteenth century its progressive power seemed about exhausted. It had made no great territorial advancement after about its first half century, and in the eighteenth century the Historical Criticism and Rationalism arose, and, with the prevailing popular demoralization, threatened, as Burnet affirms, not only the Anglican Church, but "the whole Reformation." It had become necessary that some new development of Christianity should take place. It was a providential necessity, and God provided for it. At this very period of apparent danger Christendom was in the travail of a new birth. The American and French Revolutions were drawing near. The most important phases of the civilized world were to be transformed. Science, commerce, government, religion were to pass into a new cycle, perhaps their final cycle. The revolution in religion was to be as conspicuous as any other change in the grand process. The rights of conscience were to be more fully developed; the separation of the Church from the State, and the "voluntary principle," were to be introduced. For the first time in recorded history was about to be seen the spectacle of a great nation without a State religion. Medieval dogmatism was to be more fully thrown into abeyance; ecclesiasticism and hierarchism to receive a shock under which they might still reel for a while, but only to fall, sooner or later, to their proper subordination or desuetude. The permanent, essential principles, not so much of theology (so called) as of religion, were to revive with the power of their apostolic promulgation. Missions, Sunday-schools, Bible societies, popular religious literature, all those powers which I have affirmed to have arisen with Methodism, were to come into activity in the religious world co-ordinately with the new energies of the secular world. The Church, in fine, was anew to become a living, working organism, and to be not only the Church of the present, but, probably, the Church of the future. The old questions of rationalistic biblical criticism and of ecclesiasticism were not to be immediately laid, but they were to become only occasional incidents to the Christian movement of the new age. Colenso and the Essayists, Pusey and the Oxford Papal tendencies, were yet to appear, but not seriously to obstruct the march of evangelical truth. Methodism had its birth at the date of Rationalism in Germany. The biblical criticism of Colenso and the Essayists was anticipated in the writings of Bolingbroke and other English authors before Methodism had fairly started. That criticism is much older. Spinoza's Politico-Theological Treatise is almost entirely made up of it—in many respects a much abler discussion than modern English doubt has produced. We know not how far this critical skepticism may yet go; we know not what, if any, demonstrations it may reach; but one thing we absolutely know, that the ethical purity which speaks in the Gospel—the spiritual life which filled the primitive Church with saints, heroes, martyrs, and which is now filling the Christian world with good works, sanctified homes, and peaceful death-beds—can never be overthrown; that against a living, loving, working Church the gates of hell can never prevail; and that the very existence of such a Church presupposes the coexistence of all essential theology. The production of such a Church was the special providential appointment of the eighteenth century, a "continuous revival" of spiritual life, as Wesley was able to say after fifty years, in the Old World; a still continued "revival," as we are able to say to-day, after a hundred years, in the New World. If we may not venture to affirm that Methodism, distinctively so called, is this modern development of Christianity, we need not hesitate to say, with Isaac Taylor, that the religious movement of the eighteenth century, called Methodism—Calvinistic and Arminian—is its true historical exponent—"the event whence the religious epoch now current must date its commencement."

Such was the providential origin of Methodism, such the primary condition of its success. But what was its other chief, or proximate cause?

The "Holy Club" was founded at Oxford, and the title of Methodism given to it in 1729, ten years before the recognized epoch of the religious movement which it was to introduce. The Wesleys, Whitefield, and other mighty men were then or soon after in it; but they had no notable success, for they had not yet received "power from on high." The Wesleys came to America, and labored faithfully here, but still without success, and they returned home defeated. Something was yet needed. They preached and suffered in England, but still without appreciable effect. As Methodism was to be the next great stage of religious progress, after the Reformation, it was to have affinity with the Reformation. The salient doctrinal fact of the Reformation was justification by faith. Wesley had been feeling after this as in the dark during all these ten years; but now, by the very writings in which Luther had declared it at the Reformation, he was to find it. On the 24th of May, 1738, sitting in a little religious meeting in Aldersgate-street, and listening to the reading of Luther's preface to the Epistle to the Romans, the great truth flashed upon his soul. "I felt," he writes, "my heart strangely warmed; an assurance was given me that He had taken away my sins, even mine, and saved me from the law of sin and death." Here is the proximate cause of all the Methodism in the world to-day, for this was the "dispensation of the Spirit," which has since continued in a baptism of fire upon the Churches. On that memorable night genuine Methodism had its birth. What would have been Wesley's theological opinions without this quickening of the Spirit?—Tenets only of the brain, exciting him to unavailing struggles, as they had for ten years. What his practical system, had he even been able to devise it, but a wretched failure, from which he and his people would soon have recoiled, as from a burden intolerable to be borne? This new spiritual life, this "strange" warmth of the heart, made his theology vital, his system practicable; gave power and demonstration to his preaching, and spread like contagion through his assemblies. It intoned their hymns, and kindled their prayer-meetings, band-meetings, classes, and love-feasts. The manner of its inspiration, the time of its experience, its effects and evidences, and the extent to which it could be perfected, became the themes of discourse in their meetings and in their familiar converse all through the British realm. Conversion, the Witness of the Spirit, and Sanctification, were but its corollary truths. It inspired men to enter the ministry, it inspired their preaching, and produced the peculiar power of their preaching, and of all their denominational methods, as witnessed throughout the world. Without it almost everything else that is characteristically Methodistic would have been not only ineffective but impracticable. The multitudes, the very mobs, recognized this power of personal religion, this divine power and glory of the regenerated man in the representatives of the new movement; they saw it in their countenances, in their tears, and heard it in their tones. It was the magical power by which they controlled riots, and led persecutors in weeping processions from the highways and market-places to the altars of their humble chapels. It it be inquired what has been the one chief force in the success of Methodism, and what is the chief power for its future success, I reply, it is this "power from on high," this "unction from the Holy One."

Such, I think, were the primary and proximate conditions of its success. There were also many others doubtless: its catholicity; the subordination, not to say insignificance, to which it reduced all exclusive or arrogant ecclesiastic pretensions; the importance which it gave to good and charitable works while insisting on a profound personal, if not a mystic piety; the unprecedented co-operation of the laity with the clergy in, at least, religious labors which it established; the activity of women in its social devotions; these, and still more.

I mention further but one, and particularly because it affords an important admonitory lesson—the character of its chiefs. And I mean not merely their greatness. They were indeed great men, as the world is beginning to acknowledge: Whitefield, the greatest of modern preachers; Wesley, the greatest of religious organizers; Asbury, unquestionably the greatest character in the ecclesiastical history of this hemisphere, judged by the results of his labors. But it was not so much by their great abilities, as by qualities in which all may share, that they made Methodism what it is. Its leaders were its exemplars, and that fact expresses more of the philosophy of its history than any other except that of the "baptism from on high." There is no human power above that of character. The character, not the genius, of Washington has made him chief among the military or civic sons of men. The character of a military leader can make a whole army an array of heroes or a melee of cowards. The army of the Shenandoah was rolling back shattered and hopeless; but when its chief arrived on his foaming steed, after that long and solitary ride, it stood forth again invincible; the drawing of his single sword before it, flashed lightning along all its bayonets and banners, and it dealt back the blow which sent the enemy reeling irrecoverably to destruction. The greatest of talents is character, and character is the most attainable of talents.

Had John Wesley, when his cause was somewhat established, retired from his self-sacrificing labors, and acted the dignified, well-endowed prelate in City Road parsonage, his whole system would soon have fallen through. By traveling more, laboring more, and suffering more than any of his preachers, he kept them all heroically traveling, laboring, suffering. Asbury kept Methodism astir throughout this nation by hastening from Georgia to Massachusetts on horseback, yearly, for nearly half a century, preaching daily. None of his preachers exceeded him in even the humblest labors of the ministry. His power was military, and he used it with military energy; but, as has been shown, he imposed on the ministry no task that he did not himself exemplify. Under his command the Conferences moved as columns in the field of battle, for they knew that their leader would be in the thickest fight, would be chief in suffering and labor as in authority and honor. Asbury's daily life was a challenge to the humblest of them to endure all things. It became a point of chivalric honor among them to evade no labor or suffering; they consented to be tossed from Baltimore to Boston, from Boston to beyond the Alleghanies. How would all this have been changed if Asbury, at his episcopal ordination, had housed himself in Baltimore, reposing on his dignity, and issuing his commands, without exemplifying them! The Church should understand, then, that its great men must be great workers in whatever sphere they occupy; that this is a requisite of the age, and has always been a requisite of Methodism. An itinerant superintendency or episcopacy has ever been a favorite idea of its people. They have instinctively perceived its importance; and the founders of the Church declared in its constitutional law that the General Conference shall not "change or alter any part or rule of our government so as . . . to destroy the plan of our itinerant superintendency." The unity of the denomination, the fellowship of the Churches, their co-operation in great common undertakings, and the self-sacrificing spirit of the ministry generally, have been largely attributable to this fact of their system, a fact peculiar to Methodism among Episcopal Churches.

With changes of time must come changes of policy, if not changes of what have been deemed fundamental opinions. Methodism has, through most of its history, been taking on new adaptations. Unrestricted by any dogmatism whatever in ecclesiastical polity, and less restricted, as we have seen, by theological creeds, than any other evangelical Church, it stands unshackled for its future career. That it will change, that it has changed, cannot be doubted; but devoting itself, as it has been increasingly, to the elevation of its people, to education, literature, liberty, civil and religious, missions, the amelioration of its own acknowledged defects, and all charitable works, there would seem to be, not only possible, but feasible to it, a destiny hardly less grand than its history.

Here we may appropriately drop the curtain of this singular religious drama. Its every page has been suggestive of lessons, and it needs no further epilogue. It demonstrates one obvious and sublime fact, that Christianity, thrown back upon its primordial truths and forces, cannot fail, in its very simplicity, humility, charity, and power, to attain the mastery of the human soul, to wield the supremacy of the moral world. This lowly Methodistic story is but the reproduction, in substance, of the apostolic history; and presents, in full vitality, that original, that only, example of evangelical propagandism, which, when all dogmatic conflicts and hierarchical pretensions, with their wasted passions and pomps, are recorded as historical failures, will bear forward to universal triumph the ensign of the Cross by a catholic, living, working Church of the common people.

APPENDIX.

WAS THE EPISCOPAL ORGANIZATION OF AMERICAN METHODISM IN ACCORDANCE WITH WESLEY'S DESIGNS?

THIS has been made a grave and persistent question by opponents of the denomination, especially by writers in the Protestant Episcopal Church. As presented in the preceding record, the founders of American Methodism were men of singular integrity and purity, and their great "works do follow them." A suspicion that there was anything surreptitious in their proceedings, at its very organization, would be a grave detraction from both them and the Church, and should be conclusively corrected.

Wesley had been providentially preparing for the new and momentous measure by that gradual development of his personal opinions which I have traced in another work.* Bigoted even, as a High Churchman, at the beginning of his career, he was, year after year, reaching more liberal views of ecclesiastical policy. Nearly forty years before his ordinations for America, he had, after reading Lord King's "Primitive Church," renounced the opinion that a distinction of order, rather than of office, existed between bishops and presbyters. Fifteen years later he denied the necessity, though not the expediency, of episcopal ordination. Bishop Stillingfleet had convinced him that it was "an entire mistake" that none but episcopal ordination was valid. † Henceforth he held that presbyters and bishops, identical in order, differing only in office, had essentially the same right of ordination. It was not possible for a man like Wesley—keen, quick, fearless, and candid—to remain long in

* History of Methodism, etc., 3 vols., *passim.*

† A Letter to a Friend, Works, vol. vii, p. 301.

any ecclesiastical prejudice now that he was on this track of progressive opinions. He soon broke away from all other regard for questions of Church government than that of scriptural expediency. And as early as 1756, when in his maturest intellectual vigor, he declares: "As to my own judgment, I still believe 'the episcopal form of Church government to be scriptural and apostolical;' I mean, well agreeing with the practice and writings of the apostles; but that it is prescribed in Scripture, I do not believe. This opinion, which I once zealously espoused, I have been heartily ashamed of ever since I read Bishop Stillingfleet's 'Irenicon.' I think he has unanswerably proved that 'neither Christ nor his apostles prescribe any particular form of Church government, and that the plea of divine right for diocesan episcopacy was never heard of in the primitive Church." *

It was then by no new assumption in his old age—in his imbecility, as some of his critics allege—that he now met the necessities of American Methodism by ordaining men to provide for them. His keenest-eyed associates could as yet detect no declension of his faculties; and if they could, still his course in this case was in accordance with the reasonings of his best days, and he but repeats his long-established opinions when he now asserts: "I firmly believe I am a scriptural *episcopos* as much as any man in England, for the uninterrupted succession I know to be a fable, which no man ever did or can prove." †

Methodism, as we have seen, had spread rapidly in America, notwithstanding the war of the Revolution. The Revolution had not only dissolved the civil, but also the ecclesiastical relations of the colonies to England. Many of the English clergy, on whom the Methodist societies had depended for the sacraments, had fled from the land, or had entered political or military life, and the Episcopal Church had been generally disabled. In Virginia, the center of its colonial strength, it had rapidly declined, morally as well as numerically. At the Declaration of Independence it included not more than one

* Letter to Rev. Mr. Clarke, Works, vol. vii, p. 284.

† "On the Church," Works, vol. vii, p. 312.

third of the population of that province.* At the beginning of the war the sixty-one counties of Virginia contained ninety-five parishes, one hundred and sixty-four churches, and ninety-one clergymen. At the conclusion of the contest many of her churches were in ruins, nearly a fourth of her parishes "extinct or forsaken," and thirty-four of the remaining seventy-two were without pastoral supplies; twenty-eight only of her ninety-one clergymen remained, and these with an addition, soon after the war, of eight from other parts of the country, ministered in but thirty-six parishes.† In the year in which Wesley ordained an American Methodist bishop, "memorials" to the Virginia legislature for the incorporation of the "Protestant Episcopal Church in Virginia," and for other advantages to religion, were met by counter petitions that "no step might be taken in aid of religion, but that it might be left to its own superior and successful influence."‡ The memorials were postponed till the next session, and then rejected; but a bill for the "Incorporation of all Religious Societies which may apply for the Same" was adopted. In other parts of the country the English Church never had been numerically strong, and its existence was now precarious, except in two or three of the cities.

Under these circumstances the Methodists demanded of their preachers the administration of the sacraments. Many of the Societies had been months, some of them years, without them. The demand was not only urgent, it was logically right; but by the majority of the preachers it was not deemed expedient. The prudent delay which Wesley, notwithstanding his liberal ecclesiastical principles, had practiced in England, afforded a lesson which their good sense could not disregard. They exhorted their people, therefore, to wait patiently till he could be consulted. In 1779 the question occasioned a virtual schism, the preachers of the South being resolute for the administration of the sacraments, those of the North still pleading for

* Burk's History of Virginia, vol. ii, p. 180. Hawks (Contributions to the Ecclesiastical History of the United States of America, vol. i, ch. ix) doubts Burk's estimate. Dr. Hawks's volume needs important emendations, especially in respect to Methodism.

† Hawks, Contributions, vol. i, ch. x. ‡ Journals of Virginia Assembly, 1784.

patient delay. The latter met in Conference at Judge White's residence, the retreat of Asbury, in Delaware; the former at Brokenback Church, Fluvanna county, Virginia, where they made their own appointments, and proceeded to ordain themselves by the hands of three of their senior members, unwilling that their people should longer be denied their right to the Lord's supper, and their children and probationary members the rite of baptism. At the session of 1780 Asbury and others were authorized to visit the Southern preachers, and, if possible, conciliate them. He met them in Conference; they appeared determined not to recede, but at last consented to suspend the administration of the sacraments till further advice could be received from Wesley. The breach was thus happily repaired, but must evidently soon again be opened if redress should not be obtained.

What could Wesley do under these circumstances? What but exercise the right of Ordination, which he had for years theoretically claimed, but practically and prudently declined? He had importuned the authorities of the English Church in behalf of the Americans. In this very year he had written two letters to Lowth, Bishop of London, imploring ordination for a single preacher, who might appease the urgency of the American brethren, by traveling among them as a presbyter, and by giving them the sacraments; but the request was denied. If there was any imprudence on the part of Wesley in this emergency, it was certainly in his long-continued patience, for he delayed yet nearly four years. When he yielded, it was only after the triumph of the American arms and the acknowledged independence of the colonies; and not then till urged to it by his most revered counselors. Fletcher of Madeley was one of these.

Fletcher was present with Wesley and Coke at the Leeds Conference of 1784, and there, with his assistance,* the question was brought to an issue. Wesley had previously consulted with Coke respecting it. He represented to Coke that as the Revolution had separated the United States from the

* Coke's Letter to Wesley, Smith's History of Wesleyan Methodism, vol. i, book ii, chap. vi.

mother country, and the Episcopal Establishment was utterly abolished in the States, it became his duty, as providentially at the head of the Methodist Societies, to obey their demand and furnish for them the means of grace. He referred to the example of the Alexandrian Church, which, at the death of its bishops, provided their successors through ordination by its presbyters—an historical fact exemplified during two hundred years. Recognized as their founder by the American Methodists, required by them to provide for their new necessities, and unable to induce the English prelates to do so, he proposed to ordain Coke that he might go to the American Societies as their superintendent or bishop, ordain their preachers, and thus afford them the sacraments with the least possible irregularity. Coke hesitated, but in two months wrote to Wesley accepting the office.* Accordingly, accompanied by James Creighton, a presbyter of the Church of England, Coke met him at Bristol, and on the second of September, 1784, was ordained *superintendent or bishop of the Methodist Societies in America;* an act of as high propriety and dignity as it was of urgent necessity. Richard Whatcoat and Thomas Vasey were at the same time ordained presbyters; and on the third of November, attended by his two presbyters, (the number necessary to assist a bishop in ordination, according to the usages of the English Church,) Coke arrived in the Republic, and proceeded to ordain Francis Asbury, first as a deacon, then as a presbyter, and finally as a bishop; and to settle the organization of American Methodism, one of the most important ecclesiastical events (whether for good or evil) of the eighteenth century, or indeed since the Reformation, as its historical consequences attest.

The Colonial English Church being dissolved by the Revolution, its dwindled fragments were yet floating, as had been the Methodist Societies, on the stormy tide of events. Methodism preceded it in reorganization, as I have shown. The Methodist bishops were the first Protestant bishops,† and

* Drew's Life of Coke, chap. v.

† Unless some occasional and obscure Episcopal appointments in the few local Moravian communities of the colonies may be deemed exceptions.

Methodism was the first Protestant Episcopal Church of the New World; and as Wesley had given it the Anglican Articles of Religion, (omitting the seventeenth, on Predestination,) and the Liturgy, wisely abridged, it became, both by its precedent organization and its subsequent numerical importance, the real successor to the Anglican Church in America.

Of course this extraordinary but necessary measure met with opposition from Charles Wesley. He still retained his High Church opinions; he denounced the ordinations as schism; with his usual haste he predicted that Coke would return from "his Methodist Episcopal Church in Baltimore" to "make us all Dissenters here." The poet was no legislator; he became pathetic in his remonstrances to his brother. "Alas!" he wrote, "what trouble are you preparing for yourself as well as for me, and for your oldest, truest, best friends! Before you have quite broken down the bridge, stop and consider! If your sons have no regard for you, have some for yourself. Go to your grave in peace; at least suffer me to go first, before this ruin is under your hand." He did soon after go to his grave in peace, except the alarms of his imaginary fears, and the only evidence of the predicted "ruin" is seen to-day in the prevalent and permanent success of Methodism in both hemispheres.

The next year after the ordination of Coke, Wesley records in his Journal: "I was now considering how strangely the grain of mustard-seed, planted about fifty years ago, had grown up. It spread through all Great Britain and Ireland, the Isle of Wight, and the Isle of Man; then to America, through the whole continent, into Canada, the Leeward Islands, and Newfoundland. And the Societies in all these parts walk by one rule, knowing religion is holy tempers, and striving to worship God, not in form only, but likewise in spirit and in truth." His policy becomes more and more liberal as he now finds it necessary to fortify his cause before his approaching death. The following year (1786) he ordained six or seven more preachers, sending some to Scotland, and others to the West Indies,* but he ordained none as yet for

* Jackson's Charles Wesley, chap. xxvi.

England, where he and his clerical friends could partially supply the sacraments. Three years later he ordained Mather, Rankin, and Moore.* About a score of lay preachers received ordination from his hands, and for no other purpose but that they might administer the sacraments in cases of necessity. Thus did providential events give shape and security to Methodism as its aged leader approached his end.

No act of Wesley's public life has been more misrepresented, if not misunderstood, than his ordination of Coke, and the consequent episcopal organization of his American societies. Churchmen, so called, have especially insisted that he did not design to confer upon Coke the character of a bishop; that Coke's new office was designed to be a species of supervisory appointment, vague and contingent—something widely different from episcopacy, however difficult to define; and that, therefore, the distinct existence of American Methodism, as an episcopal Church, is a fact contrary to the intention of Wesley. No extant forensic argument, founded upon documentary evidence, is stronger than would be a right collocation of the evidence which sustains the claim of American Methodism respecting this question. All Methodist authorities, British as well as American, support that claim; its proofs have been more or less cited, again and again, but they have not usually been drawn out in detail. Presented in their right series they become absolutely decisive, and must conclude the controversy with all candid minds. It is appropriate to review completely the argument once more. In stating the facts which compose it, in their successive relations one to an-

* "To administer the sacraments of baptism and the Lord's supper, according to the usages of the Church of England," says the certificate of ordination; (see it in Life of Henry Moore, p. 134, Am. ed.;) and yet a living Churchman (Dr. Pusey's Letter to the Bishop of Oxford, p. 151) says that "Wesley reluctantly took the step of ordaining at all;" and that "to the last *he refused, in the strongest terms, his consent that those thus ordained should take upon them to administer the sacraments.* He felt that it exceeded his powers, and so inhibited it, however it might diminish the numbers of the Society he had formed." The biographers of Wilberforce (vol. i, p. 248) also say: "Nor were any of his preachers *suffered during his lifetime to attempt to administer the sacraments of his Church.*" It is high time that such fictions should cease among English Churchmen. It seems that they have yet to learn how thorough and noble a heretic Wesley really was.

other, some repetition will be necessary; but the highest logic—mathematical demonstration itself—is that in which not only the postulates, but the successive proofs, most often recur to strengthen the advancing demonstration.

It has been seen that, as before the American Revolution the two countries were under one government, the two Methodist bodies were also. Wesley's "Minutes" were the Discipline of the American as well as the British Methodists; and Asbury represented his person in America, vested with much greater powers than have since belonged to the American Methodist bishops. Thus was the American Church governed, for years, by the paternal direction of Wesley. It has been further shown, that, in meeting its demands, Wesley ordained and sent over Dr. Coke, with episcopal powers, under the name of superintendent, to ordain Francis Asbury a "joint superintendent," and to ordain the preachers to the offices of deacons and elders. He sent also a printed liturgy, or "Sunday Service," containing, besides the usual prayers, forms for "ordaining superintendents, elders, and deacons," the "Articles of Religion," and "A Collection of Psalms and Hymns." Coke also bore from him a circular letter stating reasons for the new measures, the chief one being the demand of the American Societies. When he arrived, the preachers assembled in Baltimore to receive him and the new arrangements borne by him from Wesley. The adoption of the provisions thus made by Wesley, at the request of "some thousands of the inhabitants of these States," is what is called the "organization" of the Methodist Episcopal Church. The "Minutes," which had before been the law of the Church, were continued, with such additions as were required by these new arrangements. There was no revolution of the Church polity, and no new powers were imparted to Asbury, except authority to ordain. Everything proceeded as before, except that the Methodist Societies no longer depended upon the Church of England for the sacraments, but received them from their own preachers. Thus, then, it appears that the so-called "organization" of the Methodist Episcopal Church at Baltimore was simply and substantially the adoption of the system appointed by Wesley. In respect to the very term "episcopal" itself, the Conference of Baltimore said, in their "Minutes" of the so-called organization, that, "following the counsel of Mr. John Wesley, *who recommended the episcopal mode* of Church government, we thought it best to become an episcopal Church."* The Minutes containing this declaration were, six months afterward, in the hands of Wesley, and were published in England without a word of disapprobation from him; and when Coke was attacked in an English pamphlet for his doings at Baltimore, he publicly defended himself by declaring that he had "done nothing without the direction of Mr. Wesley." This he did in a publication under the eye of Wesley.†

It should be frankly admitted, however, that Wesley, while he established the American episcopacy, did not approve the use of the title of "bishop," because of the adventitious dignities associated with it. But let it be borne in mind that the American Societies had been in existence nearly four years under the express title of an "Episcopal Church," with the uninterrupted approbation of Wesley, before the name bishop was personally applied to their superintendents.‡ Not till this term was so applied did he demur. He then wrote a letter to Bishop Asbury, objecting strongly to his being "called a bishop." And it is on this letter, more than anything else, that the opponents of Methodism have founded their allegation that Wesley did not design to establish the American Methodist episcopate, but that Coke and the Baltimore Conference exceeded his intentions in assuming it. Quotations from this letter have been incessantly given, in a form adapted only to produce a false effect, for the letter can be rightly comprehended only by the aid of the historical facts of the case.

Did Wesley, then, design, by his ordination of Coke, to

* Emory's History of the Discipline, pp. 25, 30.

† Drew's Life of Coke, chap. vi. His assailant is supposed to have been Charles Wesley. Etheridge's Coke, book ii, chap. vii.

‡ It had been used, however, in the Minutes as explanatory of the word "superintendent." The Minutes say that, "following the counsel of Mr. John Wesley, who recommended the episcopal mode of Church government, we thought it best to become an episcopal Church, making the episcopal office elective, and the elected superintendent, or *bishop*, amenable to the body of ministers and preachers." Minutes, vol. i, p. 22. New York, 1840.

confer on him the office of a bishop, and to constitute the American Methodist Societies an episcopal Church? Three things are to be assumed as preliminary to this inquiry:

1. That Wesley was a decided Episcopalian. What man was ever more attached to the national episcopacy of England? I have already cited proofs that he believed the "episcopal form of Church government to be scriptural and apostolical," that is, "well agreeing with the practice and writings of the apostles;" though that it is prescribed in Scripture he did not believe.

2. That Wesley, while he believed in episcopacy, belonged to that class of Episcopalians who contend that episcopacy is not a distinct order, but a distinct office, in the ministry; that bishops and presbyters, or elders, are of the same order, and have essentially the same prerogatives; but that, for convenience, some of this order may be raised to the episcopal office, and some of the functions originally pertaining to the whole order, as ordination, for example, may be confined to them; the presbyter thus elevated being but *primus inter pares*—the first among equals—a presiding officer.*

3. That the words *episcopos*, (Greek,) *superintendent*, (Latin,) and *bishop* (English) † have the same meaning, namely, an overseer.

With these preliminaries we recur to the questions, Did Wesley appoint Coke to the episcopal office? Did he establish the American Methodist episcopate? Let us look at the evidence.

1. Wesley mentions, in Coke's certificate of ordination, as a reason for ordaining him, that the Methodists in America desired "still to adhere to the doctrine and discipline of the Church of England." ‡ That Church in America was dissolved by the Revolution; he therefore appointed Coke, with an episcopal form of government, a ritual, and articles of religion, to meet the exigency. If Coke was appointed merely to some

* See his circular letter to the American Societies, given in chap. v.

† Bishop (Saxon, *bischop*) is a corruption of the Latinized Greek word *episcopus*. Its analogy to the second and third syllables of the latter is obvious.

‡ Drew's Life of Coke, chap. v.

such indefinite and contingent supervisory office as "Church" writers allege—if he possessed not the authoritative functions of episcopacy—wherein did his appointment answer the purpose mentioned by Wesley—"the discipline of the Church of England?" Wherein consists the main feature of the discipline of the English Church? In its episcopal superintendence. Wherein does American Methodism resemble it? Certainly not in class meetings, itinerancy, and other characteristic peculiarities, but in its episcopal regimen. Wesley's language is without sense if this is not its meaning.

2. Why did Wesley attach so much importance to the appointment if it was of the secondary character alleged? He says in his circular letter, respecting Coke's ordination: "For many years I have been importuned, from time to time, to exercise this right by ordaining part of our traveling preachers; but I have still refused, not only for peace' sake, but because I was determined as little as possible to violate the established order of the national Church to which I belonged. But the case is widely different between England and America. Here there are bishops who have a legal jurisdiction. In America there are none, neither any parish ministers; so that, for some hundred miles together, there are none either to baptize or administer the sacrament. Here, therefore, my scruples are at an end!"

Scruples! What could have been his "scruples" about sending Coke on such a secondary errand as the opponents of the Methodist episcopacy assert? He had already sent Asbury and others to America, and to Asbury he had actually assigned such a special yet secondary office, but unaccompanied with the ordination and authority of episcopacy. This he had done years before, without any scruple whatever; but during all this time he had been scrupling about this new and solemn measure, till the Revolution relieved him by abolishing the jurisdiction of the English bishops in the colonies. There is certainly sheer absurdity in all this if Wesley merely gave to Coke and Asbury a sort of indefinite though special commission in the American Church, not including in it the distinctive functions of episcopacy. We can conceive of nothing in the nature of such a commission to excite such scruples—a commission which had long since been given to Asbury.

Again, when Wesley proposed to Coke his ordination to this new office, some six or seven months before it was conferred, Coke "was startled at a measure so unprecedented in modern days," and doubted Wesley's authority to ordain him, as Wesley himself was not a bishop.* Wesley recommended him to read Lord King's Primitive Church, and gave him time to reflect. Coke passed two months in Scotland, and, on satisfying his doubts, wrote to Wesley accepting the appointment, and was afterward ordained, with solemn forms and the imposition of hands, by Wesley, assisted by presbyters of the Church of England. What could have possibly been the pertinency of all these former scruples of Wesley, this surprise, and doubt, and delay of Coke, this reference to ecclesiastical antiquity, and to a book which demonstrates the right of presbyters to ordain bishops in given cases, and these solemn forms, if they related merely to the alleged species of appointment, especially as this very species of commission had already existed for some years in the person of Asbury?

3. It is evident, beyond all question, that Wesley did not consider this solemn act in the subordinate sense of an appointment, but as an "ordination," using the word in its strictest ecclesiastical application. In his circular letter he says: "For many years I have been importuned . . . to exercise this right by *ordaining* a part of our traveling preachers; but I have still refused . . . because I was determined as little as possible to violate the established order of the national Church. . . . Here my scruples are at an end." Here the word ordaining is expressly used; and if the new appointment was not a regular "ordination," but a species of nondescript commission, solemnized by the mere forms of ordination, how could it be an interference with the "established order of the national Church?" How, especially, could it be such an interference, in any important sense different from that which Wesley had already, for years, been exercising without "scruple," in sending to America his unordained preachers? It was clearly an ordina

* Drew's Life of Coke, chap. v.

tion, in the ecclesiastical sense of the term; but there have been only three ordinations claimed in the Christian world, namely, to the offices of, 1. Deacons; 2. Elders or presbyters; and, 3. Bishops. If, then, Coke was ordained by Wesley, and was not ordained a bishop, it becomes at once a pertinent but unanswerable question, To what was he ordained? He had been a presbyter for years. To what, then, did Wesley ordain him, if not to the next recognized office?

Let it be remembered that Whatcoat and Vasey were ordained elders for America at the time of Coke's ordination, but by a distinct act. If Coke did not receive a higher ordination, (that is, episcopal, for this is the only higher one,) why was he ordained separately from them, though on the same occasion? And why did Wesley, in his circular letter, declare to the American Methodists that, while Whatcoat and Vasey were "to act as elders among them," Coke and Asbury were "to be joint superintendents over them?"

4. Wesley, in his circular letter, appeals to Lord King's Sketch of the Primitive Church to show that he as a presbyter, had a right, under his peculiar circumstances, to perform these ordinations. Lord King establishes the second of the above preliminary statements, and the right of presbyters to ordain. And Wesley cites particularly his reference to the Alexandrian Church, where, on the decease of a bishop, the presbyters ordained his successor. Why now this reference to Lord King and the Alexandrian Church—proving that presbyters could ordain—in justification of Wesley's proceedings, if he did not ordain? And if he did ordain Coke, it may again be asked, as Coke was already a presbyter, to what was he thus ordained, if it was not to the only remaining office—the episcopate? And still more pointedly may it be asked, What propriety was there in Wesley's justifying himself by referring to the ordination of bishops by the presbyters of Alexandria if he himself had not ordained a bishop?

5. Wesley prepared at this time a Prayer Book for the American Church—an abridgment of the English Liturgy—to be used under the new arrangement. It contains the forms for the ordination of, 1. Deacons; 2. Elders; 3. Superintendents;

and directs expressly that all preachers elected to the office of deacon, elder, or superintendent shall be presented to the superintendent "to be ordained." Let it be remarked, then, 1) That here the very word ordain is used. 2) We have here the three distinct offices of the ministry stated in order, according to the understanding of Wesley and of all Episcopalians throughout the world. 3) That not only is the name of bishop changed to that of superintendent, but the name of presbyter, or priest, to that of elder—the new names being in both cases synonymous with the old ones. If the change of the former name implies a difference in the office also, why does not the change in the latter imply the same? 4) These forms of ordination were taken from the forms in the English Liturgy for the ordination of deacons, presbyters, and bishops, the names of the latter two being changed to synonymous terms, namely, elders and superintendents. The opponents of the Methodist episcopacy readily grant that elder means presbyter, yet, as soon as superintendents are mentioned as bishops, they protest. 5) These forms show that Wesley not only created the Methodist episcopate, but designed it to continue after Coke and Asbury's decease: they were printed for permanent use.

6. By reading Coke's letter to Wesley, consenting to and directing about his proposed ordination, it will be seen that Whatcoat and Vasey were ordained presbyters at Coke's request, because "propriety and universal practice," he says, "make it expedient that I should have two presbyters with me in this work." * That is, Coke requests, and Wesley grants, that two presbyters shall be ordained to accompany Coke in his new office, because "propriety and universal practice" require that two presbyters assist a bishop in ordaining; and yet Coke was not appointed to the office of a bishop! Coke, in this letter, let it be repeated, requests that these two men should be made "presbyters;" Wesley complies; and yet, in the forms of the Prayer Book, or Discipline, they are called "elders." The name only was changed, therefore, not the thing; why then is not the inference just, that the other change in these forms, that of bishop to superintendent, is

* Smith's History of Methodism, vol. i, book ii, chap. vi, p. 541.

only in the name, not in the thing? The rule certainly ought to "work both ways."

7. Charles Wesley was a rigid High Churchman, and opposed to all ordinations by his brother. The latter knew his views so well that he would not expose the present measure to interruption by acquainting him with it till it was consummated. Though Charles Wesley was a presbyter of the Church of England, and in the town at the time, yet other presbyters were summoned to meet the demand of "propriety and universal practice" on such occasions, while he was carefully avoided. Now why this remarkable precaution against the High Church prejudices of his brother respecting ordinations, if he did not in these proceedings ordain? If it be replied, that Charles was not only opposed to his brother's ordaining a bishop, but equally to his ordaining to the other offices of the ministry; and, therefore, the ordinations might have been confined to the latter, and yet such precautions be proper, it may then be asked again, How can we suppose Coke to be now ordained to these lower offices when he had already received them, and had exercised them for years?

8. As soon as Charles Wesley learned these proceedings he was profoundly afflicted. His correspondence with his brother* shows that he understood them in the manner that the American Methodists do, and Wesley never corrected this interpretation. He defends himself, but never denies the facts. Charles Wesley speaks of Coke's "Methodist Episcopal Church in Baltimore," alluding to the name assumed by the American Church at its organization in that city. Wesley, in his reply, utters not a word in denial or disapproval of this title, but simply vindicates the necessity of his course in respect to the American Methodists. Charles Wesley, in response, speaks of the doctor's "ambition" and "rashness." Wesley, though he knew the Church had been organized at Baltimore with the title of "Episcopal," says: "I believe Dr. Coke as free from ambition as covetousness. He has done nothing rashly that I know." Charles Wesley, in his letter to Dr. Chandler, a clergyman about to sail for America, speaks

* Jackson's Charles Wesley, chap. xxvi.

of his brother having "assumed the episcopal character, ordained elders, *consecrated a bishop*, and sent him to ordain our lay preachers in America;" showing thus what the office really was, though the name was changed. Evidently it was only the appellation of bishop, applied to the superintendents in person, that Wesley disapproved.

9. The Conference at which the Church was organized terminated January 1, 1785. The Minutes were published by Coke with the title, "Discipline of the Methodist Episcopal Church in America." The Minutes, as has been stated, expressly say that the American Societies were formed into an Episcopal Church, and this, too, at the "recommendation" of Wesley. By July, Coke was with Wesley at the British Conference. By the 26th of the preceding June, his own Journal, containing this phrase, was inspected by Wesley. Coke also took to England the American Minutes, and they were printed on a press which Wesley used, and under his own eye. The Baltimore proceedings were therefore known to Wesley, but we hear of no remonstrance from him. They soon became known, by the Minutes, to the public; and when Coke was attacked publicly for what he had done, he replied, as we have seen, through the press, that "he had done nothing but under the direction of Mr. Wesley." Wesley never denied it. How are all these facts explicable, on the supposition that Coke and Asbury had ambitiously broken over Wesley's restrictions?

10. One of Charles Wesley's greatest fears was, as we have noticed, that the English preachers would be ordained by Coke. He had prevailed upon his brother to refuse them ordination for years. He now writes, with deep concern, that "not a preacher in London would refuse orders from the doctor." "He comes armed with your authority to make us all Dissenters." Now, why all this danger of a sudden disposition of the English preachers to receive "orders from the doctor," if it was not understood that he had received episcopal powers, and they despaired of ever getting ordination from the national bishops? If it is replied, they believed, with Wesley, that, under necessary circumstances, presbyters could ordain, and

therefore desired it from Coke, not in view of his new appointment, but because he was a presbyter of the Church of England, then it may be properly asked, Why did they not seek it before, for Coke had been a presbyter among them for years? Why start up with such a demand all at once as soon as they learned of the new position of Coke? And how could Charles Wesley say, in this case, "He comes armed with your authority?" for his authority as a presbyter he obtained from a bishop of the English Church years before he knew Wesley.

11. The term bishop was not personally applied in the Discipline to the American superintendents till about three years after the "organization" of the Church, and Wesley's objurgatory letter to Asbury was not written till four years after it. During all this interval, however, the American Societies were called an "Episcopal Church." Six months after adopting the name, its Minutes were, as stated, inspected by Wesley, and published under his auspices; their title included the phrase "The Methodist Episcopal Church in America;" yet, as has been shown, during this long interim, Wesley never uttered a syllable against this assumption! When his brother writes him, accusing Coke of rashness, he replies that "the doctor has done nothing rashly;" and when Coke is accused through the press, he declares, under Wesley's eye, and without contradiction, that "he had done nothing without the direction of Mr. Wesley." What now do all these incidents imply? What but that Wesley did approve the American episcopate—that it was established by his direction? Yet four years after, when the appellation of bishop was applied personally to the American *episcopoi*, this letter of Wesley was written. What further does this imply? What but that it was not the thing he condemned, but the name; the thing had existed for years uncondemned, nay, defended by him; the very name "Episcopal," so far as it applied to the Church collectively, he did not condemn; but the personal title of bishop he disapproved, because of its objectionable associations. Is it possible to escape this inference?

Finally, Wesley himself admitted that "he had invested persons with the episcopal character and sent them to America."* Jones of Nayland asked him the direct question and received an affirmative reply, with justificatory reasons for the measure.† Thus we see that, whatever view we take of the subject, we are compelled to one conclusion: that Wesley did create and establish the American Methodist episcopacy. The man who gainsays such evidence must be given up as incorrigible. There can be no reasoning with him.

And now, what is the sum of this evidence? It has already been presented with sufficient detail; but let us retrace the successive and decisive steps of the argument. Here we have Wesley proposing to establish "the Discipline of the Church of England" among the American Methodists, and to do so he ordains for them bishops, and gives them an episcopal regimen; yet, according to their antagonists, he never designed them to be a distinct Church, but only a "society" in the Protestant Episcopal Church! Wesley and Coke have "scruples," delays, references to antiquity, imposition of hands, and other solemn forms, conforming to the "universal practice" of episcopal ordination; and yet all concerning some nondescript appointment, analogous to that which is conferred upon a missionary, in charge over his brethren in a foreign station! Wesley speaks of it as "ordaining," and of his refusing to use the right before the Revolution because it would have interfered with the "established order of the national Church;" and yet a mere secondary commission of Coke, such a one as had existed in the person of Asbury for years, is the momentous interference with the established order of the national Church—though there was nothing in that order with which it could interfere, the national Church never having had any such appointments! Wesley solemnly "ordains" Coke; and yet it is not to the episcopal office, though he had been ordained to all the other offices to which ordination is appropriate years before! Wesley ordains two other men to the office of elders, and at the same time separately and formally ordains Coke, who had already borne this office; but still Coke's new office is not the only remaining one that could be conferred upon

* Hawks's Contributions, etc., p. 169.

† Life of Bishop Horne, by Jones of Nayland, pp. 143–145.

him! Wesley refers to the ordination of bishops by the presbyters of Alexandria, in justification of his ordination of Coke, and yet he does not ordain Coke a bishop! Wesley prepares for the American Church a Prayer Book, abridged from that of the Church of England, prescribing the English forms for the three offices of deacons, presbyters, and bishops; the two former are admitted unquestionably to be what they are in England, and yet the latter is explained into something new and anomalous, answering to nothing ever heard of in the Church of England or in any other episcopal Church! In these forms the old names of two of the offices are changed to new but synonymous appellations, that of presbyter or priest to elder, that of bishop to superintendent; in the former case the change of the name is not for a moment supposed to imply a change of the thing; and yet, in the other case, the change of the name invalidates entirely the thing, without a particle more evidence for it in the one case than in the other! Charles Wesley, being a High Churchman, is kept unaware of his brother's proceedings till they are accomplished, though he is in the town at the time of the ordination; and yet it is no ordination, but a species of appointment against which he could have had no episcopal prejudice whatever! When he learns the facts he is overwhelmed with surprise, and in his correspondence exclaims against his "brother's consecration of a bishop," and "Dr. Coke's Methodist Episcopal Church" at Baltimore; and Wesley, in his replies, never denies these titles, but simply vindicates his ordinations, and says that Coke had "done nothing rashly;" yet there was no bishop, no episcopal office appointed, no distinct episcopal Church established, but Coke had fabricated the whole! When the preachers in England, trained under episcopacy, hear of Coke's new office, they are, to the great alarm of Charles Wesley, suddenly seized with a desire to be ordained by Coke, though they fully know that he is no bishop, but the same presbyter that he had been among them for years! In six months after the organization of the American Church Coke publishes its Minutes, with the title, "Methodist Episcopal Church in America," in London, under the eye of Wesley, but no remonstrance is heard from Wesley! When Coke is condemned through the press for his proceedings, he publicly replies that he had done "nothing without the direction of Mr. Wesley;" no rebuke follows from Wesley, but Coke goes on as usual, active in his Conferences, and maintained in his new position; and yet his American proceedings were an ambitious plot, contrary to the will of Wesley! The American Methodists had borne the title "Episcopal Church," with Wesley's full approval, for four years, when, on the use of the personal title of bishop, Wesley writes his letter to Asbury; and yet it is not the mere personal title he condemns, but the office which, for four years, he had left uncondemned, nay, had vindicated!

And now, looking again at this series of arguments, will not the American Methodists be acquitted of presumption when they assume that they may here make a triumphant stand, surrounded by evidence accumulated and impregnable? The ecclesiastical system under which it has pleased God to give them and their families spiritual shelter and fellowship with his saints, and whose efficiency has surprised the Christian world, is not, as their opponents would represent, an imposition of their preachers, and contrary to the wishes of Wesley, but was legitimately received from his hands as the providential founder of Methodism.

If Wesley's strong repugnance to the mere name of bishop had been expressed before its adoption by the American Church, it would probably not have been adopted. Still, the American Church was now a separate organization, and was at perfect liberty to dissent from Wesley on a matter of mere expediency. The Church thought it had good reason to use the name. The American Methodists were mostly of English origin. The people of their country among whom Methodism was most successful, were either from England or of immediate English descent, and had been educated to consider episcopacy a wholesome and apostolical government of the Church. The Church approved and had the office, why not, then, have the name? especially as, without the name, the office itself would be liable to lose, in the eyes of the people, its peculiar character, and thereby fail in that appeal to their long established opinions which Methodism had a right, both from principle and expediency, to make? The English Establishment having been dissolved in this country, and the Protestant Episcopalians not being yet organized on an independent basis, and the episcopal organization of the Methodists having preceded that of the Protestant Episcopalians, the Methodist Church had a clear right to present itself to the American public as competent to aid in supplying the place of the abolished Establishment, having the same essential principles without its peculiar defects.

May not the circumstance of the assumption of an episcopal character, nominally as well as really, by the American Methodists, be considered providential? Episcopacy, both in America and England, has reached an excess of presumption and arrogance. The moderate party, once declared by Bishop White, of the Protestant Episcopal Church, to include a large majority of American Episcopalians,* has nearly disappeared. Was it not providential, under these circumstances, that a body of Christians should appear, exceeding every other in success, and nominally and practically bearing an episcopal character, without any of its presumptuous pretensions? Amid the uncharitable assumptions of prelatical Episcopalians, the Methodist Episcopal Church stands forth a monument of the laborious and simple episcopacy of the early ages; its success, as well as its humility, contrasting it signally with its more pretentious but feebler sister. It has thus practically vindicated episcopacy as an expedient form of ecclesiastical government, and assuredly it needs vindication in these days.

Such, then, is the evidence which should, with all men of self-respectful candor, conclude decisively the question of Wesley's design and agency in the organization of American Methodism.

Driven from this ground, objectors retreat to an equally untenable one, by alleging that the episcopal organization of the Societies in America is to be attributed to the influence of ambitious counselors over Wesley in the imbecility of his old age. His biographers show that he as yet betrayed no such

* Case of the Protestant Episcopal Church in the United States, etc., p. 25.

imbecility; but it has still more conclusively been demonstrated that the ecclesiastical opinions which sanction this great act were adopted in the prime of his manhood. They were the well-considered and fully demonstrated convictions of twoscore years, before he yielded to the unavoidable necessity of giving them practical effect. Few facts in the history of Methodism are more interesting and instructive than the gradual development of Wesley's own mind and character under his extraordinary and accumulating responsibilities. No possible ground of argument remains against the Methodist episcopate but the prelatical charge against its legitimacy, founded in the traditional and exploded ecclesiasticism of obsolete ages. Methodists are content, with Wesley, to pronounce the apostolic succession "a fable which no man ever did, or ever can prove," and believe that, in this age, they need not anxiously challenge any advantage which their opponents can claim from a pretension so incompatible alike with the letter and the charity of the Gospel, as well as with the Christian enlightenment of modern times.*

* Wesley was in good company among Churchmen in his denunciation of the "fable" of the succession. Chillingworth said, "I am fully persuaded there hath been no such succession." Bishop Stillingfleet declares that "this succession is as muddy as the Tiber itself." Bishop Hoadley asserts: "It hath not pleased God, in his providence, to keep up any proof of the least probability, or moral possibility, of a regular uninterrupted succession; but there is a great appearance, and, humanly speaking, a certainty, to the contrary, that the succession hath often been interrupted." Archbishop Whately says, "There is not a minister in all Christendom who is able to trace up, with approach to certainty, his spiritual pedigree."

STATISTICS OF THE M. E. CHURCH.

MEMBERSHIP BY DECADES.

I am indebted to Rev. W. H. De Puy, of the "Christian Advocate," New York, for the following important calculations. In the text I have given the membership of the Church by decades, from 1800, corresponding to the decades of the century. They are here given from its origin, 1766, and present a much more striking result.

By examining the official returns of the Conferences for the whole century, and comparing them by decades, from 1766, we have the following table:

Year.	Traveling Preachers.	Increase of Preachers.	Members.	Increase of Members.
1766	....	....	....	....
1776	24	24	4,921	4,921
1786	117	93	20,689	15,768
1796	293	176	56,664	35,975
1806	452	159	130,570	73,906
1816	695	243	214,235	83,665
1826	1,406	711	360,800	146,565
1836	2,928	1,522	650,103	289,303
1846	3,582	654	644,229*	Dec. 5,874
1856	5,877	2,295	800,327	156,098
1866	7,576	1,699	1,032,184	231,857

* By the withdrawal and separation of Southern Conferences in 1844, organizing the Methodist Episcopal Church. South, the Methodist Episcopal Church lost 1,345 traveling preachers, and 495.288 members; and yet so rapid was her growth during the decade, that at its close (two years after the separation) there was a net gain of 654 preachers, and a lack of only 5,874 members of making up the number lost.

RETURNS TO JANUARY 1, 1867.

I. Annual Conferences.—Of these there are 64, an increase of four over the previous year.

II. Preachers.—The number of traveling preachers is 7,576, an increase over the previous year of 401. Of these 6,287 are effective, (that is, taking full work, to which they are assigned by the bishops,) 881 are superannuated, and 408 are returned supernumerary. During the year 77 traveling preachers located and 80 died, and 639 were admitted on trial. The number of local preachers is 8,602, an increase during the year of 209. The total ministerial force, not including the bishops, is 16,178, being a net increase of 610.

III. Membership.—The total membership reported is 1,032,184, an increase during the year of 102,925, *over eleven per cent.* The number of baptisms stands thus: adults, 47,419; children, 35,536; total, 82,955: being an increase of 18,269 adults and 2,645 children, or a total increase of baptisms of 20,914. During the year 12,214 members died. These are not included above. If we add this number to that showing the increase, we find that during the year at least 115,139 persons united with the Methodist Episcopal Church.

IV. Church Edifices and Parsonages.—The number of churches (houses of worship) is 10,462, being an increase of 420. The estimated total value is $29,594,004, an increase of

$2,843,502. The number of parsonages is 3,314, valued at $4,420,958—an increase of 171 in number, and of $24,277 in value. The total value of Church edifices and parsonages is $34,014,962, being an increase of $2,867,729.

V. Benevolent Collections.—The following are the summaries of the contributions for the principal benevolent causes, *omitting all receipts from legacies:* for Conference claimants, (worn-out preachers, and widows and orphans of ministers who have died in the work,) $107,892—an increase of $14,743; for Missionary Society, $671,090—an increase of $69,025; for Tract Society, $23,349—an increase of $1,026; for American Bible Society, $107,238—an increase of $5,495; for Sunday-School Union, $19,850—an increase of $782. The total contributions for these causes is $929,221.

VI. Centenary Returns.—Up to July 10, 1867, *twenty-seven* Conferences had reported to the Central Centenary Committee at New York a total of $4,342,899 17. From unofficial figures reported from the remaining Conferences, the secretary estimates the entire sum contributed as Centenary collections at *six millions of dollars.*

The above returns complete the statistics of the Methodist Episcopal Church for the *Century.*

RETURNS TO JANUARY 1, 1868.

The official returns of the Methodist Episcopal Church to the close of 1867, *the first year of the second Century*, present the following interesting and encouraging figures: Annual Conferences, 68—an increase during the year of 4; traveling preachers, 7,991—a net increase of 415; local preachers, 8,935—an increase of 333; total members, 1,144,864—a net increase, after deducting 12,583 deaths, of 112,680; church edifices, 11,138—an increase of 676; parsonages, 3,570—an increase of 256; value of church edifices, $35,854,714—an increase of $6,260,710; value of parsonages, $5,316,115—an increase of $895,157; total value of church edifices and parsonages, $41,170,829—an increase during the year of $7,155,867.

THE END.

www.ingramcontent.com/pod-product-compliance
Lightning Source LLC
LaVergne TN
LVHW021100110826
845150LV00001B/129

* 9 7 8 1 4 2 5 5 6 6 1 3 5 *